INTRODUCTION TO
STATISTICAL
DATA PROCESSING

Prentice-Hall
Series in Automatic Computation
George Forsythe, editor

BATES AND DOUGLAS, *Programming Language/One*
BAUMANN, FELICIANO, BAUER, AND SAMELSON, *Introduction to ALGOL*
BOWLES, *Computers in Humanistic Research*
CESCHINO AND KUNTZMAN, *Numerical Solution of Initial Value Problems*
DESMONDE, *Computers and Their Uses*
DESMONDE, *Real-Time Data Processing Systems: Introductory Concepts*
EVANS, WALLACE, AND SUTHERLAND, *Simulation Using Digital Computers*
FIKE, *Computer Evaluation of Mathematical Functions*
FORSYTHE AND MOLER, *Computer Solution of Linear Algebraic Systems*
GOLDEN, *FORTRAN IV: Programming and Computing*
GOLDEN AND LEICHUS, *IBM 360: Programming and Computing*
GRUENBERGER, *Computers and Communications*
HARTMANIS AND STEARNS, *Algebraic Structure Theory of Sequential Machines*
HULL, *Introduction to Computing*
LOUDEN, *Programming the IBM 1130 and 1180*
MARTIN, *Design of Real-Time Computer Systems*
MARTIN, *Programming Real-Time Computer Systems*
MINSKY, *Computation: Finite and Infinite Machines*
MOORE, *Interval Analysis*
SAMMET, *Fundamentals of Basic Computer Languages*
SCHULTZ, *Digital Processing: A System Orientation*
SNYDER, *Chebyshev Methods in Numerical Approximation*
STERLING AND POLLACK, *Introduction to Statistical Data Processing*
STROUD AND SECREST, *Gaussian Quadrature Formulas*
TRAUB, *Iterative Methods for the Solution of Equations*
VARGA, *Matrix Iterative Analysis*
WILKINSON, *Rounding Errors in Algebraic Processes*
ZIEGLER, *Time-Sharing Data Processing Systems*

PRENTICE-HALL INTERNATIONAL, INC., *London*
PRENTICE-HALL OF AUSTRALIA, PTY., LTD., *Sydney*
PRENTICE-HALL OF CANADA, LTD., *Toronto*
PRENTICE-HALL OF INDIA PRIVATE LTD., *New Delhi*
PRENTICE-HALL OF JAPAN, INC., *Tokyo*

INTRODUCTION TO STATISTICAL DATA PROCESSING

Theodor D. Sterling
Seymour V. Pollack

DEPARTMENT OF
APPLIED MATHEMATICS AND COMPUTER SCIENCE
WASHINGTON UNIVERSITY, ST. LOUIS, MISSOURI

Prentice-Hall, Inc., Englewood Cliffs, New Jersey

© 1968 by
PRENTICE-HALL, INC.
Englewood Cliffs, N.J.

Current printing (last digit):

10 9 8 7 6 5 4 3 2

Library of Congress Catalog Card Number 68-19037
Printed in the United States of America

PREFACE

Automation and computers present similar opportunities and problems wherever they are used. Ideas on statistical manipulations and experimental design have undergone many subtle changes (and some that were not so subtle) as the ubiquitous computer and the instrument complex controlled through it have forced a unification of fundamental data processing problems in many otherwise widely different types of enterprises. It is possible, therefore, to address a single text to students and investigators in all fields in which basic statistics and data processing are applied. In fact, the contents of this text, their organization, and the manner of presentation were developed through teaching two very different groups of students in biology, botany, and medicine and in the social sciences.

Teaching new concepts and usages in data processing along with proved statistical techniques represents a number of problems, and this text has been designed to deal with them. At the same time we thought it desirable to aim for as much flexibility as orderly presentation of content permits because of the many possible approaches and tastes of instructors or backgrounds and preparations of students who are now being introduced to the field. Materials are arranged so that the instructor has a choice of areas to emphasize or to slight. For students with adequate preparation, cursory skimming of some of the material will be sufficient. For others who know little if anything about computers or logical structures or about the many opportunities for automatic data acquisition or flexible display, a more thorough grounding in basic principles will be required. All materials are presented in an ascending order of difficulty (in each chapter) so that the instructor can break off at any desired level of proficiency, depending on the student's background and ability and on the purpose of the course. The detailed outline of topics given with each chapter can be used as a guide by the instructor, the student, or the investigator who wishes to gain acquaintance with modern data processing techniques.

There is one topic which, although very important, is nevertheless peripheral to the purposes of this course. This is the minimum amount of mathematics necessary for the student or investigator in the empirical sciences who wishes to avail himself of these modern data processing techniques. To aid those whose mathematical background is insufficient or who need review we have included a short treatment of basic "computer arithmetic" in Appendix A. This appendix makes no pretense of teaching mathematics. It reviews necessary procedures in notation, techniques of flowcharting, estimation of values of functions, a number of practical uses of calculus, and solution of systems of equations, and it introduces the computation of probabilities. This appendix may be used to review a number of fundamental ideas which the students are lacking or it may be used by the investigator to refresh his memory.

The text is designed for a three-hour-a-week, two-semester course. There are natural divisions in the materials which permit them to be divided into two-semester or three-quarter sequences. For a two-semester course we recommend that the initial six chapters (including the necessary parts of the mathematics appendix) be taught during the first semester and the remainder of the book during the second semester. This permits some students to leave the course halfway yet with enough knowledge about hardware and software and data preparation techniques to participate in data collecting undertakings and simple descriptive endeavors. For a three-quarter course we recommend that the first quarter cover through data preparation (Chapter 4), the second quarter be used to cover description, summary, and display of data and introduction to hypothesis testing (Chapters 5, 6, and 7) and the last quarter be utilized to cover as much of description of deterministic and probabilistic functions and multivariate analysis as indicated. For students with strong backgrounds in mathematics as well as computers, the materials in the first section of this book can be largely eliminated and the course can be taught in one semester.

Much attention has been devoted to example problems for all major analytic techniques, and a large number of practice problems have been included which are easy to work by hand or with semiautomatic calculators. The student is encouraged to use flowcharting techniques throughout the book. This is equally good practice for students who do and students who do not know how to program. If a good program library is available, the student can use it to analyze actual data along with the example problems given in the book. (The instructor who wishes to use practice problems and actual processing of data along with or instead of homework problems is referred to our discussion of "Use of the Computer to Teach Introductory Statistics," *Communications of the ACM*, Vol. 9, No. 4, April, 1966.)

The changes from conventional statistics to modern data processing and the addition of topics relevant to a course in this subject are reflected in our outline of chapters.

Chapter 1 introduces the problems and opportunities of automation against the background of experimental design and statistical analysis. It seeks to create a frame of mind which ties the efficiency of experimental designs to the capabilities of high-speed information processing as well as to the automation in data collection.

Chapter 2 describes "hardware" for the collection of data, the display of information, and processing procedures. It covers in great detail instrumentation for automatic collection of data, as well as the many peripheral devices that may be used for displaying information, but is concerned less with the structure of processors. This emphasis was chosen because modern techniques of data processing require a thorough knowledge of input and output opportunities. Chapter 3 is devoted to a description of logical structures, so-called "software," which are necessary to convert an instrumentation-processing complex into a useful data handling tool. Students who understand the underlying problems in construction of software and how they are solved develop an easy understanding for heuristic solutions to multivariate processing problems. (Chapters 2 and 3 may be skipped by the student who has a strong background in instrumentation and programming.) An understanding of the subject matter of Chapters 2 and 3 enables the investigator to optimize his experiment with respect to data collection and input and his analysis of results with respect to display and action of processing equipment. Organization of data so that they can be accepted by automatic processing equipment is extremely important. Costs of experiments can be decreased decisively and available information made immensely more usable by organizing the acquisition of data with an eye toward processing from the very beginning. Chapter 4 deals exclusively with problems of data preparation.

Chapters 5 and 6 bear testimony to the immensely increased possibilities of describing data through a variety of peripheral display devices supported by adequate processing hardware and logic. Description of data is treated in these two chapters. Chapter 5 deals predominantly with displays. The exploitation of graphic and tabular data summaries are covered in detail, and uses of two or three multidimensional display schemes are presented. Chapter

6 covers the more conventional numerical descriptions and summaries of data. To aid the student in understanding better the subsequent expansion from numerical description to statistical inferences, a discussion of sampling and a more rigorous definition of "expectations" have been included. A discussion of the statistical concept of expectation can take the place, to some extent, of a more thorough discussion on probability. (The discussion and development of expectation may be bypassed by the instructor who is concerned less with mathematical derivations and more with intuitive grasp of fundamental concepts.)

Chapter 7 discusses test of hypotheses of small and large samples. It includes an introduction to the special problems arising from the comparisons between large data files on many different measurements. Tests of multiple comparisons are introduced at the end of this chapter.

The description of associations is usually discussed in texts on statistics under a heading of "regression analysis." The vastly expanded possibilities for evaluating linear and nonlinear associations are acknowledged by a separate discussion of orderly linear and nonlinear functions in Chapter 8. Since computers make it possible to fit mathematical expressions to a wide variety of curves, this chapter also lends itself to a thorough discussion of curve-fitting techniques.

Chapter 9 treats the more conventional statistical approaches of regression and correlation and of multiple regression and multiple correlation. Discriminant functions are also introduced, since they are very similar to regression analyses.

The mathematical support of Appendix A can be used to good advantage in teaching Chapters 8 and 9. The student will find that the review of expansions of series and simple differentiation and integration will aid in understanding Chapter 8 and that a review of matrix algebra will be useful in covering some of the material in Chapter 9. A part of Appendix A has been developed especially to deal with these two chapters so that the review of necessary computer arithmetic is very simple and consumes very little time.

New ideas for multivariate analyses, especially those using heuristic techniques are introduced in Chapter 10. This chapter may be dealt with in detail or may be treated predominantly for the ideas presented in it, depending very much on the sophistication and/or the needs of students.

Probably no single statistical techniques has been so much affected by high-speed calculation as the *analysis of variance*. Chapter 11 pulls together the major uses of analysis of variance necessary for the understanding of experimental design. The student is brought as quickly as possible to complex designs and the use of the analyses with missing and misshapen data. This chapter should be viewed as laying a practical foundation for a thorough look at analysis of variance.

Chapter 12 introduces the student to the expanded possibilities of evaluating experimental results and aggregates of observations by inspecting data, trying some analyses, inspecting the results, and so finding a way through a complex series of analytic procedures. Although the state of the art is such that relatively few students will have an opportunity for easy access to the computing equipment necessary for man-machine interaction in the next decade, it is the dominant trend in hardware and software development and eventually will make this mode the preferred method of analysis. This chapter should be explored for the ideas which it represents and used to prepare the student for possibilities which will be opened to him shortly.

Modern ideas of data processing and of experimental design are undergoing a violent transition. Yet at any one period of time in this process, the old and the new merge in a sensible fashion. The difficulties in teaching these materials probably lie more with the instructor, who has to develop a new point of view, than with the student, who does not have any perspective yet. Therefore, the instructor will welcome the certain amount of freedom this text provides to select topics and materials for emphasis or to use an approach that is more comfortable for him. We have also attempted to furnish the investigator who has some statistical sophistication with a ready reference to many of the new and expanded techniques available to him.

In writing this text we were aided by so many colleagues and students that it would be difficult to mention them all. We are very much indebted to Messrs. Jay Weinkam and Ram Ganesan for proofreading large parts of the manuscript. We thank George Forsythe for many valuable editorial suggestions. We are beholden to Mrs. Baker, Miss Burroughs, Mrs. Swenson, Mrs. Schwartzkopf, and Mrs. Ward for typing, typing, and retyping. Above all, we wish to thank the many students in different subjects who had to suffer through experimental approaches to teaching (which were not all equally successful). A similar acknowledgement of a large debt is tendered to our colleagues on the faculty whose intellectual endeavors were often used as experimental materials to probe for better statistical and data processing techniques.

T. STERLING
S. POLLACK

St. Louis, Missouri

CONTENTS

*Italic entries refer to major headings, which appear centered on the type page in the text.

**7 INTRODUCTION TO
STATISTICAL HYPOTHESIS TESTING**   **266**

**8 DESCRIBING
DETERMINISTIC ASSOCIATIONS**   **328**

11 THE ANALYSIS OF VARIANCE

INTRODUCTION TO
STATISTICAL
DATA PROCESSING

INTRODUCTION TO
STRUCTURED
DATA PROCESSING

1 SCIENCE IN THE WORLD OF COMPUTERS

Members of the newly formed Invisible College (which later, long after Cromwell's death, became the Royal Society) gathered by the light of a full moon around the stump of a freshly felled oak tree. A circle of what was supposed to be powdered horn of unicorn was drawn on the stump of wood and a spider was placed in the center. The minutes of the meeting showed that the insect crossed the powdered substance without undue hesitation.

This scene took place about 300 years ago. It is illustrative of the naïvete accompanying the humble beginnings of modern experimentation. It also illustrates the confusion that so often is impressed on the observer by the endless variety of nature. Indeed, it is our great misfortune that nature does not publish textbooks. Man must grope blindly in the world about him, sometimes guessing, always testing, and constantly deciding what the meanings of his observations might possibly be. It would be so much easier if nature would offer a reference work to lean on in times of uncertainty. Culling "new" knowledge from whatever observations nature presents is a terribly difficult and often frustrating undertaking. But, at the same time, the rewards following scientific discoveries are immense.

Bacon, in his monumental *Novum Organum*, very clearly promised in the seventeenth century that carefully controlled acquisition of information somehow would convert itself into what he called picturesquely "the golden apples," or the fruits of man's industry by which he substantially improves his lot. Yet, in the beginning of what we might think of as orgainzed information gathering, man's thoughts were still directed toward the gold and silver that he could force out of captive peoples rather than on the goods and services that a burgeoning technology could give him so much more easily. From these beginnings, as humble as they may have been, we have come to a period during which large quantities of monies and support are made available routinely for the exploration of the unknown. The wealth and future of a nation rests on its technology, and the growth of the technology depends to a large extent on what is "factually" known.

Although the motivation toward exploration of the unknown has crystallized during the last three hundred years, the precise sequence of events by which knowledge is gained seems in many ways as mysterious as ever. Because of the importance of the subject, some of man's best hands and heads have made the understanding of this process their life's work. It is not easy to understand just how a new idea becomes part of the storehouse of established thought. If it is new, it has no precedents. Where does it come from? How is it amalgamated with other views and facts? When and by what route are old views ever abandoned? Answers to these questions have ranged all the way from the notion that everything is really known, so learning and remembering are actually one, to the proposition that ideas are results of very definite conditions which themselves may be a subject of study. Does man accumulate new knowledge because, at some stage of development, certain new ideas become obvious or does he add to his storehouse because the world that exists around him presents to him at frequent regular intervals observations that reflect certain fundamental associations? One might think that a study of the history of discovery would shed light on the process by which the new is gathered to the old. Unfortunately, this is not the case. There is such a variety of ways in which man has made discoveries that almost any point of view about the process of discovery can be defended. Often, too, memory is at fault, and even the discoverer is hard pressed to tell exactly how he made his discovery. Confusion is also spread by the irresistible temptation to tell stories. Did Newton really discover the laws of motion because an apple fell on his head? Did the great biologist, Koch, really discover how to grow bacteria on a solid medium by forgetting his lunch? On the other hand, how many well-reasoned models have been presented by scientists who did not wish to confess that their discoveries were accidental? Yet we know from past experience that we can develop valid approaches toward asking questions and evaluating answers without understanding very well the process of inquiry in which we are engaged. After all, man has been doing this for many years. He has created practical knowledge for himself and understanding of his environment without being too certain of the best format of his own activity. It is true that sometimes he has burnt his home to roast a pig. Often, however, he has shown the cleverness of a Charles Lamb in converging upon nature's secrets despite his own ignorance on how he derives many of his answers.

But just because the origin of the initial creative act is not well understood does not mean that the gathering and developing of new knowledge is a haphazard process. Quite to the contrary. No single activity of which man is capable is so circumscribed by rigorous rules and procedures as are the methods by which ideas about nature are tested once they have been formulated. This rigor in methods and procedures is not motivated by any medieval monasticism but by bitter experience and example. Whenever method was lacking, madness and confusion entered by the front door. The organization of observations, their evaluation, and the substantiation of hypotheses must be organized in a logical model that can converge upon useful conclusions from original ideas. Medicine and its history very often serve as a good subject with which to demonstrate the value of rigorous scientific method, because the price man has paid for his own ignorance, superstition, and sloppiness has been so very high, and the rewards for proper scientific behavior have been so great. However, there is not a single topic of scientific inquiry in which the failure to establish sound methods and logical procedures of experimental design and evaluation of results has not been followed by dire consequences of one sort or another.

Method is the servant of those who create useful knowledge. True, it is noncreative. However, there is no useful synthesis without it. Methods by which we organize, classify, generalize, and in general manipulate observations are also among the more important and difficult subjects of study. These are not simple matters at all, nor are they dry and brittle pursuits. To the contrary, the study and debate on merits of methods has written some of the most interesting chapters in modern science.

Method by itself is, of course, a very large topic. Until recently the methods used by the scientist have been divided into and treated as a number of different subjects. There are instruments which he uses, experiments which he designs, and the conventions by which he processes and classifies information. There are many other activities which might fall under the general heading of methods. Now the computer is forcing us to re-evaluate notions about methods by which creative thinking is tested and exploited. We are handicapped by the short time that has elapsed since the computer made its first impact on the knowledge-gathering enterprise. It is quite possible that our ideas will change as we go along and as we discover ways by which the technological advances in automation and computation will modify our thoughts about the scientific enterprise. At present though, we must clarify some of the ground rules by which we can proceed in formulating new knowledge and modifying the old.

THE PRACTICAL AIMS OF SCIENCE

The orderly production of knowledge is usually assigned as the province of science. Because of the intensive preparation needed, the grasp of previous accomplishments that has to be attained, and the specific attitudes that appear to be so helpful to him, the pursuit of this complicated task has left a great deal of leeway to the investigator and a considerable penumbra of uncertainty around what he actually does. There is very little agreement among scientists as to what they are doing or what science really consists of. It does not help, of course, that scientists, like any other collection of human beings, are subject to all the myths, rituals, superstitions, and self-delusions that are the common lot of all mankind. Yet an orderly point of view towards science is possible and can indeed be attained. We shall not concern ourselves, therefore, with whether science consists of "understanding nature" or of "collecting facts" mindlessly as opposing extremes would have us believe; rather, we shall seek to define a substrate common to all discussions that is suitable for obtaining an orderly view. We also need a reasonably stable point of departure to understand better why changes are forced on scientific procedures by improved instrumentation, automation, and computers. Not only is such a discussion useful; often it is good fun as well.

THE RELATION BETWEEN ANTECEDENTS AND CONSEQUENCES

The end result of any scientific activity ought to be a statement about conditions that exist in nature and how these conditions are associated with each other. From a very pragmatic point of view we might write this statement as

$$CRA$$

where A is equal to a set of antecedent conditions;

C is equal to a set of consequent conditions;

R denotes rules by which, for any given state of A (i.e., of the antecedent conditions) a particular type of C (consequent conditions) may be observed.

From a very practical and pragmatic point of view the meanings of antecedent and consequent conditions are clear as long as they refer to a specific set of instruments, methods, and the operations which create the conditions or their measurements rather than to the terms by which they may be known. This means that such terms as *class*, *status*, or *blood pressure* refer to a very concrete set of procedures. Anyone performing these procedures in precisely the way in which they are stated will make comparable judgments. In this way, it is possible to avoid not only the lack of clarity due to the use of imprecise day-to-day language but also most of the controversies aroused by the very mention of "operationism."

A precise description of the state of affairs given by **CRA** is, in many ways, the fundamental precursor of any actions that the scientist or the man of practical affairs would like to take. If a set of antecedent conditions calls forth a particular consequence, it is usually possible to manipulate this state of affairs in such a way that the consequence may be enhanced or may be prevented from occurring. A scientist can call out certain situations which he needs or suppress those which he does not in pursuit of his work and, by similar manipulations, the man of practical affairs can bring about a state in the world that will be of benefit to him or others. For instance, **CRA** is the sort of statement on which most of practical medicine is based. Observing a particular set of symptoms and signs, the physician can "diagnose" a disease by referring back to his knowledge of how these symptoms and signs may be consequences of specific antecedents which either have occurred in the past or exist at the time the patient is present but that need special instruments for observation. Conversely, the physician guides the treatment of the patient by his knowledge of the conditions that will create or be followed by specific consequences. Likewise, the skilled artist wishing to achieve some envisioned color effect calls upon his experience to devise a mixture of basic pigments which will bring about the desired result. In similar respects, statements of **CRA** find their uses in engineering and in all applied disciplines and arts. For the theoretical scientist, the certainty with which statements about **CRA** can be made serves predominantly to verify the product of his thinking and activities.

Certainty of a scientific statement connecting antecedent to consequent conditions has really nothing to do with infallibility. Some investigations may lead to scientific assertions that can be made with a great deal of confidence. Others may lead to conclusions which, while tenable, are held with less confidence by the scientific community.

If pebbles are dropped from balconies at different heights (for instance, from different levels of the Leaning Tower of Pisa), it would be relatively simple to develop a precise equation that connects the length of time it takes pebbles to fall with the height from which they start and the initial velocity with which they are propelled. Many observations can be collected in a short period of time and at a relatively small cost. Also, the relationship between antecedent and consequent conditions is uniform, and, what is more important, it is invariant. Duration of fall is simply not affected by too many other conditions or is not affected by them too markedly. It is true that the precise height or distance from the center of the earth of the balconies, the prevailing wind velocity, the shape of the pebbles, and perhaps even the position of the moon and the stars have some effect on falling time. Yet these and many other factors contribute such small changes to measurements that they can be discounted for all practical purposes. This is especially true if the instruments used to measure are crude. A good fit to nature can be expressed in the form of an equation that predicts with good accuracy how long it will take a pebble to fall, if the height at which it was released and its initial velocity are known. The same situation does not hold true for the relationship that exists between such antecedent factors as diet and such consequent conditions as weight. Although individuals who eat more do tend to weigh more and those who eat less do tend to weigh less, the relationship is by no means clear-cut. The weight of an individual depends in many ways on the weight of his ancestors, his own state of health, malfunctions of certain glandular structures, the composition of his diet, the amount and kind of activity he engages in, and on many other factors. Because of the multiplicity of the variables involved, it would be rather difficult to determine precisely the weight of an individual if only the weight of the food he consumes during the day is known. It may still be possible to develop an equation describing the weight of an individual as a function of the weight of his food intake. However, it is quite clear that this equation would predict weight very inaccurately. This type of relationship is marked by its inherent variability (i.e., it is stochastic) and by the many variables which determine the final outcome of any observation (i.e., it is multivariate). The justification for ignoring boldly the effects of other possible variables varies with types of sciences. In natural science, especially physics, it is very often possible to make an oversimplified model of the working of nature. The sensitivity of measuring instruments relative to the variations due to contributing extraneous variables may be so small that they can be ignored with an easy heart. Unfortunately, this is very seldom true for the biological and social sciences. Here the multivariate case is much more common, and as a consequence the association between antecedent and consequent conditions tends to be stochastic rather than deterministic.

From the point of view of the certainty or confidence which the scientist has in his results or in his ability to make a scientific statement, it matters very little whether variability stems from the phenomenon itself or resides in the instruments of measurement. What is important is that, the statement CRA is augmented by an assessment of the probable error with which this statement may be wrong or may not hold true on closer inspection or may not occur on repetition of conditions A. In practice this uncertainty in the stochastic situation takes on two forms of adjustment. In one case the scientist might be interested in the likelihood that his statement CRA is correct. In the other case he might be confident that a statement CRA is basically plausible and that knowledge about it is useful but that any estimate of C on the basis of A may carry a large error with it. Since the occurrence of such an error is not predictable, he speaks of an error of prediction. We shall see later that different methods and approaches toward the two types of uncertainty are involved.

Methods and procedures necessary to making statements of the form CRA by and large were developed in a world in which computers not only did not exist but in which many problems were very prominent precisely because the help of computing machines could not be marshalled to solve them.

A WORD ABOUT FUNCTIONS

William James, who defined a number of important features in the association between antecedent and consequent conditions as an end product of science, used the word *function* rather than *relation*. We prefer the term *relation*, however, because it describes better the variable and sometimes rather vague association between antecedent and consequent conditions that is true for many statements of empirical science, whereas *function* has a more limited mathematical definition. In its more precise mathematical context, function stands for rules that may exist between collections or sets of numbers.

We can present the outcome of an observation, measurement, event, or judgment by a *variable*. A variable is really a symbol that may take the place of a number or judgment. Generally, X_i and Y_j are variable names standing for the ith and jth observation of measurements or procedures X or Y.

These symbols or variables may take on any given value from the domain of real numbers The interval over which these numbers may vary may be open ($a < X < b$) or it may be closed ($a \leq X \leq b$) between the values of a and b, depending on the situation in which measurements are taken. In this way, a variable may stand for a number from a given domain or range of values.

Suppose now that with each value of one variable there is associated a single number of another variable. If this state of affairs exists, we say that two variables are associated with each other, or, knowing the value of one variable, we can say something about the value of the other variable.

If the definition of the set of values over which a number of variables may range is exact and if rules exist by which a single value of one variable is "associated" with or corresponds to a single (or only very few values) of another variable, we speak of a mathematical function

$$Y = f(x)$$

The statement denoting the existence of such a function is written usually in this form and indicates that there exists a precise *rule* which assigns a value to Y depending on the number or value of X. This relation (and function is a very precise relation in our sense) might be an algebraic expression such as

$$h(t) = \tfrac{1}{2}gt^2$$
$$g(p) = \log_{10} p$$

where h or g denote different rules.

It is customary to talk about a single-valued function if the rule is such that for each value in the domain of X there exists only a single value in the range of Y, and of a two- or many-valued formation if for any value in the domain of V there are two values in the range of W.

There are instances in which for any value of X there might occur multiple numbers and values of Y. Many important relationships and associations exist in the empirical sciences that are considered to be quite generally "true" even though they may be at best represented by multivalued functions. For instance, there is a definite relationship between age and height. Six-year-olds are usually taller than five-year-olds, who are usually taller than four-year-olds. There are instances, however, in which a four-year-old child might be taller than many children who are two or three years older. We shall see later on how these multivalued functions may be reduced to single-valued functions.

One good way to look at a function or relation is as a machine. If we feed one number into one end of this machine we obtain another number (or a small choice among numbers) at the other end. The workings of such a machine may be represented by a flow diagram.

$$f(x) = \log_{10} X + 5$$

The diagram of Figure 1.1 is usually referred to as a *flow diagram*. Note that this flow diagram may include steps calling for the determination of other functions. A rule must be given by which the value of $\log_{10} X$ can be obtained, for instance.

There are a number of ways by which such functions can be determined. The student is probably most familiar with looking up $\log_{10} X$ in a table of log values. Another way of reading off the value of $\log_{10} X$ for any given value of X is by means of a graph. There are, of course, many inaccuracies

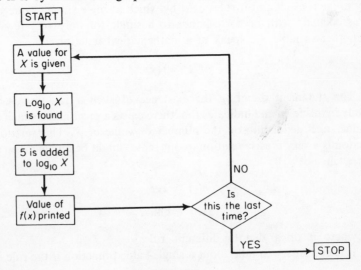

Figure 1.1

in such a graph, since graphic display, even for those equipped with the best of eyes, may not be good enough for very accruate determinations. One easy way to determine the value of $\log_{10} X$ is by means of a mechanical "device." The slide rule, one of the first forms of a many-purpose analog computer, is one example of such a device, consisting essentially of movable scales. It suffers, of course, from a similar drawback to that of graphic representation. Finally we may look for a digital machine "function" that will "map" a number in the range of $\log_{10} X$ given a value in the domain of X. Such a function is usually referred to as *numerical approximation*. It is not always possible to invent a completely accurate rule, but it may be accurate enough for practical purposes. For instance, a good approximation for $\log_{10} X$, providing that $1 \leq X \leq 10$, is given by

$$\log_{10} X = .5 - .86304\left(\frac{X - 3.16228}{X + 3.16228}\right) + .36415\left(\frac{X - 3.16288}{X + 3.16288}\right)$$

When such an equation is used to approximate the value of a more complex function, we are almost certainly forced to use an electronic computer. We shall have more to say about numerical approximations at a later point.

SCIENTIFIC DATA AND INSTRUMENTATION

The final judgment on any unit of data is made by a scientist on the basis of a sensory discrimination. Regardless of how data are produced, the element of sensory discrimination is always present (or at least had to be until logic circuitry came onto the scene). Events may impinge directly upon the sensory modalities of the scientist or they may be translated by a series of instruments and result in the reading of a dial, a picture, a color, an auditory signal, or what have you. For example, if we wish to determine the temperature of a pot of water that has been heated on the stove for periods of time, we could develop data in a variety of ways. One method would be to ask the investigator to stick his finger into the water. His reaction could be labeled as hot, cold, warm, and so on. As an alternative an electronic probe could be dangled into the water and could convert differences in movement of molecules into the readings on a dial. There are quite a number of obvious differences between the two procedures, although both result in data. Yet in each case a sensory discrimination is made. The first is perhaps in terms of pain and the second in terms of the visual reading of an instrument. But data resulting from both methods are products of discrimination.

Depending on the kind of discrimination, the numerical properties of data may vary widely and, with them, the possible alternatives for analysis.

Using the finger to measure the temperature of water results in a scale that is relatively insensitive to increases and decreases in temperature. A change of quite a number of degrees must occur before heat or pain receptors will be able to make a differential judgment between warm and hot. Because this sensory measuring scale is so very vaguely defined, it has few properties which lend themselves to manipulation for analytical purposes other than perhaps counting. Also, this type of judgment is very much dependent upon the egocentric point of view of the measurer. An Eskimo might find the water warm under almost any conditions. On the other hand, a person brought up in a very hot climate might find the same water cold which the Eskimo finds hot. Thus, both the replicability as well as the public nature of the data may be brought into question.

Many of these problems are eliminated by use of a measuring instrument. It is true that an entirely new series of errors might slip in here. The instrument might function so that it is insensitive to change or so that it presents readings which are influenced more by malfunction than by the actual changes in temperature in the pot of water. Also, the dial might be constructed in such a way that its reading may lead to errors on the part of the discriminator. Yet, although instruments represent many problems of their own, it is quite clear that the public nature of science and replicability of observation depend largely on instrumentation-assisted discrimination. Computer-based automation, which is really ultimate instrumentation, brings with it many additional advantages.

SENSITIVITY

There are two ways in which the sensitivity of instruments adds substantially to the scientific process.

Instruments give usually a finer measure of increments of change than is possible for unaided sensory judgment.

But instrument sensitivity may imply a much more important property than just giving a finer increment. Many events in the environment are not observable unless instruments exist to aid man's basic discriminatory powers. Bacteria, viruses, the structure of crystals, and other features of the microcosmos cannot be discriminated without the aid of microscopes. There are radarscopes and powerful lenses with which the astromomer scans the universe and X-rays by which the radiologist sees the inside of the body. Very often the development of a new sensitivity may lead to an entirely revised body of knowledge. Science is very much bound up with instrumentation and the invention of a sensitive instrument. The increase of man's ability to discriminate among events in his environment may have the most far-reaching consequences for his science and for his way of life.

ERROR VARIABILITY

The variability of observations depends very much on the sensitivity of discrimination. For instance, if an individual were "measured" by asking judges to guess at his height, the results would vary considerably. If a physical scale were used to measure the individual, the answers would vary a good bit less. Similarly, if the amount of heat in a gas jet were to be regulated by turning a crude device which opens and closes the opening for the jet, a final statement of the relationship between the temperature in a pot of water and the amount of heat delivered to it might be rather variable on repetition. However, if the amount of heat delivered to the pot is measured by sensing the flame through heat elements, variablity will be considerably reduced.

Decreasing variability may have more import than just reducing errors. When a point is reached at which improvements in instrumentation are not accompanied by further reduction in variability and error of measurement, revision in theory and concepts are called for. For instance, as long as the trajectory of the planet Neptune was measured rather crudely, its motions were seen to coincide with an eight-planet structure of the solar system. When measurements were refined to the point that errors in describing the orbit of Neptune became so large that they could not comfortably be adjusted by referring to crudeness of measurement, it became necessary to change the number of planets thought to exist in the solar system to nine. Such an unsuspected planet was discovered eventually, and called Uranus. There are many such examples in the history of science. As a consequence, it is quite clear that widening the range of use of instruments and increasing their sensitivity may lead to rather surprising changes in the organization of knowledge. Also, as instrumentation changes, it becomes difficult to compare data accumulated by older instruments or discriminations to data obtained through newer or different instruments.

PROPERTIES OF NUMBERS

The measurements or judgments that make up data lend themselves to different types of analyses depending on their properties, or more exactly, on how well their properties can be aligned with mathematical prerequisites and properties of numbers. Proper instrumentation may not only result in a full exploitation of data but also in a less costly experimental design. In general, the more closely the results of discrimination can be related to properties of the real number scale, the wider is the choice of mathematical manipulations that can be applied to their analysis. The more complete becomes mathematical exploitation of data, the *fewer* observations are required. As a consequence, the efficiency of experiments is very much related to the kind of numbers they generate.

DISTANCE BETWEEN PHENOMENA AND OBSERVER

The interposition of instruments increases a psychological distance between data and phenomena and sometimes creates a question about what it is that is actually measured. There are quite obviously a great number of instrumentation problems that must be solved to insure that what is received as "data" is indeed something that has to do with the phenomenon to be measured rather than with the caprice of instruments. More to the point, given the complexity of instruments, it is not always easy to maintain the meaning of the thing that is to be measured.

Instrumentation problems do become resolved if adequate thought and effort is given to them. One serious problem raised by instrumentation is that of the cooperation and dialogue between the "science" and the "engineering" contained in the instrument. Modern sciences have come to a point where a simple relation of the scientist to his subject matter is sometimes not possible any more. The convenience of instrumentation and its ability to reduce the cost of the experiments and give more information for the same amount of money (which sounds as if it were the same but really is not) are such that biologists and social scientists are increasingly encouraged to make use of advances in engineering and computation. A satisfactory solution to instrumentation problems implies, however, that the social scientist or biologist become well enough versed with engineering and computing sciences that they can control their own instruments or that they can maintain, at least, an adequate discourse or dialogue with engineers and mathematicians. Many an understanding has floundered on this obstacle.

What we have said so far is true by and large for a world in which computers do not exist. However, differences in emphasis and, above all, differences in methods are introduced when automation concepts come into the picture. We shall turn now toward gaining a better understanding of what automation is and what it means to the scientific process.

IMPACT OF AUTOMATION AND COMPUTERS
ON PLANNING EXPERIMENTS AND PROCESSING DATA

Sciences are classified by their intellectual contents and subject matters rather than through their procedures. Astronomers concern themselves with planets and stars, and chemists with molecular behavior. Although such a classification of knowledge is, of course, perfectly adequate and acceptable, it tends to slight the tremendous extent to which the knowledge and subject matter of a science is bound to instrumentation and method. Although it is true that the astronomer will concern himself with heavenly matters regardless of the instruments he uses to probe the skies, the precise nature of his information, the structure of his experiments, and his concepts of the universe will depend very heavily on the type of instruments that he finds useful in his exploration. Most scientific instruments are neither known nor understood well outside the narrow confines of their use. However, some of them have had effects so profound on all of our lives and have been so universal in their applications that their influences are common knowledge.

The history of the microscope is probably the best example of the effect an instrument can have on knowledge. Over the many years of its use, its impact on our knowledge has, if anything, increased. Basically the microscope does a simple task. By a system of lenses and lights it extends the power of the human eye to distinguish among tiny patterns and shapes. It is predominantly a tool for visual discrimination. It permits discrimination among objects and forms too small to be seen with the naked eye. However, it is not the simplicity of the task but its place in the scheme of things which is important. By enlarging the basic discriminatory ability of man it also has enlarged his data sources. It is indeed a mighty producer of data in a very general way, and the effect of the constant addition to the variety of data on knowledge is a constant force for change.

The history of developing knowledge around the microscope demonstrates clearly that the first and obvious uses of a tool are formed from the vantage of the information that exists at the time the instrument is introduced. In the case of the microscope this took the form of describing that part of the universe that had been poorly visible, but visible to some extent, prior to its invention. Descriptions were obtained of practically anything at which the microscope could be aimed. Leeuwenhoek, who discovered how to grind incredibly powerful lenses, took great delight in describing in minute detail the leg of a bee or the eye of a fly or the pistil of a flower. Sometimes the microscope was aimed at sights where it was thought certain observations should be found which actually did not exist or existed in a form quite different from expectation. It was believed that the embryo in a tiny way represented the completed adult in the ovum and just grew after fertilization. Thus it was thought, for instance, that microscopic examination of an ovum should enable the viewer to differentiate between males and females. One ambitious scheme for which the microscope was to be used was to count the number of generations that could be found in an ovum, in the naive belief that in this way the time remaining until Judgment Day could be assessed. It is a credit to man's imagination that not only were some investigators able to differentiate the yet unformed eggs into "male" and "female," but others were actually able to count the number of future generations contained in the confines of the ovum.

Sometimes the aimless inspection of the environment through the eyes of the microscope yielded very surprising results. Acids were seen to be crystalline in nature. They had definitely shaped forms and grew very much like large crystals. Tissue, whether of humans, animals, or plants, seemed to be constructed of building blocks that, at close inspection, had some very definite morphological features. Drops of water were populated by tiny vegetables and animals of such variety as to stagger the imagination. These and many other brand-new discoveries were made in the universe which was too small to be differentiated by the human eye. However, these sensory discriminations were instrument-dependent. Neither the existence of microbes nor that of cells nor that of many other phenomena in the world around us could have been detected without this instrument.

New discoveries upset the status quo of what is or is believed to be known. They must be integrated with other discriminations about phenomena. Perhaps here lies the hardest test for science, because discriminations made possible by instruments such as microscopes lead to a thorough revision of thought about the surrounding world. This constant dynamic interaction between established knowledge and data produced by old and new instruments never ceases. Only recently it was possible through new microscope techniques actually to see the chromosomes of cells. To everyone's surprise the human complement of chromosomes was not 48, as had been maintained, but 46. Despite the fact that this discovery was made only recently, it has already led to a fundamental revision in biochemical genetics.

Quite similar careers can be traced for such instruments as cloud and bubble chambers (which make it possible for the physicist to trace movements of particles), X-ray machines (which have many different uses in displaying the insides of materials besides being able to affect them directly), or the humble stethoscope (which permits the physician to make an auditory discrimination between the workings of different parts of the body). In each case the role of the instrument ranges from simple application to certain obvious tasks to the making of new discoveries which in turn lead to fundamentally new syntheses of knowledge.

It should not be a surprise to learn, therefore, that the computer has already revised the way in which we perform or think about experiments and not just our approach to data processing. However, although the instrument itself, that is, the computer, is a relatively simple affair, the sorts of things it does are not as simple as enlarging a visual image. The simple task that is usually associated with computers, namely, computing, is done only in a very narrow sense. In the wider sense, computers are instruments of over-all process control, and calculating is really only a minor part of their activity. Process control involves a wide range of fully automated and semi-automated instruments and depends only in part on the physical characteristics of what is commonly called the computer. More critical is the logic with which the circuitry of the computer is made to control processes and react to outside activities. We must therefore direct our attention to the total instrument-computation-logic complex on which the processing capabilities of the computer rest.

COMPONENTS OF THE INSTRUMENT-COMPUTATION-LOGIC COMPLEX

The instrument-computation-logic complex consists of many pieces. Some of them have been around for some time, whereas others are newly invented. Some of them stand still; others move around and may be as far away as outer space or as hidden as an electrode can be in a living organism. Man also enters into this complex at many levels and in many ways. The total process starts with the discrimination of states of the environment and ends with some action that brings about a change in this state or preserves it the way it is. The process to be controlled might be only a segment of a wide range of possible activities or all of them. The total instrument-computation-logic complex consists thus of many parts.

SENSORS

On one end of the total complex are instruments and methods that respond to changes in the environment—however the environment may be defined. Of course, the most versatile instrument is the human nervous system. It can respond to mechanical, chemical, electrical, and even social changes, so that human responses may be taken as the basic instrument for differentiation. Over the years, instruments have been built which were originally intended to extend man's discriminatory abilities but which, themselves, can be viewed as sensing instruments or sensors in their own right. These devices respond to mechanical, chemical, or electrical changes in the environment by moving a pointer on a dial, changing the color of a display device, drawing a line in response to mechanical pull, making a noise, or even creating a smell or taste. Although these instruments are thought of usually as aids to human discrimination, it may not be necessary to involve a living observer directly. Modern methods make it possible to record events of interest automatically either in the form in which they occur or in some refined form or to record all the responses of a sensing instrument or only selected readings. The automatic recording of environmental events is one of the most important features of the total instrument-computation-logic complex.

From the perspective of the total process of automatic data gathering, it is useful to expand our view of the kinds of informations that may be sensed by instruments. Anything that gathers data and responds to information in the environment is a "sensor." Processes which extract automatically information already available on "records" may be classified as sensors. Written records have posed one of the big problems to scientific research, since abstracting information from them could be done heretofore only by man and then with difficulty and usually at a great cost. However, if written records are accumulated from the beginning in such form that they may be scanned or read automatically, then extracting data from them can be done easily and inexpensively.

Automation of records may be achieved in a number of ways. They may be organized and coded for easy transference onto Hollerith cards and then preserved on magnetic tape. Another method that is becoming increasingly valuable is the organization of records in such a form that they can be scanned by special instruments, usually referred to as *optical scanners*. If the many written documents of human activity can be made easily accessible by automatic sensing procedures, it will vastly enlarge the data base for many disciplines, such as sociology, psychology, or medicine, which now depend on a laborious evaluation of such records.

Advances in instrumentation also makes it possible to broaden the kinds of information that can be gathered automatically by specially devised sensors. If it would be valuable for sociologists to trace the movement of subjects, it is possible for instance, (although very expensive) to attach specially built instruments to the clothing of a study population which would then send out a constant stream of signals. These signals could be used to locate each subject at any moment. Many aspects of social interaction could be studied by keeping track of the physical location of individuals. Automatic sensing enlarges the study possibilities in many areas of health research, where special devices can be implanted into almost any organ or tissue of the anatomy, which is then permitted to function either normally or under stress. In this way the behavior of organs can be studied under conditions at which they usually could not be observed.

Finally, it should be kept in mind that man is constantly and variously involved in sensing activities. It is quite possible to think of a mode of recording changes in the environment in which an instrumental response initiates a reaction of a human observer, who then records some quality of his response in such a way that it can be recorded and subsequently recovered automatically. Another way in which man enters the semiautomatic sensing process is by making an adjustment to one or more sensing instruments in response to environmental changes.

TRANSMISSION

Information that has been gathered in the field or during the course of experiment must be recorded and transmitted to the location at which it is to be analyzed and/or where action is taken, depending on its import. Transmission is important because the observed changes of the environment may occur in places at which the analysis of the collected data is not convenient or not possible or the action that ought to be effected on the basis of the data occurs at a different place from where data is gathered.

The oldest mode of semiautomatic transmission was of course by messenger, of which the carrier pigeon is probably one of the most picturesque examples. The concept of sending information by messenger has been rapidly broadened with the invention of fast methods of transportation. Bits of paper or, more usefully, decks of punched cards and rolls of magnetic tape may be sent from one location to another quickly and at a small cost. Even faster transmission may be had by the use of direct communication devices such as the telephone and the radio. It is thus possible to record information or data by an automatic sensing instrument on the spot and to transmit them to a central location for analyses and action.

EFFECTORS

Man has invented a wondrous technology to do work for him. A variety of actions may be started by pulling a lever, pushing a button, rotating a wheel, or by some other means that switches on a preprogrammed complex of machine tools. All of these actions can also be initiated by special devices which may push buttons, pull levers, or rotate wheels automatically. In this way a simple response or a simple command can set off a complex series of actions that could send a probe to the moon, or control the aeration of blood in an artificial lung or the elimination of waste products from the blood in an artificial kidney.

PROCESSORS

What holds the sensor-to-effector network together and makes it work is the constant processing of information and initiation of alternative actions done by man. Processing and deciding is done on many levels. During sensing, decisions must be made on whether more data ought to be collected or whether the amount of information accumlated is sufficient. Also, the format of the data must be determined and, if necessary, information accumulated in one mode must be transferred to a different mode. Transmission of information involves constant decisions on what, how much, in which form, and at what speed it ought to be sent. Execution of activities, of course, involves not only a decision to initiate an action, but the activity itself may demand constant control during execution through evaluation of ongoing performance.

Processing as we understand it then, implies the analysis of information through display, calculation, and comparison, and finally the initiation of an action based on the result of the analysis. Usually it is possible to state well-defined rules by which analysis and decision functions are to be executed.

There are also elements in processing which are not subject to clearly defined rules. It is this part of data processing which cannot be automated.

The computer enters this constant feedback among sensing, transmitting, processing, and executing activities at various levels. The circuitry of which it consists is capable of manipulating information, that is, of calculating. Results of these calculations can be compared to previously stored values. Depending on the outcome of these comparisons, alternate circuits may be activated. These new circuits in turn may trigger further calculations, or they may be used to activate instruments which themselves will send information or signals to other instruments or initiate some other action. Hence the computer acts as a control instrument in the sensing transmission-execution sequence. It is this ability to "control" which makes computers such powerful tools and accounts for the rapid rise of computer-based technology. The term *computer* is a misnomer and tends to mislead. Computing is often the least important activity of computers. They are rather, instruments for process control. It is for this reason that they are referred to usually as *central processors*.

TYPES OF COMPUTERS OR PROCESSORS

The concept of a computer is certainly not completely new. Analog computers, such as the scale, have been around for a long time. Even the digital computer could be thought of as having its roots in such mechanical devices as the abacus. Computers were built during World War II by combining clerks and desk calculators into specific action sequences. Each clerk did very routine calculations, and results were passed back and forth on pieces of paper. These semiorganic computers were used predominantly to solve large systems of equations. A number of mechanical devices were also built during that time to replace the human operator and semiautomatic calculator for similar pruposes involving the inversion of large matrices. However, the central processor as we know it did not become possible until the early 1950's, when circuitry began to approach the reliability and efficiency we enjoy today.

To the layman the computer is a confusing collection of circuits and wires. Indeed, this is precisely what processors are. They are arrays of circuits that can do specific tasks rapidly and effortlessly. The tasks themselves are relatively simple.

Exploiting the basic ability to store and retrieve large amounts of information in the form of discrete numbers or other strings of characters, digital computers are equipped with logical circuits which allow them to manipulate stored information in several basic ways. First, the digital computer can count very rapidly and by capitalizing on its counting circuits, it can add, subtract, multiply, and divide. Second, it can shuffle information around in its electronic memory, rearrange it, destroy part or all of it, move it in or out of the processor, and generate new information. Third, and most intriguing, this machine can compare two strings of characters (be they letters, numbers, symbols, or any mixture thereof) and select alternate paths of subsequent action dictated by the equality or inequality of these strings.

Equipped with high-performance amplifiers, fast-acting switches and extensive control circuits, analog computers are able to perform mathematical operations on data transmitted to them as continuous voltage signals. In addition to the basic arithmetic operations (addition, subtraction, multiplication, division) analog computers are routinely equipped to produce time integrals and derivatives directly and can be designed to produce an outgoing voltage signal whose magnitude is related in any arbitrary (but consistent) manner to that coming in. Although these operations are all direct and, for all practical purposes, instantaneous, their use in processing analog data cannot be augmented by logical decision functions in the sense that such augmentation is possible on a digital system.

HYBRID COMPUTERS

The computers of the future are most likely the hybrid computers, in which the speed of analog computation and the ease of the digital computer in control of logic and decision making are combined. For the layman the distinction among digital, analog, and hybrid is largely meaningless. He really cares little whether a differential equation is evaluated or a data file classified and sorted through digital, analog, or hybrid methods, as long as the answer he gets is accurate and can be obtained rapidly and at a small cost. Arguing about the merits of analog, digital, or hybrid processors betrays unnecessary partisanship. For the outsider the problem is really restricted to specifying calculational and logical rules. How these logical and calculational tasks are best realized are problems for special breeds of engineers and computerniks.

COMPUTERS AS ORGANIZERS AND CONTROLLERS

Viewing the computer as collections of circuits and electronic switches is, of course, only a small part of the total story. The physical component of the machine, generally referred to as *hardware*, are capable of shuttling electrical current back and forth, turning switches on and off, and changing the charges on magnetic particles. This hardware is converted into the instrument of process control by sequencing the shuttling back and forth of electrical currents so that not only does its activity result in meaningful answers to complex problems but it also enables man to exercise control over the very activity of this circuitry with relative ease and through a language-like command structure. The logic that is used to elicit meaningful and effective actions and functions from the hardware and to control it is referred to as *software*.

To say that computers are guided by "programs" is one of the most magnificent understatements. Circuitry can understand only one language, that built from the wiring diagram. Providing direction for a large number of cohesive and relatively complex series of actions from a computer via the language of the wiring diagram would be forbiddingly expensive and slow, since it could be done practically only by those individuals who had been trained in electronic engineering. What makes the computer a useful tool, however, are layers upon layers of software which allow the establishment of effective and inexpensive control over the wiring in languages that can be mastered with relatively little effort by almost all intelligent individuals.

Two different types of software packages may be distinguished. Although similar in structure, they differ widely in function. The first package is that of translator languages. Because it is so terribly difficult and costly (both in terms of time and salaries) to instruct computers in the language that they understand (i.e., machine language), the logical abilities of the computer and its processing speed are utilized to write programs that translate statements, made more or less in the vernacular, to machine language format. The computer equipped with such a translator is used to "assemble" the program written with mnemonic commands and referring to variables by names rather than as specific circuit addresses. This type of program is called an *assembler*. A step further and another layer of software away from machine languages is the *compiler*. In this program a single statement sets off a series of responses, so that a single command in the vernacular will cause the assembly of a program which executes a number of steps. In its simplest form such a compiler statement might be $Y = \log X$, and the compiler would assemble the program that would take the log of whatever value X was as well as assemble a machine language program in which Y and X would be referred to in terms of addresses rather than variable names. The concept of compilers can be extended immensely, since translating programs can be written to assemble any complex series of steps and then to rewrite them in the machine language in response to a single command. When a compiler language becomes so complex that total units of analyses can be called out by a single command, it is referred to as a *programming environment*.

Compilers save immense amounts of time for qualified programmers (including scientific users who know how to program) in describing the sort of process they wish the computer to execute. They have intricate logic and are difficult and expensive to write. It is, therefore, no surprise to anyone that programs have been invented that enable the systems programmer to specify and write compilers. These compiler-writing languages are called *compiler-compilers*, or *meta-languages*, and we may carry this into further complexities by thinking of "compiler-compiler-compilers," and so on.

The need for writing programs in a simple user or problem-oriented language has not been the only motive for extending software concepts. Since it is obviously expensive to operate computers, it becomes very important that the machine should be usefully occupied with processing as much as possible. Only in this way can the cost per unit of computation be reduced. The big cost factor in exploiting the power of the computer is caused by the slowness of most devices that transmit information to or from the processor relative to internal processing speeds. Included most prominently in these devices are human operators, whose actions are slow and whose errors may and usually do cause large wastes of useful computer time. There appears to be little sense in purchasing time on a machine capable of performing 500,000 calculations a second and letting a human operator fumble with a deck of cards for five minutes prior to submitting a correct sequence of program and data to the input source. Cost of computation would be immense if the procedure of shuffling information to and from the processor did not occur at speeds near those of processing. To achieve desirable speeds, input and output are usually regulated by a smaller computer subservient to the larger machine or by part of the computer's circuitry set aside for this purpose so that the main processor is used to take information for computation from tape or disc or other fast-access peripheral devices and put answers back on them. In this way the expensive part of the computer complex can be occupied mostly with processing, while the cheaper peripheral instruments can prepare programs and data in a form that can be quickly absorbed and quickly worked upon by the main processor. In this sequence it is, of course, necessary to replace the human operator as much as possible and to leave decisions as to when a program will execute, when it will not execute, when it will need a particular part of the programming system, when the next program should be called in, etc., up to the machine.

The control over the workings of the machine and the complex of peripheral and central equipment calls for very sophisticated layers of software which guide the computer at near computer speed through its different monitoring, sequencing, and decision tasks.

There exists a dilemma here which has not been easy to deal with. The need to decrease the cost and time of writing programs and to make it possible for programming to be done on a broad scale as well as the needs of decreasing computing time and costs require the preparation of such a tremendous amount of sophisticated software that most of the talent and skills that can deal with these programming problems are now occupied and will continue to be so within the foreseeable future. Thus initial cost of adequate software is very large, and unless this is recognized the business or scientific user may not get the desired service from the computer.

Although the construction of the sophisticated logic, lumped under the prosaic name of software, may have been motivated by the mundane needs to cut cost and replace hard-to-come-by programmers, this effort has led to important advances in the utilization of computers. The existing software, that is, the programming packages that control writing of programs and their execution, demonstrate two important features in the computer-logic complex.

1. It is possible for the computer-logic complex to interpret a command given in almost any type of language and to translate it to a sequence of commands or a series of actions in some other mode.
2. The computer-logic complex can replace the human hands, eyes, and brains when alternatives to different situations can be expressed as precise rules. Just as with differences in circuitry that distinguish types of computers, the user should not be concerned too much with the distinction between hardware and software. It is possible and often desirable to replace useful software packages or features by hardware. In this way the speed of computation and processing is again increased considerably. It is not really the concern of the user whether a command is executed by specifically designed circuitry or by logical manipulation of general-purpose circuitry. But what the user must know firmly is the kinds of controls that processors can exercise over their own actions and, by extension, over the action of other instruments. Only in this way can he understand the role computers can play in the total experimental situation and exploit their power.

A soft landing on another planet, as done by the Surveyor device, is possible only because its sensing instruments are controlled by a processor which evaluates the information sensed by them instantaneously and controls the fire of retro-rockets in the pattern that makes it possible for the device to land. Note that landing a spacecraft involves a series of actions which a human would perform perhaps by the seat of his pants (as the saying goes in pilot circles). This demonstrates again that many human actions can be reduced to logical sequences leading to a choice of alternatives according to rules. These can be made to work even though the human nervous system is not direclty involved.

The instrument-processing-logic complex is capable of a large variety of actions and controls, involving choices, decisions, flexibility, and communications with humans at various levels. Such a complex can be looked at as a semi-intelligent servant. We may think of this total complex as the robot of science fiction come to life. The conglomeration of consoles and sensing probes, some of them perhaps whirling in space or embedded in flesh, may not look like the tin man of science fiction vintage. Nevertheless, a good working perspective for scientists, businessmen, military leaders, theoreticians, or men of practical affairs would be to look at the aid provided by this total complex as coming from a clever servant who, in a tireless way and without errors, is capable of aiding at any intellectual or physical task— limited only by our ingenuity to make it operate at the desired level of sophistication.

THE INESCAPABLE FORCE TO USE THE
INSTRUMENT-PROCESSING-LOGIC COMPLEX

There are three compelling motives for undertaking the expenses and troubles involved in constructing robot systems and shedding the sweat necessary to learn how to control them.

1. *The instrument-processing-logic complex can do things man cannot do.* It can perform actions man is either incapable of doing himself or that would be too expensive or risky to perform in any other than an automated fashion. Sending a probe to the moon is one example. Analyzing signals from an electrode inserted into the heart or kidney of a living organism is another. Some jobs that could be done by hand are nevertheless so time-consuming that they could not be done in practice without automatic processing. Inverting a 100×100 matrix or matching all income tax returns to bank deposits and dividends for the country as a whole are actions that are possible in theory but not in practice without automation.

2. *The instrument-processing-logic complex can do most comparable actions at a considerably lesser cost than can man.* This is sometimes not so obvious since once the automation complex is built and the power of the computer is available, we usually attempt to perform activities which are not comparable to the sort of things done when computers were not available. However, a point-for-point comparison of particular types of operations shows clearly that the expenses in letting the processor do it are very often a tiny fraction of the expenses in letting a human do it. Of course, such cost comparisons are restricted to the sort of things computers can do. There are certain actions that are cheaper if done by man and probably will remain that way.

3. *The instrument-processing-logic complex has the ability to exercise "control" over a complex series of activities.* In this way the executive, the scientist, the military leader, and others can obtain an overview of their enterprises and can control the many complex actions involved in their execution. In many ways, possibilities for over-all process control may be the most crucial quality added by computers to our world.

EXPANDING THE SCOPE OF DATA PROCESSING

It is quite clear that the total automation complex provides a multitude of data from faraway or difficult to reach places which heretofore had not been available. New additions to the fund of knowledge do not necessarily compel changes in methods of evaluating them. There are, however, new and interrelated aspects consequent to the automation of acquisition of information which do force considerable expansion of and modification in our views of how information is to be processed.

INCREASING THE NUMBERS OF OBSERVATIONS

Complexity and cost of experiments tended to hold the total number of observations down to a "reasonable" quantity before automation reached its present stage of efficiency. Investigators were limited in many ways in providing themselves with adequate numbers of observations. The cost for an additional unit of observation usually went up. For instance, questionnaires could be handled without a big organization if the sample of respondents was kept small. Large numbers of individuals sampled for questioning demanded the construction of a combine devoted to coordinating the activities of many interviewers. This is not true where information can be obtained automatically or even semiautomatically. There are instances today in which records from many sources and about many individuals may be available already in a form that is "IBM compatible" (i.e., a form that can be read automatically) so that large information sources may be searched automatically for relevant data. Also, optical scanning and other aids in translating records can reduce the cost of analyzing large numbers of questionnaires to a fraction of what it was formerly.

Observations in experimental sciences often had to be prepared carefully and laboriously by hand. This is especially true for the science of physiology. Prior to observing factors in the regulation of blood pressure and heart activity, it was necessary to "prepare" an animal for observation by going through complex surgical procedures. The number of observations that could be obtained after the preparation had been finished were relatively few, since the animal did not survive long, as a rule, and since the duration of an experimental action (like drawing a sample of blood) lasted for some time. At present it is possible to insert electronic probes into living tissue and obtain a constant stream of signals representing perhaps very much the same information that can be obtained from a "preparation," but, since the animal lives longer and since each signal may represent the equivalent of what used to be the result of a long and tedious physical or chemical procedure, the number of observations available per animal has increased immensely. There are other examples in which continuous records, such as electrocardiograms or electromyograms, had to be laboriously digitized by hand and actual numerical values assigned by visual interpolation. This is a slow and expensive process, yielding questionable accuracy. With automatic translation and digitization procedures, it is possible and relatively inexpensive to obtain as many as 100,000 digital values per second of recorded response.

The ability to obtain large samples inexpensively not only requires new techniques and approaches to process them, but also has very real consequences for sampling procedures. Obviously, the need to make estimates about average pulse pressure disappears if numbers of observed pulse pressures are extremely large. When such is the case, the computed average pulse pressure is no longer so much an estimate but constitutes rather the real value of pulse pressure, so that the need for statements describing the confidence of the estimate based on the size of the sample might largely disappear (but not the need for defending the confidence in the validity of the sampling procedure). In general, many of the summarizing procedures of which classical statistics avail themselves become insensitive when large data files are used. Finally, modern display devices open new doors for inspection and review of information. These may eliminate the necessity in many instances to make additional estimates of population parameters based on small numbers. It turns out to be more helpful to the investigator to inspect and study many different graphic displays showing the data in all their richness than to reduce this wealth to a few summary numbers, such as the average.

MULTIVARIABILITY

Even more important than sheer number from the data processing point of view is the ability to include, with little additional effort or cost, observations on many variables during the course of the experiment or observational effort. It is quite clear that so long as the investigator had only enough time to make a small number of measurements, he tended to limit himself to those observations that were central to his problem and had neither time nor ability to obtain observations about correlated variables in which he might have been interested, but which, under the circumstances, he had to ignore. With automation this picture is markedly changed. A number of electrodes placed in the animal at various places might give the experimenter simultaneous information on blood flow, oxygenation, pulse pressure, temperature, electrical activity in the cortex, and about many other variables which he thinks may be of importance to him. These observations can often be obtained without increasing the cost of the experiment. Modern recorders, for instance, make it possible for the scientist to record on many different channels simultaneously. In addition, multiplexing and the ability to let the computer unscramble mixed data files enlarge the number of variables on which simultaneous observations can be made continuously without an appreciable parallel increase in cost.

The same multivariable possibilities exist in the realm of the social sciences. Records are being accumulated through many sources. These may be governmental agencies, insurance companies, accounting offices, businesses, and many more. It may thus be possible to combine and search through various large record files to obtain observation on individuals from many points of view. Sociologists could have access to observations of such multiple variables describing the interaction between humans in a greater richness than may be possible through the usual laborious data accumulation techniques.

It ought not to be a shocking surprise to learn that we are not as yet able to deal satisfactorily with the multivariate situation. The numerical techniques called for in dealing with multivariate data are extremely complex. A few methods which had been developed before the time of computers had to be based on many numerical shortcuts and required a highly motivated experimenter who was willing to undergo laborious computations on semiautomatic machines. This circumstance hardly served as a stimulus for the development of new multivariate analyses. Also, the occasions to use multivariate analyses were relatively restricted. Experiments just did not accumulate large masses of multivariate data. Now we are presented all of a sudden with the necessity of dealing with large and multiphasic data files without really having adequate tools in the armamentarium of classical analysis. In most ways, multivariate analysis is still more of a potential than an actuality.

REDUCING THE COST OF ERRORS

We have already pointed to the change in the utility of the additional observations on the same variables or of an addition to the number of variables on which observations are sought. This utility can be viewed not only in terms of money or cost, but also in time and effort of the experimenter. There are yet other aspects of utility, namely, the costs of errors of observation and analysis.

As experimenters become tired or distracted, their readings may be incorrect. Transferring readings from the laboratory notebook to a sheet on which calculations are done may lead to errors. These errors are costly in that they make demands on the funds and time needed to obtain other useful experimental results. If the answer he gets should be wrong because of investigator or calculation error, it may lead the scientist to devote time and effort to another experiment or analysis which is completely uncalled for.

This does not mean that computers and automated data gathering systems do not make errors. However, there are so many cross checks and double checks possible in automating data acquisition, transmission, and analysis that the likelihood of error is largely decreased. Also, if computers make errors they will usually be large and easy to spot. On the other hand, investigators' errors are usually small and difficult to ferret out.

One other source of extremely costly error resides in the memory factor and the use of records. Data gathered from interviewing informants are necessary for both medical and social science research. In both cases one large area of bias is the posssibility that a subject fails to remember exactly the diseases he had or the way he reacted in a particular situation. Sometimes records are available in profusion (as may be the case in medicine), but abstracting information from them may be extremely costly and in addition may give rise to the possibilities of many different errors. If these records are in a form that enables them to be read automatically, much of this type of error may be eliminated, or interviewers' veracity and reliablity may be established.

AUTOMATION AND ANALYSIS

The time needed to complete a particular mathematical procedure or the time needed to permit other types of comparisons, accumulation of tables, and other means by which data can be evaluated may be simply forbidding if the task must be done through human labor. Computers and available peripheral display devices can do many of these jobs in a short period of time and so enlarge immensely the possibilities for analyses at the investigator's disposal.

The ability to analyze data at a lower cost and with a smaller error means, of course, that a variety of procedures and approaches to analysis can be devised and exploited which were simply not possible without computers. Classical statistical and applied mathematical procedures very often had to be designed with an eye toward simplicity of calculation. Analytical techniques designed to sift out scientific information had to compromise and make assumptions about linearity or homogeneity of observations or about other properties of data that were sometimes actually known to be wrong. However, these assumptions had to be made because computational procedures for nonlinear and inhomogeneously distributed observations were simply so forbidding that they could not be undertaken realistically by hand. Scientists thus settled for a compromise that is not necessary now, since they can proceed, at least in theory, with analytic techinques that meet the scientific necessity of their situation.

CONTROL OF ANALYSIS

The increase in complexity of large multivariate data files produced through the process of automating experimentation represents an increase in experimental power only if these multitudes of data can be explored for what meanings might be contained in them. Even the most carefully planned experiments seldom result in answers that are so clear-cut that further analysis is unnecessary. Interpretation of the outcome of experiments is often difficult. When events are influenced by many different interacting and interdependent antecedent conditions, when variability not only is the rule but is often unpredictable, when precision of measurement is unusually poor, in short, when the normal processes and problems of empirical science prevail, the investigator is usually confronted by considerable puzzles which he has to put together. Screening of results and exploiting them is a task that calls for considerable skill and ingenuity.

The computer offers powerful tools to the investigators. Analyses that have proved their worth and usefulness are placed at his fingertips to be consulted without undue labor. It does not really matter whether the analyses were terribly laborious or easy to perform manually. So far as the investigator is concerned, once they are properly programmed, he may call for them as needed and not as he has the time to devote to their execution. Beyond conventional analytic practices or relatively simple statistics, the investigator can utilize with equal ease analyses that are based on complex mathematical procedures. Such techniques have been eschewed by empirical scientists in the past partly because their execution was terribly involved and time-consuming and partly also because the lack of familiarity with the language of mathematics prevalent among biologists and social scientists often made it impossible for them to utilize such very convenient tools. With the computer, the obstacle of complexity is largely resolved. It might be replaced by a problem of cost, since complex techniques could be expensive to program and may consume more computer time than it is within the power of the experimenter to purchase. However, if the purposes of the experiment are legitimate, the proper funds for the analysis of its data ought to exist.

ANALYSIS USING DISPLAY DEVICES

A variety of output devices exist that permit the investigator to call for "graphic" or "pictorial" display of data from a single variable or from many variables in some combined form. Such displays can be obtained from high-speed printers very inexpensively and very conveniently and also, at a greater cost, from on-line electronic scopes. The investigator need not wonder what the distribution of values for a variable might look like. He can call for the computer to display this distribution to him in the form of a picture. He need not hesitate to look at a number of graphs combining two or three variables or at multiple breakdowns and classifications in tabular form. The ease with which he can obtain graphic displays vastly enlarges the possibility for the investigator to make decisions about the sort of analyses he should want done on his data. But perhaps more importantly, as the investigator gains experience with pictorially manipulating a number of variables through visual displays, a process which was not possible as long as pictorial representation of data was so costly to produce, he develops brand-new techniques.

EXPANDING THE VARIETY OF NUMERICAL SOLUTIONS

The great ease with which numerical methods can be applied has sparked the most obvious applications of computers to the analyses of data, so that routine numerical techniques are within easy grasp of the experimenter. There exist program libraries that will do most statistical routines regardless of missing data and other shortcomings. Best known of these are probably BMD, MEDCOMP, and STATPAK, but many other fine libraries of computer programs for statistical data manipulation, can also be obtained.

An important expansion of numerical methods is into the realm of experimental controls. Procedures are being devised by which confounding among variables can be resolved through mathematical means. The techniques that must be used may have to be fitted to the individual circumstance of the experiment. However, once this has been determined, a large amount of investigators' time and experimental funds may be preserved by relying heavily on proper mathematical manipulations rather than purely on more costly experimental controls. In most instances the proper uses of numerical techniques in place of experimental controls will demand a greater sophistication in the area of applied mathematics from the empirical investigators than many of them possess now.

Finally, there is the benefit that all experimenters will reap from the intense work that has been going on since computers were invented in the development of new and better computational procedures for existing numerical methods. These benefits show up in the forms of shorter computer time, more precise approximations, solutions for cases with complex distributions or for defining multiple relationships that lack linearity or other mathematical niceties.

HEURISTIC SOLUTIONS

The numerical techniques that were used in the past were derived predominantly from formal mathematical developments. This is only natural since formal postulational methods may permit the mathematician to derive simple numerical solutions as theorems from more general statements. In this way simple calculational formulas were devised which provided answers to such questions as what the slope of a best-fitting line was or what weights should be assigned to a series of interacting factors.

The computer now makes possible a particular type of technique which may be thought of fundamentally as "trial and error." Those who have used trial and error as a powerful method to solve some problems are aware of the laborious work involved which often makes trial and error impractical. The speed of computers, however, combined with logical and systematic guidance, make it quite possible to resolve complex numerical and non-numeric problems by trial and error techniques, which are sometimes referred to also as brute force methods and which constitute the approach underlying so-called *heuristic* solutions. Such techniques may be used when formal mathematical or even clean numerical solutions may not be possible at all, such as finding clusters of variables that are associated in large data files.

SIMULATION

Simulation is actually the building of a model that has the properties (in a simplified form) which we think exist in some aspects of the world around us. Results of simulated processes can be compared to results of experiments. Simulation enables the investigator to clarify in his own mind what variables might have decisive effects on a particularly complex phenomenon that he wishes to evaluate. The geneticist may build himself a variety of models of different degrees or complexities of "heterogeneity" and "incomplete penetration" to see which would most closely resemble the type of distribution of inherited characteristics which he has observed. The use of modeling in general has not received nearly as much attention as it ought to in the world of social sciences and biology, not only because the sufficient knowledge of mathematics was not present in these two disciplines. Simulation without either an analog or a digital computer is a terribly difficult undertaking. It is true that many engineering problems were resolved by simulation without recourse to computers. Simulation could be used to study the dynamics of fluids by connecting series of pipes and running a fluid through them. Such techniques are of lesser value and usefulness to the social sciences and to biology, although they help demonstrate the value of the general approach.

AUTOMATED SEARCH TECHNIQUES

Perhaps the most important development in the control of data analysis is the invention of programming systems that sift data through a sequence of steps, making decisions along the way of what analysis to perform next, and communicating the results of this process to the investigator in a form that guides him on subsequent steps This ability of computers to "look" at data and to report to investigators on what might possibly be most "interesting" to them is a process which has yet to be studied very intensely. However, a number of very useful data screening processes are already available, and their value in culling important relations from experimental and observational results has been demonstrated. Through the use of the many automatic aids the investigator can apply more of his creative abilities to the analysis of data as he is freed from the sheer drudgery that is involved in the manipulation of numbers and symbols. The investigator also gains better perspective of the richness and variety of his data. Of course, it again requires application of creative power to devise improved methods and means by which this wealth can be tapped. The investigator who learns to control the instrument-processing-logic complex will play a crucial role in this exiting work.

TOWARD THE MODERN POINT OF VIEW

It must be kept in mind that we are just emerging from a world in which computers (or rather, central processors) and robots (the total complex of instrument-computation-logic) did not exist. The armamentarium with which the scientist approached data was designed to help him in a world in which his powers of analysis were rather limited. It would be unreasonable to expect that this large complement of needed products that can be created only by large amounts of human ingenuity and sweat would rise overnight, as Venus from the foam, as soon as computers came on the scene. The wealth of programmed processing techniques that exists today is misleading. We must remember that many of these techniques are simply carry-overs from precomputer days and have been programmed because it is more convenient to use computers for them than not to. Really new advances and expansions of the universe of analytic methods are relatively few. We may expect that during the next century ideas of how to deal with data will be changing constantly. Some dominant features of this change are apparent already, and it is unlikely that these will change in the future.

1. The preparation of scientific investigations must be such that they produce data in a form capable of being processed automatically. This is not really a question of convenience any more, nor does it appear to be a question of choice. The scientist has a a moral obligation to produce for the same amount of investment, however cost may be defined, an optimal amount of information. He may not be the one who needs all this information, but the group of investigators of which he is a part may. A serious moral question can be raised about the scientist who does not avail himself of techniques that exist so that the results of his work are relatively meager when compared to what they could and ought to be.
2. It is necessary to review constantly and evaluate critically the available practical tools of data analysis. This is true not only for mathematical techniques but also for new hardware developments which make it possible to revise systems of analytic procedures. One excellent example

comes from the field of radiation therapy. As long as distributions of doses resulting from treatment could not be properly displayed to the radiotherapist, there was really to need for him to go through complex computational procedures unless he dealt with a very perplexing case. However, with the development of on-line consoles and visual display devices which permit the therapist to sketch his treatment plan and immediately obtain a three-dimensional view of the resulting dose distribution, he would be terribly remiss if he were not to avail himself of this tool for his patients on an individual basis. The same holds true for the investigator who now finds that he can evaluate his data very quickly and easily by making use of new hardware and software possibilities.

3. Finally, there is the new concept of letting the logical and computational abilities of the processor screen data when we do not have the time or ability to do this ourselves. This leads of necessity to a renewed and rigorous examination of the rules underlying crucial decisions in the analysis of data.

PROBLEMS

1. State examples and sketch a graphic presentation of a single and a multivariate function.

2. Which statements would you call mathematical functions, and which ones would be relations in our sense?
   (a) $Y = 3X + 5$.
   (b) $Y > X$.
   (c) Height is a function of nuitrition.
   (d) Son is related to mother.
   (e) The distance traveled by a car is a function of road conditions and traffic.

3. You have coded a questionnaire on a patient's history.
   (a) Compare differences between numbers used for (1) identification of subject, (2) defining sex, (3) describing daily temperature, (4) giving age.
   (b) Can you draw graphs among all the four items in (a)? Would all graphs you draw look the same?

4. List examples of "instruments" used by physicians, sociologists, psychologists, economists, geneticists, and other scientists. Compare the "numbers" resulting from the application of these instruments with each other.

5. List sources of errors that can influence a scientific observation. Compare man as an error source to errors produced by instruments.

6. List all general steps that have to be followed to control the flow of work from the inception of an experiment to its final execution and the analysis of its data. Suggest how automation can be of help for different steps.

7. Is psychodrama simulation? Give examples of simulation in biological or sociological research.

2 COMPUTING HARDWARE

Note to the Reader: This chapter may be omitted by the reader already familiar with the existing instrumentation for automatic collection of data, with the manipulation of data, and with the many peripheral devices that may be used to display information. Parts of this chapter may also be bypassed by the reader whose needs tend to be more computational and numerical.

It is misleading to attach any particular visual image to the term *computer* or *computing system*. With today's constantly shrinking subminiature circuits and continually improving long-distance communications techniques, the computing system may be a compact console sitting on a desk or an octopus of interconnected electronic gear reaching tentacles onto various continents and perhaps onto a vehicle streaking towards Mars. Tomorrow a computer may be a small metal box in somebody's pocket. Despite their diversity, the multitude of systems lumped under the name "computer" can be examined quite adequately in general terms. All of these systems share a commonality of basic functions which can be categorized sequentially as the sensing of a phenomenon and its transmission in proper form to a central component (processor) which manipulates it in some known and predetermined manner, sending it on to some effecting mechanism which acts on the results of such manipulations. (A general representation of this sequence is shown schematically in Figure 2.1).

DIGITAL COMPUTING SYSTEMS

The vast majority of information processing machines in use today are classified as digital computing systems in that they are designed to handle

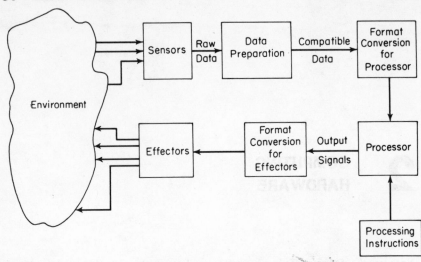

Fig. 2.1. Schematic representation of information acquisition and processing.

data in the form of individual numbers or characters, represented by discrete electronic pulses. Although these pulses are very short in duration and follow each other at intervals measured in mere billionths of a second, each piece or unit of information is still a separate and distinct entity and is handled as such. This mode of operation is basically different from one in which information is received and negotiated as continuous currents (analog mode), an area which is discussed separately.

THE CENTRAL PROCESSOR

Many people often misuse the term "digital computer" when actually referring to the central processor. For our purposes, we shall define the central processor as that component of a digital computing system (regardless of whether the separation is physical or conceptual) in which is contained the logical circuitry that allows the system to be implanted with the ability to execute a particular type of processing assignment. This capability is made possible by two basic properties of central processors: an internal memory or storage which can retain information in some coded form indefinitely, and the mechanism for locating and retrieving any and all of this information at any time or in any order, at the request of the user. *Information* in this context consists not only of data to be operated on but also instructions defining the exact nature of the manipulations to be performed. Once a particular set of instructions has been implanted in a portion of the processor's memory, activation of the processor causes these instructions to be executed in a prearranged sequence that can be repeated any number of times until such instructions are replaced with another set.

Fig. 2.2(A). Ferrite core memory (4096 16 bit words). *Courtesy Electronic Memories Inc.*

Fig. 2.2(B). Thin film memory. *Courtesy Fabritek Corporation.*

35

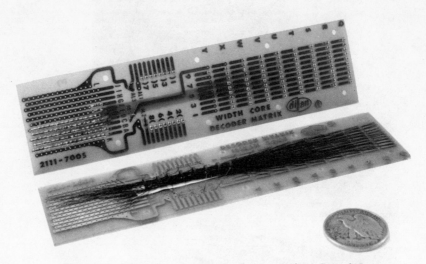

Fig. 2.2(C). Magnetic rope memory. *Courtesy DI/AN Controls Inc.*

MEMORY

Information is represented and stored in a processor as a series of electronic pulses applied to electromagnetic elements called *bits*. Physically, these bits may be tiny doughnut-shaped ferrite cores, a tiny particle or thin film of magnetic substance deposited on a flat surface, or a minute length of specially plated wire (Figure 2.2). Each bit is supported by accompanying circuitry that causes it to react to incoming pulses by being magnetized in one of two alternate directions. An element acting in this fashion is said to be *bistable* and in this respect is directly analogous to a spring-loaded light switch which can be positioned "on" or "off" with no intended ability to represent any other status. (In fact, the two states of a bit of memory are also represented in this manner.) By linking these bits together in groups, it becomes possible to devise a coding system wherein each character (numeral, digit, or symbol) is represented by a unique sequence of "ons" and "offs." Once processor designers define such a code, they can devise the accompanying circuitry that will send the proper set of pulses to a desired string of bits in memory. Although a number of such codes are presently in use, newer equipment is designed to use one of the two codes shown in Figure 2.3. In these systems a series of eight bits (referred to as a *byte*) is used as a standard string and every legally acceptable character is represented by some combination of eight bits. This provides the ability to recognize as many as 256 different characters by assigning each to a unique combination. (In earlier models a byte having a length of six bits was standard, thus limiting the character set to 64.)

Another more systematic way of representing the status of each bit in

Figure 2.3. Internal computer representation of written characters. *Courtesy IBM Corp.*

SYMBOL	ASCII Representation	EBCDIC Representation
blank	0100000	01000000
0	0110000	11110000
1	0110001	11110001
2	0110010	11110010
3	0110011	11110011
4	0110100	11110100
5	0110101	11110101
6	0110110	11110110
7	0110111	11110111
8	0111000	11111000
9	0111001	11111001
A	1000001	11000001
B	1000010	11000010
C	1000011	11000011
D	1000100	11000100
E	1000101	11000101
F	1000110	11000110
G	1000111	11000111
H	1001000	11001000
I	1001001	11001001
J	1001010	11010001
K	1001011	11010010
L	1001100	11010011
M	1001101	11010100
N	1001110	11010101
O	1001111	11010110
P	1010000	11010111
Q	1010001	11011000
R	1010010	11011001
S	1010011	11100010
T	1010100	11100011
U	1010101	11100100

SYMBOL	ASCII Representation	EBCDIC Representation
V	1010110	11100101
W	1010111	11100110
X	1011000	11100111
Y	1011001	11101000
Z	1011010	11101001
a	1100001	10000001
b	1100010	10000010
c	1100011	10000011
d	1100100	10000100
e	1100101	10000101
f	1100110	10000110
g	1100111	10000111
h	1101000	10001000
i	1101001	10001001
j	1101010	10010001
k	1101011	10010010
l	1101100	10010011
m	1101101	10010100
n	1101110	10010101
o	1101111	10010110
p	1110000	10010111
q	1110001	10011000
r	1110010	10011001
s	1110011	10100010
t	1110100	10100011
u	1110101	10100100
v	1110110	10100101
w	1110111	10100110
x	1111000	10100111
y	1111001	10101000
z	1111010	10101001
!	0100001	01011010

SYMBOL	ASCII Representation	EBCDIC Representation
"	0100010	01111111
#	0100011	01111011
$	0100100	01011011
%	0100101	01101100
&	0100110	01010000
'	0100111	01111101
(	0101000	01001101
)	0101001	01011101
*	0101010	01011100
+	0101011	01001110
,	0101100	01101011
-	0101101	01100000
.	0101110	01001011
/	0101111	01100001
:	0111010	01111010
;	0111011	01011110
<	0111100	01001100
=	0111101	01111110
>	0111110	01101110
?	0111111	01101111
@	1000000	01111100
[	1011011	01001111
\	1011100	01011111
]	1011101	01101101
^	1011110	01101111
_	1011111	01111111
←	10100000	01001100
↑	10111011	01001111
↓	10111100	01011101
¢	10111101	01101101
{	10111110	01101111
≥	10111111	01111111

the processor's memory is to use "0" and "1" in lieu of OFF and ON. With this type of nomenclature the status of each bit in a string of bits can be considered as a value in a numerical system in which the operating base is 2. This *binary* number system is in every way analogous to our standard decimal base with regard to the construction of numerical values and magnitudes. For example, if we write the three-digit number 110 as an ordinary decimal number, we are implying the following:

$$110_{10} = 1 \times 10^2 + 1 \times 10^1 + 0 \times 10^0 = 100 + 10 + 0$$

These same three digits (110) when used in the binary system have the same representation, except that instead of the base being 10, we substitute 2:

$$110_2 = 1 \times 2^2 + 1 \times 2^1 + 0 \times 2^0$$

Thus, the three-digit binary number 110 would have a decimal equivalent value of $4 + 2 + 0$, or 6.

Processor Size. The amount of memory, that is, the number of characters that can be stored at any one time, serves as the index of processor size. The three categories given below are in present use:

Classification	Memory size
Small	Less than 5000 characters
Medium	5000–131,000 characters
Large	Greater than 131,000 characters

Capacities exceeding one million characters are in current use, and sizes running into the tens of billions are well under development.

Cataloguing and Retrieving Stored Information. The processor can find any or all of the informations stored in memory by being designed so that its memory is permanently subdivided into pigeonholes, with each individual memory unit having its own assigned location (*address*). For some machines, each byte has an individual address. For others, several bytes (ranging from two to as many as twelve) are strung together to form *words*, and a unique address is assigned to each word. Depending on the type of usage, each form of memory organization has its advantages. Processors with individually addressable bytes are more versatile in that any number may be linked together by the user and referred to by a single name (*variable word length*). On the other hand, a fixed word length machine, in which each address always refers to a constant number of bytes, may operate more efficiently for many types of computation because of its basic ability to handle several bytes simultaneously instead of one by one in sequence. Each permanent location is designated by a specific number (*absolute address*) which is basic for that machine in that it is built right into logical circuitry. Thus, any reference to a given absolute location in a processor, for example, will always direct the logical circuitry to the same physical string of bits in the memory assembly. In large processors, it is more convenient to use a multilevel scheme for structuring the assignment of memory locations so that the entire storage area is divided into segments (*pages*) and each permanent location is designated by a page number and the location within that page. This type of organization is particularly useful for processing systems designed to handle multiple jobs such that information from more than one source could be in memory at a particular instant in time.

Retrieval of Stored Information. The logic supporting a processor's memory is such that the time required to find data stored at a given location is a function only of the physical characteristics of the system and has nothing to do with the location in memory which is being referenced. This attribute is known as *random access* and the "access time" is used as a general indicator of a processor's speed. Most present day commercially available processors have access times ranging from 1 to 15 microseconds. A number of large processors, used primarily for the solution of nuclear and aerospace problems, are built with access times as low as 100 nanoseconds (.1 microsecond), and custom hardware having even greater speed can be obtained.

Logical Circuit Construction. The thousandfold growth in processor speed over the past ten years is due in large measure to the revolutionary advances in the design and physical construction of logical circuitry. The first available processors were built with vacuum tube circuits (such as in Figure 2.4a), which limited processor speed because of their high inertia. A medium-sized processor required several thousand of these tubes and, therefore, was subject to frequent breakdowns. When solid state technology was developed, tubes were supplanted by transistorized printed circuits (as in Figure 2.4b), resulting in a marked increase in speed, reliability, and

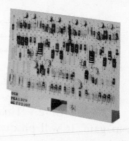

Fig. 2.4. Digital computer logic components. *Courtesy IBM Corp.*

tolerance to ambient operating conditions. Startup and shutdown became virtually instantaneous, and processor malfunction decreased to a point where the down time (time during which the computing system was unavailable for use because of malfunction) was largely dependent on the reliability of the electromechanical peripheral components rather than that of the processor itself. More recently, monolithic integrated circuits (see Figure 2.4c) have been introduced and are being used in virtually all of the newer processing systems. This third basic change in processor structure (referred to by many as a third generation of computers) has allowed processing speed to increase to a point where the time required for an electronic pulse to traverse the short length of wire connecting two neighboring circuits can, in many cases, no longer be neglected. Efforts to overcome this barrier are under way, and one of the major solutions being explored is the development of circuit groups which are stacked on one another so that the distance between adjacent circuits is several molecules wide rather than fractions of a millimeter.

BASIC LOGICAL FUNCTIONS

Logical components in a digital processor are usually built up from a relatively small number of well-tested basic circuits. Although the pulses transmitted to and from the circuits may vary in type and size, most of them are bistable, so that their state can be represented by 1 or 0. In a particular circuit, 1 might represent some specific positive voltage and 0 a particular negative value. In other components, 1 might mean a pulse, and 0 the absence of a pulse.

The AND *Gate.* This circuit (depicted schematically in Figure 2.5) is designed to receive input from several sources and transmit only one set of output signals. The state of the output signals will always be 0 unless the state of all of the input signals is 1.

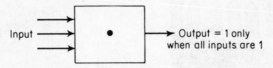

Fig. 2.5. Representation of AND gate.

The OR *Gate.* This circuit (Figure 2.6) is the logical opposite of the AND gate. It will produce output pulses representing the 1 state unless all of the input pulses coming through the circuit represent their respective 0 states.

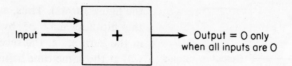

Fig. 2.6. Representation of OR gate.

The Inverter. This logical circuit (schematically shown in Figure 2.7) produces an output pulse whose state is the inverse or complement of the input. Thus, for example, if 0 volts represents the 1 condition and −5 volts is considered to be the 0 condition, a −5 volt input will produce a 0 volt output, and vice versa.

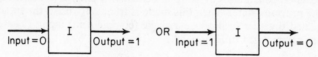

Fig. 2.7. Representation of inverter.

Delays. It is often desirable to control the transmission of a signal so that it reaches a certain point at a particular instant. A typical example is one in which two signals generated at the same time must arrive at a particular circuit simultaneously. If the route of one of the signals is more direct than that of the other, it will get there sooner unless some type of delaying action is introduced. The electromagnetic delays used for this purpose can be very carefully timed and range from several nanoseconds to 100 milliseconds or more. The longer-acting ones are particularly crucial in processor components which must synchronize with the activity of peripheral equipment.

Flip-flop Circuits. The basic building block for many logical circuits is the bistable multivibrator, more popularly known as the *flip-flop* or *toggle* circuit. Its basic construction consists of two transistors or their equivalents set up so that the output of each one is coupled to the input of the other. This feature, when used with supporting circuit components, provides a system which operates only in one of two conditions; when one transistor is conducting, the other cannot. The status of the flip-flop is determined by a pulse applied at the input and transmitted as a steady signal at the output. Even if the input pulse does not have sufficient strength to change the state of a flip-flop circuit, its components make it act like an electronic spring and then will allow the state change to occur.

The flip-flop is equipped with two input and two output terminals (as shown in Figure 2.8) with one of the latter designated to define the current status. Once the outputs are so designated, the inputs are also named (as

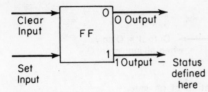

Fig. 2.8. Nomenclature for flip-flop circuit.

the figure shows). Thus, even though the flip-flop may be by definition in the zero state, the second output will at the same time be transmitting the opposite signal, which is also available for use.

The simplest type of flip-flops are designed to react to negative input pulses in three basic ways:

1. A pulse at the *set* input places the flip-flop in the 1 state.
2. A pulse at the *clear* (reset) input places the flip-flop in the 0 state.
3. Simultaneous pulses at both inputs cause a change in state, regardless of the previous state. When this mode is frequently used, the inputs are connected together to produce a single (complement) input. (These functions are summarized in Figure 2.9.)

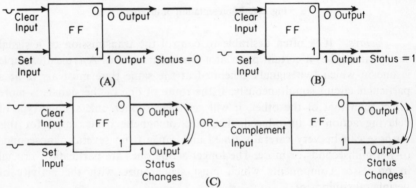

Fig. 2.9. (A) Flip-flop with pulse at *clear* input. (B) Flip-flop with pulse at *set* input. (C) Flip-flop with both inputs pulsed.

These changes of state can be made to occur very rapidly, and flip-flops capable of several million changes per second are in common use.

Binary Counters. By combining a number of flip-flops, it is possible to produce a logical circuit network that can count the number of pulses it receives and transmit a record of the total at any given instant, expressed as a binary number. The capacity of such a counter (that is, the number of binary digits it can store) depends on the number of flip-flops used.

As an example, let us construct a counter using four flip-flop circuits. This setup will allow the recording of up to 1111_2 (15_{10}) counts. (Such a counter is represented schematically in Figure 2.10. Each binary digit is stored by a flip-flop whose inputs are connected together for complementation. Each input pulse is brought to the rightmost flip-flop and to the first AND gate, which passes or inhibits the pulse, depending on the state

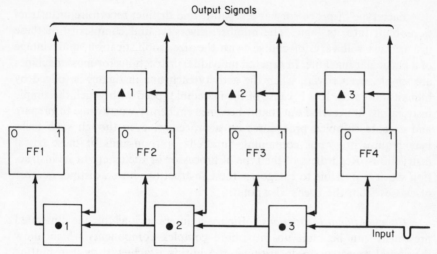

Fig. 2.10. Binary counter operation.

of each flip-flop. Suppose the counter's current contents is 0101 (or 5). The 1 indication currently coming from FF4 and going through the delay to AND gate 3 will allow pulse transmission to FF3. (The delays are included so that the signal which reaches the AND gate reflects the state of the flip-flop *immediately before* the input pulse is applied.) Since FF3 has a status of 0, gate 2 is inhibited, thus preventing transmission to FF2 and, in turn, to gate 1 and FF1. Thus, the next pulse coming in will complement (flip) FF4, and pass through gate 3, flipping FF3. FF2 and FF1 will remain unchanged, since gate 2 is still inhibited. The final status of the four flip-flops would then be 0110, representing a count of 6. When all of the flip-flops are at 1, the counter is at capacity. An additional pulse would zero the first flip-flop, which in turn would zero all the rest, since there is no additional capacity for carrying counts forward.

PROCESSOR INSTRUCTIONS

A portion of the digital processor's logical circuitry consists of controls and special memory registers that are used to trigger selected circuits and transmit selected patterns of pulses. These designate different types of activity within the processor according to a code built into the basic design. Each type of signal received by the control circuits causes them to instigate some logical acitvity of a particular type in the processor and in this sense constitutes an instruction to the processor. It is these instructions in proper sequence (called a *program*) which, when imprinted in the processor's memory, provide it with the training to carry out a particular type of task and to repeat that task as many times as desired.

Each type of processor has a separate and distinct repertoire of instructions built into its logic. The number, diversity, and complexity of these instructions will vary, of course, with the size, sophistication, and vintage of a particular machine. In general, individual instructions for most machines are simple, even trivial, when the activity each one instigates is judged by human standards. It is because of the incredible speed with which the simple instructions are carried out that it becomes eminently worthwhile to prepare and execute complex procedures on a processor, even though such tasks may require programs containing hundreds or thousands of these trivial instructions. Regardless of the type of processor or the extent of its instruction set, it is possible to categorize these instructions into a distinct number of classes from the user's viewpoint.

Computational Instructions. Binary counters such as the one illustrated previously can be built up into more complex components which allow the digital processor to do arithmetic. Addition is achieved by transmitting counts to other counters. Subtraction in the processor is performed as complementary addition, multiplication as successive additions, and division as successive subtractions. Other basic operations (such as powers and roots) and more complex calculations must then be synthesized by the user as a sequence of these instructions. (Some processors even lack multiplication and division hardware, requiring special programs for these functions.)

Manipulative Instructions. Included in the processor's instruction set is a series of commands that allow information to be shifted internally in the processor. The contents of one location may be duplicated anywhere in memory, destroying the previous contents of that second location. Depending on the type of processor involved, these instructions may allow the transfer of single bits, bytes, words, or long strings of words. In many machines these instructions can be augmented by a group of so-called *protect* instructions which can be used to put a figurative lock on any location in memory. With this lock in place, the particular portion of memory (usually no smaller than an individual byte) may be used only as a source of information and not as a repository for it (i.e., information can be read out, but not modified without special instructions). This feature is quite handy in complex systems in which the user wishes to retain certain information for repeated reference (called *read only*) and seeks to prevent any unintentional destruction of the information. In some processors, a number of instructions are actually built as part of the hardware and stored in special read only memory, so that they can be referenced by the user but not changed.

Input-output Instructions. These crucial instructions implement and control the flow of information between the processor and the peripheral devices connected to it. Operationally, they are among the more complex commands built into a processor, since an instruction to transmit information to or from an attached piece of apparatus must include with it information as to which apparatus is involved. Also, it must instigate an extensive conversion process which mediates between the representation code in the peripheral device and the internal code used in the processor. The natural categorization of these instructions is dichotomous, viz., transmission to the processor (reading) and transmission from the processor (writing).

Data-generating Instructions. The processor's input/output instruction subset is supplemented by commands which cause letters, numbers, and other data symbols to be produced internally and stored anywhere in memory as specified by the user. Once such information is generated it may be moved, destroyed, protected, transmitted to some external device, or manipulated in any other fashion.

Decision Instructions. These are by far the most intriguing instructions and constitute, indirectly, the major stimulus for much of the fever regarding thinking machines, learning machines, and other intelligent automatons. The basic decision ability consists of circuits which enable the processor to compare two pieces of information stored in its memory and to decide whether or not they are equal. Similarly, two numbers (or sets of numbers) can be compared for relative magnitude. Furthermore, the processor can change its course of action on the basis of the outcome of one or a series of such comparisons. One set of instructions is followed when number A is greater than number B, for example, and another set is followed if A turns out to be equal to or less than B. Two names may be compared and one path of instructions followed if the names are equal or another pursued if they are not. The user can synthesize more involved decisions in his program by constructing a string of comparisons in any manner that suits his purpose. Regardless of the complexity of such decisions, it should be emphasized that the alternative courses of action for each basic decision must be clearly defined and the criteria for choosing each alternative must be carefully and precisely specified. The processor will not "ad lib." If, through some oversight, a situation arises that does not match any of these decision criteria provided in the program, there will be no decision. Instead, the processor will sit and wait for further instructions to cover the unanticipated contingency. In order to prevent such interminable humming, many programs are designed with an escape clause for each decision network which consists of a catchall instruction forcing the processor to stop or proceed to a special routine if such a situation should arise.

When viewed in this context, it is proper to say that, outside of a mechanical or electrical malfunction, the processor implanted with training for a specific task which includes some decision networks, will never make an incorrect decision. "Correct" has been very specifically defined in terms of a finite number of possible situations and a corresponding finite number of resultant actions, each of which is followed to a desired end.

Parallel Processing. Although processing speeds appear to be quite staggering, some areas of applications have generated problems of such scope that their solution, when a method of solution is available, requires even faster machines. (One fruitful way to get around this is to seek new methods of solution, as discussed in the text.) A more immediate remedy than faster memories and logical circuits appears to be the use of parallel processing. In this mode of operation, the processor, traditionally equipped with a single set of control and arithmetic logic, is designed to include multiple sets so that its instructions, instead of being executed one at a time in sequence, can be divided among the sets of control logic to allow simultaneous execution of several commands. Thus, although the processing speed for a particular instruction has not changed, the apparent speed of the processor has multiplied. It will be seen in later sections that this same organizational concept, when combined with sophisticated programming, can produce an over-all system in which the number of such control circuit networks, sharing a common memory, work simultaneously on instructions from different jobs.

Bulk Memory. Just as some problems have outgrown present processor speeds, there are many applications that require greater storage than is usually provided. A solution has been made available by the recent development of auxiliary memories. These logical assemblies are constructed exactly like processor memories, having bytes or words with permanently assigned addresses that can be referenced in random fashion. The basic difference is that these locations are not supported with as complete a set of logical circuits as is used for main memory and therefore cannot communicate with all of the control components. A program in main memory can move information in and out of bulk storage, but any machine instructions contained in bulk storage are treated as data and must be brought into main memory by another section of program already there before they can act like instructions.

Access time for bulk storage is somewhat slower than, but still comparable to, main processor memories. The capacity of these units is very large, running into hundreds of millions of bytes. Some processors can be equipped to accept several such units, thus giving them a potential capacity of several billion characters, and work is well under way on bulk storage units holding 10^{11} bytes. However, these units are quite expensive, and only a few of the more recently developed processors are built for them.

PERIPHERAL EQUIPMENT

The wide array of processors presently in use or being manufactured is completely overshadowed by the bewildering assortment of devices that can be appended to them. Such gear may be installed as an integral part of the central unit or, as is true in most cases, may be a free-standing apparatus either connected directly to the processor through cables or remotely attached by telephone, microwave, or other means of communication. The business of producing such peripheral equipment is so diverse that it has attracted a large number of manufacturers who are not necessarily engaged in developing and building central processors.

PERIPHERAL EXTENSIONS OF MEMORY

Because of the great expense and still limited applicability of bulk storage, these units do not really constitute a universal solution to the problem of insufficient storage. A more practical answer is presently offered through a variety of peripheral memory extension units. Such devices, acting very much like scratch pads, serve as repositiories for information that does not always have to reside in memory during the performance of a data-processing job. They are directly connected to the central processor (either locally or via communication lines), but they differ in structure from internal memory in that the individual locations on the device are not permanently assigned as part of the hardware design. Instead, they place large general storage areas under control of the processor. The user allocates this storage according to the needs of his particular problem.

Although these memory extending units differ in type, speed, and capacity, they share two basic properties:

1. A device may serve as both an input and output unit during the same data-processing procedure. For example, a processor may be called upon to do an extensive series of calculations, some of which use results calculated during an earlier portion of the job. These intermediate results could be written on an external device, thus freeing storage space in memory. At the proper time, the device acts as an input instrument, transmitting the required results to the processor. Similarly, if a program is so long that its total inclusion in storage would tie up too much memory, it could be segmented so that the initial instructions were placed in memory while a subsequent group was read into the processor and immediately written on an external medium. After execution of the first group of instructions, some supervisory program causes the next group to be read from that external device into the memory positions previously occupied by the initial instructions.

2. External extensions of memory all use a basic storage medium that consists of a magnetic coating deposited on some flat surface. Information is written on and read from these devices by means of the same basic method

used for audio and video recording, except that the electronic signal is a series of discrete pulses rather than one or several continuous voltages. The recording head through which such pulses are transmitted to the magnetic surface is a multichannel assembly consisting of as many tracks as there are bits to the byte for that particular processing system, plus an additional track for internal circuit checking. (Thus, seven or nine tracks would be used for the standard six or eight bit bytes previously referred to. A number of typical recording heads are shown in Figure 2.11.) The relative motion of the recording surface with respect to the head

Fig. 2.11. Recording heads used on computing equipment. *Courtesy Ferroxide Corporation of America.*

assembly is very carefully controlled through synchronous motors and, by means of logical circuitry built into the unit, is timed precisely with the arrival of pulses at the recording head so that the distance between sets of magnetized particles on the recording surface is kept consistent. Thus, when a particular bit in a particular character being transmitted is in the "on" status, a pulse is sent to the corresponding track of the recording head, which in turn magnetizes a spot at a particular position along the width of the segment of surface passing the recording head. (The layout of magnetized particles for one such recording surface is shown in Figure 2.12.) When information is transmitted from tape (playback), the sequence is reversed, i.e., the section of tape passing the playback head induces momentary currents through the head in those tracks where magnetized spots are present on tape.

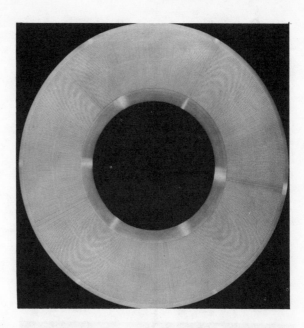

Fig. 2.12. Representation of data storage on a disk. *Courtesy IBM Corporation.*

Magnetic Tape.   The most commonly used memory-extending medium is magnetic tape of the same construction but of much higher quality than that used for audio or video recordings. Widths of $\frac{1}{2}$ and $\frac{3}{4}$ in. are standard. The drive on which such tape is used (Figure 2.13) is equipped with record and playback heads, and with regulatory circuits which control the winding and unwinding of tape. The columns seen in the figure are evacuated reservoirs to provide an indirect pathway for the tape from reel to reel so that sudden stops will not stress the tape unduly. By careful control of tape transport speeds and pulse timing, it is possible to store adjacent characters on the tape very closely together. Standard *densities* are 200, 556, 800, and 1600 characters per inch, and work is continuing to provide even greater densities.

The amount of information that can be stored on a given length of tape at a given density depends on how the processor is instructed to write that information. Each command to transmit output to a particular magnetic tape unit includes information as to the amount of data to be written and its location in memory. When all of the specified data have been found in memory and written on tape, the tape transport logic automatically treats that information as an entity (a *logical record*) and signifies its end by leaving a standard length of blank tape (.75 inch and .6 inch are most commonly used) called an *interrecord gap*. A 2400-foot-long reel of tape written at a density of 800 characters per inch and having record lengths (number of characters between interrecord gaps) representative of those commonly

Fig. 2.13. Digital tape transport units. *Courtesy IBM Corporation.*

used may contain 15,000,000 characters of information. (A widely used seven-track code is shown schematically in Figure 2.14.) Since these tape reels are realtively inexpensive and very easy to change on a tape drive, they also serve as a very good and economical repository for computer compatible information as well as a memory-extending medium. Thus, it is very common practice to produce information on magnetic tape, remove that physical tape from the tape drive, and save it for further use. In fact, many installations maintain libraries of data on thousands of tape reels.

Magnetic tape is, of course, a sequential storage device in that information located on a particular portion of the tape can be accessed only by searching through all of the information preceding it. Hence, a good portion of data-processing time is often spent rewinding and searching for a par-

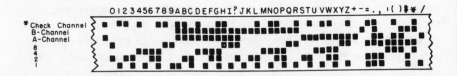

*A magnetic impulse is generated in this channel so that all characters are represented by an even number of impulses (even parity).

Fig. 2.14. Coding of digital data on magnetic tape.

ticular record from the start of a tape. Even with very high tape speeds (150 inches per second is the present standard limit) the rate at which information can be written on or read from a magnetic tape falls far below the internal data-handling abilities of most processors. Although many computing systems are designed so that internal processing can continue while the tape is being manipulated (*overlapped operation*), there are a large number of processors that do not have this capability. Consequently, a crucial factor in planning data-processing procedures is often the mimization of tape manipulation. For this reason, processing systems using tape usually have several tape drives connected to increase flexibility of transmission.

Once a data tape is produced, it is often desirable to protect it so that the data will be available for future input and inadvertent writing on the tape, which can destroy the information already there, will be prevented. For this purpose, all tape reels are equipped with a special plastic ring, which, when removed, makes it impossible to write on that tape but does not inhibit the read capability.

Tape Strip Recorder. Efforts to overcome the sequential limitations of magnetic tape without substantial penalties in cost have resulted in the production of devices (such as the one in Figure 2.15) where several strips

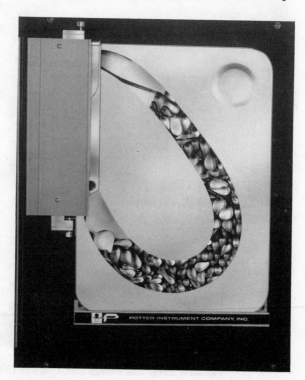

Fig. 2.15. Auxiliary storage service using tape strip. *Courtesy Potter Instrument Corporation.*

are provided, each with its own set of read and write heads. With this arrangement, it then becomes possible to refer to a particular strip and a sequential searching operation is restricted to that strip instead of the entire unit.

Peripheral Random Access Devices. In an effort to bring peripheral information transmission rates somewhat closer to internal processing speeds, a number of hardware units have been developed with random access abilities.

The most commonly used of these devices is a storage unit (Figure 2.16) in which a number of magnetically coated discs, with recording surfaces on both sides, are mounted on a common shaft. Each surface, containing up to several hundred concentric tracks, is associated with its own set of heads which can be moved towards or away from the center of the disc. The supporting logical circuitry is such that the processor can be instructed to read or write information at a particular location by selecting a disc and signaling the corresponding head assembly to bring the head to the appropriate radius (or track). Since this assembly is constantly revolving, it cannot take longer than one revolution of the disc for the proper piece of infor-

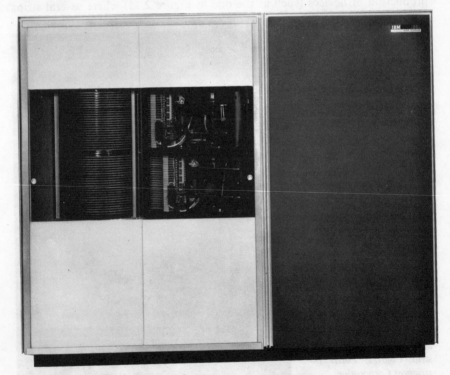

Fig. 2.16. Large disk storage unit. *Courtesy IBM Corporation.*

mation to be found once the reading head has been positioned at the appropriate radius. The time required to locate a particular piece of information on a rotating disc is in the neighborhood of .1 second, although it varies with the size and rotating speed. If the information to be transmitted from the disc to the processor is a fairly long string of characters, the transmission rate can exceed 100,000 characters per second, once the initial location has been found. Large units (such as the one shown in Figure 2.16) can

Fig. 2.17. Drum storage unit. *Courtesy IBM Corporation.*

store hundreds of millions of characters at a time, but small units are also available with the disc assembly itself removable, thus providing data files with random access ability that can be permanently stored in a library and used as needed.

A variation of the discs is a device in which the magnetic coating is placed on the rotating surface of a cylindrical drum (Figure 2.17). The recording tracks are laid out as circles around the surface and are served by a number of heads along the periphery. The diameter of the drum is very large, and the access time can be decreased by using more heads around the circumference so that once the proper set of tracks is found, it need not take a full revolution of the drum to reach the exact desired location and effect the subsequent transmission of information to or from it. As with the disc assembly, some drum models provide replaceable data storage elements.

A third type of apparatus makes use of a stationary sensing head in conjunction with movable cards coated with magnetic film. When a signal

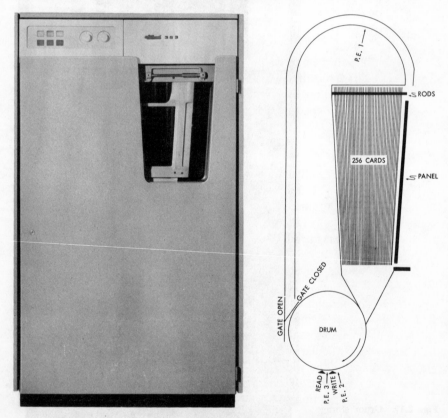

Fig. 2.18. Magnetic card storage unit. *Courtesy National Cash Register Co.*

is transmitted to read the information from a particular part, it is mechanically retrieved by a set of metal fingers which find the part along the stack, lift it up and bring it to a nearby set of heads (Figure 2.18). After the information is transmitted, the card is automatically replaced among the stack. If more than one card is to be used in succession, over-all access time can be minimized by overlapping the operation so that the second card is being accessed and positioned while the first card is still being used. Here again, the entire data storage assembly (in this case, a single card or a whole cartridge of cards) may be removed and replaced.

Most processing systems include logical circuitry which allows a number of these random access units to be tied to the central processor. As higher character densities and more flexible use of peripheral devices become commonplace, it will not be unusual to obtain systems capable of making billions of characters of stored information directly available to a central processor.

INPUT PERIPHERY

In contrast to memory-extending units which can receive information from processors, store it, and allow it to be read in again, a number of devices are in use whose exclusive function is to deliver input to the central processor. This bridges the gap between information presented on some physical medium and its counterpart converted into coded impulses for internal storage.

Punch Devices. The most widely used process for preparing computer-compatible input of soft data involves the representation of the data as a series of punched holes on a medium in much the same way that a series of magnetized bits are used on magnetic tape. In one respect the design of central processors was tailored to match these punched media, since their use had preceded the introduction of electronic computers by a good number of years.

The ubiquitous punched card (Figure 2.19) in its present standard form was designed for use in the 1890 census. (There were, of course, no computers, but sorting and counting machines were made available.) The card is designed so that a single character of information can be stored in each of the 80 columns across the length. A code has been devised and standardized so that a particular combination of holes punched in one or more of twelve rows across the width of the card represents a particular character. A keypunch (Figure 2.20), operated very much like the typewriter, is used to transcribe information onto punched cards.

In many instances a roll of paper tape (Figure 2.21) is used in lieu of cards to contain punched information. This medium has also seen extensive

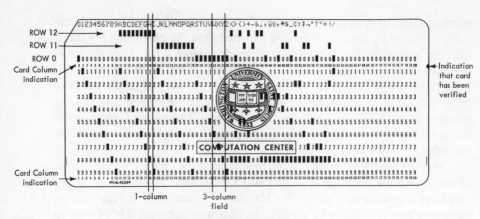

ROW 12
ROW 11
ROW 0
Card Column indication

Card Column indication

Indication that card has been verified

1-column   3-column field

Fig. 2.19. Punched card. *Courtesy Columbia Press.*

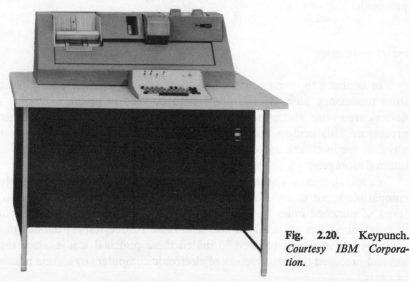

Fig. 2.20. Keypunch. *Courtesy IBM Corporation.*

use in precomputer years, primarily in telegraphic work. A number of different codes are in use, requiring five, six, seven, eight, or in some special instances as many as 25 tracks across the width of the tape. Here again, a typewriterlike device is used for punching and, in many instances, double purpose units are used (Figure 2.22) with which it is possible to prepare a paper tape while producing a conventional typewritten document.

Information is read from punched cards or tape with an apparatus no different in principle from that used in player pianos. Sets of metal fingers are provided on each side of the card or tape passing between them, which sense the presence or absence of holes, and close or open corresponding

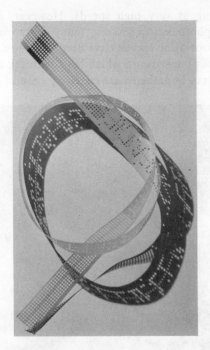

Fig. 2.21. Punched paper tape.

circuits, sending appropriate signals to the processor. The maximum speed of such mechanical units is presently in the neighborhood of 1000 cards per minute for card readers and 500 characters per second for tape readers. It is not likely that these rates will increase appreciably because of the excessive cost imposed by the requirements of precisely dimensioned moving

Fig. 2.22. Flexowriter for punching simultaneous typewriter program and punched tape. *Courtesy Friden Corporation.*

parts operating at very high speeds. However, by replacing mechanical fingers with photoelectric sensors, many of the moving parts can be eliminated and operating speeds have been roughly doubled.

A form of punched card which has found use in very large-scale studies where the data to be gathered are relatively simple (such as polls and surveys)

Fig. 2.23. Port-a-punch card. *Courtesy IBM Corporation.*

is the so-called *port-a-punch card* (Figure 2.23), in which the positions where holes are to be punched have been partially perforated so that they can be punched with a pencil point, paper clip, or other such instrument. Because of handling considerations, only every other column is available for data, thus limiting the number of characters to 40. Since such cards are generally prepared by untrained personnel, the usual practice is to preprint the instructions on the actual card.

Conversion of Input Information. Even if the fastest available reading equipment is used, input transmission rates from punched media are inordinately slow compared to internal processing speeds ($\frac{1}{1000}$ or less). The inequity is such that the operating time for many data processing procedures is strictly a function of the input transmission rate (*input bound*). When very large amounts of data are being handled, it is often more economical to use a smaller, "slow" processor to read cards or punched tape and transcribe the information onto some memory extension device (usually magnetic tape). The output thus produced serves as the input to the larger processor and can be read into it at a rate at least fifty times as great as that possible with the data in their original form.

Fig. 2.24. Magnetic tape keypunch. *Courtesy Mohawk Data Corp.*

A special device (Figure 2.24) for direct manual transcription of raw data onto magnetic tape has been developed in an effort to eliminate the satellite processor. The unit is used in much the same way as an ordinary keypunch and produces a data tape compatible with most processors.

Mark Sense Devices. An alternate medium to punched cards or tape is provided by devices that are designed to recognize and determine a series of marks made with special pencils. (Multiple choice answers on many standard aptitude and achievement tests are recorded in this way.) In this case, the actual source document (either a card whose size and shape is identical to that of the standard punched card, or an entire page) also serves as the initial medium for automatic data processing. This document, be it a questionnaire, lab sheet, or other source of data, is imprinted with the data outline (see Chapter 4) and the boundaries of the spaces (usually elongated slots or circles) where the marks are to be made. Once the information is thus recorded, it can be scanned automatically by a device that either can transcribe the markings to corresponding information on punched cards or can transmit it directly into a central processor.

Optical Scanning Devices. In an effort to preserve the traditional forms for recording data and at the same time provide direct data transmission to the central processor from such forms, much work is going into the development of equipment that can read printed information of various types. A number of such devices are presently being marketed, but their cost limits their use to specific installations (such as large libraries). These devices are capable of scanning and interpreting documents prepared in specific type, and a number of the more elaborate ones will accept a variety of type faces. Many workers who direct their efforts towards the development of more versatile and less expensive optical scanning devices maintain that there are no theoretical deterrents to the invention of a device which will not only "read" and interpret information from a wide variety of typewriting and printing devices, but will also handle handprinted and perhaps handwritten characters as well.

Direct Data Input. In many applications it is desirable to use a digital computer to process data immediately as they are generated by establishing a direct link between the instrument producing the data and the memory of the processor itself. Many automatic measuring instruments which are designed to produce discrete readings and record them on strip charts, cash register tapes, etc. (see Chapter 4) need only slight modifications to produce these readings as a series of pulses acceptable by digital machines. Correspondingly, many of the current digital processor types include, or can be supplemented with, a feature which allows such pulses to be transmitted to internal memory as if they were emanating from one of the standard input units. Although direct data input is not generally necessary, it is crucial in applications in which the course of an ongoing process is dictated by the nature of computed results. Frequent examples of this type of usage may be seen in almost every phase of aerospace work. Most dramatic of these is the type of system wherein information from satellites and other space vehicles is transmitted directly into a digital processing system. Calculated results are then produced in time to signal the nature of corrective action, should it be required. (Some systems are sufficiently sophisticated so that the results of processing are, in themselves, signals which trigger corrective action such as positioning of an antenna, turning a thruster on or off, etc.) Since the amount of time elapsed during processing corresponds to the amount of time elapsed during the actual occurrences, this type of information handling is known as *real time* data processing.

ANALOG DATA PREPARATION FOR DIGITAL PROCESSING

Quite often, automatically generated data are produced in analog form, i.e., as continuous signals rather than as a sequence of individual pulses. Before such signals can be handled by a digital processor, they must be

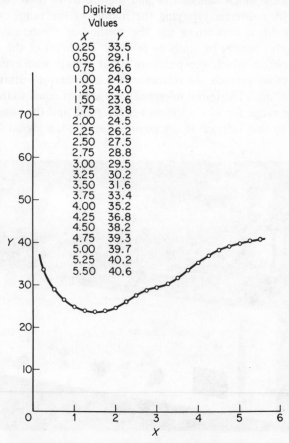

Digitized Values	
X	Y
0.25	33.5
0.50	29.1
0.75	26.6
1.00	24.9
1.25	24.0
1.50	23.6
1.75	23.8
2.00	24.5
2.25	26.2
2.50	27.5
2.75	28.8
3.00	29.5
3.25	30.2
3.50	31.6
3.75	33.4
4.00	35.2
4.25	36.8
4.50	38.2
4.75	39.3
5.00	39.7
5.25	40.2
5.50	40.6

Fig. 2.25. Representation of manual digitization process.

converted into sequences of discrete readings which, when taken in total, still preserve the shape and integrity of the original signal. This conversion process, called *digitization*, involves the periodic sampling of a continuous signal and reporting the results as a table of separate readings. Since the automatic sensing and recording of continuous signals preceded the development of instruments to digitize them, this function was initially performed by hand. A typical example is shown in Figure 2.25.

A/D Converters. A variety of electronic instruments are available to sample continuous voltages at desired time intervals and to produce a series of electronic pulses which constitute some coded representation of the magnitudes of those voltages. The designs of these instruments [called *analog-to-digital* (A/D) converters] vary widely, ranging from slow, fixed-rate units capable of converting several hundred samples per second to elaborate models which can sample and digitize more than 100,000 times per second. (A converter typifying the middle of the range is shown in Figure 2.26.) Most converters use the method of "successive approximation," which operates basically as follows: The heart of the system is a comparator circuit which compares an input voltage with some reference level. If the input exceeds the reference, the comparator's status is "on;" otherwise it is "off." The initial reference voltage is set equal to the midpoint of the voltage range for which the unit is designed, and the sample reading is compared to this voltage. If the comparator is on, a signal is sent to a

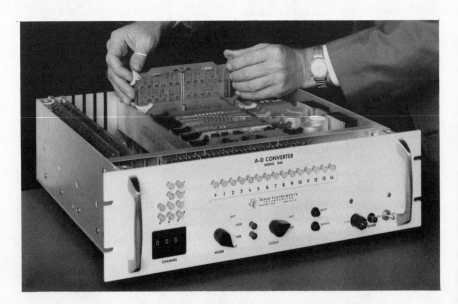

Fig. 2.26. A-10 converter. *Courtesy Texas Instrument Corporation.*

counter and a new reference voltage is applied, this time equal to the midpoint of the upper half of the range. Conversely, if the comparator is off, the new reference voltage is set equal to the midpoint of the lower half of the range. A second comparison is made and the range is split in half again, and so on. The final digitized representation is then a function of the number of "on" signals received from the comparator, and the number of significant digits in it is directly controlled by the number of comparisons made. Since these approximations are done sequentially, the speed of conversion attainable by a given physical set of circuits is related inversely to the number of significant digits produced in the output. Most converters are designed to produce fixed-length binary numbers, with the available range being from 2 to 16 binary digits. Some models can be obtained with facilities for varying the number of bits in the output as well as the conversion rate.

Multiplexers.   When several analog signals are generated simultaneously, it is an expensive proposition to connect an A/D converter to each analog source. Instead, a multiplexer is installed directly ahead of a single converter. These fast-acting multiple switches are built to connect the converter to each of the analog signals in turn, maintaining the connection just long enough for the sample reading to be picked up. This cyclic operation (represented schematically in Figure 2.27) is repeated automatically. The range of obtainable switching speeds is such that the converter need never be held up waiting for the next connection to be made. Units having virtually any number of terminals are available, with the sequencing operation being fixed or variable. In the latter case, a wiring board is provided so that the user can "patch in" any sampling sequence he desires, including so-called short cycles, which do not involve all of the input terminals on the switch. Similarly, uneven sequences can be arranged in which certain terminals are accessed more often than others (e.g., if terminals 1 through 5 are being sampled, the input to the A/D converter might conceivably be in the order 1, 2, 1, 3, 1, 4, 1, 5, 1, 2, 1, 3, etc.).

Sample and Hold Circuits.   Usually the time elapsed between successive sampling in a multiplexing sequence is small enough so that the user can consider his samples as being obtained simultaneously. However, the conversion system can be equipped with a set of *sample and hold* circuits which do exactly what their name implies. Each of these circuits, connected to an individual analog signal source, consists of a capacitor and supporting components. When the analog signals are sampled, their instantaneous values are retained as charges for a long enough period without significant loss so that the multiplexer can get to them and send them on to the converter, thus providing it with a set of samples which were obtained simultaneously. (This is schematically depicted in Figure 2.27.)

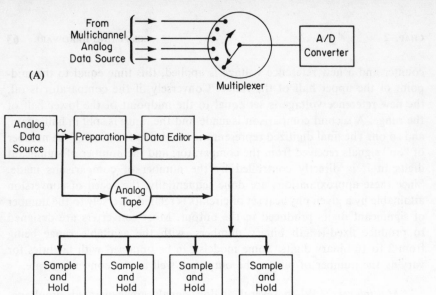

Fig. 2.27. (A) Action of multiplexer. (B) Representation of simultaneous analog sampling. *Courtesy Columbia Press.*

Digitized Output. Once the digitization has occurred and the actual binary number representing the sample value has been formed, it can be transmitted to virtually any medium fast enough to accept it, including the memory of the processor itself. Digital magnetic tape is the usual repository for such output.

OUTPUT PERIPHERY

A number of devices are available for the display of processing results in forms that can be easily read and interpreted by users, or that can be resubmitted for subsequent processing. The actual display of the results is preceded by a decoding step in which information of internal storage is converted to whatever code system is employed by the output device.

Output on Punched Media. Punched cards or paper tape, discussed previously as input media, also serve conveniently for intermediate output.

When a number of programs are required to complete a given processing procedure on a system not equipped with magnetic tape, it is the usual practice to produce punched cards or paper tape at the end of each stage or input to the next one.

Printing Devices.   Two basic types of printer are used to produce output in permanent readable form from digital processors. The more common of these is the high-speed line printer, which is almost universally used to display charts, tables, graphs, pictures, texts, and an endless variety of other processor-generated information. A typical model (Figure 2.28) operates with several copies of the available character set mounted on a constantly moving drum or chain. At the instant the desired characters are about to approach the proper locations along the line as designated by the user's program, signals are sent to the print mechanism and the paper is momentarily pushed against the type, producing an entire written line. Printers are available with lines up to 160 characters wide, and are built to operate at speeds as high as 1500 lines per minute.

The second type of printer, known as a nonimpact line printer, operates by setting up a pattern of minute electrostatic charges on specially prepared paper, which is then fed past a reservoir of powdered ink, from which it attracts enough material to form the readable images. Because of fewer moving parts and lower operating inertia, these devices, presently in limited

Fig. 2.28. Line printer. *Courtesy IBM Corporation.*

use, already promise much higher speeds. The paper industry has responded to the versatility of automatic printers, and a large number of business forms specifically designed for these devices are in common use.

The line printer has recently been put to an entirely new use. With proper programming and control of the operating pressure, the printer can be made to produce output in braille of sufficient quality to allow unhindered reading by the blind (Figure 2.29). This has placed the blind individual in direct communication with computers and has therefore opened the computer profession to them. Furthermore, with the increasing availability of computer-compatible information, the availability of written material to the blind is widening as well.

As is the case with paper tape and card readers, the electromechanical nature of printing mechanisms limits their operating speed to but a small fraction of that exhibited by processors (at least several hundred to one). Consequently, it is common for large computing systems to produce output on magnetic devices and then use a separate processor for formatting and printing.

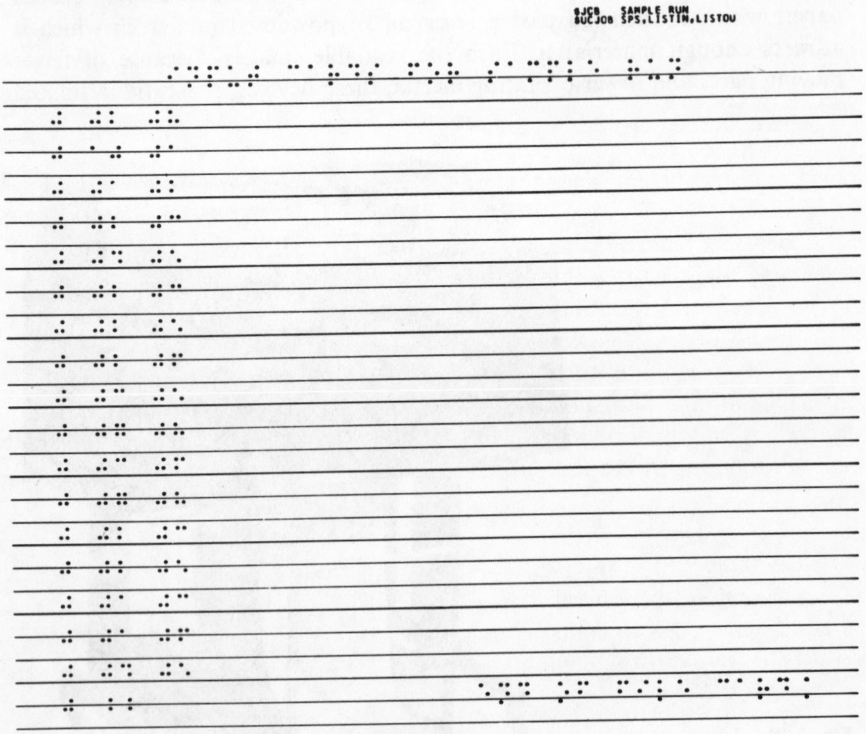

Fig. 2.29. Braille output on line printer.

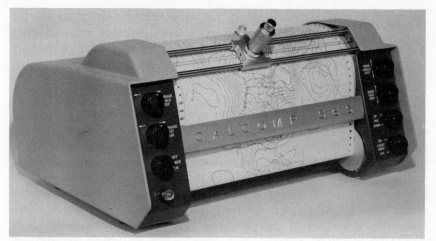

Fig. 2.30. Digital X-Y plotter. *Courtesy California Computer Products Co.*

Graph Plotters. When data processing applications demand greater sensitivity and more intricate written detail than can be provided by the line printer, use is made of the digital graph plotter (Figure 2.30). Output is produced on ordinary graph or drawing paper by a recording pen whose motion is controlled by the processor. In some models a single sheet of paper is mounted on the plotting surface and the recording pen moves back and forth or up and down. In other types, the pen is mounted on a fixed track and can be moved only back and forth, while the paper can be moved up and down. Since the resolution attainable on such plots is very high (up to $\frac{1}{200}$ inch), the output produced on such devices is not limited to graphs. They can be supplemented with explanatory notes, labels, dimensions, and other written information. This is especially useful in automatic design procedures resulting in actual engineering drawings.

Plotters are even slower than line printers. Consequently, an installation making frequent use of such a device can produce representations of graphs on magnetic tape and submit that tape to a special plotter-magnetic tape drive complex which operates separately (offline). Also, fairly good graphs can be produced by the line printer.

TERMINALS

Although all peripheral devices are terminals in a sense, we refer here to the specific class of units in which the user has the capability of interacting directly with the computer system.

Typewriters. Use of the typewriter as an output device has been standard since the advent of computers. They are attached to many of today's systems, but have broader usage in that an increasing number are serving as input devices as well. With proper instructions, the processor can display results on the typewriter and then stop, awaiting the next move on the part of the user. After examining the results, the user is able to enter additional data or instructions via the typewriter, causing processing to resume. (A terminal of this type is shown in Figure 2.31.)

Since maximum automatic typing speed is in the range of 10 to 15 characters per second and the human typing rate is well below that, the operating speed of such devices is exceedingly low. Add to this the inevitable time delay incurred while the user examines the results, makes his decision, and implements it, it is seen that this mode of operation is highly inefficient in terms of utilization of a high-priced computing system. To overcome this discrepancy and at the same time allow users to "converse" with computers, a number of configurations have been designed which allow many terminals to be connected to a single system. By turning the attention of the processor to each of the terminals in sequence for a short length of time (very much like multiplexing), the effect is achieved wherein each user operates as if he were the only one connected to the system and, while he is deliberating his next move, the other terminals are being serviced. This concept, known as *time sharing*, is discussed further in Chapter 3.

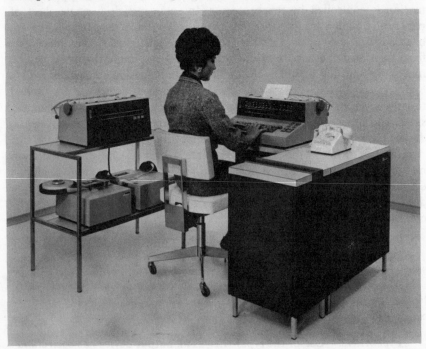

Fig. 2.31. Remote access terminal. *Courtesy IBM Corporation.*

Cathode-ray Terminals. A more recently introduced terminal device offers the familiarity of the typewriter coupled with a most versatile display medium whose use has been extended to include input capabilities. In this apparatus (Figure 2.32) output from the processor is displayed on a television-type cathode-ray tube (CRT) instead of a typewritten sheet. Since no moving parts are involved, it is possible to produce and change displays very rapidly. Some units can display up to a million characters per second and as many as five thousand characters at any one time. For each character, the processor transmits a signal to the display unit, giving the location on the screen and the type of character to be shown. The actual characters are formed either by a mechanism within the display assembly itself or are "drawn" by an appropriate program in the processor. To give the illusion of stability, each signal to the CRT is reinforced (40 times per second is standard). With many such devices a small special memory built into the unit itself is used to store the information for the picture currently being

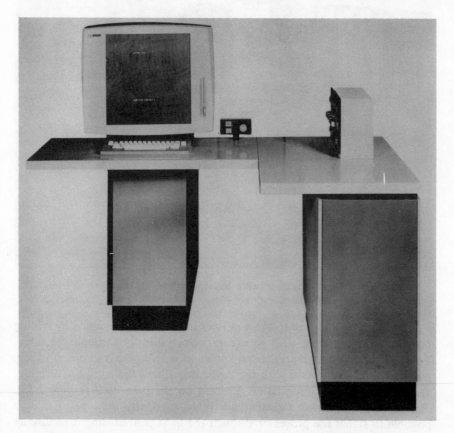

Fig. 2.32. Cathode-ray display and input device. *Courtesy IBM Corporation.*

displayed so that it can be reinforced automatically without tying up a part of the processor's memory. Only when the image is to be changed need the processor transmit a new set of signals.

Growing interest in the usefulness of such devices has brought their price down, and they can now be obtained as standard units for many computing systems. In some cases (Figure 2.33) such a display is built into the central processor as the system's integral output unit. To extend its use as a communication device, the CRT is usually accompanied by a typewriter keyboard so that the user, having observed a table, graph, picture, or other diagram produced by the processor, may easily change some input conditions by entering new data directly through the keys. This sequential process by examination, modification, and re-examination (heuristic analysis) has already found successful use in optimization work.

Fig. 2.33. Central processor with built-in cathode-ray display. *Courtesy Central Data Corporation.*

An exciting addition to these devices has been implemented by adding provisions for entering data to the processor directly through the CRT. To do this, an electric marker (also known as a *light pen*) is provided which, when used in conjunction with the keyboard, allows the addition, deletion, and modification of information depicted on the tube itself (Figure 2.32), thus using the device as a sketch pad. When used with the typewriter, it is possible to signal the processor through the light pen, causing it to display any desired character at the location on the screen pointed to by the pen.

On many units special provisions may be incorporated to allow the user to draw lines, curves, and two-dimensional representations and have their coded equivalents enter into the processor. As with other periphery, a number of these units may be attached to a given computing system with the remoteness of their location strictly a function of the availability and quality of transmission equipment.

More Powerful Terminals—the Programmed Console.   When a number of terminals are connected to the same computing system, it is often of great advantage to equip some or all of them with storage ability and logical circuitry so as to imbue them with a certain amount of processing capability. With this arrangement and appropriate software, the over-all processing can be divided so that the terminal's "computer" does much of the work necessary to prepare the input in the form best suited for the main program and edit and format the output for convenient display, thus restricting the use of the central processor to those portions of the task which demand its larger memory, greater speed, and extended logical capabilities.

Such a terminal is the programmed console (Figure 2.34) developed by the Biomedical Computer Laboratory at Washington University. The CRT is supported by a small memory (4096 words) and a set or logical circuits that provide machine instructions allowing the user to do arithmetic, shift information around in the small memory, and transmit information to and from the central system. A special communications link is included so that the programmed console can be connected to a variety of central

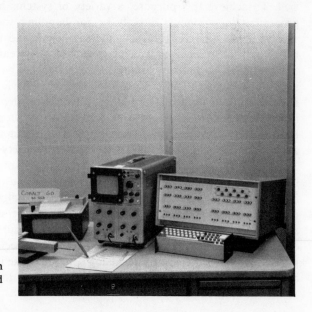

Fig. 2.34.   Washington University programmed console.

processors with a minimum amount of modification. A typical sequence of events on this console is as follows:

1. The user reads in his console program, followed by his input in a form most convenient to him.
2. The console program does some preliminary calculations and arranges the input in a form most convenient for the central processor, at which point it refers to the main program.
3. The supervisory routines in the processor bring in the main program from external storage, which reads and processes data from the console.
4. The main program initiates transmission of output to the console and then refers to the supervisory routines which may or may not go on to the next job, depending on the time elapsed.
5. The console program takes over, constructing the output display and rearranging the data accordingly.
6. The display is produced and "frozen" until the user decides to erase or change it. At this point he can decide that he is through or he can introduce new input and/or instructions to start the sequence again.

ANALOG COMPUTING SYSTEMS

When data are generated in the form of continuous signals, it is often desirable to analyze these signals without the necessity of sampling and digitizing them, and to produce the resulting output in continuous form as well. To achieve this purpose, a variety of systems have been devised for processing these signals directly or for handling some other, more convenient signal that fluctuates in the same way and otherwise follows the behavior of the phenomenon being generated. A system designed to duplicate the action of some time-varying phenomenon is known as an *analog* and need not necessarily be an electric or electronic device. Electrical networks have often been studied by building water flow systems (hydraulic analogs) in which current is represented by water flow, electromotive force (voltage) by pressure drop, and resistance by friction. Pneumatic and mechanical analogs are also in common use to explore a variety of problems.

When the capability exists for transforming some continuous signals into a voltage whose variation reflects that of the original phenomenon, it is possible to augment the resulting electrical analog with a wide variety of circuits and networks which can manipulate the signal in virtually any desired way, producing a functionally related output. In contrast to most other analog devices, which have to be designed especially for the particular problem at hand, the electronic analog computer, like its digital counterpart, can be set up to handle one type of problem and then easily adapted for completely different assignments. In this respect the electronic analog computer is very much like a more familiar analog computer, i.e., the slide rule, in which distance along a particular scale may represent length in one problem, weight in another, force in a third, and so on.

General-purpose analog computers (electronic being implied) have come into increasing use in recent years because of the development of a wide variety of instruments for transforming basically nonelectric signals into continuous voltages. Reliable devices (generally referred to as *trans-ducers*) are now available for transforming such signals as pressure, deflection, sound, light, or heat into electrical representations whose variations with time mirror that of the actual data signal.

ANALOG PROCESSORS

The equipment used to handle and manipulate continuous voltages is not a tightly integrated system of many logical circuits as is the digital processor. Instead, it is a rather loose assemblage of large building blocks, with each major component capable of performing an entire mathematical operation that would require a large number of circuits in the digital machine. Instead of writing a program which, when stored in memory, presents a sequence of trivial instructions for a particular job, the analog processor is prepared by actually restructuring the hardware, that is, rearranging the order in which its building blocks are connected so that the voltage is routed through the processor as the user desires. Direct physical access is provided to the input and output connection for each building block by means of a patch panel (see Figure 2.35) so that the implementation of a particular "program," once the desired sequence has been defined, is relatively simple.

OPERATIONAL AMPLIFIERS

The elemental building block in the electronic analog processor is a highly reliable, low-noise, D/C amplifier capable of high gain (ratio of output to input voltages) and sustained operation. A number of such amplifiers are available with standardized performance characteristics, and a variety of processors are commercially available in which such amplifiers, together with control circuits, are combined into an integral design. Since the amplifier is so basic to the analog processor, it serves as the criterion for assessing a processor's relative size. Small systems are available with as few as ten amplifiers, whereas some military and aerospace installations require complex configurations having several hundred.

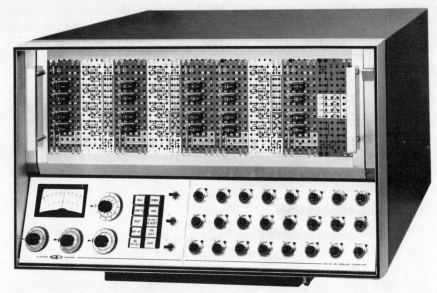

Fig. 2.35. Analog computer. *Courtesy Systron Donner Corporation.*

With the amplifier itself acting as a nucleus, various types of circuit elements (such as resistor-condenser networks) can be added, converting the basic amplifiers into operational amplifiers capable of performing an extremely wide array of mathematical manipulations. In addition to the more basic ones outlined below, network designs have been published for converting basic amplifiers to operational components for many desired mathematical manipulations.

Multiplication by a Constant.   Sending an input voltage E_1 through this type of amplifier will produce an output voltage E_2 whose relative magnitude follows the function

$$E_2 = -KE_1$$

where K is a constant greater than 1. (This is schematically shown in Figure 2.36). A basic characteristic of all such amplifiers is that they reverse the sign of the input voltage regardless of the operation performed. Where necessary, this is compensated for by placing additional amplifiers in the circuitry which do nothing but invert the sign. When multiplication by a

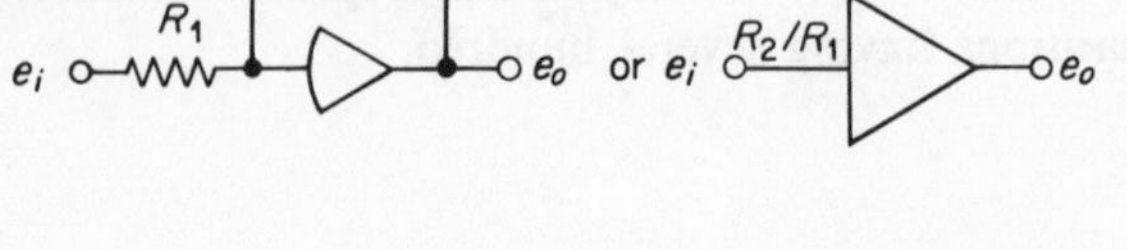

Fig. 2.36. Operational amplifier for multiplication by a constant.

constant less than 1 is required, it is cheaper and easier to use a potentio-
meter in which a dial can be set to the appropriate factor.

The Summing Amplifier. Input to this component consists of several
voltages $(E_1, E_2, E_3, \ldots, E_n)$. The output voltage E_0 represents the negative
algebraic sum

$$E_0 = -E_1 - E_2 - E_3 - \cdots - E_n$$

A simple variation of this component is one which combines this function
with that of the multiplying amplifier, thus producing an output voltage
representing the sum of the input voltages multiplied by some constant
(Figure 2.37).

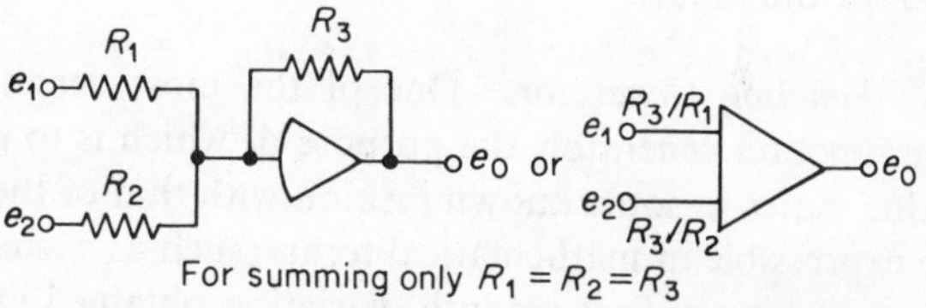

Fig. 2.37. Operational
amplifier for summing.

For summing only $R_1 = R_2 = R_3$

The Integrating Amplifier. By proper inclusion of a condenser in an
operational amplifier circuit, it is possible to create a component that has
the ability to store a charge accumulated over a time interval. When the
condenser discharges, the output voltage thus produced represents the time
integral of the input voltage, i.e.,

$$E_2 = -K_1 \int_{t_0}^{t_0+\Delta t} E_1 \, dt + K_2$$

where K_1 is a characteristic constant of the circuit and K_2 represents
some residual charge. (This amplifier is schematically shown in Figure
2.38.) As in the previous case, the input voltage may be singular or plural
with the amplifier producing the integral of the summed voltages if the
latter is true. Furthermore, a single amplifier may be constructed which will
multiply each of several input voltages by its own constant, sum them
together and produce the time integral of that sum.

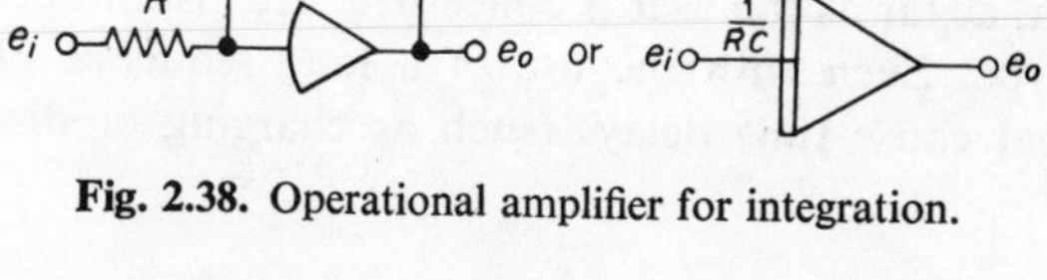

Fig. 2.38. Operational amplifier for integration.

Multipliers and Dividers. With some additional complexity it is possible to produce combinations of operational amplifiers which, when acting as a unit, will produce an output voltage that is the product of two input voltages, i.e.,

$$E_3 = E_2 E_1$$

or a ratio for two input voltages,

$$E_3 = \frac{E_1}{E_2}$$

Slight adaptations of this type of amplifier will produce components in which the output is proportional to the square of the input or to the square root of the input.

Function Generator. One of the most versatile types of networks is the function generator, the purpose of which is to produce an output whose value varies in some known fashion with that of the input. Its variation may be expressible in mathematical terms (such as cosine or logarithm) or it may be an arbitrary (but smooth) variation obtained experimentally or by some other means and expressible only as a graph or a table of values. When such a function is fairly standard (such as a sine curve), a fixed-function generator can be designed for this purpose and units are, in fact, available for such more common functions. If the relationship is nonstandard but frequently used in an installation, a fixed-function generator can be custom designed for it. Otherwise, variable-function generators are used and changed as required.

OPERATIONAL CHARACTERISTICS OF ANALOG PROCESSORS

Because the analog processor operates on one or more continuous input voltages, is not equipped with an extensive memory, and does not follow a stored sequence of minute instructions, it is not meaningful to describe the operation of these devices in terms of the digital processor. Consequently, the various functional characteristics are outlined below with no comparison implied.

Operating Speed. The analog processor handles continuous voltages at speeds which, as far as the user is concerned, are instantaneous regardless of processor type. Even with the use of a long sequence of circuits and components that cause time delays (such as charging or discharging condensers), the holdup is sufficiently small so as to be unnoticeable. Consequently, it is possible to process a large variety of problems in real time (where one second on the processor actually corresponds to one second of problem time).

Analog Decision Capability.   The facilities for making logical decisions using predetermined criteria exist on the analog processor but only to a very limited extent. Certain types of decisions can be made by means of electronic comparators, whose basic operation is as follows: The input consists of two voltages, one of which is a constant value generated in the processor itself and the other of which is time-varying input. At the instant the two voltages are equal, a switch is triggered on the output side, causing (or inhibiting) some further action. In this sense, the analog processor can be considered a logical device, with more complex decisions being synthesized by using multiple comparators and switches. Most standard processors are equipped with only a few such circuits.

Operating Range.   Since even the best operational amplifiers exhibit a certain amount of instability, especially at the extremes of their operating ranges, the over-all voltage range of the analog processor must be limited. Thus, inexpensive models are usually designed to operate between -10 and $+10$ volts, and the range of even the more elaborate types is restricted to -100 to $+100$ volts. Since it often happens that a particular sequence of analog operations can produce intermediate and/or final output voltages well beyond this range, the user must know enough about the system he is studying so that such contingencies can be anticipated and averted. This is usually done by multiplying or dividing by appropriate scale factors along the processing pathways so that all values remain within the operating range and yet are not excessively compressed so as to sacrifice sensitivity. By keeping track of the various scale factors, the user is then able to readjust his output to attain the correct magnitude. This usually involves a trial and error procedure.

Precision.   The basic structure of operational amplifiers also places a restriction on the precision with which analog processors can be used and still be practical Most models are accurate to 1%, and improvement to $.1\%$ is usually accompanied by a substantial increase in cost. The design and construction of a configuration capable of producing voltages accurate to $.01\%$ is considered by most experts to be an ultimate level whose projected cost is far beyond realistic considerations. As a result, the scope of problems handled by an analog processor must be such that input and output expressed to the nearest volt (or .1 volt at best) is satisfactory.

PERIPHERY FOR ANALOG COMPUTERS

The choice of devices available to transmit voltages to and from analog processors is much more limited than the tremendous array designed for digital systems. The basic reason, of course, is that much analog information is generated "naturally" as voltages or signals that can easily be converted to voltages, so that elaborate circuitry to mediate between data generating devices, input or output devices, and processors is not necessary. In fact, the use of analog processors as online devices in which the raw data expressed as voltages are introduced directly to the processor constitutes a considerably greater proportion of over-all analog use than is true in the digital case.

Magnetic Tape. When analog data are not processed online, by far the most common medium for storing them is magnetic tape. Although tape of the same composition and quality is used as for digital devices, the recording and playback mechanisms are designed for continuous signals rather than discrete pulses. The method of recording analog data is basically the same as for digital pulses (Figure 2.39). The signal is introduced as a varying current to the winding around the recording head, which consists basically of a magnetic core having a very small nonmagnetic gap. During the recording process, the moving tape is brought into contact with the head at the gap. Finely divided magnetic particles on the tape surface act to close this gap, thus completing the magnetic pathway in the recording head. This enables the current in the winding to produce magnetic flux whose

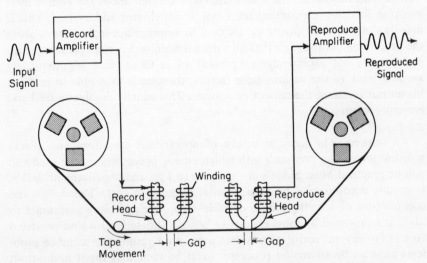

Fig. 2.39. Schematic representation of analog recording process. *Courtesy Columbia Press.*

magnitude is proportional to the current in the winding. During playback, the process is reversed, in that the magnetized tape sets up a flux in the core which produces a proportionate voltage in the winding around the playback head. This voltage reflects the rate of change of flux as the tape passes the head.

Most analog data are recorded in frequency modulated (FM) mode, because of inaccuracies inherent in direct recording. The basic technique involves the use of a reference signal (carrier frequency) which is used to represent zero input. The level of an incoming signal is then reflected as a deviation in frequency from the carrier level. Before playback, FM signals are demodulated to return them to their original form.

Recording units may range from a portable model with four tracks and the recording speed to an elaborate console capable of recording as many as 14 signals simultaneously and operating at as many as eight different speeds. In many cases the unit can be equipped with a variety of amplifiers to prepare raw signals for efficient recording.

Display. Analog information is usually displayed as permanent ink traces or on a cathode ray screen. When only one time-varying parameter is of interest and the range is sufficiently limited, use is made of an analog plotter whose basic design and operation are very similar to those used in some digital X-Y plotters. While several variables are being measured simultaneously, a written trace of these parameters may be obtained with the multichannel oscillograph (Figure 2.40), with versions available for the accomodation of as many as 14 variables. Here a continuous roll of graph paper is brought past a number of pens at a regulated speed (which can be changed to suit the sensitivity of the signal), and the pens move up and down in accordance with the amplitude of each signal. When greater sensitivity is desired, oscillographs may be purchased in which the recording paper is photosensitive and beams of light are used instead of pens to reduce inertia and increase response. Traces thus produced are semipermanent in that they will become illegible after a short time unless chemically treated.

A variety of cathode ray oscilloscopes are available for the display of analog data, ranging from small battery units to consoles with screens as large as television sets, with capability of displaying four signals simultaneously. (A widely used model is shown in Figure 2.41.) When users require it, many of these oscilloscopes can be equipped with polaroid cameras to obtain permanent records of particular displays.

Use of these devices is, of course, not restricted to displaying output from analog processors. Such units are commonly connected directly to the data source or may be used to display previously collected data stored on magnetic tape.

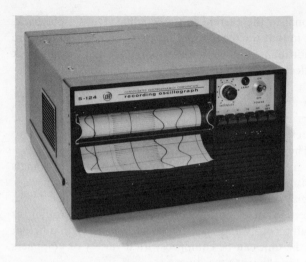

Fig. 2.40. Multichannel oscillograph. *Courtesy Consolidated Electrodynamics Corp.*

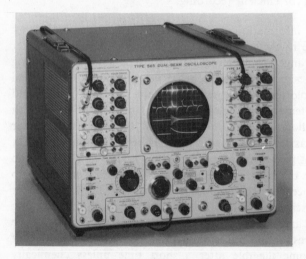

Fig. 2.41. Multichannel oscilloscope. *Courtesy Tektronix, Inc.*

HYBRID COMPUTING SYSTEMS

A number of configurations have been built in which it is possible to process data in both analog and digital modes. Two basic types of systems are presently used. The first of these consists of a complete analog processor augmented by digital logic circuits and memory components. Input and output terminals are available for transmission of data in either mode, and converters are included to change modes as the user requires. Access to the digital circuitry is provided in much the same way as for the operational amplifiers so that the user can wire his data flow paths once they have been defined.

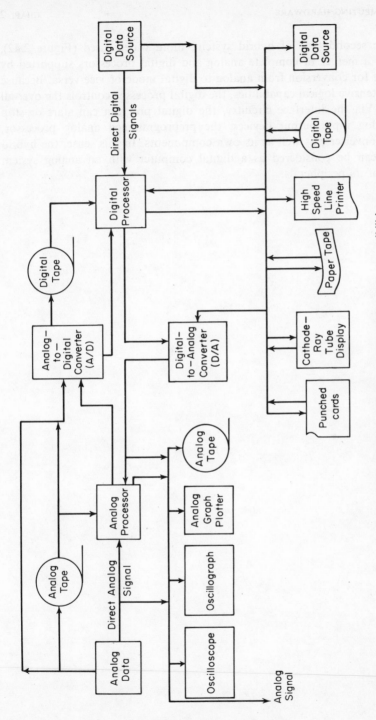

Fig. 2.42. Schematic of hybrid data-handling system possibilities.

The second type of hybrid system, more widely used (Figure 2.42), is really a merger of complete analog and digital processors supported by interface for conversion from analog to digital mode or vice versa. Because of its extensive logical capabilities, the digital processor controls the over-all system. Via the interface circuitry, the digital program can start or stop the analog input-output devices, the preprogrammed analog processor, or the converters, as well as its own components. In this sense, the hybrid system can be considered as a digital computer with an analog system as one of its peripherals.

3 COMPUTER SOFTWARE

Note to the Reader: This chapter may be omitted by the reader who is familiar with the logical structures which are necessary to convert an instrumentation-processing complex into a useful data handling tool, especially for the heuristic solution to multivariate problems. Parts of this chapter may also be omitted by the reader whose needs are predominatly computational and numerical.

It is obvious from our discussion that the implantation of proper training in a digital processor is crucial in transforming the computer into a robot and requires a level of ingenuity and creativity matching that demanded of the hardware innovator. Furthermore, this "training" begins rather than ends with a single program. Underlying the operating success of such programs is an extensive foundation of logical structures that make this program much easier to write and perfect, expand its operating scope, and allow it to be executed much more efficiently and economically. The efficacy of this supporting logical network of programs, known as software, determines the extent to which the full power of a given hardware configuration is available to the user, and therefore is the key to effective exploitation of this instrument. Recognition of this truth by knowledgeable users has moved them to invest funds in software development which match and in most cases exceed those expended for the actual hardware.

The growth of digital robots can be traced as a series of major developments prompted by user demands for more powerful systems. As this growth progressed and each demand was met, a level was added to the robot's over-all capability which, when amalgamated with existing levels, either expanded its processing capability or increased its degree of automation.

THE BASIC PROGRAM

The first step in the metamorphosis from a digital computer to a digital robot is, of course, the design and implementation of one sequential set of instructions which, when stored in the processor's memory, imbue it with the wherewithal to perform one specific data processing task. Though in the over-all view this constitutes the smallest step in the evolutionary process, its realization involves the successful completion of several phases, none of which can be considered trivial.

THE ALGORITHM

The design of a program to handle a particular data processing procedure or solve some mathematical or logical problem must be preceded by the formulation of a method of solution for that problem which can be expressed as a sequence of computer operations. The complete statement of such a method represents the initial state of program preparation and is called an *algorithm*.

As a simple example, we shall construct a computer-oriented algorithm around the determination of the modulus of elasticity (a strength property) of a circular section of material. As part of this algorithm we shall incorporate a logical decision based on the calculated magnitude of the modulus.

The modulus of elasticity E is defined by the ratio

$$\frac{P/A}{D/L}$$

where P is the magnitude of the stretching force in pounds.

A is the cross-sectional area in square inches.

D is the deformation or change in length due to the stretching force, expressed in inches.

L is the initial length of the test sample in inches.

Once this calculation is made, it is desired to test its value against a range which is to be defined as "normal." Should the value turn out to be less than 24,000,000 pounds per square inch (psi), it is desired that a message be printed together with the value indicating that it is below normal. If the value should exceed 36,000,000 psi, a message should appear together with the value indicating that it is above normal. Input information available to the processor for each set of calculations consists of the force in grams p, the diameter of the sample in centimeters s, the initial length in centimeters i, and the deformation in millimeters d.

From this information it is seen that the calculation of the modulus of elasticity must include additional steps to calculate area from diameter and to convert metric into English units so that all of the dimensions are consistent. When these considerations are incorporated into the over-all procedure, the algorithm can be expressed as a sequence of the following steps:

1. Read p, s, i, and d into the processor.
2. Convert the d from millimeters to inches:

$$D(\text{inches}) = \frac{d(\text{millimeters})}{25.4}$$

3. Cross-sectional area A (square inches)
$$= 3.14159 \left(\frac{s}{2}/2.54\right)^2$$

4. $P(\text{pounds}) = p(\text{grams})/453.6$.
5. $L(\text{inches}) = i(\text{centimeters})/2.54$.
6. Modulus of elasticity $E = (P/A)/(D/L)$.
7. If E is below 24,000,000 psi, write the value of E together with the message "modulus is below normal." If E is above 36,000,000 psi, write the value of E together with the message "modulus is above normal." For all other values of E write the value of E together with the message "modulus is in normal range."

For many problems or portions of problems there may be more than one algorithm that will yield a solution. (For example, Appendix A shows several ways to calculate the square root of a number.) The particular algorithm to be used for a program is selected on the basis of accuracy, consistency with the over-all program, duration in terms of processor operating time, and the number of instructions required for the algorithm (i.e., amount of memory used for storing these instructions). Special areas of interest have grown around the development of methods for selecting algorithms and the formulation of algorithms specifically designed for advantageous use on computers.

THE BLOCK DIAGRAM

Once a satisfactory algorithm has been selected and expressed as a sequence of distinct operations (where an operation in the descriptive sequence does not necessarily correspond to an operation on the processor), it is necessary to restate and expand the algorithm in terms of a series of events occurring within the processing system itself. The functional block diagram (or flow chart) serves as an extremely useful vehicle for expressing this chronology, just as it does in many other fields. For the user, it represents a documentation of the processing procedure, giving him an overview of the flow of data and logic. The programmer (who may not necessarily be the

Fig. 3.1. Input-output symbol in program flowcharts.

user) uses it as a communication link with the user and as a starting point of departure; the same basic flow diagram may be used to produce a given program for a variety of processor types. When a particular type of processing job calls for an extremely large program, the flow chart provides a convenient and effective means by which preparation of such a program can be divided into several well-defined portions, each of which can be assigned to a different individual without undue effect on consistency or continuity. (It is not unusual to find some very large programs requiring the efforts of a dozen or more

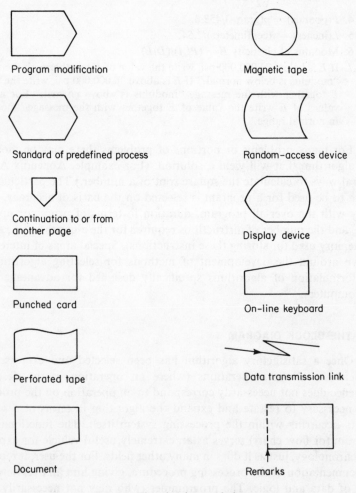

Program modification

Magnetic tape

Standard of predefined process

Random–access device

Continuation to or from another page

Display device

Punched card

On-line keyboard

Perforated tape

Data transmission link

Document

Remarks

Fig. 3.2. Flowcharting symbols.

individuals.) In addition, a clearly designed block diagram serves as an effective means of conveying the design intent and structure of a given procedure to others whose familiarity with computing ranges from the skilled programmer to the interested but casual user.

To facilitate the synthesis of block diagrams and universalize their form, a number of standard symbols and conventions have been adopted to represent the various processing functions and types of equipment assigned for their execution. The basic symbols are the same as those defined in Appendix A for flowcharting general information handling procedures (see Figure A.1). The slot (Figure A.1c) has the added meaning of representing

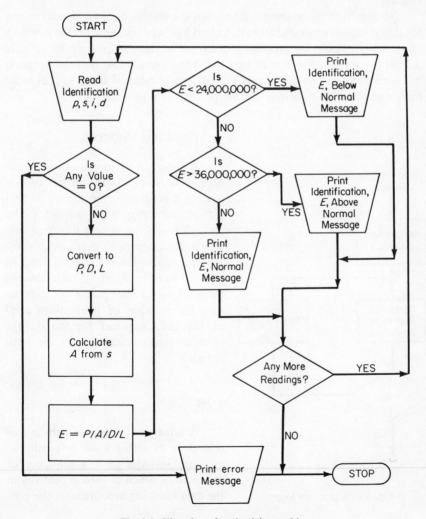

Fig. 3.3. Flowchart for elasticity problem.

an intentional pause in the program to allow operator action (e.g., changing a tape reel). Added to these is the trapezoid (Figure 3.1) which is used to depict the transmission of information to or from the processor.

A number of other symbols are in common use (see Figure 3.2), although the five basic ones are adequate for most purposes. It is seen that this set of symbols does not restrict the scope of the diagram to functions and operations performed by the processing system per se. It is, in fact, possible to depict the flow of information and logic for an entire data processing procedure, including generation of the source document, communication between components, production of the final results, and their routing.

To illustrate the relationship between the statement of an algorithm and the flow diagram generated from it, a chart has been prepared for the modulus of elasticity calculation procedure described in the previous section (Figure 3.3). It is seen that the flow of logic has been amended so that the program has been given the ability to repeat itself any number of times so that more than one set of calculations can be performed continuously.

PROGRAM MODULES

It is very easy to run out of available processor storage when one is writing a program, even though at first glance there may have seemed to be enough room for almost any purpose. When this happens, it may be necessary for the programmer to spend time in finding ways in which to compress his program or to manipulate his data so that the number of instructions and/ or the area required for the storage of input and calculated data are both reduced.

LOOPS

A substantial source of help in this regard is available when a particular program includes in it a sequence of instructions which is used repeatedly in the data handling procedure. If the pro-

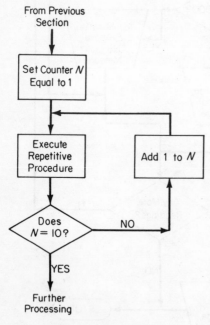

Fig. 3.4. A program loop.

grammer knows in advance how many times that particular sequence is to be repeated, or if he can devise some indirect way of determining when the repetition is to cease, he may exploit the processor's decision-making ability by incorporating these criteria into the program. Thus, for example, if a sequence of instructions is to be executed ten times in succession, the programmer need not write a string of ten sequences. Instead, he can count the number of times these instructions are executed and, as long as that number does not exceed ten, he can repeat those same physical instructions. As soon as the ten cycles are completed, the decision can be implemented to change the path of operations. A segment of flow chart symbolizing this type of technique, called *looping*, is given in Figure 3.4.

SUBROUTINES

In many instances a particular type of calculation or data handling procedure finds use in more than one portion of the same program. By using a programming technique somewhat more complex than looping, it is possible to prepare a set of instructions for this procedure and to make the same set available to two or more portions of the program. The ability to write it just once and refer to it from several places in the program could represent a considerable savings in memory requirements. This economy is achieved by writing the often used sequence of instructions as a separate entity, known as a *subroutine*. This module, usually placed at the end of the main program, is equipped with special instructions that allow the main program to reference it at one or more points along the way. Basically, this special logic keeps track of these references (calls) so that after the instructions in the subroutine are executed, the flow returns to the proper place in the main program.

The savings in memory and programming time realized by using subroutines extend beyond the individual program. Once a subroutine is written for a particular type of procedure, that subroutine can be used with any other program written for the same processing system. The utility of the subroutine technique is generally recognized, and most well-developed libraries include a series of subroutines for their special but frequently used procedures as well as for the standard calculations (such as square root, logarithm, and trigonometric functions). In some of the more advanced computing installations, effort has been extended to modularize data processing procedures to a maximum extent so that a good number of the required main programs can be synthesized at least partially by combining subroutines already written and part of the program library.

LANGUAGES

Translation of an algorithmic procedure into a workable sequence of machine instruction is usually not a straightforward proposition. Languages used by computing systems are not directly related to those used by humans, and much of the effort in software development is devoted to bridging this gap.

MACHINE LANGUAGE

Since all information is stored in a processor's memory as a series of binary numbers, instructions must also be presented to it in this form. Consequently, each type of processor is designed to accept particular combinations of 1's and 0's and interpret them as specific instructions. The repertoire of such instructions built into a processor's logical design is called its machine language, and the so-called *power* of a computer is often assessed by the number of different instructions available in its machine language and how complex an operation each one instigates.

The general form for machine instructions is as follows:

OPERATION	OPERAND(S)

The command inplied in this structure is "Perform this operation on the information stored at such and such location."

SINGLE ADDRESS MACHINES

Some computers are designed to perform all processing in special registers. This means that the processing of a particular piece of information involves moving it from its stored location to a special register, operating on it, then putting it back or moving it to some new location. Such processors are called single address machines, since their instructions require only one operand. Suppose we wanted to add two numbers together (one from location 511 and the other from 446) and place their sum in some new location (say 632). An English representation of the required command sequence for a single address machine would be:

1. Duplicate the contents of location 511 in the special register (accumulator).
2. Duplicate the contents of location 446 and add that quantity to what is currently in the accumulator.
3. Store the result in location 632.

At the end of this sequence, locations 511 and 446 would still contain what they had before, 632 would contain their sum, and so would the accumulator. In one type of single address computer, the machine language sequence would appear as follows:

PLACE IN ACCUMULATOR   CONTENTS OF 511

000101000000000000000   000000111111111

ADD TO ACCUMULATOR   CONTENTS OF 446

000100000000000000000   000000110111110

PLACE CONTENTS
OF ACCUMULATOR   IN LOCATION 632

000110000001000000000   000001001111000

DOUBLE ADDRESS MACHINES

In these processors the instruction form uses two operands, so that the commands required for the example above would be:

1. Duplicate the contents of location 511 in location 632.
2. Add the contents of location 446 to those in location 632.

The contents of the three locations at the end of the sequence would be the same as in the previous case. If we were not interested in preserving the number in location 446, the single command, "Add contents of location 511 to the contents of location 446," would have sufficed, since 511 would be unchanged and 446 would now contain the sum of its previous contents and those of 511. This instruction, when written in the machine language for a particular processor, would appear as:

ADD   CONTENTS OF 511   TO CONTENTS OF 446

110001   00010100000100000   000100000100000110

TRIPLE ADDRESS MACHINES

In one- and two-address machines, the logic organization is such that once a particular instruction is executed, the instruction reference next will be the one stored in the next location in memory. The exception, of course, occurs when an instruction is of the decision type, which causes a jump to occur, and a sequence starting at some other location is executed.

The triple address machine is organized so that each instruction can point to the next one. The addition shown in the previous example would be represented in this case as:

Add contents of 511 to contents of 446 and reference location xxx for the next instruction.

This type of command structure is not generally used in newer processors.

ASSEMBLY LANGUAGE

Writing programs in machine language is obviously an arduous business. Added to the tedium of learning and using binary numbers that bear no resemblance to the names of the operations they trigger is the necessity of assigning specific locations for storing these instructions as well as for the data on which they will operate. Because present and projected hardware technology requires machine languages to be structured as outlined, any efforts to provide programmers with more equitable languages must manifest themselves as software.

The first step in language simplification is the synthesis of a command structure in which each instruction has a machine language counterpart but the code for the instruction is mnemonic in nature and therefore more meaningful to the user. Furthermore, the operands can be symbolic; i.e., the locations to be referenced can be named rather than numbered. An instruction to add two quantities in a double address machine can be written something like

$$\text{ADD} \quad \text{X} \quad \text{Y}$$

instead of in the form shown previously, using labels (such as X, Y, TIME, etc.) for addresses in memory.

This type of language is called a machine-oriented, symbolic, or assembly language. A program in such a language is, of course, not directly acceptable by the processor but must instead be transformed into machine instructions. The software that does this is itself a program (called an *assembler*) written originally in machine language. In addition to translating instructions, the assembler performs the following tasks:

1. It assigns storage locations to each instruction.
2. It replaces symbolic names with actual storage locations so that the user can name his variables as well as his instructions as is convenient to him. The assembly language command

$$\text{SUM1} \qquad \text{ADD} \qquad \text{X} \qquad \text{Y}$$

would thus be a signal to the assembler to assign unique locations for X and Y and to record the fact that the location containing this instruction is to be called SUM1. Then, when these names (i.e., X, Y, SUM1) are used anywhere else in the program, the assembler will substitute the proper addresses in the final machine language version.

3. It generates special machine instructions which identify the end of the

program. If these were not present, the processor would have no way of differentiating between stored instructions and stored data. The combination of 1's and 0's representing a divide instruction might be the internal symbol for a K. Thus, when a logical circuit accesses a memory location and finds a K there, it has to know whether that is a divide instruction or just a piece of data which happens to be a K. Consequently, the assembler organizes memory as follows:

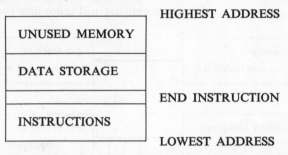

4. The assembler also generates a special little program called a loader as part of the final machine language program. Its instructions cause the processor to erase the current contents of memory and read the user's program, placing each instruction in its assigned location. When the signal indicating the program end is encountered, the logic is triggered to access the location containing the user's first instruction. That instruction is then examined and executed, and processing is under way.

The action of an assembler is schematically shown in Figure 3.5.

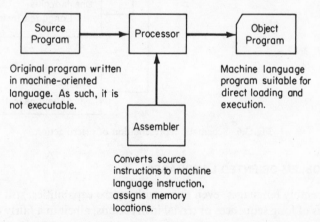

Fig. 3.5. Schematic representation of assembler function.

THE MACRO ASSEMBLER

A more advanced version of an assembler provides the user with an expanded language containing some instructions which follow the normal assembly language format but do not correspond to individual language commands. Instead, they cause the assembler to generate a particular string of machine language instructions (Figure 3.6). Since this automatically produced sequence can be quite long, involving dozens or even hundreds of instructions, this capability is a considerable convenience to the user. In some macro assemblers it is possible for the user himself to write a sequence of instructions, which he then defines by a single, newly created command. Subsequent references to the new command will reproduce that sequence.

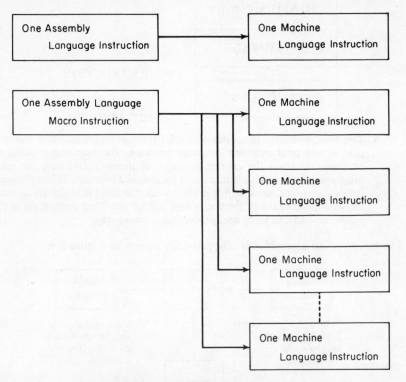

Fig. 3.6. Schematic representation of macro action.

PROBLEM-ORIENTED LANGUAGES

Assembly languages, even those with macro capabilities, still require the synthesis of long sequences of trivial instructions, albeit in a fairly convenient form. Consequently, much work has gone into producing languages that would remove the user from a particular machine syntax and would move him closer to his own vernacular. The result has been a proliferation of problem-oriented languages in which the command structure available to the user is not at all similar to the processor's internal organization. These languages are called problem-oriented because many of them have been structured with some broad application in mind. COBOL, for example (COmmon Business Oriented Language) is intended for writing business and financial data processing programs; FORTRAN (FORmula TRANslation) is oriented towards algebraic problems involving extensive computation.

The software underlying such a language consists of a large complex program called a *compiler*, whose function it is to scan each source language statement and produce a list of machine-type instructions that will duplicate the activity implied by the single command. It is generally too cumbersome for a compiler to produce an executable machine language program directly from one written in one of these high-level languages. Instead, most compilers generate a program in machine-oriented language which is passed on to an assembler which completes the job. This is done and out comes a directly executable object program. The underlying action is schematically shown in Figure 3.7.

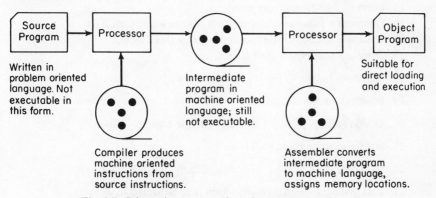

Fig. 3.7. Schematic representation of computer function.

To establish a more specific picture of a compiler's action, let us go back to the previous example in which modulus of elasticity is calculated. Steps 2 through 7 of the procedure outlined therein can be summarized in the algebraic expression

$$E = \frac{\frac{(p)}{(453.6)} / \left[\frac{3.14159}{4}\right]\left[\frac{s}{2.54}\right]^2}{\left(\frac{i}{2.54}\right) / \left(\frac{d}{25.4}\right)}$$

This same expression can be written as one statement in one problem-oriented language (FORTRAN) as follows:

```
E = (SMALLP/453.6)/((3.14159/4.0)*(SMALLS/2.54)**2)/(SMALLI/2.54)/(SMALLD/25.4)
```

The instructions generated by the compiler to fulfill the requirements of this one statement can be represented somewhat as follows:

1. Generate a value of 453.6 and store it somewhere (say location b).
2. Calculate $p/453.6$ (divide contents of p by those in b).
3. Store p/b in some location (call it c).
4. Generate the value of 3.14159 and store it somewhere (say w).
5. Generate the value of 4.0 and store it somewhere (say f).
6. Calculate 3.14159/4 (w/f).
7. Store w/f in a new location (say g).
8. Generate a value of 2.54 and store it somewhere (say h).
9. Calculate $s/2.54$ (divide contents of s by those of h).
10. Square s/h and store the result somewhere (say j).
11. Calculate $\dfrac{w}{f}\left(\dfrac{s}{h}\right)^2$ (i.e., multiply g by j).
12. Store $g(j)$ in a new place (call it k).
13. Calculate $i/2.54$ (divide contents of i by those in h).
14. Store i/h somewhere (say m.)
15. Generate a value of 25.4 and store it somewhere (call it n).
16. Calculate $d/2.54$ (divide contents of d by those in n).
17. Store d/n somewhere (call it r).
18. Calculate $(p/b)/\left[\dfrac{w}{f}\left(\dfrac{s}{h}\right)^2\right]$ (divide c by k).
19. Store c/k in some location t.
20. Divide $(p/b)/\left[\dfrac{w}{f}\left(\dfrac{s}{h}\right)^2\right]$ by $i/2.54$ (divide t by m).
21. Store t/m somewhere (call it u).
22. Calculate $p/b/\left[\dfrac{w}{f}\left(\dfrac{s}{h}\right)^2\right]/(i/2.54)/(d/25.4)$ (divide u by r).
23. This gives the desired result, which is to be stored in E.

Since the syntax of problem-oriented languages is not machine-oriented, the opportunity presents itself to make a particular language machine-independent, something which is impossible at the assembly level. This is exactly what has happened. Several languages have become sufficiently popular to prompt the development of compilers for a variety of processor types. Consequently, a user with one type of computer can take a source program originally written for some other machine and process it through the compiler for his machine. This flexibility is schematically illustrated in Figure 3.8.

PROCEDURE-ORIENTED LANGUAGES

By expanding the scope of a compiler it is possible to design a programming language in which the single statement or command can trigger the generation of a string of machine instructions for an entire data processing procedure. For example, a procedure to find the best-fitting parabola of the

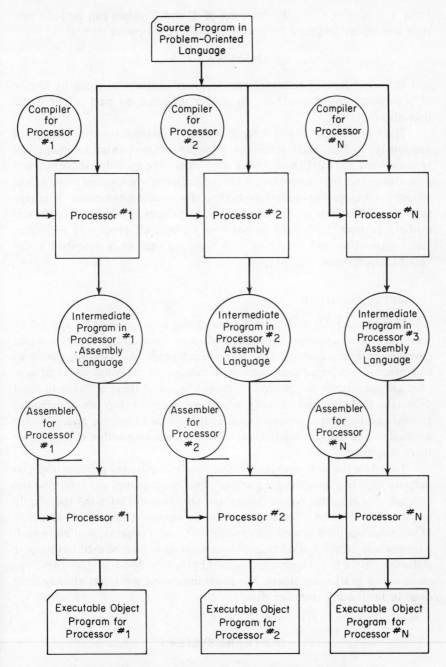

Fig. 3.8. Representation of problem language flexibility.

form $Y = a_0 + a_1 X + a_2 X^2$ for a set of X and Y values can be built into such a compiler and used by a source language statement such as

PARABOLA (Y, X)

and the compiler will reference the program instructions from its library of procedures and insert them, in proper sequence, as part of the users' over-all program.

These procedures do not differ in concept from the subroutines described previously. In fact, each statement in a procedure-oriented language can be considered as a call to a very large subroutine. The main difference between procedure- and problem-oriented language lies in the organization of the software. Besides the actual compiler, the procedure-oriented language support must include a number of logical structures to handle the data and mediate between procedure modules in an over-all processing sequence. The organization and nature of such software support is described under robot environments.

META-LANGUAGES

The considerable savings in programming time achieved by the use of powerful source language has motivated many computerniks to design and develop compilers oriented for their special needs. As a result, problem- and procedure-oriented languages now number in the hundreds, and new ones are continually announced. Although many of these are akin to local dialects in that they find use only in one installation, others are of sufficient general use to arouse interest outside their place of origin, and it is not unusual to find many computer establishments working with a half-dozen or more languages.

To reduce the large amount of effort usually required to produce a special purpose high-level language, a number of software groups are exploring the concept of a language whose design and structure are intended specifically as a medium in which other languages can be conveniently written. This type of language has been named a *meta-language*, and a program written in such a language is, in effect, a compiler, since it would in turn be used to interpret statements in the target language designed by the user. Meta-language development is still in its early stages, but some impressive work has already been done in facilitating compiler design.

SOFTWARE SYSTEMS

Production on a computing system can be considered to consist of a series of data processing jobs, each consisting of a program and input data.

When the flow of a job is handled manually, i.e., by operating personnel who remove the program, input, and output of a completed job and load the next one, much of the efficiency that was carefully built into an individual program is often washed out by the physical process of job handling. This limitation is of sufficient magnitude to counteract many hardware improvements in faster machines. Consequently, a major portion of software effort is devoted to developing supervisory programs capable of minimizing operator intervention.

THE PROCESSING MONITOR

The most basic type of supervisory software is a monitor that can automate the flow of production by recognizing the end of each job and bringing in the next one. Each job setup includes special signals to the monitor for this purpose, so it can assume and relinquish control as required; the operator's task becomes one of preparing the job stream (which can and often is a full day's computer production), loading the monitor, and introducing the first job, and separating the output after the last job is processed.

The monitor described above is conceptually complete, but its design unrealistically assumes that every job in a batch will be properly set up and will run smoothly. Quite often a mistake in the input format or an undiscovered logical error in the program will produce wrong results. Worse, it can cause the processor to stop in the middle of a job or to get hung up in an endless loop, executing the same sequence of instructions over and over. Hence, the monitor must include logical features which will recognize such conditions, terminate the job, and bring on the next one. On processing systems equipped with built-in timers, endless loops are often handled by providing the user with the ability to specify the maximum allowable processing time as part of the input data. Special signals are also included for a variety of other error conditions. In all cases, the operator can, if necessary, manually terminate a job and transfer control to the monitor. When a job runs completely but wrongly, it is, of course, strictly a matter of output inspection to detect such errors.

THE OPERATING SYSTEM

Computer activity in most installations is not restricted to production processing. An appreciable portion of the operating time is spent in assembling, compiling, and checking out new programs. The monitor being used as a basis, additional executive routines can be added to create a software system that incorporates handling capabilities for several languages and treats compilations and assemblies as ordinary members of a job stream.

THE BATCH PROCESSING SYSTEM

The monitor for such systems is designed to recognize and act on user requests ranging from straightforward execution of programs to the processing of input consisting of a source program in a high-level language followed by a set of data. In the latter case, the monitor must bring in the proper compiler from the software library and, at the proper time, follow it with the corresponding assembler. If conversion to an object program is successful, the monitor is automatically signalled, whereupon it clears memory of those software components no longer needed, and loads the newly created object program, which then proceeds with the processing. A schematic design depicting this process is shown in Figure 3.9.

The batch operating system can also be equipped with a permanent but expandable library of programs and subroutines so that the user need only submit his data together with signals referencing the appropriate program and/or routines. The final object program produced in such cases will include the necessary references to bring the routines into memory as required. To support these added responsibilities, the operating system monitor is given the added capability of accepting instructions to change the contents of the library, add a compiler, replace utility routines, etc. Also, a set of diagnostic statements is built in so that the user can be notified as to the nature of various types of compiling and operational errors. (Logical errors are still the user's business.)

This entire assemblage of software is carefully organized so that the user is only minimally aware of its presence. An executive nucleus, built as compactly as possible, permanently resides in memory and calls in other components as they are needed from the tape, disk, drum, or other device on which they are stored. Even with the concerted effort to make as much memory as possible available to the user, it is often the case that one-fourth to one-third of memory may be required for systems programs.

MULTIUSER SYSTEMS

With many of the larger and faster computers, a batch processing system may be inadequate in terms of harware utilization. This is especially true for installations servicing users with remote online terminals in addition to those who bring their work in. To handle an inflow of jobs from various sources efficiently, the operating system must be capable of stacking jobs into a composite "waiting line" (called a *queue*) regardless of their source, processing them in stride, and routing the output to the appropriate place. Furthermore, data from certain users may require immediate processing, thus necessitating the interruption of whatever is in progress, storing it and resuming work on it when the urgent job is finished.

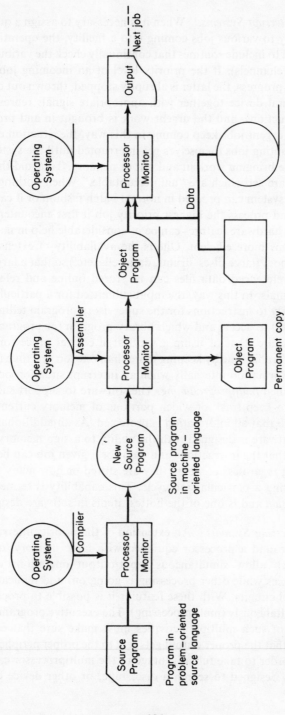

Fig. 3.9. Schematic representation of processing monitor function.

Program in
problem-oriented
source language

Source program
in machine -
oriented language

Permanent copy

Compiler

Assembler

Next job

Priority Interrupt Systems. When it is necessary to assign a quantitative relative urgency to various jobs coming into a facility, the operating system can be designed to include routines that continually check the various physical input sources (channels). If the priority level of an incoming job is higher than the one in progress, the latter is abruptly stopped, thrown out of memory onto a peripheral device together with appropriate signals representing resumption instructions, and the urgent work is brought in and processed. If enough highly urgent jobs keep coming in this way, the situation could arise wherein interrupting jobs themselves get interrupted until the system spends most of its time bringing work in and out of memory. To avoid this, certain priority levels are set which are "uninterruptable." When nothing urgent is coming in, the system can proceed in normal batch fashion or it can scan the entire queue and process the highest priority job it first encounters.

Two basic hardware features can be of considerable help in making such interrupt systems more efficient. One is the availability of extensive online peripheral memory (large discs, drums, data cells, etc.) so that a large number of frequently referenced data files can be stored online and referenced by appropriate signals. In this way, the input submitted for a particular job can be limited merely to instructions for the supervisory program telling it which data file (or files) to access and which library program (or programs) to use. The second feature, that of using a very large central processor memory, can save considerable time by keeping more than one job at a time in memory and shifting information internally when an interrupt situation occurs. This capability is called *multiprogramming.* The software to support such activity must be able to keep track of which portions of memory currently belong to which job, so that all information is protected. As an additional improvement, some software is designed with the ability to assign memory locations in such a way that the instructions and data for a given job can be triggered into processing regardless of where they are stored or how many times they are shifted during a particular job cycle. This capability is termed *dynamic memory allocation* and is one of the hottest items in software design.

Multiprocessing Systems. An extension of the priority interrupt system can be built around a processor equipped with large memory, overlapped channels (which allow simultaneous input/output operations on several peripheral devices while other processing is going on) and replicated sets of internal control circuits. With these features it is possible to process several jobs truly simultaneously (multiprocessing). The executive programs required to keep track of such multiple activities must make sure that each job is protected and that the proper output gets sent to the proper peripheral device. Moreover, in order to take full advantage of the multiprocessor capabilities, the software is designed to search a disc, tape, or other device containing a queue of waiting jobs and to select a combination having fairly high priority and the ability to fit in the available memory. This search and selection process continues as processing is completed on various jobs and differing portions of memory become free.

Time-sharing Systems. The area of software development receiving perhaps the greatest amount of attention at present is the one concerned with servicing a number of online users at the same time. If several people at remote terminals are engaged in the type of work which requires continuous interaction between user and program (e.g., a cyclic process in which each set of input is dictated by previous results), it becomes a plausible proposition to devise a system of software which will give a user his output and go on to process other jobs while he ponders and prepares his response. By the time he is ready for the next phase in his processing, the system has got around to him again and, as far as he is concerned, he is and has been the only one on the machine. This general concept, known as *time sharing*, offers the possibility of making considerably more use of available processing time while providing apparently simultaneous access for many users.

In general, a time-sharing system operates in a cyclic fashion, processing input from each terminal for a prescribed length of time and going on to the next one. Even more than is the case with batch processing or priority interrupt systems, time-sharing software is highly individualized. Operating characteristics such as the time alloted to each time-sharing user in a given cycle, whether or not to provide multiple access to the same data file, the number of priority levels, and whether to set up one or more waiting lines depend strongly on the job mixture and number of terminals to be accessed. For example, an optimum compromise must be made between the conflicting parameters of fast response time and excessive processor time tied up in moving jobs in and out of memory. For some installations it may be much more efficient to assign unequal time intervals to various users rather than to allot equal slots as is usually done. For installations in which interactive (also called *conversational*) processing is not the typical operating mode for all terminals at all times, it is advantageous to maintain a batch queue of jobs for fill-in, to be worked on until the monitor detects some activity at the terminals. (This is called a background batch.) For installations which are batch oriented and where there is little call for immediate response, time sharing may not be appropriate in any form, and a less complex priority interrupt system may suffice. There is some confusion with regard to time sharing in that some people misconstrue it as a universal replacement or an improvement over other supervisory systems. As exemplified above, the advantages and benefits of such procedures must be evaluated carefully for each individual setting.

ROBOT ENVIRONMENTS

A new concept in supervisory software is being explored which promises greater power and flexibility for the user by providing him with a very powerful command structure for executing highly complex analytical, numerical, logical, and graphical processing tasks. The languages available through such systems allow the user to build entire chains of procedures, using a small number of relatively simple commands, as described in the section on procedure-oriented languages.

These software systems are called *robot environments* because implied in their structure is the ability to synthesize and carry out decision-making networks regarding the automatic manipulation of data files as well as programs. Whereas a standard type of monitor is built to process requests by accessing and retrieving specific routines for each of a sequence of jobs, the executive programs for a robot environment must decode users' requests and decide which programs are required, in what sequence, and when they should be brought into memory. Furthermore, it is the system's, rather than the user's, responsibility to make sure that the data required for the next procedure in a chain of procedures are made available at the proper time, in the proper place, and in the form expected by the routines for that procedure.

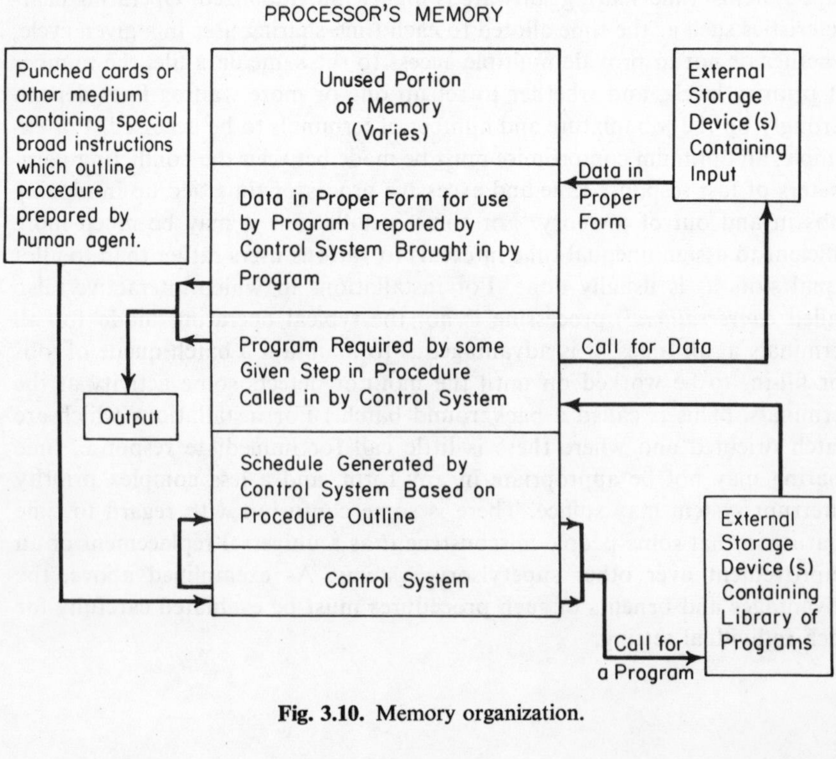

Fig. 3.10. Memory organization.

The basic components of a robot environment include a compiler that decodes procedural requests in the user's language and constructs a set of scheduling instructions. A scheduling routine uses these instructions to build a detailed table describing the sequence of routines and data files required for the procedures. Once this is prepared, it is continually consulted by information handling routines which bring the various packages in and out of memory as required. Output produced by the various library programs is transmitted via the information handling routines to a report writing structure that formats the results and produces the actual displays. The entire network operates under a monitor that mediates between jobs (Figure 3.10).

Although the robot environment concept was initially conceived for use in a batch processing setting, it is not limited to that mode. There are no forseeable barrier problems which prevent its inclusion in a time-shared or other multiuser operating system, and some work towards this end is in progress.

4 ORGANIZATION AND COLLECTION OF DATA

Since the introduction of computers has instigated basic changes in the techniques and scope of data processing, it is to be expected that over-all procedures involved in the generation, collection, and preparation of data would undergo fundamental changes too. Some of these, in fact, have already taken place. We are tending toward universal collection of computer-compatible data in two basic ways. First, methods for collecting and preparing manually generated data are being modified to produce information that is properly coded and formatted for computer use. Second, more and more automatic sensing devices are being introduced which are designed to provide a direct bridge from the data source to the computer. Concurrently, computer manufacturers and allied industries are engaged in a continuing program to develop peripheral hardware that will accept input from a widening spectrum of instruments. With the gradual convergence of these broadening technologies, the over-all volume of data still unreadable by computing systems will inevitably lessen to a point where the inaccessibility of data will no longer be a valid reason for not using automatic processing techniques and procedures.

MANUALLY GENERATED DATA

Regardless of the extent to which instrumentation technology grows, there will always be certain information which will be recorded and collected manually. Besides normal human stubbornness, there are two compelling reasons for manual data gathering. There always will be instances for which the price for automation cannot be justified. If the volume of data to be recorded is small or the required automating components are complex, it may often be cheaper and no less reliable to use the human as observer and recorder. More basically, circumstances do and always will exist wherein information relating to certain areas can only be obtained as the result of human decision processes or through circumstances in which the human observer must act as the measuring instrument. When these processes cannot be articulated to the extent that a machine can be devised to parallel them, there is no choice but to record and collect data manually. This situation is especially common in the biological and behavioral sciences, where much can be learned from interviews, remarks, observations of attitudes, and other similar sources.

PREPARATION OF MANUALLY COLLECTED DATA

The conversion of manually collected data to computer-compatible form is based on the fulfillment of two distinct requirements, physical and organizational. Achievement of physical compatibility is, of course, a fairly straightforward matter. The information must be made available on some medium from which a particular computing system is able to read. Thus, digital information recorded on punched cards, punched paper tape, mark sense cards or on digital magnetic tape satisfies the requirements for physical compatibility.

The organization of data for computer processing, that is, the achievement of logical compatibility, is tied in closely with the basic mechanism by which processors handle data. Since each information handling procedure is represented in the processor's memory by a series of specific and very detailed instructions in which there can be no uncertainties, the data to be processed according to these instructions must be equally consistent and equally unambiguous. Consequently, the codes used to represent manually collected data and the forms on which such data are recorded (whether they be questionnaires, lab sheets, sales reports, or other data documents) must strive to present as orderly and concise a picture of the data as possible. Experience with the design of computer-oriented data collection forms has brought to light a number of techniques that insure that these features are present.

NUMERICAL DATA

When a variable is expressed as a quantitative reading, measurement, or score, i.e., some actual number which reflects the magnitude or intensity of the observed phenomenon, the investigator must express that variable in the same form every time he records it. This means that he has to establish the expected range that the variable might cover in the course of his observations and the degree of accuracy with which it is to be recorded. Once the range and accuracy have been defined, this variable is reported as a quantity containing a specific number of digits. No subsequent observation of the variable should then exceed the prescribed number of digits, and those not requiring the full field length should be supplemented by zeros.

As an example, let us suppose that the observer wished to report "body temperature" of human subjects as one of his observed variables and he expects information to be available to the nearest tenth of a degree Fahrenheit. In this case he knows he will need three digits to report the integer portion of the reading (since temperature could exceed 99) and an additional digit for the decimal place. The portion of his questionnaire where temperature would be recorded would then appear somewhat as follows:

Temperature, °F   ☐ ☐ ☐ ☐

An observed reading of 103.2 would be recorded as

1	0	3	2

and a reading of 98.8 would appear as

0	9	8	8

Note that since the decimal point is usually not punched onto cards, it need not appear on data gathering sheets except as a convenience. If the investigator knows in advance that all of the readings for a particular variable will be positive numbers, the assignment of a field length (number of digits) is adequate as described above. Should the possibility exist however, for the appearance of a negative reading, a digit must be reserved for the minus sign, even if it should occur only once in several hundred readings. If, for example, a voltage of 17.6 is recorded in the following established format

1	7	6

it is poor practice to represent a voltage of −4.4 in the same experiment or study as

−	4	4

Instead, an extra digit should be allocated in the field for the sign (this can usually be left blank if the number is positive).

| 1 | 7 | 6 |　　| − | 0 | 4 | 4 |

QUALITATIVE DATA

When the design of a data collection sheet must include provisions for coded qualitative observations, it often places an organizational burden on the investigator, since he must make sure that the alternative attributes to be used in expressing a particular variable of this type are given clearly distinguishable codes and that each of them represents a unique condition. For example, if a sociologist is working with a group of subjects who receive their incomes from employment or from city welfare and he wishes to record the source of income as one of his variables, the following assignment of alternative categories would not be sufficiently clear:

Sources of Income
1 = From employment
2 = From city welfare

The insufficiency lies in the fact that this distinction does not make allowance for those subjects who receive their income from neither source, from both sources, or from some other source. The category assignments shown below represent a more complete and unambiguous spectrum of choices:

Sources of Income
Blank = No visible source of income
1 = From employment
2 = From city welfare
3 = Employment and city welfare
4 = Other than employment or city welfare
5 = Employment and other
6 = City welfare and other
7 = Employment, city welfare, and other

In this particular instance some of the alternatives could be eliminated if the investigator knows in advance that only two sources of income are to be considered. At all times the choices must be exhaustive and excluisve. Untold difficulties may be created if the investigator finds cases that do not fit in his classification scheme. If he had deleted the choice "employment and city welfare" from above and he finds individuals who do have both sources of income, it may be very difficult to add this category. Take the instance in which the investigator starts with ten alternatives, which he numbers 0 to 9, and discovers an eleventh choice midway through the study. He may be forced into a costly modification of his data recording media.

One crucial error to be avoided is the failure to provide mutually exclusive categories. If the investigator has failed to provide choice 3 above and finds individuals with sources of income from employment and from city welfare, he cannot record both by punching a 1 and a 2 in the same column of the card. Most automatic reading input devices will balk at double punches and refuse to read them, or they will interpret the double punch as an alphabetic or other type of character. If classifications are not exclusive, provisions must be made to record each choice separately. For instance, if a patient can have more than one symptom, choices could be recorded as follows:

Symptoms	Yes	No
Headache	1	2
Toothache	1	2
Flat feet	1	2

etc.

When recorded on the questionnaire or laboratory sheet, it is certainly possible but very cumbersome to use the actual wording for the particular choice. Instead it is much easier for the person filling out the data collection sheet to employ a concise code to represent the appropriate alternative (as well as being much more economical in terms of processor's memory usage). The assignment of a number to each alternative is the most obvious coding scheme and usually works best. For ordered variables, the codes can be identical with the scale assignments so that they reflect the observed degree of magnitude or intensity. Where more than ten alternatives exist for a given variable, a multidigit numeric code or one consisting of one or more letters may be used. Thus, for example, many observers represent the months of the year by codes 01 through 12 (for January through December, respectively), while others, interested in more compact coding, use the letters A through L for the same purpose. (In general, the internal circuitry of most digital processors is such that it is somewhat easier to handle numbers than letters.) Wherever possible, it is a good idea to keep the maximum number of available coded alternatives as small as possible. Although the investigator may be tempted to classify according to minute details, he should keep in mind that the greater the fragmentation of his data, the more limited he will be in using methods of multivariate analysis. When a variable is used with a very large number of inherent choices (such as diagnosis, occupation, or crime, all of which have standard lists containing many thousands of choices), it is necessary to define a series of major categories, each encompassing a set of choices appropriate to and consistent with the intent of the particular study. In the case of medical diagnosis, for example, such grouping may be delineated by major body systems or by suspected relation to a given environmental condition, such as air pollution. In the case of occupation, the categorical combinations may be made on the basis of income, amount of education, relative number of people in that vocational area, etc. In the event that the investigator cannot decide upon a simplified classification scheme, he could provide a number of alternate classifications. For instance, if he is unhappy about grouping diagnoses by physiological systems or by possible effect of air pollutants, he could use both classifications and, in fact, add any number of other schemes to them. In any case, the search of literature and/or conscience required to produce such a combined grouping makes this an arduous but necessary task.

Once a set of mutually exclusive and unambiguous choices have been defined for a numeric or qualitative variable and the corresponding code designations have been established, the physical placement on the data collection sheet is fairly straightforward. To facilitate preparation of the sheet and reduce the amount of time and skill required to handle it, it is usually best to state each choice clearly, accompanied by its corresponding code designation so placed that it can be easily circled or underlined. For example, if the twenty-third question in a political survey is concerned with an individual's attitude toward a candidate, its form on the questionnaire might look as follows:

23.   Over-all attitude toward candidate (circle only one)
        Blank = Opinion unknown
            0 = No opinion
            1 = Decidedly hostile
            2 = Unfavorable
            3 = Somewhat negative; cold
            4 = Neutral; indifferent
            5 = Somewhat positively impressed
            6 = Favorable
            7 = Very enthusiastic

Note. When data are not available for a variable, it is best to leave that column blank rather than to indicate that by a special code.

IDENTIFICATION

When sets of observations are to be recorded for a number of subjects (or experiments), a place must be included on the questionnaire for some identifier such that each experimental entity is uniquely distinguished. The simplest and most effective method is to assign successive numbers to the subjects in any convenient fashion. Even if a study is concerned with human subjects and the name is included on the data collection sheet, it is a good idea to assign a subject number as well, since the latter is less cumbersome for a processor to handle and overcomes possible sources of inconsistency due to spelling errors, name changes, etc. Furthermore, distinguishability of subjects is assured in studies of a confidential nature where the names have to be suppressed. (When data for such studies are transcribed onto punched cards, it is good practice to produce two sets of cards with one containing the data, identified only by subject number, and the other being a key set for limited access in which each subject number is linked with the corresponding name.)

Assignment of identification numbers is usually governed by the anticipated size of the study. Thus, for example, if it is expected that a particular investigation will involve several thousand subjects, a four-digit numerical identifier is used from the very start (i.e., the first subject is assigned number 0001, etc.). The importance of adhering to this practice will become clearer when we discuss the transcription of data from collection sheets to punched mediums. In certain instances the identifying number can serve a double purpose by designing it so that it conveys some additional information. As a case in point we can consider a questionnaire used for a survey of college students. Several thousand individuals were involved, but it was known beforehand that there would be no more than 1000 from any given year. Since the investigators were interested in how students of a particular year responded to various questions, the data collection sheets were prenumbered with a four-digit identifier in which the first digit was used to denote the year. Thus the freshmen were handed sheets numbered from 1000 to 1999, the sophomores received questionnaires numbered 2000 through 2999, and so on.

Efforts are being made to devise "standard" identifications for individuals which can be used universally for a variety of data collection purposes. The name is intrinsically unreliable (and even variable) and inefficient. A favorite identifier gaining wide acceptance is the nine-digit social security number, since it is unique. A person receives it relatively early in life and carries that number until his death and its retirement. Urban planners and sociologists wishing to study family movements and other time-varying family phenomena are experimenting with an extension of the social security identifier to link family data together and overcome the objection that not everyone has a social security number. The plan is to augment an individual's social security number with a code indicating his position in his household and to carry along his social security number with that of the head of the household. This presumes that there is at least one person in a given household with a social security number. A household relation code might look as follows:

Status in Household

Blank = Unknown
   1 = Head
   2 = Spouse
   3 = Son or daughter
   4 = Grandson or granddaughter
   5 = Parent
   6 = Sister or sister-in-law; brother or
       brother-in-law
   7 = Niece or nephew
   8 = Other relative
   9 = Unrelated

Thus, Mary Smith with identification given as

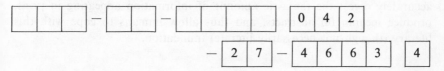

is a son or daughter of 054-26-7961 and her own Soc. Sec. No. is 066-14-2097.
Similarly, little Murray Jones' identification might be

which indicates he is a grandson or granddaughter belonging to 042-27-4663's
household but has no social security number.

   Another unique identifier being used in a number of studies consists
of a composite of abbreviations taken from various attributes: First and last
letter of first name (this is far less likely to change than the last), date and
place of birth, sex, and race. Thus, Thomas Bellows, a white male (code 1),
born in Arizona (coded as AZ) on January 4, 1939, would be assigned the
identification TS010439AZ1, or the day of birth might be omitted, leaving
TS0139AZ1. Experience with this type of identifier in one project has produced no duplicates in over 5000 subjects.

EDITING OF MANUALLY COLLECTED DATA

   The nature of some investigations, particulary in the management, behavioral, and social sciences, is such that data can be collected only in narrative

form (taped interviews, transcripts of trials or meetings, books and articles, etc.). When this happens, the processes of recording observations and devising codes for them must, of course, be preceded by an editing stage in which the salient points and quantitative and coded features are extracted from the mass of narrative. Although this is a time-consuming and arduous task, it is certainly not a new one generated by the advent of computers. Actually, it represents a more disciplined version of a procedure as old as data gathering itself. It has generally been found that once an investigator becomes accustomed to editing narrative information for mechanized data processing purposes, he will tend to construct subsequent studies such that his useful and interesting data can be obtained as scalable observations.

In this connection it is interesting to note that one of the most active areas of computer applications research concerns itself with the exact nature of such editing processes. A number of techniques are being explored whereby some narrative material (usually but not necessarily a technical article) available on some appropriate medium is scanned by a processor in whose memory is stored a set of linguistic rules. The intent is to develop a logic which is sufficiently comprehensive and effective, so that, by finding key words and phases, the processor can piece together a satisfactory summary or abstract of the material it scans. Since a great deal of parallel effort is going on to develop sensing mechanisms that allow computers to scan printed texts, the ultimate aim, of course, is to build a robot that can speedily and accurately digest the fantastic amount of information appearing in print, produce meaningful abstracts, and thus allow humans to cope with this literary (though not necessarily literate) inundation.

TRANSCRIPTION OF MANUALLY COLLECTED DATA

Once the content of the data collection sheet has been defined by establishing ranges for quantitative variables and appropriate coding for qualitative information, the relative ease with which such data can be transcribed onto some machine-compatible medium will depend on the physical layout of the sheet and how closely its design has been coordinated with the properties of the medium to be used. A carefully constructed layout can appreciably reduce the time, cost, and errors in transcription; at the same time, it will present no serious compromise to the investigator collecting the data or the personnel filling out the sheets.

Two basic media presently compete with each other for use as receptacles for manually produced information. Although punched paper tape has a number of features which make it attractive as a convenient repository for source information, the familiar and seemingly ubiquitous punched card is and will continue to be by far the most widely used medium. Consequently, in our discussion of transcription techniques and considerations, we shall concern ourselves primarily with punched cards as the end product.

Because of the processor's requirements for consistency, a fixed relationship must be established for a given study between the data on the lab sheet and its placement on the punched card. This correspondence is effected through the use of a well-designed card outline on which is specified the name of each variable in the experiment or study, its assigned column location(s) on the punched card, and the form in which it is to be punched. Such an outline, set up cooperatively by the investigator and computer personnel, serves several useful functions:

1. It is a clear and permanent record of the type of data being collected and used for a given study. As such, it provides a convenient summary of the project for interested parties, who can use it as a point of departure for subsequent discussion.

2. It also provides information for setting up appropriate processing. Thus, for example, if a card outline for a given study specifies that the variable "attitude toward candidate," coded as a single digit, is assigned to be punched in column 55 of the card for that particular subject, the processor can be instructed to "look" in column 55 for attitudes towards candidate with the assurance that the attitude will always be found in that column and in no other place on the card; furthermore, the number found in that column will always represent "attitude toward candidate" and nothing else for that study.

The assignment of card columns to the variables in a study or experiment is quite arbitrary and should be governed by convenience. If there is some preferred sequence of variables that is more useful or meaningful to the investigator, then the column assignments on the punched cards can follow that order. In some studies it may be useful to keep certain types of variables together because they normally form a cluster as a result of commonality of content or source. In biomedical studies involving patients, for example, physical characteristics, laboratory findings, and treatment variables commonly form three such clusters. Since the keypunch, like the typewriter, operates sequentially from left to right (columns 1 through 80), the most efficient physical layout of a data collection sheet is one in which the order of the variables corresponds to that on the punched card. Consequently, the assignment of columns is often really decided by the investigator's preference for the placement of variables on his data collection sheet.

When columns are being assigned to variables containing decimals, it is not necessary to leave room for the actual decimal point to be punched. Instead, the placement can be implied and handled during the processing. All well-designed general programs are equipped with instructions that determine the number of decimal places in a variable. (This must be consistent for a given study.) The same holds for other symbols, so that a data item written as $3,729.81 is punched as 372981 and the program is instructed accordingly so that the final results will have the dollar sign, the comma, and the decimal in their proper places.

Many investigators are under the mistaken impression that they are restricted in the number of digits of data they can make available for computer processing by the number of columns on the punched card. In fact, many have kept their studies off the computer for this reason, feeling that it places an undue constraint on the scope of analyses that could be performed. Others have simply ignored certain variables already recorded so that they could fit a set of data on one card. This, of course, is like telling an author that he has one page in which to express himself, or limiting an artist to so many square inches of canvas. With proper organization, there is no practical limit to the number of cards which may be used for a set of variables in a given study. (Just as there is no conceptual limit to the number of pages for a questionnaire or other data collection document.) In no event should the number of available columns on a card seriously compromise the scope of the data to be collected.

When it is necessary to use more than one punched card for a set of observations, care must be taken to provide space for enough information on each card so that all of the cards belonging to a set of observations (such as the same subject or experiment) can be grouped together and each individual card can be distinguished from the others. The former contingency is most conveniently handled by repeating some identifier (usually the subject or experiment number) on each card, the same columns being used each time for organizational consistency. Distinguishability of individual cards for a given set of observations is achieved by allocating a certain column (or columns, if necessary) on each card for a card number. Although it makes no difference in terms of computing procedures or mechanics, it is usually most convenient for the design of the data collection sheets to place such card identification in the last (rightmost) column or columns.

The observation of a large number of variables is not the only reason for requiring a multicard data file. Many studies are of the type in which a basic set of data is collected, followed by a prescribed or unpredictable number of repetitions of part of that set. Typical of such studies is the chronic disease investigation in which each subject, after having been brought in for an initial interview and examination, is called back periodically to determine his progress. In such studies the set of variables are divided into those that are basic to the patient (such as sex, initial diagnosis, age at initial examination, etc.) and those that will be observed at each subsequent examination or interview. The data file is then organized by allocating a card for the basic parameters (not all of the columns in the card need necessarily be assigned) and an additional card (called a *trailer card*) for those observations that will be repeated at each subsequent visit. Thus, at any given point in time, the record for a particular individual may consist of the initial card followed by any number of such trailer cards. If a large number of variables are to be recorded for each followup visit, there need be no limit, of course, to the number of cards used for each followup visit or episode as long as proper identification is provided. Thus, it is perfectly reasonable to have a single card containing basic data followed by a number of three-card sets reflecting the observations recorded at a succession of visits. Since it is necessary to maintain consistency in such sets, they must be organized to accommodate the maximum number of anticipated variables even though certain areas may be left blank most of the time. In such studies it is also useful to include the date as part of the information on each trailer card (or cards) so that all kinds of chronological calculations can be done as part of the data processing (e.g., current age, elapsed time from initial diagnosis, length of hospitalization, etc.). Another useful gimmick in the design of data files for followup studies is to include, where applicable, a place on each trailer card (or set of cards) where the date of the next examination or interview or billing can be recorded. By making such information available to the processor, periodic followup lists can be generated automatically by having the processor search the entire data file and extract those with the appropriate date. Followup processing is

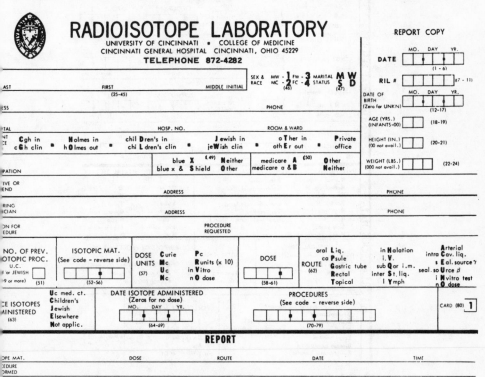

Fig. 4.1. Data form for radioisotope patient file—initial portion. *Courtesy Radioisotope Labratory, University of Cincinnatti.*

CARD #2 - Results, Interpretation, and Miscellaneous Data

(1 - 6)		(7-11)		(12-17)	
DATE	SAME AS CARD # 1	RIL #	SAME AS CARD # 1	DATE OF BIRTH	SAME AS CARD # 1

ASSESSMENTS — PHOTOSCANS (Not Scinti-Photos)

SCAN - REGION I			SCAN - REGION II		
n 0 scan			n 0 scan		
Blank in boxes 18-33 (18-33)			Blank in boxes 26 - 33 (26-33)		
SITUATION (18)	Normal no Rmal & abn.ext. Ectopic tissue Abn.	a Bn. & ectopic in Det. or irrel. or Gan absent	SITUATION (26)	Normal no Rmal & abn.ext. Ectopic tissue Abn.	a Bn. & ectopic in Det. or irrel. or Gan absent
SIZE (19)	Small Border. sm. Normal	bo Rder. lge. Large in Det. or irrel.	SIZE (27)	Small Border. sm. Normal	bo Rder. lge. Large in Det. or irrel.
SHAPE (20)	Normal Assym. (abn.) i Rreg.	Unusual in Det. or irrel.	SHAPE (28)	Normal Assym. (abn.) i Rreg.	Unusual in Det. or irrel.
EDGES (21)	Well def. Adeq. def.	Poorly def. in Det. or irrel.	EDGES (29)	Well def. Adeq. def.	Poorly def. in Det. or irrel.
UNIFORMITY (22)	Uniform Non uniform in Det. or irrel.		UNIFORMITY (30)	Uniform Non uniform in Det. or irrel.	
HOT AREAS (23)	Single Multiple None in Det. or irrel.		HOT AREAS (31)	Single Multiple None in Det. or irrel.	
COLD AREAS (24)	Single Multiple None in Det. or irrel.		COLD AREAS (32)	Single Multiple None in Det. or irrel.	
TECHNICAL QUALITY (25)	Good Poor Adequate		TECHNICAL QUALITY (33)	Good Poor Adequate	

NUMERICAL RESULTS

RESULTS (Percent) n 0 t applicable n 0 code	Blanks in boxes 34-41	ie UPTAKE LOSS RECOVERY RETENTION ABSORPTION ETC.	GROUP - 1 (34-37)	GROUP - 2 (38-41)
RESULTS (Time or Quantity Units) n 0 t applicable n 0 code	Blanks in boxes 42-49	ie MINS. HRS. GMS. LITERS ETC.	GROUP - 3 (42-45)	GROUP - 4 (46-49)
RESULTS (Rates) n 0 t applicable n 0 code	Blanks in boxes 50-57	ie MGM/100ML LITERS/MIN. ETC.	GROUP - 5 (50-53)	GROUP - 6 (54-57)

RESULTS (Ratios) n 0 t applicable n 0 code	Blanks in boxes 58-69	GROUP - 7 (58-63) : 1	GROUP - 8 (64-69) : 1

MISCELLANEOUS DATA

INTERPRETATION OR TECHNICAL EVALUATION		DIAGNOSTIC SPECIAL TECHNIC	
Normal range	Abn. found (70)	I (71)	II (72)
Normal result	Spurious (biol.)	n 0 t applicable	n 0 t applicable
Minor abn.	s Purious (tech.)	None	None
Border. high	in Com. or unsat. study	Solid st.	Solid st.
High (abn.)	no in Terpretation	Gamma cam.	Gamma cam.
bo Rder. low	Good tech. proc. (ther.)	Hippo	Hippo
Low (abn.)	sat. t Ech. proc. (ther.)	Liq. scin.	Liq. scin.
Unsct. or incomp. tech. proc.(ther.)		Wbc	Wbc

CLINICAL OR (73) PATHOLOGICAL DIAGNOSES	INTEREST (74)	PURPOSE OF PROCEDURE (75)	
To be rec. on "dx fu form"	Routine	Clinical	Other research
Not yet made	Teaching	Survey	s P ecial
Previously rec.	Unusual	Formal research	
no Diagnosis		Therapeutic	

PURPOSE (76) (Ther. Procedures)		FOLLOW-UP MONTH (77)		
n 0 t applicable		Jan	i Une	Nov
Rad. curative	" P rophylactic"	Feb	ju L y	Dec
Ablative	T o induce remission	March	au G	n 0 f.u.
Local control	ad J uvant	Apr	S ep	
Disease suppressive		ma Y	o Ct	
Symptomatic benefit				CARD (80) 2

Fig. 4.2. Data form for radioisotope patient file—supplementary portion. *Courtesy Radioisotope Laboratory, University of Cincinnatti.*

118

performed routinely in a number of areas where the automatic production of followup lists is augmented by computer-produced letters to each individual calling him in. Figures 4.1 and 4.2 show the data collection forms used for initial examination and followup in one such project.

This type of multicard data file is assuming growing importance in epidemiological, demographic, economic, and other studies involving large amounts of information. Data file designs of the type described above, when properly developed and implemented, permit the effective planning of projects concerned with such areas as population morbidity, usage of public service facilities (such as hospitals, nursing homes, and social centers), and long-term family histories.

CUSTOM-DESIGNED PUNCHED CARDS

When a study or project is of sufficient size to justify the cost, it is often very convenient to produce special punched cards in which the column assignments are imprinted on the cards themselves. If the number of variables is reasonably small and the coding for the ordinal and nominal ones is not extensive or complex, it is possible to include sufficient information in the printed design so that the card itself will carry adequate documentation that fulfills most of the functions and conveniences of the card outline. A typical example of such specially prepared cards is shown in Figure 4.3.

In some specific instances, where only small amounts of information are being recorded, it is possible to imprint the card in such a way that it serves as the initial questionnaire (Figure 4.4). After the appropriate information is filled in, the keypunch operator reads it and punches it right on that card. In general, this is a fairly tenuous practice and is best avoided, particularly when such cards get out of the hands of the staff immediately concerned with

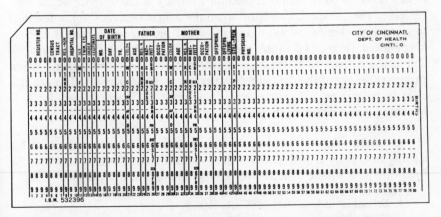

Fig. 4.3. Preprinted punched card containing code designations. *Courtesy Department of Health, City of Cincinnatti.*

the study or project. The now well-recognized admonition not to tear, fold, staple, spindle, or mutilate is in many instances an invitation to tear, fold, staple, spindle, or mutilate.

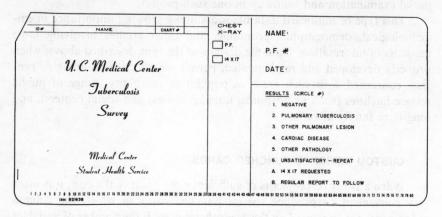

Fig. 4.4. Preprinted punched card serving as source document. *Courtesy Student Health Service, University of Cincinnatti.*

FINALIZATION OF DATA COLLECTION SHEETS

Once the card outline is complete, the appropriate column assignments can be indicated next to the corresponding variables on the data collection sheet so that the keypunch operator is furnished with a built-in guide and need make no external reference. When the volume of data to be collected is such that the forms are to be printed rather than produced on some office duplicating device, the column assignments can be displayed in boldface type or in a different color than that used for the body of the form for added convenience. This is especially helpful when the data collection sheet is designed to serve a number of functions and not all of the information on it is to be keypunched. (Figure 4.5 shows such a form which is printed on heavy stock and becomes part of a permanent record file after keypunching.) When permanent filing of the data sheets is necessary, some may find it more efficient to prepare each questionnaire in duplicate and send the copy for keypunching while retaining the original for their files.

Example. It is desired to prepare a questionnaire and card outline for a study to explore growth patterns in school children. Towards this end, the following data will be collected for a large number of individuals:

    1. School identification   (86 schools)

    2. Date of birth   (month, day, year)

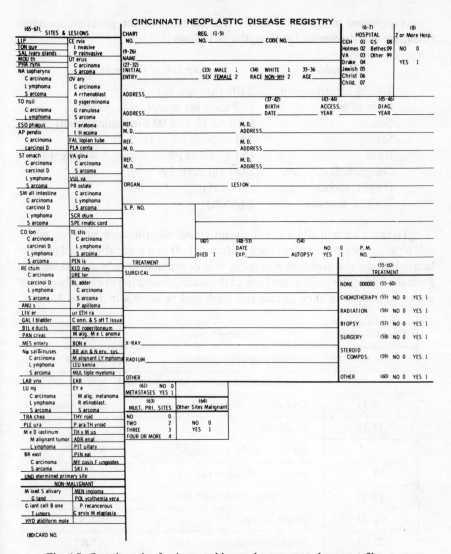

Fig. 4.5. Questionnaire for keypunching and permanent document file.

3. Grade   (kindergarten through twelfth grade)
4. Sex   (male, female)
5. Race   (white, negro, and others)
6. Geographic division   (29 divisions)
7. Height   (inches, to the nearest half inch)
8. Weight   (pounds, to the nearest pound)

It is expected that 10,000 individuals will participate in the study.

Assignment of Card Columns.   On the basis of the problem specifications, we can determine field lengths as follows:

Variable	*Number of Columns*
School identification	2 (01 through 86)
Date of birth	6 (2 each for month, day, year)
Grade	2 (01 to 12 and 00 for kindergarten)
Sex	1 (1 = male; 2 = female)
Race	1 (1 = white; 2 = negro; 3 = other)
Geographic division	2 (01 through 29)
Height, inches	3 (XX.X)
Weight, pounds	3 (XXX)

To these we will add a five-digit individual identification number, which will be at the beginning of the card (columns 1–5) and a one-digit card number located at the end (column 80). Also, it is convenient to add a variable that gives the age of the child at the time of the study. Assigning the variables listed above in order, we then obtain the card outline shown in Figure 4.6.

Card Columns	Variable Name	Format
1–5	Student indentification no.	XXXXX
6–7	School identification (01–86)	XX
8–13	Date of birth (month, day, year)	XX XX XX
14–15	Grade (00–12)	XX
16	Sex (1 = male; 2 = female)	X
17	Race (1 = wh.; 2 = neg.; 3 = other)	X
18–19	Geographic division (01–29)	XX
20–22	Height, inches	XX.X
23–25	Weight, pounds	XXX
26–27	Age, years	XX
80	Card number	1

Fig. 4.6. Student growth study card outline.

DESIGN OF QUESTIONNAIRE

Once the card columns have been assigned, the layout of the data collection sheet is fairly straightforward (Figure 4.7).

Variable	Columns
Student identification number	1–5
School identification number	6–7
Date of birth (month, day, year)	8–13
Grade (00 = kindergarten)	14–15
Sex (1 = male; 2 = female)	16
Race (1 = white; 2 = negro; 3 = other)	17
Geographic division	18–19
Height, inches	20–22
Weight, pounds	23–25
Age, years	26–27
Card number	80

Figure 4.7. Student growth study questionnaire.

MACHINE-COMPATIBLE DATA COLLECTION SHEETS

For certain very large-scale data collection projects, particularly those in which data come in from many sources and are collected by a large number of untrained individuals, it may be economical to design mark sense data collection sheets so that the transcription step is automatic, or in the case of newer processing systems, eliminated. Where a small number of variables are involved, it is feasible to imprint the questionnaire directly onto a punched card (Figure 4.8) which can then be filled in and submitted to an offline device

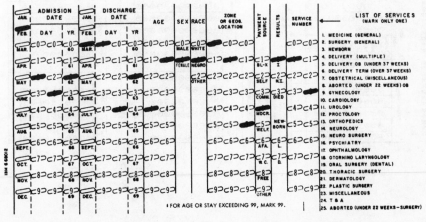

Fig. 4.8. Mark sense data card. *Courtesy Cincinnatti Hospital Council.*

SCIENCE RESEARCH ASSOCIATES, INC.   SIDE 1
MEDICAL INDEX AND RECORDS ANALYSIS—FORM I

1. PATIENT NUMBER
3. DATE ADMITTED
4. DATE DISCHARGED
5. HOW ADMITTED
6. SEX
7. RELIGION
8. RACE
10. AGE ON ADMISSION
11. HOSPITAL SERVICE
12. DISCHARGE STATUS
13. AUTOPSY
14. MEDICAL CONS
15. SURGICAL CONS
16. INSURANCE

JAN. FEB. MAR. APR. MAY JUN. JLY. AUG. SEP. OCT. NOV. DEC.

5. HOW ADMITTED: MOR, EMR, PV, CIN, OTH

SEX: MALE, FEMALE

RELIGION: CATHOLIC, PROTESTANT, JEWISH, OTHER, UNKNOWN, NONE

HOSPITAL SERVICE: GENERAL, CARDIOLOGY, DERMATOLOGY, EAR-NOSE-THROAT, NEUROLOGY, OPHTHALMOLOGY, ORTHOPEDICS, PEDIATRICS, PLASTICS, PROCTOLOGY, PSYCHIATRY, THORACIC, UROLOGY, SPECIAL, GYNECOLOGY, OB—NORMAL, OB—NOT DEL, OB—ABORT, OB STILLBORN, NEWBORN, TERM, IMMATURE

DISCHARGE STATUS: RECOVERED, DIAGNOSIS ONLY, NOT TREATED, TRANSFERRED, IMPROVED, NOT IMPROVED, DEATH—UNDER 48, DEATH—OVER 48

AUTOPSY: NONE, HOSP, CORONER; Performed By: HOSP, CORONER

INSURANCE: BLUE CROSS, COMMERCIAL, PERSONAL, WORKMEN'S COMP, GOVT. AGENCY, CHARITY, OTHER

SRA MEDICAL INDEX AND RECORDS ANALYSIS—FORM I

2. RECORD STATUS: COMPLETE, INCOMPLETE, ADDITION, TWO OR MORE RECORD FORMS

1. USE A SOFT LEAD PENCIL
2. MARK ONLY IN THE CIRCLES PROVIDED
3. DO NOT STAPLE OR FOLD

PHYSICIANS AND DIAGNOSES

17a. PHYSICIAN   17b. CONSULTANT
18a. FIRST   18b. SECOND   18c. THIRD   18d. FOURTH   18e. FIFTH   18f. SIXTH
19. MANIFESTATIONS
20a. ADDITIONAL PHYSICIANS   20b.
21. TRANS-FUSIONS
22. TUMOR: NONE, MALIG, N-MAL

SURGEONS AND OPERATIONS

23a. SURGEON   23b. CONSULTANT
24. INFECTION
25a. FIRST   25b. SECOND   25c. THIRD   25d. FOURTH   25e. FIFTH   25f. SIXTH (TIS, ANA)
26a. ADDITIONAL SURGEONS   26b. 26c.

which scans the card and punches it appropriately, or to a newer apparatus which can be used online to transmit information directly to the processor's memory. Mark sense cards, when used to full capacity, will accomodate a maximum of 54 characters or digits of data. For larger sets it is possible to design page-sized questionnaires (such as in Figure 4.9), and special equipment is available to scan such documents. In general, mark sense media are best suited for data collection projects in which the variables are numbers or easily understandable codes (e.g., multiple choice questions). Furthermore, the size of the data file must be sufficient to tolerate certain numbers of erroneous transcriptions, since most scanning equipment is sensitive to pencil smudges, sloppiness, misalignment of cards or pages, etc.

The ultimate objective, of course, is to produce equipment that will mediate between the source document, in virtually any form, and the computing system. Towards this end, extensive and widespread effort is under way to perfect optical scanning equipment that will recognize a variety of standard characters. A number of such instruments with limited capabilities are already available and in use.

AUTOMATICALLY GENERATED DATA

One of the most fruitful areas of technological growth in the burgeoning electronic industry has been the development of interfaces. Electronic systems engineers have become very adept at designing and building "black boxes" which successfully combine diverse pieces of apparatus from different manufacturers and allow them to function as an integrated unit. Many computing system manufacturers routinely buy peripheral equipment intact from other manufacturers and design interface components to link them with their central processors. So successful is this area that an increasing number of computer users are configurating systems having components from different sources and requiring special interfaces.

This surge has also made its mark in the instrumentation field, where a large variety of interfaces are now available to link automatic sensing instruments with producers of machine-readable output. In many kinds of apparatus, the interface has become a standard part of the basic instrument, so that the user has the option of connecting his sensing device to a computer-oriented output unit instead of or in addition to his usual recording medium.

DIGITAL DATA

A large number of experiments are conducted in which observations are recorded as individual readings at predetermined time intervals. These readings may represent "instantaneous" values as in the case of a temperature

Fig. 4.10(A). Cobalt irradiation unit positioned over water tank containing movable sensing probe.

Fig. 4.10(B). Dose plotting and recording unit with A/D converter and paper tape output.

recorder, accumulated values over a given time increment as in the case of radiation counters, or average values over that period of time as with some wattmeters. In other types of studies, individual observations are sensed and recorded in which the decisions to record are not based on elapsed time from the last reading but on some other parameter. For example, the radiation dose plotting mechanism shown in Figure 4.10 has a sensing element that is automatically moved a preset distance and allowed to stablize, at which point a signal is transmitted to the recording component. When the rate at which such observations are made is low enough to allow the use of a conventional recording device (such as a strip chart or cash register tape), it is just as convenient to use a paper tape punch as the recording medium. (A number of devices are hooked directly to keypunch units, but paper tape is much more popular because of the compactness of its punch unit.) With setups of this type it is possible to produce as many as 300 characters per second. The recording rate in actual readings per second would depend, of course, on the number of digits required for each variable to be observed. Although it is possible to route these observations directly into an online digital processor, the great disparity between processing and data acquisition speed makes this very uneconomical and limits its use to those areas such as process control, where results must be available immediately. Situations in which the required sampling and recording rate exceeds that of electromechanical digital recording instruments (whether computer-oriented or not) must be treated as analog phenomena and handled by means of A/D converters, as discussed shortly.

DATA PREPARATION AND FORMATTING

Arrangement for automatically generated digital data is substantially more straightforward than for manually collected information, since the number of digits assigned to each variable, the order in which the variables are read (sequencing of data on punched tape) or the assignment of card columns, if punched card equipment is attached, are operations usually controlled by the instruments themselves. For specialized devices permanently attached or assigned to an experiment the preparation and formatting logic is incorporated as part of the basic equipment design. It is also possible to make this logical circuitry flexible (by means of a wiring board or similar device) so that the operating parameters can be changed from experiment to experiment and the recording device can be attached to various sensing instruments. The scheme used with the spectrometer shown in Figure 4.11 typifies such preparation and formatting. This instrument is used to measure and record the radioactivity of a number of samples fed to it sequentially. Each sample is measured over a predetermined time interval, and its intensity, expressed as a total number of counts, is punched on paper tape as a six-digit number. The logical circuitry is set up such that zeros are filled in where necessary to keep the field length constant. Each reading is followed by a specially punched signal that is interpreted as a separator between observations. (On punched cards such separation can be achieved by skipping a column or going to a new card.)

The user's key to the data format is still a data outline prepared in the same way as described previously for manually collected material. There is one difference in that some of the identifying information is implicit in the order in which the variables appear on the punched cards or tape rather than being physically included as part of the data set. An example will help clarify this distinction: Suppose a sensing device picked up readings in ten different channels and expressed each reading as a six-digit number. If this information were collected manually and placed on punched cards, each card, aside from normal identification (such as experiment number and/or date), might have the following layout:

Column no.	Item	Format	
10–11	Channel no.	XX.	(decimal points are
20–25	Reading	XXXXXX.	not actually punched)

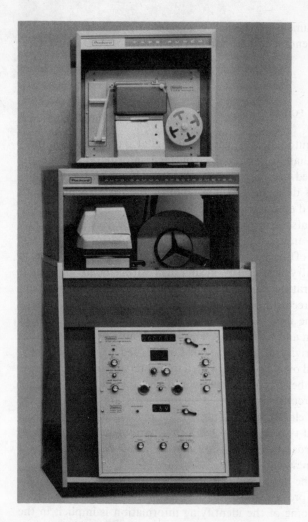

Fig. 4.11. Spectrometer equipped with paper tape outlet. *Courtesy Hewlett-Packard.*

(Column numbers were selected arbitrarily.) On the other hand, if the data were recorded automatically on an online keypunch, a single card might be used to record all ten channels for a given set of observations, and the format might look as follows:

Column no.	Item	Format
8–13	Reading for Channel 1	XXXXXX.
15–20	Reading for Channel 2	XXXXXX.
22–27	Reading for Channel 3	XXXXXX.
29–34	Reading for Channel 4	XXXXXX.

and so on. Although this second format appears to have a decided advantage in that it uses considerably fewer cards per data set, it does require some additional data preparation in the processor for most types of analyses. For example, if one wished to plot a graph showing reading vs. channel number, the channel number would have to appear explicitly as part of the data so that the graph program could make appropriate coordinate assignments.

When such information is automatically generated, proper identification must be added manually. This is usually done either by hand punching the appropriate information on each card before the data are generated or, in more sophisticated equipment, by dialing the identification on the instrument and letting it be punched as part of the data set.

ANALOG DATA

Means for the automatic collection and recording of continuous electronic signals preceded the ability to analyze them automatically by a good number of years. Consequently, the processing of such data rarely exceeded visual inspection and calculations based on a certain number of measurements tediously obtained by hand. However, the extremely rapid growth of aerophysics, bioelectronics, and other technologies in which large amounts of continuous electronic signals are generated has stimulated the perfection of a variety of analog computers and supporting equipment for the preparation and processing of such data (see Chapter 2). Although the history of the application of such techniques is a relatively short one, some very worthwhile contributions have already been made in a variety of areas which in turn are spurring additional interest, so that the gap between the amount of data being collected and that being explored analytically is gradually narrowing.

Although analog signals may reflect a variety of activities ranging from communications signaling to muscular contractions, the final form for purposes of automatic recording and/or processing must be that of a continuous varying voltage. When some type of change is required to obtain this final form, a device must be used to sense the signal as it is generated and produce from it a voltage that mirrors this signal's variation directly. A variety of such energy converters (transducers) are in routine use for a variety of data forms (such as temperature, pressure, chemical concentration, sound, and light, among others) and can be microminiaturized to the point that their use to monitor functions of internal organs is no longer uncommon.

Unlike digital data, for which there is a wide choice of machine-compatible recording media, analog information is universally recorded and stored on magnetic tape. Since considerations of convenience, economy, sensitivity, and reliability have virtually ruled out possible competing methods for analog data storage, development effort in this regard is concentrated on producing improved recorder designs offering greater flexibility and reliability at less cost.

PREPARATION OF ANALOG VOLTAGES

Conversion of an analog signal from its original form to a voltage by means of an appropriate transducer must usually be followed by one or a series of further preparatory steps in order to improve the quality of the signal and/or to alter its form in some consistent way so that it is compatible with the recorder or analog computer.

Amplification. The development of analog recorders has proceeded along a decidedly more uniform pathway than has been the case with most digital equipment. Consequently, such basic features as recording/playback

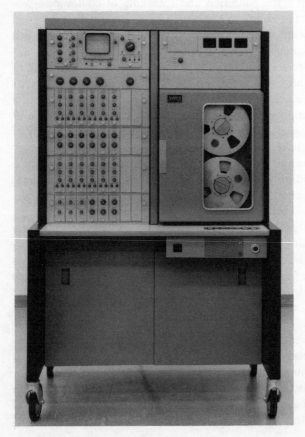

Fig. 4.12. Analog recording complex equipped with biological amplifiers. *Courtesy Ampex Corporation.*

speeds, tape widths, and track sizes are standardized, and a tape produced on one manufacturer's unit can usually be played on someone else's. The operating voltage range has also been standardized so that most recorders are designed to respond best to voltage levels around 1 volt. As a result, it is necessary to alter the magnitude of input data (usually upward) for peak efficiency of recording and subsequent playback. Some similar adjustment is also required for input to analog computers. The degree of amplification needed for such preparation varies widely and depends, of course, on the data source. Some signals may have to be doubled in magnitude. Others, like many biological traces, require amplification by a factor of several thousand. Still others may require reduction (de-amplification) to bring them into proper range. When a particular type of signal is used frequently (such as the electrocardigram), production amplifiers are available for it, and many recorders are designed for such modules to be plugged in and taken out as usage dictates. An analog recorder with facilities for interchanging such amplifiers is shown in Figure 4.12.

Noise Reduction. It is usually impossible to design and install a sensing element that will pick up nothing but the pure signal of interest. A portion of the input will invariably consist of a mixture of extraneous signals (noise) emanating from the power lines or the data producing mechanism itself and varying at different frequencies. (For example, the heartbeat is a common source of noise when trying to obtain "clean" electroencephelograms.) The total effect of this mixture of signals is to produce a wave which often bears no resemblance at all to the phenomenon being studied. With many weak signals, as is the case in much bioelectronic work, the noise is often as strong as the signal. Consequently, amplification of the signal will amplify the noise as well. Careful design and placement of the sensor, together with the use of special amplifiers, alleviate the situation but only to a minor extent.

The bulk of noise reduction is usually accomplished with the use of electronic filters. These components are designed to reduce the voltage of signals in a given (unwanted) range of frequencies without appreciably changing the values of other frequencies. Combinations of these filters are often used when it is desired to weaken (attenuate) extraneous signals above and below some frequency range. Figure 4.13, in which a signal is depicted before and after filtering, shows the amount of distortion which may be produced by the presence of noise. "Purity" of a signal is often assessed by the amount of voltage due to data versus that due to noise (signal-to-noise ratio). Levels above 50:1 are usually considered satisfactory.

Editing. The relative ease with which it is possible to record large amounts of analog data often works against the investigator rather than in his favor. It is an unfortunate fact that many experiments producing analog data yield only a small portion of data that might be termed "technically interesting." Moreover, there is often no way of knowing when in the course of an experiment such interesting information will be generated. A satellite transmitting signals back to earth may send hour after hour of routine (and therefore useless) information indicating no activity in a particular variable before something eventually occurs (such as the approach of meteoric particles, a change in ambient radioactivity or some other noteworthy happening). When such an event does occur, the investigator wants not only a full description of it in terms of the data but also a detailed identification of the time at which it took place relative to some base point, so that it could be linked to other information. One way to handle this, of course, is by recording everything and defining and retaining the "interesting" portions by some manual or automatic means as part of the subsequent processing procedure. This is satisfactory for experiments of short duration. However, when data must be collected over a long time period there is a practical limit to the amount that can be retained, dictated by the length of tape available and by recording speed (Table 4.1), and means must be sought to examine the data and eliminate superfluous portions prior to permanent recording. (If the experiment is online, the problem by definition disappears, since the data are processed directly by the computer as they are generated and provisions can be included to record only the "interesting" output, properly identified.)

A useful device for screening analog data is available in the form of a

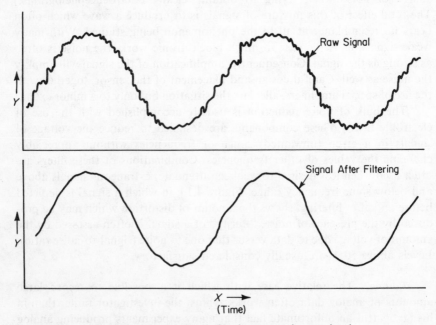

Fig. 4.13. Effect of electric filtering on continuous signal.

recording loop (Figure 4.14) which, when combined with an ordinary analog recorder and an oscilliscope or other display device, allows the user to look at his data and decide whether he wants them or not. In this apparatus, data are recorded on an endless (closed) loop of tape which, after having run its full length, begins to record over the previous contents, thus destroying them. This continuing recording, erasing, rerecording process goes on until the user presses a signal button that activates the regular recorder connected to the loop mechanism so that information from the loop is transferred to the recorder tape reel just before that part of the loop comes around again for rerecording. Between the time data are recorded on the loop and the time they are destroyed, the user is able to look at the display and decide

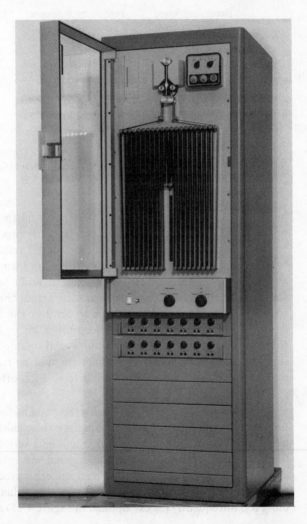

Fig. 4.14. Analog loop recorder. *Courtesy Ampex Corporation.*

whether to begin permanent recording. The length of time he has is governed by the size of the loop and the recording speed. Some mechanisms allow loops up to 150 feet in length, thus permitting up to four minutes lag time at the normal recording speed. When criteria for determining "interesting events" can be defined with sufficient rigor (e.g., expressible as a maximum voltage, critical change in frequency, etc.) logical circuitry can be devised to check for these automatically and activate the recorder accordingly. In a sense, this constitutes a special-purpose analog computer and may very well be more economical than a loop recorder.

Table 4.1. AVAILABLE RECORDING TIME FOR VARIOUS SPEEDS
(STANDARD REEL)—FM RECORDING MODE

Recording Speed (inches/second)	Frequency Response (cycles/second)	Time (minutes)
$1\frac{7}{8}$	0–625	256
$3\frac{3}{4}$	0–1250	128
$7\frac{1}{2}$	0–2500	64
15	0–5000	32
30	0–10,000	16
60	0–20,000	8

PREPARATION OF ANALOG DATA FOR DIGITAL PROCESSING

Because of the analog processor's inherent memory limits and its inability to render a large number of decisions and to operate with high levels of precision, investigators find it necessary to process much of their data originally collected as analog signals on digital systems. When this is called for, the data acquisition and preparation equipment must be augmented by an analog-to-digital conversion system. In addition to the hardware that samples the analog data and performs the actual conversion to digital form, such a system requires special logic to arrange the digitized results in some desired form compatible with the computer on which it will be processed. If conversion is to be performed on several analog signals being generated simultaneously, additional components would be required to accommodate these data and distinguish the signals from each other.

A/D Converters. The A/D converter used as the heart of such preparation systems must be capable of sampling the analog signals with sufficient frequency so that the resulting output will be a series of points which constitute a faithful representation of the original wave form. The selection of an adequate sampling rate is usually a trial and error procedure in which compromise is reached between the possibility of losing valuable information by sampling too infrequently (as exemplified in Figure 4.15) and the risks of inundat-

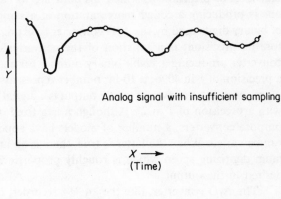

Fig. 4.15. Analog signal with insufficient sampling.

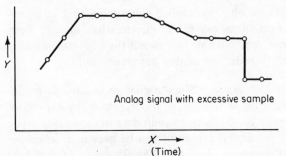

Fig. 4.16. Analog signal with excessive sample.

ing even a fast digital processor with more data than it can handle at a time, of collecting redundant information for a signal whose regularity requires less frequent sampling (Figure 4.16) and of oversampling a regular but noisy signal so that a record of the distortion is acquired right along with the data (as in Figure 4.17).

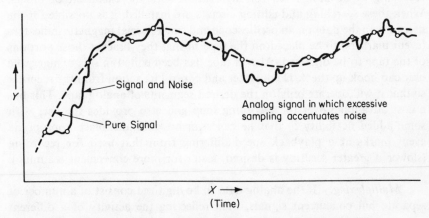

Fig. 4.17. Analog signal in which excessive sampling accentuates noise.

In addition to sampling frequency, the user may wish to select a particular level of precision at which his data are to be digitized. That is, when one is producing a coded representation of a sampled voltage, the number of binary digits used by the A/D converter to express that voltage (and therefore its precision) is a function of the converter's design. For instance, a converter producing a 12-bit binary number for each digitized sample yields a precision of 1 in 4096; a 10-bit number represents a precision of 1 in 1024; more generally, a converter whose output is a digital number of n bits operates with a precision of 1 in 2^n. Although n is a fixed quantity for most general purpose converters, a number of models have appeared recently in which it can be varied. When the latter is true, there is an attendant penalty in maximum digitizing speed which is roughly proportional to the number of bits desired in the output.

The A/D converter, like the analog recorder, is designed to accept and operate on continuous voltages with the implied assumption that all necessary signal conditioning (amplification, filtration, etc.) has already been performed. Once this is true, it is possible to connect the converter directly to the data source, analog recorder, or analog computer output.

Editing Data for A/D Conversion. Since digital processing is intrinsically slower than data handling in the analog mode, which, by definition, is instantaneous, it is generally good practice to edit data in the analog mode before digitization so that the digital processor can be presented whenever possible with the smallest necessary data file. The flexibility of the A/D converter in accepting either online or previously recorded input offers opportunities for data editing and screening in addition to the ones available prior to recording, as described earlier. Should the experiment or process be of such duration to allow its complete recording, it is possible to equip the analog recorder with components that will allow certain portions of that recording to be designated for digitization with the exclusion of others. When these searching and editing circuits are installed, it is possible for the user to scan the data on an oscilloscope and cause special magnetic indicators (event markers) to be placed on the tape so that they bracket those portions of the tape to be digitized. After a tape has been edited in this manner, the user can hook up the A/D converter and control its action from the recorder so that it will operate only on the desired segments of analog tape. This has a cost advantage over the recording loop and also provides the user with some added flexibility in that he can scan his data and place appropriate event marks at a playback speed differing from that used for recording (slower if greater scrutiny is desired, faster for more convenient scanning).

Multiplexing. If the analog data to be digitized consist of a number of separate but concurrent signals, each reflecting the activity of a different variable, the conversion system must include an appropriate multiplexer that allows the converter to sample each of these signals in sequence. This is decidedly less expensive than using a separate converter for each signal, and multiplexers of sufficient speed can be obtained such that the amount of time spent in going from one signal to the next is, for most applications, small enough that a set of sampled readings obtained for one full cycle of the multiplexer can be treated as being simultaneous.

Sample and Hold Circuits. When the variation of a given set of analog signals is sufficiently sensitive, the user may find that the time delay caused by even the fastest multiplexing switch is intolerably large. In order to assure a much closer approximation to true simultaneity in sampling, the user may have to resort to sample and hold circuits. When such components are incorporated in his conversion system (one between each data signal and the multiplexer), the signal to start the multiplexing cycle (that is, to sample the data on the first channel) will also trigger all of the sample and hold circuits, so that instead of obtaining the signal itself, the multiplexer will obtain its input from each sample and hold circuit. Thus the signal sent to the converter from any data channel will represent the value of the data at the same instant that the other values were captured from their respective channels.

Formatting of Digitized Data. As stated previously, the output of an A/D converter is basically a binary number that represents the magnitude of the voltage digitized. At this point the universality of A/D conversion systems ends, in that additional logic must be provided to produce output that is compatible with the digital processor for which the data are intended. In many cases the installation has the flexibility of dividing this task between hardware and software (part but not all of it can be done with software), with the division criteria being basically economic ones. The necessity for such formatting is present whether the digitized data will be used directly online or whether they will be stored on some digital device (usually magnetic tape). If the latter is true (and in most cases it is), additional logic circuits are required as part of the conversion system. Such data are stored on magnetic tape or any other medium in normal fashion, that is, as a succession of digits with one (or at the most two) digit across the width of the tape. Thus a set of readings consisting of one sample from each analog channel is stored as a sequence of digital numbers rather than as a set of simultaneous signals across the tape width as in the analog case (Figure 4.18). It is therefore essential that some type of identification be included with each digitized signal to indicate the channel from which it came and at what time it occurred.

Since many analog recorders include recording of time as part of the original data set, its subsequent inclusion with the digitized signals is already assured. Additional information must be generated by the conversion system

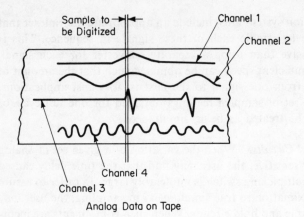

Sample to →||← be Digitized

Channel 1

Channel 2

Channel 4

Channel 3

Analog Data on Tape

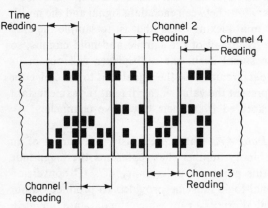

Time Reading

Channel 2 Reading

Channel 4 Reading

Channel 3 Reading

Channel 1 Reading

Digitized Data on Tape (4 digits per reading)

Fig. 4.18. Comparison of data storage methods (not to scale).

itself, however, so that each complete set of readings is written on digital magnetic tape in some standard sequence. The sequence generated by the conversion system logic usually begins with the time indication followed by each of the digitized signals in the order in which they are multiplexed, and supplemented by a special signal, generated by the conversion system. This signal, set and known by the user, is supplied to the digital computer at the time of processing as a separate part of the input or is built into the digital program, so that the digitized data are expected in a prearranged sequence.

Although digitized magnetic tape is by far the most commonly used output unit for A/D conversion, it is not necessarily the only medium available for such use. When the required conversion rate is very low, it can be considerably more economical to use a keypunch or paper tape punch as the output storage device. Some formatting and reorienting logic is, of course, still required, but the end result is more flexible because of the relative universality of punched cards and paper tape.

DATA FROM AUXILIARY SOURCES

Automatic data processing techniques are presenting investigators with the opportunity to conceive and implement studies whose dimensional scale is basically different from any that could be considered previously. First and most obvious is the prospect of research undertakings in which the amount of information to be examined and analyzed is no longer limited by the mechanics of collecting, storing, and accessing it. And, with the present concerted effort directed toward developing adequate multivariate analytical techniques, the number of observed parameters will present no constraint either. The manifold advantages of examining and working with full data networks versus samples have been explored in the previous chapter and require no further discussion. Moreover, we have seen in preceding sections that relatively simple, effective, and surprisingly economical means are established for the acquisition of such information networks.

The scope of data gathering enterprises is also extended in another, quite different direction, with resulting prospects that are as exciting as the removal of size limitations. With more data becoming available in computer-compatible form, one can now speak realistically about conducting studies in which the data files are composites consisting of newly collected observations supplemented by excerpts or entire files of existing information accumulated previously. The synthesis of such files is not limited to amalgamations of data sets originally collected for purposes that are identical or even similar. Sets extracted from census files, for example, are being used in studies by planners of such diverse things as hospitals, supermarkets, breweries, and boy scout troups. Recently, a thorough and revealing analysis of urban air pollution effects was conducted in which the merging of two separate data sets played a most crucial role. By combining pollutant concentration data collected for this study with existing hospital admission data for the same city gathered and used initially for financial analysis, it was possible to reproduce a data structure which proved very useful in establishing meaningful relationships for the first time.

This critical element in the successful amalgamation of data from various existing collections is the extent to which the identifying parameters of one file can be linked to those of others. When such linkages are directly established through the common use of one or more identical variables, creation of the amalgamated file becomes fairly straightforward, involving at most some manipulation of formats and sequences of variables to produce a consistent composite. Depending on the nature of the study, the common identifier may take on a variety of forms. For some files, observations for events may be linked together as having occurred on the same date, or in the same place. In others, different sets of attributes may be merged into a single sequence on the basis of their having been observed for the same general population, as defined by some geographic identifier (such as state, city, census tract, etc.) or by one of a myriad of other designators, (school, hospital, socioeconomic index, diagnosis, and so on). As data collection becomes more universally standardized, the extraction and combination of information from a number of sources, a capability confined to data files containing summary information usually in the form of totals, will be extended to information on specific individuals through the use of standard identifiers (such as those described earlier), which are more reliable than the name. When this becomes the case, combining of information such as employment, banking, and tax records for a particular person will be a fairly routine process.

When common identifiers are not available in identical form, it may still be possible, though considerably more difficult, to produce a legitimate composite data file. In most cases the type and amount of manipulation required to reconcile the differences in identifiers is such that the resulting amalgamation will be less precise than any of its components. As an example, let us consider what is perhaps the most common type of inconsistency in present data files. Suppose we wished to produce a data file containing detailed summary information about a city's population, extracted from three currently available files. The first of these, from which income data are to be extracted, contain data categorized by census tract; the second, to be the source of basic health and medical data, has its contents grouped by health district; the third file, which is to supply voting rate summaries and other political information, has such statistics stored by electoral precinct. Thus, before any combining can be achieved, it is necessary to produce a superposition of these geographic distribution schemes on a map of the city to determine the appropriate correspondence. One of these schemes, or an entirely new one, has to be selected as a standard to which the files can be referred and converted. Complications set in when one is defining a conversion process since there is virtually no commonality, either in size or in placement, among these various geographic divisions. Consequently, some method has to be established for apportioning segments of a given geographic division which happens to divide itself between several divisions in the standard scheme (as typified in Figure 4.19). The most common way of doing this is to assume that the total population in the geographic section to be apportioned is uniformly distributed so that the amount assigned to each of the new standardized sections is prorated according to the area falling into that region. The inaccuracy incurred by assuming such proportionality will depend not only on the general population distribution in that area, but also on its distribution

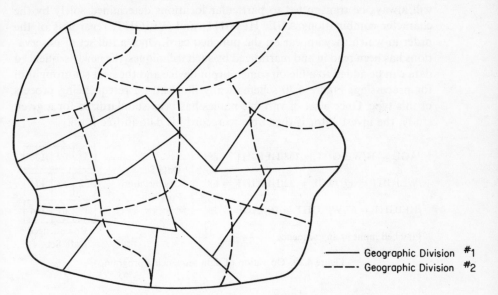

Geographic Division #1
Geographic Division #2

Fig. 4.19. Division of an area by two hypothetical sets of boundaries.

with respect to the specific attributes of interest. (For example, the total population may be fairly equally distributed throughout a district, but the higher income groups may be concentrated in one corner of it.)

If a particular study can tolerate inaccuracies of the type described above or if there is no other choice, it is possible to implement such conversions and adjustments and make them generally available to anyone wishing to make use of the resulting data files. As more investigators, planners, and other potential users recognize the advantages of data file organization for computer processing, the development, introduction, and acceptance of standard designations will accelerate and greatly facilitate the synthesis and use of cross-sectional files.

THE GENERALIZED (FREE FORM)
CARD OUTLINE

Some very promising exploratory work is under way to develop logical techniques for the automatic organization of data from collection sheets that do not follow any particular format. These techniques are based on the processor's internal coding structure, which represents each type of character by a unique binary number. If it is assumed that each variable in a set of data has a distinctive name, a logical structure can, in principle, be designed to use the name to assign a location in memory to each observed variable.

Thus, for example, observations labeled AGE, HEIGHT, and WEIGHT will always be transmitted to particular locations determined solely by the character combinations AGE, HEIGHT, and WEIGHT, regardless of the order in which they appear on the punched card. Once a full set of observations has been read in and rearranged by such techniques, the newly sequenced data can be added to a file on some output device and the next set brought in for processing. Figure 4.20 schematically illustrates a resequencing process of this type. Once a set of variable names has been standardized for a given study, the investigator is then able to record his data in free form.

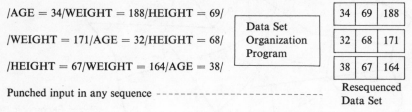

Figure 4.20. Operation of data sequencing program.

ORGANIZATION OF DATA FILES

As is the case with any system of documents, the evolution of related though independent sets of observations into a cohesive file requires considerations which transcend the immediate purpose for collecting the data. With the data already in machine-compatible form, there is a tremendous opportunity to break away from the concept (unintended, perhaps, but there nonetheless) of collecting data, looking at them in some specific way for some particular purpose, and then, for all intents and purposes, discarding them (figuratively) as having fulfilled their use.

There is no uniquely "correct" way to organize and maintain a data file. In fact, one is hard pressed to define the point (if indeed there is such a point) at which a file ceases to be merely a collection of related punched cards. It is profitable, however, to examine the attributes that have contributed to the usefulness of files already in existence and from them derive and develop guide lines which can be stated in general terms.

ACCESSIBILITY OF FILES

The evaluation of how well a data file is organized can best be made in the light of criteria which, though self-evident, should be restated with a view towards the realized and potential power of computing hardware-software complexes.

Foremost among these, of course, is the attribute of accessibility. It should be possible (in fact, relatively easy) for anyone to obtain part or all of the information contained in a file without requiring more than a description of the file and standard data handling utility programs for extracting information, rearranging variables, etc. The most accessible files are usually those whose arrangements are simple and straightforward. For example, it is much easier, less time consuming, and in the long run considerably more economical to use two punched cards for each set of observations and keep the code designations simple than it is to work out some fantastically clever (and equally cumbersome) scheme for compressing codes to save six columns. The time and effort involved in deciphering and unwinding such data usually negates any savings that might have been realized during their preparation. When the file is sufficiently large (say, over 5000 cards) it is transferred to magnetic tape, disc, etc., anyway, so the number of cards used for a set of readings or observations is only of operational interest.

A crucial measure of a file's accessibility is the extent to which it retains fundamental data, i.e., information in the form it was originally keypunched. The initial user might find it convenient, or even necessary, to develop some other expressions for a particular variable and work with the derived form. For instance, an age category rather than the age itself might be more useful to an investigator. Should this be the case, it would be extremely shortsighted to categorize the age as a coded variable and enter that on the data card to the exclusion of the actual age. Suppose a poll were taken by city hospital planners to determine the public opinion of a medical facility. The investigators might be interested in determining whether there is a difference in feelings between people under 65 years of age and those 65 or over. If, as a result, the recorded age for each person polled has 1 (for under 65) or 2 (for 65 or over) without including his or her age in years, the file may be virtually useless once this study is concluded. A political analyst interested in the same type of opinion survey and wishing to divide the individuals into categories corresponding to voting age or nonvoting age would not be able to do so. If a number of different issues are explored on a given opinion survey, it is plausible to think of a large number of users for it, each of which would benefit most by a different type of age classification.

The same holds true in any study for other variables such as height, weight, number of years of schooling, income, IQ, diagnosis, occupation, etc. It is but a small matter to supplement any data file with additional coded variables representing some grouped derivatives of original observations. With adequate utility programs such groupings can conveniently be done for each study starting with the basic data file and producing from it an augmented one appropriate to the needs of the individual user.

Physical accessibility of files, though a lesser consideration, is also important, particularly since the computing hardware industry is not famous for successful standardization. Because there are only two basic types of punched cards, 80- and 90-column types (and the use of the 90-column variety is rapidly diminishing, so the percentage of such users is becoming virtually negligible), data on punched cards are more easily accessible to the widest population of users. Almost all general-purpose digital computers will accept punched card input and can be easily instructed to prepare a new file on whatever medium may be appropriate to the task at hand. However, this has the obvious disadvantage of being bulky and inconvenient to ship, and magnetic tape is used whenever possible. The computer manufacturing industry has recently begun to recognize the tremendous payoff in making data files generally available and is consequently making a concerted effort to standardize the operational characteristics of magnetic tape units. Even where incompatibilities still exist, manufacturers can often convert one type of magnetic tape file to another by means of special interface devices. Punched paper tape is generally not a popular vehicle for data files. Although compact, it is somewhat inflexible, and many people prefer not to use it because of slow input rates and a multiplicity of standards. Despite efforts to develop economical equipment that will accept several types of paper tape codes, an investigator can still spend many futile weeks or even months trying to find equipment that will read and interpret paper tape he has received from a colleague.

SEQUENCING OF DATA SETS IN FILES

The order in which sets of observations are placed in a data file is determined primarily by the nature of the intended use of the file. For some files there may be no particular order that is more convenient or efficient that any other, and it is easier to keep the entries in the order in which they were submitted. In most cases, however, there is enough prior knowledge of the general questions to be answered so that some type of sequencing emerges as being advantageous. In many biological, social, and behavioral science research endeavors, much of the processing is concerned with producing summaries and lists of selected portions of a data file. The requests for such processing are typically of the form "Select all individuals (or subjects) who have the following attribute(s) in common and list the data for those subjects." Or, the request might be to count that subset, or to calculate average values for some of the variables in that selected population. When the investigator knows in advance which attributes he is likely to use as group categories, his data can be arranged accordingly with a resulting simplification in programming and a savings in processing time. As an example, let us suppose that an investigator wishes to keep a monthly record of the number of people treated in the emergency room at each of five hospitals. Information for each person consists of a punched card containing his name or other identification, hospital identification, date treated, type of treatment (coded), and results of visit (coded). If the data file were to be kept in its original order (that is, the order in which the entries were made available to the file) a program to produce the desired monthly record would have to check each entry, determine the month and hospital to which it belongs, increment the appropriate counter, and go on to read the next entry. Each of the five hospitals in our hypothetical study would require a counter for each of the 12 months, thus necessitating a total of 60 counters. The basic flow chart for such a program is shown in Figure 4.21, with a grand total thrown in for good measure. Processing is simplified somewhat by arranging the file so that all entries belonging to a particular hospital are grouped together. With the data sequenced in this manner, the entries for an entire hospital are completely processed before data for the next hospital are brought into the processor. Consequently, only 12 counters are needed (one for each month), since these can be used again after the sums for the preceding hospital are printed. The flow chart for this program appears in Figure 4.22. Of course, the simplest type of program for this study would be one for which the data file was arranged by hospital and within each hospital by month. Under those circumstances only one counter would be required.

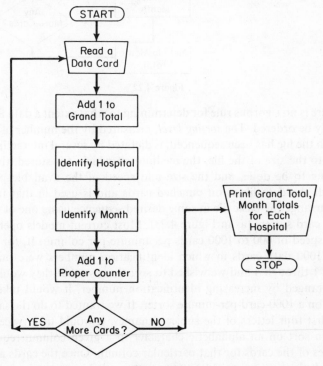

Figure 4.21

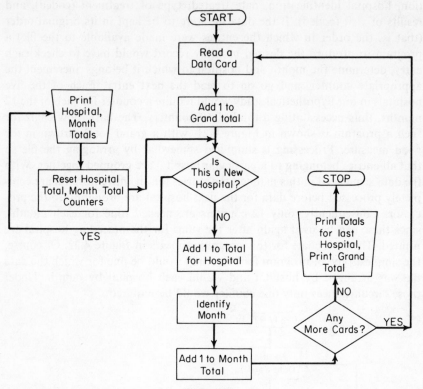

Figure 4.22

There is no rigorous rule for determining to what extent a data file should optimally be ordered. The *sorting level,* measured by the number of variables for which the file has been sequenced, is dictated by several interacting factors relating to the size of the file, the medium on which it is stored, the type of processing to be done, and the size and speed of the available processing system. If the data file is on punched cards and is used in that form, it is easy to arrange the basic file in some desired sequence using one of the many types of card sorters (as in Figure 4.23). Most current models operate at an average speed of 600 to 1000 cards per minute per column. If, for instance, we had 1000 data cards in which identification numbers were punched in columns 1 through 4 and we wished to sort them so that they would end up being arranged by increasing identification number, it would take us four minutes on a 1000-card-per-minute sorter. If we wanted to do the same thing on the first four letters of the subjects' names, it would take twice as long, because a sort on an alphabetic character in a given column requires two full passes of the cards for that particular column. Once the cards are sorted as desired, the process of adding new cards to their proper places in the file is as straightforward as with any other set of documents. Thus, although a

Fig. 4.23. Punched card sorter. *Courtesy IBM Corporation.*

card sorter is convenient and relatively inexpensive, it does require constant attention, and the amount of time required for sorting accumulates rapidly. When a file is large enough so that it becomes more convenient to transcribe it onto magnetic tape, it is usually more economical to sort it in that form. Tape sorting is many times faster than card sorting. The actual sorting takes place in the processor's memory, and therefore the relative speed of the operation depends on how much of the data can be placed in memory at any one time.

On the surface it would appear that the best thing to do is to submit the data file in any order and let the processor do all the sorting as part of the processing procedure. If we were to use the example above as a criterion, the amount of programming effort and operating time saved by using a file presorted on two levels (hospital, and month within hospital) versus a completely unsorted file is certainly nothing to get excited about. With a processor having room in memory for 100,000 characters and capable of performing 300,000 additions per second, who cares if we are able to reduce the number of required counters from 60 to 12, or even from 60 to 1? However, most questions investigators ask of their data are not nearly so simple. More realistically, our investigator might want to know the number of cases treated at each of five hospitals for each of 12 months for each of 100 diagnoses for men and women separately. Now we need 12,000 counters, and their reduction by sorting the data in such a way that all entries for a given month are together, regardless of hospital, becomes important. If the output produced by a particular data processing job consists of actual data listings instead of summary information such as totals, averages, and the like, the data file must be in some prearranged order to allow useful processing to occur at all. A typical case in point is one in which an automated library submits an input data file in which there is an entry for each book currently in circulation, giving its name, call number, borrower, and the date it was taken out. As output it is desired to produce a listing of all books that have been out for more than a prescribed length of time, with said listing being arranged in order of call numbers and containing for each entry the name of the borrower. With this type of situation it is virtually unavoidable that the file be sorted in order of call number before any further processing is done. Once this is so, the processing is very simple, requiring merely that the take-out date on each entry be checked against the date of the current run and if the elapsed time exceeds a given amount, the data entry is printed. If not, it is ignored and the next one is read.

A large number of flexible utility programs are or should be available at the user's computing facility to enable him to produce any desired juxtaposition of variables within a data set or of data sets within a data file. Chapter 12 discusses the techniques that can be marshalled to provide such flexibility. For our purposes it is best to state that should a presorted file appear more desirable than an unsorted one, the nature of such arrangements should be dictated primarily by immediate and local utility.

FILE DOCUMENTATION

When a collection of similar observations is being organized into a data file, the file itself assumes certain properties that must be documented along with the description of the actual data in it. Such information, relating to the size of the file and the nature of its organization, is helpful to the investigator when he determines the types of analyses to be performed, and is indispensible to the computernik in planning and executing the actual data processing operations.

DESCRIPTION OF DATA SETS

For a punched card file, the detailed description of the individual data set already exists (or should exist) in the form of a card outline or code sheet, as discussed in the previous section. When the data are transferred to tape, disc, or other magnetic medium, there may be a reorganization which requires documentation. If the transfer is straightforward and each tape record is a direct and exact representation of a single punched card, the record is termed a *card image* and the original card outline provides a sufficient description. However, this need not be the case. If a full set of observations on an individual subject requires a full punched card and part of a second card (say the first 20 columns), it would not be necessary to transfer all of the 160 card columns to tape. Instead, only those columns actually designated for use would be written on tape, and each tape record would contain 100 characters. (Some of these characters might be blank, of course, corresponding to missing data.) The same could be done for files in which each data set (*logical record*) is less than 80 characters long. The documentation describing such storage is usually recorded on a layout form analogous to a card outline. (Figure 4.24 shows one used for tape.) An additional code sheet may be required to explain some of the designations, or they may be indicated on the layout form itself.

RECORD FORMAT

Application __Cross-Cultural Interaction Study__ Record Name __Individual Subject Record__ By __

FIELD NAME	Subject No.	Subject Name	Sex/Race Code	Date of Birth	Educ. Code	Occ. Code	No. of Dependants	Height In.	Weight Lbs.
CHARACTERISTICS*	XXXX	Last, F. M.	X	Mo/Day/Yr	X	X	X (9= >9)	XX	XXX
RELATIVE POSITION	1 - 4	5 - 26	27	28 - 33	34	36-36	37	38-39	40-42

FILE DESCRIPTION

RECORDING MODE: 7 Channel BCD
Records per Block: 18
Characters per Record: 48
LABEL: FHWUSO660054CROSS-CULTURE:
SUBJECT RECORDS
File Number: 0471
No. of Reels: 1
Creation Date: 6/14/66
Retention: Permanent
Sorted by Increasing Subject No.

Fig. 4.24. Magnetic tape record layout.

DESCRIPTION OF FILES

Transcending the detailed information regarding the contents of a file is a description of the file itself: What kind of information does it contain, how much of it, and in what way, if any, is it sequenced? The most straightforward method of providing such material is to publish a guide which identifies the file (name of study, investigator's name, etc.) and notifies the reader as to the physical form in which the file is available and how it is sorted. The number of records in the file may or may not be meaningful, depending on how actively the file is being augmented or depleted, so that its inclusion as part of the file description is optional. Identification is usually simplified by assigning some type of project number to the file so that it can be linked directly to a corresponding card or tape layout, code sheet, original data collection form, etc. The project number may in itself be descriptive, being a coded representation of the investigator's department, the project date of origin, and/or other pertinent data. If a particular project generates more than one file, appropriate differentiation can be included as part of the file identifier.

For taped files it is very convenient to include descriptive information as a physical part of the file. This is done in the form of a *tape label* which is punched on one or more cards depending on its form and added to the file before taping. It may precede data (in which case it is called a *header label*) or follow them (*trailer label*) and contains whatever information is felt to be of use. Programs for processing the data are routinely designed to expect such labels and if appropriate, extract information from them. When necessary, it is a simple matter to devise a program that takes an existing tape file and punched label information and produces a new labeled tape file. Most computing installations standardize their tape label formats (and their project numbering system as well) so that a general program which looks for and uses label information can expect to find it in the same way and in the same place on any file generated at that installation. Since most data files do not require a full tape reel to accommodate them, it is customary to store several files on a single tape, especially when the files are closed (not expected to be augmented). When this is done the use of proper tape labels is essential so that the program used to retrieve a file for subsequent processing can distinguish it from others on that tape and insure that the desired file is being obtained.

FILE MATRICES

An effective way to organize data files for efficient processing and simplified documentation treats the collected data sets as members of a two- (or multi-)-dimensional array. When handled in this manner, each full data set (i.e., for one subject) is a row in this matrix and each attribute is a column. ("Column" and "row" here correspond to matrix dimensions and not actual punched card rows and columns.) An example of such a matrix is shown in Figure 4.25 for a hypothetical file containing five subjects. In this matrix row 1 consists of all measurements on subject 1, row 3 consists of all observations on subject 7, column 3 contains height measurements for all subjects,

Subject No.	Age (yrs.)	Height (in.)	Weight (lb)	Eye color	Sex
01	22	66	141	1	1
02	28	68	166	2	2
07	27	70	—	1	2
09	29	67	170	1	1
14	31	68	177	3	1

Fig. 4.25. Representation of data file in matrix form.

etc. Although this organizational concept requires no physical changes in the way the data are keypunched, it allows for more efficient generalization of processing programs for producing file subsets and data summaries. A single program can be designed to handle any file in matrix form, presuming its layout is known. Requests to such a program are stated in terms of column or row numbers (e.g., "Produce all rows for which column 3 contains a value of 70 or more."). Matrix operations in a processor are very efficient in that it is easier and more convenient to read in a number of rows (subjects) at a time (the number being dependent on available memory) and process them all via a program loop before reading in the next group.

An additional convenience is provided when the file documentation is included on tape with the data matrix in the form of a table. The information thus provided (see Figure 4.26) allows the user to phrase his request in more

Matrix Column No.	Item	Format	Code
1	Subject no.	XX	
2	Age (yr)	XX	
3	Height (in.)	XX	
4	Weight (lb)	XXX	
5	Eye color	X	1 = blue/2 = brown/3 = other
6	Sex	X	1 = male/2 = female

Figure 4.26. Representation of built-in documentation for file matrix in Figure 4.25.

familiar terms and lets the processing program determine which columns are to be checked. If we reword the request previously given, it would now read "Produce all rows for which height is 70 inches or more."

FILE SUMMARIES

A more recently introduced concept, not yet in common use, is that of including a data summary as part of the over-all file description. In some cases, this may give users other than the initial investigator much of the information they need. In most cases, the availability of such information as part of the file can simplify or obviate part of the processing that may be called for.

The file summary, stored together with the data and labeling information, contains commonly used quantitative descriptions of the variables in the data. For continuous parameters, this would include information such as ranges, means, standard deviations, and numbers of observations. For qualitative and coded variables, summary information might be limited merely to a reporting of the numbers of observations, or it could include a frequency breakdown for each alternative category in each variable. Although no information is available to indicate the frequency with which such summary figures are requested and used, it appears more economical to produce these summaries routinely as part of the file generating procedure than to prepare them each time (or nearly each time) the file is processed.

LARGE SCALE DATA FILES

The size and scope of data processing ventures that people are willing to undertake have increased dramatically during the past ten years. Earlier successes with modest-size projects, coupled with the introduction of vastly more powerful hardware-software symbiotes, have encouraged many to embark on more ambitious projects involving much larger data aggregates. In other instances, rapid increases in the amounts of data that have to be maintained and controlled by various groups are making overwhelming demands on manual information handling systems and there may be no choice but to automate these procedures. Regardless of the motivating reason, a large number of current data collecting and processing enterprises are concerned with files containing hundreds of thousands or millions of records.

The criteria for well-organized files, discussed in the previous section, hold true regardless of the file's size. There are, however, certain areas which require special consideration when files become very large.[1] Those problems having to do with the effect of very large files on actual processing techniques and considerations are not of direct concern at present, and their detailed description is inappropriate at this point. It should be stated, however, that for the most part they hinge around the fact that processing speed and time become major considerations. Savings of a millisecond per record, obtained through more complex program design or by reprogramming, may appear inconsequential for a 5000-record file, but looms as being eminently profitable

---

[1] As with so many of these terms, the criteria for "largeness" vary with a number of factors including processor size and speed, available periphery, and how frequently the file is handled. For no more precise reason than orientation, let us say that any file containing more than 50,000 records is a large file.

for a file containing 10 million records. Similarly, the cost differential between processing time saved and added equipment expense for random access periphery may swing in favor of the equipment and justify its procurement. No quantitative statement can be made relating the choice of random access equipment to the size and characteristics of data files to be organized and processed. Instead, it must suffice to say that enough information can be calculated or estimated to allow a competent systems designer to construct a cohesive and dependable case for the choice of particular constellations.

Of more immediate concern to us is the fact that the use of large-scale files is often accompanied by unique organizational problems which must be recognized and handled. Proper solutions for such problems are often the prerequisites for the implementation of efficient (or even adequate) processing methods.

THE LARGE SINGLE FILE

One direction of growth in files has been a straightforward increase in the number of data sets without corresponding lateral expansion in the type of data collected. The primary cause for this type of increase is simply population growth, and projects most affected, of course, are those in which information on entire populations, rather than samples, must be accumulated and maintained. Typical of these are the census, insurance files, Internal Revenue, motor vehicle registration, Social Security, customer records, parts inventory, and a myriad of other public or private files. The organization of such files involves essentially an extension of techniques used for smaller collections with additional attention being given to their division into subfiles. When a single file becomes very large, certain divisive categories emerge as logical lines along which these files break into smaller entities. Each resulting file is then a self-standing unit which can, in fact, be meaningfully processed by itself if desired. Collections of data at the national level naturally divide by states. Birth or death records for a large city divide by year. Educational records may divide by school or by grade. Such logical division is carried over into actual terms by relegating subfiles to separate physical storage units. Thus, data for each state in a national file are started on a new tape reel, though this invariably leaves a number of reels only partially filled.

The price tag for such "waste" is very small and decreases even more with data aggregates in which each subfile fills several reels. Even if there is no reason, in terms of the data themselves, to handle large single files as a group of segments, there are compelling processing reasons for doing this. Consideration must be given to the logistics of computing center operation. An example will clarify this. Suppose we had a file of 20,000,000 records, each containing 100 characters of information (not at all unusual) which have to be processed by examining each record and adding something to it or not adding something to it based on some conditions ascertained from the contents of the records. Furthermore, let us say that the processing is sufficiently simple so that the input transmission rate is not decreased because of internal processing time, i.e., the procedure is input bound. Our file is on several reels of tape, and the available periphery can transfer data into the processor at a rate of 90,000 characters per second (fairly typical). If we neglect the amount of time it takes to remove a reel of tape from a drive and replace it with the next one, then the number of reels used for our file is irrelevant. Moreover, if we make hypothetical use of an overlapped processor in which input and output can occur while internal processing is going on, then the processing time can be calculated merely by determining how long it takes for all of the characters to be brought into the processor.

This is simply

20,000,000 records $\times$ 100 characters/record $\times$ 1 second/90,000 characters $=$ 22,000 $+$ seconds

or something over 6 hours of processing time. Although this is certainly an impressive rate for data handling, it is, for many computing installations, an intolerably long period of time to devote to any one job. This is especially true if a number of such files must be processed frequently and must compete with other jobs handled by the center. Over-all scheduling is facilitated greatly if each subfile could be processed as a separate job. This is most easily done if the processing of a particular record does not affect the contents or status of any other record (such as pay status in a social security file). When the processing involves some interaction between records in the file, sufficient summary information can be written for each subfile to provide carry-over from one segment to the next.

When it is possible to absorb long processing runs into the over-all schedule of the computing installation (the common practice is to perform them during the night shift) the division of files into more or less independent subsets assumes somewhat less importance from a processing viewpoint and is dictated more by the usefulness to the investigator of processing a subfile separately. If he has occasion to make frequent reference to a particular state, year, age group, or whatever key is used to divide his file, initial effort involved in creating and arranging such divisions may well be worth the time savings realized by not having to search the entire file and create the subsets during processing. In no case, however, should the user feel that his scope of processing is necessarily constrained because of the existing order or segmentation of his file. As with smaller data collections, the file can be rearranged in any way or any subset of the file can be extracted to suit a particular purpose by an appropriate utility program.

THE MULTICOMPONENT FILE

Successful synthesis and use of composite data files has given many investigators the opportunity to discover that the computer-based information system involving input from several sources can be designed to carry its major handling functions considerably beyond the processing stage. When enough is known to articulate the exact relationship between data processing results and the various decisions stemming from them, this facility can be made a part of the over-all computerized system, thus endowing it with the ability to control as well as process. Although this intriguing extension of automated information handling was at first considered a luxury (and of those who recognize its existence, many still consider it as such), a large number of projects could not be conceived without depending on it. Moreover, a growing number of investigators are finding that the natural expansion of their projects has increased the number of decisions to be made and the rate at which they must be available for implementation to a point where, if they continue to rely completely on manual methods, they will lose all ability to control and manage their systems.

This situation naturally led to the formulation and development of central repositories for the storage, maintainence, and processing of a variety of integrated data files relating to some general entity. The underlying body might be a corporation, government, or any other organization with occasion to collect and process diverse files to obtain a picture of its current status, identify over-all trends, or perform other analyses. In addition, such depots are becoming centralized private or public information sources to a community of users with a variety of needs and questions whose nature is not precisely known and can only be generally anticipated. The answers to such diverse inquiries may be derived from data in a single file or may require reference to several sources and generation of a temporary composite data structure for subsequent processing. Suppose such a central repository were established for a manufacturing concern. A request for some particular item in inventory would instigate processing involving only the inventory file, such processing consisting of depleting the total for that item and, if it reached some critical minimum, writing the actual order for restocking. Furthermore, the physical document authorizing withdrawal of the item could be prepared as part of the procedure. On the other hand, the data center might receive a request from production control who, after having established the necessity of a new warehouse, wishes to determine its optimum size, location, and contents. Fulfillment of such a request might require reference to the sales file to determine who buys how much of what, to the production file to obtain timing schedules for various items, to traffic files for shipping and receiving scheduling information, and to accounting files for cost and pricing data. The summary picture gleaned from these files, together with externally supplied land, building, and labor cost data, would then serve as a basis for defining the desired optimum. If we take this a step further, the optimization process itself could be automated, presuming the availability of all the data to the computer.

INTERACTION AMONG FILES

The establishment of a central computing facility to handle the data processing needs for a corporation, university, hospital, etc. is certainly not an uncommon practice. In fact, it is fast becoming a universal one. What is uncommon, however, is the realization that a central facility can mean substantially more than a concentration of equipment and a collection of data files. The efficiency (and therefore the cost) with which complex requests such as the one described in the preceding paragraph can be filled is related directly to the extent of development of linkages among the various files. More basically, when no effort is made to define and construct such logical connectives, data processing does not occur at the multifile level except by specific design, and the users throughout the organization have no stimulus to expand their developmental thinking in such directions.

The basic principles for organizing each individual file have already been discussed and still apply here. It is necessary at this point only to re-emphasize the desirability of retaining quantitative data in their original form and identifying each individual set of observations as fundamentally and uniquely as possible. This can free potential users from arbitrary constraints that may impede their investigations and, perhaps more importantly, can provide users with the maximum opportunity to establish intimate relations between observations in various files by aligning data for the same population and/or individuals.

The additional techniques to be discussed here concern the identification of files for the specific purpose of linking them to other files in a general collection. Although this is done in a sense by publishing adequate systems documentation describing the contents of the various files in a central repository, the type of linkages referred to herein imply the existence of some connectives that are part of the actual file structures and are therefore available to the computer. An effective technique towards this end entails the use of a set of auxiliary identifiers called *pointers*. Each file, in addition to its own labeling, is augmented by a table of similar identifiers for each of the other related files. The usefulness of such supplementary information is dictated, of course, by the amount of detail supplied, which may range from a simple list of the exact file labels to a complete table for each file (such as in Figure 4.25) giving the names of the variables in the file, as well as their order and format. If the latter is used, utility software to service such integrated file libraries can be designed to accept a list of desired variables, specified by actual name, consult a master table to determine which files must be accessed, sort the names so that they are grouped by file, consult another table to determine a physical catalog number for each file to be accessed, print the appropriate instruction to the operator so that he can get the file and make it ready for input, and prepare a new composite collection containing the variables requested by the user. A flow chart for this type of program is shown in Figure 4.27.

The process of creating specialized data files to service user requests is greatly simplified when a series of files individually contain sufficient corresponding identification to allow the creation of a single unified data matrix. Thus, if the individual person were the unit for which observations were collected, there would be a record in the combined file for each person in the observed population consisting of identifying variables (such as name, social security number, sex, birth date, marital status, blood type, etc.) followed by a sequence of his observed attributes or properties (e.g., bank name and account number, employer code, driver's license number, coded medical history, and so on). This sequence would be standard for the entire population, so a single generalized utility program could be used to generate any desired subfile quickly and economically.

PROTECTION OF DATA FILES

Despite the high reliability of today's processing systems, components still malfunction, especially where electromechanical parts are involved, with the result that a data tape occasionally snaps in two or gets partially erased, or some cards get chewed up by the card reader. The time and effort to rebuild such data files make this a costly loss. It is fairly easy to minimize the impact of such misfortunes by maintaining a duplicate set of data files in a location remote from the computing installation just for such contingencies. Once a taped data file is generated, it takes but a few minutes to duplicate it, and such a procedure can save much money and trouble.

The possibility of such catastrophes has prompted the appearance of data processing insurance which is designed to cover the costs incurred in recreating a data file. A typical calamity for which this insurance is sought is one in which a new file is being generated as the result of a seven-hour processing run and the tape mechanism mangles the data tape with 15 minutes left to go in the run. At $600 per hour of processing time, the loss is not inconsequential.

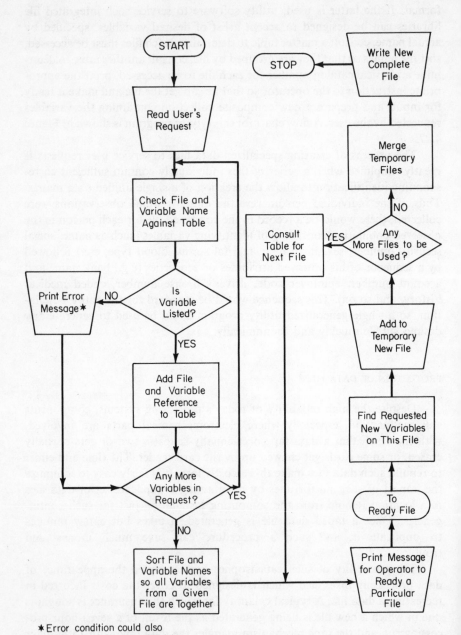

*Error condition could also
be handled by terminating job

Fig. 4.27. Flowchart for a data file search program.

THE DATA BANK

Although many variables are universally recorded and collected in fairly standardized ways, it is unrealistic to expect that data coming into a center from a variety of independent sources for a variety of purposes will generally be so consistent as to permit extensive amalgamation into a single cohesive logical structure. Obviously, the most effective way to maximize such compatibility is to extend control by the central repository to include the collection of data as well as the organization and processing of files. Repositories having such over-all cognizance (*data banks*), though recently emergent and still few in number, are already beginning to demonstrate their ability to cope successfully with large masses of data. Furthermore, they can provide a level of data processing services which demonstrates that central organization of data collection makes much more information available to the individual investigator without really compromising the structure of his own project. In addition, it costs him less for a variety of reasons.

One of the most powerful of these lies in the elimination of redundancy, a very common phenomenon which occurs at two distinct levels. The more frequently encountered type occurs at the level of individual variables, usually identifiers. It is not unusual, for example, for a particular person to be included in a number of different data files. His birth record will be in a health department file; his cumulative school record will be part of a board of education file; if he owns an automobile an appropriate record will be found in a motor vehicle bureau registration file; if he is a home owner, a record so indicating will be part of a land title file, and on and on. It is certain that each of these files includes at least one identifying variable (e.g., name, birth date) that is replicated in all the other files, and it is highly likely that there are several such replicated variables. A rarer occurrence, but still prevalent enough to be noted and corrected, is the duplicate collection and recording of virtually identical data files by different groups or agencies who are not aware and have no easy way of finding out that the data in which they are interested have already been collected. Information about the physical characteristics of a particular single family dwelling, for instance, could very plausibly be of direct and immediate interest and therefore could be collected independently several times by utility companies, the census bureau, the fire department, the tax office, building inspectors, and some psychiatrist studying the affect of architecture on oedipal behavior. When duplicate data are collected under the aegis of a data bank, subsequent additions to the central data file automatically eliminates such redundancies, resulting in a compact file that is easier to maintain and takes considerably less time to search and manipulate. More basically, the data bank's responsibility for organization of files and data collection system includes dissemination of detailed communications to all interested parties in which are described the current contents of the data bank, together with directions for accessing them. Once the investigator, administrator, analyst, or other user is confident in both the existence and accessibility of the information in the bank, he could either restrict his data gathering enterprise to those variables not already available, thus reducing that portion of the over-all cost, or he could avail himself of the opportunity to collect additional data that may be of interest to him but had to be bypassed for economical reasons.

Appreciable cost savings can also be realized by designing the data bank's file organization programs with the ability to check for certain types of inaccuracy and, where possible, to correct them automatically or bring them to somebody's attention. Inconsistencies in the data due to errors in keypunching, coding, or recording of the data can be defined in many cases in sufficient detail to allow their restatement as a set of processor decision functions. Some of these inconsistencies are strictly mechanical in nature and can be spotted easily enough. For example, a code may appear for a given variable for which there is no specification in the data outline (such as a letter appearing in a field which is supposed to have only numbers). Such entries are by definition "illegal" data that could easily interrupt and curtail a processing procedure which had already been running for some time. Consequently, the discovery of such an error would result in the substitution of blanks for that particular observation, with the production of a corresponding message to that effect so that the user would know that a particular observation on a particular record was erased, together with the reason for its erasure. He could then introduce the necessary correction if he desired. More complex errors, having to do with the logic of the data, can be handled with decision rules based on the rather simple principle of reasonableness.

There are certain values for variables which, although plausible as absolute magnitudes, are impossible or highly unlikely in the context of the particular study for which they were collected. For example, a registered patient in a children's hospital with a birth date which would make him 81 years old, or an 11-year-old mother of four constitute implausible situations which could be detected and singled out for further scrutiny. In some cases, the control facility could be added to these programs so that when a certain type of contradiction or inconsistency is detected, the program itself would substitute the most likely correction. For example, a tumor registry record showing a male patient with cancer of the cervix could be recognized as an inconsistency which, in all likelihood, was caused by an erroneous sex designation on the questionnaire, and the appropriate substitution could be made, with or without an accompanying message relating what was done. (Obviously, such corrective routines could also be built and would be equally useful for independent individual files.)

The major economy, of course, resides in the extended services a data bank can offer to all of its users because of the controlled and purposeful fashion in which its contents are collected and maintained. In many cases the payoff can be measured in specific terms as day-to-day cost reductions in the operations of a plant, or services rendered by an agency. In others, the benefits are long-term, and may not be as assessable in terms of profit made or money saved, as in the case of a police chief who is able to change the deployment of his available officers in response to geographic crime distribution data made available to him in convenient summary form on request. In this respect the installation and development of a data bank at the municipal level promises to be a most fruitful endeavor. Consolidation of administrative, health, financial, commercial, educational, regulatory, recreational, and other such data, together with their availability to a wide variety of interested users constitutes not only a convenience for maintaining current operations but a necessity for planning future ones.

STRUCTURE AND FUNCTIONS OF A DATA BANK

Organization of a data bank, be it for a corporation, city, state, or single government agency, must begin with a careful and detailed examination of the types of data to be collected, the population of users who will avail themselves of this resource, and the scope and nature of their usage. Although only a portion of this information can be defined in any detail (after all, one of the underlying purposes for a data bank is its ability to handle a variety of unanticipated data processing requirements), a consciencious scrutiny will produce sufficient detail regarding type and volume of data, number of users, and frequency of requests to allow specifications to be drawn up for the organization of data files and the type of hardware/software required.

One general requirement that applies to virtually all data banks is that the processing hardware must include the capability to support a software structure which allows certain types of requests to interrupt others already being processed based on a preassigned priority ranking. With very rare exceptions, a certain portion of data banks' day-to-day activities will consist of fulfilling requests in which the user requires some part of a file or the result of some calculations to be made available to him immediately (say within five minutes). An unconscious but identified person brought into a hospital emergency room might prompt an urgent request from the attending physician to determine whether that person's medical records show any specific drug allergy or other special considerations that might influence the nature of his treatment. Along similar lines, a police officer might require an immediate description of an automobile and identification of its owner, given its license plate number. Since such requests may come in at any time in any number, the computing system must be able to handle them in some way even though other requests are being filled at that instant. The way this is usually handled is to assign a particular priority to each known general type of request, based on its source. The software can then check on the priority rating for the request coming in, compare it with that of the job presently being processed and decide what to do. If the current job carries a higher priority than the incoming one, the latter is transmitted to a temporary file (queue) on which is stacked a line of requests waiting to be processed. If the opposite is the case, the processing is interrupted abruptly and the contents of that portion of memory being used for the job are transmitted to another temporary file (this takes only a fraction of a second). Once the high-priority job is executed and finished, the supervisory software programs access the temporary file on which the job was stored, thus allowing it to resume from the point at which it was interrupted. If the two jobs being compared are of equal priority, the incoming one is placed last on the queue and the current job is finished. The supervisory software can then consult the queue and select from it the highest-priority job closest to the first entry in the queue and begin processing it. Machines are presently available with inherent capability of assigning dozens and even hundreds of different priority levels.

If immediate response for certain types of requests is a requirement for a particular data bank, it is highly likely that the sources making frequent inquiries will want an online terminal of some kind through which they can communicate directly with the system. Thus the hardware to be used must be capable of accepting input from such terminals (usually keyboard devices) and sending output to them. Supporting software design would provide prescribed formats for entering requests through the terminals, together with a supporting set of executive programs for handling interruptions, adding and discharging jobs from the waiting list, finding necessary files, and negotiating their transmission between peripheral devices and the processor's memory. Subservient to these routines would be the utility programs which organize and maintain the actual files and the library programs which are referenced by the supervisory software to execute the particular processing called for in response to user inquiries. It should be pointed out that the scope of direct inquiries available to the user working through a terminal is not limited to requests for processing which produce some result or set of results transmitted back to him. In addition to such basic activity, it is possible for the user to perform such utility functions as adding data to his file or generating new files. If this is done frequently with large amounts of data which must be entered quickly, and if the user is far enough away from the data bank so that it is not convenient to hand-carry the data, that particular terminal, rather than being limited to a keyboard or keyboard/cathode ray display, may instead be a terminal complex including a faster input device (such as a card or paper tape reader) or even a small processing system such as a programmed console.

File organization for a data bank is really no different from that for any large information center. Where completeness of identification permits, a maximum amount of information is consolidated into a single data file and redundant variables are eliminated. Data for which such amalgamation is not feasible for technical or other reasons are maintained as separate files. In this respect, the primary distinction between a data bank and any other type of large multifile center lies beyond the file organization level and rather in the unified control of data collection and formatting.

The existence of a complete and well-organized data bank does not always eliminate the necessity for storing original source documents. The basic reason for this, of course, is that such material usually contains information that cannot as yet be represented economically on a mechanized data file. Although special equipment is becoming available for such purposes, the storage and retrieval of information such as that contained in texts, pictures, and drawings is still less expensively done in the original form with appropriate linkages to a data file on which such information is described and indexed. Another type of document which must be kept in its original form is one in which the contents may be directly and economically transferable to a machine-compatible medium, but not the meaning. An obvious example of such information would be a contract in which clauses and stipulations could be obtained from a taped data file but whose validity would still have to be checked by examining the signatures on the source document.

SOCIAL IMPLICATIONS OF DATA BANKS

There is no longer any reason to dispute that the rapid growth of automatic data collection and processing is leading inevitably to a state of affairs in which a great deal of information about each individual will be available on either a large file in some data bank or dispersed among several such files. There is, however, some very heated dispute that is going on and will continue to go on about whether the economic, procedural, and research gains made possible by such availability is really worth the accompanying serious curtailment of individual freedom and deprivation of a person's right to privacy. What a hell of a world this will be, many people say, when each person's soul is laid bare on magnetic tape for all to see and handle! And to make matters worse, the improved organization of data banks will make this material just that much easier to get at. These statements cannot be shrugged off, because it is undeniably true that an increasing amount of information about individuals is indeed becoming easily accessible and the price for retrieving it is steadily coming down. Consequently, such fears have a very real basis and must be given more serious attention than the hogwash concerning machines taking over and the like.

In order to discuss this problem properly, it is necessary to make a rather universal distinction and particularize it with respect to data banks and other automated information networks. We must recognize that the difference between accessible data and the data that are being accessed is a most crucial one which can be likened to the one which exists between the availability and use of any powerful tool, weapon, idea, or force. The fact that certain data are stored in an easily accessible file does not automatically produce the corollary that such information will be obtained immediately and exploited for questionable purposes. Intervening is man's sense of responsibility, conscience, strength of character, or whatever popular name is currently being used for his ability to keep his hands off what does not belong to him. The unfortunate fact that this ability is not a universal one will cause some abuses just as it has in every other field. The point is that there is no reason to expect these abuses to be any more extensive than they are for some other technological improvement, say the telephone.

There is a corollary worth considering here which is every bit as universal as the distinction made above. Man has always acknowledged a tendency to do something nasty if it is made sufficiently easy for him. Consequently, he has continually attempted to erect a variety of stumbling blocks and inconveniences to help his weaker fellows stay out of trouble. The structure of data banks is no exception in this regard in that one of the prime concerns of system designers is maintenance of confidentiality of files. Two major types of precautions are taken to prevent unauthorized access to the various components of a data bank. The first of these is an obvious legislative precaution familiar in defense and business circles as the "need to know" policy. This is a long-used and basically simple scheme in which the person or agency generating a particular network of information defines the extent of its accessibility to others. Detailed specifications of the form and contents of such files are still available to all potential users, but actual accessing of the information must be preceded by some type of authorization from the controlling agency to the data bank before such files may be released. This is no different in principle from the privileged communication policy followed by physicians, attorneys, etc. in their dealings.

The second level of precaution is a more sophisticated one, prompted by the advent of remote access systems in which the data bank personnel may not have a direct way of knowing which user is sticking his fingers into what file. The most widely used method of coping with this situation is to include a special identification variable or "password" as part of the over-all file identification, with the nature of a particular password known only to the data bank personnel and the user immediately concerned with that file. Authorization to use a file protected in this manner constitutes divulgence of this identification to the appropriate party, who can then gain access to the file by identifying it in his request. If necessary, similar but more extensive provisions can be built into the over-all file system such that parts of a file may be protected, various levels of protection may be assigned, etc. Thus, the notion that availability of extensive data in a centralized bank places mankind in a fishbowl is a rather naive one, predicated on the notion that man has not learned anything about himself.

PROBLEMS

1. A study is being undertaken to summarize and evaluate voting records of Federal legislators. Towards this end, the following information will be collected for each individual:

   1. Name.
   2. Membership (House or Senate).
   3. How many years in office (including present year).
   4. Party.
   5. Date of birth.
   6. Age at time of study.
   7. Education.
   8. Marital status.
   9. Previous occupation.
   10. State represented.
   11. Total number of bills voted on.
   12. No. of times voted with majority.
   13. No. of times voted with minority.

   Design a card outline for such a study.

2. A city health department wishes to maintain an updated file that reflects the current geographic distribution of physicians throughout the area, indicates their age, shows what their specialty is, how long they have been in practice, and their hospital affilation. Assuming there are roughly 4000 doctors, 31 hospitals and 28 standard specialty designations, design a card outline and questionnaire for such an undertaking.

3. It is desired to evaluate a new series of achievement tests for school children. The method to be employed is to take a sample of roughly 27 pupils from each grade (kindergarten through grade 8) for each of 118 schools and test them. Sometime later during the year, these same children will again be tested, a different exam being used. (Those who had the new test first will get the "standard" one later, and vice versa.) Assuming all the tests for all the grades are scored 0–760, design a questionnaire and card outline showing what information would be collected and in what form.

4. Suppose that the study in Problem 3 were to be expanded so that each pupil is tested in this manner every year through the eighth grade. Assuming that no pupils in the sample left the school in which they started, show what the questionnaire and card outline would now look like.

5. A smoggy city wishes to embark on an air pollution study during which 12 stations will be set up to measure daily concentrations of the following materials:

Item	Maximum Expected Value
Carbon dioxide	12.0 parts per million
Sulfur dioxide	15.0 parts per billion
Nitrogen dioxide	55.0 parts per billion
Other oxides of nitrogen	90.0 parts per billion
Carbon monoxide	20.0 parts per billion
Solid particles	5.0 parts per million
Other gaseous pollutants	40.0 parts per billion

In addition, temperature (to nearest .1°F), humidity (percentage of saturation), wind speed (miles per hour), and wind direction (eight compass points) will be recorded together with date and day of week. Develop a card outline and a lab report form for this investigation.

6. Design a suitable tape record for the study in Problem 5.

7. The manager of a bank, who is also an amateur socioeconomist, wishes to study the banking habits of his depositors. He installs automated equipment that operates in such a way that each transaction (deposit or withdrawal) is recorded in machine-readable form as the teller enters it on the regular record. Assuming the availability of any required program for reorganizing the data, enumerate the pertinent variables and develop a suitable tape file for the study.

8. It is proposed to investigate marriage age trends among various socioeconomic groups by accumulating data for a large number of individuals (roughly 15,000) over a span of ten years. The following files are available in machine-compatible form:

   (a) Marriage Bureau records.   (b) Internal Revenue records.   (c) Census data.

   Construct a composite file from the above data, enumerating the variables you consider pertinent. Show the final file layout including provisions for storing "labels" for variable and classification names.

9. A chemical company maintains the following information for each of a series of insecticides:

   (a) Code name (a three-digit number).
   (b) Molecular weight (to two decimals, never exceeds 400).
   (c) Density (lb/cu ft, to nearest .1 ft^3; all are lighter than water).
   (d) Price ($/gallon; nothing ever exceeds $1.50).
   (e) Toxicity rating (scaled as integers from 0 to 10) for each five insect types (A,B,C,D,E) and humans.

10. As each engine leaves the assembly line in an aircraft engine factory, it is accompanied by a punched card containing:

    a. Engine type (a three digit code)
    b. Engine serial number (five digits)
    c. Engine weight (to the nearest lb, with no engine $>$ 8000 lb.)
    d. Assembly completion data (month, day, year)

    Each engine proceeds to final testing where, at a particular air flow (in lb/sec to the nearest lb, always $<$ 700 lb/sec), the crew measured thrust in lb., ± 1 lb, always $<$ 5000). These items are recorded on another punched card, along with the test date.
    Prepare outlines for each of the punched cards described above.

11. When a number of engines (see Problem 10) have been tested, their cards are matched against a file of assembly cards and, for each engine, a new card is produced showing its identification, dates of assembly completion and testing, air flow, weight, thrust, and ratio of thrust to weight.

    a. Propose an outline for the new card.
    b. Assuming a computer which can perform the necessary operations, prepare a flow chart for an appropriate program.

5 DESCRIPTION AND SUMMARY OF DATA: DISPLAY TECHNIQUES

The immediate results of experimentation consist of large numbers of records made up of numbers, words, sentences, pictures of graphic traces, and even audio tape recordings or just impressions imprinted in the minds of observers. Having completed his research, the investigator is then faced with two problems of some consequence. Somehow he must distill the information that he has gathered and compiled in such varied forms that he or his colleagues can fathom what actually has been observed. He must be able to describe what he has observed for himself and for others. Insofar as he did (or should) undertake the investigation for some purposes, he is also faced with the necessity of drawing inferences or conclusions for his observations. Obviously, the way in which he will describe or summarize what he has observed will exert considerable influence on the conclusions that can be drawn from his data.

Before turning to the more traditional methods of numerical summaries and statistical indices, we shall explore a new world of possibilities which has been very much neglected so far. Pictorial summaries of phenomena, multiple relationships, and patterns and shapes of events all form an important substrate on which the ideas and intuitions and the serendipity and creativity of scientists thrive and prosper. The insurmountable cost and time limitations existing when such summaries must be prepared by hand have so far prevented any serious investigation of their use as convenient tools. A new vista has now opened for feeding back the substance of his findings to the investigator. What the yield of this tool will be is hard to assess until it has been used for some time.

We may surmise with confidence, however, that pictorial display can serve as a valuable basis for scientific understanding. The constant and intense use of microscopes, X-rays, area presentations, and the many other forms in which data are rendered pictorially supports the contention that such presentations are found useful by scientists. The history of science also tells us of many instances where valuable insights and findings were produced by manipulation of images, graphs, pictures, and so on. For instance, the Italian scientist Grassi identified the Anopheles mosquito as the carrier of malaria by superimposing the location at which different mosquitos were found over a map of Italy on which the areas of high malaria incidence had been clearly marked. Similarly, during the London cholera epidemic in 1820, Snow was able to show that one of the five water supply systems was responsible for the spread of the disease through the city simply by superimposing locations of cholera outbreaks over a map of London on which water supply routes were drawn. Another famous incident concerns Kepler, who plotted the orbit of Mars around a number of possible geometric shapes until he found that an elliptical shape would account for all data points each time.

There seems to be no question but that representing data in the form of images and manipulating them may serve as valuable sources for scientific insight. Where these images can be produced quickly and easily they are indeed used in profusion. Examples are X-rays, scans of radioisotopes, pictures of particle pathways and collisions in bubble and cloud chambers, enlargement of microscopic pictures, anatomical slides, and on, and on. The accumulation of data into summaries in the form of easily handled images has been a less prominently used scientific tool only because of the immense amount of labor involved in producing such summaries. The proliferation of flexible output devices and increased central processor versatility has now changed this picture.

The fantastic speed at which processors are able to perform extensive and complex calculations has often obscured the fact that they are extremely versatile instruments for preparing an endless variety of displays. There are many different varieties of devices on which output in the form of print, line drawings, or some patterns of shapes and forms can be produced. Programs for converting results into such displays are complex and would not be possible to produce without considerable sophistication of hardware and software. The writing of program packages and systems that regulate display generation make up a constantly growing percentage of the over-all effort expended to make the information processing "robot" the useful slave it ought to be. Many users have been so preoccupied with employing computers for calculating numbers from other numbers that systems are often designed with only casual regard to input-output speeds, on the basis of the contention that the amount of time spent in reading and writing would almost always be a small portion of that spent in actual computing. As a result, it has been only recently that concerted attention has been given to the exploitation of the computer's descriptive power. Conventional periphery is being employed in many imaginative ways, and new equipment is rapidly being introduced specifically for presenting the user with the results of data processing procedures in directly interpretable form. Furthermore, these applications to describe and portray, in which actual mathematical computation plays a secondary role or is altogether absent, now constitute a substantial portion of total computer usage.

As emphasis on producing comprehensive output takes hold, an increasing number of investigators are shifting their concepts of computer usage from calculation to display. Experienced users are expanding the scope of their applications to include more comprehensive and meaningful display of results. Others, who stayed away from computers previously because they felt their work involved an "insufficient" amount of calculation, are exploring the potentialities of display as a tool for decision.

The techniques developed by these explorations are not necessarily antithetical to procedures involving extensive computation. Because of the general usefulness and versatility of these displays, it is not uncommon to find the same techniques employed as the final steps in a wide variety of computation procedures or as independent processes entailing little or no data manipulation outside of the actual output preparation.

DOCUMENT DISPLAYS

One of the most widely used procedures involves no calculations at all (although it may entail fairly complex programming problems). It consists instead of the retrieval and display of data from a stored file. In its simplest form, this procedure includes no provisions for selectivity, its function being merely to find, read, arrange, and produce the entire contents of a file on some suitable output device. The most common use for such straightforward processing is the generation of virtually an endless variety of lists. A society may require a set of name and address labels for a mass mailing to its membership; a library wishing to produce and disseminate an updated roster showing available periodicals can print such listings directly on master sheets from which any number of copies can be reproduced. A very helpful version of this procedure is often encountered at meetings or conventions. The registration forms filled out by the attendees are collected periodically and brought to a local service bureau, where their contents are keypunched. The newly produced cards are added to the existing batch and the enlarged file is sorted into alphabetical order and then printed. Copies of the resulting list are brought back to the convention site and posted at some strategic locations. This process can be repeated virtually as frequently as is desired, with the only possible limitation being the availability of sufficient keypunch operators for really large gatherings. In most cases hourly updatings are sufficient.

The utility of a list-producing process increases, of course, when provisions are added for extracting and displaying certain portions of a data file based on one or more attributes specified by the user. Thus a clinic working with a complete patient file can extract from it a list of individuals to be brought in for followup examinations during a particular month. Similarly, a health officer working with the same file could obtain a printout listing patients from a particular geographic area. To insure versatility, such procedures usually allow the user to restrict the display to a desired subset of each record which meets his criteria for inclusion. For example, the information displayed in a list of patients to be called in for followup examinations would most likely contain the patient's name and address, attending physician, and, perhaps, the type of treatment. Listing of all other data in the record would be suppressed. The flow chart for a general listing program of this type is depicted in Figure 5.1.

Record identification and display procedures basically similar to those described above are also applicable to the retrieval of information consisting of pages of text rather than sets of observations. A request for the display

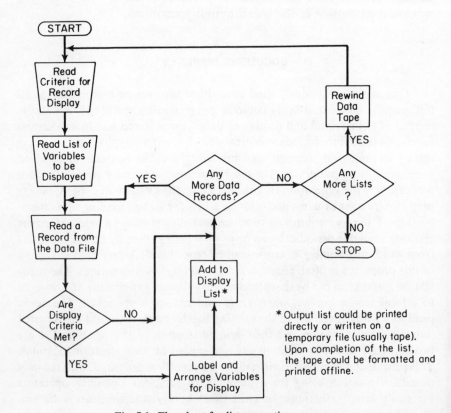

Fig. 5.1. Flowchart for list generating program.

of such data would include a proper file identification (e.g., name of book or article) and specifications as to which page or pages are to be displayed. The program would process the request by searching the tape, disc, or other medium on which the files are stored, locating the required material, and displaying it on some output device (usually a printer or cathode-ray tube). A large amount of material is already available in machine readable form and more is constantly being added, so that a growing library is becoming accessible in this fashion. Although at first glance it appears that the retrieval and display of information in this manner, though possible, is hardly economical, the usefulness of such document displays is becoming evident in a number of areas. Obvious among these is the increased availability of large amounts of information from a central location to a number of remotely located terminals. This is especially useful when speed of dissemination is desirable. The practicality of such complexes is increasing rapidly with the growing availability of very high capacity storage devices. If we add various types of processing steps between access and display, the potential usefulness becomes virtually immeasurable. Such processing, for example, may consist of a set of routines which scan the document and produce a meaningful abstract or summary, translate the entire document into another language, or convert its contents to Braille or some other special display form.

RETRIEVAL OF INFORMATION

One of the most actively pursued computer problems and potentially one of the most useful applications is that of information retrieval. It grew out of more complex variations of requests for information display described above. Instead of displaying particular documents specified by the user, one of the primary aims of automated library techniques is to allow the user to define the type of content desired and from this information to identify those members of a larger array of documents which come closest to matching the user's requirements. The output from such procedures may be a list of document identifications which can then be used to find the proper information by hand, a display of document summaries selected from a stored array of summaries which can then be viewed to determine whether the documents themselves will be of interest, or a display of the documents themselves.

Crucial in the development of such automated retrieval techniques is the creation of an effective set of attributes (sometimes called *descriptors*) for a given library of documents. This vocabulary, whose compilation is extremely arduous and complex, must be sized so as to offer the user an efficient yet not cumbersome system that, for a given request, will retrieve a maximum percentage of the available relevant documents and a minimum amount of extraneous material. Such compilations of attributes usually take the form of dictionaries of key words or phrases. Each document in the library is described by a combination of several of these key words whose selection is based on frequency of appearance in the abstract or body, nature of the title, and/or various other criteria. The master data file, then, is a listing of each document in the library, together with its attributes. Figure 5.2 gives a schematic representation of one method for constructing such a file for a library containing n documents and a vocabulary of m possible descriptors. In this scheme an n by m matrix is constructed whose form is identical to the general data array shown in Figure 4.23. Each element indicates the presence or absence of a particular attribute for a specific document. A typical request

	Attribute 1	Attribute 2	Attribute 3 ... Attribute m
Document 1	1 (present)	0 (absent)	1 ...
Document 2	1	1	0
.	.	.	
.	.	.	
.	.	.	
Document n	0	1	1

Figure 5.2. Document retrieval matrix.

in this arrangement consists of a list of attributes which may or may not be weighted according to their relative importance to the user. Each document (row in the array) is scanned to determine how many of the desired attributes are present, and some type of relevance score is compiled for that document. If it equals or exceeds some minimum score specified by the user, that document is listed in the output. A number of other organizational arrangements are also in use or under development, and some conspicuous successes have been achieved, notably in specialized libraries.

Aside from the basic task of defining a good vocabulary of descriptors, dictionary thesauri, and so on, operational considerations such as updating (adding or retiring documents or worse, adding a descriptor), defining the most effective type of relevance score, or reducing the time, effort, and cost involved in attaching descriptors to a new acquisition pose very serious problems for which no general solutions exist. The potential payoff is so great that much work is going into the exploration of algorithms for automatic compilation of key-word vocabularies and similar endeavors. With this scope and challenge ahead of it, automatic information retrieval has become a large and separate field of inquiry.

REVIEW OF RAW DATA

Any collection of data in a sense is a document. We may think of an electrocardiogram, a fever chart, a succession of aerial photographs, and other instances as "documents" of particular sorts. Very often the data aggregate in document form (in this case in raw document form) is not viewed because its production for the human eye as well as its analysis would be too time consuming. However, there are a variety of new techniques possible which have as yet to be explored thoroughly, but seem potentially of value.

For instance, it is possible to obtain a continuous record of electrocardiograms, pulse, blood pressure, temperatures, chemical events, and so on for patients on the critical list. Most of these data may not be of any interest at all to the investigator. On the other hand, when a patient takes a sudden turn for the worse or for the better, the investigator may be curious to see whether any events heralded this turn in patient status. When recordings have been taken routinely, he can play back the data documents for previous periods of time. He may even be interested in readjusting time scales for different variables so as to check for covariations separated by time lags.

This type of recording and recovery of data documents is still in its infant stage. We may expect to investigate uses of such automatic data review aids more intensely in the future as the cost of automatic recording of complex events decreases.

GRAPHICAL DISPLAYS

Regardless of his field of inquiry or the degree of sophistication he ultimately brings to bear on the analysis of his data, the investigator has always welcomed the opportunity to display them in such a way that their full content is available for a convenient overview. The general impressions which can be gleaned from such scrutiny are extremely valuable, often serving as a crucial factor in dictating the direction of subsequent analyses. Since the purpose of such display is to give the user a look at his data without the loss in content inherent in any kind of summary, its preparation, involving all of the data, is necessarily tedious. As a result, the investigator faced with the task of manually preparing such displays has often been forced to limit them by selecting in advance those which he feels will be most revealing. Since this is not always easy to predict, the collection of interesting data without accompanying adequate scrutiny has not been uncommon.

With the development of automatic techniques for producing such displays quickly and economically, it is possible for the investigator to obtain whatever type and number of displays he may deem useful for assessing the nature of his data. Furthermore, the procedures producing such displays can be augmented by logical structures that imitate the user's decision processes in determining which displays are interesting. (We shall talk about this in great detail later on.)

There is yet one more reason for emphasizing good display. Reports often contain a large number of graphs and tables, which are expensive and tedious to produce by hand. These can be generated automatically in well-labeled form directly suitable for publication. The investigator may find that money thus saved from art work may well pay for a part of the statistical analysis of his data.

GRAPHS AND SCATTERGRAMS

If sets of observations on two variables can be expressed along continuous scales, there is no more revealing summary of their activity relative to each other than a graph. Besides providing strong visual indication of the presence or absence of a relationship between the variables being displayed, the graph presents the experienced viewer with valuable clues as to the type and strength of such relationships, the variability of the measurements, and the possible identification of spurious observations.

There are two general types of graphical displays for continuous data. The more basic one, called a *scattergram* (also *scatterplot* or *scatter diagram*) is intended to give the user an initial look at the distribution of his data. Its construction, therefore, involves the display of each data point, as shown in Figure 5.3. In this example, produced on a line printer, the useful convention is followed in which coincident points (those having identical sets of coordinate values) are denoted by special symbols so that the viewer has some notion as to the density of the data points. In contrast to the scattergram, the graph

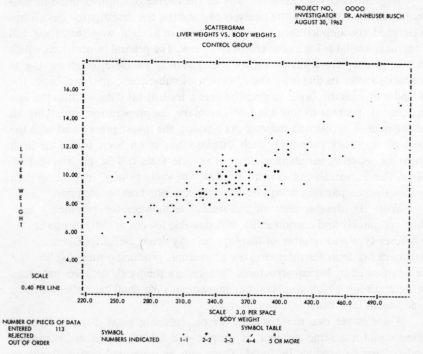

Fig. 5.3. Scattergram produced on a line printer. *From MEDCOMP Library.*

presents a continuous curve or line, if it is presumed that the data points are connected in some known way.

Programs for the generation of such scattergrams on computers can range from fairly straightforward procedures for producing single displays to very large and complex structures that are systems in themselves for automatically turning out multitudes of combinations without user intervention. In its simplest form, designed for small computing systems, this type of program operates on a single set of coordinate data with the assumption that the ordinate (Y) values are already prearranged in descending order of magnitude. The display is of a fixed size that is built into the program logic. For example, when the output is to occupy a single page on a standard line printer, it is convenient to use a vertical dimension (measured along the Y axis) of 40 printer spaces and a horizontal dimension (measured along the X axis) of 100 spaces. As part of the input, the user specifies the magnitude and identification of the scales to be affixed to each of the axes for his particular scattergram. (In more powerful versions, scaling and sorting are done automatically.) In order to specify the scales, the investigator must know the range of his data, so that none of the points will be deleted from the display. At the same time the range of data must be chosen such that the output will not be compressed beyond the limitations imposed by the size of the graph. To understand some of the procedures better, let us consider an example for which the investigator has to specify scales.

Let us say that a user wishes to prepare scale specifications for a scattergram depicting height in inches Y versus age in years X. The program available to him produces a standard size display having 100 spaces along the X axis and 40 spaces along the Y axis. Ages of the subjects in the investigator's data range from 2 to 85 years; minimum height is 22 inches, while the maximum is 78 inches.

Horizontal Scale: Since he has 100 spaces available for age, it is obviously most convenient to set the lowest X value on the scattergram to 0 and the highest to 100. This gives him a horizontal scale factor of $(100 - 0)/100$, or one year per space.

Vertical Scale: The choice of a vertical scale factor is somewhat less straightforward. As a possibility, he could set the minimum Y value on the scattergram at 20 inches and the maximum at 80. This gives him a scale factor of $(80 - 20)/40$, or 1.5 inches per space. The resulting scattergram is shown in Figure 5.4. Although maximum use is made of the vertical space available, it may be rather awkward for an investigator to read. As an alternative he can drop the minimum value along the Y axis down to 0 while maintaining the maximum at its previous level of 80 inches. This gives him a new vertical scale factor of $(80 - 0)/40$, or 2 inches per space, as shown in Figure 5.5. The vertical scale can be modified further for centering purposes by shifting the minimum value upward from 0 to 10, with a corresponding shift in the maximum level. Note that this does not alter the scale factor from

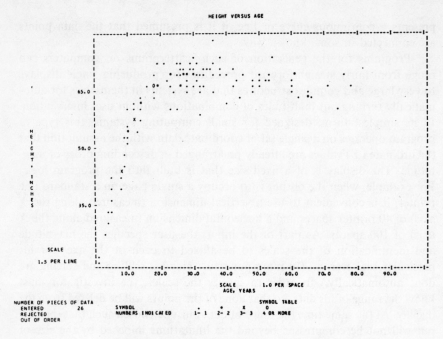

Fig. 5.4. Scattergram (shifting vertical scale).

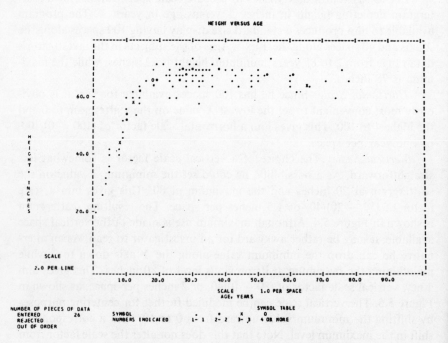

Fig. 5.5. Scattergram (shifting vertical scale).

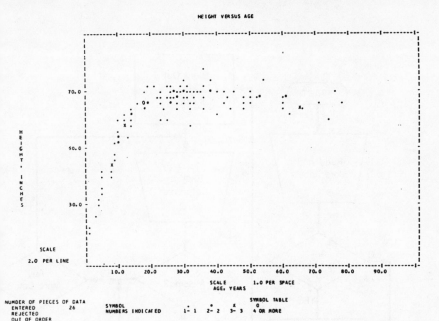

Fig. 5.6. Scattergram (shifting vertical scale).

its previous value $[(90 - 10)/40 = (80 - 0)/40 = 2$ inches per space]. This modification is depicted in Figure 5.6.

Armed with such scale specifications, the scattergram can then determine the range of X and Y values to be assigned to each horizontal and vertical position of the scattergram, respectively. An area of storage is set up to represent a single horizontal section of the scattergram (including borders). This is called a *line image* which, for the scattergram size specified above, would be composed of 100 cells plus borders. Each cell is initially blank. The program then reads in the data points in sequence and compares each Y value to the range for the first (topmost) line of the scattergram. If the point falls within that range, the proper location along the horizontal axis is determined by comparing the X value to the horizontal range. When the proper cell is found, a symbol is placed in the appropriate cell of the line image. This is repeated with succeeding data points until a point is read in which the Y coordinate falls below the range previously determined for the topmost line. When this occurs, that line is printed, the cells in the line image are reset to blanks, and the range is changed to that for the second line of the scattergram. This process continues until there are no more data, at which point the final lines of the scattergram, together with appropriate bottom labels, are printed. A more complete flow chart for this basic type of scattergram program is shown in Figure 5.7. It is essential in this type of program that scales be predefined and the data be introduced to it with the highest Y value first, and so on; it is thus presumed that some type of sorting operation took place before execution of the scattergram generating procedure.

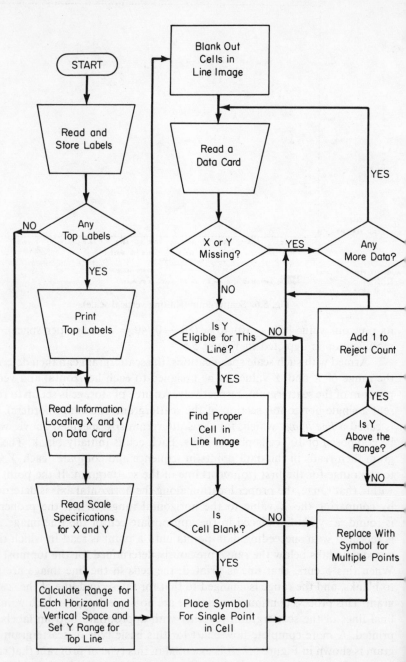

Fig. 5.7. Flowchart for basic scattergram program.

AUTOMATIC SCATTERGRAM GENERATORS

When larger computing systems are available, it is possible to design more powerful and much more convenient programs that can prepare and produce any number of graphs or scattergrams from a particular data file

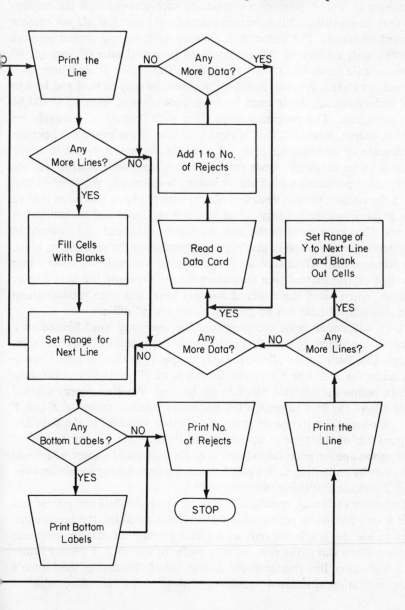

in a continuous run activated by very simple specifications from the user. As a minimum, he need only supply the names of the X and Y variables for each display to be generated. Using this input, the program can scan the data file for each variable to determine its range and use this information to set the horizontal and vertical scales for each scattergram or graph. The algorithms required for automatic scale setting are not as straightforward as they might seem at first. A primary constraint on such techniques is the requirement that the resulting settings be convenient for the user (i.e., do not contain awkward divisions). For instance, if an automatic scaling procedure were presented with a range of 200 to 55,480 to be scaled into 40 lines (or 40 classes), a scale factor of 13.87 would emerge. This factor or scale interval is extremely awkward. Printout and display should be easy to read and lead to quick understanding. An interval between lines of 14 or even 15 would be much preferable. The programs to produce such "pleasant" intervals are far from simple, however. This is especially true if the processor operates in a domain of numbers far removed from the decimal notation in which output is to be produced. Once scaling factors have been determined, the technique for preparing an individual display is essentially the same as that used in the simpler version described above, with the basic exception that an entire graph image rather than a line image is produced and maintained in memory. Thus each point in the data file can be examined and assigned to its proper cell on the graph or scattergram regardless of the sequence in which these points appear. Once such an internal image is completed, it can either be printed or transmitted to a temporary output tape and the next display prepared. When all of the required displays have thus been produced and stored, the output tape can be printed, either on- or offline.

With additional input specifications, the user may avail himself of a number of convenient options that instigate the preparation of more complex displays. One such option allows the user to specify minimum and/or maximum values for X and/or Y variables for any or all of the displays, thus causing data points outside this range to be ignored. Another more involved option allows the user to request the display of selected values of X and Y based on restrictions in one or more of the other variables in the data file. A typical use of this type of option would be to request a scattergram of height versus age for male subjects only; or the user could impose additional restrictions by requesting such a plot for male subjects having weight between A and B pounds and living in census tract C.

In certain instances, specifically those in which the data are precise and reflect a very consistent relationship between two variables, the investigator wishes to use the graph not only as a visual display but also for reference purposes. When this is the case, he may prefer to use an X-Y plotter rather than a high-speed line printer as the display vehicle because of the former's greater resolution (increased sensitivity). Most units can place adjacent points sufficiently close to each other to produce a closer approximation to a continuous line (Figure 5.8) than the points generated on the printer (Figure 5.9). In those installations where a large number of graphs are routinely generated and scrutinized, of which a small number are to be retained for permanent use, it may be more appropriate to install a cathode-ray display

Fig. 5.8. Graphical display on an X-Y plotter. *Courtesy Hewlett Packard Corp.*

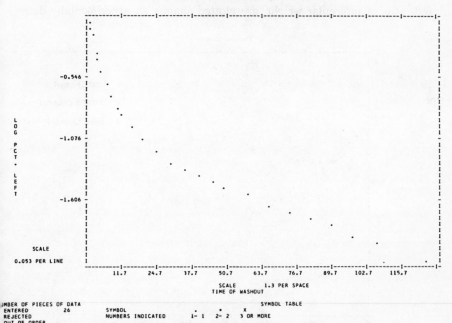

PROJECT NO. MPHC630154-ANALYSIS OF MUSCLE WASHOUT-04/14/64
DR. LIPICKE, DR. BRYANT   EXP. 030   GOAT NO. 236M   X

Fig. 5.9. Graphical display on a line printer.

device equipped with the facilities for producing permanent copies of those graphs to be retained. In certain cases, such scrutiny and selection can be made online. Techniques of on-line search will concern us later on when we discuss man-machine interaction.

MULTIVARIATE GRAPHS

Computer-generated graphs need not be limited to displays of single pairs of variables. By incorporating some rather straightforward modifications to the graphing algorithm it is possible to devise effective procedures for producing a variety of very useful displays in which the actions of several dependent (Y) variables are depicted relative to a specified independent (X) variable. One of the most common multivariate displays is the one in which the fluctuations of a number of observed and/or calculated phenomena are portrayed against the progress of time. Frequent examples can be found in medical work, when such displays may range from multiple lead electrocardiagram readings against time in tenths of a second to histories of various chemical or hematological measurements taken over a period of days or weeks. The common abscissa can, of course, be any continuously measured variable to which the others are known or suspected to be related. A case of this type is seen in Figure 5.10, where three calculated parameters, each a separate indicator of molecular weight, are plotted against an experimentally deter-

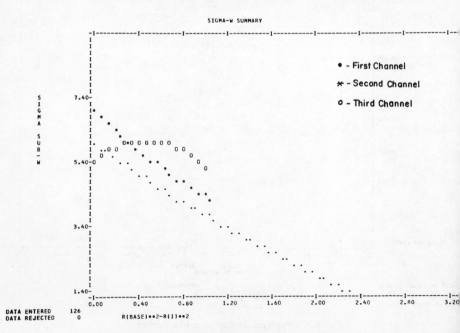

Fig. 5.10. Production of multiple graphs on a line printer.

mined figure reflecting a radial distance measured from the center of a centrifuge instrument.

The design of a successful procedure for producing multivariate graphs hinges on the ability to formulate routines that will generate different symbols for the different dependent variables. The major logical problem with such graphs, the same as the one encountered when plotting them manually, is the selection of a vertical scale that is optimum for all of the dependent variables to be depicted. This is especially true in those situations where the user does not specify the scales, leaving their determination to the scaling routine in the program. The possible danger here is that one or two points in one of the ordinate variables may force the routine to extend the range of the vertical scale to a degree which excessively compresses one or more of the other dependent variables. A way to get around this is to devise a program that actually produces several small graphs on the same page, as is shown in Figure 5.11. This type of program is quite complex to design and prepare and, in most cases, efforts are made to circumvent its necessity.

A second type of multiple display is obtainable when values of the dependent variable can be segmented according to some third variable. For exam-

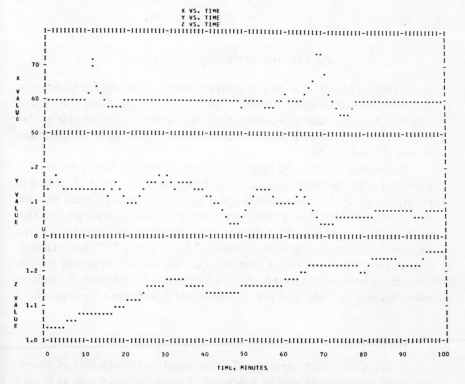

Fig. 5.11. Multivariate graphs with common abscissa and separate ordinate scale.

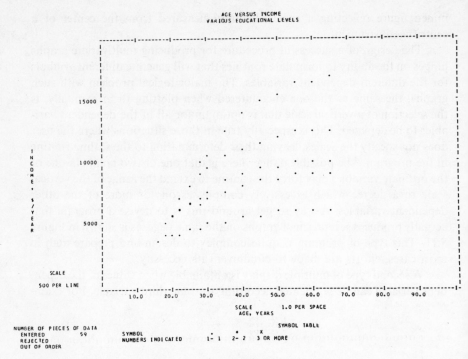

Fig. 5.12. Multivariate graph of curve family.

ple, Figure 5.12 shows a display of average income versus age for groups that are separable according to number of years of education. Since this type of output represents a family of curves, it can be considered as a multiple display only if the third variable produces considerable and consistent differences among the subgroups.

Regardless of type, the output from a multivariate display program is generated with the implication that the user is confident that his data will result in a set of distinguishable graphs. Specifically, it is assumed that the dependent variables have a minimum number of common points and that each of the variables to be displayed has only one data point for a given value of the common independent variable. Thus, if Figure 5.12 showed individual income versus age rather than averages, the distinction among various educational levels would have been considerably less discernible or might have been obscured entirely, and the display would have been a scattergram.

HISTOGRAMS

Histograms, which serve as effective visual representations of simple frequency distributions, can be generated in much the same way as is used for producing graphs. As a matter of fact, the histogram can be considered a specific type of graph in which the abscissa is any continuously measured variable while the ordinate always indicates either the actual or relative number of occurrences of a given abscissa value or, more usually, a range of abscissa values.

Construction of a histogram begins with the division of the over-all range of abscissa values into a number of smaller intervals. In the great majority of instances the intervals are set to be of equal size for a given histogram. The use of unequal intervals is, of course, possible, but such divisions produce a display that is difficult to read and easy to misinterpret. The size and number of intervals to be used, dictated mainly by the range of the data and the total number of observations available, must be an effective compromise between excessive fragmentation of the data, tending to produce many intervals with one or no occupants, and insufficient division, which can obscure important dispersions in a set of measurements. This happy medium must often be determined by trial and error. General experience with a variety of data files has shown that the use of 10 to 12 intervals provides adequate

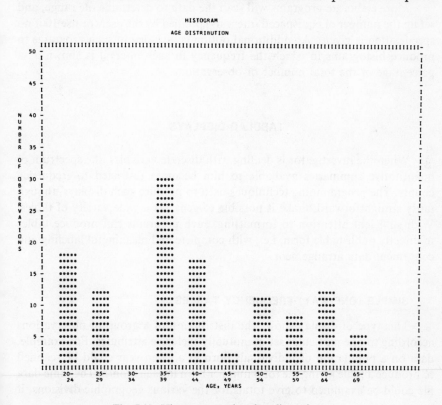

Fig. 5.13. Histogram produced on line printer.

but not excessive division in most cases. A good procedure is to request a numeric breakdown first (such as shown in Figure 5.15) and use the information given there to specify an appropriate number of intervals.

The construction of a program for generating histograms parallels that of a grapher: In a basic version, the number of intervals is fixed (usually 10) and the user specifies the range of the data or the interval size. Furthermore, the vertical scale is fixed so that there is some prescribed limit on the number of observations in a given interval (usually 50 or some multiple thereof). On the basis of the input information, the program can set the intervals and proceed to examine the data. A counter is set up for each interval and initialized (set to zero). Each observation is classified, and the appropriate counter is incremented. When all the data have been scanned and classified, the display is produced. As with the grapher, a histogram is generated either a line at a time or in its entirety, depending on machine size. The form of the display (as exemplified in Figure 5.13) is produced by carrying the succession of points in each interval from its frequency value down to the zero level. The flow chart for such a program is given in Figure 5.14.

More elaborate programs will scan the data to determine the range, and set up the number of equispaced intervals specified by the user (or use 10 if no specification is given). An additional option is included in such programs to produce histograms in which the frequency in each interval is shown as a percentage of the total number of observations.

TABULAR DISPLAYS

When the investigator is dealing with discrete variables, the spectrum of quantitative summaries available to him becomes restricted to frequency counts. The programming techniques used to produce such displays, though fairly straightforward, make it possible to generate a wide variety of tables. With sufficient attention to formatting, such programs can produce tables in directly publishable form, i.e., with complete and meaningful labeling and convenient data arrangement.

SIMPLE (ONE-WAY) FREQUENCY TABLES

This type of display shows the distribution of a group of observations according to one particular set of mutually exclusive attributes. For example, data on a population of individuals born in a given year could be scanned to produce a table giving the total number born in each month. The same data file could be examined to give totals for the various geographic divisions, if

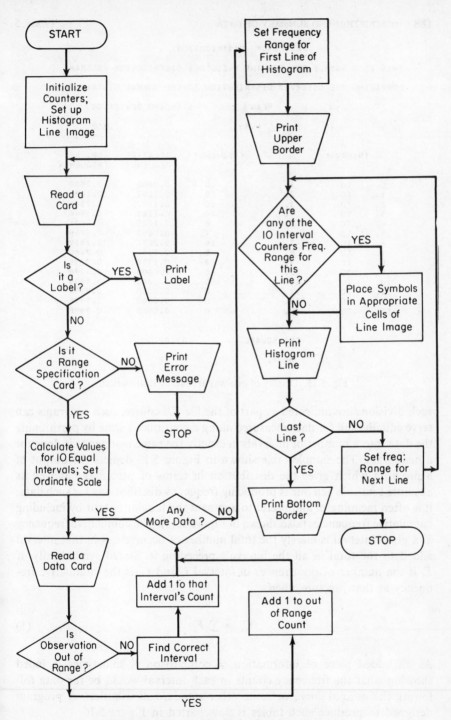

Fig. 5.14. Flowchart for basic histogram program.

187

FREQUENCY DISTRIBUTION

THIS IS A SAMPLE RUN FOR THE FREQUENCY DISTRIBUTION PROGRAM,

COMPARING THE OBSERVED DISTRIBUTION TO THE NORMAL DISTRIBUTION

N	MEAN	STANDARD DEVIATION
78	4.53	2.350

INTERVAL			FREQUENCY	RELATIVE FREQUENCY	CUM. REL FREQUENCY
0.	TO	1.	0	0.0000	0.0000
1.	TO	2.	10	0.1282	0.1282
2.	TO	3.	10	0.1282	0.2564
3.	TO	4.	10	0.1282	0.3846
4.	TO	5.	8	0.1025	0.4871
5.	TO	6.	7	0.0897	0.5768
6.	TO	7.	16	0.2051	0.7819
7.	TO	8.	5	0.0641	0.8460
8.	TO	9.	12	0.1538	0.9998
9.	TO	10.	0	0.0000	0.9998
10.	TO	11.	0	0.0000	0.9998
11.	TO	12.	0	0.0000	0.9998
12.	TO	13.	0	0.0000	0.9998
13.	TO	14.	0	0.0000	0.9998

CHI SQUARE	43.02
D. F.	11

Fig. 5.15. Display of one-way frequency distribution.

such divisions are indicated as part of the file. Of course, such programs can serve equally well for data measured along a continuous scale by partitioning the data into a number of intervals in exactly the same manner as is done for a histogram. The sample table shown in Figure 5.15 depicts the output of a program which gives the distribution in terms of percentage as well as absolute totals. When one is producing frequency distributions for such data, it is often meaningful and useful to augment the tabular output by including cumulative frequencies (also shown in Figure 5.15). The cumulative frequency at a given interval is merely the total number of occurrences in that interval added to the total in all the intervals preceding it. Stated symbolically, if F_i is the number of occurrences in interval i, and C_i is the cumulative frequency at that juncture, then

$$C_i = \sum_{i=1}^{i} F_i \tag{1}$$

As an added piece of information, a comparison is sometimes included showing what the frequency counts in each interval would be for data following the normal curve or some other standard distribution. A program designed to produce such tables is flowcharted in Figure 5.16.

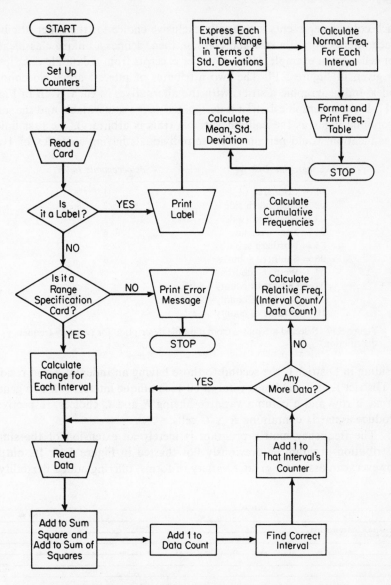

Fig. 5.16. Flowchart for simple frequency distribution procedure.

JOINT (TWO-WAY) FREQUENCY TABLES

When a group of observations is classified by two sets of attributes, the resulting frequency distribution takes the form of a matrix in which each row represents a particular alternative for one attribute or property and, similarly, each column represents a mutually exclusive choice for the other attribute. Each intersection of a row and column, then, defines a unique classification (or cell). As an example, let us consider excerpts from a data file description as given in Figure 5.17. The two attributes of interest are socioeconomic index and geographic district, with the alternatives in each given in Figure 5.17. If the geographic district is designated as the row variable and the socioeconomic index as the column variable (this is arbitrary), the first unique classification would pertain to those individuals having an Index of 1 and

Geographic District	*Socioeconomic Index*
01 = Core area	1
02 = Near north side	2
03 = Near south side	3
04 = Near west side	4
05 = Northern suburbs	5
06 = Southern suburbs	6
07 = Western suburbs	
08 = Outside of county—north	
09 = Outside of county—south	
10 = Outside of county—west	

Figure 5.17. Selected attributes from data file description for two-way frequency distribution.

residing in District 1, the second to those having an Index of 2 and residing in District 1, etc., yielding a total of 60 such unique intersections. In general terms, a row and a column variable having R and C choices, respectively, produce a matrix containing $R \times C$ cells.

The frequency matrix program is merely an extension of the simple distribution program as previously flowcharted in Figure 5.16. Its output, however, can assume a greater variety of forms, offering added flexibility to

07/14/66 TABLE NO. 2

ROW VARIABLE ECONOMIC STATUS
COLUMN VARIABLE AGE

	01	02	03	04	05	06	07	08	09	10	11	12	ROW TOTAL
AED	0.	0.	1.	1.	1.	2.	6.	8.	5.	7.	6.	5.	42.
0	0.	0.	0.	0.	0.	1.	4.	5.	8.	1.	1.	1.	21.
A.B.C	0.	0.	0.	0.	1.	1.	1.	1.	1.	2.	0.	0.	7.
D	0.	1.	0.	0.	1.	4.	3.	3.	3.	0.	0.	0.	15.
COLUMN TOTALS	0.	1.	1.	1.	3.	8.	16.	17.	17.	10.	7.	6.	85.

DEGREES OF FREEDOM = 12 CHI SQUARE = 21.018776

CHI SQUARE SIGNIFICANT AT .0501 LEVEL

Fig. 5.18. Display of two-way frequency distribution. *From MEDCOMP Program Library.*

the user. As an addendum to the basic frequency matrix, the display usually includes row and column totals (Figure 5.18). Optionally, the cell frequencies can be expressed as percentages of row totals, column totals, or grand totals. In addition, the output may include the results of a statistical test in which the relative uniformity of the distribution is assessed.

HIGHER LEVEL FREQUENCY DISTRIBUTIONS

There is no conceptual limit to the number of attributes that can be used to define a unique classification, nor is there any great difficulty in expanding the scope of corresponding display programs. The usefulness of the resulting frequency distributions, however, may be severely limited by two practical constraints. First, there is the problem of fragmentation, caused by the rapid increase in the number of possible cells as we include more attributes to define a cell. If, for example, we add age as a third cell-defining variable to the pair used in Figure 5.17, and there are ten age groups, the number of possible cells jumps from 60 to 600. Unless a very large data file is available, many of these cells will be empty and many others will have only one or two occupants. As a result, the user often runs out of data well before any clustering effect becomes noticeable.

The second limitation is an operational one, centering around the awkwardness inherent in displaying such large arrays in convenient form. Although the excerpt of a four-way frequency tabulation shown in Figure 5.19 represents perhaps the most effective available display format for mul-

THYROID STUDY

MENSES FOR FEMALES
  TREMOR AND SLEEP
    GLAND PALPATION
      I-131 INIT UPTAKE

PURPOSE OF THERAPY

Menses	Tremor and Sleep	Gland Palpation	I-131 Init Uptake	OTHER	NOT DETMD	DIFF HYPER THYR	TOX NOD GOITER	CANCER	ANGINA PECT	CONG FAIL	PULM EMPHYS	P O GOITER	SUM
OTHER	TREMOR	DIFF ENLARG	70-100	–	–	8 (100.0)	–	–	–	–	–	–	8
NORMAL	TREMOR	DIFF ENLARG	70-100	–	–	2 (66.6)	–	–	–	–	–	1 (33.3)	3
NORMAL	TREMOR POOR SLEEP	DIFF ENLARG	70-100	–	–	3 (100.0)	–	–	–	–	–	–	3
DECR	TREMOR	DIFF ENLARG	70-100	–	–	2 (66.6)	–	–	–	–	–	1 (33.3)	3
MENOPA	NONE	MULTI NODULE	70-100	–	–	–	4 (100.0)	–	–	–	–	–	4
MENOPA	TREMOR	DIFF ENLARG	50-59	–	–	3 (100.0)	–	–	–	–	–	–	3

Fig. 5.19. Display of four-way frequency distribution.

tilevel distributions, it is evident that the user receiving a full table of this kind must prepare himself for a lengthy process of scrutiny. (We will have more to say about this in Chapter 10, Robot Data Screening.)

PATTERN DISPLAYS

A very interesting type of display is produced by using various symbols to form a visual pattern. Unlike a graph, on which the coordinates may represent any pair of continuous variables, the symbolic pattern is basically a geometric display in which the coordinates always represent or imply distances and the symbols themselves represent changes in some property of the data. This is closely akin to the familiar map in which color changes are used to denote bodies of water, mountains, deserts, etc. The user working with such displays is generally more interested in the distribution of values over the surface under scrutiny than he is in individual readings at particular points.

CONSTANT MAGNITUDE DISPLAYS

One of the most effective forms developed for the depiction of such data patterns is a display in which the area is divided into regions of constant magnitude or intensity and each such area is clearly delineated and labeled. The user looking at such a display can immediately detect the location, shape, and extent of an area exhibiting a particular level. One way of identifying these regions is to outline their boundaries by locating points of equal intensity and connecting them. The techniques involved in this procedure can be exemplified by Figure 5.20. This display represents a surface which has been exposed to radioactivity from several point sources, and the strength of the dose has been recorded at a number of points. The respective intensities are denoted on this display as three-digit numbers that express the local dose as a percentage of some reference number. Lines connecting equal dose levels (isodose lines) have been drawn in by hand to show the formation of boundaries. Automation of this technique obviates the necessity of displaying the actual values (unless, of course, the user wishes to see them). The arrangement of the points on the surface under consideration, their scrutiny, and the subsequent formulation of the boundaries can all be done internally, with the output being restricted to the actual border lines. In Figure 5.21 we see a display of this type in which is depicted the isodose line pattern characteristic of the area surrounding a single source of radioactivity.

When such constant intensity patterns are produced frequently and repeatedly for a standard display area, a significant dimension of convenience

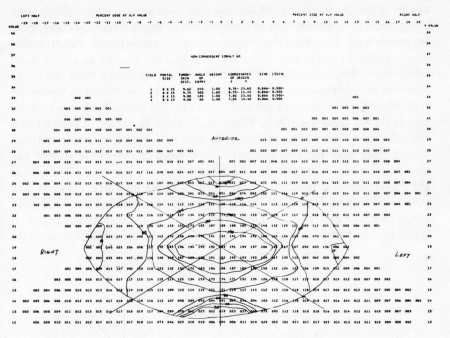

Fig. 5.20. Printout of numerical dose distribution with isodose lines superimposed.

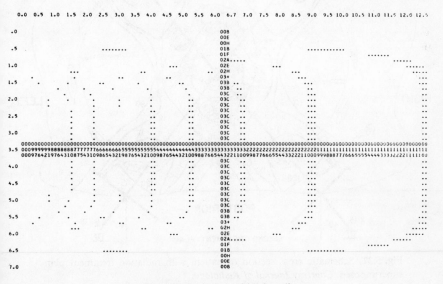

Fig. 5.21. Printout of isodose lines.

can be added by preparing the display area with some reference landmarks upon which the constant lines of intensity can be superimposed. This supplies the viewer with immediate orientation so that he can interpret a distribution of intensities properly and conveniently. Thus the display in Figure 5.20, which shows the distribution of radioactive intensity over a cross section of a human patient receiving radiation therapy, can be supplemented by images representing the various organs and tissues in that plane. Such a superposition is shown schematically in Figure 5.22. Since the plane of interest to a radiotherapist is very likely to change for each patient and, in fact, from treatment to treatment for a given patient, it is more convenient to display the dose distribution automatically and superimpose the anatomical features of the display surface by hand. In other applications the reference surface is sufficiently standardized that it becomes practical to preprint it on the display sheets (if a line printer or graph plotter is used as the display device) or to generate it as part of the over-all display program. Typical of such displays

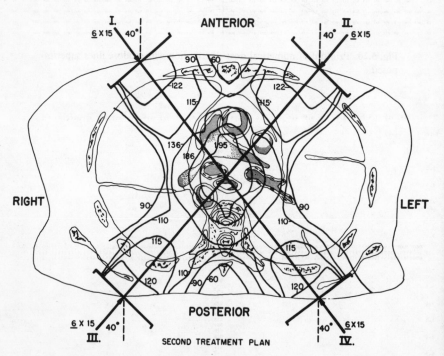

Fig. 5.22. Schematic cross section of patient with radiation treatment plan superimposed. *Courtesy Journal of Radiology.*

is the familiar meteorological map for which the standard background is a particular geographic area, and the varying display consists either of lines connecting constant temperature points (isotherms) or similar lines connecting points at which the atmospheric pressure is constant (isobars). Similarly, fluctuations in population densities in large regions could be visualized by connecting areas of equal densities by lines and producing what one might call "isopops."

An alternate method of showing areas of varying magnitude or intensity is to devise a code whereby a particular symbol stands for a particular range of values. The display is then produced by covering the entire output surface with symbols. Figure 5.23 shows such a display for the radioactive dose distribution described previously. In this particular printout each character stands for a dose value rounded to the nearest multiple of 10, and blanks are used as symbols to depict values below a minimum (threshold) level. The detail exhibited in such displays implies, of course, that correspondingly

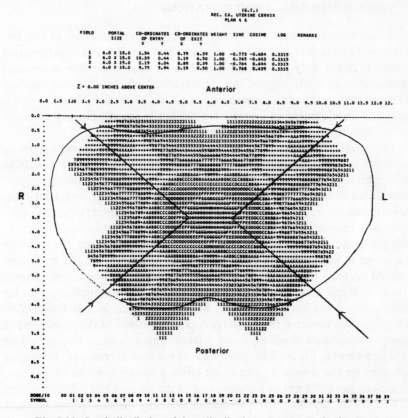

Fig. 5.23. Symbolic display of dose distribution. *Courtesy Columbia Press.*

detailed data are available to produce them or that data trends are sufficiently consistent to allow meaningful interpolation to be used for the calculation of additional points.

If the hierarchy of symbols is selected so that greater values are represented by darker symbols, this visual correspondence provides the viewer with a display that he can scan and interpret almost intuitively. Such representations have long been used to depict a wide variety of situations, ranging from maps showing relative amounts of rainfall to geographic distributions of uranium. Automation of the generation of such displays has not only facilitated the production of familiar ones but has introduced the possibility of providing new types of displays in which the phenomena to be depicted are sufficiently transient that an adequate updating rate would have been impossible by manual means.

THREE-DIMENSIONAL REPRESENTATIONS

Experimentation with various symbol coding has resulted in the formulation of hierarchies of darkness of print which produce combinations and patterns that not only yield striking and easily comprehensible summaries but may even strongly suggest three-dimensional effects. The investigation and use of these techniques (known as *gray shading*) has stimulated the exploration and development of systems for the automatic production of visual images, with some striking results already in evidence.

In general, such display systems are structured around an optical device that is set to scan the object under consideration and transmit signals at predetermined distance intervals, with the intensity of the signal being proportional to the density (average degree of darkness) over that particular area. These signals are recorded on some external storage medium (punched cards, paper tape, magnetic tape, etc.) or directly in a digital processor's memory. Once the data for an entire scan are available to the processor, the signal at each point is adjusted by expressing it as a percentage of the maximum observed intensity for the entire scan. The results are then classified by comparison to standardized intensity intervals, for each of which a particular display symbol has been designated. Successive search in a stored symbol table allows the program to assign appropriate symbols to the points on the display image, which is subsequently printed. This procedure is summarized in the flow chart in Figure 5.24. Although the range of darkness of the various characters on the standard print chain offers a certain amount of contrast, it is usually not sufficient to portray some of the more subtle differences that are well within the sensitivity of optical scanning devices. Many types of digital processing systems have line printers equipped with a feature which allows a line to be printed without subsequent advance of the carriage to the

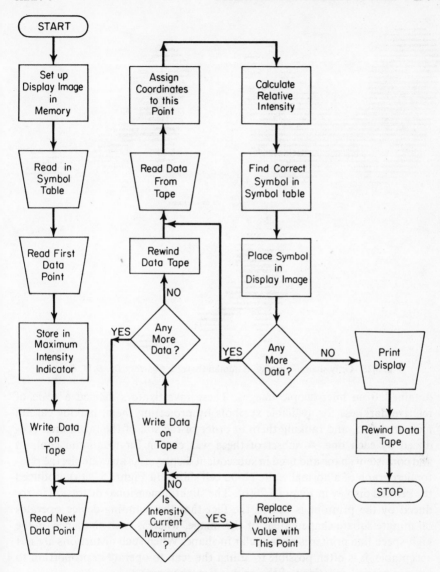

Fig. 5.24. Basic flowchart for image displays.

next line (this is called a *space suppress feature*). This property makes it possible to overprint, thus adding a number of available "symbols" to the dark end of the display spectrum. The effectiveness of such scanning/display procedures can be seen in Figure 5.25, which shows the representation of a thyroid scan resulting from a technique developed by D. W. Brown at the University of Denver. A similar procedure, developed by Mendelson at the University of Pennsylvania, evaluates and displays representations of scans

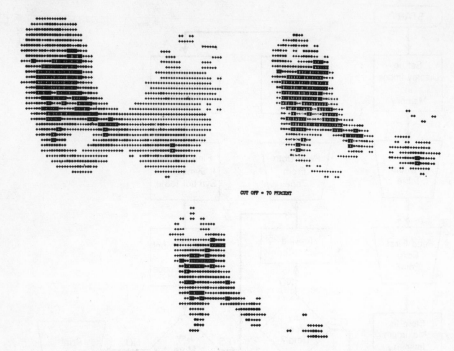

Fig. 5.25. Gray shading display of human thyroid. *Courtesy Dr. D.W. Brown.*

obtained from microscopic images. These investigators defined a scale of relative darkness for available symbols by projecting them, making careful measurements, and ranking them in order of the size of the inked area produced by each one. A subset of these was chosen for maximum contrast and consistent shape and used in subsequent displays. As an example, the photomicrograph of a normal white blood cell shown in Figure 5.26(a) produced the printed display in Figure 5.26(b). The slight dimensional distortion introduced by the printout is due to the fact that the scanning device operates on minute square-shaped areas of the image, whereas each character on the high-speed line printer is rectangular in shape. When such distortions are not acceptable, it is often possible to adjust the scan to operate in proportion to the geometric limitations of the printing mechanism.

When a particular application requires greater sensitivity, nonstandard dimensioning, or other special consideration, it may be justifiable to use the sensing-processing complex in conjunction with special display equipment. A striking example of such display generation is the procedure developed at the California Institute of Technology Jet Propulsion Laboratory for reconstructing the pictures transmitted by the Mariner IV spacecraft. This vehicle, which passed within 6000 miles of Mars, was equipped with a television camera and A/D converter. The result of the scanning and conversion process

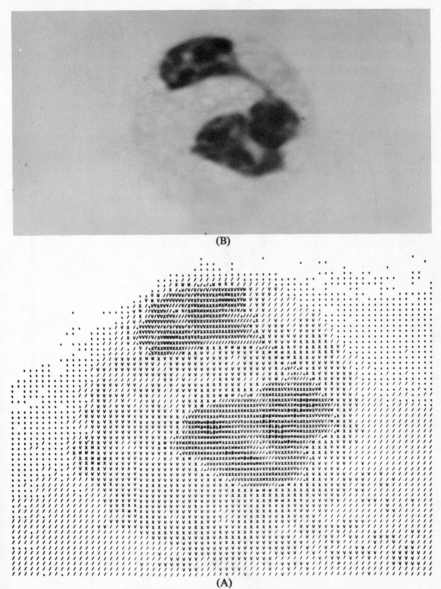

(B)

(A)

Fig. 5.26. (A) Photomicrograph of white blood cell. (B) Digital representation of white blood cell. *Courtesy Dr. M. L. Mendelson.*

was a series of digital signals, each of which represented a dot along a scan line. A typical picture was composed of 200 scan lines, each containing 200 such dots. These signals were recorded as binary numbers on a digital magnetic tape in the vehicle. The value of the binary number was a direct indication of

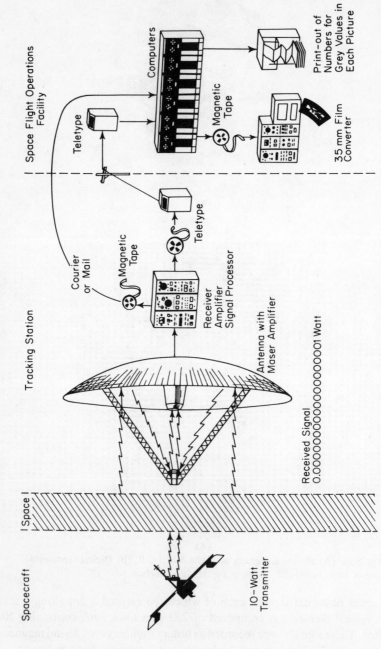

MARINER IV TV TRANSMISSION AND RECORDING

Fig. 5.27. Mariner IV TV transmission and recording system. *Courtesy Jet Propulsion Labs.*

the degree of intensity for that particular dot. These binary numbers were then radioed by the vehicle's transmitter to earth, where they were amplified and sent on to the digital processor. Once available to the processor, the data for each picture could be decoded and formatted in final preparation for reconstruction. The refined output was written on magnetic tape, which was then used with a special film scanner which sends a tiny beam of controlled light across a piece of 35 mm film. The amount of exposure at each point along the beam's trajectory is carefully controlled by the signals on the output tape, thus reconstituting the visual image that was scanned initially. A flow diagram of this processing system is shown in Figure 5.27, and a typical result is shown in Figure 5.28.

Successful reconstruction of scanned visual images, though an interesting and imaginative technique, is not primarily an end in itself. It is, rather, a demonstration that a particular procedure has rendered visual data in machine readable form without seriously altering their content. Quite to the contrary. Very often an instrument-generated picture has certain distortions in it which mar its clarity. (e.g., television pictures taken at a distant location are usually distorted at the periphery of the lens.) These distortions can be removed by appropriate corrections based on experimentation. But processing of these images need not be limited to correction of distortions. Algorithms are under development for the internal scrutiny of such scan representations to determine the presence or absence of certain patterns, identification of certain geometric features, or the recognition of some other attributes that will lead to some classification or other conclusion about the image. Such

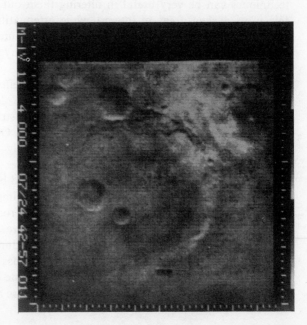

Fig. 5.28. Display of Mariner IV Mars photograph —altitude is 7800 miles. *Courtesy Jet Propulsion Labs.*

techniques are already being used in a wide variety of applications ranging from the suppression of visual "noise" in particle physics photographs to classification of chromosome type to location and mapping of brain tumors.

IMAGE ENHANCEMENT

Three-dimensional display through gray shading is only one method by which an image may be made more understandable. There are other instances in which the image may be enhanced to yield a better understanding of the phenomenon of which it is, after all, a collection of data points.

Very often a picture of an event or a summary of events brought together in graphic form tends to be confusing. Details may obscure some of the image features that are of interest. Also, some of the patterns and shapes for which the investigator searches may be hidden or masked by stronger components. For instance, soft tissue marks on an X-ray are difficult to spot, being obscured to a great extent by shadows thrown by hard tissues such as bone and cartilage. Similarly, the details and shadows of blood vessels, minor calcifications, and so on, tend to obscure each other to some extent. By the same token, a scan of radioactivity of a patient, when translated through a photosensitive instrument into a picture visible to the human eye, very often represents a confusion of points in which the details pointing towards the location of lesions or tumors may be hidden.

These visual obstructions are sources of noise in exactly the same sense as are extraneous currents in electrocardiograms, and image enhancement techniques can be very useful in filtering them out. One way to approach this is to darken areas of interest while attenuating surrounding regions, thus increasing the contrast. If it is desired, unwanted surroundings may be entirely deleted. In addition, areas of interest may be enlarged for further scrutiny.

The techniques of superposition may also be effectively applied to image enhancement processes by producing composite displays. In sociological areas, for example, representations of income distribution and crime incidence for a given region can be viewed together. Other such combinations can be synthesized by extensions of the basic algorithm shown in Figure 5.24.

A time or a depth variable may be introduced by presenting a sequence of pictures in rapid succession. This may give the impression of "animation" by which events may be viewed as they change. From a very practical point of view, the investigator could sit in front of a screen depicting a picture of traffic arteries in which the frequencies of traffic during successive times are presented by increased or decreased light intensities (or gray shading intensities) over the course of a day or a year, or some other period. Similarly, it may be possible to follow the distribution of dose in an irradiated medium by representing slice after slice of dose distribution calculated for a succession of parallel planes. We shall discuss techniques of this type in greater detail in Chapter 12, Man-machine Interaction.

OTHER PICTORIAL PATTERNS

A separate phase of display generation has developed around the production of pictures composed of printed symbols. The technique of producing these pictures involves virtually no data manipulation insofar as the processor is concerned, consisting instead of a straight listing of a point-by-point layout which was prepared manually (Figure 5.29). Although the uses of such displays are basically recreational or promotional, some very clever output has been prepared. The technique serves as an illustration of the versatility of output devices when put to imaginative use. For example, the same sequence of pictures mentioned before may be prepared in such a way that the rapid viewing of the sequences produces an animated movie.

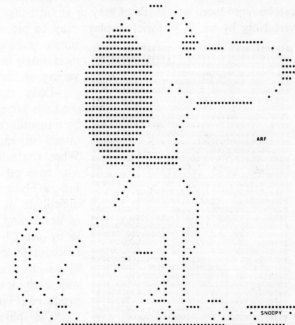

Fig. 5.29. Pictorial display on printer.

COMPUTER-GENERATED ART

Experimentation with various algorithms and output devices directed towards improvement and expansion of data display techniques has produced a variety of patterns with esthetic content. Some of these were generated as regular geometric patterns formed by representations of known, continuous mathematical functions, whereas others were displays of uncontrolled points, lines, and shapes synthesized randomly by a variety of programs. As a result, a number of groups are investigating the possibilities of generating displays primarily for this purpose.

A lively controversy has grown over the question as to whether such output should be considered art and exhibited as such. Proponents claim such displays to be artistic because their esthetic value has been recognized, with source being a secondary consideration; those against such forms base their argument on the contention that art by definition must directly involve a human in its creation. Furtherance of one side or the other is irrelevant here.

A FURTHER WORD ABOUT GRAY SHADING

We have already described the general technique by which a numerical value standing for some density, amount of light, or other quality or quantity can be reproduced as a shade of gray or an intensity of light. Because of the versatility by which pictorial displays may be presented to a viewer, this simple technique has taken on an increasingly important role in a wide variety of instances.

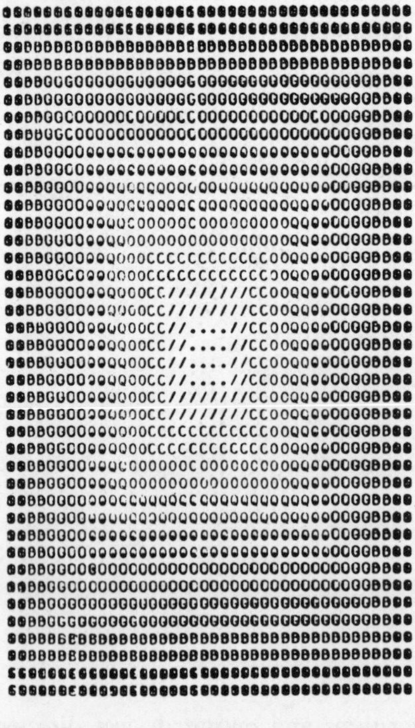

Early representations of gray shadings were done predominantly by estimating the amount of ink contained in each printed character. When characters are superimposed over each other, then the amount of ink or blackness produced is more difficult to obtain. One simple way of developing a gray shading scale is by actually measuring the light reflection (or decrease in it) produced by combinations of letters. In this way, a physical scale of gray can be produced (Figure 5.30).

The physical scale, however, while very useful, does not answer all requirements of pictorial display. The utility of the display is that it leads to an increased ability to discriminate between patterns. Therefore, a scale designed to evaluate

```
●●●●●●●●●●●●●●●●●●●●●●●●●●●●●●●●●●●●●●●●●●●●
●●●●●●●●●●●●●●●●●●●●●●●●●●●●●●●●●●●●●●●●●●●●
●●B●BB●BD●DB●BB●BB●BB●B●BB●BB●BB●BB●BB●BB●●●
●●BB●BB●BB●BB●BB●BB●BB●BB●BB●BB●BB●BB●BB●●●●
●●BB●QGQGQQGQQGQQGQGGGQGQQGQQGGQQGQOGB●●●
●●B●QGQGGQGGQGGQQGGQGQGGQGGQGGQGOGB●●●
●●B●QGCOOOOCCOOQOCCOOOOOOOOOOCCOOOQGBD●●●
●●BB●GCOOOOOCOOOOOOOOOOOOOOOOOOCQGGB●●●
●●BB●QOOOO●●OQCOOOOOOOOOOOOOOOQOCQGBB●●●
●●B●QOCOOOOOQCOOOOOOOOOOOOQOQOOOCQGGB●●●
●●B●QOOOOOQUCCQOOCOOQUUUQUQOUO●OCQGGB●●●
●●B●QOOOOOQUQCQOOCOOQQOQQQQOQQOOCQGB●●●
●●B●QOOOOQUUCOOOOCOOOOOOOOOQQQOOCQGBB●●●
●●B●QOUOQOQQUOOOOOOOOOOOOOOOOQQOOOQGBB●●●
●●B●QOOOOQQOOOCCCCCCCCCCOOQQOOOQGBB●●●
●●B●BOGCOQOQOOOCCCCCCCCCCCOOQOOOQGGB●●●
●●B●BOOOOQOQOOCC////////CCOOQQOOCQGGB●●●
●●B●BGOOOQOQUOCC///////CCOOQQOOOCQGBB●●●
●●B●BOOOOQOQOOCC//....//CCOOQQOOOCQGBB●●●
●●B●BOOOOQOQOOCC//....//CCOOQQOOOCQGBB●●●
●●B●BUOOOQOQUOCC//....//CCOOQQOOOCQGBB●●●
●●B●BOOOOQOQUOCC//....//CCOOQQOOOCQGBB●●●
●●B●BGUOOQOQUOCC///////CCOOQQOOOCQGBB●●●
●●B●BOGOOQOQUOOCC///////CCOOOCQOOOQGBB●●●
●●B●BOOOOQOQOOOCCCCCCCCCCOOQQOOOQGGB●●●
●●B●BOGCOQOQOOOCCCCCCCCCCOOQQOOOQGGB●●●
●●B●BOOOOQOQUCOOOOOCOOOOQOQOOOCQGGB●●●
●●B●BOOOOQOQOOOOOOOOOOOOOOOOOOCQGBB●●●
●●B●BOOOOQOOCCUUQOCCQOOQUQUQQOQOOOQGBB●●●
●●B●BOOOOUQUUCQQQUQQQQQQQQQOQQOOOQGBB●●●
●●B●BOOOCOOQOCOOQQQQOOCOOQQOOOOOCQGGB●●●
●●B●BOOOOQOOQOOOQOCOOQQOOOOOOOOOCQGB●●●
●●B●BOOOOQ●OOOOOOOOQOOOOOOOOOOOOOQGBB●●●
●●B●BBOGCOOOOOOOOOOCOOOOOOOOOOOOOOQGBB●●●
●●B●BOOOOOOQGUOGGGGGGGGGGGGGGGGGGGQGBB●●●
●●B●BOGCGOGOOGGOOGGGGGGGGGGGGGGGGGGGGB●●●
●●BBB●GEBBBBBBBBBBBBBBBBBBBBBBBBBBDDGB●●●
●●BBBB●BBDDBBBBBBBBBBBBBBBBBBBBBBBBBBB●●●
●●●●●●●●●●●●●●●●●●●●●●●●●●●●●●●●●●●●●●●●●●●●
●●●●●●●●●●●●●●●●●●●●●●●●●●●●●●●●●●●●●●●●●●●●
```

Fig. 5.30. Gray shading scale produced with overprinting.

gray shadings in terms of human discriminability or the ability of an observer to differentiate one shade from another is more important than a physical sensitivity scale. It is well known that human discrimination varies with the actual magnitude of an environmental event.

A psychological gray shading scale can be produced by measuring the amount of overlap in discriminability that can be obtained by different combinations of letters on a print chain. Because the pictorial manipulations and discriminations of gray shadings are so important, combinations of letters, their physical intensity or grayness, and their psychological discriminability are represented as a set of arbitrary scale values in Table 5.1.

Table 5.1. CHARACTER COMBINATIONS FOR A GRAY
SHADING SCALE ON A LINE PRINTER

Relative Darkness	Character(s)
10 (darkest)	O$
9	DB
8	UG
7	UC
6	O.
5	Q
4	O
3	C
2	/
1	o

DIAGRAMMATIC DISPLAYS

Imaginative application of these various techniques has led to the development of a number of extremely useful applications in which the output consists of one or a number of pictures. In contrast to the procedures described above, which dealt with the scanning and reconstruction of existing visual images, these pictorial techniques are concerned with the generation of new diagrammatic material produced from trivial processes that merely retrieve and display stored diagrams, or they may be the culmination of extremely complex logical and mathematical manipulations whose end products are a set of specifications that are subsequently used to generate the visual output.

DRAWINGS AND DIAGRAMS

The techniques for generating pictorial and diagrammatic displays stem from the procedures used for producing patterns, as discussed in the previous section. We are still concerned basically with the logical placement of symbols on the display surface such that the over-all visual aspect of the resulting output will be organized and meaningful. There is a departure, however, from the relatively free form of the pattern drawing or visual image display in that we seek the automated construction of a more rigidly organized output whose appearance and content is dictated by a set of criteria specified by the user. Because of this increased control, the utility of the diagrammatic display lies in the specific information imparted by its components rather than in the visual effect and stimulation produced by its shape and/or convolutions.

The programming techniques used to produce such displays reflect this increased systematization. Whenever possible, program modules are developed to generate standard diagrammatic components, and the formulation of the display is achieved by a synthesis of these components.

AUTOMATED PRODUCTION OF DIAGRAMS

An application which typifies the use of such techniques is the generation of program flow charts. This automated documentation is accomplished by means of a program whose logical structure provides the user with a set of routines for constructing various types of flow chart elements. The mechanisms for calling these routines and supplying them with detailed information respond to a set of statements that define each box of the flow chart, specify its type (process, decision, etc.) and contents, and indicate its relative placement in the over-all stream of program logic. Thus, in actuality, the flowcharting program provides the user with a special command language so that his specifications for a given flow chart constitute a set of program instructions in that language; similarly, the input portion of the flowcharting logic acts as a compiler, transforming the user-oriented commands (which are necessarily broad) into appropriate strings of machine instructions. The result is a diagram (as in Figure 5.31) which not only presents a readable account of a program's organization but also provides a flexible document that can be modified very easily and conveniently to reflect changes and additions to the procedure it describes.

Experience with compilers of flowcharting programs is providing computerniks with valuable knowledge which is helping to direct the design of more sophisticated versions. The eventual goal is a logical structure that will produce efficient and meaningful flow charts by obtaining the specifications from the user's program itself.

Along similar lines, a number of programs have been developed to produce logic and wiring diagrams for various electrical and electronic circuits. These are in fairly common use, primarily by computing system manufacturers, who find this to be a most expedient method for supplying their inspection and maintenance personnel with system and component diagrams. The command language made available to the user via such programs allows him to construct circuits by specifying each component (e.g., transistor,

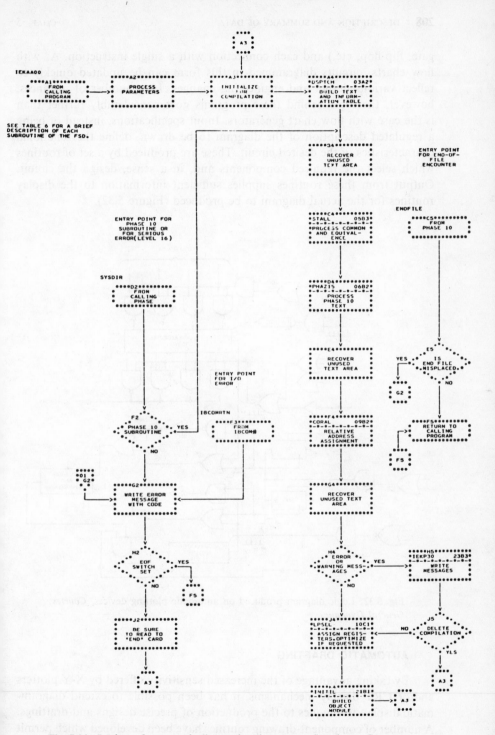

Fig. 5.31. Section of automatically produced program flowchart. *Courtesy IBM Corp.*

gate, flip-flop, etc.) and each connection with a single instruction. As with flow charts, circuits diagrammed in this form can be updated quickly to reflect various design and engineering changes. In a number of instances, however, the logic behind these programs goes considerably further than is the case with flow chart generators. Input specifications, instead of being a regulated description of the diagram to be drawn, define the functional characteristics of the desired circuit. These are produced by a set of routines which select the required components and, in a sense, design the circuit. Output from these routines supplies sufficient information to the display routines for the actual diagram to be produced (Figure 5.32).

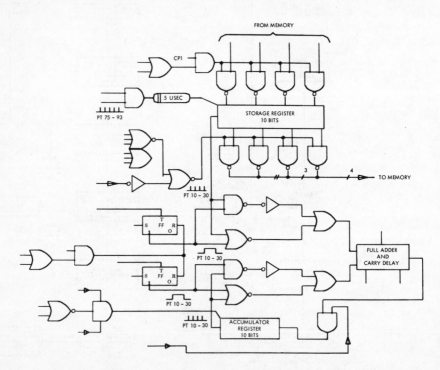

Fig. 5.32. Logic diagram produced on automatic plotting devices. *Courtesy General Dynamics.*

AUTOMATIC DRAFTING

By taking advantage of the increased sensitivity offered by X-Y plotters and/or CRT display mechanisms, it has been possible to extend diagrammatic display techniques to the production of precise designs and draftings. A number of component-drawing routines have been developed which permit the user to specify such elements as line segments, circular arcs, and labeling symbols with simple commands so that the synthesis of complex designs is appreciably facilitated. The results of such programs can be used exactly as conventional draftings (i.e., they can be blueprinted, scaled, used as manufacturing drawings, etc.). When usage justifies it, output plotters can be installed for generating very large drawings. If the production of such drawings involves some type of optimization procedure during which a number of alternatives are examined, it may be more appropriate to conduct these explorations with a cathode-ray display system equipped with a photographic or other image processor for making a permanent copy of the final version. The importance of this diagramming technique to biological and social science is far from realized. Methods available for such exploratory work form a large and separate data processing area in themselves and will be discussed as such, together with a number of major potential applications, in the chapter on man-machine interaction.

SPECIAL DISPLAY FORMS

When mention is made of computer output displays, one automatically and understandably thinks of the production of visually oriented material. There is, however, a small but very interesting group of techniques in use and under development whose primary purpose is the generation of displays aimed at other senses. Although some of the work in these areas can still be categorized as esoteric intellectual pursuit, a number of techniques are already operational and have far-reaching practical implications.

AUDIBLE DISPLAYS

Several applications have developed in which the processor-generated output signals are used to activate some type of device for the production of audible signals. These displays, and the techniques to generate them, fall into two basic classifications; the first of these is basically a variation of the document retrieval and display technique discussed in the initial section of this chapter. In this case the "library" of reference information consists of spoken messages or other data recorded and stored on some appropriate device. The program accompanying this system operates very similarly to the one outlined in Figure 5.1 in that it reacts to input queries by finding and retrieving the proper recorded response and activating some type of playback mechanism to produce it. Such audible displays may consist of sentences constructed from a vocabulary of stored words or a selection of one or more stored phrases. Although the latter type of structure is considerably more redundant, it is in more common use since the responses produced by it sound more natural. This type of system has been set up and is in use for stock quotation inquiries. A central processor which receives immediate notification of each stock transaction is designed with additional input capabilities so that users can submit requests for latest prices, volume, etc., on any particular issue being traded. The processor, after determining the pertinent values, accesses the proper recorded output from a stored vocabulary (in this case a combination of a stock name and a price) and causes that verbal combination to be played back.

The second basic type of audible output, produced by direct transformation of processor-generated signals, is at present a much more experimental endeavor. Several groups of investigators are engaged in some very interesting research to define the signal patterns produced by spoken words so that understandable audible output can be synthesized from signals internally generated in a processor by an appropriate program. Realistic duplication of certain musical instruments has already been accomplished with synthesized signals, and some speech pattern elements have been identified. (Incidentally, along similar lines, work is being pursued to develop reliable sensing instruments that will convert spoken input into stored information, thus making the human voice a machine-compatible input medium.)

The ability to transform internal signals into audible output has prompted a number of individuals and groups to utilize this process as a new form of musical expression. A variety of programs have been designed to generate patterns of such signals which are recorded on magnetic tape. The composer then combines this with other signals or with recordings of sounds made with conventional instruments, or otherwise edits the output to produce the final work. As is the case with computer-generated art, many maintain that music and composer, especially the latter, should be written surrounded by quotation marks. Again, it suffices to point out that this controversy exists.

TACTILE OUTPUT

A most interesting type of computer-generated display produces output in readable Braille. The basic techniques make use of a conventional high-speed line printer whose operating pressure is increased to a point at which the hammers striking the paper produce an embossment. A translation program converts internally stored information to dots, asterisks, or other appropriate symbols which, when printed at this increased pressure, produce symbol patterns meaningful to the touch. (An example of such a printout is seen in Figure 5.33.) Simpler versions of the translating program produce a character-for-character conversion (known as grade I Braille), whereas more sophisticated algorithms yield a more advanced display (grade II

Fig. 5.33. Brailled flow-chart. *Courtesy Communications of the ACM.*

Braille) which uses a variety of shortened forms and contractions. Braille generated from internally stored information is also being produced on several special devices that have been designed to be electronically acceptable as computer output periphery. Imaginative combinations of brailling technique with the output generating procedures have produced some unique displays, such as the Braille flow chart shown in Figure 5.33.

Since a growing amount of information is becoming available in machine readable form and work is progressing toward the development of scanning instruments that will increase this availability even more rapidly, the impact of computer-produced Braille is twofold: First, it is causing revolutionary changes in the amount and range of information becoming available to the blind. Further work is being directed toward the perfection of hardware and software to decrease the cost of such Braille conversion. Second, since Braille conversion programs can operate on any type of information stored in a processor's memory, the results of any information handling procedure can be made available to the blind in readable form. As a result, qualified blind individuals are now presented with the opportunity to train and work competitively in a variety of computer-related professions.

Along similar lines, work is progressing on the development of online devices which translate processor-generated output signals into a series of coded vibrations or mechanical movements that a blind individual can "read." Although the development of such devices is still in progress, indications are that they will provide an effective and economical access to information for the blind in those situations where a permanent copy of the information is not necessary.

PROBLEMS

The data given below were obtained for individuals residing in a particular area.

Subject No.	Sex†	Race‡	Date of Birth	Resident Since	Marital* Status	Income**	Height, (in.)	Weight, (lb)
001	1	1	08/07/89	03/07	4	$3400	65	150
104	1	1	04/21/94	12/21	4	6700	64	141
027	2	1	04/04/14	01/30	2	6400	61	104
061	1	1	07/18/06	07/06	4	4500	67	175
004	2	2	09/16/22	05/39	2	5200	64	123
019	2	1	12/30/08	04/18	1	4100	62	117
171	2	1	05/11/29	06/36	2	6100	65	181
074	1	1	02/01/91	02/31	4	3200	66	145
036	2	2	04/12/02	01/10	4	3500	68	153
090	2	2	10/24/11	04/20	2	4000	64	124
008	2	2	10/16/18	10/18	2	6400	69	172
014	2	2	03/03/16	11/22	2	5800	70	190
021	1	1	11/06/24	11/24	2	6600	66	183
002	1	1	09/17/31	09/31	1	7000	64	117
031	1	1	02/26/96	08/14	4	3200	60	104
032	2	2	07/20/90	07/90	4	3600	59	098
033	2	2	12/08/21	04/40	2	5800	69	193
034	2	2	11/14/08	02/18	4	4100	62	111
035	2	2	07/26/19	03/27	5	5400	70	204
037	1	1	07/03/96	05/27	4	2900	68	187
038	2	2	05/06/30	05/30	1	6500	61	110
039	1	1	06/24/11	06/11	2	6800	63	135
144	2	2	05/18/04	07/18	4	4200	64	116
003	2	2	08/11/20	08/20	2	5900	67	212
004	1	1	01/16/07	10/11	4	4800	69	188
005	2	2	01/18/03	03/21	4	3600	61	109
006	1	1	03/12/01	01/18	4	3700	63	112
007	1	1	01/17/16	01/16	2	4400	60	104
009	1	1	12/24/22	08/40	2	6200	71	202
010	2	2	09/04/27	09/27	2	7000	70	196
020	1	1	10/29/29	11/33	2	7100	68	189
022	2	2	10/06/12	11/19	2	6500	64	114
061	1	1	12/02/14	12/14	2	6700	69	177
023	2	1	01/06/30	01/30	2	7100	64	114
024	1	1	04/30/24	07/44	2	6600	68	181
025	1	2	07/31/17	09/22	5	6400	67	182
026	2	1	08/07/11	11/46	4	5800	63	120
028	2	2	11/17/26	04/30	2	6200	62	118
040	2	2	11/21/29	12/30	2	6000	62	124
057	1	1	12/24/22	12/22	2	5900	70	195
101	2	1	12/08/19	12/19	4	6800	63	111
045	1	2	09/08/09	04/27	4	4400	69	184
029	2	2	09/03/27	09/27	2	5400	71	205
052	2	2	05/19/31	07/33	1	5800	64	114
042	1	1	04/21/07	08/34	4	4100	68	184
127	2	2	10/24/16	10/16	4	4000	69	177
030	1	1	08/20/21	08/44	2	4800	61	101
208	1	1	05/08/20	03/27	2	5100	61	112
059	2	2	03/06/11	07/41	2	5000	63	108
081	1	2	06/04/17	10/32	2	5600	70	198
047	2	1	06/24/24	06/24	2	5800	65	131

† 1=male, 2=female
‡ 1=white, 2=nonwhite
* 1=single, 2=married, 3=separated, 4=widowed, 5=divorced
** Income is in $/year

1. Flowchart a program that will list the data for all males 40 years old or older who have been residents of the area for a period exceeding half their lives.

2. A scattergram program is available which gives a display having dimensions of 50 lines (vertical) by 100 lines (horizontal). Specify convenient horizontal and vertical scales, together with corresponding scale factors, for the following scattergrams, referring to the above data:

(a) Weight (vertical) versus height.
(b) Weight (vertical) versus age (use this year as a reference).
(c) Income versus age.
(d) Income versus age at arrival in this area.

3. Repeat Problem 2, assuming that the display area is 40 lines (vertical) by 80 lines (horizontal).

4. For a scattergram of 40 lines (vertical) by 100 lines, specify the vertical and horizontal scales and scale factors that would be used to display a multivariate graph showing average height and average weight versus age for the above data.

5. A histogram program is available which is designed to accept ten equispaced intervals for a set of data. Specify the ten intervals that would be used for the following histograms:

(a) Age.
(b) Weight.
(c) Height.
(d) Income.
(e) Years of residence.

6. If a very flexible histogram program were available, such that any number of intervals could be used, specify what you would consider to be the optimum number and size of intervals for each of the histograms in Problem 5.

7. Flowchart a program for displaying the absolute and relative frequency tables for marital status.

8. Using the intervals defined for Problem 6, flowchart a procedure for constructing a two-way frequency table showing the distribution of height by weight.

6 DESCRIPTION OF DATA BY STATISTICAL SUMMARIES

When the results of observations under similar or identical experimental conditions are not the same from instance to instance, it is obviously necessary to observe repeatedly. The actual numbers of observations that have to be made depend largely on the variability of the phenomenon. If the outcome of a particular procedure varies widely, then the assessment of trends or constancies that may be contained or hidden within these variations would take more observations than when the results are more constant. The first fundamental problem facing the investigator in an empirical science, then, is to describe the universe with which he deals in such a way that, despite its variations, he obtains for himself a picture of what it looks like (as well as he is able to draw).

In certain instances, variability can be reduced by proper instrumentation. However, when the phenomena observed are the result of interplay between many events that are not under the control of the investigator, variations in quality and quantity are part and parcel of his results.

If it is within the power of the investigator, he would like to distinguish between these two basic effects by dividing the description of the population variability into a component due to error of measurement and to another component due to the stochastic nature of the phenomenon itself. The latter serves as a measure of his "ignorance" about conditions that have an effect on the phenomenon with which he is concerned and is, in fact, called the "unexplained" variation. We shall see later when and how variations can be partitioned into explained and unexplained components. However, in most instances, the investigator may not be able to make such a distinction. At any rate, he is always faced with the problem of describing a variable phenomenon.

Not only is the world of empirical science variable, stochastic, probabilistic, or however one wishes to describe this fluctuating behavior, but it is also multivariate. By this we mean that the instances in which phenomena in it are determined by one or two variables are rare. Such instances do exist, and we shall describe some of them. Most often, however, many variables work together in relative intricate fashions to produce a particular result. Each of these variables, of course, has its own stochastic properties. In seeking a solution to these and in devising adequate description techniques, we shall be guided by two criteria:

1. Any summary of data represents a loss of the richness and variety of results which have been observed. In a way this loss represents an error, and the method of condensation used, whatever its form, ought to be such that the error due to summarization is minimal and, if possible, the size of the error should be known.

2. In selecting descriptive indices we must not lose sight of the necessity of eventually drawing conclusions from them. Whatever indices are used to describe the stochastic and multivariate universe of empirical science, they must also lend themselves to drawing of conclusions and inferences.

The investigator has two basic choices in choosing a method for summary. Unfortunately, these choices were somewhat at odds until now. He can portray data pictorially. Such pictorial representations are easy to understand and can be made to convey a good bit about the wealth and richness of data. Unfortunately, they do not lend themselves at all to an assessment of error introduced by summary (in fact, they can distort findings quite easily), and all pictorial representation seldom if ever lends itself to the drawing of inferences. The other alternative, that of summarizing results in the form of numbers, suffers from the shortcoming that numerical summaries are difficult to understand and do not easily convey meaning to the untutored. Intimate knowledge of the derivations, properties, and limitations of numerical indices are very necessary; otherwise, numerical representations lose all meaning or can be seriously misinterpreted.

THE DISTRIBUTION OF A SINGLE VARIABLE
AND ITS NUMERICAL PROPERTIES

The basis of numerical description is derived from properties of distributions in which results of experiments may be arranged. If these distributions are of numbers obtained from repeated observations, we call them *frequency distributions.* They may describe a single variable, or they may be the results of simultaneous interaction of a set or collection of variables. When these distributions show regularity of form, they can be described

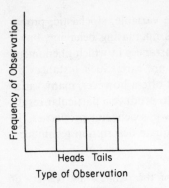

Fig. 6.1. Rectangular frequency description.

mathematically. The numerical terms or factors that determine the mathematical properties of such regular forms are called *parameters*. Since observations or experiments really represent samples from a total universe of possible observations, the parameters that are calculated from experimental results are treated as estimates of the true parameters of the universe and its distribution.

For instance, if we toss a coin, we may expect to observe heads half of the time and tails for the other half. The distribution of heads or tails would be rectangular if half of the outcome were heads and the other half tails (see Figure 6.1). However, this expectation is based on the assumption that the coin we toss is perfectly balanced. If we toss a particular coin a number of times, we may not find that exactly half the outcomes are heads. If in one thousand tosses of a coin we observe 502 heads, then our best estimate of the parameter "per cent heads" in the distribution of outcomes for this specific coin would be 502 divided by 1000, or 50.2 per cent.

One numerical method of summarizing data, then, is to make an estimate of the parameters that would best describe the distribution of results. In these estimates we must also include, whenever we can, a statement about the error incurred by making this estimate and the variation around the estimate which the data exhibits. A complete numerical description of results, then, consists of an estimate of the parameters describing the distribution of results and an estimate of the variation with which this parameter could have taken on different values at repeated sampling. The latter statement is usually referred to as an *estimate of confidence*, and we shall discuss it at a later point.

SPECIFIC METHODS FOR
CONSTRUCTING DISTRIBUTIONS

Ordering observations into arrays provides a simple way to begin the analysis of any distribution. An array is an arrangement of results according to size. For instance, we could make arrays of observed weights by building a table in which weights would be given in 20-pound intervals from 20 to 400 and the number of individuals in each category simply listed. If we view the interval 1–20, 21–40, . . ., 81–100, . . ., 401–420 as class intervals and simply state the number of cases that fall into each of the intervals, we obtain a frequency distribution. The only difficulty in devising a frequency distribution is in the determination of useful interval sizes.

Each observation loses its identity once it is placed in the class interval. To identify each observation more easily and to give it an actual value if computation is called for, we use the midpoint of the interval. If the intervals are 1–20, 21–40, . . ., 81–100, . . ., 401–420, then the corresponding midpoints are 10.5, 30.5, . . ., 90.5, . . ., 410.5. In practice we would set the size of a class interval as a compromise between the desire to let as much of the variability of the data as possible come through and the need to have a meaningful number of observations in each interval. Also, in constructing these intervals care must be taken so that class intervals do not overlap. This is usually accomplished by using fractions. For instance, we could restate the above-mentioned class intervals from 0–19.99, 20–39.99, . . ., 80–99.99, . . ., 400–419.99. In this case, the class midpoints would be in multiples of 10, a number much easier to work with than 10.5 (see Table 6.1).

Table 6.1. FREQUENCY BREAKDOWN OF WEIGHTS OF 8490 SCHOOL CHILDREN FROM CINCINNATI SCHOOLS

Class Interval	Interval Midpoint	Interval Frequency	Per Cent Frequency	Cumulative Frequency	Per cent Cumulative Frequency
–39.9	35	163	1.9	163	1.9
40–49.9	45	965	11.4	1128	13.3
50–59.9	55	1297	15.3	2425	28.6
60–69.9	65	987	11.6	3412	40.2
70–79.9	75	767	9.0	4179	49.2
80–89.9	85	678	8.0	4857	57.2
90–99.9	95	592	7.0	5449	64.2
100–109.9	105	668	7.9	6117	72.0
110–119.9	115	651	7.7	6768	79.7
120–129.9	125	526	6.2	7294	85.9
130–139.9	135	417	4.9	7711	90.8
140–149.9	145	277	3.3	7988	94.1
150–159.9	155	195	2.3	8183	96.4
160–169.9	165	106	1.2	8289	97.6
170+	175	201	2.4	8490	100.0

There are a few rules that need to be followed in developing meaningful frequency distributions. The determination of the number of useful class intervals is always the biggest problem. It is obvious that if too many are adopted then a summary of the summary is needed, and if too few are used the summary itself loses its usefulness. In selecting a meaningful class interval, it is often useful to have the computer first print out the frequency with which numbers for a particular variable occur in the data file. This very detailed distribution can then serve as a guide to determine the optimal usable number of divisions (see Table 6.2). Another useful guide in determining the number of groups is to keep in mind the size and capability of a display device to represent the frequency distributions conveniently to the investigator. This consideration is not a minor one at all. It does not matter what fancy and flexible system may be used to make up frequency distributions if they are not made readily available for the investigator or anyone else who wishes to inspect them. This is especially true when the investigator wishes to look at possible alternative combinations between many variables.

Table 6.2

FREQUENCY BREAKDOWN OF WEIGHTS OF 8,490 SCHOOL CHILDREN FROM CINCINNATI SCHOOLS

WEIGHT IN LBS.	FREQUENCY OF OCCURENCE	WEIGHT IN LBS.	FREQUENCY OF OCCURENCE	WEIGHT IN LBS.	FREQUENCY OF OCCURENCE	WEIGHT IN LBS.	FREQUENCY OF OCCURENCE
25	1	77	58	126	42	175	9
29	2	78	64	127	50	176	3
30	1	79	56	128	45	177	9
31	2	80	77	129	46	178	5
32	3	81	64	130	58	179	6
33	5	82	72	131	54	180	7
34	6	83	67	132	37	181	5
35	14	84	61	133	41	182	5
36	28	85	69	134	40	183	7
37	33	86	58	135	42	184	7
38	29	87	72	136	39	185	2
39	39	88	77	137	41	186	4
40	78	89	61	138	29	187	7
41	64	90	72	139	36	189	8
42	72	91	64	140	36	190	6
43	84	92	64	141	34	191	5
44	86	93	39	142	29	192	2
45	106	94	47	143	29	193	2
46	121	95	75	144	38	194	4
47	118	96	52	145	29	195	6
48	120	97	65	146	27	196	3
49	116	98	52	147	19	198	2
50	192	99	62	148	22	199	1
51	118	100	69	149	14	200	1
52	140	101	75	150	34	201	2
53	101	102	63	151	23	203	1
54	137	103	64	152	15	205	4
55	161	104	78	153	16	206	2
56	114	105	79	154	21	207	2
57	101	106	58	155	22	208	2
58	112	107	70	156	21	210	2
59	121	108	46	157	17	211	2
60	127	109	66	158	10	212	1
61	94	110	79	159	16	213	2
62	112	111	70	160	11	214	3
63	87	112	74	161	11	215	2
64	85	113	57	162	10	217	1
65	141	114	53	163	13	218	1
66	79	115	77	164	8	219	1
67	94	116	57	165	17	222	2
68	93	117	72	166	7	223	2
69	75	118	56	167	13	224	2
70	106	119	56	168	6	229	1
71	75	120	68	169	10	234	1
72	78	121	65	170	14	244	1
73	69	122	50	171	4	252	1
74	90	123	46	172	9	261	1
75	91	124	51	173	8	263	1
76	80	125	63	174	10	264	1

GRAPHIC DISPLAY OF FREQUENCY DISTRIBUTIONS

Although the definition of a frequency distribution is completely exhausted by giving the number of cases that fall in any class interval (i.e., have a particular midpoint) it is customary and also very useful to represent the frequency distribution in the form of a graph.

Two basic types of graphs are available. The first is a histogram. Frequency distributions can be plotted as histograms by marking off class intervals on the abscissa and frequencies on the ordinate. A bar or rectangle is erected over the class interval to the height indicated on the ordinate. The resulting bar graph may be represented in a number of forms. Values on the ordinate could be actual frequencies (Figure 6.2) or they could be in percentage of total frequencies (Figure 6.3). In the latter case, the ordinate is marked off from 0 to 100 per cent and the height of a bar over a class interval indicates the total percentage of observations which fall within that particular class interval. Frequency distributions may also be prepared in the form of frequency polygons by connecting the midpoint of the bars (or the class midpoints) by straight lines (Figure 6.4). Again the frequency polygon may represent actual frequencies or percentage of total frequency corresponding to each class interval (Figure 6.5). Histograms and frequency polygons can also be cumulative. In this case, each bar represents the additional increment of cases found in the next class interval in the sequence (Figures 6.6 and 6.7). Similarly, cumulative histograms and frequency polygons can express percentages of the total (Figures 6.8 and 6.9). In this case, the percentage of acses found in a particular class interval is added to the percentage of cases up to the class interval, and the total bar graph or frequency polygon becomes asymptotic to 100 per cent of all observations.

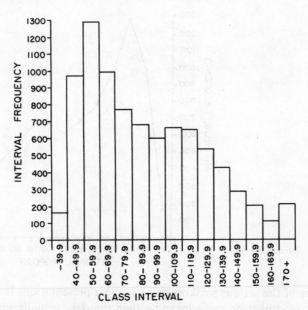

Fig. 6.2. Frequency histogram.

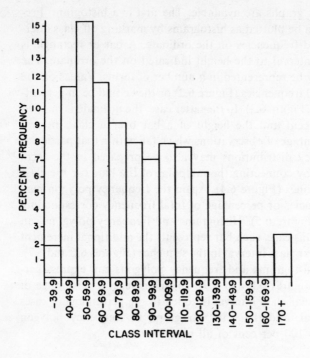

Fig. 6.3. Per cent frequency histogram.

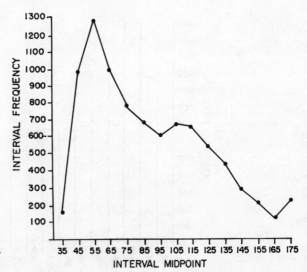

Fig. 6.4. Frequency polygram.

One of the serious weaknesses of graphic presentations is that they run the risk of conveying more meaning then the data actually imply. By judiciously squeezing a bar graph together, elongating it, or making it shorter, the investigator with an axe to grind can exaggerate small differences between

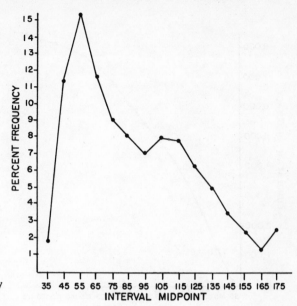

Fig. 6.5. Per cent frequency polygram.

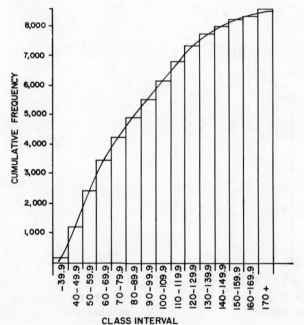

Fig. 6.6. Cumulative frequency histogram.

adjacent class intervals or, conversely, make it appear that large differences are really very minor. If data are to be presented in pictorial form, extreme care should be taken that unintended biases are avoided. The introduction of biases through pictorial display may be a fair-sized problem if the investi-

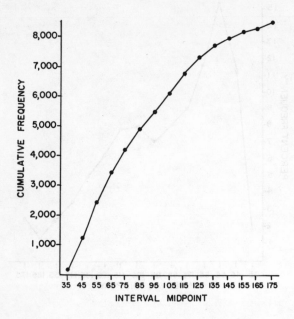

Fig. 6.7. Cumulative frequency polygram.

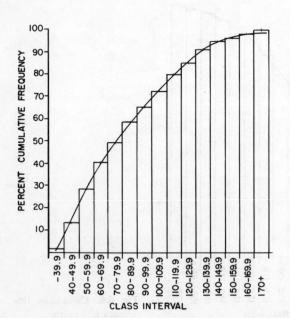

Fig. 6.8. Per cent cumulative histogram.

gator makes intense use of an automatic display device. Visual display should be used to look for hints and trends rather than in place of numerical analyses.

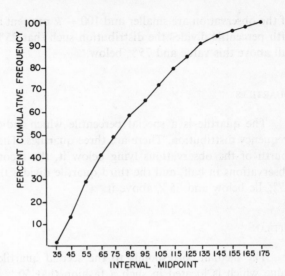

Fig. 6.9. Per cent frequency
cumulative polygram.

DESCRIBING A FREQUENCY DISTRIBUTION
BY NUMERICAL PARAMETERS

The simplest way to describe a frequency distribution is to choose some number representing a typical, central value or weight, and another number that describes the variation around this central value. It is customary, therefore, to speak of parameters of central tendency and parameters of variation.

DESCRIPTIVE INDICES OF CENTRAL TENDENCY

MODE

The mode is defined as that typical number or value describing a class interval or midpoint of a distribution for which more observations occur than for any other such value. Sometimes a distribution is such that several class intervals have the same largest frequency of observations. In such cases there is more than one mode. By and large, the mode is a relatively useless measurement. However, as we shall see later on, its value in relation to other parameters might be of some importance.

PERCENTILES

The percentile is a positioned measurement in a distribution. The kth percentile marks that point or that value for which approximately k per cent of the observation are smaller and $100 - k$ per cent are larger. The seventy-fifth percentile divides the distribution such that 25% of the measurements fall above this value and 75% below.

QUARTILES

The quartile is a special percentile which indicates fixed points of a frequency distribution. There are three quartiles. The first quartile has one-fourth of the observations lying below it, the second quartile divides the observations in half, and the third quartile divides the observations so that 75% lie below and 25% above it.

MEDIAN

The median corresponds to the second quartile. It is defined as that value which is located in such a fashion that 50% of the observations lie below it and 50% lie above it. It is the most important of all percentile measurements, since it is not only a position average, but also a very useful index of central tendency or typicality. As such, it lies in the middle of the distribution in the sense that it is that value which divides the total frequency distribution into two equal parts.

The median is easily computed. Observations are first arranged in size, either in an increasing or decreasing order. If there is an even number of observations (say n), then the median is halfway between the two middle observations, the $(n/2)$th and $(n/2 + 1)$th observation. If there is an odd number of observations (say k) then the median is the mid or $[(k - 1)/(2 + 1)]$th observation.

When data are in a data file, a program can be written to pick the median without using class intervals. If class intervals are chosen and computation is done by hand, then the computation of the median becomes somewhat more involved.

The data shown in Table 6.2 can be used to illustrate the various descriptive indices.

Mode.   The most "typical" value in this distribution is 50 lb, since there are more individuals having that weight than any other.

First Quartile.   Since there are 8490 individuals in this data file, the first quartile will be that value having 25% or 2123 values below it. Since there are 2091 values below 57 lb, and 2192 values below 58 lb, the first quartile lies between these two weights.

Median (Second Quartile).   Similarly, the weight at which the data divide into two halves is between 79 and 80 lb.

Third Quartile.   The weight which exceeds the value exhibited by 75% (i.e., 6368) of the subjects lies between 112–113 lb.

ARITHMETIC MEAN

The arithmetic mean is defined as the sum of the values of all the observations divided by the number of observations. This number is not only descriptive but has some very important mathematical properties. It is useful to notice that the median and mean are affected quite differently by extreme observations. The median is not influenced at all by the actual size of observations on either side of it. On the other hand, the mean is very sensitive to them. For this reason, quite different central tendencies or "average" values can be obtained if extreme values are involved by choosing the mean or the median as a typical value of the population. Thus the median of roughly 79.5 lb obtained for the data in Table 6.2 differs widely from the mean of 100.98 for the same data.

$$\text{Arithmetic mean} \quad \mu = \frac{\Sigma X_i}{N} \tag{1}$$

The relationship between mean, median, and mode may give a useful indication of whether the distribution is symmetrical or skewed negatively (to the left) or positively (to the right). In a symmetrical distribution the mean, median, and mode coincide. If the distribution is skewed negatively, then the mode represents the largest number, the median is in the middle, and the mean is the smallest of these three numbers. The sequence is reversed with the mode the smaller and the mean the larger number when the distribution is skewed positively (Figure 6.10). Besides giving information on the skew of the possible distribution, differences between the mode, the mean, and the median have been exploited in the past for a pleasant pastime entitled *How to Lie With Statistics*. The student is referred to a book by this title by Darrell Huff (W. W. Norton & Co., New York, 1954).

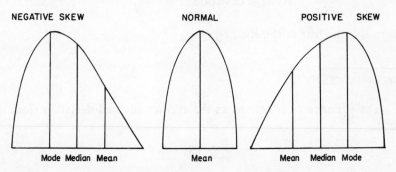

NEGATIVE SKEW   NORMAL   POSITIVE SKEW

Mode Median Mean   Mean   Mean Median Mode

Fig. 6.10. Different skewed frequency curves.

INDICES OF VARIATION

Any statement of central tendency which is used to describe a distribution is, of course, inadequate unless some understanding is given to the extent the values found in the distribution vary about this tendency.

THE RANGE

This measure of variation gives the extreme values in any set of numbers. The range may be given by reporting the lowest and highest number or by giving the spread between them (25 to 264 or 239 for the data in Table 6.2). The actual size of the range is not constant, but depends to some extent on the number of observations which have been taken in a population. For this reason it is a poor index of a population's variability.

INTERQUARTILE RANGE

This is the difference between the first and third quartiles. If the first and third quartile are given, then the interquartile range is immediately defined. This range gives no information about the extremes of the distribution, since it really describes only the mid 50% of measurements (55 lb for the data in Table 6.2).

THE AVERAGE OR MEAN DEVIATION

A measurement that is seldom used because it has few, if any, merits is the absolute average deviation around either the mean or the median. It indicates, as its name implies, how much on the average an observation may be expected to vary from the mean or the median. It is computed by the following expression.

$$\text{Average deviation} = \frac{\Sigma \,|(X_i - \mu)|}{N}$$

where μ is the true arithmetic average.

THE VARIANCE

The variance σ^2 is defined as the average squared deviation from the mean.

$$\sigma^2 = \frac{\Sigma \,(X_i - \mu)^2}{N} \qquad (2)$$

Each observation is measured as a deviation from the mean, and this value is squared. The sum of the squares is divided by the number of observations.

THE STANDARD DEVIATION

The standard deviation is defined simply as the square root of the variance.

$$\sigma = \sqrt{\sigma^2} = \sqrt{\frac{\sum (X_i - \mu)^2}{N}} \tag{3}$$

The standard deviation is important for instances where the distribution has a specific form (normal or bell-shaped) and also enters importantly into procedures for drawing scientific inferences. It will be discussed in greater detail later on in this chapter.

Example. Compute the mean, variance, and standard deviation for the scores (of a complete population) given below.

$$1, 3, 4, 6, 2, 1, 4$$

If we set up our data systematically, we obtain

X	$X - \mu$	$(X - \mu)^2$
1	-2	4
3	0	0
4	1	1
6	3	9
2	-1	1
1	-2	4
4	1	1
$\sum X = 21$	$\sum (X - \mu) = 0$	$\sum (X - \mu)^2 = 20$

$$\text{Arithmetic mean} = \tfrac{21}{7} = 3$$

$$\sigma^2 = \tfrac{20}{7} = 2.87$$

$$\sigma = \sqrt{2.87} = 1.69$$

COEFFICIENT OF VARIATION

It is sometimes interesting to the investigator to get some idea of how his variations relate to the magnitude of numbers that he observes. He may want to compare groups of similar observations or observations taken at one time with observations taken at some other time. He may also be concerned with increases and decreases in variability as the actual volume of numbers increases. Does the increase in variability result purely from the fact that larger numbers are involved, or is there another element added? For this reason, the coefficient of variation is defined as the ratio of the standard deviation to the arithmetic mean and is commonly expressed as a percentage by multiplying it by 100.

$$CV = \frac{\sigma}{\mu} \times 100 \qquad (4)$$

The coefficient of variation is very useful in comparing variables of different units of measurement. However, for more rigorous tests between sizes of variations, direct comparisons of a coefficient are not fruitful.

COMPUTING WITH GROUPED DATA

Prior to the advent of computers a great deal of time in numerical analysis and statistics courses was devoted to techniques of computation from grouped data. Grouping techniques were necessary when the high-speed data processing possibilities of the computer were not available. They are not discussed here any further, since it is assumed that the student will have a computer available for his purposes. When such is not the case and when he needs to compute data on large data files, computation formulas using groupings can be obtained from almost any statistics book published before 1955.

NUMERICAL PROPERTIES OF THE
NORMAL DISTRIBUTION

So far we have looked at indices that describe a distribution in terms of some typical value and a spread around this value and have not been concerned with what the form of the distribution is. We shall now turn to the study of a particular distribution.

There are two compelling reasons for establishing and employing specific distributions. The forms of the distributions of observations in nature tend to be constant. Most of the data collected in empirical science can be made to fit one of a surprisingly small number of distributions. In addition, one of the most important questions asked by the investigator who wants to draw an inference from a sample of observations is: What would have happened if he had subsequently taken repeated samples from the same population? He would gain immeasurably if he knew something about the behavior of parameters computed from samples drawn repeatedly from different types of population distributions. Therefore, since there is a relatively small number of distributions of interest to begin with, study of the properties of repeated samples from these distributions makes it possible to find ways of generalizing from a single sample to the parent population.

SAMPLING

We must detour for a moment and consider the problem of sampling. It is obviously not possible to observe all cases in any distribution of measurements. For instance, if we are interested in the height or weight of the population, it would be neither practical, feasible, nor necessary to measure all instances of heights or weights. What we need, obviously, is to measure heights on a "representative sample" of the population. If the sample selected represents the distribution of heights in the total population, then whatever we say about the sample also holds true about the parent population.

The problem, however, is to find the best method of selecting a sample from the population in such a way that whatever measurements are taken from the sample reflect properties of the parent population. This is apt to be rather difficult. The physical processes of selection may single out a subgroup of measurements that do not happen to reflect the distribution of all measurements of interest in the general population. For instance, we may be interested in such a simple problem as to find the average height of teenagers in University City. There obviously are too many teenagers in the city, so that measuring them all would be rather difficult and certainly very expensive. Also, while we are conducting our research, time will have passed during which new teenagers enter the population and old teenagers leave it, so in many ways the population of teenagers is practically endless. Of course, we do not have to measure all teenagers. A representative sample might be all we need. But how do we find it?

One simple solution to finding a sample of teenagers easily might be to go to a place where teenagers congregate. Such places are a swimming pool, a pool hall, a library, a dance, and so on. However, each one of these locations might also attract a "particular" type of teenager. For instance, the swimming pool might be the place in which the more athletic teenagers are found. Height of teenagers at the swimming pool might not reflect the height distribution of a total population of teenagers, but rather those of the more athletic individuals. Similarly, the library might be a place where teenagers of a more studious attitude assemble. It might be that the lack of sunshine and exercise affects the height of the studious fellow in some way.

The selection of samples from a location in which they are easily available has with it the imminent danger that such samples may be *biased*. By bias it is meant that the manner of selecting or the manner by which part of the sample congregates at the particular place for selection is such that it touches only a specific part of the population which differs from the rest, so that estimates based on measurements of the sample do not reflect the properties of the population itself.

There is one method, however, by which one can assure oneself that the sample will be representative of the total population. If one selects a sample using a method by which each individual or instance in the parent population has an equal chance to appear in the sample (random selection), then in most instances the distribution of observations in the sample will be a true reflection of the distribution of measurements in the total parent population. There are certain disadvantages to random sampling, and it is not always true that a random sample will be a reflection of the "true" properties in the reference population. We shall deal with these problems in a later chapter. Here we shall assume for the time being that the sample selected by whatever method used is an unbiased reflection of the population.

EXPECTED VALUES

Let us begin by studying the fate of large samples of size n taken at random from a population. Each of these samples will reflect approximately the true distribution of the measurement of interest in the population. We shall concern ourselves with two parameters of the sample as well as of the population. One is the mean of all the observations in the population noted by μ. Where X_i denotes some observation of interest, μ was defined by

$$\mu = \frac{\sum X_i}{N}$$

The other index of description with which we shall concern ourselves is the variance, σ^2. The variance was defined as the average squared deviation of the measurement from the mean, viz.,

$$\sigma^2 = \frac{\sum (X_i - \mu)^2}{N}$$

The two values, μ and σ^2, are constant characteristics of the population. That is, if we could measure all of the parent population, then we would obtain single values for μ and for σ^2, said value being characteristic of that population. However, if we take samples, then the values of μ and σ^2 computed from each sample would be expected to vary somewhat about the true value of μ and σ^2. If the samples are random, the variation is obviously due to chance and may be expected to follow the laws of chance.

We shall use different symbols to distinguish between a fixed parameter of the parent population itself and the estimate of the same parameter obtained from a sample. Greek letters will be used to label values of parameters that are literally "true" for the total population and the more conventional English alphabet to indicate measurement based on samples. A sample mean will be defined by $\bar{X}$, where

$$\bar{X} = \frac{\sum X_i}{n} \tag{5}$$

(Note that the mean of the sample is computed exactly as μ. We denote the size of the sample by n and the number of cases in the total population by N.)

The variance of a sample, s^2, used to compute the best estimate of the true variance is calculated somewhat differently from σ^2:

$$s^2 = \frac{\sum (X_i - \bar{X}_i)^2}{n-1} \tag{6}$$

We subtract one from the denominator and divide by $n-1$ rather than by n, because otherwise s^2 would be an underestimate of σ^2. We can see intuitively that this is true by noting that the unusually small or unusually large observation may easily be missing from a sample precisely because such values represent unusual instances. Thus, $\sum (X_i - \bar{X})^2/n$ would be expected to be smaller than $\sum (X_i - \bar{X})^2/N$ whenever n is smaller than N. It turns out that for reasons shown more precisely below, $n-1$ will give an adequate correction for the estimate of σ^2 in the long run.

It is important to grasp the idea that $\bar{X}$ and s^2 are estimates of μ and σ^2. We do not explore a sample for its own sake, but rather for what it can tell us about a reference population. In this population there is a "true" value for each of the quantities μ and σ^2. The sample values of $\bar{X}$ and s^2 offer estimates that vary with the actual values comprising the observed sample. Thus, $\bar{X}$ and s^2 are "variables" that may take on different values depending on the procedures used during sampling and on the vagaries of chance. Some notion of how samples of different sizes behave can be derived from studying Table 6.3. This table shows the distribution of means of samples of different sizes selected from the same reference population. Table 6.4 shows the distribution of variances for the same set of samples. These 10,000 samples were selected, incidentally, by a computer program, indicating that the computer may be used to study the behavior of variables under certain conditions. (We shall use these tables again later.)

Often much more valuable than the study of tables is the proof that a variable will behave in a particular way in the long run. What will happen to sample means and variances when we sample frequently is very important. The next section takes a more detailed look at the expectations that we may form about estimates calculated from samples.[1]

---

[1] This section on expectations may be omitted if the student is familiar with estimations or is willing to take our word for some of the properties of estimates. It is included because it furnishes the justification for much of statistical reasoning.

Table 6.3. FREQUENCY DISTRIBUTION OF MEANS OF SAMPLES OF DIFFERENT SIZES

Class Interval	Interval Midpoint	.... Interval Frequency of Means of Sample Size N ..					
		$n = 2$	$n = 4$	$n = 9$	$n = 16$	$n = 25$	$n = 36$
–39.9	35	15	0	0	0	0	0
40–49.9	45	415	50	0	0	0	0
50–59.9	55	1054	431	68	1	0	0
60–69.9	65	1247	1046	595	202	66	7
70–79.9	75	1357	1933	2087	1764	1357	998
80–89.9	85	1508	2138	3120	4150	4845	5523
90–99.9	95	1362	1920	2594	2968	3247	3230
100–109.9	105	1120	1243	1135	809	468	238
110–119.9	115	761	725	323	103	17	4
120–129.9	125	523	330	72	3	0	0
130–139.9	135	338	128	6	0	0	0
140–149.9	145	153	46	0	0	0	0
150–159.9	155	94	9	0	0	0	0
160–169.9	165	39	0	0	0	0	0
170+	175	14	1	0	0	0	0
Over-all Mean of Means		87.15	87.75	87.14	87.19	87.26	87.23
Over-all Variance of Means		647.45	328.73	147.93	81.55	52.74	36.77

Table 6.4. FREQUENCY DISTRIBUTION OF VARIANCE OF SAMPLES OF DIFFERENT SIZES

Class Interval	Interval Midpoint	.. Interval Frequency of Variance of Sample Size N ..					
		$n = 2$	$n = 4$	$n = 9$	$n = 16$	$n = 25$	$n = 36$
0.– 999.9	500	6112	4735	3665	2838	2189	1650
1000.– 1999.9	1500	1697	3729	5002	6297	7241	8028
2000.– 2999.9	2500	874	1218	1107	800	550	320
3000.– 3999.9	3500	540	480	190	59	19	1
4000.– 4999.9	4500	306	153	30	4	0	0
5000.– 5999.9	5500	189	79	4	0	0	0
6000.– 6999.9	6500	110	29	0	0	0	0
7000.– 7999.9	7500	54	15	1	0	0	0
8000.– 8999.9	8500	39	5	0	0	0	0
9000.– 9999.9	9500	21	5	0	0	0	0
10000.–10999.9	10500	21	2	0	0	0	0
11000.–11999.9	11500	7	0	0	0	0	0
12000.–12999.9	12500	11	0	0	0	0	0
13000.–13999.9	13500	4	0	0	0	0	0
14000.+	14500	15	0	0	0	0	0
Over-all Mean of Variance		1290.53	1331.37	1299.05	1309.33	1311.33	1309.57
Over-all Variance of Variance		$0.34E\,07$	$0.12E\,07$	$0.44E\,06$	$0.24E\,06$	$0.16E\,06$	$0.11E\,06$

EXPECTATION

Suppose that we select some value X_i at random from the population and do so repeatedly. By definition of random selection, each X_i has the same chance of being selected as any other X_i in the long run, and we can see intuitively that the average of these X's will approximate the average of the population. It would be reasonable, therefore, to estimate the true mean value of the population μ from the mean value of the sample $\bar{X}$. We shall denote this process of estimating by the symbol E which means simply: "in the long pull the average value of" or "the expected value of" or "the mathematical expectation of." The statement $E[X] = \mu$ means that in the long run the expected value of X is equal to μ. Since $E[X]$ is equivalent to μ, we may replace one by the other.

Associated with each observation X_i there is also a squared deviation $(X_i - \mu)^2$. The variance is defined as the average value of all squared deviations. The expected value of (on the averaged) the squared deviation will be given by $E(X_i - \mu)^2 = \sum (X - \mu)^2/N = \sigma^2$. These two statements are equivalent, so $\sum (X - \mu)^2/N$ can always be replaced by $E[X_i - \mu]^2$. Because E stands for a particular type of manipulation, it is usually referred to as the *operator*. It is handled essentially in the same manner as the symbol $\sum$. Whereas $\sum$ stands for a process of summing, E stands for an averaging process. That is, $E[X]$ means that we shall take a number of values of X, weigh them by their probabilities or relative frequencies of occurrences, and add them together.

SOME ELEMENTARY RULES

1. $$E[X_1 + X_2 + \cdots + X_K] = E[X_1] + E[X_2] + \cdots + E[X_K] \qquad (7)$$

    This expression indicates that the expected value of a sum of variables is equal to the sum of the expected values of the individual variables. The identity results from the simple operation of adding and averaging.

2. If c is a constant, then it is true that

    $$E[c] = c \qquad (8)$$

    and

    $$E[cX] = cE[X] \qquad (9)$$

    which indicates that the average value of a constant is still obviously the same constant and that the long range average of a constant times a value is the same as the product of the constant times the average of the values.

3. $$E(-X) = -E(X) \qquad (10)$$

    from which it follows that

    $$E(A - B) = E[A + (-B)]$$
    $$= E(A) + E(-B) = E(A) - E(B) \qquad (11)$$

ESTIMATING VARIANCE AND MEAN

An important relationship binds together the variance σ^2 and its estimate s^2. The relationship between these two is important enough that we shall digress and explore its nature.

We said before that the estimate of the variance of a population is computed from the sample by

$$s^2 = \frac{\sum (X_i - \bar{X})^2}{n - 1} \tag{12}$$

Let us ignore the denominator $n - 1$ for the moment and just consider the numerator, which is called the *sum of the squares* (ss, for short).

$$ss = \sum (X - \bar{X})^2$$

It turns out that we can write this sum of squares as follows:

$$\sum (X - \bar{X})^2 = \sum X^2 - \frac{(\sum X)^2}{n} \tag{13}$$

We said that the symbol $E[X]$ stands for the expected value of X and is the result of an averaging process. If we now take a random selection of values of X from a large population of measurements so that the values we observe are $X_1, X_2, \ldots, X_n$, the n values of X represent a sample. Let us now assume that there are many such samples, each consisting of n values of X. Let us label all the X's in each sample in a completely arbitrary (and random) fashion. It does not really matter how. Then, if we were to look at the expected value of all the X's that we have called X_1, and all the X's that we have called X_2, it would be true that

$$E[X_1] = E[X_2] = \cdots = E[X_n] = \mu \tag{14}$$

Since we have n expected values of the variable X, if we add these n values together, we end up with the quantity $n\mu$. (Why?)

$$E[X_1 + X_2 + \cdots + X_n] = n\mu \tag{15}$$

Similarly, it is true that the expected value of a product between any of these subscripted X's is

$$E[X_i X_j] = E[X_i]E[X_j] = \mu\mu = \mu^2 \tag{16}$$

Of course, this is true only if the drawing of a particular value of X_i is completely independent of drawing any other value of X_j. When this happens we say that the X's are results of random sampling, that they are selected with the same probabilities, or that they are statistically independent, or that they are not correlated.

Next let us take a look at the expected value of X^2. This may be found from our definition of the variance

$$
\begin{aligned}
\sigma^2 &= E[X - \mu]^2 \\
&= E[X^2 - 2\mu X + \mu^2] \\
&= E[X^2] - 2\mu E[X] + \mu^2 \\
&= E[X^2] - 2\mu^2 + \mu^2 \\
&= E[X^2] - \mu^2
\end{aligned}
\tag{17}
$$

From (17) follow two important results. In the first place, the expected value $E[X^2]$ is actually equivalent to an averaging process, so $E[X^2]$ is equal to $\sum (X^2)/n$. Hence it follows that

$$
E[X^2] - \mu^2 = \frac{\sum X^2}{n} - \frac{(\sum X)^2}{n^2}
\tag{18}
$$

As one consequence of (18) we can derive a computation formula that is very convenient to calculate sums of squares on semiautomatic machines and incidentally furnishes a rationale for the identity in (13).

$$
\text{ss} = ns^2 = n\left[\frac{\sum (X - \bar{X})^2}{n}\right] = \sum X^2 - \frac{(\sum X)^2}{n}
\tag{19}
$$

Since $\sum (X - \bar{X})^2$ over a sample is an estimate of $\sum (X - \mu)^2$ over the whole population, the computation procedure or $\sum (X - \bar{X})^2$ given in (13) makes it the most convenient way of obtaining the ss.

The second important result is

$$
E[X^2] = \mu^2 + \sigma^2
\tag{20}
$$

which shows that the expected value of the square of a variable has two components, the square of the mean and the square of the variance.

If we now wish to resolve what the expected value $E(X - \bar{X})^2$ is, we will have to find the expected values of the quantities $\sum (X)^2$ and $(\sum X)^2/n$. Let us first look at the expected value of $(\sum X)^2$.

$$
\begin{aligned}
&E[X_1 + X_2 + \cdots + X_n]^2 \\
&= E(X_1^2 + X_2^2 + \cdots + X_n^2 + 2X_1X_2 + 2X_1X_3 + \cdots + 2X_{n-1}X_n)
\end{aligned}
\tag{21}
$$

But if we take repeated samples of X at random and label each X_1, X_2, $\ldots$, X_K as we described before,

$$E[X_1^2 + X_2^2 + \cdots + X^2] = E(X_1^2) + E(X_2^2) + \cdots + E(X_n^2)$$
$$= n(\mu^2 + \sigma^2) \tag{22}$$

Since we know from (20) that

$$E(X^2) = \mu + \sigma^2$$

the remaining portion of (21), i.e.,

$$E(2X_1X_2 + 2X_1X_3 + \cdots + 2X_{n-1}X_n)$$

can be rewritten

$$2E(X_1X_2 + X_1X_3 + \cdots + X_{n-1}X_n)$$

Since $E(X_i) = \mu$ and there are $n(n-1)/2$ product terms, $2E(X_1X_2 + X_1X_3 + \cdots + X_{n-1}X_n) = [2(n)(n-1)/2](n\mu) = n(n-1)\mu^2$ so that

$$E[(\textstyle\sum X)^2] = n(\mu^2 + \sigma^2) + n(n-1)\mu^2 = n^2\mu^2 + n\sigma^2 \tag{23}$$

Dividing by n gives

$$E\left[\frac{(\sum X)^2}{n}\right] = E[n\bar{X}^2] = n\mu^2 + \sigma^2 \tag{24}$$

and if we divide (23) by n^2

$$\frac{E[(\sum X)^2]}{n^2} = E[X^2] = \mu^2 + \frac{\sigma^2}{n} \tag{25}$$

We now wish to find the best expectation for

$$E(X - \bar{X})^2 = E(X^2) - E\left[\left(\frac{\sum X}{n}\right)^2\right] \tag{26}$$

but we saw from expression (22) that

$$E[\textstyle\sum X^2] = n\mu^2 + n\sigma^2$$

and we saw from expression (24) that

$$E\left[\frac{(\sum X)^2}{n}\right] = n\mu^2 + \sigma^2$$

The difference between expression (22) and (24) is equal to

$$E[\textstyle\sum X^2] - E\left[\frac{(\sum X)^2}{n}\right] = (n-1)\sigma^2 \tag{27}$$

so that our best expectation of variance computed from a sample is the sum of squares divided by $n - 1$.

$$E\left[\frac{\sum (X - \bar{X})^2}{n-1}\right] = E[s^2] = \sigma^2 \tag{28}$$

The quantity s^2 is called the sample variance. For each sample of size n there is a corresponding value of s^2. If we take repeated samples of size n and compute a variance each time, then the average of these variances is an unbiased estimate of the variance of the total population, provided the samples are taken at random. (See again the distribution of means and variances in Table 6.3.)

It is much easier to show that a mean $\bar{X}$ computed on each sample represents in the long run an unbiased estimate the true value of μ. The quantity $\bar{X}$ is not a constant but a variable. If we take a random sample for a population, then we may expect the means to vary for each sample. If we look at the expected value of $\bar{X}$, that is, the value that would be the result of an averaging process of many $\bar{X}$'s, we can make the following statement based on expression (15) and the definition of $\bar{X}$, namely,

$$E[\bar{X}] = \frac{1}{n} E[X_1 + X_2 + \cdots + X_n] = \frac{1}{n}(n\mu) = \mu \tag{29}$$

A sample mean is then an unbiased estimate of the true mean of a population (providing it is based on a random sample).

A very important statement can be made about the variation of sample means. It is clear that if we take successive random samples of n observations each, then the mean of each sample will vary because of the workings of chance. How large will the variation of the means be? Intuitively it would seem that this variation will be smaller when the number of observations on which each mean is based is large. This can easily be shown to be the case. It is clear that the variance of the means, which we shall denote as $\sigma_{\bar{x}}^2$, is defined as

$$\sigma_{\bar{x}}^2 = E(\bar{X} - \mu)^2 \tag{30}$$

or it is defined the same way as the variance σ^2 except that we are interested now in expected squared deviation of a sample mean from the true mean of the population.

If we treat each sample mean as a value of its own so that a collection of sample means would be a collection of values, then we can use expressions (17) and (26) from before to say that

$$\sigma_{\bar{X}}^2 = E[\bar{X} - \mu]^2 = E[\bar{X}^2] - \mu^2 \tag{31}$$

and since

$$E[\bar{X}^2] = E\left[\frac{\sum \bar{X}^2}{n^2}\right]$$

it follows that

$$E[\bar{X}^2] - \mu^2 = \mu^2 + \frac{\sigma^2}{n} - \mu^2 = \frac{\sigma^2}{n} \tag{32}$$

or, if we have samples of size n, then the mean of these samples may be expected to vary as the variance divided by the number of observations in the sample mean. Or the variance of the mean is equal to the variance of the population divided by the number of observations in the sample (see Table 6.3). We have now defined the function that ties together the variance of the means and the variance of the population with the number of observations on which each mean is based. As we shall see, the relation is extremely important.

$$\sigma^2_{\bar{X}} = \frac{\sigma^2}{n} \tag{33}$$

where n is equal to the number of observations on which $\bar{X}$ is computed and is of the population of all measurements. (The student should again inspect Table 6.3 or multiply the variance of sample means by the proper value of n.)

Example.   A numerical example may help to clarify the concepts demonstrated here. Let us say we have a large population of numbers consisting of 0's, 3's, and 6's. For this population, $\mu = 3$ and $\sigma^2 = 6$ (why?), and we take random samples of $n = 3$ from this population. If we extract a large number of such samples, we should obtain all combinations of 0's, 3's, and 6's in about equal numbers. Below is a listing of these possible samples.

In this section we have made a number of statements that will turn out to be extremely important for the understanding of inferences that can be drawn from populations which are normally distributed. Since populations of sample means tend to be normally distributed even if the original populations are not, the inference that can be drawn about the distribution of all or most sample means takes on a tremendous importance in the numerical analysis of data. Although we may not be able to make certain inferences about the sample itself if the sample is not normally distributed, we may still be entitled to make inferences with respect to the mean of the sample and the variance of the mean because the means themselves may be and probably are normally distributed (see Figure 6.11).

Possible Combination of Sample Values			For each sample we can compute			
			$\sum X$	$\bar{X}$	$\sum (X - \bar{X})^2$	$(\bar{X} - \mu)^2$
0	0	0	0	0	0	9
0	0	3	3	1	6	4
0	0	6	6	2	24	1
0	3	0	3	1	6	4
0	3	3	6	2	6	1
0	3	6	9	3	18	0
0	6	0	6	2	24	1
0	6	3	9	3	18	0
0	6	6	12	4	24	1
3	0	0	3	1	6	4
3	0	3	6	2	6	1
3	0	6	9	3	18	0
3	3	0	6	2	6	1
3	3	3	9	3	0	0
3	3	6	12	4	6	1
3	6	0	9	3	18	0
3	6	3	12	4	6	1
3	6	6	15	5	6	4
6	0	0	6	2	24	1
6	0	3	9	3	18	0
6	0	6	12	4	24	1
6	3	0	9	3	18	0
6	3	3	12	4	6	1
6	3	6	15	5	6	4
6	6	0	12	4	24	1
6	6	3	15	5	6	4
6	6	6	18	6	0	9
Long run average			9	3	12	2
Corresponding to			$n\mu$	μ	$(n - 1)\sigma^2$	$\dfrac{\sigma^2}{n}$

Fig. 6.11. Frequency distribution for different sample sizes.

SOME PROPERTIES OF A NORMAL DISTRIBUTION

It is important to realize that one of the reasons why it is possible to utilize the properties and shapes of distributions to describe results of experiments and at the same time to use the parameters of description for inference lies in the rather convenient fact that experimental results tend to fall in most cases into a very small number of distributions. Of these distributions, the one that occurs the majority of times is the so-called *normal* distribution.

If X is the numerical value of a variable that may take on values $-\infty < X < +\infty$ and if it is also true that the determination of any particular value of X is the result of the interaction of many random factors, then the frequency distribution with which values of X will occur will most likely be approximately "bell-" or "normal-" shaped (as in Figures 6.12, 6.13, and

6.14). The fact that random variables form this type of frequency distribution was already observed by the ancient Greeks. In more recent times, Gauss, Bernoulli, and others recognized the importance of this distribution for scientific investigations. From the point of view of the analysis of data, this distribution is most important for detailed study.

The normal distribution is almost universal for instances in which many chance factors combine during selection of a sample from a large domain of numbers. Let us take an object, such as an orange. There are a number of ways in which we could measure things about it that would result in numbers. We could squeeze it and measure the amount of juice obtained. We could measure the thickness of the skin. We could throw the orange at a target and measure the distance of each miss. We could weigh the orange. We could measure its largest diameter. We could have individual judges rate the color of several oranges on a scale of "orangeness" ranging from 0 to 10. We could determine the price at which the orange sells at different locations, or we could measure the number of oranges eaten during the year by individuals under the age of ten. As a matter of fact, we could develop an almost infinitely large number of measurements around this orange, limited only by the amount of imagination we can bring to bear on the subject and the amount of available oranges.

Now if we were to measure a large number of instances of such variables and determine the frequency distribution each time, it would turn out that all of them would have approximately the same basic shape, that of the normal distribution. The reason for this is that the various measurements are determined by a large number of factors, each one of them interacting at "random" with others. It turns out that the basic shape of the normal distribution itself can be described by an equation.

$$\text{Fr}\,(X) = \frac{1}{\sigma\sqrt{2\pi}} \int_{-\infty}^{x} e^{-\frac{1}{2}\left(\frac{x-\mu}{\sigma}\right)^2} \tag{34}$$

where Fr(X) is the frequency, X is a continuous variable which may take on values $-\infty < X < \infty$, π and e are the well-known physical and log constants, respectively (π is usually taken as equal to 3.1416 and e to 2.7183). The quantity μ is the arithmetic mean, and σ is equal to the square root of the variance and is referred to as the *standard deviation*.

The normal distribution is characterized by two parameters, the mean μ and the standard deviation σ. Because of the universality of this equation we may think of the normal distribution as a "natural law." The value for the mean μ and the standard deviation σ (or rather the variance which is the square of the standard deviation) now takes on somewhat more meaning. The arithmetic mean locates the center of the distribution. The standard deviation describes the dispersion of values around that center. We may think

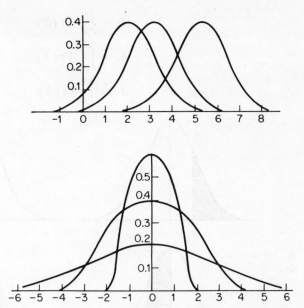

Figure 6.12

of the normal distribution as having two handles for manipulation. One of these handles is the mean μ, which may be thought of as determining the point on the scale of real numbers at which the distribution will find its center. The second handle is the standard deviation σ, which may be considered as determining the "stretch" or elongation of a curve around this mean. (Figure 6.12 shows a number of alternative shapes of the normal distribution.) It cannot be emphasized enough that the normal distribution will "fit" the largest imaginable variety of circumstances. It may fit the distribution of sizes of bacteria as well as that of weights of locomotives. The differences between these two distributions lie exclusively in the values of μ and σ that define each one of them.

Let us assume that we do know that some variable X is distributed normally. We estimate μ and σ by taking a random sample and calculating $\bar{X}$ and s. We can now estimate the location and form of the normal curve that can be drawn over the frequency distribution encompassing all instances of X. The area under this curve represents all instances of X. If we let the total area under the curve be equal to unity and express any part of it as a fraction or as a decimal number, we can express the relative frequency or proportion of time with which X may be expected to take on values in the interval $(a \leq X \leq b)$ by the equivalent area or segment of area under this curve. Let us say that we are interested in finding the relative frequency with which X will take on the values shown by shaded portions of the curve in Figure 6.13. Let the relative frequency represented by the shaded value be denoted by A. Then we will have

$$A_1 = \int_{-\infty}^{X_1} \text{Fr}\,(X) \tag{35a}$$

$$A_2 = \int_{X_2}^{+\infty} \text{Fr}\,(X) \tag{35b}$$

$$A_3 = \int_{M}^{X_2} \text{Fr}\,(X) \tag{35c}$$

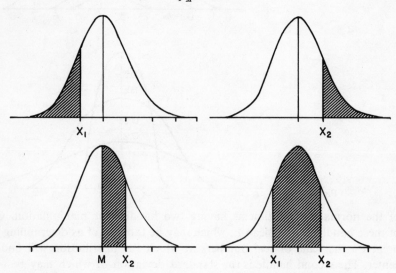

Fig. 6.13. Areas under the normal curves for the examples.

and

$$A_4 = \int_{X_1}^{X_2} \text{Fr}\,(X) \tag{35d}$$

where Fr (X) is defined by expression (34). If we know the values of μ and σ, then all we have to do to find the relative frequency with which X takes on certain values is to evaluate the integral in expression (34).

We can take one more important step by computing the likelihood with which we may select any particular value of X_i in the interval $(X_1 \leq X_i \leq X_2)$ by using the frequency distribution of X as a probability distribution. In this sense the normal distribution is a probability distribution with the total area under the graph equal to unity or equal to the certainty that X will take on any value. Probabilities associated with various specific values of X may be represented as areas under the normal curve corresponding to these values. The probability that X_i will take on values between two points of the interval Fr $(X_1 \leq X_i \leq X_2)$ is determined in exactly the same way in which we determine the relative frequency with which X_i appears in this interval.

The student should note here that we are equating probability and relative frequency. We do so to make it easier to understand something about the notion of probability. If a variable can take on a value X_i between two bounding conditions X_1 and X_2 with a given relative frequency and if we were to select instances of X from all possible values by some random process, then the observed values would indeed fall between X_1 and X_2 a given proportion of the time. We can say equally well that the probability that X_i will take on a value between X_1 and X_2 corresponds to the proportion of times that such values exist in the population of numbers from which X_i is a sample.

STANDARDIZING THE NORMAL DISTRIBUTION

The evaluation of the integral in expression (34) is laborious. If we are going to make frequent use of the characteristics of the normal curve to evaluate relative frequencies or probabilities, then it would be very desirable to simplify the evaluations of areas under the curve. This can be done by developing a standard form of the normal curve and representing different area segments in the form of tables.

To obtain the *standard normal distribution*, a normal curve is constructed such that its mean is set at 0 and its standard deviation is 1. Each value of X_i is then rescored as a departure from zero, where the extent of departure is expressed in units of standard deviation. The resulting standardized score Z_i is thus related to X_i by

$$Z_i = \frac{X_i - \mu}{\sigma} \quad \text{or} \quad \frac{X_i - \bar{X}}{s} \tag{36}$$

(The distribution of Z is shown in Figure 6.14.) Next we present the relative

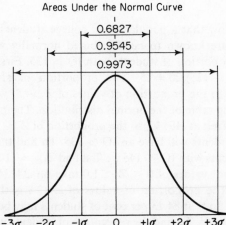

Areas Under the Normal Curve

Figure 6.14 -3σ -2σ -1σ 0 $+1\sigma$ $+2\sigma$ $+3\sigma$

frequency with which Z takes on different values in tabular form so that observed values for a normal distribution with known (or estimated) μ and σ can be read off with ease.

TABLES OF AREAS OF NORMAL DISTRIBUTION

The relative frequencies with which values of certain Z's may be found is given in the table of the normal distribution (Table 7, Appendix B). In this table column 1 represents values of Z (standardized scores). Column 2 represents the proportion of the area that falls between μ and any particular value of Z. To use the table we convert all values of X to their corresponding Z's, and obtain approximate relative frequencies of Z in the interval of interest. Let us denote the area to be found as A and find the areas of A_1 to A_4 of expressions (35a) to (35d).

First we convert X_1 and X_2 scores to Z_1 and Z_2.

$$Z_1 = \frac{X_1 - \mu}{\sigma} \quad \text{and} \quad Z_2 = \frac{X_2 - \mu}{\sigma} \tag{37}$$

Where T_i is equal to the value of the segment of the normal curve between the mean and Z_i as given in the table. The expressions (35a) to (35d) are evaluated as follows:

$$A_1 = .5 - T_1 \tag{38a}$$

$$A_2 = .5 - T_2 \tag{38b}$$

$$A_3 = T_2 \tag{38c}$$

$$A_4 = T_1 + T_2 \tag{38d}$$

Example. We know that a population of college students has a mean IQ of 125. The IQ's are known to be distributed normally with $\sigma = 20$. We want to find the proportion of students with IQ > 135. First we find the value of $Z_{135} = (135 - 125)/20 = .5$. The proportion of students with IQ > 135 corresponds to the proportion of values of $Z > .5$, which we can obtain by consulting the table of the normal distribution. The proportion of values $0 \leq Z \leq .5$ is given as .19146, so the proportion of $Z > .5 = .31854$, or 31.85 per cent of students will have an IQ > 135. To find the percentage (or proportion) of students with IQ < 145 we first find $Z_{145} = (145 - 125)/20 = 1.0$. Next we find that values of $0 \leq Z \leq 1.0$ take up .34134 of the area of the normal curve. The proportion of values of $Z \leq 1$ is then equal to $.5 + .34134$, or .84134, so that 84.13 per cent of students may be expected to have an IQ smaller than 145. To find the percentage of students with IQ ≤ 95

we find $Z_{95} = (95 - 125)/20 = -1.5$. The negative value of Z_{95} means only that this value is found on the left side of the distribution. Since the normal curve is symmetrical, we can use the same table, imagining all values of Z to be preceded by a minus sign. The proportion of the normal curve for $-1.5 \leq Z \leq 0$ is equal to the proportion $0 \leq Z \leq 1.5$, or .43319. Thus $Z < -1.5$ has associated the proportion of .06681, or 6.68 per cent of students have IQ's of less than 95.

To find the percentage of students with IQ's between 105 and 155 we first find Z_{105} and Z_{155}. Next we find the proportion of the normal curve that lies between $-1 \leq Z \leq +1.5$. However, our table does not permit us to read off this value directly. Instead, we find the two proportions for $-1 \leq Z \leq 0 = .34134$ and $0 \leq Z \leq +1.5 = .43319$ and add them together. Thus, 77.45 per cent of the students have IQ scores between 105 and 155. To find the percentage of students who have IQ's between 145 and 155 we again find Z_{145} and Z_{155}. Next we find the proportion of the area under the normal curve for $+1.0 \leq Z \leq +1.5$. However, we can not read this value directly from our table. Instead, we find the proportion for $0 \leq Z \leq 1.0 = .34134$ and subtract it from the proportion for $0 \leq Z \leq 1.5 = .43319$, so the percentage of students with IQ between 145 and 155 is given as 8.18 per cent. (Note that these percentage values are approximations and will estimate the true percentage of students falling in any IQ interval as closely as the distribution of IQ values approximates the normal curve.)

USING OTHER DISTRIBUTIONS

There are a number of important distributions which are near enough to the normal curve so that its properties can be used to answer questions concerning them. These distributions are generated by variables that are not really continuous numbers but can take on a large enough range of values that the resulting distributions of observed samples are nearly normal. Two of the most useful of these are the binomial and the Poisson distributions.

BINOMIAL DISTRIBUTION

There are many cases in which the observed variable can be judged to be in one of two states. For instance, we think of sex being in the states of male or female. A particle may or may not be present at any particular period of time as we count emission from radioactive materials. When we pull a particular colored marble from a bag containing marbles of many colors, the marble selected could be red or some other color (i.e., not red). These types of situations are called *dichotomous*. We may also dichotomize (or truncate) observations that are actually continuous. For instance, we might think of persons to be either older or younger than 33 years. Similarly, we could give a distance as longer or shorter than 25 meters.

In a dichotomous situation we can assign a value of 1 for one outcome of our observation and a value of 0 for the alternative. If we now collect n such observations, the result will be a series of 1's and/or 0's. Let us denote those states for which X is equal to 1 as X_1 and the other states for which X is equal to 0 as X_0. Then the sum of all X's will equal the sum of all the X_1's.

$$\sum X_i = \sum X_1 \tag{39}$$

and the sum of squares of X^2's will also equal to the sum of X_1^2

$$\sum X_i^2 = \sum X_1^2 \tag{40}$$

since the square of 1 is 1 and the square of 0 is 0. The mean of the sample of n observations will be

$$\bar{X} = \frac{\sum X_i}{n} = P \tag{41}$$

Note that $\bar{X}$ is really a ratio, namely the proportion of time P for which X is equal to 1 out of n observations of 1's and 0's. (It does not really matter to which observations we assign the value of 1 and to which we assign 0.) It is obvious that to every $\bar{X}$ or P there corresponds another mean or proportion Q for which

$$P + Q = 1 \tag{42}$$

To compute the variance of this distribution we go back to equation (12). The sum of squares, ss, is given by

$$ss = \sum (X_i - \bar{X})^2$$
$$= \sum X_i^2 - \frac{(\sum X_i)^2}{n}$$

so that the ss of a binomially distributed variable

$$ss = nP - nP^2 = nP(1 - P) = nPQ \tag{43}$$

and finally the variance is given by

$$\sigma^2 = PQ \tag{44}$$

The binomial distribution corresponds more and more closely to the

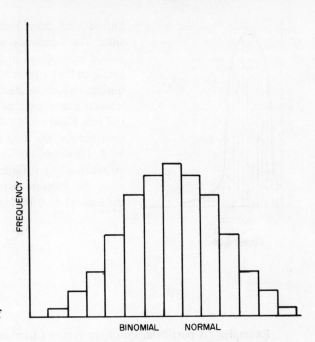

Fig. 6.15. Histogram of binomial normal.

normal distribution as n increases. This means that if the sample is relatively large (say 100 observations) we can get an excellent fit to the normal distribution (see Figure 6.15). Of course, for any sample of n observations from a dichotomous universe, the value of P describes the population completely. The quantity P in this case would stand for the proportion of times in which one outcome was observed relative to another. The importance of fitting the binomial distribution to the normal is not to describe a single sample but to describe the sampling distribution of many samples of size n. We are mainly interested, therefore, in the variance of the mean

$$\sigma^2_{\bar{P}} = \frac{PQ}{n} \tag{45}$$

Example. A bag contains 20 per cent black and 80 per cent white beads. Thus, $P = .2$, $Q = .8$, and $\sigma^2 = (.2)(.8) = .16$ and $\sigma = .4$. If we take many samples of $n = 20$, then $\sigma^2_{\bar{P}} = .4/20 = .02$.

THE POISSON DISTRIBUTION

If the frequency with which X takes on alternative values of 1 or 0 is very, very small, then the resulting distribution has a peculiar shape in that its mean would be very close to 0 or 1. This makes for a normal-like distri-

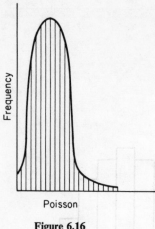

Poisson

Figure 6.16

bution that may have a long tail to one side. The frequency with which occurrences would be observed in this tail would be very small, so that a good fit for this type of distribution, called the *Poisson distribution*, to the normal curve obtains despite the one-sided tail (see Figure 6.16). Just as in the binomial distribution, the best estimate of μ is given by P. However, unlike the binomial, the best estimate of the variance is given by P. Otherwise, the Poisson distribution is treated like the normal distribution.

$$\sigma^2 = P \qquad (46)$$

and

$$\sigma_{\bar{P}}^2 = \frac{P}{n} \qquad (47)$$

Example. A particular symptom occurs 1 time in 100 patients. Average occurrence is thus given by $\bar{P} = .01$ with $\sigma^2 = .01$ also.

NORMALIZING

The investigator may very often observe that the values that he has found in his distributions are not quite normal. Nevertheless, there is a great convenience in using the normal distribution to describe experimental findings. We shall see later on that it is even more convenient to use a normal distribution and its parameters for inferences. Therefore, it is useful to make the data conform more closely to the mathematical model (in this case the normal distribution). Since we can legitimately reason that the shape of a distribution may be due to a particular number scale, which may be chosen quite arbitrarily, it should be possible to change scales of measurement, if, by the choice of a convenient scale, it should turn out that the resulting numbers assigned to our observations are distributed in a more desirable form. It is important to remember, however, that in transforming from one scale of measurement to another, the investigator must act as if he had originally taken his measurements in the transformed scale. The most common and useful type of transformations have been from the real number scale of measurements to logarithms, square roots, sines, cosines, and other transcendental forms. One particularly useful transformation is to *probits*, a set of measures based on the normal curve. This transformation deals best with percentages, especially those of mortality rate.

One aspect about normalizing should be remembered at all times. The shape of a particular distribution is inherent in the data. The fact that the distribution is not normal indicates that some elements or forces are in operation that contribute sufficiently in determining the outcome of observations that they may counterbalance many random factors. To normalize for the sake of convenience may be appropriate for a particular analysis. However, the fact that the distribution is not normal may be of greater significance than any other analysis that could possibly be performed by transformation.

There is no reason, however, not to find a proper equation to cover a distribution that is regular, albeit not normal. A number of important non-normal distributions are found in nature quite frequently. Foremost of these are exponential types, which are found when variables go to an *asymptote* (see Figure 6.17). Asymptotic curves usually describe distributions of variables that approach a limit. This is exhibited by many attributes, especially those of an organism. These exponential curves are described by a number of simple expressions. Many of them are determined by the choice of models rather than a simple statement about the shape of a curve. There are other curves that are also found with some

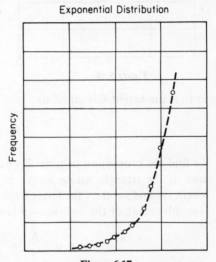

Figure 6.17

frequency. For instance, counting radioactivity during decay is a function that is not approximated by a single curve going to an asymptote but rather by two processes, both exponential, that combine. Examples of this type are very numerous. When they occur it is better in principle to develop a mathematical model to describe them than to handle them by curve fitting. However, for descriptive purposes, there is no reason why a simple curve could not be fit to the observed distribution of values and this curve used very much like the normal or other well-known distributions have been. It does require, however, that the investigator have a firmer grasp of mathematics than is usually found in the empirical sciences.

In principle, the treatment of a distribution to which a curve is fit is the same as that for the normal curve. We shall take as an example a case in which a distribution is found to be simply linear. Let us say that we can describe a distribution by a simple expression

$$Fr(X) = a_0 + a_1 X \qquad (48)$$

Triangular Distribution

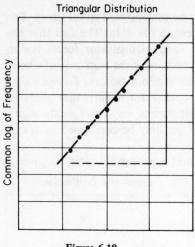

Figure 6.18

where a_1 is a slope and a_0 is an intercept. (A picture of such an unusual triangular distribution is given in Figure 6.18.) Let us find the relative proportion with which X falls into any interval with boundaries designated by X_1 and X_2.

Let the area of the triangle formed by our distribution in Figure 6.18 be equal to 1. The length of the base of the triangle b is given. The height of the triangle can be deduced from the equation of the area of triangles

$$\text{Area} = \frac{bh}{2} = 1 \qquad (49)$$

so that the height h is equal to

$$h = \frac{2}{b} \qquad (50)$$

To find the proportion of time X would fall between X_i and X_j we find the area of the triangle whose length is j and the area of the triangle whose length is i and subtract the latter from the former. To find h_i and h_j we could take advantage of the well-known law of similar triangles.

$$\frac{h_i}{i} = \frac{h_j}{j} = \frac{h}{b} \qquad (51)$$

When the triangular distribution is met frequently enough we could standardize it and represent area segments as a set of tables just as we did for the normal distribution. This would be unlikely, however, because a triangular distribution does not occur very frequently in nature.

The triangular distribution is rather unusual. The more complex curves that are found more frequently can be treated exactly the same way as was the triangular distribution. This is important especially for a number of distributions used by the statistician which are of great value for making inferences. These frequency distributions, (such as χ^2, t, r, F, etc.) resulting from special manipulation of measurements have a number of important properties that we shall meet later.

EXPANDING DESCRIPTIVE PARAMETERS: MOMENTS AND SKEW

The parameters that define a frequency distribution serve as a very convenient vehicle for conveying a good bit of information. Obviously the "goodness" of the resulting description depends to a large measure on how well the population or its sample distributes relative to how the equation to which the data have been fitted say they should. The mean and standard deviation are excellent descriptors of a distribution that fits the normal curve. However, the goodness of the description of this population's distribution as given by the mean and standard deviation will be increasingly poorer as the actual distribution of the parent population deviates from the normal.

There are basically two avenues open to the investigator to handle lack of "fit" of the data to his descriptive indices. In the first place he can "normalize" his distribution and so make it fit better. The investigator claims in essence that if he had used a different number scale for measurement (and who is to say what number scale is the proper one) the data would very conveniently fit a particular type of distribution for which, it just so happens, some very useful descriptive indices exist (and, as we shall see later on, many analytic procedures also). A second possibility open to the investigator is to use additional parameters that convey something about the deviation of the actual distribution from the normal model. This is useful, providing that additional information is more valuable than an improvement in the goodness of fit. Such is the case when knowledge of deviation of data from normal curve characteristics may point to the possibility that sampling procedures were such that they ignored dominant determinants of the phenomenon.

The deviations from normalcy which are encountered very frequently are *skew* and *kurtosis*. Skew indicates a concentration of observations away from the center. It is a situation in which more than 50 per cent of the values are either smaller or larger than the mean. Kurtosis is a condition in which the spread of observations under the curve does not conform to the percentages met with in the normal curve. The observations can be concentrated very close together, or they could be spread over a larger interval. If a curve is more pointed than a perfectly normal curve it is called *leptokurtic;* if it is flatter than the perfectly normal curve, it is called *platykurtic.*

In describing deviation from normalcy we might think of the normal curve as a balance very much like a lever in equilibrium. Deviation from this curve tends to disturb the balance and can be expressed in terms of moments about a fulcrum. Since the "fulcrum" in our case is the mean, we can express various properties of the curve by so-called moments about the mean. Moments are defined as the average distances or deviations from the mean or fulcrum taken to a power. For a mean μ of a population of N cases,

$$m_1 = \frac{(X - \mu)}{N} = 0 \qquad \text{(first moment)} \qquad (52a)$$

$$m_2 = \frac{(X - \mu)^2}{N} = \sigma^2 \qquad \text{(second moment)} \qquad (52b)$$

$$m_3 = \frac{(X - \mu)^3}{N} \qquad \text{(third moment)} \qquad (52c)$$

$$m_4 = \frac{(X - \mu)^4}{N} \qquad \text{(fourth moment)} \qquad (52d)$$

THE FIRST MOMENT

The first moment around the mean is equal to 0. The mean or average deviation is actually a derivation of the first moment.

THE SECOND MOMENT

The second moment about the mean is known as the variance. It describes the tendency toward dispersion.

THE THIRD MOMENT

The value of the sum of the cubed deviations from the mean reflects the preponderance of left or right scores by being either smaller or larger than 0. The direction of skew is shown by the sign and the amount of skew by the value of the third moment.

THE FOURTH MOMENT

Any sum of differences taken to the fourth power will always be positive, so the degree of kurtosis can be assessed only by comparing it with the average kurtosis for the normal curve, which turns out to be 3. If the measurement of kurtosis of a set of data is larger than 3, then the distribution may be thought of as leptokurtic. If it is smaller than 3, then the distribution is platykurtic.

ROUNDOFF ERRORS IN COMPUTATION

High-speed processing of data, especially when general-purpose programs are used, carries with it the danger of inadvertently introducing errors of calculation. These errors occur because numbers often have to be truncated on the right.

Let us take $\sqrt{2}$ for instance. This number is an endless decimal, and we must cut it off at some place so that it can fit into the memory of the machine, or onto a piece of paper for that matter. Depending on the physical space we have available we may write $\sqrt{2}$ as 1, 1.4, 1.41, 1.414, 1.4142,

1.41421, etc. Obviously the error incurred in truncating on the left will be always larger than that incurred by truncating to the right. If we must restrict $\sqrt{2}$ to three places, then 1.41 is our best approximation rather than .414.

Roundoff errors are not restricted to finding square roots. Whenever large numbers are developed as products, quotients, or sums, it may be necessary to round them off—that is, to drop all digits to the right of a given position. For instance, the mean is obtained by summing scores and dividing by the number of observations. The estimate of the mean, limited to a reasonable number of decimals, is necessarily an approximation. The true mean equals the observed mean plus an error, which we shall call e. In computing sums of squares for moments and, generally, in summing deviations or their squares, we use the estimate of μ containing this error,

$$\bar{X} = \mu + e \tag{53}$$

We can then look at the sum of the deviations of scores from the mean taken to any power k as the sum of the deviation taken to that power plus the summed error taken to that power. Regardless of whether the error is positive or negative, the summing and squaring operation adds an increment of error expressed as a positive number to each accumulation of the sum, so the final sum of the deviation taken to the kth power contains in it ne^k. When the number of observations n is large this error may amount to an appreciable quantity.

There are a number of ways by which roundoff errors may be reduced. Well-designed computer programs are written with enough precision that the number of places carried along throughout calculation are sufficient to keep the error to a minimum. However, regardless of the method for minimizing approximation errors, when the number of observations becomes very large or when the physical size or number of significant digits increases, then any program may introduce inadvertent calculation errors. (The student should remember to examine the program he plans to use for precision.)

One problem in calculating statistical parameters is that safeguards against roundoff errors are not necessarily the same for automatic processing and for hand calculation using semiautomatic calculators. For instance, if we want to compute $\sum (X - \bar{X})^2$ and are using a hand calculator, our best method is to use the identity $\sum (X - \bar{X})^2 = \sum X^2 - (\sum X)^2/n$.

The advantages are that we use only one division in the whole process. Furthermore, we compute the sum of deviations from the mean without using the value of $\bar{X}$. The errors of calculation that may be produced on the right-hand side by adding or subtracting large positive numbers are of no concern during hand calculation, where we see numbers and make automatic adjustments to preserve accuracy on the right when the length of numbers increases toward the left. But for completely automatic computation, especially if all data are stored internally, it is often safer to adjust to the left.

The structure of calculations to avoid roundoff on computers is a complex topic. Because the student will make some calculations by hand, we shall give optimum procedures for hand calculations. The student has to keep in mind that the best procedure for hand calculations is often not identical to the best procedure for computers.

Below are given the best formulas for hand calculation of moments about the mean.

$$\frac{\sum (X - \bar{X})^2}{n} = \frac{n \sum X^2 - (\sum X)^2}{n} \tag{54a}$$

$$\frac{\sum (X - \bar{X})^3}{n} = \frac{n^2 \sum X^3 - 3n \sum X \sum X^2 + 2(\sum X)^3}{[n \sum X^2 - (\sum X)^2]^{3/2}} \tag{54b}$$

$$\frac{\sum (X - \bar{X})^4}{n} = \frac{n^3 \sum X^4 - 4n^2 \sum X \sum X^3 + 6n(\sum X)^2 \sum X^3 - 3(\sum X)^4}{[n \sum X^2 - (\sum X)^2]^2}$$

$$\tag{54c}$$

Note that in these hand computation formulas the amount of division has been held to a minimum. There is only one quotient developed in each formula.

DESCRIPTION OF THE
ASSOCIATION BETWEEN VARIABLES

To determine associations, observations are made when two or more conditions may be expected to exert a joint influence on the observed variable. Probably the simplest and most frequent type of joint conditions studied are repeated observations to see whether a phenomenon changes in the course of time. A more complex multiple situation is presented by the question of whether and to what extent the heights of sons are determined by the heights of fathers, mothers, grandparents, by diet, illness, and so on. Again we need a simple way of presenting results so that the investigator may evaluate his data and convey whatever his findings are to the scientific community at large.

There are a number of graphic and pictorial displays possible. The data can be arranged in tables in which columns represent subcategories in one variable and rows represent subcategories in another variable. The individual cell entries can be actual frequencies or they may be percentages of

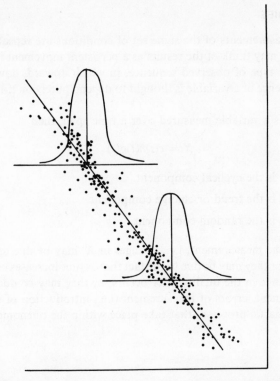

Fig. 6.19. Pictorial representation of a joint distribution of two tables.

the total number of observations or of row or column frequencies. When the variables are continuous, the data may be depicted on a graph. A smooth graph would result in instances in which a consequence varies very consistently as a result of varying the antecedent condition. If the range of consequences associated with any single antecedent condition is large, we can still represent the results in the form of a graph, but now we refer to it as a *scattergram* (see Figure 6.19).

It is desirable and often necessary to represent the joint effects of many variables in a descriptive summary form. Instead of a table, the investigator may be interested in a single parameter that expresses the quality of association between variables. Such a parameter representing the association found in a joint frequency table is known as *chi square* (χ^2). When the vehicle for display is a scattergram, the parameter indicating the degree of association is a number referred to as a *correlation coefficient*. We shall see in later chapters that the problems and solutions in describing the character of joint distributions are not really different from problems and solutions in describing the distribution of a single variable, although they are usually more complex.

TIME SERIES

When measurements of the same set of conditions are repeated periodically, then we may think of the results as a persistent movement in the same direction. This type of observed sequence, in which upward, downward, or cyclical persistence of a variable is thought to depend purely on time, is called a *time series*.

When X is a variable measured over a time span, then

$$X = c(t)h(t)g(t) \tag{55}$$

where $c(t)$ is the cyclical component.

$h(t)$ is the trend or change component.

$g(t)$ is the random component.

The result of the measurement, i.e., changes in X, may be due to a cyclical phenomenon, or they may be due to the fact that as time increases or decreases a constant change in the quality of X occurs, or they may be due to simple random movement, errors of measurement (i.e., introduction of extraneous noise), or stochastic processes that take place within the phenomenon itself.

TRENDS

Two general methods of isolating trends have been used. The assumption can be made that the trend is linear, i.e., it represents a constant rate of increase or decrease. When this is done, the method of fitting regression lines is used. A regression line is in essence the best-fitting straight line that can be drawn through the data of the form

$$X = [a_0 + a_2 \, (\text{time})] + e \tag{56}$$

where X is the best trend estimate for X (refer to Figure 6.20). The term in the parentheses is the linear expression, and e is the error term around the best-fitting line (usually represented by the standard error of estimate). This regression line is found by the least square method of calculation and by definition is that line from which the squared deviation of all observed points is a minimum. (Finding "best fits" will be discussed in a later chapter.)

A generalization of the mathematical procedure to determine trends is to find the actual curve of the best fit rather than to make the assumption of linearity. Before computers came onto the scene the advantages of assuming linearity were so great for purposes of hand calculations that this assumption was almost always made. In fact, nonlinearity still presents such considerable computational problems that even where computers are easily available, it is still most convenient to make the assumption that trends are actually linear if it can be defended. The form of a trend is not necessarily apparent from a simple inspection of data. More often than not, data points are widely distributed either because of random variation, because of pronounced cyclical effects, or both. These effects have to be dampened or smoothed out before trend analysis can proceed.

CYCLES

Many phenomena are cyclic. One of the best known of these is ambient temperature, which varies over the year and also over the days, so that a temperature versus time graph shows a large cycle for seasonal changes and smaller cycles for daily changes (see Figure 6.20). Generally the cyclic component is found by dividing through by the trend component

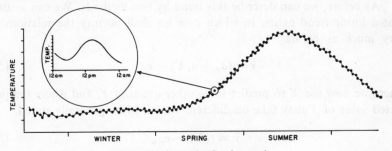

Fig. 6.20. A graph of a time series.

$$\frac{X}{h(t)} = \frac{c(t)g(t)}{h(t)} = c(t)g(t) \tag{57}$$

so that variations due to trends can be eliminated. One method to determine cycles in temperature would be to take all temperatures of the same day of the year measured at the same time of day. Variations around the trend line would then make themselves apparent as a curve representing the cycle for day and for season.

RANDOM COMPONENTS

It is terribly important to differentiate both cycles and trends from random components. This is not always simple and often may be altogether impossible. Natural variation by itself is cyclic. Since variation occurs between two extremes, the long-run tendency will be for low values to follow high values and for high values to follow low ones. Insofar as that is by definition cyclic, then any smoothing process within random values will result in cycles. The best way to deal with cycles is to find an *à priori* theoretical content for them. The existence of daily and seasonal temperature cycles finds substance through the rotation of the earth around its axis and revolution around the sun. No such reasons, on the other hand, may be adduced to give sense to variations of the stock market or of the Gross National Product.

JOINT DISTRIBUTIONS OF TWO STOCHASTIC VARIABLES

Trends may also be observed when two variables, each one of which is permitted to vary over a range of numbers, are associated with each other. The difference between a time series or a graph of repeated measurements and a joint distribution of two variables is that we cannot connect the points in the latter to obtain a smooth line. Rather, a trend has to be adduced from the scatter of isolated points.

As before, we can describe this trend by two methods. We can assume that a linear trend exists, in which case we shall portray the relationship very much as before:

$$\tilde{y} = (a_0 + a_1 X) \pm e_{y|x} \tag{58}$$

where we now use X to predict some other quantity Y, and where the predicted value of Y may take on different values. More generally stated,

$$\tilde{y} = f(X) + e_{y|x} \tag{59}$$

where $f(X)$ may be any mathematical expression. In general, many different forms of mathematical description may be used to summarize the association between X and Y. Techniques and methods of obtaining such expressions will be discussed in a later chapter.

CORRELATION

The correlation coefficient is a special measure and probably one of the best expressions available to describe a relationship between two variables. The best-known correlation coefficient is the so-called *Pearson product moment correlation coefficient*, usually referred to as r. The meaning of the correlation coefficient rests in the error reduction realized when variable X is used to predict variable Y as compared to the error that would be incurred if variable X were not used to predict variable Y.

Let $e_{y|x}$ be the expected error of prediction when X is used to estimate Y and let e_y be the expected error in the situation in which we do not use the variable X to predict Y. The meaning of the correlation coefficient (or rather of its square) is given by

$$\text{Square of correlation coefficient} = \frac{e_y^2 - e_{y|x}^2}{e_y^2} \tag{60}$$

and can thus be seen to be a proportion of the decrease of the squared expected error that is obtained when a prediction equation involving X on Y is used. It is in this sense that correlation actually does describe the relationship between two variables. Note that the limits of the correlation coefficient are ± 1 (when a prediction equation eliminates all the error) and 0 (when a prediction equation eliminates none of it). Hence correlation serves as a scale expressing the amount of relationship that may be found between two variables.

We shall save the rest of the discussion of regression, correlation, and the mathematical description of two variables for Chapter 9. At this time, however, it is important to point out that the assignment of descriptive indices such as r, a_0, a_1, and $e_{y|x}$ makes very little sense unless we can also test the hypothesis that these attributes observed in a sample are not due just to the working of chance but reflect a real quality contained in the parent population. Of course, as far as the description of data is concerned, these tests are of lesser importance. However, descriptive indices should be accompanied by an indication of the confidence that may be placed in their veracity.

NOISE ELIMINATION

When a data input stream consists of one or more variables that have been observed and recorded repeatedly for a particular subject over a time span, the analysis of such networks for trends and tendencies may often be impeded by noise. This interference, which tends to obscure consistent trends in such time series, stems from a number of sources that are usually beyond the control of even the most careful investigator. For cases in which such data are automatically generated as direct or transduced electronic signals, and the noise represents the effect of electrical disturbances or unwanted auxiliary signals, it is often possible to eliminate much of it by appropriate filtering circuits and other attenuating devices. There are, however, a number of distortion effects which cannot be treated successfully in this way and must be handled by software techniques.

STANDARDIZATION

A universal source of noise which often thwarts comparison between experimental subjects is the prima facie difference which exists between individuals, regardless of treatment. For instance, a normal pulse rate for one person may be suspiciously high for another. Consequently, a direct comparison of the raw numerical data may be inconclusive or misleading.

One way to compensate for this type of variation is to express the results as relative quantities, based on some reference or standard value. As an example we may start with a situation in which a drug designed to reduce blood pressure is tested by administering it to a group of patients with high blood pressure. Another group, also with high blood pressure, is given a placebo. Readings for each individual are recorded for several days before the administration and for a number of days afterward. The results are as shown in Figure 6.21. As is seen on this graph, the individual variations make it extremely cumbersome to interpret the comparative results. In this instance, the data can be normalized to reflect the pressure change of the

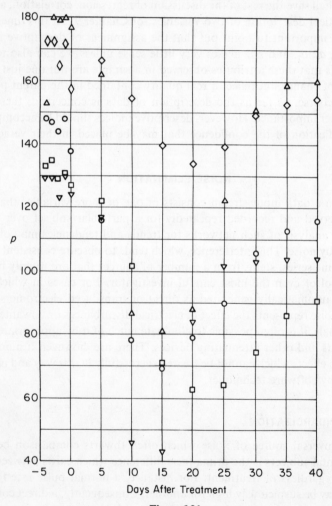

Figure 6.21

individual patient relative to his state before the drug or placebo was administered.

If n_{i0} is the number of readings recorded for patient i before he received the drug, P_{i0} is one of the pressure readings for patient i before drug administration, and P_{ij} is a pressure reading for patient i on one of the days j after administration, then we can transform each of the test readings into a more consistent measurement by referring it to the average value of that individual's pressure before he received the drug. This measure, which we shall call P'_{ij}, the relative pressure for patient i on some given day j after administration, is calculated as

$$P'_{ij} = \frac{P_{ij}}{\sum P_{i0}/n_{i0}} = \frac{P_{ij}}{\bar{P}_{i0}}$$

The modified graph resulting from such transformations is shown in Figure 6.22. Similar manipulations are possible for a wide range of variables. For example, the effect of temperature, which often distorts the direct comparison between aircraft velocities at different altitudes, is eliminated by expressing the velocities as ratios, relative to the respective velocities of sound at the particular altitudes in question.

This internal standardization technique can work equally well for variables in which the timing is inconsistent. In electrocardiography, for example, the time duration for a particular portion of the cardiac cycle is of

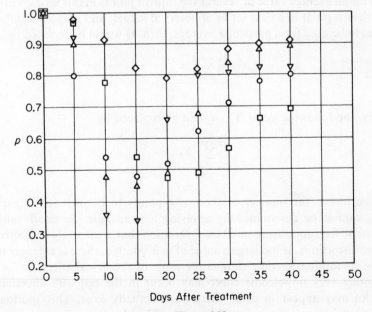

Days After Treatment

Figure 6.22

clinical interest. The inconsistency in heart rate extends not only from patient to patient but also exists within the individual himself, since it is fairly unlikely that he will produce two successive heartbeats whose length will appear the same to most modern measuring instruments. Consequently, the time for a heartbeat, whose beginning and end are easy to identify, is defined as 100 per cent, and any component thereof is proportioned accordingly. The same thing is done for the amplitudes of such waves, which are also subject to extensive variation. (That is, the value for each digitized reading is converted to a percentage of the highest amplitude for that heartbeat).

DATA FILTERING

When the distortions in an observed time series do not respond to electronic signal conditioning and are not relieved by normalization techniques, it may be possible to alleviate much of this distortion by means of data filters. These data processing techniques are aimed at smoothing the minor bumps and ridges in time series.

MOVING AVERAGES

This smoothing technique operates by replacing each point in the time series with an average value of several subsequent points in this series. Thus, if Y_i is the ith point in a time series of observed values, and m is the number of points to be used for a particular average, then Y_i would be replaced by

$$\frac{\sum_{j=i}^{j=i+m-1} Y_j}{m}$$

Similarly, the following point Y_{i+1} would be replaced by

$$\frac{\sum_{j=i+1}^{j=i+m} Y_j}{m}$$

The value for m, the number of successive points to be included in each average, cannot be determined by applying a fixed rule. A small value of m is useful for suppressing small local variations but is relatively ineffective for larger distortions. If too large a value of m is selected, there is a danger of excessive smoothing, thereby eliminating some of the actual effects.

Another very unwelcome effect may occur in the opposite direction, i.e., cycles may appear in data where none actually exist. This spurious phenomenon is sometimes referred to as the *Slutzsky-Yule effect*.

Furthermore, as m becomes larger, an increasing number of observations towards the end of the time series cannot be smoothed, since there are no subsequent data points available for use in calculating a moving average. This type of filtering technique is usually restricted to those time series in which observations are recorded at equal time intervals.

PARABOLIC FILTERING

The moving average technique, although very simple to apply, may, in certain situations, provide more smoothing than is really needed. When more sensitivity is desired, the parabolic filtering technique can be used instead. For this procedure, m is selected as an odd number of consecutive points in the time series. The point to be replaced y_i is located in the center of these m points. The best parabola is fitted to these points by means of the least squares technique (see Chapter 8), and the pivotal or central point y_i is replaced by the corresponding point $\tilde{y}_i$ on the derived parabola. The process

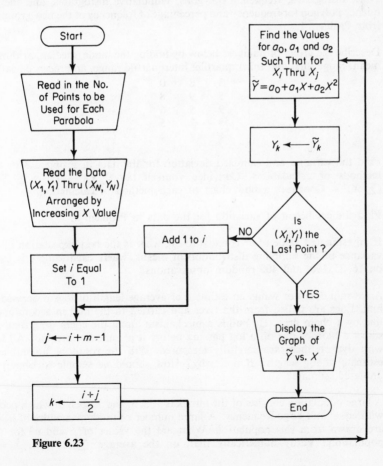

Figure 6.23

is repeated by shifting the center point to the next one in the time series, dropping the earliest point, and adding one more at the far end. Thus, for example, if $m = 7$, our first parabolic fit would occur when points 1 through 7 in the time series are used, with $\tilde{y}_4$ replacing the fourth point. We would then perform the same type of fit for points 2 through 8, with $\tilde{y}_5$ being used, and so on until the seventh point in a group used for a parabolic fit was the last point in the time series. Figure 6.23 shows a flow chart for such a procedure. Again, as in the case of moving averages, it is necessary that successive points in the time series be spaced at equal time intervals.

PROBLEMS

1. Group the data in Table 6.2 into 15 lb class intervals. Arrange the data as in Table 6.1.

2. Draw histograms, frequency polygons, cumulative histograms, and the frequency polygon for frequency and percentage of frequency of the new groupings from Problem 1.

3. Describe the group of numbers below by finding the mode, median, arithmetic mean, range, first and third quartile, interquartile range, and mean deviation.

3	8	0
5	9	8
9	5	6
5	2	5
4	7	4

4. Find the variance and standard deviation for the data in Problem 3 by two methods of calculations. Convince yourself that $\sum (X - \bar{X})^2 = \sum X^2 - (\sum X)^2/n$. Construct a flow chart of each method of calculation.

5. Find the coefficient of variation for the data in Problem 3.

6. If an estimated value of σ^2 is equal to 50, what is the best expectation of the variance of the sampling distribution of means, where each sample is based on 16, 25, 100, and 400 random observations?

7. A sawmill operator wants an estimate of average length of logs processed by him. Logs are pulled from the river and carried to the mill in a continuous line by a chain drag. He builds a mechanism along the chain drag that will squirt a blob of dye on a log passing before it at random intervals. All logs with dye on them are carefully measured. Will the result be an unbiased estimate of log length? If not, why? How should he sample to obtain an unbiased estimate?

8. A large population consists of the numbers 1, 3, 5, and 7, each of which occurs with equal and large frequency. A large number of random samples of $n = 4$ are drawn from this population. What are the values of μ and σ^2 for this population? Verify numerically that, on the average, $\sum X = 4\mu$, $\bar{X} = \mu$,

$\sum (X - \bar{X})^2 = 3\sigma^2$ and $(\bar{X} - \mu)^2 = \sigma^2/4$. The interested student might also attempt to prove that $\sum (\bar{X}^2) = \sigma^2/n$ and verify this result again numerically.

9. A variable X is distributed normally with $\mu = 50$ and $\sigma = 10$. Find these proportions.

   (a) $X \geq 62.5$ (f) $40 \leq X \leq 45$
   (b) $X \geq 57.5$ (g) $40 \leq X \leq 52.5$
   (c) $X \leq 62.5$ (h) $47.5 \leq X \leq 55$
   (d) $X \leq 42.5$ (i) $55 \leq X \leq 57.5$
   (e) $X \geq 37.5$

10. A variable X has a distribution that is known to be triangular (as in Figure 6.24) with base $b = 8$. Find the proportion of values of X such that

    (a) $X < 6$
    (b) $X > 3$
    (c) $2 \leq X \leq 5$
    (d) $2 \leq X \leq 7$

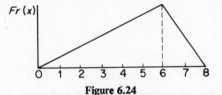

Figure 6.24

11. A variable X has a distribution known to be as follows:

$$X = \begin{cases} 0, & \text{for } x < 0. \\ \dfrac{6x^2}{15}, & \text{for } 0 \leq x \leq 3. \\ 0, & \text{for } x > 3. \end{cases}$$

    Find the proportion of values for X such that
    (a) $X \leq 1$
    (b) $1 \leq X \leq 2$
    (c) $X \geq 2$

12. A variable X is known to be distributed like half a circle with radius $= 4$ and center at $\mu = 10$. Find the proportion of values for X such that
    (a) $X \leq 8$
    (b) $9 \leq X \leq 12$
    (c) $11 \leq X \leq 13$

13. Compute the third and fourth moments for the data in Problem 3.

14. If the student has a program for moving averages available, he can perform an illuminating experiment. Select a series of numbers from a table of random numbers and compute a moving average, using varying length intervals (from 3 to 10). For some intervals, definite cyclical patterns will be observed in many instances.

15. If there is a good library of descriptive programs available, the student should try to obtain a multivariate data file and use the available programs to describe a sample of findings.

7 INTRODUCTION TO STATISTICAL HYPOTHESIS TESTING

Prior to the advent of computer-based automation, the cost of additional observations usually became increasingly larger as more observations were obtained. Thus the smaller the number of observations required, the easier it was to perform an experiment. As a consequence, the mathematical properties of distributions has immediate and important consequences. Since the investigator was going to summarize his findings by computing the parameters describing the distribution of his results and since he was going to test hypotheses on these parameters, it was always advantageous and often necessary for him to collect only that number of observations that would suffice to give him a reasonably accurate estimate of these parameters. If he was using μ and σ to describe his results, then he needed a number of observations n no larger than that necessary to make a fairly accurate estimate about the mean $\bar{X}$ and standard deviations of his population. The idea of "sufficient" statistics was engendered by this type of thinking. Data processing, in large part, applied statistical methods of estimating parameters of different distributions and establishing inferences and confidence statements about them. At the same time the design of experiments was influenced very much by the existence of these methods.

It turns out, as we may reasonably suspect, that some of these methods of estimating parameters, drawing inferences, and making confidence statements require fewer observations than others and still yield results as reliable as those based on less efficient designs. Thus one way of designing an experiment or testing hypotheses can be said to be more "efficient" than another, because it requires fewer observations. Since the design of experiments is often contingent on the techniques available for evaluating its results, the efficiency and therefore the preferability of a particular design over some

266

alternative may be dictated by the applicability of such important techniques.

Whenever results are not obtained by automatic means, efficiency is still a primary consideration. Observations that are costly in terms of time and money, as is true for many biological, sociological, or economic problems, or that are not obtainable in large numbers, as is very often true in medical areas, should be collected in such a way that optimum use can be made of their smallest number during final analysis. Experimental designs always ought to be aimed at the use of optimum analytic methods. Computers enter into such designs only secondarily in that they make computation problems, which are often severe, somewhat easier to bear. In studying such a problem as leukemia, where the population is small to begin with and might be reduced by deaths during the testing of a new drug or where individuals take unexpected turns for the better, severe computational problems may be created in evaluating results of a study that had been designed with an eye toward efficiency. At this point the possibilities opened by the computer become very important.

With the introduction of automation, sufficient statistics have been deprived of much of their importance, and the drive for the most "efficient" experimental designs has lost much of its momentum, or more to the point, efficiency has been considerably redefined. There are many instances in which data can be accumulated quite easily and cheaply and in large numbers. There already exist today numbers of large data files describing the health, economic, political or social factors for large population groups. Similarly, instrumentation makes it possible to observe many, many responses from individuals in very inexpensive ways. The physiologist furnishes a striking example. He now finds that preparing an animal for observation may require only the insertion of a few electrodes in crucial spots in the animal's anatomy rather than the use of large surgical incisions. As a consequence, the animal survives for a longer period of time and can be observed continuously. Add to this the fact that he can now obtain thousands of exact measurements for each second of observation, and the problem of "insufficient numbers" somehow becomes less pressing.

In this way automation has developed separate requirements for different types of research. In instances where the cost of observations is high or observations are not available in large numbers, the design of experiments and analysis of data must proceed along traditional statistical lines, and problems of inference raised by small samples ought to dominate the thinking of the experimenter. On the other hand, where observations are relatively inexpensive and simple to obtain, the considerations determined by the opportunities offered by automatic data processing should prevail. This is especially important for multivariate situations where the investigator has automatic data gathering opportunities available. Yet we shall also have to learn something about statistical inference. In the first place, statistical inference in some form or the other will always be relevant to analyses of large data files. In the second place (and this may seem a contradiction but really is not) the inappropriate application of certain types of statistical inference to the analysis of large data files easily leads to misleading conclusions. In the third place, the analysis of some experiments, designed to conform with traditional requirements of statistical efficiency, often requires automatic processing of data because of the complexity of calculation. Finally, although this book is not concerned with experiments based on small samples, the student ought to know enough about statistical inference so that he can turn to an appropriate text if he must design an experiment for instances where the numbers of observations can be expected to be small.

CERTAINTY OF CONCLUSION

The major purpose of an experiment is to enable the investigator to make a statement about a large population of instances from which his experimental sample is drawn as a subset. The chemist who works with sulphur atoms addresses his conclusions to all of sulphur and not just to the few grams of substance with which he experimented. Similarly, the purpose of an observation on a few dogs is not to describe these dogs in detail, but to say something about the larger population of dogs and perhaps even the larger universe of mammals. The same is true for experimentation on tissues, small groups, industrial complexes, economic situations, and so on. An experiment is a tiny slice, an isolated situation, selected for detailed scrutiny to enable us to draw conclusions not only about the state of affairs, the value of certain parameters, the existence of relationships, and other factors that have been observed in this small sample of observations, but it is implied that these conclusions ought to hold true for the larger population from which the experimental sample was drawn.

There are two related questions that have to be asked about any conclusions reached on the basis of observing a sample:

1. How accurately do the results estimate the true properties of the larger population? How close is the observed proportion, mean, mean-difference, correlation, etc., of the sample to the true proportion, mean, mean-difference, correlation, etc. of the total population?

2. One of the major purposes of the experiment is to make statements concerning cRa. When it is true that observations fall closely on a well-defined and invariant curve, it is often not difficult at all to decide that an association between consequences and antecedent conditions exists, as well as to define what this relationship is. However, many relations or associations in the biological and social sciences are more in the nature of trends than of single-valued functions. This leads to the legitimate question of how

small and vague an observed trend can be before we may want to conclude that it is an accidental observation rather than a reflection of a true trend in the reference population. As a corollary to this question we may ask what the possibility is of missing a trend that exists in the reference population (although perhaps it is only a relatively casual association) because the sample is too small to allow its detection?

Actually these two questions are related. We can view the decision about the existence or nonexistence of a trend as a problem in estimating the parameters that describe it. The question of whether or not a trend exists may then become a question of determining the size of the slope of the function associating an antecedent condition with a consequence and on the certainty with which we can make a statement that the value of the true slope in the total population is different from zero.

SAMPLING AND ACCURACY

Whether or not our conclusions concerning the reference populations are correct or in error will depend exclusively upon the situation that exists in the sample and not on the true state of affairs in the reference population. We must keep uppermost in mind that conclusions can be based only on whatever observations are made in the experimental situations and not on the conditions that actually exist in the reference universe. Thus, accuracy of results depends largely on whether or not the conditions of the world outside are faithfully reflected in the experimental sample. (The student will find it profitable at this point to review the discussion on sampling in Chapter 6.)

Inaccurate results, and, consequently, erroneous conclusions arise from biased samples. In a biased sample, selection of observations is influenced by conditions in the reference population, so that the result is not so much a reflection of the state of affairs that reigns in the population as a reflection of sampling method. We pointed out before that the one way by which assurance could be had that the sample reflects the properties of the general population is to sample at random.

Unfortunately, a random sample will furnish a good estimate of parameters existing in the population with *great certainty* only if it is a large enough sample.

But what is a large enough sample?

It is true that if we toss two tons of coins by some completely random process and if these coins are not biased, we may expect roughly a ton of heads and a ton of tails. However, if we toss only five coins and even if the coins are not biased and our method of tossing does not favor either heads or tails, it is still possible that all five coins could come up heads or tails or in any combination of heads and tails. If we toss a coin five times and come up with four heads and one tail, are we justified in concluding that this coin is biased and will come up 80 per cent heads and only 20 per cent tails if tossed any number of times? In considering how we make decisions about this type of outcome, we shall always assume that our sampling has been unbiased and that any deviation from the true state of affairs is due to random sampling error.

Note that bias of a sampling procedure cannot be corrected by making a sample larger. A biased sample will lead to inaccurate estimates of the values of parameters, and these inaccuracies will only tend to stabilize if the sample is made very large. Random sampling error, on the other hand, will also lead to inaccurate estimates, but these inaccuracies can be decreased or eliminated by enlarging the number of observations.

THE FUNDAMENTAL DECISION MODEL

The true state of nature is reflected, hopefully, in the outcome of an experiment. However, other factors may be and usually are also involved in this outcome. Even when all variables that may influence the end result of an experiment in some spurious fashion are eliminated, there still remain the vagaries of chance.

Say we observe that an animal expired within a day after having been fed on food containing a specific chemical compound. Two alternative explanations can be advanced for this event:

1. The animal's death was due to the ingested chemical.
2. The animal was due to expire anyhow (as all animals do sooner or later) and was picked accidentally for the experiment.

The choices available to us are shown in the simple decision model of Table 7.1.

With this representation the "true" state of affairs in any well-controlled experiment reduces to at least two alternatives; the workings of chance vs. the effects of the antecedent condition. These alternatives are stated in the left column of Table 7.1.

The experimenter must now make a decision. He may ascribe the observed results to chance or to the antecedent manipulations. It is important to understand, however, that he can base his decision only on what he observes, not on what the true state of affairs is. If the true state of nature is that the animal's death was determined by chance, he will observe an event that does not necessarily reflect the effect of the experimental condition but will be mistaken for that effect nevertheless. Thus, his alternative decisions, which are given in the top row of Table 7.1, must be considered as separate

Table 7.1. DECISION MODEL FOR A ONE-ANIMAL EXPERIMENT WITH
DECISION RULE OF "EFFECT" IF THE ANIMAL DIES AND
"NO EFFECT" IF THE ANIMAL SURVIVES

If it is true that	And we decide that	
	The animal's death was due to chance	The animal's death was due to the chemical
The animal's death was due to chance	We will have made the correct decision	We will have made an incorrect decision
The animal's death was due to the chemical	We will have made an incorrect decision	We will have made the correct decision

from the true state of nature. The consequences of the interaction between "truth" and "decision" may be that he is right or wrong, as shown in the body of the table.

The only reasonable way to resolve the problem of which choice to make is to find the probabilities associated with those events that will lead us to make correct and incorrect decisions under whatever circumstances may be assumed to be actually existing in nature.

Let us assume that the investigator uses a single animal for his test. He decides to use the following "reasonable decision rule:"

1. If the animal dies within 24 hours after having fed on the chemical, he will conclude that the chemical is harmful.
2. If the animal survives 24 hours after having fed on the chemical, he will conclude that the chemical is harmless.

Let us first consider a true state of affairs in which the chemical is *harmless* and assume that the endemic death rate in the colony from which the experimental animal was selected is 1/10,000. The probabilities associated with the outcome of the experiment are as follows:

A. The correct conclusion will be drawn (i.e., the chemical is harmless) if the animal survives 24 hours. In the long run 9999 out of 10,000 animals will survive for this length of time. Hence the probability of drawing the correct conclusion will be .9999.
B. The incorrect conclusion will be drawn if the animal fails to survive 24 hours. In the long run, 1 out of 10,000 animals chosen at random from the colony will die within this period of time. But the investigator has adopted the rule to conclude that the chemical is harmful if he observes death. Hence the probability of drawing the incorrect conclusion is .0001.

The investigator then stands to make the error of rejecting the alternative of "no effect" when it is true with probability .0001. This error is referred to usually as a Type I error, and the value of the probability associated with it is commonly given the symbol of α.

Let us now assume that the chemical is *harmful*, i.e., an animal feeding on it will die usually within 24 hours. However, we also assume we know (although the investigator does not) that 5 out of 100 animals in the colony are not susceptible to the chemical. The probabilities associated with the outcome of the experiment now are as follows:

A. The correct conclusion (i.e., the chemical is harmful) will be drawn if the animal dies within 24 hours. In the long run, 95 out of 100 animals selected at random from the colony will die within 24 hours after ingesting the chemical. Hence the probability of drawing the correct conclusion is .95.

B. An incorrect conclusion will be drawn if the animal survives 24 hours. In the long run, 5 animals out of 100 selected at random from the colony will survive the feeding of the chemical. But the investigator has adopted the decision rule that the chemical is harmless if he fails to observe death within 24 hours. Hence the probability of drawing an incorrect conclusion is .05.

The investigator stands to reject the alternative of "effect" when it is true with probability .05. This error is referred to as Type II error, and the value of the probability associated with it is commonly denoted by β.

The decision model for these alternatives is summarized in Table 7.2. In Table 7.3 the same decision model is given for the condition in which the investigator uses two animals and adopts a decision rule of calling the chemical harmless if at least one of the two animals dies within 24 hours.

The number of deaths on which hinges our conclusions is referred to as a *random variable*. The exact value at which we decide to change from one type of conclusion to another is referred to as the *point of rejection* because

Table 7.2. DECISION MODEL FOR A ONE-ANIMAL EXPERIMENT WITH DECISION RULE OF "EFFECT" IF THE ANIMAL DIES AND "NO EFFECT" IF THE ANIMAL SURVIVES

If it is true that	*And the conclusion is drawn*	
	"No effect" because the animal survives	"Effect" because the animal dies
The chemical is harmless	The correct conclusion is drawn with $P_1 = .9999$	Type I error: The incorrect conclusion is drawn with $\alpha = .0001$
The chemical is harmful	Type II error: The incorrect conclusion is drawn with $\beta = .05$	The correct conclusion is drawn with $P_2 = .95$

Table 7.3. DECISION MODEL FOR A TWO-ANIMAL EXPERIMENT WITH DECISION RULE
OF "EFFECT" IF AT LEAST ONE OF THE TWO ANIMALS DIE
AND "NO EFFECT" IF BOTH ANIMALS SURVIVE

If it is true that	And the conclusion is drawn	
	"No effect" because both animals survive	"Effect" because at least one animal dies
The chemical is harmless	The correct conclusion is drawn with $P_1 = .9998$	Type I error: The incorrect conclusion is drawn with $\alpha = .0002$
The chemical is harmful	Type II error: The incorrect conclusion is drawn with $\beta = .0025$	The correct conclusion is drawn with $P_2 = .9975$

we usually frame our question around a hypothesis that we decide to accept or reject depending on the precise value of the random variable. For this reason the values of the random variable for which a hypothesis will be rejected or accepted are referred to as *region of acceptance* and *region of rejection*.

In general, an experiment must have the following elements before its results can be evaluated:

1. A public and repeatable method of assigning a measure or value to the observation or outcome of the experiment must exist.
2. All spurious factors that would restrict the range of resulting measures must be eliminated so that the outcome of the experiment may be due only to one of two factors:
   (a) The experimental condition.
   (b) Chance.
3. The probabilities with which different measures may be observed must be known for at least one of the alternative hypotheses.

The simplest and most reliable method of insuring against the presence of spurious factors is to randomize with respect to all but the experimental conditions. In that way observed differences can be assumed to be due either to the workings of the experimental variable or to chance. However, randomization is often seriously restricted in empirical situations. For instance, in evaluating the effect of low dose diagnostic radiation on subsequent neoplasia, one has to compare individuals who were radiated with those who were not. However, individuals are not selected at random for radiological diagnostic workup. The same conditions that select patients for the radiologist may also predispose them toward or against the subsequent development of neoplasia. Such a dual effect of selection procedures is called *confounding*. Elaborate control conditions have to be devised when randomization is not feasible, and sometimes it is not possible completely to eliminate confounding. In the latter instance there is very little to be gained from performing and reporting an experiment, since no conclusions can be drawn from it.

When randomization over all spurious factors is adequate, there automatically exist two alternative hypotheses about the underlying causes of the experimental outcome.

H_0: The absence or presence of the experimental conditions has no influence on the outcome of the experiment. Any observed differences or deviations from expectation of the resulting measures are due to chance factors.

H_1: The absence or presence of the experimental condition has a differentiating effect on the outcome of the experiment. Any *lack* of observed differences among resulting measures is due to chance factors.

As we have seen, two errors may be made in interpreting experimental results. The first is to conclude that an experimental condition has an effect when it really does not (Type I with $P = \alpha$), and the second is to conclude that an experimental condition does not have an effect when it really does (Type II with $P = \beta$). Whether one or the other of these errors may occur depends upon the elements of chance alone. At best we are limited to estimating the probability that, for a given decision, an error of the first or second kind has been made.

It is easier, usually, to compute the probability distribution for the different values of experimental measures under the assumption that H_0 is true. However, for optimum procedures, the investigator should strive to evaluate the probabilities of risking either of the two errors.

The probability of risking either error depends on the rule, adopted by the experimenter, of when and for what value of the experimentally obtained measure or measures he will decide for H_0 or for H_1. For any rule there exist probabilities for making either of the two errors. These probabilities can be computed. Changing the rule for decision changes these two probabilities such that when one increases, the other decreases. It is not ever possible to derive a rule that will completely eliminate the risk of making any error at all. In selecting a particular rule on which to base his decision, the investigator must be guided, therefore, on factors of scientific judgment that are completely extraneous to the experiment itself. Such factors are the consequences of a correct or incorrect decision on the future management of a disease, on subsequent experimental work, or on the career of the investigator and are not easily reduced to a set of rules. Let us illustrate with a simple example.

Example. Our aim is to decide whether a drug reduces mortality from a specific disease. The mortality rate without the drug is known to be 50 per cent of infected individuals and it is claimed that the drug will reduce mortality to 20 per cent. Ten infected individuals are treated and the mortality among them observed.

EXPERIMENTAL MEASURE: X = number of individuals who die.

HYPOTHESES:

H_0: The drug has no effect. Probability of death after treatment with the drug P_0 is the same as probability of death without it and is equal to .5.

H_1: The drug reduces mortality. Probability of death after treatment with the drug P_1 is equal to .2.

Table 7.4 gives the probabilities with which X may take on values between 0 and 10 under the two conditions postulated by H_0 and H_1. (These values were taken from the table of binomial probabilities.)

Table 7.4. PROBABILITIES WITH WHICH X MAY TAKE ON VALUES BETWEEN 0 AND 10 FOR MANY SAMPLES OF 10 OBSERVATIONS EACH

If it is true that $X =$	0	1	2	3	4	5	6	7	8	9	10
$p = p_0 = .5$	.001	.010	.044	.117	.205	.246	.205	.117	.044	.010	.001
$p = p_1 = .2$	.107	.268	.302	.201	.088	.026	.006	.001	.000	.000	.000

Values of X

We will not examine the risk engendered by incorrect decisions.

RULE A: Accept H_0 if $X \geq 4$.

Accept H_1 if $X \leq 3$.

An incorrect decision will occur under the following conditions:

i. H_0 is true and 3 or fewer deaths are observed.

ii. H_1 is true and 4 or more deaths are observed.

The probability of an incorrect decision in the case when H_0 is true hinges, therefore, on the likelihood of drawing a sample at random that contains fewer than four susceptible individuals and on nothing else. Similarly, the probability of an incorrect decision in the case when H_1 is true hinges on the likelihood of drawing a sample at random that contains four or more individuals who are susceptible to the disease but do not respond to the drug.

When α is the probability of an incorrect decision when H_0 is true, then

$$\alpha = P_0(X = 3) + P_0(X = 2) + P_0(X = 1) + P_0(X = 0) = \sum_{i=0}^{3} P_0(X = i)$$

$$= .117 + .044 + .010 + .001$$

$$= .172$$

When β is the probability of an incorrect decision when H_1 is true, then

$$\beta = \sum_{i=4}^{10} p_1(X = i) = .088 + .026 + .006 + .001 + .0 + .0 + .0$$

$$= .121$$

The resulting decision model is summarized in Table 7.5.

Table 7.5. DECISION MODEL FOR RULE A

	Accept H_0 if $X \geq 4$	Accept H_1 if $X \leq 3$
If H_0 is true so that $p_0 = .5$	probability correct $p_c = 1 - \alpha$ $= .828$	$\alpha = .172$
If H_1 is true so that $p_1 = .2$	$\beta = .121$	$p_c = 1 - \beta$ $= .879$

RULE B: Accept H_0 if $X \geq 3$.

Accept H_1 if $X \leq 2$.

An incorrect decision will occur under the following conditions:

i. H_0 is true and 2 or fewer deaths are observed.

ii. H_1 is true and 3 or more deaths are observed.

$$\alpha = \sum_{i=0}^{2} p_0(X = i) = .001 + .010 + .044 = .055$$

$$\beta = \sum_{i=3}^{10} p_1(X = i) = .322$$

The resulting decision model is summarized in Table 7.6.

Table 7.6. DECISION MODEL FOR RULE B

	Accept H_0 if $X \geq 3$	Accept H_1 if $X \leq 2$
If H_0 is true so that $p_0 = .5$	$p_c = 1 - \alpha$ $= .945$	$\alpha = .055$
If H_1 is true so that $p_1 = .2$	$\beta = .322$	$p_c = 1 - \beta$ $= .678$

RULE C: Accept H_0 if $X \geq 5$.

Accept H_1 if $X \leq 4$.

An incorrect decision will occur under the following conditions:

i. H_0 is true and 4 or fewer deaths are observed.
ii. H_1 is true and 5 or more deaths are observed.

$$\alpha = \sum_{i=0}^{4} p_0(X = i) = .377$$

$$\beta = \sum_{i=5}^{10} p_1(X = i) = .033$$

The resulting decision model is summarized in Table 7.7.

Table 7.7. DECISION MODEL FOR RULE C

	Accept H_0 if $X \geq 5$	Accept H_1 if $X \leq 4$
If H_0 is true so that $p_0 = .5$	$p_c = 1 - \alpha$ $= .623$	$\alpha = .377$
If H_1 is true so that $p_1 = .2$	$\beta = .033$	$p_c = 1 - \beta$ $= .967$

Note that α and β change in opposite directions when the rule for deciding between alternative hypotheses changes. Any decrease in α automatically increases β and vice versa. The only way to decrease both α and β simultaneously would be to increase the number of observations.

It is unlikely that the investigator will be able to state an alternative hypothesis H_1 as precisely as is stated in this example. Exact limits for p_1 and p_0 are common in certain engineering, quality control, and economic problems, but outside of these types of situations, a statement of exact values is usually limited to p_0. Thus an expectation for H_1 (i.e., the drug reduces mortality to 20 per cent) is not realistic. A more likely claim for the drug would be that it merely decreases mortality.

The hypotheses now become somewhat changed:

H_0:   Same as before (i.e., $P_0 = .5$).

H_1:   The drug reduces mortality. Probability of death after treatment with the drug P_1 is smaller than .5 (i.e., $P_1 < .5$).

When H_0 is true, the probability distribution for the event X is the same as before. On the other hand, when H_1 is true, the probability distribution of X depends on the precise value of P_1 which, of course, is unknown. However, if H_1 is true, then P_1 takes on some value between zero and .4999. This means that for any decision rule, the value of β will depend on the value of P_1. Thus β will not be a single value but rather a continuous function of P_1. This function can be determined and graphed and is called the *operating characteristics* of a specific rule or test.

DETERMINING THE OPERATING CHARACTERISTICS

RULE A (as before):   Accept H_0 if $X \geq 4$.

Accept H_1 if $X \leq 3$.

As before, an incorrect decision will occur under the following conditions.

i. H_0 is true and 3 or fewer deaths are observed.

ii. H_1 is true and 4 or more deaths are observed.

The value of α is computed as before:

$$\alpha = \sum_{i=0}^{3} P_0(X = i) = .172$$

To find the possible values of β, we must evaluate β for a number of possible values of P_1. Again we use the table of binomial probabilities to find

$$\beta_a = \sum_{i=4}^{10} p_1(X = i) \qquad \text{for Rule A}$$

$$\beta_b = \sum_{i=3}^{10} p_1(X = i) \qquad \text{for Rule B}$$

$$\beta_c = \sum_{i=5}^{10} p_1(X = i) \qquad \text{for Rule C}$$

Table 7.8 summarizes the results. We can graph values of β from Table 7.8 against possible values of P_1 to get a better picture of the relation between them. This is seen in Figure 7.1.

The study of the values of β as a function of P_1 permits the following conclusion: If it is true that P_1 does not differ very much from P_0 (or if the drug has only a very small effect on reducing mortality) the probability is large of rejecting H_1 when it should be accepted. If P_1 differs considerably from P_0 (or if the drug brings about a pronounced decrease in mortality), then the probability is small of rejecting H_1 when it should be accepted. This relation holds for any decision rule, albeit the rate at which β approaches small values depends very much on the kind of rule adopted.

Table 7.8. Probabilities for Decision Rules Using Various p_1 Levels

		Rule A	Rule B	Rule C
If $p_1 = .4999$	then $\beta =$	.8282	.9454	.6231
If $p_1 = .45$	then $\beta =$	.7240	.8905	.4856
If $p_1 = .40$	then $\beta =$	.6178	.8328	.3670
If $p_1 = .35$	then $\beta =$	.4862	.7384	.2485
If $p_1 = .30$	then $\beta =$	.3503	.6171	.1502
If $p_1 = .25$	then $\beta =$	.2241	.4744	.0781
If $p_1 = .20$	then $\beta =$	.1209	.3222	.0328
If $p_1 = .15$	then $\beta =$	.0499	.1797	.0098
If $p_1 = .10$	then $\beta =$	.0128	.0702	.0016
If $p_1 = .05$	then $\beta =$	.0011	.0116	.0001
If $p_1 = .00$	then $\beta =$	0	0	0

Since an error in decision would be less important the more alike P_1 and P_0 are and, more important, the more P_1 and P_0 differ, we may be guided in setting an adequate decision rule by three criteria:

1. By the magnitude of the minimum effect we want to detect.
2. By the magnitude of the maximum error we are willing to risk in failing to detect such an effect.
3. By the magnitude of the maximum error we are willing to risk in ascribing an effect to the drug when none exists.

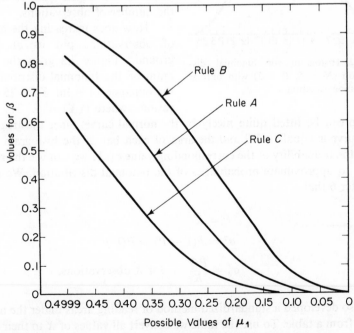

Fig. 7.1. Curve of operating characteristics for Rules A, B, and C.

For instance: If the minimum effect we want to detect is a reduction of the mortality rate from 50 per cent to 25 per cent and we are willing to live with $\beta \leq .10$ and $\alpha \leq .4$, then Rule C would be quite adequate. However, if we would have liked to detect a minimum reduction in the death rate from 50 per cent to 40 per cent with α and β both smaller than .05, the experiment would not have yielded a satisfactory answer for any decision rule. It is possible, however, to compute how many animals would be needed to permit a decision at those levels of sensitivity and risks.

INCREASING THE NUMBER OF OBSERVATIONS

We considered the case for which there were only 10 subjects available for study. Such instances are, of course, quite possible. However, from a realistic point of view, we would hesitate to make a judgment on the effec-

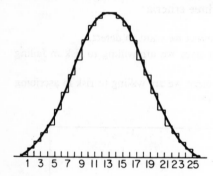

tiveness of a drug if such relatively large probabilities for errors are contingent upon any decision we make. Of course, sometimes no more subjects are available and our decisions will just have to be made with cognizance of the risks involved. Usually, however, we would want to increase the number of observations.

How does increasing the number of observations put us on firmer ground? Figure 7.2 gives the histogram of the binomial distribution of the outcome of event X for 25 obser-

Fig. 7.2. Histogram for binomial distribution ($N = 25$, $P = .5$) with normal curve approximation.

vations, where $P(X) = .5$. The distribution can be fitted quite nicely by the normal curve. Since the area under this curve is equal to 1.0 and the area of each bar of the histogram represents the probability of the corresponding value of X, we can use the normal curve to approximate probabilities of the binomial distribution. We saw in Chapter 6 that

$$P = \bar{X}$$

$$\sigma^2 = P(1 - P) = PQ$$

$$\sigma_{\bar{x}}^2 = \frac{PQ}{K} \qquad \text{for } K \text{ observations.}$$

We also developed a standardized method of reading areas under the normal curve from a table. To use the table we convert all values of X to their corresponding standardized Z values and obtain the approximate relative frequencies with which a variable may take on various values between X and μ by looking up approximate value of Z in the table.

$$Z = \frac{X - \mu}{\sigma}$$

When X is a proportion and we want to find the probability that it takes on values between P and X_i, we first find

$$Z_i \simeq \frac{X_i - P}{\sigma_{\bar{x}}}$$

Note that we divide by $\sigma_{\bar{x}}$ because a proportion is based on a number of observations. Thus the correct divisor is the standard error of the mean $\sigma_{\bar{x}}$, which really should be called the standard error of the proportion.

Actually we must modify our approximation of Z because X is based on discrete numbers. We can have any number of deaths such as 1 or 2 or K or $K + 1$ but no values in between. Thus our best approximation for Z is given by

$$Z \simeq \frac{(X \pm .005) - P}{\sigma_{\bar{x}}}$$

Let us now re-examine the drug example for 25 observations.

The alternative hypotheses are as before:

$H_0: \quad P_0 = .5$
$H_1: \quad P_1 < .5$

Since we now have a larger number of observations, we must modify our rules under which we will accept one hypothesis or the other as true. Let us choose the following rule

RULE A: Accept H_0 if $X \geq 8$.

              Accept H_1 if $X \leq 7$.

As before, an incorrect decision will occur under the following conditions:

   i. H_0 is true and 7 or fewer deaths are observed.
   ii. H_1 is true and 8 or more deaths are observed.

We compute the value of α as before:

$$\alpha = \sum_{i=0}^{8} P(X = i)$$

However, this would be too cumbersome. Instead we shall make use of the fact that we can approximate the binomial distribution by the use of the normal curve.

APPROXIMATIMATING THE BINOMIAL DISTRIBUTON

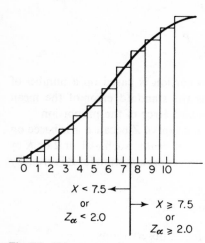

Inspecting Figure 7.2, we see that the probability of observing seven or fewer deaths represents a portion of this curve. This portion starts midway between eight and seven deaths because we obviously can only expect either a number of eight or larger or seven and smaller but no value in between, even though the normal curve assumes that such values exist. Therefore, we divide the normal curve into two regions: One for which we accept H_0 and one for which we reject it and accept H_1 (see Figure 7.3).

$X < 7.5$
or
$Z_\alpha < 2.0$

$X \geq 7.5$
or
$Z_\alpha \geq 2.0$

Fig. 7.3. Using normal curve to approximate binomial distribution. For rule: reject h_0 if $x < 7.5$.

We may restate the conditions under which an incorrect decision will occur in terms of proportions:

  i. H_0 is true and the observed proportion of deaths is .30 or less.
 ii. H_1 is true and the observed proportion of deaths is larger than .30.

Note that X, the proportion of deaths, has become our random variable.

With $X = .3$, $P(X) = .5$, and $K = 25$ (Figure 7.2), α can now be approximated from

$$Z_\alpha = \frac{.3 - .5}{\sqrt{\dfrac{.5(1 - .5)}{25}}} = \frac{.3 - .5}{\pm .1} = \pm 2$$

so that the probability of making the incorrect decision when H_0 is true is equal to .0455.

To find the possible values of β, we must evaluate β for a number of possible values of P_1. Again we can use the normal curve to approximate the binomial distribution for finding probabilities of β where

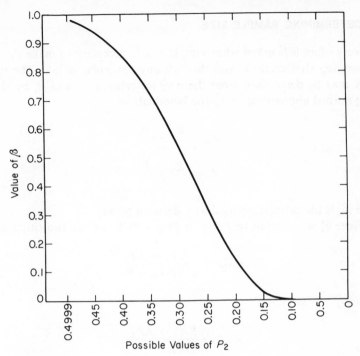

Fig. 7.4. Curve of operating characteristics for rule: Reject h_0 if $\times$ 7.5 for $p = .5$, $p < .5$, and $N = 25$.

$$Z_{\beta_i} \simeq \frac{X_i - P_1}{\sigma_{\bar{x}_i}}$$

The curve of operating characteristics is shown in Figure 7.4. If we compare the curve of operating characteristics for our tests, we can quite properly conclude that as the number of observations increase, the probabilities of making an error for any fixed rule decrease sharply. As a corollary, we can see that as the number of observations increase, we can make a decision rule discriminate between finer and finer differences. This means that if we had 10,000 observations and were satisfied with a given value of α and β, we could establish a decision rule that would decide between H_0 and H_1 for a very small difference in observed proportion. If we take this reasoning to its ultimate conclusion, we come to a somewhat unhappy statement that if we make the number of observations large enough, a very, very small deviation from expectation may become statistically meaningful, and yet such a small difference could be without practical consequence. Thus, although a certain amount of association exists between statistical and practical effects for a relatively small sample, when large numbers of observations are used this parallelism is largely lost.

DETERMINING SAMPLE SIZE

Very often it is asked what sample size is necessary to make the curve of operating characteristic pass through any particular points. The sample size K may be determined from the way we compute α and β, by the use of the normal approximation to the binomial.

$$Z_\alpha = \frac{X_d - P_0}{\sigma_{\bar{x}_0}}$$

$$Z_\beta = \frac{X_d - P_1}{\sigma_{\bar{x}_1}}$$

where X_d is the proportion used as a decision point.

Since $\sigma_{\bar{x}}^2$ was seen to be PQ/K or $P(1 - P)/K$, we can substitute so that

$$-Z_\alpha = \frac{KX_d - KP_0}{\sqrt{KP_0(1 - P_0)}}$$

Similarly,

$$Z_\beta = \frac{KX_d - KP_1}{\sqrt{KP_1(1 - P_1)}}$$

Rearranging, we have

$$KX_d - KP_0 = -Z_\alpha\sqrt{KP_0(1 - P_0)}$$

$$KX_d - KP_1 = Z_\beta\sqrt{KP_1(1 - P_1)}$$

Subtracting the lower equation from the upper and changing signs, we obtain

$$K(P_0 - P_1) = Z_\alpha\sqrt{KP_0(1 - P_0)} + Z_\beta\sqrt{KP_1(1 - P_1)}$$

$$= \sqrt{K}\,[Z_\alpha\sqrt{P_0(1 - P_0)} + Z_\beta\sqrt{P_1(1 - P_1)}]$$

From this expression,

$$K = \left[\frac{Z_\alpha\sqrt{P_0(1 - P_0)} + Z_\beta\sqrt{P_1(1 - P_1)}}{P_0 - P_1}\right]^2 \tag{1}$$

The proper value for X_d may be found by substituting back into the original equation.

One very useful program to have for the computer, therefore, is one which gives different readings of acceptance and rejection as well as curves of operating characteristics and number of observations required for tests at a given level of Type I and Type II errors. Figure 7.5 shows the printout from such a program. To use this program, the investigator must make a number of decisions. First he must select that smallest or largest value of P_1 for which he would not like to make the incorrect decision (i.e., reject H_1 in error). Next he must state the values for α and β which represent acceptable risks to him. The printout will then tell him the least number of subjects to use in his experiment and the location of the regions of rejection and acceptance of his decision rule.

For example, an investigator wants to determine the effectiveness of anthrax vaccine for cows. If the mortality of cows from anthrax is known to be half the infected cows, his hypotheses would look like

$$H_0: \quad P_0 = .5$$
$$H_1: \quad P_1 < .5$$

Without further specifications he would be at a loss as to how many cows to choose for his experiment and what decision rule to adopt. Although it would be unreasonable at times to require a specific value for P_1, the investigator will be able, in most instances, to state a limiting value for P_1 beyond which he would like to reduce his error as much as possible. In the present instance, he could specify that he would not like to make the incorrect decision if $P_1 < .4$ with probability greater than .025 and would not like to reject H_0 erroneously if $P_0 = .5$ with probability no greater than .05. This query now becomes: Find N and the rule for the test so that if H_0 is true then $\alpha \leq .05$ and if H_1 is true (and P_1 is equal to or less than .4) then $\beta \leq .025$. The program in Figure 7.5 will then show him that he will

ESTIMATICN FOR NUMBER OF OBSERVATIONS NEEDED

AND DECISION RULE.

INVESTIGATOR,   TEST RUN

INITIAL CONDITIONS,

ALPHA =	0.05000
BETA =	0.02500
P ZERO =	0.50000
P ALTERNATE =	0.40000

FOR THESE CONDITIONS,

N =   318

Figure 7.5   DECISION POINT =   144

need approximately 318 animals for his test, and his rule will be

$$\text{Reject } H_1 \text{ if } X > 144; \text{ otherwise accept } H_1$$

Interacting with this program, the investigator can then derive a reasonable estimate of the cost (in terms of time and money) that is needed to yield an answer to his experiment with acceptable certainty. The program format can help in this decision not only by calculating on the basis of the requested values of P_1, α, and β but also by showing results that would be obtained by use of adjacent values. How the dialogue between investigator and computer can be enhanced further will be the subject of Chapter 12.

PROBLEMS

1. An investigator tests "knowledge of foreign affairs" through a questionnaire that consists of ten multiple-choice questions. Each question asks about some recent event in a foreign country. The respondent checks off one of four possible choices as the correct answer.

    In evaluating each respondent, the investigator decides first if the respondent is "informed" or "uniformed." A respondent is considered informed when the number of correct answers selected by him is greater than that which would result from chance selection of answers.

    State H_0 and H_1 for such a test.

2. Assume that the investigator adopts the rule (where X is equal to the number of correct answers):

> *Reject* the hypothesis that the subject is informed if $X \leq 3$; otherwise *accept* the hypothesis.

State the value for α for this rule. What would have been the value for α if the same decision had been made for $X \leq 4$ or ≤ 2?

3. Compute enough points to sketch the curve of operating characteristics for the rules in Problem 2. Compare the values of β for the three rules for a subject who is informed enough to answer correctly (in the long run) 50 per cent of the questions.

4. If the investigator had used 25 questions, what would be the values for α for these rules:
    (a) Reject $H_{\text{(informed)}}$ if $X \leq 8$.
    (b) Reject $H_{\text{(informed)}}$ if $X \leq 9$.
    (c) Reject $H_{\text{(informed)}}$ if $X \leq 5$.

5. How many multiple-choice questions would have to be used if the investigator would want to run a risk no larger than $\alpha \leq .01$ and $\beta \leq .05$ and when the minimum level of "informed" to be detected is a long-run proportion of 30 per cent correct answers? What would be the rule for this test?

6. Assume that it is known that 90 per cent of modern men are right-handed. An anthropologist finds a cave with skulls of animals killed by Cro-Magnon man. He assumes that a skull crushed from the right indicates a right-handed hunter and a skull crushed from the left a left-handed hunter. He finds that of nine skulls, five were crushed from the right and four from the left. What is the probability that this sample came from a population of Cro-Magnons who were right- and left-handed as is modern man? Test the same hypothesis for the case that five out of 30 heads were crushed on the left side. How many skulls would the anthropologist need to be sure that errors of rejecting the hypothesis (that Cro-Magnon's hand preference was similar to modern man's) versus the alternative (that more Cro-Magnons were left-handed than we are) with $\alpha \leq .05$ and $\beta \leq .01$ for the case that at least 80 per cent of Cro-Magnons were right-handed?

TESTING HYPOTHESES ON
DISTRIBUTIONS WITH MANY CATEGORIES

The principles of hypothesis testing which were developed around approximations of the binomial distribution can be extended to instances involving distributions across more than two categories. In fact, our most frequent interest lies in multiple classifications of this type.

There is a very useful measure for the discrepency between observed and expected frequencies which is called χ^2 (Chi square). The quantity χ^2 is given as

$$\chi^2 = \sum^c \frac{(O - E)^2}{E} \tag{2}$$

where O is the observed frequency in each subclass or cell.

E is the expected frequency in each subclass or cell.

C is the number of cells in distribution.

$\sum\limits^c$ is the sum of all values taken over the C number of cells.

Thus, χ^2 is not a very obvious measure. We may look at it in one of two ways. From an intuitive viewpoint the evaluation of a discrepency by looking at the squared difference between observed and expected frequencies weighted by the number of the expected cases makes good sense. We can see that when the difference between the observed and the expected values are small, χ^2 tends to be very small, if not equal to zero. On the other hand, if the discrepencies between observed and expected frequencies are large, then χ^2 becomes increasingly larger as the difference between 0 and E relative to the number of observations becomes larger. It turns out that the probability density function of numbers that are distributed as χ^2 is relatively easy to compute.

As we increase the number of categories, the value of χ^2 will tend to increase. This is true even if differences between the observed and expected frequencies are due only to random chance. Hence one of the important parameters of the χ^2 distribution is the number of cells over which summing takes place. This probability distribution of χ^2 is characterized by a parameter that has been called *degrees of freedom*, or d.f. We shall discuss the concept of degrees of freedom in greater detail later. Here we shall simply accept this as a parameter whose value influences the distribution. Figure 7.6 shows examples of three distributions of χ^2 for different numbers of degrees of freedom.

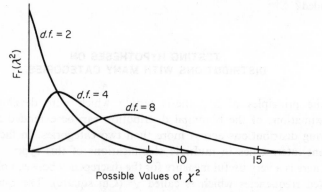

Fig. 7.6. Distributions of χ^2 for different d.f.

For simplicity's sake, values of χ^2 around which one ordinarily rejects hypotheses of difference are commonly summarized in tables. In the probability table labeled "Percentiles of the χ^2 Distribution" (Appendix B, Table 6) each row is for the proper degrees of freedom. Since the values of χ^2 do not change very rapidly with increases in the number of degrees of freedom, it is possible to omit some and limit the table to only relatively few rows. We read the table of χ^2 values as follows: For any given number of degrees of freedom, each row in the table represents the value of χ^2 that is frequently used as a decision point, or to mark a region of rejection. The actual probabilities associated with each of these rejection or decision points is given in the top row of the table.

In this way, if χ^2 is computed for ten degrees of freedom, enter the appropriate row in the table. We find that χ^2 values of 18.31 and larger tend to occur by chance no more frequently than five times in 100, or values of χ^2 of 23.21 or larger tend to occur by chance no more frequently than one time in 100. Since there is a limitation to the number of lines that can be kept in a useful table, it is always better to develop a subroutine that computes the value of χ^2 for a number of common regions of rejection and incorporate it in any program that develops frequency distributions. There is a simple formula by which this value can be obtained.

$$\chi_d^2 = K\left(1 - \frac{2}{9K} + Z_\alpha\sqrt{\frac{2}{9K}}\right)^3$$

This formula represents a simple numerical method by which a value of χ^2 for a particular region of rejection may be approximated for any number of degrees of freedom K. The quantity Z_α is the value of the now familiar normal deviate corresponding to the probability α for which a region of rejection is to be computed.

For instance, if we wish to find a value of χ^2 such that would occur by chance no more frequently than five times in 100 for 10,000 degrees of freedom we would compute its value by

$$\chi_{.05}^2 = 10,000\left(1 - \frac{2}{90,000} + 1.645\sqrt{\frac{2}{90,000}}\right)^3$$

The quantity χ^2 is used to set up tests in two rather different situations. In the first instance, the values of expected frequencies are known; in the second instance, expected frequencies are not known but are derived from the data. We shall discuss each of these uses separately.

USE OF χ^2 WITH A PRIORI EXPECTATION

There are instances in which expected distributions can be deduced from prior considerations. For instance, if we toss a coin we can expect it to fall heads 50 per cent of the time. If the coin is tossed 100 times our expectations would be 50 heads and 50 tails. Similarly, if we toss two dice and sum the values on their faces, there are 11 different values that may be obtained in different ways and can be expected with somewhat different frequencies. When these dice are honest, the frequencies with which different values will occur are known.

These examples all are of instances in which classifications into cells occur in one dimension. And indeed, in most instances, the testing of hypotheses on distributions for which exist *a priori* expected values turns out to be just such a single classification problem with K cells. The degrees of freedom parameter, which is crucial for determining the shape of the χ^2 distribution in any of these instances, is simply given as $K - 1$.

The most common use of χ^2 tests has been around genetic problems. Let us say that a geneticist expects a cross-fertilization of an F_2 generation of peas to yield four phenotypes, A, B, C, and D. His expectations are

Phenotype	Expected Proportions
A	.5633
B	.1875
C	.1875
D	.0617
	1.0000

The discerning student will recognize this as the 9: 3: 3: 1 expected ratio of frequencies.

Let us say that these four phenotypes, A, B, C, and D, are different-looking peas. When our geneticist harvests these peas the expectations are that their frequencies will be distributed as the ratios or proportions given above. However, he is well aware that in planting, some peas get more light or sun or are better conditioned to growth than others, that he is not quite sure how well he has kept various vermin and pests out of his pea patch, and finally, that the accuracy of graduate students in collecting and counting peas is proverbially open to question. He does expect to observe values that are closely in line with the proportions given above but may not be exactly like them.

He may then set up the following hypotheses:

H_0: The observed ratios or proportions of different types of peas are chance deviations from the expected ratios or proportions.

H_1: The observed ratios come from a distribution of pea types which is different from the one deduced from prior principles as 9: 3: 3: 1.

We can use the values of χ^2 as the random variable around which a decision model is built. The parameter of degrees of freedom equals $(K - 1)$, or 3 in this case. Since we will use the known distribution of χ^2 values for our tests, we reformulate the alternative hypotheses:

H_0: The computed value of χ^2 is an estimate of the true value of $\chi^2 = 0$. Any deviation from 0 is simply due to chance.

H_1: The computed value of χ^2 is an estimate of a true value of χ^2 that is larger than 0. If a value of χ^2 approaches 0, it will do so only because of chance.

In our previous examples it made a good bit of sense to set a region of rejection according to the number of dead or survivors that were observed. Setting a value of χ^2, which has no immediate intuitive meaning with respect to data, as a rejection point may not appear equally sensible. However, the probability with which certain errors are incurred consequent to decision does have meaning. We can thus build a decision model around the investigator's ability to tolerate a particular error in making incorrect decisions.

We have two errors to choose from. We could let either the Type I or Type II error decide where we will set up our region of rejection. For Type I error (i.e., for the proposition that H_0 is true) we have a specific expectation about how the distribution of χ^2 should look and what its expected value should be. On the other hand, if our expectation about H_0 is wrong, then any number of distributions is possible and we do not have a single fixed and expected value for χ^2. Rather, we would have to examine the operating characteristics of as many distributions as we can deduce as likely alternate hypotheses or give up the idea of the curve of operating characteristics (O.C. curve) altogether. It is much simpler, therefore, to let the probability of commiting a Type I error determine the region of rejection. If the geneticist decides that he would want to be incorrect no more often than one time in 100 in rejecting H_0, then he would select the value of $\chi^2 \geq 11.34$ (for d.f. = 3) and set up a decision rule as follows:

i. Reject H_0 if $\chi^2 \geq 11.34$.
ii. If $\chi^2 < 11.34$, accept H_0 and reject H_1.

Which value the geneticist will actually choose in accepting or rejecting H_0 will depend largely upon the circumstances of the experiment, the importance of his theory, and on many other factors.

Let us consider two possible outcomes of the genetic experiment. In the first instance, results are as follows:

Phenotype	Number Observed	Number Expected
A	460	479
B	181	159
C	136	159
D	72	52
	849	849

$$\chi^2 = \frac{(-19)^2}{479} + \frac{22^2}{159} + \frac{(-23)^2}{159} + \frac{20^2}{52} = 14.84$$

The value of $\chi^2 = 14.84$ could be expected by chance no more frequently than one time in 1000. In this case, there is certainly no question that he would want to reject H_0 or at least very seriously re-examine the premises along which he has evolved his original expectations.

However, let us take a look at the second instance. Let us now say that our geneticists harvest peas of the following categories:

Phenotype	Number Observed	Number Expected
A	463	479
B	178	159
C	139	159
D	69	52
	849	849

Then

$$\chi^2 = \frac{(-16)^2}{479} + \frac{(19)^2}{159} + \frac{(-20)^2}{159} + \frac{(17)^2}{52} = 10.88$$

Here the value of χ^2 is smaller than the one he had decided to use as a point of rejection but close enough to it that he may pause and think about it. He may look at this value in one of two ways. He could say that in performing many, many experiments, he always uses that point of rejection for which he stands to be wrong no more often than one time in 100 in rejecting H_0 when it is true. In this way, he can expect to be correct 99 times in 100 in making this decision. Since these are the odds at which he wishes to play the game, he will simply follow this rule and will not be shaken at all by a value of χ^2 that falls close to his region of rejection but does not quite reach it.

On the other hand, he might view this marginal value as "suggestive," since it is large enough to occur by chance no more frequently than one time in 20. The decision that the investigator might make in this case will depend very strongly on the number of times he performs experiments, the conviction he has about the theory from which he has drawn his original proportions, the confidence he has in his methods of planting and reaping peas and controlling his total experiment, and on his personality and disposition as well.

The one serious mistake the student may make is to view the region of rejection of statistical tests as hard and fast rules along which scientific decisions must be made. To reach a decision in science is sometimes a very painful process resting on a careful evaluation of evidence, motives, and consequences rather than on a particular value of χ^2.

MAKING A DECISION ABOUT THE SHAPE OF A DISTRIBUTION

We have already seen that we can base descriptive indices and inference techniques on knowing what sort of distribution we are dealing with. It is also quite obvious that the distribution of results can tell us a good bit about the phenomena of interest.

Let us look at the distribution of weights of school children given in Chapter 6 and ask if they are normally distributed. Our sample contains a variety of different age groups and with it also youngsters in different stages of puberty. The sample also contains males and females, whites and non-whites, and members of different economic and social strata. We might ask ourselves whether in view of the many different groups sampled the total population of weights still can be expected to be distributed normally.

When weight is the random variable designated by W, we wish to test the hypothesis that W is distributed normally. The two parameters of the normal distribution, μ_w and σ_w of W, are unknown, but we can use our sample of 8490 cases to estimate them by computing $\bar{W}$ and s_w.

To find the number of cases expected to fall within each subclass classification of the sample we would find the proportion of cases which would be expected to fall within any two values of Z_i and Z_j, where Z_i and Z_j are, of course, the standardized normal variate Z, for class intervals designated by limits i and j. Since $\bar{W} = 87.55$ and $s_w = 36.16$, we can find the values of the standardized normal variate Z for each of the boundaries of class intervals, from 39.9 lb to 170 + lb as given in Table 6.1. The proportion of total cases that are expected to fall within the interval Z_i and Z_j are then multiplied by the total number of cases in the sample to give the expected number of cases in any particular class interval.

The number of observed and expected values, together with their difference, are summarized in Table 7.9. We can then compute χ^2 for the hypothesis that the weights are distributed normally.

Table 7.9. FIT OF NORMAL CURVE TO WEIGHT DISTRIBUTION OF TABLE 6.1

Class Intervals	Z Values of Class Intervals	Expected Proportion	Expected Frequency	Observed Frequency	$\frac{(0-E)^2}{E}$
less than 39.9	less than −1.32	.0934	793	163	500
40– 49.9	−1.32 to −1.04	.0559	474	965	509
50– 59.9	−1.04 to −0.76	.0744	632	1297	700
60– 69.9	−0.76 to −0.49	.0844	751	987	74
70– 79.9	−0.49 to −0.21	.1047	889	767	17
80– 89.9	−0.21 to 0.01	.1111	943	678	74
90– 99.9	0.07 to 0.34	.1051	892	592	101
100–109.9	0.34 to 0.62	.0993	843	668	36
110–119.9	0.62 to 0.90	.0836	710	651	5
120–129.9	0.90 to 1.17	.0630	535	526	0
130–139.9	1.17 to 1.45	.0476	404	417	1
140–149.9	1.45 to 1.73	.0325	276	277	0
150–159.9	1.73 to 2.00	.0182	154	195	11
160–169.9	2.00 to 2.28	.0115	98	106	1
170–	2.28 or more	.0113	96	201	11
					2040

$X^2 = 2040$

For how many degrees of freedom is this value of χ^2 to be evaluated? While there were $K = 15$ classifications, a number of parameters had to be estimated from the sample. These were the mean and standard deviation of the distribution, which also have to be subtracted from the total number of classifications available. In general, χ^2 for the normal curve is evaluated for $K - 3$ degrees of freedom, where K is the number of classifications.

Evaluating our computed value of $\chi^2 = 2040$ for 12 degrees of freedom, we find that we must reject our hypothesis that the distribution is normal. The probability that a deviation as large as observed is due to chance only is smaller than 10^{-8}.

We mentioned before that although the original distributions may not be normal, the distribution of means of a given sample size will tend toward normalcy. We can see this trend toward normalcy by inspection of Tables 6.2 and 6.3. Although the distribution of weights is almost rectangular, the distribution of mean weights based on larger samples tends toward the typical normal distribution. The samples based on as few cases as 36 are still too small to distribute normally, but at their ends we can see the peaking process that takes place. (The student should compute the number of expected means in the class interval 80 to 89.9 and compare it to the number of observed means in that interval.)

The general solution to test the fit to the binomial distribution is given by

$$\chi^2 = \frac{n \sum\limits_{i=1}^{k} (\bar{X}_i - p)^2}{p(1 - p)} \qquad (3)$$

where p is the probability that an event will happen.
$\bar{X}_i$ is the proportion for the class interval i.
n is the number of cases.
K is the number of classifications examined.
χ^2 is evaluated for $K - 2$ degrees of freedom if p is estimated by

$$p = \frac{\sum \bar{X}_i}{K} \qquad (4)$$

When p is extremely small, we prefer the Poisson distribution (as pointed out in Chapter 6). The χ^2 test for the Poisson distribution is given by

$$\chi^2 = \frac{\sum\limits_{i=1}^{k} (\bar{X}_i - np)^2}{np} \qquad (5)$$

where np is estimated by

$$np = \frac{\Sigma \, X_i}{K} \qquad (6)$$

and χ^2 is evaluated for $K - 2$ d.f.

Next in importance to fitting data derived from biological and sociological experiments to normal and normal types of distribution is a comparison to exponential shapes. Exponential distributions are most commonly met in economic data, but they also occur very often in such areas as nuclear medicine, quality control studies, and many biochemical instances in which a behavior is asymptotic to a fixed limit. A general formulation used very frequently to fit an exponential for test purposes is

$$f(X_i) = \left(\frac{n}{\bar{X}}\right) e^{-X_i/\bar{X}} \qquad (7)$$

where n is the number of observations.

X is the random variable.

$\bar{X}$ is the mean for the random variable.

In using the exponential theory, the proportion for each class interval is developed very much like fitting the normal curve, and the computed value of χ^2 is evaluated for $K - 2$ degrees of freedom.

In general, any possible distribution can be evaluated by the use of χ^2 as long as expectations about frequencies can be formulated.

χ^2 FOR INSTANCES WITHOUT A PRIORI EXPECTATION

Let us assume an investigator evaluates a breakdown of frequency of hospitalization of a sample of individuals covered by Blue Cross of Los Angeles by day of week and by sex. He notices that the number of hospitalizations occurring during the weekend fall well below those accumulated during the week. There are many obvious reasons for this. The question that interests him now is whether or not women are affected similarly to men by these factors. If he knew something about the expected frequencies with which males, females, or people in general are hospitalized by day of week he could develop a decision model using χ^2 again as the random variable. However, these theoretical expected frequencies do not exist.

A method may be used instead by which expected frequencies are derived from a sample based on the hypothesis that there is no difference between the rate of hospitalization of males and females with respect to day of week. If it is true that no difference really exists between males and females, with respect to hospitalization trends, then the observations we have are actually of "people" and of the frequencies with which they are hospitalized. Using the proportional breakdown for people (i.e., into males and females) as our best expectation, we would then assign to males and females the number of hospitalizations which we would expect to take place if no difference would exist between them. The number of cases expected, for each cell is given by

$$E_{rc} \frac{T_r}{T} \times T_c \tag{8}$$

where T_r is the row total.

T_c is the column total.

T is the total number of cases.

E_{rc} is the expected frequency for the cell in the rth row and cth column.

The number of degrees of freedom for which the value of χ^2 from such a test is evaluated is given by $(C - 1)(R - 1)$, where C is the number of columns and R is the number of rows. Although this type of test is used very frequently, it has a number of difficulties that ought to be examined.

In the first place, the value of χ^2 depends to some extent on how the groupings in the columns and rows are done. The investigator can increase or decrease the resulting value of χ^2 in many instances by a judicious manipulation of categories. Another problem is that with large numbers of row and column categories and a large number of observations χ^2 tends to significance at any level at which one wishes to test a hypothesis that a chance relationship does indeed exist. There is the additional difficulty that in multivariate situations the number of tables that can be potentially inspected is so very large that those few that are selected because they seem to yield some insight or relationship may do so not because they reflect true relationships but because in developing many breakdowns, some are bound to be better than others by chance alone. (The problems thus created for testing hypotheses are discussed in greater detail at the end of this chapter and in the chapter on robot data screening.)

In writing a general program that computes χ^2 as part of a table of frequency breakdown (as shown in Chapter 6), care must be taken that the program eliminate columns or rows with very low frequencies. These tend to bias the value of χ^2. The best method of meeting this problem is to use an algorithm that eliminates all columns or rows for which the number of observations are fewer than the numbers of rows and columns, respectively. Symbolically stated, if a table initially contains R rows and C columns, and K_{ij} is the number of observations in the cell at the juncture of the ith row and jth column, then

$$\text{Eliminate row } i \text{ if } \sum_{j=1}^{c} K_{ij} < C$$

$$\text{Eliminate column } j \text{ if } \sum_{i=1}^{r} K_{ij} < R \tag{9}$$

In general, however, χ^2 should not be used if the average number of expected frequencies per cell is less than 5. A correction factor is usually introduced when the number of expected values tends to be less than 20. This correction factor (known as the Yates correction) consists of subtracting .5 from each difference between observed and expected frequencies prior to squaring this value:

$$\chi^2 = \sum_{\text{all } K} \frac{(0 - E - .5)^2}{E} \tag{10}$$

Testing for an average number of expected values per cell and introduction of a proper correction do not represent a particular problem for a general table of frequencies and χ^2 program.

Example. An insurance company wishes to determine if intense classroom training in driver safety is of value. Experimental classes are held in a number of schools, involving 1,142 students who were selected for these classes purely at random. Another 1,078 randomly selected students serve as controls. They receive the usual safety instructions. After three years, experimental and control subjects are divided into three groups: those who had accidents and were found to be at fault, those who were involved in accidents but not through their own fault, and those who were not involved in accidents at all. The number of individuals for each group were:

	Received Intense Safety Training	Received Routine Safety Training	All Subjects	Per Cent of Total
Accident, driver at fault	223	255	478	21.5%
Accident, driver *not* at fault	269	233	502	22.6%
No accident	650	590	1,240	55.9%
	1,142	1,078	2,220	100.0%

The company must decide now if the differences in distributions between experimental and control groups could have resulted from chance.

If H_0 (i.e., the hypothesis that the true distribution of subjects after intensive and routine training is the same) is true, then the investigator observed a total of 2,220 drivers of which 21.5% had accidents through their own faults, 22.6% were involved in accidents but not through their own faults, and 55.9% were not involved in accidents at all. These percentages now form the basis for the expected number of subjects in each accident cagegory. The expected distribution would now look as:

	Intense Training	Routine Training
Accident, driver at fault	245.5	231.8
Accident, driver not at fault	258.1	243.6
No accident	638.4	602.6
	1,142.0	1,078.0

We can now compute χ^2 as:

$$\chi^2 = \frac{(-22.5)^2}{245.5} + \frac{(11.9)^2}{258.1} + \frac{(11.6)^2}{638.4} + \frac{(23.2)^2}{231.8} + \frac{(-10.6)^2}{243.6} + \frac{(-12.6)^2}{602.6} = 5.86$$

For $(3-1)\cdot(2-1) = 2$ degrees of freedom, a value of χ^2 of 4.61 or larger would be expected to occur by chance 1 time in 10 and a value of χ^2 of 5.99 or larger would be expected to occur by chance 1 time in 20. The observed value of $\chi^2 = 5.86$ is large enough so that we would be tempted to reject H_0 (the hypothesis that differences were due to chance) and accept its alternative.

2 × 2 TABLES

Very often the investigator wishes to examine a number of dichotomous situations which can be summarized by 2 × 2 tables, such as sex by race. It is also convenient very often to reduce data that have more than two categories to 2 × 2 tables to do a rapid check for possible relationships.

A method for determining whether the probability for differences in 2 × 2 distributions could come from a random selection process is given by Fisher's exact test. In this test the probability for obtaining observed differences when H_0 is true is computed directly by

$$P = \frac{(a+b)!(c+d)!(a+c)!(b+d)!}{N!\,a!\,b!\,c!\,d!} \tag{11}$$

where N is the total number of observations and a, b, c, and d are given as in Table 7.10. This exact test has been used before only for small numbers

Table 7.10. 2 × 2 CONTINGENCY TABLE

Variable I

Variable II	a	b	Row sum $(a+b)$
	c	d	$(c+d)$
Column sum	$(a+c)$	$(b+d)$	$N = a+b+c+d$

of observations, since the difficulties for computing factorials of large numbers are rather severe. With high-speed processors these computational difficulties are relieved, making Fisher's exact test preferable to χ^2 for 2 × 2 contingency tables.

Example. Compare two methods of stacking cement bags in railroad cars. In Method A, cement bags are arranged to lie lengthwise; in Method

B alternate layers are used. On arrival, shipments are judged on whether damage to cement bags was excessive or not.

Method A: 8 with acceptable damage	5 with excessive damage	= 13 total
Method B: 4 with acceptable damage	1 with excessive damage	= 5
Total 12	6	18

If A and B work alike, the distribution of damages for each should be the same. Fisher's Exact Test computes the probability of observing a combination of cell frequencies as extreme or more extreme than the one observed.

In this example, the cell and marginal frequencies are small and can be computed quite easily by hand. The probability of a distribution as extreme or even more extreme than observed is given by p where

$$p = \frac{13! \times 12! \times 6! \times 5!}{18! \times 8! \times 5! \times 4! \times 1!} = .35$$

The direct method of calculation (writing out factorials and then cancelling in numerator and denominator) becomes cumbersome with larger cell frequencies. Values of $N!$ up to 100! are given in Appendix B, Table 12. Another quick method of calculation is to make use of logs.

log p = log (of factorials of all marginal frequencies)
           − [log $N!$ + log (of factorial of cell frequencies)]

Tables for log factorials are given in Appendix B, Table 13.

Let us assume that we had the following data from our experiment.

Method A: 24 with acceptable damage	15 with excessive damage	= 39
Method B: 16 with acceptable damage	6 with excessive damage	= 22
Total 40	21	61

A direct method of calculation would be too cumbersome. However, we can use logs of factorials in the appendix and compute the log of the probability so that.

log p = (46.30959 + 21.05077 + 47.91165 + 19.70834)
        − (83.70550 + 23.79271 + 12.11650 + 13.32062 + 2.85733)
        = 134.98035 − 135.79266

Since probabilities are less than one, the log of p will be negative. Presuming that the student knows the dodge of adding and subtracting a constant to and from the logs of a number, we find p by

log p = (135.98035 − 1) − 135.79266 = .18769 − 1

so that

$$p = .154$$

TESTING DIFFERENCES BETWEEN TWO CUMULATIVE DISTRIBUTIONS

It is very often important to know whether two cumulative distributions differ from each other. In the use of χ^2 no assumption is made about a particular direction of scaling factor underlying a phenomenon. Very often such a scaling factor, however, does exist. For instance, the distribution of death by age is along a scalable dimension, i.e., age. The quantity χ^2 turns out to be relatively insensitive to changes in distribution with age, since as far as the test is concerned it is immaterial whether any particular number of differences in the age at death distribution of two groups is grouped at one end of the distribution or occurs randomly throughout the table.

A suitable test can be evolved for evaluating the extent of differences in the cumulative frequency distribution of two variables as they progress along a scale.

Let us say we are interested in evaluating if one of two populations dies "younger" than the other. We could compare the frequency of death for different age groups by using a χ^2 test for independence. However, there are two drawbacks here. The proposition examined by use of χ^2 is that the two groups "differ" but not that they differ in some systematic way. Also, a slight but systematic difference in patterns of death may be significant if the direction of change is considered along with differences in frequencies but this slight difference fails to yield a convincingly large value of χ^2 if the systematic trend is not part of the test.

Let us take an example. In comparing age at death of males who worked regularly and for many years in the steel production industry with that of other males living in the same region of the country, we compare a highly selected group of individuals with the general population. Steel workers by and large must be physically robust, since their work is arduous and demanding. Thus those suffering from chronic diseases such as tuberculosis are almost automatically excluded from this occupation. Since the work itself is somewhat dangerous, it demands habitual carefulness on the part of the "surviving" workers. A carry-over of habits of circumspection to such other potentially dangerous activities as driving a car or working around the house may be expected. As a result, fewer steel workers die an accidental death from automobile collisions or from falling off the roof of a house, etc. Being also steadily employed (by definition) has implications for age at death. Steady workers may be expected to be more stable persons; hence their rate of death from homicides and suicides should be less than that for the general population. Then there are such factors as regular hours, good nutrition, adequate medical care, and others that would all contribute to the survival of a population.

All these selection factors may contribute a slight difference in the overall age at death pattern but not enough to indicate a difference in distribution if a progression by age as a scale factor is ignored.

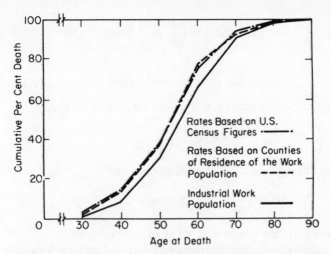

Fig. 7.7. Comparison of cumulative death rates of an industrial population with cumulative death rates of U.S. and county of residence populations. From T.D. Sterling "Epidemiology of Diseases Associated with Lead," *Arch. Envir. Health* **8** (1964), pp. 333–348.

However, if we compare the cumulative distribution function of the two populations we could hypothesize that the cumulative function for age at death of the general population will be larger for every age group than that of the population of steel workers (see Figure 7.7). If X is the age of death of male steelworkers and Y the age of death of males in the general population and $F(X)$ and $G(Y)$ are cumulative distribution functions, the variable Y may be said to be stochastically smaller than X if $F(a) \leq G(a)$ for every age a, with a "more than" relation holding for some a. This is really saying that individuals in the general population tend to die at a younger age than do steelworkers.

We wish to examine the hypothesis, therefore that $G(a) = F(a)$ for all a against the alternative that Y is stochastically larger than X.

To do so we take the sum of the differences between $F^*(a_i) - G^*(a_i)$ or the two sample cumulative distribution functions.

$$z_i = G(a_i) - F(a_i)$$

where a_i are α arbitrary points defining the $\alpha + 1$ intervals into which the m and n sample values fall. If H_0, the hypothesis of no difference between $F(X)$ and $G(Y)$, is true, then

$$E(z_i) = 0$$

$$E(z_i)^2 = \left(\frac{1}{m} + \frac{1}{n}\right) p_i q_i$$

$$E(z_i z_k) = \left(\frac{1}{m} + \frac{1}{n}\right) p_i q_k$$

where

$$p_i = F(a_i) = G(a_i) \quad \text{and} \quad q_i = 1 - p_i$$

A. W. Marshall constructed a test on the statistic $S = \sum_{i=1}^{i} z_i$.

$$Z_\alpha = \frac{S}{\sqrt{\text{Var}(s)}} \tag{12}$$

where Z_α is the now familiar normal deviate and

$$\text{Var}(s) = \left(\frac{1}{m} + \frac{1}{n}\right)\left(\sum_{i=1}^{i} p_i q_i + 2 \sum_{i=1}^{i-1} \sum_{k=i+1}^{i} p_i q_k\right) \tag{13}$$

where m and n are the cumulative totals of the two groups.

The method of calculation is demonstrated on data from a study in which the onset of a specific disease was recorded for all cases. All individuals who had had a history of this disease in their family were put into one group and the remaining individuals in the other. We test the hypothesis H_0 that age of onset is identical for both groups versus the possibility that individuals with a positive disease history will get the disease at a younger age. Table 7.11 shows the results of the stochastic test based on a large sample test of the hypothesis that one of two random variables is stochastically larger than the other (computed by the MEDCOMP library program). The number of cumulated cases by age of onset of disease are shown for the two classes of individuals—those with and those without positive family history—as well as all relevant results.

The quantity S is given by

Table 7.11. DISTRIBUTION OF AGE OF ONSET OF DISEASE FOR TWO POPULATIONS DIVIDED ACCORDING TO POSITIVE AND NEGATIVE FAMILIAL DISEASE HISTORY

Age of Onset	(1) Cumulated Positive Cases	(2) Cumulated Negative Cases	(3) Pooled Sample (1)(2)	(4) p_i	(5) q_k
0–49	12	32	44	.0176	.9824
50–54	28	93	121	.0484	.9516
55–59	64	242	306	.1223	.8777
60–64	118	495	613	.2450	.7550
65–69	175	850	1025	.4097	.5903
70–74	276	1276	1552	.6203	.3797
75–79	360	1664	2024	.8090	.1910
80–84	399	1942	2341	.9357	.0643
85–over	415	2087	2502		
	1847	8681			

$$S = \frac{1847}{415} - \frac{8681}{2087} = .291$$

To compute Var (S) we find

$$\frac{1}{m} + \frac{1}{n} = \frac{1}{415} + \frac{1}{2087} = .00289$$

$$\sum_{i=1}^{8} p_i q_i = 1.0477$$

$$\sum_{i=1}^{7} \sum_{k=2}^{8} p_i q_k = 1.2183$$

(Note that the program multiplied and summed $p_1 q_2 + p_1 q_3 + p_1 q_4 + \cdots + p_7 q_8$)

$$Z_\alpha = \frac{.291}{.1005} = 2.90$$

Looking up this value for Z_α in the table of the normal curve, we find that the probability for a chance difference in stochastic size of the two distributions is equal to .002. Hence we would be very tempted to reject H_0.

The format for a computation or printout of this test may be tailored to satisfy the user. The point is well worth noting that many powerful tests exist that are not frequently used because of computational difficulties.

PROBLEMS

1. What are the following probabilities?
   (a) $P(\chi^2 > 40.26 | \text{d.f.} = 30)$.
   (b) $P(22.31 < \chi^2 < 30.58 | \text{d.f.} = 15)$.
   (c) $P(\chi^2 < 11.07 | \text{d.f.} = 5)$.

2. A geneticist expects a $9:6:1$ ratio of markings in crossing two heterozygote earthworms. The expectations are 9 (no markings for), 6 (spotted), and 1 (striped). He observes

No markings	155
Spotted	141
Striped	24
	320

   How likely is the $9:6:1$ ratio?

3. In a study on superstition, the investigator spills a salt shaker as by accident in front of a subject. The investigator observes if the subject responds with

a stereotype (such as throwing salt over his shoulder). Of 100 male and 150 female subjects, the following results are observed:

	No response	Stereotype response	
Males	38	62	100
Females	37	113	150

Would you reject the hypothesis that women are more superstitious than men? Why?

4. A furious argument on bull shooting between Ivy League schools and the Big Ten is to be settled by an experiment. Teams consisting of the best bull shooters from the two sets of rival schools meet in competition and obtain the following scores:

	Kill the animal	Wound the animal	Miss completely	
Ivy League	158	72	18	248
Big Ten	103	41	26	170
	261	113	44	

Is it likely that these skills are equally represented by both types of school? Why?

5. Make a flow chart for a program that generates an M by N table, computes expected frequencies and a value of χ^2. Build in precautions for small frequencies of row and column.

6. Make a flow chart for a program that tests for goodness of fit of a frequency distribution to the normal curve. Build in the precaution to pool frequencies on each tail of the distribution.

7. Throw a pair of dice 100 times and record the sum of their face value at each toss. Test the hypothesis that the dice are unbiased by comparing the number of observed instances with the number of expected instances where the sum of their faces, X, has the value
   (a) $X \leq 5$
   (b) $6 \leq X \leq 8$
   (c) $X \geq 9$

8. Below is the distribution of an amount of lead found in the urine of refinery workers. Determine if it is reasonable to assume a normal distribution?

Microgram of lead per sample	Frequency	
.02–.0249	185	
.025–.0299	707	$\bar{X} = .038$
.030–.0349	1835	
.035–.0399	2493	$S = .0065$
.040–.0449	2123	
.045–.0499	824	
.050–.0549	283	
	8450	

(If you use a table of the normal distribution rather than a program, use linear interpolation to find the best estimates for proper areas under the normal curve).

TESTS BETWEEN MEANS

We saw that the elements of a scientific decision were as follows:

1. A random variable that reliably measures an observation or the outcome of an experiment.
2. Sets of alternative hypotheses: H_0, H_1, etc.
3. Knowledge of at least one of the probability density distribution of outcomes that would result if one of the alternative hypotheses were true.

Statistical reasoning will then result in an estimate of the probabilities of making an error for any specific rule of deciding between alternative hypotheses.

When results are normally distributed, knowledge of the properties of the normal distribution can be used to supply the necessary probabilities for possible outcomes of the experiment under the assumption that one of the alternative hypotheses is correct (i.e., point 3 above).

Example. The average survival time for rats is known to be 420 days with a known standard deviation of 20 days. A single rat is selected at random and given 50 r of whole body radiation during the first week of life to test the hypothesis that radiation after birth will increase the lifespan of the animal.

We will consider two possible outcomes of the experiment:

(a) The animal survives for $X_a = 470$ days.
(b) The animal survives for $X_b = 440$ days.

The experimental measure (or the random variable) is the number of days the animal survives.

HYPOTHESES

H_0: Radiation during the first week of life does not lengthen the life-span. Average survival time after treatment is equal to average survival time without treatment is equal to μ_0. Any observed deviations from 420 are due to chance.

H_1: Radiation during the first week of life increases the lifespan to μ_1 such that $\mu_1 <_{,} \mu_0$. Any observed deviation from μ_1 is due to chance.

Since survival times are normally distributed, the possible outcomes for X_a under hypothesis H_0 are known. For instance, the probability that the animal will survive more than 400 days is equal to .84. We obtain this probability by first finding Z_{400} and consulting the table of the normal distribution.

$$Z_{400} = \frac{400 - 420}{20} = -1$$

The probability that the animal will survive more than 400 days is equivalent to the proportion of the area of the normal curve to the right of $Z = -1$.

We can now consider the consequence of a specific rule. Let us say an animal is treated and survives for 470 days, i.e., $X_a = 470$. We must decide on rejecting or accepting H_0 or H_1 with this as the only evidence. We must consider the consequences of the following rule:

Reject H_0 and accept H_1 if $X_a \geq 470$;
Otherwise accept H_0.

If H_0 is true, then the probability of observing, by chance alone, a survival time of 470 days or more is equal to .0062 or 62 times in 10,000 observations. (Why?)

An incorrect decision for our rule under the condition that H_0 is true will occur only if we had picked, at random, an animal that was slated to survive 470 days or more to begin with. The probability of this happening is .0062, so for our test $\alpha = .0062$. This probability is low enough so that in most instances we would reject H_0 and accept H_1 and conclude that radiation during the first week of life does have an effect on survival.

To compute the curve of operating characteristics of our tests, we assume that the true average survival time for animals who have had 50 r of body radiation in the first week of life takes on values of 420.001 days or more. But, it is obvious, the curve of operating characteristics will depend not only on the actual true mean survival time but also on the standard deviation of the distribution of survival time. If we assume that the experiment does not

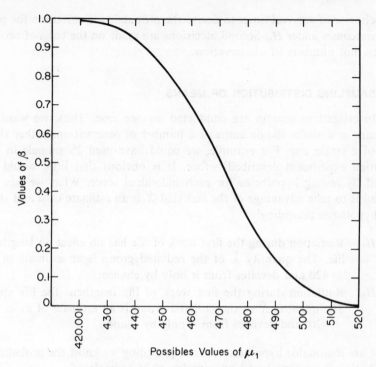

Fig. 7.8. Curve of operating characteristics for rule.

affect distribution of survival time, we can sketch a curve of operating characteristics. Such a curve is given in Figure 7.8.

If the outcome of the experiment had been $X_b = 440$ days, our rule could have been as follows:

Reject H_0 and accept H_1 if $X_b \geq 440$;
Otherwise accept H_0.

If H_0 is true, then the probability of observing, by chance alone, a survival time of 440 days or more is equal to .1586, or 16 times in 100 observations. (Why?) An incorrect decision for our rule under the condition that H_0 is true will occur only if we had picked, at random, an animal that was slated to survive 440 days or more. The probability of this happening is .1586, so for our test $\alpha = .1586$. This probability is large enough so that in most instances we would accept H_0 and reject H_1, concluding that radiation during the first week of life has no effect on survival. The O.C. curve would be computed as before.

The student should not be fooled by the fact that decisions were reached on the basis of a single observation. First, a good bit had to be known about the behavior of survival times to derive the probability distribution for possible outcomes under H_0. Second, decisions are made on the basis of probabilities, not numbers of obsservation.

SAMPLING DISTRIBUTION OF MEANS

Investigations seldom are conducted on one case. Thus, we want to compare or describe the outcome of a number of observations rather than that of a single one. For example, we could have used 25 animals in the radiation experiment described before. It is obvious that little would be gained by testing hypotheses for each individual score. What we can do instead is to take advantage of the fact that $\bar{X}$ is an estimate of μ and state our hypotheses accordingly:

H_0: Radiation during the first week of life has no effect on length of life. The quantity $\bar{X}$ of the radiated group is an estimate of μ_0 = 420 and deviates from it only by chance.

H_1: Radiation during the first week of life lengthens the life span. The quantity $\bar{X}$ of the radiated group is an estimate of $\mu_1 > (\mu_0$ = 420) and deviates from it only by chance.

These are reasonable hypotheses to test, providing we know the probability distribution for means based on samples of 25 animals.

The distribution of means based on samples of size n obviously differs from that obtained from single scores. Each sample mean tends toward the true mean μ of the total population, so means distribute much tighter about μ than do single scores. Also, the larger the number of cases on which means are based, the more tightly is their distribution clustered around the true mean μ.

We saw in Chapter 6 that

$$\sigma_{\bar{x}} = \frac{\sigma}{\sqrt{n}}$$

That is, to obtain the standard error of the mean for a distribution of means based on a sample size n, we simply divide the standard deviation by the square root of n.

In our example, $\mu = 420$, $\sigma = 20$. If means are obtained from many samples of 25 observations each, these means would still distribute about μ, so μ is the mean of the means as well as the population mean. The standard error of the distribution of means would be

$$\sigma_{\bar{x}} = \frac{20}{\sqrt{25}} = 4$$

(The student may profitably review the discussion on $\sigma_{\bar{x}}$ and empirical examples of Chapter 6.)

Thus we can use $\sigma_{\bar{x}}$ exactly as we used σ previously. Approximately 68 per cent of the observed *means* (not single scores) will lie between $\mu \pm 1\sigma_{\bar{x}}$ and approximately 95 per cent of the observed means will lie between $\mu \pm 2\sigma_{\bar{x}}$. The probability of obtaining, by chance, a mean of greater than a given value is obtained again by finding Z_α and looking up the appropriate probability in the table of the normal distribution.

Example. We continue our previous example for which $\mu = 420$, $\sigma = 20$. We observe a sample of 25 animals that were picked at random and given 50 r during the first week of life. We observe a mean survival time, $\bar{X} = 428$ days. The hypotheses for this case have already been stated before. The rule we evaluate now is as follows:

Reject H_0 if $\bar{X} \geq 428$;
Otherwise accept H_0.

If H_0 is true, then the probability of observing, by chance alone, a mean survival time of 428 days or more is given the proportion of the normal curve that lies to the right of $Z_\alpha = +2$, where

$$Z_\alpha = \frac{\bar{X} - \mu}{\sigma_{\bar{x}}} = \frac{428 - 420}{4} = 2$$

The probability corresponding to this proportion of the normal curve equals to .0228, or roughly 1 time in 50.

An incorrect decision for our rule under conditions that H_0 is true will occur only if we had picked, at random, a group of 25 animals that were slated to survive on the average 428 rather than 420 days. The probability of this happening is the one computed above: namely, .0228. This probability is low enough so that in most instances we would reject H_0, accept H_1, and conclude that radiation does have an effect on survival.

If the outcome of the experiment had been $\bar{X} = 424$ days, our rule would have been

Reject H_0 and accept H_1 if $\bar{X} \geq 424$;
Otherwise accept H_0.

If H_0 is true, then the probability of observing by chance alone, an average survival time of 424 days is equal to .1586 or roughly 16 times in 100. This probability is large enough so that in most instances we would accept H_0 and reject H_1.

If we compare our decisions when using a single case with those using

n animals we see that the problem and its solution as far as the decision model is concerned remains unchanged. What does change is the sensitivity of the experimental design to detect a difference or an effect of a given magnitude. The larger the number of animals, the smaller may be the effect that can be spotted with a fixed certainty, or the larger the number of animals, the greater the certainty with which an effect of fixed magnitude may be spotted. Note that "certainty" actually means a value of α, or the probability of rejecting H_0 erroneously.

Table 7.12 shows the differences in regions of rejection that could be used in the long run for different values of α and different-sized samples. Note that as n increases for each α, the region of rejection for H_1 becomes smaller and smaller. This corresponds to saying that, the larger the sample, the better the chance that the test will pick up a difference due to experimental conditions if it exists. It also means that as n becomes very large, the test will spot differences due to experimental conditions that are extremely small and perhaps even trivial. This latter conclusion becomes troublesome.

Because of automation in data acquisition, sample sizes become extremely large in some instances. Does that mean that differences that were insignificant with samll samples take on new importance when samples are large? There is one area where the introdution of automation and computers has led to a serious re-evaluation of what the crucial elements of scientific decisions are.

Table 7.12. DEPENDENCE OF TYPE I AND II ERRORS ON n FOR ANY FIXED DECISION RULE*

N	$\sigma_{\bar{x}}$	α	β
1	20	.48	.44
4	10	.46	.38
16	5	.42	.27
25	4	.40	.23
100	2	.31	.07
400	1	.16	.001
1000	0.6	.04	.0000003
10000	0.2	.0000003	.0000000

*For $H_0 : \mu_0 = 420$
$H_1 : \mu_1 > 420$
and where $\mu_0 = 420$, $\mu_1 = 424$, $\sigma = 20$ and the decision rule is: Reject H_0 if $\bar{X} > 421$.

USING s TO ESTIMATE $\sigma_{\bar{x}}$

The statistic Z_α can be used only when σ is known. Unfortunately, this is not usually the case. What is true instead is that n observations are taken, $\bar{X}$ and s are computed, the observed value of $\bar{X}$ is used to estimate μ and the observed value of s to estimate σ. Since σ can be estimated from the observed value of s, it would appear reasonable to use the same method as before to test hypotheses on $\bar{X}$, and indeed it is. However, we shall now use a statistic t, which is defined like Z except s instead of σ is used to calculate $\sigma_{\bar{x}}$.

Since σ is estimated by s, $\sigma_{\bar{x}}$ is estimated by $s_{\bar{x}}$, where

$$s_{\bar{x}} = \frac{s}{\sqrt{n}}$$

and the statistic t is defined as

$$t = \frac{\bar{X} - \mu}{s_{\bar{x}}}$$

The quantity t_α may be viewed, therefore, as an estimate of Z_α. However, t is not quite normally distributed unless the sample size n, on which the calculation of s is based, is very large. The reason for the difference in distribution between Z and t lies in the process of sampling. In a normally distributed universe, about 95 per cent of all observations lie between $\mu - 2\sigma$ to $\mu + 2\sigma$, and about 99 per cent lie between $\mu - 3\sigma$ to $\mu + 3\sigma$. Observations that lie more than 2σ or 3σ from the mean are relatively infrequent. Therefore, if a small sample from this universe is taken, it would be unusual if this sample were to contain observations over the whole range of the distribution. The chances are rather good that all observations occur in that part of the universe that lies within 2σ or 3σ of μ. Hence, $s_{\bar{x}}$ is an underestimate of $\sigma_{\bar{x}}$, and the smaller the sample size, the greater the underestimate. As a consequence, if one wishes to cut off the same proportion of the normal curve that is to the right of some value of Z, one has to use more than the equivalent units of t (i.e., t_α would have to be larger than 2 for the same area under the normal curve that lies to the right of $Z_\alpha = 2$). The number of units of t needed to cut off an area equal to that cut off by a specific unit of Z depends on the number of observations on which the calculation of t is based less a number of restrictions due to the need to estimate additional parameters. This number is called *degrees of freedom* (d.f.). (Assume for the present discussion that d.f. $= n - 1$).

The distribution of t for various d.f. is known and could be summarized in tables like the one for the normally distributed Z. However, a large number of tables would be needed, one for each number of d.f. Since for decision models we are interested in a relatively small number of probabilities, these tables are not really needed for most statistical purposes. Rather than loading down the investigator with large numbers of tables, relevant values of t for various d.f. are summarized in a single table (like the one entitled "Percentiles of the t Distribution." Appendix B, Table 8).

The rationale of this summary is that the investigator is usually interested in those values of t that cut off 10, 5, 2.5, 1.0, and 0.5 per cent of the normal curve. Table 8 is divided into four columns. The first column gives different values of d.f. The next three columns give the values of t that cut off .10, .05, and .01 of the area of the t distribution to the right of t_α. For example, for d.f. $= 6$, $t = 1.440$ divides the distribution of t such that 90 per cent lies to the left and 10 per cent to the right; $t = 3.143$ divides the distribution such that 99 per cent lies to the left and 1 per cent to the right. For d.f. $= 20$, the same values that cut off 90 per cent and 99 per cent of the distribution to the left would have to be $t = 1.325$ and $t = 2.528$, respectively. When d.f. becomes very large, the values of t_α needed to cut off a given part of the normal distribution approach those of Z_α. Note the row for which d.f. $= \infty$. Here it takes $t = 1.282$ and $t = 2.326$ to cut the distribution of values of t such that 90 and 99 per cent, respectively, lie to the left and 10 and 1 per cent, respectively, lie to the right. Checking the table of the normal curve, we find that these t values for d.f. $= \infty$ correspond to the same values of Z_α needed to cut off the same proportion of values of Z on the normal curve.

How likely is it that tests between means using small samples will be computed on a high-speed processer? Actually the time it takes to perform a test between means by hand, even if this test is based on a small sample, is large enough, if one also counts time for checking, recomputing, and making up for errors, that it pays to use the high-speed processer even for small samples. If in addition we have a large data file and use it to perform a test of hypothesis for two means in that file, use of the statistic t may be called for, so that both the programs using it as well as the knowledge of its interpretation ought to be at hand.

(Subsequent examples of decisions will use t rather than Z, and we will keep in mind that the value of t approaches that of Z as the numbers of observations become very large.)

TESTING HYPOTHESES ON THE MEANS OF TWO SAMPLES

We are now ready to utilize the sampling distribution of t (or Z) to test hypotheses in situations where σ is estimated by s. The discussion will examine three prototypes that correspond to three different instances of experimental design. It will be noted that these three prototypes are alike in principle.

Case 1: DIFFERENCE BETWEEN A SAMPLE AND A KNOWN OR POSTULATED MEAN

It is known, from years of observation, that the lifetime of rats of a particular strain is 420 days on the average. A random sample of 25 animals are given 50 r of whole body radiation during the first week of life to test the hypothesis that this treatment lengthens their lifespan. The average survival of the sample $\bar{X} = 426.3$ days, with standard deviation $s = 15$ days.

HYPOTHESES

H_0:   Radiation has no effect. The equation $\bar{X} = 426.3$ is an estimate of $\mu_0 = 420$. The deviation of $\bar{X}$ from μ is purely due to chance.

H_1:   Radiation has an effect. The equation $\bar{X} = 426.3$ is an estimate of the average survival time of treated animals, $\mu_1 > 420$.

We next evaluate the rule:

Accept H_1 if $\bar{X} \geq 426.3$; otherwise accept H_0.

The probability of $\bar{X} \geq 426.3$ for the condition that H_0 is true is obtained by finding the appropriate value of t and looking up the associated probability from the table of the t distribution.

Since $s = 15$

$$s_{\bar{x}} = \frac{15}{\sqrt{25}} = 3$$

and

$$t_\alpha = \frac{426.3 - 420}{3} = 2.1$$

For Case 1, d.f. is given by $n - 1$. For our present example $n = 25$, so d.f. $= 24$. Turning to the table of the t distribution, we find that for d.f. $= 20$ a value of $t \geq 1.725$ would occur with probability of .05. Hence we conclude that if H_0 were true, a value of $\bar{X}$ as large as 426.3 or larger would occur by chance alone less than 50 times in 1000 experiments. One would usually reject H_0 for such small probabilities and conclude that the treatment had the effect postulated under H_1. If the results had been that $\bar{X} = 422.7$ with $s = 15$, t would have equaled

$$\frac{422.7 - 420}{3} = .9$$

For d.f. $= 30$, a value of $t \geq 1.310$ would occur by chance with probability of .1. Hence we would have concluded that if H_0 were true, a deviation as large as 422.7 or larger would occur, by chance alone, less than one time in ten experiments. One would usually accept H_0 for such large probabilities and conclude that the treatment had no effect.

Case 1 thus follows the same procedure as our previous example for which σ was known except that t_α rather than Z_α is used to obtain the desired value of α (where, of course, α is the probability of incorrectly rejecting H_0 when it is true). Remember that for Case 1, d.f. $= n - 1$.

Case 2: DIFFERENCE BETWEEN TWO MEANS FOR MATCHED OR CORRELATED GROUPS OF OBSERVATIONS

Observations come from matched groups if they are made on the same subject or materials or from subjects and materials that are paired because they are alike.

We wish to discover if the suggestion of having taken a tranquilizer has a measurable effect. Sixteen subjects are used for the experiment. Each subject is measured for frequency of hand tremor over a five-minute period after having been given a placebo and told it is a tranquilizer. For control, each subject's frequency of hand tremor is measured for five minutes at the same time of day but at a date preceding or following the experimental trial. At the control trial the subject is given the same placebo but told it is a tranquilizer. Scores are given in Table 7.13.

Table 7.13. HAND TREMOR FREQUENCY DATA FOR
TRANQUILIZER EXPERIMENT

Subject No.	Control Score	Experimental Score
01	60	54
02	27	18
03	53	44
04	52	37
05	83	62
06	48	40
07	43	44
08	55	49
09	47	53
10	25	23
11	71	69
12	58	51
13	47	42
14	52	52
15	66	60
16	53	46

To deal with these data, we must first clarify the nature of the observations. Although we observed two scores on each individual, our interest lies in the difference between the scores obtained under experimental conditions and under control conditions. From this point of view, the data look like Table 7.14.

Table 7.14. DIFFERENCE IN TREMOR SCORES OBTAINED
IN TRANQUILIZER EXPERIMENT

Subject No.	$D = (Cont - Exp)$
01	6
02	9
03	9
04	15
05	21
06	8
07	-1
08	6
09	-6
10	2
11	2
12	7
13	5
14	0
15	6
16	7

$$\sum_{i=1}^{16} D = 96$$
$$\bar{D} = 6$$
$$s_d = 6.28$$

Next we express the expectation about the experiment in a form in which it is capable of being tested.

H_0:   The suggestion of having been given a tranquilizer has no effect on hand tremor. The equation $\bar{D} = 6$ is an estimate of a true mean difference $\mu_0 = 0$. Any deviation of $\bar{D}$ from zero is due to chance.

H_1:   The suggestion of having been given a tranquilizer has the effect of reducing spontaneous hand tremor. The equation $\bar{D} = 6$ is an estimate of a true mean difference $\mu_1 > 0$.

Reflect for a moment on the form of H_0. With proper counterbalancing of measurements and other safeguards it is obvious that *if H_0 is true*, then the sum of the differences between repeated measurements on the same subjects should be equal to zero and will approach this value if a sufficiently large number of observations are taken. In this way, we have actually reduced Case 2 to Case 1 for which the solution has been worked out already. The crux of the matter is, of course, that experimental conditions have to be arranged such that H_0 could be true and that H_1 is the only alternative. This would not be true if, for instance, the control observation had always preceded the experimental session. The observed difference could have been due to adaptation rather than suggestion. Similarly, if no placebo had been given during the control session, the observed difference could have been due to whatever was in the placebo rather than to the suggestion.

Failure to control the experiment adequately so that the final analysis is restricted to the desired hypotheses is called *confounding*. Thus the final decision model determines the experimental design rather than the other way around. This relationship should be uppermost in the mind of the investigator when he designs an experiment or evaluates a study performed by a colleague.

The final analysis of the data in Tables 7.13 and 7.14 follows the lines laid down by Case 1.

$$s_{\bar{D}} = \frac{6.28}{\sqrt{16}} = 1.57$$

$$t = \frac{\bar{D} - \mu}{s_{\bar{D}}} = \frac{6 - 0}{1.57} = 3.82$$

$$P[\bar{D} \geq 6] = P[t \geq 3.82] < .01$$

For Case 2, d.f. = n − 1. Thus if we decide to reject H_0 if $\bar{D} \geq 6$, we stand to make an error in this decision with a probability α that is less than .01. Note that our table of the t distribution does not give values beyond $t = 2.602$ for d.f. = 15. For most purposes, a value of $\alpha \leq .01$ is sufficient to reject H_0. More complete tables of the t distribution are available and can be consulted if desired.

Case 3: DIFFERENCES BETWEEN THE MEANS OF INDEPENDENT SAMPLES

Observations are considered independent of each other when one observation only is made on each subject or material and where subjects or materials are assigned at random to either of the comparison groups.

We are going to consider the same experiment as in Case 2. However, we now use two groups of 16 subjects, each formed by dividing 32 subjects into two groups by a random procedure. One group of subjects is given a placebo and told it is a placebo. One group of subjects is given a placebo and told it is a tranquilizer. Frequency of hand tremor is measured for each subject under identical conditions. Also, experimental and control subjects are tested in a random order. The results are shown in Table 7.15.

Although we cannot reduce the data to single difference scores for each subject as in Case 2, we can state H_0 and H_1 as before. If suggestion has no effect on hand tremor, then the two means $\bar{C}$ and $\bar{E}$ ought to be alike and their difference $\bar{D} = \bar{C} - \bar{E}$ an estimate of a true mean of zero. The difference between Case 2 and Case 3 lies in the calculation of $s_{\bar{D}}$, the standard error of the mean difference $\bar{D}$. In Case 2, $s_{\bar{D}}$ was computed from s_D, which, in turn, was the standard deviation of the observed difference scores. To compute $s_{\bar{D}}$ for Case 3 we take advantage of the following relationship (which we are not going to prove here).

$$s_{A \pm B} = \sqrt{s_A^2 + s_B^2} \qquad (15)$$

This relationship is true if A and B are uncorrelated or unmatched observations.

Thus,

$$s_{\bar{D}} = s_{\bar{C} - \bar{E}} = \sqrt{s_{\bar{C}}^2 + s_{\bar{E}}^2}$$

$$= \sqrt{\frac{s_C^2}{n_C} + \frac{s_E^2}{n_E}}$$

$$= \sqrt{13.025 + 10.894}$$

$$= 4.89$$

Since $\bar{D} = 6$,

$$t = \frac{\bar{D} - \mu}{s_{\bar{D}}} = \frac{6 - 0}{4.89} = 1.23$$

For Case 3, d.f. $= n_C + n_E - 2$, or, in this case d.f. $= 30$. For d.f. $= 30$, a value of $t = 1.31$ or larger would occur with $P \leq .1$. For practical purposes

Table 7.15. RESULTS OF PLACEBO TESTS ON TWO
INDEPENDENT GROUPS

Control C	Experimentals E
C	E
53	54
66	18
52	44
47	37
58	62
71	40
25	44
47	49
55	53
43	23
48	69
83	51
52	42
53	52
27	60
60	46
$\Sigma C = 840$	$\Sigma E = 744$
$s_C = \sqrt{208.4}$	$s_E = \sqrt{174.3}$

$$s_{\bar{C}} = \sqrt{\frac{208.4}{16}} = \sqrt{13.025}; \qquad s_{\bar{E}} = \sqrt{\frac{174.3}{16}} = \sqrt{10.894}$$

we can use this probability to estimate α for our test if we were to reject H_0 for $t \geq 1.23$.

$$P[\bar{D} \geq 6] = P[t \geq 1.23] \simeq .1$$

Thus if we decide to reject H_0 if $\bar{D} \geq 6$, we stand to make an error in this decision with a probability α that is slightly larger than .1. This is usually considered a borderline probability for the acceptance or rejection of H_0. Some investigators would accept H_0, some would reject it, and most would increase the number of observations and retest the hypotheses on additional data.

Compare the outcome of the examples in Case 2 and Case 3. The same data were used. However, since in Case 2 each subject served as his own control, the variation between subjects did not affect our estimate of $s_{\bar{D}}$. This was not true for Case 3. Here variations between subjects enter as part of the estimate of $s_{\bar{D}}$, so a larger variation is involved. This is one example of how some experimental designs are more *efficient* than others in evaluating a possible experimental effect. The concept of efficiency is important to keep in mind, since the more efficient the design of the experiment (i.e., the more efficient the test that can be performed on the data), the fewer observations need be accumulated.

If the numbers of observations are very small, the efficiency of the Case 3 design can be increased by pooling observations from both groups.

Suppose we had the following data:

C	E	
		$n_C = 3$
4	0	$\sum C = 15$
5	1	$\sum C^2 = 77$
6	1	$n_E = 6$
	2	$\sum E = 7$
	1	$\sum E^2 = 11$
	2	

We can obtain a pooled estimate of the value of σ for the assumption that H_0 is true, where s_p is the pooled standard deviation

$$s_p = \sqrt{\frac{\sum (C - \bar{C})^2 + \sum (E - \bar{E})^2}{n_C + n_E - 2}} \tag{16}$$

Note that this estimate of σ is independent of the value of any of the means, since $(C - \bar{C})$ and $(E - \bar{E})$ are the deviations from whatever value the mean might have. (The deviation of 3 from a mean of 10 is the same as the deviation of 3 from a mean of 10,000).

For our data

$$s_p = \sqrt{\frac{4.87}{7}} = \sqrt{.7}$$

Next we compute $s_{\bar{C}}$ and $s_{\bar{E}}$.

$$s_{\bar{C}} = \frac{s_p}{\sqrt{n_C}} = \sqrt{\frac{.7}{3}}$$

$$s_{\bar{E}} = \frac{s_p}{\sqrt{n_E}} = \sqrt{\frac{.7}{6}}$$

and from equation (15) we know that

$$s_{\bar{D}} = \sqrt{\frac{.7}{3} + \frac{.7}{6}} \simeq .6$$

To compute t we have

$$t = \frac{(\bar{C} - \bar{E}) - 0}{s_{\bar{D}}} = \frac{5 - 1.83}{.6} = 5.3$$

The value of $t = 5.3$ would then be evaluated for d.f. $= N_C + N_E - 2 = 7$.

In summary, Cases 1, 2, and 3 are proper models for testing differences between two means. There are two important questions with which we need to concern ourselves right now. Are these the proper models if we compare population on more than two means? If not, what is the proper model to use in such cases?

PROBLEMS IN USING TESTS OF HYPOTHESES BETWEEN TWO MEANS IF MORE THAN TWO MEANS ARE INVOLVED

An investigator is interested in determining whether the season of year at birth or conception in any way affects the intelligence of an individual. He obtains birth records from a school for mentally retarded children and computes the average number of individuals born during each month of the year for n years. He ends up with 12 means, each mean being the average number of individuals in the institution who were born during a particular month. It is noticed that the average number of births during the month of February has the largest mean and the average number of births during the month of October the smallest one. He then tests the hypothesis that the difference between these two means is due to chance.

Let us see whether the investigator really can proceed in this way.

First, we shall assume that the date of birth is distributed randomly throughout the year. If this is the case, then the mean for each of the 12 months corresponds to a mean based on n observations selected at random. However, by random chance alone these means ought to be distributed in such a way that some are higher and some are lower. In fact, where μ is the true average number of births and σ the true standard deviation we might expect that the population of 12 means will be distributed normally around μ with

$$\sigma_{\bar{x}} = \frac{\sigma}{\sqrt{n}}$$

If our sampling has been done truly at random (and we assume that this is the case), then we would expect 10 of these 12 means (which correspond to 83 per cent of all the means) to fall within $\pm 1.4\ \sigma_{\bar{x}}$ units from the mean. This means that the remaining two observations, those which we may expect to form the highest and the lowest mean, could be expected to be 2.4 $\sigma_{\bar{x}}$ units apart from each other by random chance alone. Thus if we observe a t_{α} equal to 2.8 or larger, we cannot conclude that we have demonstrated in this way a so-called statistically significant difference between two means. We have really observed exactly what we would expect to observe if chance had been the only criterion for selection of means.

As a general rule it is clear that the larger the number of observations, the larger the chance differences that may be expected to be included in the sample. We may link this experience to a poker game. A stranger stepping into a game with individuals whom he has never met before, drawing a hand of four aces on the first hand, and being beaten by a royal flush would be well advised to leave this game, since the chances are rather good that it is crooked The same person playing in a weekly game with his friends over a period of 25 years, drawing four aces and being beaten by a royal flush would shrug off such an event as "tough luck." The difference between these two instances is that he has only a single observation for inference in the first case, whereas in the second instance he has enough data to support his view that sooner or later somebody holding four aces will be beaten by someone else who holds a royal flush.

Prior to the advent of automation this particular problem was relatively easy to deal with. An investigator wishing to undertake a multivariate study would limit his observations to four or five variables. He could adopt a design such as the analysis of variance (which we shall look at in a later chapter) and very profitably compare multiple effects as well as interactions among a few limited variables. The observation of many different variables was limited, however, as were multiple comparisons, by the cost and effort required for them. All this has changed now. When large data files, which give many measurements for comparison between different groups (such as different patients or social classes), are used, it would be fatal to compare means of observation category by observation category and select only those for attention or report which appear to give a "striking" difference.

Let us say that we had two data files, one on individuals labeled "upper upper" and one on individuals labeled as "lower lower" class status by some instrument of classification. Let us also assume that we have measurements in this file on some 250 variables. If we were to adopt the position that a difference that would be observed by chance no more often than one time in 20 will be considered an indication of significant effect, then, if there were no differences at all underlying the measurements in our two data files except those caused by random chance, we would expect to make approximately 25 incorrect decisions by deciding that a true difference between two variables would exist. (Why?) Similarly, of course, we would make an unknown number of incorrect decisions deciding that a true difference between two variables does not exist where it actually does.

Let us assume now that we actually compare two such data files, each containing as many as 250 variables. Let us assume further that we subject each category of measurement (or variable) to a t test and reject H_0 for all differences for which $\alpha \leq .05$. Let us also say that we make this decision 33 times.

We can now take two views with respect to our findings. We could say that since we expected to make this decision 25 times even if no differences at all exist between our files and the universe of measures from which our files are random samples, the fact that we have made it 33 times fails to impress us. In fact, we can compute the probability of deciding wrongly that such a difference exists 33 times or more if none of the differences observed are really a reflection of the true difference between two variables. The chance that this will occur is roughly one in ten.

Our second position could be that there may be some differences between variables which are real and reflect a true population difference among these tests. The question is, however, which ones are they? Offhand it seems that we could solve this problem by taking additional observations. If we started with n observations and we now take another set of n observations, it would appear that we could compare the outcome of these two studies. We would accept only those "significant" differences as indicating a true difference that occur in both samples.

It is open to question if this is really a permissible procedure. On first glance it would seem that such a procedure constitutes verification. However, this is not necessarily true.

Let us start with the supposition that our sample size was $2n$ rather than n. This may very well be the opinion of an individual who is presented with all the data after it has been accumulated. We now divide our total set of $2n$ observations into two groups of n each.

If a difference resulting from sampling error exists in this population it ought to show up in both groups, providing that the only differentiation between groups 1 and 2 is chance selection. We are thus no better off than before, except that we now have a larger number of observations. On the other hand, if a difference between two variables appears time after time in successive samples, we will be forced to conclude that this reflects a real difference in the world about us.

We do not wish the student to form a firm opinion about this problem. However, he should keep in mind that such a problem does exist. Whenever multiple comparisons are made, some of them are bound to be impressively large. They cannot be evaluated by themselves by disregarding other observations that may seem to be less important.

SOME MULTIPLE COMPARISON TESTS
FOR SMALL NUMBERS OF VARIABLES

Let us return to the example in this chapter in which we compared a control group that was given a placebo and told it was a placebo with an experimental group that was given a placebo and told it was a tranquilizer (Table 7.15). Let us enlarge the number of experimental groups to five by varying the instructions given with the placebo. Group 1 is told the placebo is a tranquilizer; Group 2 is told it is a sleep producer; Group 3 is told it will relax circulation; Group 4 is told it will dampen all outside stimulation; and Group 5 is told it will bring forth pleasant memories. Amount of tremor is measured for all five groups. Let us label the mean of the control group as $\bar{X}_c$ and the means of the other five groups as $\bar{X}_1, \bar{X}_2, \bar{X}_3, \bar{X}_4$, and $\bar{X}_5$.

When the population variance is s_i^2, the variance of each mean is

$$s_{\bar{x}_i}^2 = \frac{s_i^2}{n_i}$$

where n_i is the number of repetitions for the ith measure.

The variance of the difference between any two treatment means is equal to

$$s_{d_{ic}}^2 = \frac{s_i^2}{n_i} + \frac{s_c^2}{n_c}$$

where

$$d_{ic} = \bar{X}_i - \bar{X}_c$$

When there are only two means, we would compute the Z_α or t_α by

$$Z_\alpha \text{ or } t_\alpha = \frac{d_{ic}}{s_{d_{ic}}}$$

However, we really have five comparisons:

$$d_{1c} = \bar{X}_1 - \bar{X}_c$$
$$d_{2c} = \bar{X}_2 - \bar{X}_c$$
$$d_{3c} = \bar{X}_3 - \bar{X}_c$$
$$d_{4c} = \bar{X}_4 - \bar{X}_c$$
$$d_{5c} = \bar{X}_5 - \bar{X}_c$$

It is obvious that the probability of observing a large value of Z_α or t_α increases with the number of comparisons which we are going to make.

If α is the probability with which we reject H_0, for any one of the comparisons, then $1 - \alpha$ is the probability that we will accept H_0 when we should (or make the correct decision). If we have n comparisons, the probability that *at least one* of these comparisons will yield a value of a test large enough for H_0 to be rejected is equal to

$$\alpha' = 1 - (1 - 2\alpha)^n$$

(where positive or negative differences could be accepted as significant). Thus, if we decide to reject H_0, using α as a criterion for rejection when $\alpha = .05$, and then making 5 comparisons, the probability that we will reject at least one of these five comparisons by chance alone, α', is given by

$$\alpha' = 1 - (.9)^5$$
$$= .41$$

or the probability is roughly 40 per cent that we will make the incorrect decision using this criterion.

We can overcome the problem of making the wrong decision by increasing the value of t needed to make a decision at the same level of probability as α. A t table corresponding to the number of treatments to be compared with a control group has been constructed by Dunnett. The larger the number of treatments, the larger would be the value of t selected by Dunnett's criteria to make a test at a given level of probability. (For instance, for $\alpha = .05$ and d.f. $= 20$, we would use $t_\alpha = 2.73$ rather than $t = 2.09$. A copy of this table by Dunnett is given in *Biometrics*, **20**, 1964.)

This type of procedure is limited to the situation in which the number of variables or comparisons with a control is relatively small or in which we are interested just in determining whether one of these comparisons yields a difference so large that we will want to decide there is a true difference without making a judgment about any of the comparisons.

Tukey has provided us with another multiple comparison test if these conditions do not hold. As we have already mentioned before, in any sample of means there will be a maximum and minimum value. The difference between these is commonly called the *range*. Furthermore, it was pointed out that the larger our sample, the more frequently will we expect to observe very deviant observations. (Remember this presented a problem in estimating the true value of α.) We can view the distance defined by the range as measured in units of standard deviation:

$$q = \frac{\text{Range}}{s}$$

The quantity q has been called the *studentized range*. Of course, the actual value of q, as well as its distribution, will vary with sample size and the actual magnitude of the standard deviation.

The procedure of testing all possible pairs of treatment means is based on the distribution of q. When our comparisons are all of the form

$$\bar{X}_i - \bar{X}_j$$

Tukey's T is given by

$$T = \frac{q}{\sqrt{2}} \qquad (13)$$

The probabilities associated with Tukey's T may be obtained from J. W. Tukey, *The Problem of Multiple Comparisons*, Princeton University Press, Princeton, New Jersey, 1953.

The problems raised by multiple comparisons have just began to come to the attention of the investigator. We shall see later on how they affect us in devising adequate techniques for the evaluation of large data files and multivariate data.

TESTS BETWEEN TWO VARIANCES: THE VARIANCE RATIO

There are many occasions when we want to test the hypothesis that two independent estimates of a variance come from the same population of measurements. Such a test is similar in principle to determining if two independent means are estimates from one or two separate populations but is somewhat more complex. This is so because the sampling distribution of σ^2 is changed for small numbers of observations, and the shape of this distribution depends on this number. Rather than consider the difference between estimates it was found to be more suitable to deal with their ratios. When s_1^2 and s_2^2 are two independent estimates of a variance with n_1 and n_2 observations,

$$F = \frac{s_1^2}{s_2^2}$$

is known as the variance or F ratio (F was selected in honor of the great geneticist and statistician Sir Ronald Fisher). The sampling distribution of F is given by

$$F_r(F) = \frac{\Gamma\left(\dfrac{d_1 + d_2}{2}\right) d_1^{d_1/2} d_2^{d_2/2}}{\Gamma\left(\dfrac{d_1}{2}\right)\Gamma\left(\dfrac{d_2}{2}\right)} \times \frac{F^{(d_1 - d_2)/2}}{(d_1 F + d_2)^{(d_1 + d_2)/2}}$$

(where d_1 and d_2 are degrees of freedom for estimating s_1^2 and s_2^2. This means that $d_1 = n_1 - 1$ in most cases.) From this expression a program will evaluate the exact $F_r(F > k)$ whenever required. However, as is the case with other sampling distributions, crucial values of F have been assembled in tables so that they may be looked up conveniently.

We can see from the sampling distribution of F that it depends on the two parameters d_1 and d_2. This means that there are as many different curves of this sampling distribution as there are values of d_1 and d_2 or n_1 and n_2. To make it possible at all to collate crucial values of F into a table that makes any sense, it is assumed that the greater variance has been divided by the smaller each time (so that $F \geq 1$ always), and each table is limited to only those values of F that cut off the same part of the area under the distribution curve for different values of d_1 and d_2. The resulting table is then of those values to which F would be equal or would exceed with a specific probability. Two such tables are included in Appendix B, one for $P(F \geq k) = .05$ and one for $P(F \geq k) = .01$, to which we shall refer as the five per cent and the one per cent probability tables.

The tables are arranged so that each row and column represents a specific value of d.f. Each cell entry is thus at the intersection of two values of d.f. and stands for that value which an observed F may be expected to exceed by chance five or one per cent of the time. For instance, if we have $s_1^2 = 5.72$ with $n_1 = 7$ (i.e., $d_1 = 6$) and $s_2^2 = 2.2$ with $n_2 = 21$ (i.e., $d_2 = 20$), then

$$F = \frac{5.72}{2.2} = 2.6$$

Entering the five per cent table at the column labeled d.f. = 6 and the row labeled d.f. = 20, we find that a value of F of 2.6 or larger may be expected to occur by chance alone one time in 20. (Actually, the probability in this example will have to be modified, because we divided the larger variance by the smaller so that in this case $P = .1$, not .05. But we shall see later that there are instances in which the variance in the numerator is always going to be equal to or larger than the variance in the denominator, so that the table magnitude of F will reflect the actual probability rather than half its value.)

We introduce the notion of the F ratio now because this test is useful in some instances where we want to make statements about the shape of specific curves. The major uses of F are in connection with testing hypotheses about means of groups that may differ on many levels of experimental conditions. These techniques are referred to as the *analyses of variance* (or ANOVA) and will be taken up in detail in Chapter 11.

PROBLEMS

1. The weight of Chinese females is known to be normally distributed with $\mu = 96$ lb and $\sigma = 8$ lb. Where X is the weight of a Chinese woman selected at random, find:
   (a) $P(X > 92)$.
   (b) $P(X < 96)$.
   (c) $P(X < 114)$.
   (d) $P(X > 116)$.
   (e) $P(92 < X < 94)$.
   (f) $P(98 > X > 88)$.

2. If $\sigma = 4$, answer questions (a) through (f) from Problem 1. Do the same for $\mu = 100$ and $\sigma = 8$.

3. Find the 70, 60, and 40 percentile of the three distributions in Problems 1 and 2.

4. Where $\bar{X}$ is the sample weight based on the weights of 16 randomly selected Chinese women, find
   (a) $P(\bar{X} < 98)$.
   (b) $P(100 < \bar{X} < 96)$.
   (Using μ and σ from Problems 1 and 2.)

5. Select a sample of 10, 20, and 30 single integers (i.e., 0 through 9) from a table of random numbers. Compute $\bar{X}$, and s, and estimate $\sigma_{\bar{x}}$. Compare these values with the known values of μ and σ for the population of random integers.

6. Compute the probability that a mean based on samples of 16, 25, or 64 randomly selected single integers is larger than five.

7. The average birth weight is known to be 6.8 lb with $\sigma = 1.2$.
   (a) What is the probability that a normal infant weighs more than 7.4 lb, 8.0 lb, or 8.6 lb or less than 6.2 lb, 5.6 lb, or 5.0 lb?

   (b) What is the probability that the average weight of a sample of 16 infants ($\bar{X}$) will be heavier than 7.4 lb or 8 lb or lighter than 6.2 lb or 5.6 lb?

8. Compute enough points so that you can sketch the O.C. curve for the rule:

   Reject H_0 and accept H_1 if $\bar{X} < 5.6$; otherwise accept H_0.

   for a sample of $n = 16$ and σ known to be 1.2. (Assume that when H_1 is true, $\sigma_1 = 1.2$ also.)

9. A group of identical twins are used in an experiment. One child from each pair is taught to program a computer, the other is not and serves as the control. IQ measures are obtained from each child, and the results are given below:

Pair	IQ of Child Taught to Program	IQ of Control Child
A	91	100
B	78	87
C	118	118
D	96	98
E	67	77
F	96	104
G	84	90
H	102	104
I	99	106
J	108	114
K	76	98
L	90	96
M	104	106
N	121	124
O	82	87
P	84	94

(a) Test the hypothesis that computer training hurts intelligence. Set up and state clearly alternative hypotheses and obtain the value of α for H_0.

(b) What would be the outcome of the same analysis if, instead of twins, the investigator had used two randomly selected populations of 16 children each and had obtained the same results?

10. An experiment on a sobriety drug tests the ability of a drunk to insert a key into a lock. Two groups are compared with results (in seconds) given below.

Time with Drug	Time without Drug
8	10
4	9
4	4
6	8
2	

Does the sobriety drug show a significant effect?

11. An investigator compares two groups of subjects on ten measures. If he would reject H_0 ordinarily with $\alpha = .1$, what is the probability that he will reject H_0 for at least one test in error? What is the probability that he will make the same error for at least two tests?

12. Construct a flow chart for a program that will handle the t test for Cases 1, 2, and 3.

8 DESCRIBING DETERMINISTIC ASSOCIATIONS

We have previously explored the notion that a set of rules relating the nature of a consequence C with some antecedent conditions A may often crystallize into a more precise statement or function. The conditions under which such functions can be derived are very special and, when we come right down to it, quite restrictive. In order to develop such a function, it is usually necessary for the pertinent variables to be measurable along continuous scales. The same holds true for the description of the phenomenon itself. If we wish to derive a precise (which often implies also a mathematical) statement in which the magnitude or intensity of a particular variable is expressed as a function of the magnitude or intensity of one or more antecedent variables, it must be realized that we are counting on the assumption that the behavior of the numbers parallels that of the variables they represent. In this sense, the equation is really a model of the observed system.

Such models are drawn from a highly complex universe in which the prediction of most outcomes must be qualified with a statement or estimate of the likelihood with which that outcome will occur, as opposed to some alternative. When the outcome in question can be expressed as a measure along some continuous scale, then a set of alternative consequences can be represented by a range of values along that scale, and relative likelihoods can be attached for obtaining one value in contrast to some other one for a given set of antecedent conditions. Furthermore, if the action of a particular consequent variable is dictated predominantly by one or a very small number of antecedent conditions, the resulting tendency is for the range of alternatives along the dependent variable's scale to contract, so that a particular set of antecedent values produces a particular consequent magnitude more and more consistently. When such is the case, the range of doubt

328

surrounding a particular consequent value is fairly small, so that repeated observations at a given antecedent condition are avoided in favor of a dispersion of observations over a maximum number and range of antecedent values (Figure 8.1). The error in such situations can usually be traced in great part to imprecise and/or improper experimental techniques, instrumentation,

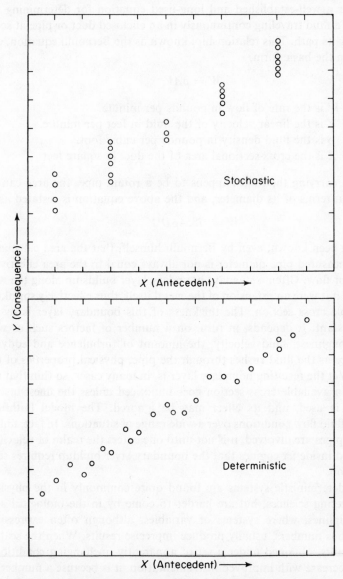

Fig. 8.1. Typical characteristics of continuous experimental data.

or measurements, and can therefore be improved by an appropriate tightening of these factors.

A system of variables in which the consistency and predictability of a consequence responds in this manner to improved instrumentation and observational techniques is said to be a *deterministic system* and is potentially expressible by a deterministic model. As an example of such a model, let us consider a well-established and long-used equation for determining the velocity of a fluid traveling continuously in an enclosed duct or pipe at some point along its path. This relationship, known as the Bernoulli equation, can be stated in the basic form,

$$W = \rho A V \tag{1}$$

where W is the rate of flow in pounds per minute.
V is the linear velocity of the fluid in feet per minute.
ρ is the fluid density in pounds per cubic foot.
A is the cross-sectional area of the duct in square feet.

If the duct carrying the fluid happens to be a round pipe, the area can be expressed in terms of its diameter, and the above equation is restated as

$$W = .7854\rho D^2 V \tag{2}$$

It has long been known, even by Bernoulli himself, that the area calculated from the measured pipe diameter is not always equal to the area effectively available for flow. Often a stagnant boundary layer builds up along the wall and acts as if it were an extension of the metal itself, thus effectively shrinking the available cross section. The thickness of this boundary layer is by no means constant. It depends, in turn, on a number of factors such as wall size and roughness, fluid velocity, the amount of turbulence and eddying taking place as the fluid rushes through the pipe, physical properties of the fluid, etc. Yet the resulting boundary layer is, in many cases, so thin that the reduction in available cross section goes unnoticed unless the finest instrumentation is used, and its effect may be ignored. The model faithfully represents fluid flow conditions over a wide range of situations. In fact, unless very small pipes are involved, it is not until one enters the realm of velocities encountered inside jet engines that the boundary layer buildup requires serious attention.

Such deterministic systems are found quite commonly in the physical and engineering sciences, but are harder to come by in the biological and social disciplines, where systems of variables, although often expressible as continuous numbers, usually produce imprecise results. When the scatter of such results, obtained under a set of apparently unchanging conditions, does not decrease with improved instrumentation, it is because a number of variables combine to produce a joint effect. The actions of many of these variables are unknown to the investigator; others may have a known effect but of such minor magnitude that they are permitted to vary freely. As a consequence, random variation is part of the biological and social phenomenon in most instances. These situations, which cannot be handled deterministically, are termed *stochastic systems*. A separate group of techniques is often necessary for their manipulation and analysis, as will be discussed in the next chapter.

EMPIRICAL EQUATIONS

Once the controlling antecedent variable or variables have been identified, the mathematical description of the form $C = f(A)$ about a particular system of interest may proceed along one of two basic pathways. In some situations, the precise form of the equation can be derived from theoretical considerations or deduced intuitively by the investigator on the basis of his observations and experience. This type of procedure leads to an equation in which the basic structure is determined and the precise values of its numerical components remain to be defined. A case in point is seen in the formulation of the relationship that describes a moving body. If a force is applied to a moving body such that it causes that object to accelerate at a constant rate (i.e., its velocity increases by a fixed amount every second), we can construct an equation for the velocity of this object at any time t by saying that this velocity would be the sum of whatever velocity it may have started out with and the velocity it managed to build up by that time t as a direct result of its acceleration. Symbolically stated, such a relationship is written as

$$V_t = V_0 + at \qquad (3)$$

where V_0 is the initial velocity, expressed in feet per second.

  t is the elapsed time since the beginning of our observation, expressed in seconds.

  a is the rate of acceleration, expressed in feet per second per second.

This relationship is depicted for a particular value of V_0 and a in Figure 8.2. Taking this a step further, we can derive an expression for the distance traveled by this moving object over some time period t. If we intuitively accept the notion that distance is the product of velocity and time, and we realize from expression (3) that velocity in this case is a varying function of time, we can reach the conclusion that the distance can be represented by the area under the line in Figure 8.2 from time zero to time t. Otherwise stated,

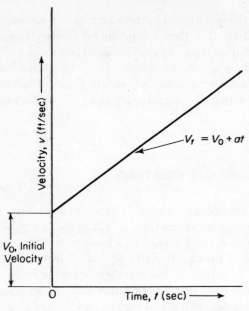

Fig. 8.2 Deterministic model relating velocity to initial velocity and time.

$$S_t = \int_0^t (V_0 + at)\, dt \tag{4}$$

This works out to be

$$S_t = V_0 t + \tfrac{1}{2}at^2 + K \tag{5}$$

The value of the constant of integration K can be determined by taking advantage of the fact that when $t = 0$, the moving body has covered no distance at all, or

$$S_0 = 0 = V_0(0) + \tfrac{1}{2}a(0)^2 + K \tag{6}$$

Thus the integration constant $K = 0$ and the expression becomes

$$S_t = V_0 t + \tfrac{1}{2}at^2 \tag{7}$$

This gives us a deterministic model for predicting the distance traversed by a moving body under constant acceleration. If the body happens to be in free fall, a special case results in which the accelerating force is supplied by gravity, and our expression becomes

$$S_t = V_0 t + \tfrac{1}{2}gt^2 \tag{8}$$

Having established this relationship, one could presumably determine the value of g by measuring the time it takes for various objects to fall from different known heights. (Elimination of the $V_0 t$ term by imparting no initial velocity simplifies such experiments considerably.) We now know that a large number of such observations would cluster around a g value of roughly 32.17 ft/sec/sec. Thus, the equation

$$S_t = 16.085t^2 \qquad (9)$$

represents a good deterministic model for depicting the activity of a body with no initial velocity in free fall on earth. The fact that this particularization of expression (7) gives accurate prediction over an extremely wide range of conditions indicates that the equation accounts for the dominating effect. Yet we know that it does not account for all of the factors. As an example, let us consider the constancy of g. Because there was no need to do otherwise, most of us ignore the fact that the value of g is dependent on the distance from the center of the earth to where it is measured. The range of distance between the deepest valley and the altitude of the highest flying plane is sufficiently inconsequential to preclude any concern about g. To people in the business of launching rockets and placing satellites in orbit, however, the variability of g looms as an important factor that must be taken into account.

In contrast to such derived equations, the empirical relation constitutes an attempt to predict C from A without any prior attention being paid to the particular form which that equation must "naturally," "intuitively," or "theoretically" assume. For example, a well-known equation in thermodynamics developed by Kistyakowsky is used to predict the amount of heat required to vaporize a particular liquid compound as a function of the temperature at which it boils under normal atmospheric pressure. The expression is

$$H_v = \frac{8.75T_b + 4.571T_b \log_{10} T_b}{MW}$$

where H_v is the heat (expressed in calories) required to vaporize one
    gram of liquid.
    T_b is the boiling point of the liquid in degrees Kelvin (degrees
    centigrade $+ 273$).
MW is the molecular weight of the compound, expressed in grams.

This equation gives excellent agreement with experimentally determined results for a wide variety of biochemical and other nonpolar liquids. However, there is no fundamental chemical or thermodynamic reason underlying either the form that the equation takes or the magnitude of the constants in it. (Attempts made to provide such reasons after the equation has been developed should not be confused with derivations made prior to the curve-fitting process.)

DEVELOPMENT OF EQUATIONS

Although there is virtually a limitless choice of forms that can be used for fitting equations to experimental data, actual usage is limited to a very small number of curve types. Unless the observed trends exhibit some special quirk, it is possible to represent the data adequately with one of a relatively limited repertoire of fairly simple functions. The amount of payoff achieved by resorting to much more complicated relations is often inconsistent with the extra effort involved and, in some cases, introduces artificial corrections that are outside the range of sensitivity of the data themselves.

CHOICE OF FORM

When there is insufficient theoretical structure, the investigator must find and utilize some other basis for selecting the particular type of equation to be used to fit his data. In some cases he is guided by previous work in which a particular type of equation was used to fit data for a similar phenomenon. In other instances, there may be no precedent to guide the selection, but the investigator may have fundamental reasons for establishing some particular point on the curve. Such a point need not even be one that has been experimentally observed. The most typical case is the identification of limiting conditions of the dependent variable Y at extreme values of the independent variable X. The fact that the distance traveled by an object at time zero $= 0$ for example [see expression (5)] is a case in point. Such limits, called *boundary conditions*, are real values on a curve and are considered as having no error attached to them. A second type of pre-established boundary value is one that sets a limit of Y that is not exceeded no matter how large X may get. For example, in certain types of curves which show the temperature rise for a material being heated by a particular source, there is a maximum attainable equilibrium temperature towards which the material tends but does not exceed, no matter how long it is heated.

When a backlog of experience is not available, the investigator has nothing to work with but the data themselves, and he must seek criteria for choice in their contents. In this endeavor he is helped by and can take advantage of the fact that each type of equation possesses a unique set of numerical properties. When such equations are displayed graphically, these characteristics become visually apparent and are sufficiently consistent that the observer can train himself to link a particular type of graph with a corresponding form of equation. With such recognition criteria established, he can inspect a scattergram and, if a consistent trend is evident, he can make a decision about the type of equation that would be most suitable for a mathematical description of his data.

In some cases the distinctions among various types of equations are sufficiently clear-cut that they can be articulated in precise terms. When this is the case, it is possible to formulate algorithms around these distinctions so that the inspection of the raw data, followed by the choice of an appropriate equation type, can be performed as part of an automatic information handling procedure. In general, these distinctions become increasingly vague when the available set of data covers only a narrow range of values. If this range is sufficiently small, there may not be enough of a trend displayed to allow the development of a particular set of operating characteristics, so that in effect the data appear to fit any one of a number of equations equally well. Under such circumstances, the use of an empirical equation to predict consequences from antecedent conditions outside of the range of observed values is a dangerous pastime and should be carefully avoided.

CRITERIA FOR GOODNESS OF FIT

Regardless of the reason for choosing a particular type of equation to represent a set of experimental data, its applicability must ultimately be assessed by some indicator which shows how well the data are represented by that equation. Such indices may be expressed in a number of ways, all of which reflect the amount of disparity between an observed value of a consequent variable and that which would be predicted by the equation at the same antecedent conditions. It is important to note that these "goodness of fit" criteria cast no light on how well the phenomenon is represented by the data. It is still up to the investigator to determine this, so that he can evaluate the error of prediction in the perspective of experimental accuracy and precision. In fact, this point serves as an additional, very useful criterion for discussing deterministic as opposed to stochastic situations. The deterministic model strives to produce a useful numerical expression for predicting $C = f(A)$ with the underlying implication that, except for small errors of measurement, the observed values reflect true magnitudes. The stochastic structure, on the other hand, treats the observed data as a series of distributions that cluster around a set of true values. Consequently, the results of stochastic analyses take the form of estimates used to predict the most probable consequences for given antecedents.

Table 8.1 gives a set of X and Y values. Inspection of these points (plotted in Figure 8.3) indicates that a straight line will provide a fairly good representation of the relation between the two variables. Such a line, shown in the figure, has the equation

$$\tilde{Y} = 1.41X + 0.67 \tag{11}$$

(The mechanism for selecting this line over other, somewhat different lines which can be drawn for the same set of data is not important for the immediate discussion, and will be taken up later. The assessment of goodness of fit, if consistent, is applicable to any such line.) It is seen that this line does

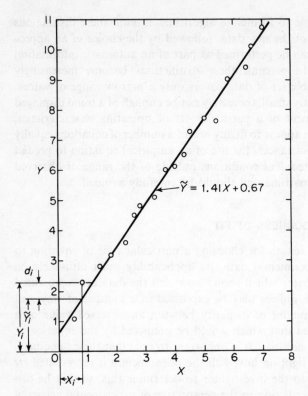

Fig. 8.3. Linear X-Y data.

not intersect with all of the data points. In fact, it is possible for a line representing a perfectly satisfactory equation to come close to but not intersect any of the observed points.

The proximity of each data point to the graph of the equation is expressed as an absolute deviation having the form

$$d_i = |Y_i - \tilde{Y}_i| \qquad (12)$$

where $\tilde{Y}_i$ is the value of the dependent (consequent) variable calculated from the equation for the value of X_i.

Y_i is the observed value of this variable at the same X_i.

This expression forms the conventional basis for all goodness of fit indices in deterministic models.

MAXIMUM DEVIATION

The simplest (and coarsest) method of indicating the goodness of fit is to report the magnitude of the largest deviation between observed and calculated Y values, with the implication that this corresponds to the largest error that can be expected when the equation is used for prediction. Thus, the inspection of the graph in Figure 8.3 reveals that the use of this equation would produce a maximum deviation of 0.7 (Table 8.1). To reflect this expected

Table 8.1 SET OF X AND Y VALUES

Point No.	X	Y	$\tilde{Y}$*	d*	%d*
1	0.5	1.1	1.4	−0.3	27.4
2	0.8	2.3	1.8	0.5	21.7
3	1.4	2.8	2.6	0.2	7.2
4	1.8	3.2	3.2	0.0	0.0
5	2.3	3.6	3.9	−0.3	8.3
6	2.6	4.5	4.3	0.2	4.5
7	2.8	4.8	5.0	−0.2	4.2
8	3.3	5.1	5.3	−0.2	3.9
9	3.7	6.0	5.9	0.1	1.7
10	4.0	6.1	6.3	−0.2	3.3
11	4.3	6.5	6.7	−0.2	3.1
12	4.5	7.3	7.1	0.2	2.7
13	5.0	7.7	7.7	0.0	0.0
14	5.4	7.6	8.3	−0.7	9.2
15	5.8	9.0	8.8	0.2	2.2
16	6.4	9.4	9.7	−0.3	3.3
17	6.6	10.1	9.9	0.2	2.0
18	7.0	10.7	10.5	0.2	1.9

Equation shown in Figure 8.3: $\tilde{Y} = 1.41X + 0.67$
Maximum deviation = 0.7
Average absolute deviation = 0.23
Average % deviation = 5.92%
Sum of squared deviation = 1.42
Standard error of estimate = 0.296

error, the prediction equation can be rewritten as

$$\tilde{Y}(\pm 0.7) = 1.41X + 0.67 \tag{13}$$

AVERAGE DEVIATION

Since in a deterministic data set the small variation obtained in observing Y repeatedly for a given value of X is largely attributable to experimental error and therefore potentially correctable by improved instrumentation, the maximum deviation is usually misleading in that it bears no consistent relation to the most likely deviation. Unless there is some peculiar type of

*Based on the line in Figure 8.3.

bias in its operation, the errors inherent in an instrument are random in nature, having a normal distribution. Consequently, a much more realistic estimate of the error most likely to be incurred by using a particular equation fit to a set of experimental data is obtained from the mean of the deviations between observed and predicted values. If these instrument errors are indeed random and the equation is properly fitted, the predicted values will exceed their observed counterparts in some cases and fall below them in others (as exemplified in Figure 8.3). Hence, the calculation of the average deviation in the ordinate, using their signs, will cause many of the deviations to cancel others, resulting in a misleading mean. To avoid this difficulty, it is necessary to modify the calculation of the average deviation by using the absolute rather than the signed values for each deviation:

$$|\bar{d}| = \frac{\sum\limits_{i=1}^{n} |Y_i - \tilde{Y}_i|}{n} \tag{14}$$

For the data in Table 8.1 this value turns out to be 0.23.

Many investigators find it more convenient to express this average deviation as a percentage rather than an absolute figure. To produce this, each individual deviation is transformed to a fraction of the observed Y value at that point, viz.:

$$\%d_i = \frac{|Y_i - \tilde{Y}_i|}{Y_i} \times 100 \tag{15}$$

and the average percentage of error is then calculated as

$$\overline{\%d} = \frac{\sum\limits_{i=1}^{n} \%d_i}{n} \tag{16}$$

These results for the data in Figure 8.3 are shown in Table 8.1.

SUM OF SQUARED DEVIATIONS

A more sensitive measure of the excursion of points from a fitted curve is obtained by squaring each deviation and using their sum:

$$D = \sum d_i^2 = \sum\limits_{i=1}^{n} (Y_i - \tilde{Y}_i)^2 \tag{17}$$

Although the numerical magnitude of the sum of squared deviations cannot easily be linked back to the data, as is possible with the average absolute deviation, this indicator is useful to many investigators interested in detecting small differences in "goodness of fit" between alternative functions for a given set of data. This value is shown as part of Table 8.1 for the sample data.

The sum of squared deviations assumes great importance as an error indicator when the investigator, after having selected a type of equation, proceeds to determine the best values for its constants. For this purpose, the most widely used criteria for "best" center around the minimization of this error indicator. The methods used in identifying equations that meet such criteria are known as *least squares* techniques and will be discussed shortly.

STANDARD ERROR OF ESTIMATE

If inconsistency in a set of observations can be attributed to random effects, the distribution of error magnitudes around "actual" values of the dependent variable will be normal. Consequently, given the characteristics of this distribution, one should be able to make some statements about the expected occurrence of a deviation having a given magnitude. A basic descriptor of this error distribution is the standard error of estimate,

$$\sigma_{y|x} = \sqrt{\sigma_{y|x}^2} = \sqrt{\frac{\sum (Y_i - \tilde{Y}_i)^2}{N}} \qquad (18)$$

The quantity $\sigma_{y|x}$ in turn is estimated from data by

$$s_{y|x} = \sqrt{\frac{D}{n-2}} = \sqrt{\sum_{i=1}^{n} \frac{(Y_i - \tilde{Y}_i)^2}{n-2}} \qquad (19)$$

where Y_i, $\tilde{Y}_i$, D, and n have their previous meanings, and $s_{y|x}$ is read as "the standard error of estimating Y, given the value of X."

This quantity operates and is used like the standard deviation in determining the probability of obtaining a particular size of error. The two indicators are conceptually analogous in that a standard deviation reflects the variability of points around a central (mean) value, whereas the standard error of estimate describes the dispersion around a line or curve representing a particular equation. For this purpose, the normal table is consulted, just as in the case of the ordinary standard deviation.

This indicator is of limited use in deterministic systems, where the dispersion is relatively small and we are not estimating "true" magnitudes. Its value is found, rather, in stochastic situations. The structure and use of this indicator and others stemming from it will be fully developed in the next chapter. Here we shall be concerned only with the use of $s_{y|x}^2$ in developing best-fitting equations.

FITTING EMPIRICAL EQUATIONS TO OBSERVED DATA— INITIAL CONSIDERATIONS

To facilitate the exploration of curve-fitting techniques we shall assume that there is no prior reason to favor one type of equation over another. Thus the assignment of specific constants for the data under consideration must be preceded by the selection of an appropriate form, based on criteria in the data themselves. In the following sections, we shall develop such recognition criteria for a number of commonly used equation types. Once the characteristics are established for a unique form, we can then explore appropriate fitting methods.

THE LINEAR EQUATION

This is the simplest function relating a set of continuous X-Y variables and therefore serves as a convenient vehicle for describing various generalized fitting techniques. The basic form for the linear equation is

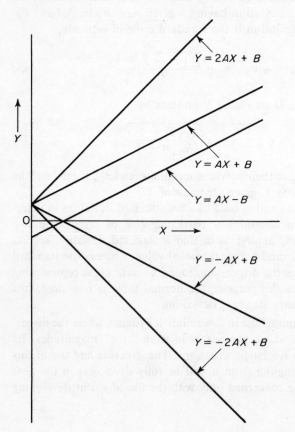

Fig. 8.4. Effect of the characteristic constants in a linear equation.

$$Y = a_0 + a_1 X \tag{20}$$

where a_0 and a_1 are characteristic constants for a given set of data or phenomena.

The action of the constants in determining the properties of the linear equation is summarized in Figure 8.4. The constant a_1, called the *slope*, represents the rate at which the magnitude of Y increases relative to X. Thus, if the slope is positive Y increases as X increases, whereas a negative slope indicates the opposite trend.

The other characteristic constant a_0 is called the *intercept*. When X has a value of zero at the Y axis, a_0 represents the Y value at the point where the line crosses that axis.

METHODS FOR FITTING LINEAR EQUATIONS

Although a number of techniques are available for developing empirical linear equations, they cannot be considered as being alternatives for one another, since the goodness of fit resulting from each method varies. In general, the trend of this variation is such that a decrease in the amount of calculations required is accompanied by an error penalty. The various methods described below have all been used routinely when the investigator has been willing to accept the additional error in order to reduce the computations. With today's general availability of computing systems, such compromises are no longer necessary. However, these methods still retain their usefulness, since they present quick and convenient means for obtaining approximate values of constants for initiating various iterative procedures.

FITTING BY VISUAL INSPECTION

The most direct method of fitting a straight line to a set of data involves virtually no calculations at all, consisting merely of selecting what appears to be the best line by eye and drawing it in.

Once the line is drawn, its constants can be determined quite easily. The intercept, a_0, is usually obtained by extending the line (if necessary) and reading off the Y value at $X = 0$. Then any convenient point (X_i, Y_i) is chosen on the line and the slope is found from

$$a_1 = \frac{Y_i - a_0}{X_i} \tag{21}$$

As crude as this method may seem, it often gives surprisingly good results, which improve, of course, with increasingly precise and consistent data. It has the obvious drawback of giving results that vary with the individual user and cannot be quantitatively predicted.

METHOD OF SELECTED POINTS

This technique is similar to but somewhat less subjective than the one previously described in that it requires the user to choose two of the data points and use their values in calculating the characteristic constants of the linear equation. Thus if P_i and P_j are the two selected points having coordinates (X_i, Y_i) and (X_j, Y_j) respectively, the slope (a_1) is immediately determinable from

$$a_1 = \frac{Y_j - Y_i}{X_j - X_i} \tag{22}$$

This result is then used in the basic equation form [expression (20)] with either of the selected points to obtain a value for the intercept a_0:

$$a_0 = Y_i - a_1 X_i \tag{23}$$

As in the previous case, this method is quite arbitrary, since there are no specific rules for choosing the points to be used. In some cases the selection may be made because of fundamental or technical reasons (such as a case in which it is known phenomenologically that when X is zero, Y is also zero). In other instances the investigator may have some information which indicates that his instrumentation is more accurate in one range of magnitudes than in another, and he will choose accordingly. When no prior knowledge is available, it is customary to choose two points at the extremes of the observed range. To illustrate this method, we can make use of the data presented previously in Table 8.1. Assuming that we have no other criteria to dictate our selection, we shall use the extreme points (numbers 1 and 18 in the table). The slope, then, is equal to

$$\frac{10.7 - 1.1}{7.0 - .5} = \frac{9.6}{6.5} = 1.48$$

and the intercept is

$$10.7 - 1.48(7.0) = 0.37$$

giving us an equation which reads

$$\tilde{Y} = 0.37 + 1.48X \tag{24}$$

Table 8.2 shows the deviations obtained with the equation, resulting in an average deviation of 0.24 and a standard error of estimate equal to 0.34.

Although the use of selected points eliminates the subjectivity of the previously discussed method, it is clear that the arbitrariness is still there.

Depending on the particular set of data under consideration, selection of different pairs of points may produce considerably different constants and deviations. For instance, if we were to use points 2 and 17 for fitting the data in the previous example, our equation would read

$$\tilde{Y} = 1.26 + 1.34X \tag{25}$$

and the average deviation and error of estimate would be 0.37 and 0.50, respectively.

METHOD OF AVERAGES

This technique results from an attempt to involve all of the data in deriving an empirical linear equation without adding unduly to the amount of calculation involved. The basic strategy here is to amalgamate the data points in such a way that two artificial "summary" points are produced for consequent use in determining the characteristic constants. The method most frequently used is to divide the data points into two halves containing the lower and higher values of X, respectively. Thus, if we have a sequence of n data points in which X_1 is the lowest X value and X_n the highest, our summary point would be obtained as follows:

Table 8.2. ERROR CHARACTERISTICS OF EQUATION (24)

Point No.	X	Y	$\tilde{Y}$	d
1	0.5	1.1	1.1	0.0
2	0.8	2.3	1.6	0.7
3	1.4	2.8	2.4	0.4
4	1.8	3.2	3.0	0.2
5	2.3	3.6	3.8	0.2
6	2.6	4.5	4.2	0.3
7	2.8	4.8	4.9	0.1
8	3.3	5.1	5.3	0.2
9	3.7	6.0	5.8	0.2
10	4.0	6.1	6.3	0.2
11	4.3	6.5	6.7	0.2
12	4.5	7.3	7.0	0.3
13	5.0	7.7	7.8	0.1
14	5.4	7.6	8.4	0.8
15	5.8	9.0	9.0	0.0
16	6.4	9.4	9.8	0.4
17	6.6	10.1	10.1	0.0
18	7.0	10.7	10.7	0.0

Maximum deviation = 0.8
Average deviation = 0.24
Sum of squared deviations = 1.89
Standard error of estimate = 0.34

$$\bar{X}_1 = \frac{\sum\limits_{i=1}^{i=n/2} X_i}{n/2}, \qquad \bar{Y}_1 = \frac{\sum\limits_{i=1}^{i=n/2} Y_i}{n/2} \qquad (26a)$$

and

$$\bar{X}_2 = \frac{\sum\limits_{i=(n/2)+1}^{i=n} X_i}{n/2}, \qquad \bar{Y}_2 \frac{\sum\limits_{i=(n/2)+1}^{i=n} Y_i}{n/2} \qquad (26b)$$

The above expressions assume, of course, that n is an even number. Should this not be the case, some ambiguity is introduced once again in that the assignment of the odd point to the upper or lower group for averaging is purely arbitrary.

Application of the method of averages to the data in the previous example produces the following values:

$$\bar{X}_1 = 2.13, \qquad \bar{Y}_1 = 3.71$$
$$\bar{X}_2 = 5.44, \qquad \bar{Y}_2 = 8.27$$

Then from (22) and (23)

$$a_1 = \frac{8.27 - 3.71}{5.44 - 2.13} = \frac{4.56}{3.31} = 1.38$$

and

$$a_0 = 8.27 - 1.38(5.44) = 0.76$$

giving the equation

$$\tilde{Y} = 0.76 + 1.38X \qquad (27)$$

Evaluation of the goodness of fit yields an average deviation of 0.24 and an error of estimate of 0.29.

METHOD OF LEAST SQUARES

This technique represents a basic departure from the others in that it is the only one in which goodness of fit is a criterion for obtaining the characteristics of the derived equation rather than a consequence of the derivation process. The indicator that dictates the selection of constants for nonlinear as well as linear functions is D, the sum of the squared deviations,

$$\sum (Y_i - \tilde{Y}_i)^2$$

with the resulting procedure being directed towards producing an equation for which this quantity is minimized. It can be shown, in fact, that there is only one such equation (of a given type) for a particular set of data, but the analytical proof of this statement need not concern us here.

The conditions under which this error term is actually at its minimum can be derived with the techniques of calculus by taking advantage of the properties of first derivatives (see Appendix A). If we can express the variation of the error term as a continuous function of the slope and intercept values, then the conditions producing the minimum will occur at the point where the first derivative of such a function is zero. In this case we need not concern ourselves with the possibility that such a point indicates the maximum, since the concept of an equation derived so as to give a maximum error is implausible.

We can develop a method around the minimization of this index as follows: If we have a linear expression that predicts the value for a particular consequence Y_i, viz.,

$$Y_i = a_0 + a_1 X_i$$

and we sum over all observed points,

$$\sum_{i=1}^{n} Y_i = na_0 + a_1 \sum_{i=1}^{n} X_i \tag{28}$$

Dividing through by n gives

$$\frac{\sum Y_i}{n} = a_0 + a_1 \frac{\sum X_i}{n} \tag{29}$$

Since $\sum Y_i/n$ and $\sum X_i/n$ are the mean values for Y and X, respectively, we can express (29) as

$$\bar{Y} = a_0 + a_1 \bar{X} \tag{30}$$

Now, we shall make use of this relationship by defining temporary variables y and x such that

$$y_i = Y_i - \bar{Y} \tag{31a}$$

and

$$x_i = X_i - \bar{X} \tag{31b}$$

If we subtract $\bar{Y}$ from both sides of our basic linear expression,

$$Y_i - \bar{Y} = a_0 + a_1 X_i - \bar{Y}$$
$$= a_0 + a_1 X_i - a_0 - a_1 \bar{X} \tag{32}$$

Substituting in accordance with (31a) or (31b), we have

$$y_i = a_0 - a_0 + a_1 x_i$$

$$= a_1 x_i \qquad (33)$$

Thus we have succeeded in eliminating a_0 from most of the subsequent manipulations. In graphical terms, we have moved our coordinate system to force our line to pass through a point $(\bar{X}, \bar{Y})$ without changing the ordinate or abscissa scales. This shift does not affect the distribution or magnitude of errors, so our individual deviation merely becomes

$$|d_i| = |y_i - a_1 x_i| \qquad (34)$$

and our error term D is now

$$D = \sum d_i^2 = \sum (y_i - a_1 x_i)^2 \qquad (35)$$

In order to minimize D, we must find those conditions under which its derivative with respect to a_1 will be equal to zero:

$$\frac{dD}{da_1} = 0 = -2 \sum [(x_i)(y_i - a_1 x_i)] \qquad (36)$$

Dividing by -2 and rewriting in expanded form, we have

$$\sum x_i y_i - a_1 \sum x_i^2 = 0 \qquad (37)$$

from which

$$a_1 \sum x_i^2 = \sum x_i y_i \qquad (38)$$

and

$$a_1 = \frac{\sum x_i y_i}{\sum x_i^2} = \frac{\sum (X_i - \bar{X})(Y_i - \bar{Y})}{\sum (X_i - \bar{X})^2} \qquad (39)$$

Having found a_1, we can go back to (30) and find a_0:

$$a_0 = \bar{Y} - a_1 \bar{X} \qquad (40)$$

When the least squares procedure is transformed into a program, the manipulative formulas are rearranged somewhat to avoid initially calculating $\bar{Y}$ and $\bar{X}$. This allows the computations to be performed with only one reading of the data instead of the two passes ordinarily required. The resulting expressions for a_1 and a_0 are

$$a_1 = \frac{n \sum X_i Y_i - \sum X_i \sum Y_i}{n \sum X_i^2 - (\sum X_i)^2} \tag{41}$$

$$a_0 = \frac{\sum Y_i - a_1 \sum X_i}{n} \tag{42}$$

Subsequent evaluation of the goodness of fit (by means of the sum of squared deviations, average deviation, etc.) is then performed in the usual way.

Because of the extensive computations involved in using this technique, it has been generally avoided in deterministic models in favor of the method of averages or even the selected points method. However, the design of a program to perform these calculations mathematically is rather straightforward, resulting in the universal adoption of this technique for routine use. A flow chart showing how such a program can be organized is given in Figure 8.5.

A most interesting alternative method for defining the least squares equation for a straight line can be developed starting from the hypothetical proposition that the tools of calculus are not available, but a very speedy and powerful computer is at our disposal. In this case we shall not derive mathematical formulations for the unique values of a_0 and a_1 but, rather, we shall evolve an iterative procedure for closing in on these values:

Step 1. Transform each X_i and Y_i to x_i and y_i, respectively.

Step 2. Select some initial trial value for a_1. (This value may be any convenient number, including 0.)

Step 3. Calculate D, using this new value of a_1.

Step 4. Increment the selected value of a_1 by some prescribed amount (say 0.1) and recalculate a new value for D.

Step 5. If the new value of D shows a decrease over the initial one, increase a_1 by 0.1. If the reverse is true, decrease a_1 by 0.1. Continue changing a_1 in the direction that decreases D until the latter begins to increase again.

Step 6. At this point, reduce the value by which a_1 is changed by a factor of 10 (i.e., to 0.01), and reverse the direction in which a_1 is being changed.

Step 7. Continue modifying a_1 by this new amount until D once again begins to increase.

Step 8. The process of reducing the increment in a_1 and reversal of direction can be repeated to whatever degree of precision is desired.

This type of algorithm is flowcharted in Figure 8.6.

Of course, this technique is not meant to serve as a practical alternative for the one based on first derivatives, simply because the latter is so much faster and easier by comparison. With most of today's computers, however,

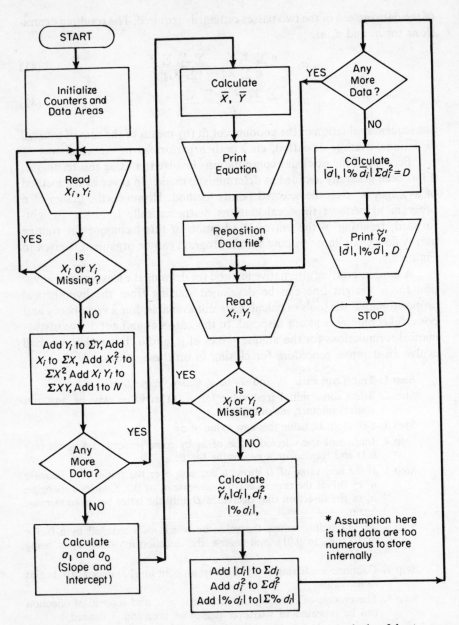

Fig. 8.5. Flowchart for a linear fit program using the methods of least squares.

such an iterative procedure is no longer unreasonable. This point is particularly significant in that it presents us with a most powerful set of "brute

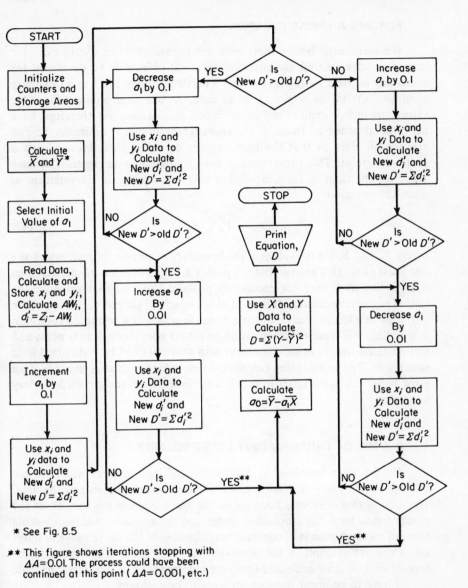

* See Fig. 8.5

** This figure shows iterations stopping with
$\Delta A = 0.01$. The process could have been
continued at this point ($\Delta A = 0.001$, etc.)

Fig. 8.6. Flowchart for linear fit program using iterative method.

force" techniques that can be applied to the solution of a variety of information handling problems (deterministic and otherwise) for which there are no analytically developed alternatives. Just how powerful an addition this is to the investigator's repertoire is just beginning to be realized, and concerted efforts are under way to explore the possibilities. The nature of such inquiries and their consequences are discussed in Chapters 10 and 12.

FORCING A LINEAR EQUATION

We mentioned before that there are occasions when the investigator knows in advance that the equation that will ultimately be developed for describing his data must pass through a particular point (such as a boundary condition). What he is saying, in essence, is that such points reflect true values, are independent of any experimental procedures, and, therefore, have no error attached to them. If the investigator deems it desirable, he can arrange his data so that the least squares equation goes through such a particular point. This is most easily done by determining the least squares value for the slope a_1 from expression (41) and solving for the intercept a_0 from the equation

$$a_0 = Y_0 - a_1 X_0 \tag{43}$$

where X_0 and Y_0 are the values at the boundary condition through which the line must pass. This insures that the point (X_0, Y_0) will lie on the derived line, but the line itself may not necessarily produce the minimum value for the sum of squared deviations. If desired, it is a relatively simple matter to include a routine in a linear equation-fitting program which, if a boundary condition is specified, will force-fit the equation so that it goes through that point and will compare the resulting error term with that obtained by a standard least squares fit. The investigator can then decide whether there is enough of an error reduction in the latter to justify a deviation from the known boundary condition.

A WORD OF CAUTION ABOUT LEAST SQUARES

The equation obtained by the method of least squares will yield the most probable value of Y for a given X based on the contents of the data. Underlying this attribute, however, is the basic assumption that all of the observations have been obtained under conditions such that the absolute error of measurement is of constant magnitude over the entire range of interest. Thus, for example, if the observations were obtained by reading some type of dial or other scale and the error incurred was a visual one, the scale would have to be linear for such an error to be constant.

Fortunately, this assumption is met or satisfactorily approximated in most situations. The notable exception is the type of instrument or experiment in which the error is a constant proportion or percentage of the observed magnitude rather than a constant absolute value. When this is the case, compensation may be introduced by applying a weighting factor to each observation in order to adjust its value. It has been found that once a "standard" Y value has been selected (i.e., a value to which a weight of 1 is assigned), the most effective weighting will be obtained by multiplying each $(Y_i - \tilde{Y}_i)^2$ by a factor whose value is proportional to $1/Y_i^2$.

The amount of discrepancy introduced by omitting the weighting procedure is usually small in the case of most empirical engineering data, but can be considerable in other situations. Since it cannot easily be estimated in advance, it may be necessary to develop empirical equations for a given type of experiment with and without weighting, so that its importance may be assessed for future use of that general situation.

NONLINEAR FORMS

Although it is highly desirable to devise linear expressions for experimentally observed phenomena, nature is singularly uncooperative in this respect. Most observed phenomena are not adequately described by straight line equations, and more complex forms must be sought. Because the development of nonlinear equations involves considerably more extensive calculation, the use of direct methods as described for the linear form is not always practical, even when such procedures are automated. Hence a number of manipulative techniques have been evolved to preprocess the raw data in preparation for simplified calculation.

GENERAL SIMPLIFICATION PROCEDURES

Methods that have been devised to handle data sets with nonlinear trends have two distinct but related objectives. The amount of computation involved to handle such equations directly may be immense, so the time required to carry them out and the chances for arithmetic and manipulative errors increase sharply. The advent of computers has alleviated this problem to a great extent but has not eliminated it completely, since some of the techniques require extremely long and complex programs for their implementation. The second objective of simplification is to overcome a difficulty that still exists with most computing systems. The computations in many direct nonlinear derivation procedures entail the evaluation of products, cross products, and their sums, all containing many factors. Except for a few very special designs, processors are generally not equipped to carry the very large number of significant digits generated by such successive multiplications, so the precision of the final results may be seriously impaired.

The indirect techniques designed to avoid these difficulties operate with two basic strategies. The first of these is to simplify the desired equation, operate on it in that form, and reconvert the results to a more complex expression. The second is a less consistent but often more expedient technique which seeks to replace the equation altogether with a simpler form that is a close approximation but usually bears no algebraic relation to the original form.

RECTIFICATION (LINEARIZATION)

A number of nonlinear functions can be algebraically manipulated so that the resulting transformed variables are linearly related to each other. The ability to make such transformations (called *rectification*) allows us to fit a linear equation to the data, a process which is usually very simple. Once the equation has been derived, it can be reconverted to a form that is consistent with that of the original data.

As an example, let us consider the set of data in Table 8.3. A plot is shown in Figure 8.7. Suppose further that we have some previous experience

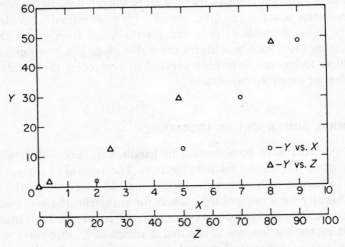

Fig. 8.7. Rectification of parabolic *X-Y* data.

Table 8.3

X	Y
0	0.2
2	1.9
5	12.6
7	29.5
9	48.5

that indicates that there is a fundamental reason for the use of an equation having the general form

$$\tilde{Y} = a_0 + a_1 X^2 \tag{44}$$

If we define a new variable W such that

$$W_i = X_i^2 \tag{45}$$

expression (44) can then be rewritten

$$\tilde{Y} = a_0 + a_1 W \tag{46}$$

which is a standard linear equation. Thus, expression (46) is the rectified form of the original function. (Table 8.4 shows the appropriate values of W, and Figure 8.7 shows the corresponding graph).

Table 8.4

W	Y
0	0.2
4	1.9
25	12.6
49	29.5
81	48.5

If we apply the least squares technique to the rectified data, we obtain the relation

$$\tilde{Y} = -0.48 + 0.61 W$$

Replacing W by X^2 gives the final form

$$\tilde{Y} = -0.48 + 0.61 X^2$$

Of course, the convenience provided by this technique becomes much more apparent when one is dealing with more complicated equations, as will be seen in subsequent sections.

APPROXIMATION BY ANOTHER FUNCTION

When an equation is of such form that rectification is impractical, the use of that form may be abandoned entirely, in favor of a function that is easier to deal with and whose values at various antecedent conditions come very close to matching those that were observed. In most cases, such functions take the form of polynomials, i.e.,

$$\tilde{Y} = a_0 + a_1 X + a_2 X^2 + a_3 X^3 + \cdots + a_n X^n \tag{47}$$

where n is the degree of the polynomial.

Such approximations, which have been worked out for a wide variety of functions, offer alternatives for rectifiable forms in some cases, but may be the only available method for handling others. Since these functions are merely computational expedients, it is inappropriate to attempt to attach any physical significance to the constants in them.

PARABOLIC EQUATIONS

This equation is actually a second degree polynomial whose general form is

$$Y = a_0 + a_1 X + a_2 X^2 \tag{48}$$

The basic shape produced by this equation, shown in Figure 8.8, indicates that two values of X can produce an identical Y value. Of course, this is because the equation contains an X^2 term that can be obtained by squaring either some value of X or its negative counterpart $-X$.

The size (steepness and width) of a parabola, as well as the direction of

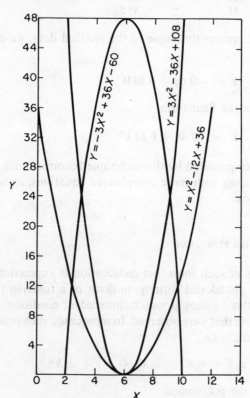

Fig. 8.8. Effect of characteristic constants on the parabolic equation.

its opening and its placement on the coordinate system, are determined by the value of the constants a_1 and a_2. The constant a_0 controls the vertical placement of the graph. Although many observed phenomena follow trends that are approximately parabolic, the range of interest is not always sufficient to allow the full development of this characteristic curve. Instead, only one side is produced, making its recognition more difficult.

Since the parabolic equation is still relatively simple to deal with in mathematical terms, the employment of indirect methods is not necessary for obtaining coefficient values. They may be used, however, as a help in establishing the appropriateness of the parabolic form.

DIRECT LEAST SQUARES FIT

The derivation of the equations for determining the least squares parabola parallels that for the linear case. In this instance

$$d_i = Y_i - a_0 - a_1 X_i - a_2 X_i^2 \tag{49}$$

and

$$D = \sum_{i=1}^{n} (Y_i - a_0 - a_1 X_i - a_2 X_i^2)^2 \tag{50}$$

This time the equation has to be minimized with respect to three constants a_0, a_1, and a_2, so that the differentiation process produces three equations, all of which have to be satisfied for minimization of D.

$$\sum Y = na_0 + a_1 \sum X_i + a_2 \sum X_i^2 \tag{51a}$$

$$\sum XY = a_0 \sum X_i + a_1 \sum X_i^2 + a_2 \sum X_i^3 \tag{51b}$$

$$\sum X^2 Y = a_0 \sum X_i^2 + a_1 \sum X_i^3 + a_2 \sum X_i^4 \tag{51c}$$

Programs designed to solve such equations for the values of least squares constants are usually structured around a matrix solution. If we look at expression (51), it is apparent that each of the multipliers of a_0, a_1, and a_2 is a constant whose value can be determined from the observed data points. Hence, this system of equations is actually a matrix of the form

$$\begin{pmatrix} n & \sum X_i & \sum X_i^2 \\ \sum X_i & \sum X_i^2 & \sum X_i^3 \\ \sum X_i^2 & \sum X_i^3 & \sum X_i^4 \end{pmatrix} \times \begin{pmatrix} a_0 \\ a_1 \\ a_2 \end{pmatrix} = \begin{pmatrix} \sum Y_i \\ \sum X_i Y_i \\ \sum X_i^2 Y_i \end{pmatrix} \tag{52}$$

The solution of this system, as outlined in Appendix A, is more efficient than performing successive substitutions. This becomes especially apparent with higher-order polynomials. (Solution of this type of system of equations is discussed more fully in Chapter 9.)

RECTIFICATION OF PARABOLIC EQUATIONS

When it is known that the desired parabola is to pass through a particular point (X_1, Y_1)[1], it is possible to rectify the equation as follows: Since (X_1, Y_1) is a point on the fitted parabola, we can say that

$$Y_1 = a_0 + a_1 X_1 + a_2 X_1^2 \tag{53}$$

Subtracting Y_1 from both sides of the general parabolic equation [expression (48)], we obtain

$$
\begin{aligned}
Y_i - Y_1 &= a_0 + a_1 X_i + a_2 X_i^2 - Y_1 \\
&= a_0 + a_1 X_i + a_2 X_i^2 - a_0 - a_1 X_1 - a_2 X_1^2 \\
&= a_1(X_i - X_1) + a_2(X_i^2 - X_1^2) \\
&= a_1(X_i - X_1) + a_2(X_i + X_1)(X_i - X_1) \tag{54}
\end{aligned}
$$

If we divide both sides of the above expression by the quantity $(X_i - X_1)$, we obtain

$$
\begin{aligned}
\frac{Y_i - Y_1}{X_i - X_1} &= a_1 + a_2(X_i + X_1) \\
&= a_1 + a_2 X_i + a_2 X_1 \\
&= (a_1 + a_2 X_1) + a_2 X_i \tag{55}
\end{aligned}
$$

Thus we now have a linear equation in which the slope is equal to a_2 and the intercept is the quantity $(a_1 + a_2 X_1)$. Determination of the characteristics of this line would then be achieved by defining a new variable W such that

$$W_i = \frac{Y_i - Y_1}{X_i - X_1} \tag{56}$$

and using this as a temporary dependent variable against X in a least squares linear fit. Once a_2 is determined, it can be substituted in the expression for the intercept value to determine a_1, following which further substitution using X_1 and Y_1 in the basic parabolic equation will yield a_0.

---

[1] Note that since the original equation is not linear we cannot use the mean values if there is no preselected point. The point $(\bar{X}, \bar{Y})$ is not a point on a parabola or, for that matter, on any nonlinear curve.

LOGARITHMIC EQUATIONS

A large number of phenomena in a variety of fields produce data that can be represented very well by an equation of the type

$$Y = aX^b \tag{57}$$

where b, the exponent of the independent variable, is any power, not necessarily an integer. Examples of this form are shown in Figure 8.9.

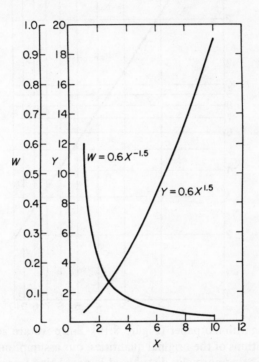

Fig. 8.9. Typical shapes of logarithmic equations.

RECTIFICATION OF LOGARITHMIC DATA

The least squares equations for this function in its basic form are very awkward to handle, either manually or automatically. Consequently, their use is avoided in favor of a rectified form: If we take logarithms of both sides of expression (57), we obtain

$$\log Y = \log a + b \log X \tag{58}$$

which describes a straight line having b and $\log a$ as its slope and intercept, respectively. This is exemplified by plotting one of the curves in Figure 8.9

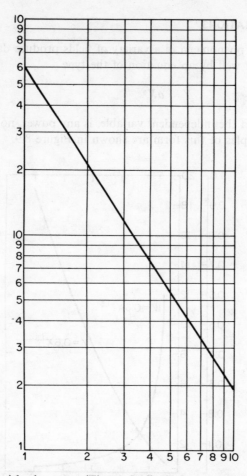

Fig. 8.10. Rectification of logarithm graph by using log paper.

on logarithmic paper (Figure 8.10). Since we are actually dealing with the logarithms of the original quantities, our assumption about the experimental error being normally distributed is now being transferred to the logarithms of those errors—a contention much more difficult to defend. As a result, we can say only that the use of the rectified form gives us an equation that may not differ substantially from but is usually not in fact the least squares fit.

Sometimes the transformation to logarithms produces a curve which is almost but not quite linear (Figure 8.11). This is often remedied by adding another constant, viz.,

$$Y = aX^b + c \qquad (59)$$

To rectify the data for such a form, a temporary variable W is defined such that

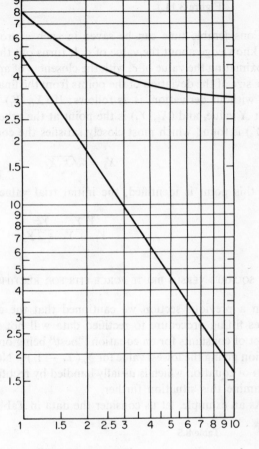

Fig. 8.11. Rectification of logarithmic data by using an additional constant.

$$W_i = Y_i - c \qquad (60)$$

Determination of the constants for this equation then proceeds by the following general technique:

Step 1. A value of c is selected and used to calculate the set of W values.

Step 2. The least squares line for log W versus log X is then determined.

Step 3. A suitable error term is then calculated. (Since this iterative method is computer-oriented anyway, it would not be more difficult to use the sum of squares of the actual deviations rather than their logarithms.)

Step 4. Change c by some prescribed increment and recalculate the set of W's.

Step 5. The procedure of incrementation and evaluation of error terms proceeds in exactly the same manner as described for the brute force linear fit until the error term is minimized to some predetermined degree of precision. (The results of such correction are shown in Figure 8.11.)

Considerable time can be saved in such a procedure if there is some prior knowledge about the value of c. It turns out that there is a method for approximating the value of c, with the closeness of approximation depending on the size of the deviation of the points from the final curve. This procedure, given without derivation, is as follows: If (X_1, Y_1) is the point having the lowest X value, and (X_2, Y_2) is the point at the other extreme, a data point (X_3, Y_3) is found which most closely satisfies the condition

$$X_3 = \sqrt{X_1 X_2} \tag{61}$$

Once this point is identified, the initial trial value for c is calculated as

$$c_0 = \frac{Y_1 Y_2 - Y_3^2}{Y_1 + Y_2 - 2Y_3} \tag{62}$$

LEAST SQUARES VERSUS BRUTE FORCE FITS FOR RECTIFIED LOGARITHMIC DATA

In a previous section we cautioned that the application of the least squares fitting procedure to rectified data will not necessarily produce the best set of constants for an equation ["best" being once again defined as that equation giving the lowest value for $\sum (Y_i - \tilde{Y})^2$]. Now that we have covered a form of equation which is usually handled by rectification, it is appropriate to examine this situation further.

As an example, let us consider the data in Table 8.5. A plot on logari-

Table 8.5

X	Y	$\log_{10} X$	$\log_{10} Y$
2.0	2.4	0.3010	0.3802
2.5	3.8	0.3979	0.5798
4.0	5.0	0.6021	0.6990
5.3	5.6	0.7243	0.7482
7.2	7.4	0.8573	0.8692
9.1	9.9	0.9590	0.9956

thmic paper (Figure 8.12) indicates that the form $\tilde{Y} = a_0 X^{a_1}$ is appropriate, and we shall proceed to operate on the rectified data. If we set

$$V = \log_{10} Y$$

and

$$W = \log_{10} X$$

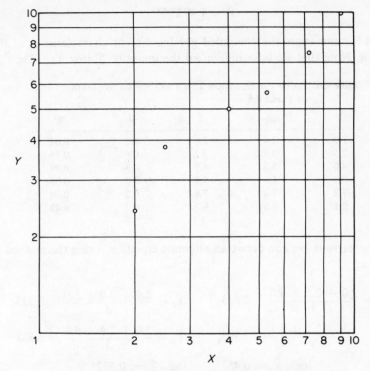

Fig. 8.12. Rectification of the data in Table 8.5.

then, from Table 8.5,

$$\sum W = 3.842$$
$$\sum V = 4.272$$
$$\sum W^2 = 2.791$$
$$\sum WV = 3.008$$

and a_1, the slope, is obtained from (41) as

$$a_1 = \frac{6(3.008) - 3.842(4.272)}{6(2.791) - 3.842(3.842)} = 0.824$$

The quantity $\log_{10} a_0$ is then calculated as

$$\log_{10} a_0 = \frac{4.272 - 0.824(3.842)}{6} = 0.173$$

The quantity a_0 itself is the antilog of 0.173, or 1.49, and our derived equation reads

$$\tilde{Y} = 1.49 X^{0.824}$$

Table 8.6 summarizes the computed goodness of fit characteristics of this equation. Note that we have minimized the quantity $\sum (\log Y_i - \log \tilde{Y}_i)^2$.

Table 8.6. FIT OF THE EQUATION $\tilde{Y} = 1.49 X^{0.824}$ TO THE DATA OF TABLE 8.5

X	Y	$\tilde{Y}$	d	d^2
2.0	2.4	2.6	0.2	0.04
2.5	3.8	3.2	0.6	0.36
4.0	5.0	4.7	0.3	0.09
5.3	5.6	5.9	0.3	0.09
7.2	7.4	7.6	0.2	0.04
9.1	9.9	9.2	0.7	0.49

$$D = 1.11$$

As a comparison, we can derive an alternate equation, using the method of averages:

$$\bar{X}_1 = \frac{2.0 + 2.5 + 4.0}{3} = 2.833, \qquad \bar{Y}_1 = \frac{2.4 + 3.8 + 5.0}{3} = 3.733$$

$$\bar{X}_2 = \frac{5.3 + 7.2 + 9.1}{3} = 7.200, \qquad \bar{Y}_2 = \frac{5.6 + 7.4 + 9.9}{3} = 7.633$$

$$\log_{10} \bar{X}_1 = 0.4523, \qquad \log_{10} \bar{Y}_1 = 0.5721$$

$$\log_{10} \bar{X}_2 = 0.8573, \qquad \log_{10} \bar{Y}_2 = 0.8827$$

Then

$$0.5721 = \log_{10} a_0 + 0.4523 a_1$$

$$0.8827 = \log_{10} a_0 + 0.8573 a_1$$

Solving these equations gives

$$a_1 = 0.780$$

$$\log_{10} a_0 = 0.219$$

from which $a_0 = 1.66$ and the equation is

$$\tilde{Y} = 1.66 X^{0.780}$$

Table 8.7 contains a summary of its computed characteristics.

Thus, despite the fact that a cruder method was used in the latter case, the resulting equation was measurably better than the least squares fit of the rectified data. Furthermore, there is no reason to suppose that the least

Table 8.7. FIT OF THE EQUATION $\tilde{Y} = 1.66X^{0.780}$ TO THE DATA
OF TABLE 8.5.

X	Y	$\tilde{Y}$	d	d^2
2.0	2.4	2.8	0.4	0.16
2.5	3.8	3.4	0.4	0.16
4.0	5.0	4.9	0.1	0.01
5.3	5.6	6.1	0.5	0.25
7.2	7.4	7.7	0.3	0.09
9.1	9.9	9.3	0.6	0.36
		$D = 1.03$		

squares fit on the actual data [i.e., minimization of $\sum (Y_i - \tilde{Y}_i)^2$ rather than $\sum (\log Y_i - \log \tilde{Y}_i)^2$] will not provide substantial improvement in the goodness of fit.

The difficulty in obtaining an adequate analytical procedure for performing a least squares fit on nonrectified data can no longer be an acceptable excuse, especially if the collection of the data entailed some effort to maximize accuracy and precision. Although rather inelegant, the brute force methods for converging on suitable equation constants (as in Figure 8.6) are quite effective and no longer uneconomical.

EXPONENTIAL FORMS

Another type of equation that seems to handle a wide variety of experimentally observed phenomena has the general form

$$Y = a_0 e^{a_1 X} \tag{63}$$

where e is the base of natural logarithms and a_0 and a_1 are the characteristic constants of the equation. Several examples of such exponential curves are shown in Figure 8.13 to illustrate their general form.

Rectification can be achieved by taking natural logarithms of both sides of the equation

$$\log_e Y = \log_e a_0 + a_1 X \tag{64}$$

Thus a linear fit of $\log Y$ versus X will produce an equation whose slope is a_1 and whose intercept is $\log_e a_0$. When graphical means are used, it is more convenient to express such equations as

$$Y = a_0(10^{hX}) \tag{65}$$

where

$$h = \frac{a_1}{\log_e 10} = \frac{a_1}{2.303}$$

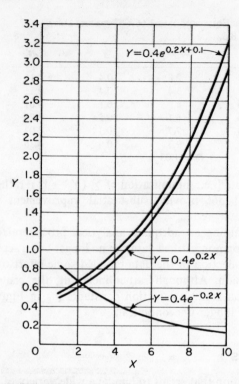

Fig. 8.13. Typical forms for exponential curves.

This allows the data to be plotted on semilogarithmic paper (Figure 8.14), where they will appear linear.

In some cases (Figure 8.15) an additional constant c is required such that

$$Y = a_0 e^{a_1 X} + c \qquad (66)$$

The transformation for handling this involves the substitution of a variable W calculated as

$$W_i = \log (Y_i - c) \qquad (67)$$

Once again, the constants can be evaluated by brute force procedures with the help of a first approximation for c:

$$c_0 = \frac{Y_1 Y_2 - Y_3^2}{Y_1 + Y_2 - 2Y_3} \qquad (68)$$

where Y_1 and Y_2 are the Y values at the lowest and highest values of X, respectively, and Y_3 is the Y value corresponding to the X closest in magnitude to $(X_1 + X_2)/2$.

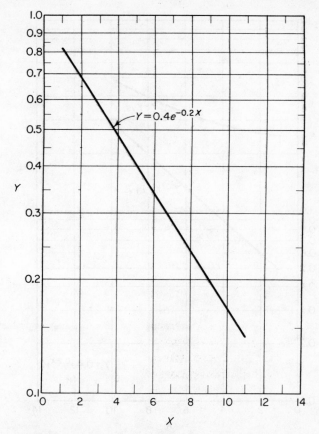

$Y = 0.4e^{-0.2X}$

Fig. 8.14. Rectification of exponential graphs by using semilog-arithmic paper.

An alternate form that may fit certain data more closely is

$$Y = a_0 e^{a_1 X + c} \tag{69}$$

Since the log transformation yields

$$\log_e Y = \log_e a_0 + a_1 X + c \tag{70}$$

the appropriate temporary variable W this time is

$$W_i = \log_e Y_i - c \tag{71}$$

so that

$$W = \log_e a + bX \tag{72}$$

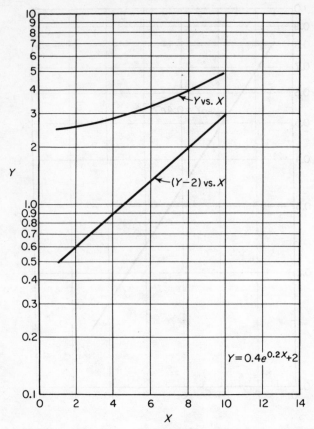

Fig. 8.15. Rectification of exponential data by using an additional constant.

We can again obtain a first approximation for c, using expression (68). If a satisfactory fit cannot be effected with the three-constant form, it is usually better to seek another type of equation than to add a fourth constant (such as $Y = ae^{bX+c} + d$).

In some cases, a better fit is obtained with the form

$$Y = a_0 a_1^x \tag{73}$$

The rectification for this type of equation is similar to the general exponential case, viz.,

$$\log_e Y = \log_e a_0 + X \log_e a_1 \tag{74}$$

The slope of the rectified line in this instance is $\log_e a_1$.

RECIPROCAL AND HYPERBOLIC EQUATIONS

A number of phenomena have been observed for which there are fundamental reasons to fit the data to an equation of the general form

$$Y = \frac{X}{a_0 + a_1 X} \tag{75}$$

Note that although this type of equation produces smooth and continuous curves for certain ranges of values (as in Figure 8.16) there is a discontinuity inherent in the form. This is illustrated in Table 8.8 for the function $Y = X/(3 + 2X)$, which is plotted in Figure 8.16. Note that as X gets larger and

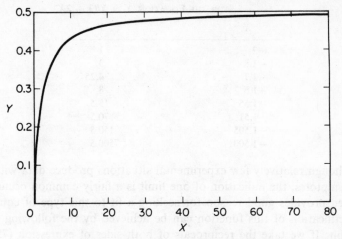

Fig. 8.16. Typical form for reciprocal data.

Table 8.8. X AND Y VALUES FOR THE
FUNCTION $Y = X/(3 + 2X)$

X	Y
0	0.0
1	0.2
2	0.29
3	0.33
4	0.36
5	0.39
6	0.40
7	0.41
8	0.42
9	0.43
10	0.44
20	0.47
100	0.49

larger, the value of Y approaches but never quite reaches the value of 0.5. This function is said to be asymptotic to $Y = 0.5$ (Figure 8.16). Otherwise stated, $Y = 0.5$ is a limiting value, which will not be exceeded no matter how large X gets. Characteristically, such equations also have a second limiting value, i.e., a value of X that is approached but never quite attained, as Y becomes infinitely large. This asymptote is quite easy to find, since, from expression (75), it exists at that point where $a_0 + a_1 X = 0$, or Y becomes infinitely large when $X = -a_0/a_1$. Thus, in the equation for the data in Table 8.8, Y rapidly becomes extremely large as X approaches $-\frac{3}{2}$ or -1.5. Table 8.9 illustrates this tendency.

Table 8.9. APPROACH TO LIMITING X VALUE
FOR THE EQUATION $Y = X/(3 + 2X)$

X	Y
−2	1
−1.8	3
−1.7	4.25
−1.6	8
−1.55	15.5
−1.51	70.5
−1.505	150.5
−1.5001	7500.5

Although relatively few experimental situations produce data with two such asymptotes, the indication of one limit is a fairly common occurrence and often provides good reason for seeking a fit to this type of equation.

Rectification of this function can be achieved by the following transformation: If we take the reciprocals of both sides of expression (75), we obtain

$$\frac{1}{Y} = \frac{a_0 + a_1 X}{X} = \frac{a_0}{X} + a_1 \qquad (76)$$

Now if we set

$$V = \frac{1}{Y}$$

and

$$W = \frac{1}{X}$$

and substitute in (76) our expression becomes

$$V = a_0 W + a_1 \qquad (77)$$

which, of course, is a straight line with slope a_0 and intercept a_1. A least squares fit on the reciprocals of the variables will not be misleading, as was the case with logarithmic transformation, since the condition for the minimum absolute difference between two quantities will also give a minimum for the difference of the reciprocals of those quantities.

Sometimes it is possible to fit such data to a simpler form, namely,

$$Y = a_0 + \frac{a_1}{X} \tag{78}$$

Rectification of this function involves only one transformation, that being

$$W = \frac{1}{X} \tag{79}$$

resulting in the linear equation

$$Y = a_0 + a_1 W \tag{80}$$

Least squares solution can then proceed in the normal fashion.

SIGMOID CURVES

There are a number of experimental situations which result in X-Y data whose graphs have the shape of an elongated "S" (as in Figure 8.17).

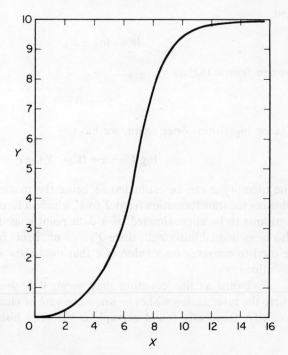

Fig. 8.17. Typical form for sigmoid data.

This characteristic is also encountered with many frequency distributions when they are expressed in cumulative form. Such graphs are called *sigmoid* and are among the most difficult regular shapes to fit with an equation.

THE GOMPERTZ EQUATION

It is sometimes possible to represent s-shaped graphs by an equation credited to Gompertz:

$$Y = ab^{c^x} \tag{81}$$

The constant a determines the upper limit of Y, the product ab defines the Y value at an X value of zero, and c regulates the rise (or fall) of the curve.

This equation can be rectified by two successive transformations, but the results can only be considered as first approximations. If we take logarithms of both sides of (81) we obtain

$$\log Y = \log a + c^x \log b \tag{82}$$

Now if we define new variables

$$V = \log Y - \log a \tag{83a}$$

and

$$W = \log b \tag{83b}$$

we can rewrite (82) as

$$V = Wc^x \tag{84}$$

Taking logarithms once again, we have

$$\log V = \log W + X \log c \tag{85}$$

The quantity a can be estimated as being the maximum value of Y, thus allowing the transformation from Y to V, which in turn permits the remaining constants to be approximated. If a data point is available at $X = 0$, b can also be estimated fairly well, since $Y_{X=0} = ab$. Brute force methods can then be used to converge on a value of c that minimizes D, the sum of squared deviations.

Awkward as this equation may seem, it is useful in those instances where the investigator wishes to know the rate of change at some particular point. (A frequently found example is the sales history of a product that starts off slowly, is accelerated steeply by an advertising campaign, and then stabilizes at some higher level.) The first derivative of this equation is fairly easy to determine, being

$$\frac{d}{dx}(ab^{c^X}) = c^x ab^{c^X} \log b \log c \qquad (86)$$

POLYNOMIAL APPROXIMATIONS

Unfortunately, sigmoid data do not always yield to a satisfactory fit by equation (81). Alternate equations that have been proposed to handle sigmoid data are also awkward and difficult to manipulate without catastrophic loss in precision.

Consequently, sigmoid data are most usually fitted by polynomial approximations in which the individual coefficients are not directly related to specific properties of the data. A very good fit of this type is given by Hastings:[2]

$$\tilde{Y} = 1 - \frac{1}{(1 + .278393X + .230389X^2 + .000972X^3 + .078108X^4)^4} \qquad (87)$$

More will be said about such approximations in a subsequent section.

SOME STUBBORN CASES

Despite valiant attempts to control the precision of instrumentation and data collection, there are instances in which a set of observations will produce an apparently smooth trend which will not succumb to any common equation type. In other cases, there may be good fundamental reasons, such as two effects of different and varying strength acting in concert, for producing data whose trend shows some discontinuity or abrupt change. When this occurs, use of the following techniques may prove helpful.

COMBINED FUNCTIONS

Sometimes a set of data produces a graph that very nearly represents a simple function but exhibits a consistent deviation from that function over part of the observed range. Such a set of points is given in Table 8.10 and plotted in Figure 8.18. Since the data appear almost linear, we can assume

---

[2] C. Hastings, *Approximations for Digital Computers* (Princeton, N.J.: Princeton University Press, 1962).

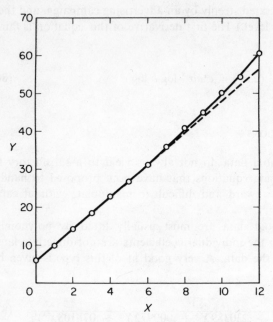

Fig. 8.18. Plot of nearly linear data from Table 8.9.

Table 8.10. A Set of Almost Linear Data

X	Y	$|Y - \tilde{Y}'|$	$|Y - \tilde{Y}|$
0	6.05	1.05	0.05
1	10.20	1.20	0.02
2	14.45	1.45	0.06
3	18.50	1.50	0.15
4	23.00	2.00	0.05
5	27.30	2.30	0.00
6	31.45	2.45	0.26
7	36.20	3.20	0.00
8	40.60	3.60	0.19
9	45.10	4.10	0.36
10	50.30	5.30	0.02
11	54.70	5.70	0.54
12	60.50	7.50	0.15

that the final function will have a strong linear component. Consequently, the first step in the curve-fitting procedure will be to treat the data as being linear. The linear equation works out to be

$$\tilde{Y}' = 5 + 4X$$

The resulting absolute deviations are shown in Table 8.10. Obviously, the deviations are sizable at the upper range of X, and we really should indicate their presence in the equation, so the previous equation is modified to read

$$\tilde{Y} = \tilde{Y}' + d$$
$$= 5 + 4X + d$$

When these deviations are plotted versus the values of X at which they occur on semilogarithmic coordinates (Figure 8.19), it is seen that the trend resembles that generally associated with the exponential curve (as in Figure 8.14). The equation fit to the deviations comes out to be

$$\tilde{d} = 2^{0.24X}$$

Substituting, we obtain the final equation

$$\tilde{Y} = 5 + 4X + 2^{0.24X}$$

Although in concept this type of procedure will work for combined nonlinear

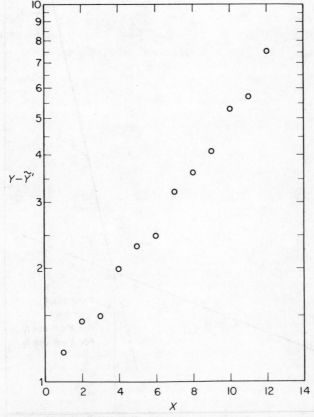

Fig. 8.19. Semilog plot of d versus X obtained from a linear fit of the data in Figure 8.18.

functions, the recognition of such trends is extremely difficult, and its use is most frequently restricted to data sets that exhibit strong linear tendencies, altered by some slight nonlinear component.

ALTERNATIVE EQUATIONS

When a sufficiently abrupt change in trend occurs in a set of data, there may be no choice but to apply one function to a particular range of the data and to express the remainder by some other equation. Symbolically we can express the use of alternative functions as follows:

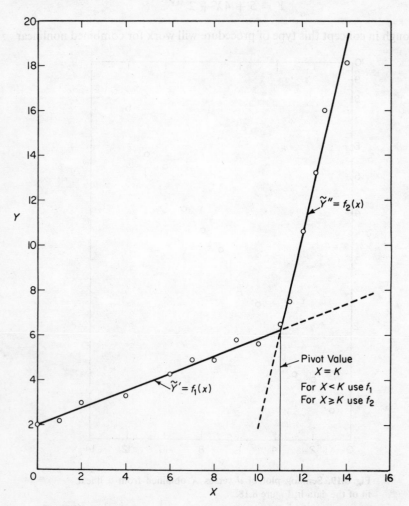

Fig. 8.20. Use of alternative linear equations to fit experimental data.

$$Y = f_1(X) \qquad \text{for } X < K$$
$$Y = f_2(X) \qquad \text{for } X \leqslant K \tag{88}$$

where K is some particular pivotal value. This type of situation is exemplified

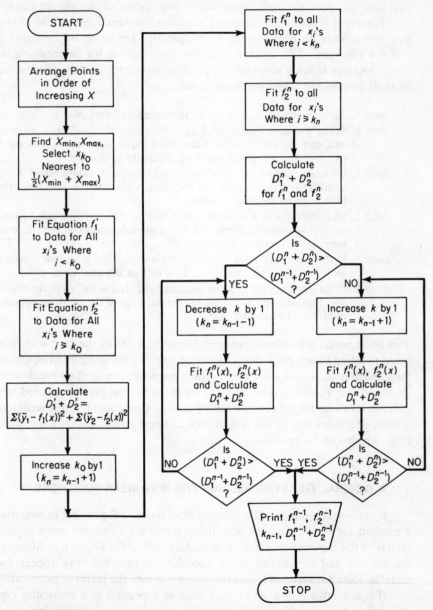

Fig. 8.21. Flowchart for a program to find the best pivot point for alternative equations.

in Figure 8.20. The abrupt change in slope indicated by these points may or may not be spurious (in many situations there is no reason to assume the former), and a single continuous function, though more convenient, may be extremely difficult to derive. Furthermore, it is quite likely that such an equation will produce high deviations in the region of the abrupt change.

The exact location of the point at which the functions should change may not always be pronounced. Consequently, any program designed to perform this type of fit must include some mechanism for determining the "best" location for this pivot point. An effective routine for this purpose can be built around the following iterative sequence:

Step 1. Arrange the data in order by increasing value of X.

Step 2. Select the initial value of K (pivotal value of X). This is arbitrary and can be set at some convenient value (say the X nearest to $(X_{min} + X_{max})/2$ unless specified otherwise by the user).

Step 3. Fit one equation to the subset of data having X values below K and another to the remainder of the data. Calculate the resulting error term (sum of the two D terms).

Step 4. Shift the value of K upward so that the first subset of data now includes an additional point. Repeat the fitting procedure and compare the error term to the previous one.

Step 5. If the error has been reduced, continue shifting K in that direction until the error term increases. This defines the final pivot point.

Step 6. If the upward shift in K has increased the error term, go in the reverse direction, shifting K and evaluating the error of the resulting equation until it no longer decreases.

This basic procedure is flowcharted in Figure 8.21. As in the case with combined functions, such procedures can be of help in producing fitted equations for nonlinear data, but their use for such purposes requires so much manipulation and transformation that the resulting loss in precision could very well produce meaningless or misleading results. Consequently, this technique is most effective when its use is restricted to linear combinations (or to functions which can be rectified).

A GENERAL ITERATIVE METHOD FOR NONLINEAR FUNCTIONS

By taking advantage of the properties of series, it is possible to construct a method for converging on best-fitting nonlinear functions more rapidly than with the incremental iteration procedure outlined in Figure 6.6. Although the amount and complexity of the calculations involved may appear formidable, their automation brings this technique into the realm of practicality.

If it is known that a set of data is to be expressed as a particular type of function, the value Y of that function for a particular value of the independent variable X can also be expressed as the sum of a Taylor series, as described in Appendix A. In this situation we have the function values (the observed Y's), the corresponding X's, and the form of the function, but not the specific constants. Consequently, we can still write the Taylor series, but in this instance it will be the equation constants that are the unknowns, rather than the Y values.

We can exploit these circumstances by creating a set of criteria that must be met by the unknown constants and structuring a solvable set of equations around them. If we are interested in fitting a function $Y = f(X)$ to a set of observed data, we can define an error function $F(X)$.

$$F(X) = f(X) - Y \qquad (89)$$

or, for some particular value X_i,

$$F(X_i) = f(X_i) - Y_i$$

The ideal situation, of course, would be one in which the constants in $f(X)$ would be such that, for any X_i, $F(X_i) = 0$. If we impose that condition as a criterion, using all of the observed X-Y points, we should be able to determine those constant values that come closest to satisfying the condition that $F(X_i)$ be zero for all X_i's. Since for many functions the Taylor series is extremely difficult to work with if many terms are included, it is usually truncated, thus giving approximate values for the best constants. These approximations can then be used in a repetition of the process until the user is satisfied that further iteration will not pay off. Thus if there are N pair of observed (X, Y) points, N Taylor series can be set up for $F_1(X)$ through $F_n(X)$, and the resulting system of equations can be solved for the constants.

An adequate general description of this procedure would of necessity be extremely lengthy and is still likely to leave some doubts as to some of its aspects. For our purposes, it will be more effective to develop the technique around a specific example.

Let us assume that we are interested in fitting the set of observed data given in Table 8.11 to a logarithmic function of the type

$$Y = aX^b$$

Table 8.11

X	Y
5.0	29.0
7.5	69.0
11.0	145.0
15.0	400.0

In expression (74) of Appendix A, the Taylor series was defined for a function $F(X)$ as

$$F(X) \approx F(X_1) + F'(X_1)(X_1 - X) + \frac{F''(X_1)(X_1 - X)^2 + \cdots}{2!}$$

where X_1 can be some value approximating X.

$F'(X_1)$ is the value of $\frac{d}{dx}[F(x)]$ at $X = X_1$.

$F''(X_1)$ is the value of $\frac{d^2}{dx^2}[F(X)]$ at $X = X_1$, etc.

From (89) $f(X)$ is aX^b and $F(X)$ is $aX^b - Y$. We shall write four expressions for this function, each involving an X-Y point and the unknowns a and b. To get started, we need approximate values for a and b. It does not matter particularly how we obtain those, so for convenience we shall use the method of selected points on the rectified form for $P_1(5.0, 29.0)$ and $P_2(15.0, 400.0)$:

$$\log_{10} 29 = \log_{10} a_0 + b_0 \log_{10} 5$$

$$\log_{10} 400 = \log_{10} a_0 + b_0 \log_{10} 15$$

Taking logs and rewriting, we have

$$1.46240 = \log_{10} a_0 + .69897 b_0$$
$$2.60206 = \log_{10} a_0 + 1.17609 b_0$$

Subtracting, we obtain

$$.47712 b_0 = 1.13966$$
$$b_0 = 2.389$$

from which

$$\log_{10} a_0 = 2.60206 - 2.80968 = .20762$$
$$a_0 = 0.6200$$

The value of D resulting from using these constants comes out to an intuitively unimpressive 2139.

If our final equation were to be a perfect fit, i.e., passing through all four points, all the deviations would be zero and the following equations would have to hold:

$$F_1(a, b) = a(5)^b - 29.0 = 0 \tag{90a}$$

$$F_2(a, b) = a(7.5)^b - 69.0 = 0 \tag{90b}$$

$$F_3(a, b) = a(11.0)^b - 145.0 = 0 \tag{90c}$$

$$F_4(a, b) = a(15.0)^b - 400.0 = 0 \tag{90d}$$

To get as close as we can to a perfect fit, we shall impose the above conditions. First, let us define a Taylor series for this general function $F_i(a, b)$. Since two unknowns are involved, we have to develop each derivative as a sum of the partial derivatives with respect to each of the variables a and b. Thus, with a_0 and b_0 as our first approximations, expression (89) would have to be rewritten to suit our specific case. Its form would then be as follows:

$$F(a, b) = a(X)^b - Y = 0 = F(a_0, b_0) + \frac{\partial F}{\partial a}(a_0, b_0)(a - a_0)$$
$$+ \frac{\partial F}{\partial b}(a_0, b_0)(b - b_0) + \frac{\partial^2 F}{\partial a^2} \frac{(a_0, b_0)(a - a_0)^2}{2!}$$
$$+ \frac{\partial^2 F}{\partial b^2} \frac{(a_0, b_0)(b - b_0)^2}{2!} + \cdots \tag{91}$$

We shall confine our illustration here to the first derivative terms. Since

$$F(a, b) = aX^b - Y$$

$$\frac{\partial F}{\partial a} = X^b$$

$$\frac{\partial F}{\partial b} = aX^b \log_e X$$

and

$$\frac{dF}{d(a, b)} = X^b + aX^b \log_e X \tag{92}$$

then, at any data point $(X_i \ Y_i)$, (91) expanded through the first derivative terms works out to be

$$F_i(a, b) = a_0 X_i^{b_0} - Y_i + X_i^{b_0}(a - a_0) + a_0 X_i^{b_0} \log_e X_i(b - b_0) = 0 \tag{93}$$

Using a_0 and b_0 from our selected points calculations, we can write the series for each (X, Y) point:

$$F_1(a, b) = .6200(5)^{2.389} - 29 + 5^{2.389}(a - .6200) + .6200(5)^{2.389}$$
$$\times \log_e (5)(b - 2.389) = 0 \tag{94a}$$

$$F_2(a, b) = .6200(7.5)^{2.389} - 69 + 7.5^{2.389}(a - .6200) + .6200(7.5)^{2.389}$$
$$\times \log_e (7.5)(b - 2.389) = 0 \tag{94b}$$

$$F_3(a, b) = .6200(11)^{2.389} - 145 + 11^{2.389}(a - .6200) + .6200(11)^{2.389}$$
$$\times \log_e (11)(b - 2.389) = 0 \tag{94c}$$

$$F_4(a, b) = .6200(15)^{2.389} - 400 + 15^{2.389}(a - .6200) + .6200(15)^{2.389}$$
$$\times \log_e (15)(b - 2.389) = 0 \tag{94d}$$

This works out to

$$0 + 46.76(a - .6200) + 29(1.60944)(b - 2.389) = 0$$
$$76.36 - 69 + 123.2(a - .6200) + 76.36(2.01490)(b - 2.389) = 0$$
$$190.66 - 145 + 307.5(a - .6200) + 190.66(2.39790)(b - 2.389) = 0$$
$$0 + 645.20(a - .6200) + 400(2.70805)(b - 2.389) = 0$$

Multiplying out and rearranging, we get

$$46.76(a - .6200) + 49.123(b - 2.389) = 0 \tag{95a}$$
$$123.20(a - .6200) + 76.360(b - 2.389) = -7.36 \tag{95b}$$
$$307.50(a - .6200) + 190.660(b - 2.389) = -45.66 \tag{95c}$$
$$645.20(a - .6200) + 1083.220(b - 2.389) = 0 \tag{95d}$$

These equations are known as the approximate equations of condition. Determination of new values of a and b from these equations proceeds as follows:

The equations of condition are transformed into a set of two equations by a succession of multiplication and additions. First, for convenience, let us substitute T for $(a - .6200)$ and S for $(b - 2.389)$. Now, each of the equations is multiplied by its respective coefficients of T and added together to produce the first of the two final equations:

$$2,186.50T + 2,296.99S = 0$$
$$15,178.24T + 9,407.55S = -906.75$$
$$94,556.25T + 58,627.95S = -14,040.45$$
$$416,283.04T + 698,893.54S = 0$$

$$\overline{528,204.03T + 769,226.03S = -14,947.20} \tag{96a}$$

The second equation is obtained in a similar fashion, by multiplying each equation in (95) by its coefficient of S and adding:

$$2{,}296.99T + \quad 2{,}413.07S = 0$$
$$9{,}407.55T + \quad 5{,}830.85S = -562.01$$
$$58{,}627.95T + \quad 36{,}351.24S = -8{,}705.54$$
$$698{,}893.54T + 1{,}173{,}365.57S = 0$$

$$769{,}226.03T + 1{,}217{,}960.73S = -9{,}267.55 \tag{96b}$$

Simultaneous solution of (96a) and (96b) gives

$$S = 0.1279$$
$$T = -0.2146$$

Substituting back for S and T gives

$$a - 0.6200 = -0.2146$$
$$b - 2.389 \;=\; 0.1279$$

So the new values of a and b are

$$a = 0.4054$$
$$b = 2.517$$

Using these with our data now gives a D value of 1557. An additional run through the procedure with a_0 at 0.4054 and b_0 at 2.517 reduces D further to 930.

If a constant c were involved, so that the required equation had the form

$$Y = aX^b + c$$

the basic expansion equation would be modified to read

$$F_i(a, b, c) = a_0 X_i^{b_0} + c_0 - Y_i + X_i^{b_0}(a - a_0) + a_0 X_i^{b_0} \log_e X_i (b - b_0)$$
$$+ c - c_0 = 0 \tag{97}$$

Similar equations can be worked out for other functions. For example, the exponential form

$$Y = ae^{bX}$$

would require the following expansion equation:

$$F_i(a, b) = a_0 e^{b_0 X_i} - Y_i + e^{b_0 X_i}(a - a_0) + X_i a_0 e^{b_0 X_i}(b - b_0) = 0 \tag{98}$$

POLYNOMIAL APPROXIMATIONS

When a particular set of data cannot be handled to the investigator's satisfaction by the commonly used equations described in the foregoing sections, the polynomial equation having the general form

$$\tilde{Y} = a_0 + a_1 X + a_2 X^2 + a_3 X^3 + \cdots + a_n X^n$$

is usually employed as a catchall. This form has the fortunate property that if enough terms are used, a fairly good fit can be developed for virtually any set of continuous data that displays a smooth graph. Furthermore, as seen in Appendix A, the polynomial is easy to differentiate so that the determination of slopes or integrals is a straightforward procedure.

EXACT EQUATIONS

If a set of observations consists of a relatively small number of points (say n) each taken at a different value of X, it is possible to develop an $(n-1)$th-order polynomial equation whose graph will pass through each of those points, producing a curve fit with an error of zero. Thus, if we have five points (X_1, Y_1), (X_2, Y_2), (X_3, Y_3), (X_4, Y_4), and (X_5, Y_5), we can set up a system of five equations as follows:

$$a_0 + a_1(X_1) + a_2(X_1)^2 + a_3(X_1)^3 + a_4(X_1)^4 = Y_1$$
$$a_0 + a_1(X_2) + a_2(X_2)^2 + a_3(X_2)^3 + a_4(X_2)^4 = Y_2$$
$$a_0 + a_1(X_3) + a_2(X_3)^2 + a_3(X_3)^3 + a_4(X_3)^4 = Y_3 \qquad (99)$$
$$a_0 + a_1(X_4) + a_2(X_4)^2 + a_3(X_4)^3 + a_4(X_4)^4 = Y_4$$
$$a_0 + a_1(X_5) + a_2(X_5)^2 + a_3(X_5)^3 + a_4(X_5)^4 = Y_5$$

Or, rewritten in matrix form,

$$
\begin{pmatrix}
1 & X_1 & X_1^2 & X_1^3 & X_1^4 \\
1 & X_2 & X_2^2 & X_2^3 & X_2^4 \\
1 & X_3 & X_3^2 & X_3^3 & X_3^4 \\
1 & X_4 & X_4^2 & X_4^3 & X_4^4 \\
1 & X_5 & X_5^2 & X_5^3 & X_5^4
\end{pmatrix}
\begin{pmatrix}
a_0 \\
a_1 \\
a_2 \\
a_3 \\
a_4
\end{pmatrix}
=
\begin{pmatrix}
Y_1 \\
Y_2 \\
Y_3 \\
Y_4 \\
Y_5
\end{pmatrix}
\qquad (100)
$$

(Solution of matrix forms will be discussed in detail in Chapter 9.)

Although this may seem to be a most effective technique, it has several serious drawbacks that limit its use. First of all, polynomials are usually restricted to no more than six or seven terms, since extension beyond that level makes for very unwieldy equations. Furthermore, the loss in precision rises sharply with the number of multiplications used, thus decreasing the reliability of derived high-order polynomials. Since sets of observations are not generally limited to five or six points, the development of an exact equation for most systems would require the use of very high degree polynomials.

Second, more significantly, the search for an exact equation presupposes that each of the data points is in itself exact, having no error associated with it. Since it is relatively difficult to deduce the shape of a polynomial equation merely from its coefficients, the development of such exact equations can produce some rather implausible results. One such situation is exemplified in Figure 8.22. The solid line represents a polynomial fit through all of the points. The path of such an equation includes convolutions whose occurrence is quite unlikely. In general, this practice is as questionable as the use of linear segments to connect successive values of X on a graph. A more plausible alternative is the curve shown as a dashed line. Although it produces a larger error term, its trajectory is much closer to what would be expected, and the investigator can use it to predict Y values with much more credibility. Thus, even when the accuracy of a set of observations is assured, it is dangerous to fit an exact equation to them without examining the resulting graph to determine whether the function's characteristics produce fluctuations that make interpolation useless.

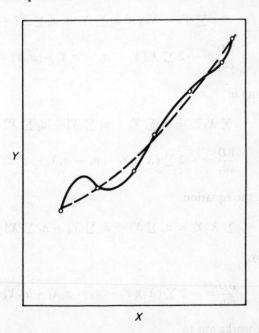

Fig. 8.22. Plot of polynomial data illustrating the implausability of an exact fit.

LEAST SQUARES POLYNOMIALS

Because of the reasons stipulated above, the polynomial fitting technique used most frequently is the least squares procedure applied to all of the observations. Its construction is exactly analogous to that shown for the linear case, as seen by the following development for the cubic form:

$$\tilde{Y} = a_0 + a_1 X + a_2 X^2 + a_3 X^3 \tag{101}$$

The individual deviation d_i is

$$d_i = Y_i - a_0 - a_1 X_i - a_2 X_i^2 - a_3 X_i^3 \tag{102}$$

and D, the sum of the squared deviations, is

$$D = \sum_{i=1}^{N} d_i^2 = \sum (Y_i - a_0 - a_1 X_i - a_2 X_i^2 - a_3 X_i^3)^2 \tag{103}$$

This time there are four unknown constants involved ($a_0, a_1, a_2,$ and a_3), and thus our function has to be minimized with respect to all of them:

$$\frac{\partial D}{\partial a_0} = -2 \sum (Y_i - a_0 - a_1 X_i - a_2 X_i^2 - a_3 X_i^3) = 0$$

from which

$$\sum Y_i = N a_0 + a_1 \sum X_i + a_2 \sum X_i^2 + a_3 \sum X_i^3 \tag{104}$$

$$\frac{\partial D}{\partial a_1} = -2 \sum X_i (Y_i - a_0 - a_1 X_i - a_2 X_i^2 - a_3 X_i^3) = 0$$

resulting in

$$\sum X_i Y_i = a_0 \sum X_i + a_1 \sum X_i^2 + a_2 \sum X_i^3 + a_3 \sum X_i^4 \tag{105}$$

$$\frac{\partial D}{\partial a_2} = -2 \sum (X_i^2)(Y_i - a_0 - a_1 X_i - a_2 X_i^2 - a_3 X_i^3) = 0$$

giving the equation

$$\sum X_i^2 Y_i = a_0 \sum X_i^2 + a_1 \sum X_i^3 + a_2 \sum X_i^4 + a_3 \sum X_i^5 \tag{106}$$

Finally,

$$\frac{\partial D}{\partial a_3} = -2 \sum (X_i^3)(Y_i - a_0 - a_1 X_i - a_2 X_i^2 - a_3 X_i^3) = 0$$

which works out to

$$\sum X_i^3 Y_i = a_0 \sum X_i^3 + a_1 \sum X_i^4 + a_2 \sum X_i^5 + a_3 \sum X_i^6$$

Equations (104) through (107) form the matrix system

$$
\begin{pmatrix}
N & \sum X_i & \sum X_i^2 & \sum X_i^3 \\
\sum X_i & \sum X_i^2 & \sum X_i^3 & \sum X_i^4 \\
\sum X_i^2 & \sum X_i^3 & \sum X_i^4 & \sum X_i^5 \\
\sum X_i^3 & \sum X_i^4 & \sum X_i^5 & \sum X_i^6
\end{pmatrix}
\begin{pmatrix}
a_0 \\ a_1 \\ a_2 \\ a_3
\end{pmatrix}
=
\begin{pmatrix}
\sum Y_i \\ \sum X_i Y_i \\ \sum X_i^2 Y_i \\ \sum X_i^3 Y_i
\end{pmatrix}
\tag{108}
$$

From this structure, we can state the system of $n + 1$ equations for the general case of an nth-order polynomial containing $(n + 1)$ constants $a_0, a_1, \cdots, a_n$:

$$
\begin{pmatrix}
N & \sum X_i & \sum X_i^2 & \sum X_i^3 & \cdots & \sum X_i^n \\
\sum X_i & \sum X_i^2 & \sum X_i^3 & \sum X_i^4 & \cdots & \sum X_i^{n+1} \\
\sum X_i^2 & \sum X_i^3 & \sum X_i^4 & \sum X_i^5 & \cdots & \sum X_i^{n+2} \\
\sum X_i^3 & \sum X_i^4 & \sum X_i^5 & \sum X_i^6 & \cdots & \sum X_i^{n+3} \\
\cdot & \cdot & \cdot & \cdot & & \cdot \\
\cdot & \cdot & \cdot & \cdot & & \cdot \\
\cdot & \cdot & \cdot & \cdot & & \cdot \\
\sum X_i^n & \sum X_i^{n+1} & \sum X_i^{n+2} & \sum X_i^{n+3} & \cdots & \sum X_i^{2n}
\end{pmatrix}
\begin{pmatrix}
a_0 \\ a_1 \\ a_2 \\ a_3 \\ \cdot \\ \cdot \\ \cdot \\ a_n
\end{pmatrix}
=
\begin{pmatrix}
\sum Y_i \\ \sum X_i Y_i \\ \sum X_i^2 Y_i \\ \sum X_i^3 Y_i \\ \cdot \\ \cdot \\ \cdot \\ \sum X_i^n Y_i
\end{pmatrix}
$$
$$\tag{109}$$

If the investigator finds himself obliged to fit a polynomial to his data, there is no quick and easy way for him to determine what order to use.[3] (Obviously, he will use the lowest order he can get away with, since he wants the equation which is easiest to use.) Consequently, many polynomial fitting programs will present the user with least squares equations for several orders so that he may decide whether the additional reduction in error warrants the use of an $(n + 1)$th order over an nth order. The Medcomp program, whose output is shown in Figure 8.23 for example, is designed to produce first- through fifth-order polynomials automatically. (The particular goodness of fit indicator used in this program is the correlation coefficient, which is related to the sum of squared deviations and will be discussed in the next chapter.) Most programs of this type are limited to fourth- or fifth-order polynomials, since experience has demonstrated that sets of data which cannot be fit by such equations are not sufficiently consistent to be represented by a predictive equation at all.

---

[3] Techniques have been developed for estimating the highest degree required by evaluating the differences between adjacent Y values, then evaluating the differences between the differences, etc. Descriptions are given in most numerical analysis texts.

```
POLYNOMIAL FIT
     SAMPLE PROBLEM


DEGREE OF                COEFFICIENT                        POWER OF X
EQUATION


   1          Y = -2.165142857 X 10 TO THE + 3   TIMES X 0
                  +1.606714285 X 10 TO THE + 3   TIMES X 1

       VARIANCE = +4.794367643 X 10 TO THE + 6
      R SQUARED = +6.987480061 X 10 TO THE - 1


   2          Y = +6.934285710 X 10 TO THE + 2   TIMES X 0
                  -1.823571429 X 10 TO THE + 3   TIMES X 1
                  +5.717142857 X 10 TO THE + 2   TIMES X 2

       VARIANCE = +5.703665901 X 10 TO THE + 5
      R SQUARED = +9.641612647 X 10 TO THE - 1


   3          Y = -7.857142900 X 10 TO THE + 1   TIMES X 0
                  +7.497619040 X 10 TO THE + 2   TIMES X 1
                  -5.862857143 X 10 TO THE + 2   TIMES X 2
                  +1.286666666 X 10 TO THE + 2   TIMES X 3

       VARIANCE = +2.022751705 X 10 TO THE + 4
      R SQUARED = +9.987290128 X 10 TO THE - 1


   4          Y = +8.857141690 X 10 TO THE + 0   TIMES X 0
                  -1.099523654 X 10 TO THE + 2   TIMES X 1
                  +1.689999852 X 10 TO THE + 2   TIMES X 2
                  -7.533332940 X 10 TO THE + 1   TIMES X 3
                  +1.699999966 X 10 TO THE + 1   TIMES X 4

       VARIANCE = +1.054944839 X 10 TO THE + 2
      R SQUARED = +9.999933713 X 10 TO THE - 1


   5          Y = +6.000020291 X 10 TO THE + 0   TIMES X 0
                  +4.999234100 X 10 TO THE + 0   TIMES X 1
                  +4.001092800 X 10 TO THE + 0   TIMES X 2
                  +2.999483210 X 10 TO THE + 0   TIMES X 3
                  +2.000098660 X 10 TO THE + 0   TIMES X 4
                  +9.999934375 X 10 TO THE - 1   TIMES X 5

       VARIANCE = +4.580299196 X 10 TO THE - 9
      R SQUARED = +1.000000000 X 10 TO THE + 0


     VARIANCE OF Y = +1.591480800 X 10 TO THE + 7
     NUMBER OF OBSERVATIONS +1.400000000 X 10 TO THE + 1
```

Fig. 8.23. Polynomial fit. Sample problem.

EVALUATION OF POLYNOMIALS

We mentioned before that the evaluation of high-order terms in polynomials (or other expressions, for that matter) can lead to serious errors because of the truncation of significant digits during successive multiplica-

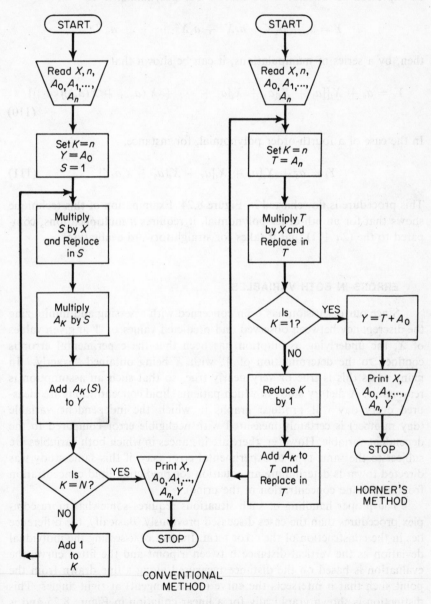

Fig. 8.24. Flowcharts for polynomial evaluation using coventional and Horner's methods.

tions. Although this situation is never completely avoided, there are techniques by which such errors can be reduced considerably.

A very effective procedure for reducing the number of multiplications required to calculate the value of a polynomial is Horner's rule, which can be expressed as follows: If we express our polynomial Y as

$$Y = a_0 + a_1 X + a_2 X^2 + a_3 X^3 + \cdots + a_n X^n$$

then, by a series of manipulations, it can be shown that

$$Y_i = a_0 + X_i\{\{a_1 + X_i\{a_2 + X_i[a_3 + \cdots + X_i(a_{n-1} + X(a_n))]\cdots\}\}\} \tag{110}$$

In the case of a fourth-order polynomial, for instance,

$$Y_i = a_0 + X_i\{a_1 + X_i[a_2 + X_i(a_3 + X_i a_4)]\} \tag{111}$$

This procedure is flowcharted in Figure 8.24. Examination of this technique shows that for an nth-order polynomial, it requires n multiplications, compared to the $(2n + 1)$ that it takes for straightforward evaluation.

ERRORS IN BOTH VARIABLES

Since our discussion has been concerned with assessing and minimizing the discrepancy between observed and predicted values of Y at given values of X, the underlying assumption has been that the experimental error is confined to the determination of Y, with X being obtained "exactly." In many cases this is true or very nearly true, so that such an assumption is reasonable. A dietary study in which patients' lipid concentrations are measured every day will produce graphs in which the independent variable (day number) is certainly measured with negligible error compared to the dependent variable. However, there are instances in which both variables are subject to the same type of experimental error (say, if this same study was directed towards determining an equation for predicting lipid concentration from creatinine concentration in the urine).

The proper handling of such situations requires somewhat more complex procedures than the cases discussed previously. Basically, the difference lies in the construction of the error term. Instead of assessing the individual deviation as the vertical distance between a point and the fitted curve, the evaluation is based on the distance measured along a line drawn from the point such that it intersects the curve (or its tangent) at right angles. This distinction is shown graphically for a linear equation in Figure 8.25 and is calculated as follows: If we express the general linear form as

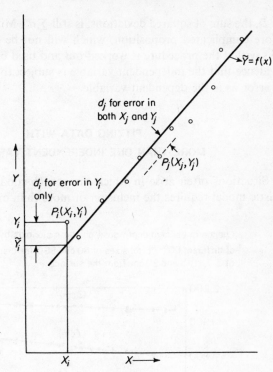

Fig. 8.25. Linear X-Y data with errors in both variables.

$$a_0 + a_1 X - Y = 0 \qquad (112)$$

and divide by a_0, we obtain

$$1 + \frac{a_1}{a_0} X - \frac{1}{a_0} Y = 0 \qquad (113)$$

If we let

$$V = \frac{a_1}{a_0}$$

and

$$W = \frac{-1}{a_0}$$

it turns out that the perpendicular distance d of any point (X_i, Y_i) from some particular line characterized by a_0 and a_1 is

$$d_i = \frac{VX_i + WY_i + 1}{\sqrt{V^2 + W^2}} \qquad (114)$$

and D, the sum of squared deviations, is still $\sum d_i^2$. Minimization of D is now a more complicated proposition, which will not be discussed here. Suffice it to say that the procedure is worked out and used occasionally when there is evidence that the independent variable is subject to at least the same relative error as is the dependent variable.

FITTING DATA WITH
MORE THAN ONE INDEPENDENT VARIABLE

Situations often arise in which the construction of a successful deterministic model requires the inclusion of more than one antecedent variable.

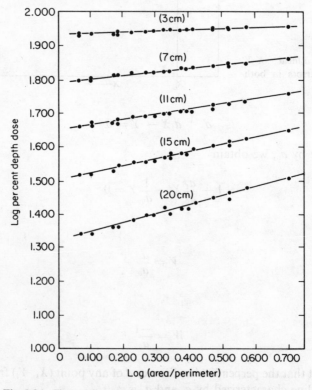

Fig. 8.26. Change in per cent depth dose on the major axis by log (area/perimeter) of different CO^{60} portal sizes at 80 cm SSD for distances of 3, 7, 11, 15, and 20 cm from the surface. *Courtesy British Journal of Radiology.*

Equations to handle such systems can be synthesized if sufficient data are available to depict the effects of each independent variable. The technique is basically analogous to the mathematical procedure of constructing a total derivative by adding together the isolated effects, represented by partial derivatives.

The nature of this procedure can be illustrated very aptly by describing an investigation directed toward defining an equation which could be used to predict the dose along the central axis of a radioactive beam of a given size at a particular distance from the beam source. The beams under consideration were rectangular in shape, with a variety of sizes in common use.

Sufficient data were collected to allow graphs to be constructed showing the variation of dose with beam size for each of a series of distances from the source. Examination of these displays indicated that each of the resulting curves exhibited a logarithmic trend that could be rectified by the appropriate transformation. When the rectangular beam size was expressed as area/perimeter (A/P), and the transformed data were plotted as a family of curves (Figure 8.26) so that a function could be derived for each particular distance from the source, the typical equation took the form

$$\log \text{dose} = a + b(\log A/P) \qquad (115)$$

Change in slope of axial per cent depth dose as function of log (area/perimeter) of the treatment field with distance below surface

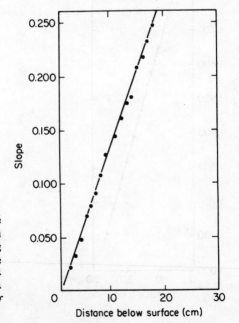

Fig. 8.27. Change in slope of axial per cent depth dose as function of log (area/perimeter) of the treatment field with distance below surface. *Courtesy British Journal of Radiology.*

where a and b were characteristic constants for a particular distance from the beam source. Use of this equation involved inserting the constants for the distance of interest, as well as the A/P, and solving for the dose value.

To consolidate the family of equations, an examination was undertaken to determine how the values of a and b varied with distance. The resulting graphs (Figures 8.27 and 8.28) showed that the variations were sufficiently systematic to allow curves to be fitted closely to these trends. This resulted in expressions for

$$a = f_1(\text{distance}) \tag{116a}$$

$$b = f_2(\text{distance}) \tag{116b}$$

so that a general equation for central axis dose could be written as

$$\log \text{dose} = f_1(\text{distance}) + f_2(\text{distance}) \log A/P \tag{117}$$

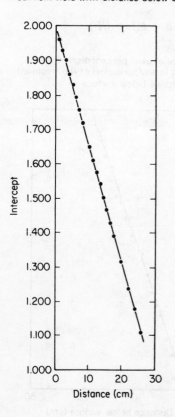

Change of intercept of axial per cent depth dose as function of log (area/perimeter) of the treatment field with distance below surface

Fig. 8.28. Change of intercept of axial per cent depth dose as function of log (area/perimeter) of the treatment field with distance below surface. *Courtesy British Journal of Radiology.*

If additional factors are involved in determining the antecedent conditions, this sequence can, of course, be extended. For instance, the constants in f_1 and f_2 of expression (117) could themselves be expressed as other functions of some additional antecedent variable. The amount of data required for such extensions, of course, rises very rapidly.

PROBLEMS

For the sets of data points given below, find the most appropriate form or function by rectification and fit an equation to the points, using the method of averages. (Use least squares if a suitable computer program is available.) The quantity Y is always the dependent variable. If more than one form appears to fit, show the values of $|\%d|$ for each.

1.

X	0.5	1.0	1.7	2.5	3.1	3.7	4.4	5.0
Y	0.4	1.3	1.9	3.1	3.6	4.5	5.2	6.1

2.

X	150	369	532	838	910	961	1049	1128	1211	1264
Y	7	219	609	790	1073	1133	1321	1683	1987	1871

3.

X	5	10	18	28	43	140
Y	6	8.5	22	26	32	113

4.

X	.01	.32	.34	.35	.54	.55	.69	.70	.90	.92	1.00	1.20	1.22	1.55	1.60	2.10
Y	111	116	110	106	109	100	101	98	94	92	91	91	90	90	88	86

5.

X	28	33	34	37	41	43	44	47	49
Y	12	14	15	15	17	20	19	23	24

6.

X	75	125	175	225	275	325	375	425	475	525	575
Y	427	339	319	239	220	219	153	119	83	54	46

7.

X	212	214	231	237	244	255	257	273	284	290
Y	199	204	216	218	224	235	238	256	264	270

8.

X	0	2	4	6	8	10	12	14
Y	−40	−36	−28	−20	−13	−11	0	4

9.

X	3	4	6	7	10	12	13
Y	−60	−110	−247	−350	−702	−1010	−1200

10.

X	11	18	22	30	36	40	45	48
Y	22	76	110	215	300	390	480	550

11.

X	.15	.3	.45	.6	.75	.9	1	1.2
Y	1	2	4	8	12	18	23	30

12.

X	100	120	140	160	180	200
Y	30,100	43,300	58,800	76,800	97,000	122,000

13.

X	1.1	2.1	3.1	4.1	5.1	6.1	7.1	8.1
Y	7	14	19	32	40	60	75	91

14.

X	2	3	5	6	8	9
Y	4	8	16	20	35	39

15.

X	10	20	30	40	50	60	70	80
Y	20	64	140	225	320	430	575	725

16.

X	5	10	15	20	25	30	35
Y	9	10	15	16	20	20	21

17.

X	25	50	75	100	125	150	175	200	250	300
Y	5.4	2.8	1.2	0.2	−1.1	−2.1	−3.3	−4.0	−5.9	−7.3

18.

X	0	1	2	3	4	5	6	7
Y	3.5	9.5	29	93	304	950	2990	9470

19.

X	4	8	12	16	20	24	28	30	35	40
Y	5	15	40	100	170	600	1530	2400	7650	24,150

20.

X	1.0	1.2	1.4	1.6	1.8	2.0	2.2	2.4	2.6	2.8
Y	10	11	18	30	35	50	63	80	115	150

21.

X	1	3	5	7	9	11	15	20
Y	.7	.25	.1	.1	.08	.07	.05	.03

22.

X	0	1	2	3	4	5
Y	4.60	5.25	5.40	5.60	5.82	5.80

23.

X	.2	.4	.6	.8	1	1.2	1.4	1.6
Y	−10	4	9	10	12	12	15	15

9

DESCRIBING STOCHASTIC ASSOCIATIONS

The precise mathematical description of relationships is associated predominantly with the natural sciences, where plotting consequent versus antecedent conditions usually gives rise to a series of points which fall on a smooth curve. The equation describing this curve may be derived from prior theoretical considerations, through empirical curve-fitting techniques or by just guessing. Possible forms of such curves and their method of description have been covered in the previous chapter.

There are yet other types of relationships which, although they clearly indicate some association between antecedent or independent variables on one and consequent dependent variables on the other, predict "in general" but with a rather pronounced error. The relationship between liver and body weight is a good example. A "trend" exists so that, in general, the heavier the individual, the heavier the liver. However, if we make a scattergram of liver versus body weight (see Figure 5.3), we can see that although such a trend does exist, there are many instances of overlap in which individuals who are heavy have livers that weigh less than those of some individuals who are lighter. Can we write a mathematical expression to predict liver from body weight or body from liver weight? (It does not matter in which direction we try to predict right now.) We can indicate the form of an equation, but there will always be large errors around such descriptions. These errors will not decrease (beyond a point) by increasing the precision by which either liver or body weight is measured. This is perhaps the crucial distinction between a deterministic and a nondeterministic model.

Where does this variation come from? Let us take the relation between height and weight as an example. Although it is true that taller individuals weigh more than shorter individuals, it is also true that individuals with a higher specific gravity weigh more than those with a lower specific gravity; individuals who exercise and build up muscles weigh more than those who do not exercise; individuals who have genetically heavy bone structure weigh more than those who do not have such inherited characteristics; individuals who have better nutrition and eat more outweigh those who do not have good nutrition or eat less, and on and on. We could even go so far as to claim that all things being equal, those who have a short haircut weigh less than those who have long hair. Thus there are a large number of variables besides height which determine the weight of an individual. The variation around whatever best prediction for weight can be based on knowledge of height will thus reflect the presence or absence of a variety of other factors that also contribute increments to the determination of weight.

We have thus come closer to an understanding of what a trend is. If we find that one variable seems to be associated with another but that this association is far from perfect, our most sensible interpretation is that the reflected relationship is only incomplete. There are a variety of other conditions that determine the outcome of the observations which vary in some more or less random fashion, so that the sum total effects are a collection of data points through which it is not possible to draw one smooth curve that contains all observations. The reasons for the additional variation lies in our own "ignorance" about what other variables determine the phenomena or in our inability to control them. When such a relationship exists it would be more appropriate to call it stochastic (or probabilistic).

Contained in this notion of stochastic is the idea that if we were able to describe the effect of the many variables that work together, we could predict or describe the outcome of an experiment to a degree of accuracy that would convert a stochastic association into a deterministic one. It is here that the computer opens an entirely new avenue of approach, which will be discussed in the next chapter. Keep in mind that the material in this chapter is a necessary prerequisite for understanding the multivariate approach to description and prediction in the stochastic world of empirical science that is in large part a proliferation of techniques developed around the description of the stochastic relationship between a small number of variables.

Despite the calculation power of the computer, we shall restrict our discussion largely to relationships that are assumed to be basically linear, because calculations involved in linear manipulations are very much simpler than those needed for nonlinear cases. Not only does their simplicity make it possible for students with less sophistication in mathematics to deal with them, but the complexities introduced by nonlinearity are often so great that they can now be handled only with the greatest difficulties. Very often, too, in terms of the additional accuracy and the decrease of error of prediction that may be entailed by forsaking the notion of linearity and going into the more complex nonlinear computation, that payoff is not really sufficient to justify the much larger efforts required. Consequently, we shall concern ourselves predominantly with a linear model and indicate ways and means to deal with nonlinear situations as they become appropriate.

SIMPLE LINEAR REGRESSION
AND CORRELATION

Where height is a variable denoted by X and weight is denoted by Y we look for a line that goes through the points $(X_i, \tilde{Y}_i)$, where X_i is the ith value of the independent variable and $\tilde{Y}_i$ is our best prediction of the dependent variable Y. The form of equation we shall consider first is

$$Y_i = a_0 + a_1 X_i$$

which, as we saw in the previous chapter, is the equation of a straight line with intercept a_0 and slope a_1. If we define

$$\tilde{y}_i = \tilde{Y}_i - \bar{Y}$$
$$x_i = X_i - \bar{X}$$

we can write the same expression as

$$\tilde{y}_i = a_1 x_i$$

thus eliminating one unknown.

In Chapter 8 we found a simple expression for the slopes of the best-fitting lines through a scatter where "best fit" was defined as that line for which the sum of the squared deviations is a minimum. This relation still holds true for the stochastic case. For that line,

$$a_1 = \frac{\sum (X - \bar{X})(Y - \bar{Y})}{\sum (X - \bar{X})^2}$$

or

$$a_1 = \frac{\sum xy}{\sum x^2}$$

and

$$a_0 = \bar{Y} - a_1 \bar{X}$$

We can then write the expression for the best prediction of Y as

$$\tilde{Y}_i = [\bar{Y} - a_1\bar{X}] + a_1 X_i$$
$$= \bar{Y} + a_1(X_i - \bar{X})$$

MEASURING THE "GOODNESS" OF REGRESSION—CORRELATION

The average squared error, better known as the variance of points around the best-fitting line, $\sigma^2_{y|x}$ is defined as before by

$$\sigma^2_{y|x} = \frac{\sum (Y_i - \tilde{Y}_i)^2}{N} \tag{1}$$

If the relationship between Y and X is "good" so that all the points in Y lie very close to their predicted values, then

$$\sum (Y - \tilde{Y})^2 \to 0$$

and

$$\sigma^2_{y|x} \to 0$$

On the other hand, when the relationship between Y and X is "poor" so that Y is *not* predicted from the knowledge of X, then for each X_i there will occur a number of values for Y_i which represent, in essence, a random sample of values of Y from the total population. When this happens, the best estimate of $\tilde{Y}$ is equal to $\bar{Y}$, so that as

$$\tilde{Y}_i \to \bar{Y}$$
$$\sum (Y_i - \tilde{Y}_i)^2 \to \sum (Y_i - \bar{Y})^2$$

and

$$\sigma^2_{y|x} \to \sigma^2_y$$

We may summarize this by saying that when the relationship described by our linear regression line is "good," $\sigma^2_{y|x}$ becomes very small. On the other hand, where the regression line does not fit, then knowing X_i will not help us, and $\sigma^2_{y|x}$ will be no better than σ^2_y.

We use this knowledge of the relationship between $\sigma^2_{y|x}$ and σ^2_y to define the goodness of a relationship. The measure we employ here is the proportion by which $\sigma^2_{y|x}$ is smaller than σ^2_y or

$$r^2 = \frac{\sigma^2_y - \sigma^2_{y|x}}{\sigma^2_y} \tag{2}$$

where r is known as the *Pearson product moment correlation coefficient*. Note that if the relationship is good, then

$$\lim_{r^2 \to 1} \sigma^2_{y|x} = 0$$

and if the relationship is poor, then

$$\lim_{r^2 \to 0} \sigma^2_{y|x} = \sigma^2_y$$

In this way r^2 takes on values between 0 and 1 proportional to the "goodness" with which we can predict Y from a knowledge of X.

The computational formula of r derived from its definition is

$$r = \frac{\sum [(X - \bar{X})(Y - \bar{Y})]}{\sqrt{\sum (X - \bar{X})^2} \sqrt{\sum (Y - \bar{Y})^2}} \tag{3}$$

or

$$r = \frac{\sum xy}{\sqrt{\sum x^2} \sqrt{\sum y^2}}$$

so that the value of r ranges between $-1 \le r \le +1$. Negative values of r indicate that the relationship between X and Y is inverse so that Y decreases as X increases, whereas positive values of r would indicate the opposite. We can rewrite expression (3)

$$\sqrt{\sum (X - \bar{X})^2} = \sqrt{N} \sigma_x$$

$$\sqrt{\sum (Y - \bar{Y})^2} = \sqrt{N} \sigma_y$$

so that

$$r = \frac{\sum [(X - \bar{X})(Y - \bar{Y})]}{N \sigma_x \sigma_y} \tag{4}$$

There are a number of important relationships between r and the variance and standard deviations of variables X and Y that we should keep in mind.

We saw in Chapter 6 that

$$\frac{d[\sum (y - a_1 x)^2]}{da_1} = \frac{-2 \sum x(y - a_1 x)}{N}$$

If we find the value of a_1 for which $\sum (y - a_1 x)^2$ is a minimum, we get

$$\frac{\sum (X - \bar{X})(Y - \bar{Y})}{N} - \frac{a_1 \sum (X - \bar{X})^2}{N} = 0$$

And using the formula for r from expression (4), we get

$$r \sigma_x \sigma_y - a_1 \sigma^2_x = 0 \tag{5}$$

so that

$$a_1 = r\left(\frac{\sigma_y}{\sigma_x}\right) \tag{6}$$

We can now write the expression of the best-fitting line in terms of standard deviations and correlation coefficients

$$\tilde{y}_i = r\left(\frac{\sigma_y}{\sigma_x}\right) x_i \tag{7}$$

or as its alternative

$$\tilde{Y}_i = r\left(\frac{\sigma_y}{\sigma_x}\right) X_i + \left[\bar{Y} - r\left(\frac{\sigma_y}{\sigma_x}\right)\bar{X}\right] \tag{8}$$

It obviously makes no difference whether we compute a correlation of X on Y or of Y on X [the student may verify this by examining equation (3)]. On the other hand, if we want to predict X from Y, then

$$\tilde{X}_i = a_0' + a_1' Y_i \tag{9}$$

since by definition

$$a_1' = r\left(\frac{\sigma_x}{\sigma_y}\right) \tag{10a}$$

and

$$a_0' = \bar{X} - a_1'\bar{Y} \tag{10b}$$

The best-fitting lines predicting X from Y and Y from X coincide only if they have the same standard deviation. Conversely, in any stochastic situation, the predictions of Y from X and X from Y take different forms. Here we have again a way of differentiating between a deterministic and a stochastic situation. In a deterministic model where $f(X)$ is known, a statement for $X = g(Y)$ can be deduced in most cases. This is not true for the stochastic situation, where $f(X)$ and $g(Y)$ must be determined separately. separately.

One other definition of the correlation coefficient is possible.

$$r = a_1\left(\frac{\sigma_y}{\sigma_x}\right) = a_1'\left(\frac{\sigma_x}{\sigma_y}\right) = \sqrt{a_1 a_1'} \tag{11}$$

when a_1 and a_1' have the meanings implied in (6) and (9), respectively.

PREDICTION AND CERTAINTY

For any level of goodness of fit, there will be a certain amount of uncertainty about the prediction of Y_1 from X_1. This uncertainty is summarized by $\sigma_{y|x}^2$. Since

$$\tilde{y} = r\left(\frac{\sigma_y}{\sigma_x}\right)x$$

$$\sigma_{y|x}^2 = \frac{\sum\left[y_i - r\left(\dfrac{\sigma_y}{\sigma_x}\right)x_i\right]^2}{N}$$

$$= \frac{1}{N}\left[\sum y^2 - 2r\left(\frac{\sigma_y}{\sigma_x}\right)\sum xy + r^2\left(\frac{\sigma_y}{\sigma_x}\right)^2\sum x^2\right]$$

(and since $\sum xy/N$ can be written as $r\sigma_x\sigma_y$)

$$\sigma_{y|x}^2 = \sigma_y^2 - 2r\left(\frac{\sigma_y}{\sigma_x}\right)r\sigma_y\sigma_x + r^2\left(\frac{\sigma_y}{\sigma_x}\right)^2\sigma_x^2$$

$$= \sigma_y^2 - r^2\sigma_y^2$$

so that

$$\sigma_{y|x}^2 = \sigma_y^2(1 - r^2) \tag{12}$$

and

$$\sigma_{y|x} = \sigma_y\sqrt{1 - r^2} \tag{13}$$

This result should not really surprise us. We started off by defining the correlation coefficient as an estimate of the goodness of a prediction. Equation (12) is just such a statement, which says that the error of prediction incurred by making use of the relationship between X and Y is a fraction of the error of prediction that would have occurred had we not made use of the knowledge of such a relationship. This fraction is defined by $(1 - r^2)$ or expressed in standard deviation form as $\sqrt{1 - r^2}$.

We may summarize now what we have learned so far. In describing the relationship between two variables which is in the form of a trend we find the best-fitting function (in our case linear) that will enable us to make a prediction of one variable from knowing the other. The error entailed in this procedure serves as the basis of a measurement of the goodness of fit or the usefulness of predicting one variable from the other by this strategy. We derived a measure called *correlation*, which describes the proportion by which a variation in the error of prediction is decreased by the use of a prediction equation. In the back of our mind there is the proposition that if we do not know the relationship between X and Y, our best prediction will be the mean of the dependent variable $\bar{Y}$, and σ_y^2 can be interpreted as that average squared error that would occur if we were to predict $\bar{Y}$ each time, regardless of what X was.

Note that in our definition, correlation does not mean causation by any stretch of the imagination. Correlation implies two concepts.

First is the concept of covariation. The quantity X becomes a predictor of Y to the extent that variations in X are paralleled by variations in Y. The covariation is actually measured by the sum of the cross products

$$\Sigma\,(X - \bar{X})(Y - \bar{Y})$$

which is actually called the *covariance*. This number will tend to be large when fluctuations of X and Y coincide (either directly or inversely).

A second point to note is that correlation defines pragmatic "usefulness" of a predictor. The degree of correlation helps us decide whether it is or is not worthwhile to use a specific predictor.

VARIANCE AND CORRELATION

The concept of correlation and the concept of variance are closely related. Not only is correlation defined in terms of variance, but from a logical point of view, they are connected as are the two sides of a coin. Variance is essentially the measurement the "unknown" or, if it suits us better, the amount of "ignorance" which we have about the workings of nature with respect to some particular phenomenon. Correlation measures how much of this ignorance or uncertainty can be removed by the use of other variables as predictors.

Very much embedded in this view is the concept that the variance of any set of events consists of many parts. Let us assume that a variable X is made up of two increments, V and W, which are contributed by different sources.

$$X = V \pm W$$

and

$$x = v \pm w$$

Let us now examine the variance of X:

$$\sigma_x^2 = \frac{\Sigma\,x^2}{N} = \frac{\Sigma\,(v \pm w)^2}{N}$$

$$= \frac{\Sigma\,v^2}{N} + \frac{\Sigma\,w^2}{N} \pm \frac{2\,\Sigma\,vw}{N}$$

and since

$$\frac{\sum vw}{N} = r_{vw}\sigma_v\sigma_w$$

we have as a result, if $X = V + W$,

$$\sigma_{v+w}^2 = \sigma_v^2 + \sigma_w^2 + 2r_{vw}\sigma_v\sigma_w \tag{14a}$$

and if $X = V - W$, our result becomes

$$\sigma_{v-w}^2 = \sigma_v^2 + \sigma_w - 2r_{vw}\sigma_v\sigma_w \tag{14b}$$

If V_i and W_i are completely independent of each other so that $r_{vw} = 0$, then

$$\sigma_{v+w}^2 = \sigma_r^2 + \sigma_w^2 \tag{15}$$

[We have now justified equation (27c) in Chapter 5, where we simply assumed that we could find the variance of the difference by summing two independent variances. Note that we can now expand our procedure to test differences between two correlated means.]

The proof that variances are additive is important. It means that if additional factors are introduced which affect the outcome of an observation, the result will be an increase in the variance of this observation. Thus, we can consider the variance of a variable to be the result of the contribution of different factors. Since variances are additive, the total variance reflects the sum of all the contributions. Consequently, each time we find a correlated variable, we reduce in effect the total variance by some increment. Correlation is thus an expression of explained variance. Let us now think of a variable Y to be made up of two parts. One part P is the increment of Y that has been predicted by the knowledge of another variable and the other is the residual E, both of whose origin or predecessors are unknown so that

$$Y = P + E$$

We then deal with a case where P and E are independent of each other by definition so that

$$\sigma_y^2 = \sigma_P^2 + \sigma_E^2$$

If we now divide through by σ_y^2 we get

$$1 = \frac{\sigma_P^2}{\sigma_y^2} + \frac{\sigma_E^2}{\sigma_y^2}$$

It is obvious that

$$\sigma_E^2 = \frac{\sum (y_i - \tilde{y}_i)^2}{N} = \sigma_{y|x}^2 \tag{16}$$

and

$$\sigma_P^2 = \frac{\sum (\tilde{y}_i - \bar{y}_i)^2}{N} = \frac{\sum \tilde{y}^2}{N} = \sigma_{\tilde{y}}^2 \tag{17}$$

so that

$$1 = \frac{\sigma_{\tilde{y}}^2}{\sigma_y^2} + \frac{\sigma_{y|x}^2}{\sigma_y^2} \tag{18}$$

where $\frac{\sigma_{\tilde{y}}^2}{\sigma_y^2}$ is the predicted proportion, and

$\frac{\sigma_{y|x}^2}{\sigma_y^2}$ is the residual or unpredicted proportion.

As before,

$$\frac{\sigma_{y|x}^2}{\sigma_y^2} = 1 - r^2$$

$$\sigma_{y|x}^2 = \sigma_y^2 (1 - r^2)$$

and

$$\sigma_{y|x} = \sigma_y \sqrt{1 - r^2}$$

It also follows that

$$r^2 = \frac{\sigma_{\tilde{y}}^2}{\sigma_y^2} \tag{19}$$

or that the square of the correlation coefficient is the predicted proportion of the variance.

The concept of dividing a measurement into parts according to their contributions can be taken a step further. If we look at the difference between the observed score and the expectation of what the value of a variable ought to be, we can divide this difference into two parts.

$$(Y_i - \bar{Y}) = (Y_i - \tilde{Y}_i) + (\tilde{Y}_i - \bar{Y}) \tag{20}$$

We now examine the sum of squares

$$\sum (Y_i - \bar{Y})^2 = \sum [(Y_i - \tilde{Y}_i) + (\tilde{Y}_i - \bar{Y})]^2$$
$$= \sum (Y_i - \tilde{Y}_i)^2 + \sum (\tilde{Y} - \bar{Y})^2 + 2 \sum (Y_i - \tilde{Y}_i)(\tilde{Y}_i - \bar{Y})$$

but

$$\sum (Y_i - \tilde{Y}_i)(\tilde{Y}_i - \bar{Y}) = 0 \tag{21}$$

(The proof for this is very simple and almost intuitively given. The student should try to derive it for himself.) As a result,

$$\sum (Y_i - \bar{Y})^2 = \sum (Y_i - \tilde{Y}_i)^2 + \sum (\tilde{Y}_i - \bar{Y})^2 \tag{22}$$

The sum of the variation of predicted scores around the mean can be rewritten as

$$\sum (\tilde{Y}_i - \bar{Y})^2 = \sum (\tilde{y} - 0)^2$$
$$= \sum a_1^2 x^2$$
$$= a_1^2 \sum (X_i - \bar{X})^2 \tag{23}$$

and since

$$a_1 = r\left(\frac{\sigma_y}{\sigma_x}\right)$$

and

$$\sum (X - \bar{X})^2 = N\sigma_x^2$$

we can substitute to obtain

$$\sum (\tilde{Y}_i - \bar{Y}) = r^2 \left(\frac{\sigma_y^2}{\sigma_x^2}\right) N\sigma_x^2 = Nr^2\sigma_y^2 \tag{24}$$

so that the variations of predicted scores for any fixed number of observations and variance of the parent population is purely a function of the correlation coefficient.

ESTIMATING THE VALUES FOR REGRESSION AND CORRELATIONS FROM SAMPLES

The relationships that we have examined so far are true for the unrestricted population. We can estimate the values of the variance and of the correlation coefficient from samples, provided that the samples are truly random.

We already know how to estimate the variance by

$$s_y^2 = \frac{\sum (Y - \bar{Y})^2}{n - 1}$$

However, to estimate $\sigma_{y|x}^2$ we must subtract two restrictions (the remainder being called degrees of freedom), since our estimate hinges not only upon sampling variable Y but also on sampling variable X. Our best estimate of $\sigma_{y|x}^2$ is given by

$$s_{y|x}^2 = \frac{\sum (Y_i - \tilde{Y}_i)^2}{n - 2} \tag{25}$$

For calculation with semiautomatic hand calculators, we have summarized some useful computing methods below:

$$\sum (Y - \bar{Y})^2 = \sum Y^2 - \frac{(\sum Y)^2}{n} \tag{26a}$$

$$\sum (Y_i - \bar{Y})(X_i - \bar{X}) = \sum XY - \frac{(\sum X)(\sum Y)}{n} \tag{26b}$$

$$\sum (Y_i - \tilde{Y}_i)^2 = \sum Y^2 - a_0 \sum Y - a_1 \sum XY \tag{26c}$$

$$a_1 = \frac{n \sum XY - (\sum X)(\sum Y)}{n \sum X^2 - (\sum X)^2} \tag{26d}$$

(We are using r, a_0, and a_1 for sample estimates of correlation, intercept, and rate of change. Using the same notation for population parameter and its estimates simplifies discussion, but the student should keep aware of the distinction. Also we shall use n for number of observations in a sample and N for all cases in the total population.)

$$r = \frac{n \sum XY - (\sum X)(\sum Y)}{\sqrt{n \sum X^2 - (\sum X)^2} \sqrt{n \sum Y^2 - (\sum Y)^2}} \tag{26e}$$

$$s_{y|x}^2 = \frac{\sum Y^2 - a_0 \sum Y - a_1 \sum XY}{n - 2} \tag{26f}$$

However, for high-speed processors these calculation methods may and usually will lead to problems with trailing digits, so the best methods of calculation are often the direct use of definition with enough precision to eliminate errors of approximation. With large memories and fast processors it is relatively easy to compute first $\bar{X}$ and $\bar{Y}$ and then develop $\sum (X - \bar{X})^2$, $\sum (Y - \bar{Y})^2$, and $\sum (X - \bar{X})(Y - \bar{Y})$ directly.

In some instances, computational methods may create unforseen problems. Single accuracy and some computational formulae may result in spurious negative variances or sums of squares. The same is true for any computational procedures (albeit not as frequently as in analysis of variance computation). Spurious negative values are possible for some sums of squares. These are easily interpreted, however, as indicating small values close to zero.

Very often, for practical reasons, the actual range of measurements of two variables X and Y cannot scan the total possible domain of available values. Thus, although we may obtain a random sample of each variable separately, we may not be able to obtain concurrent measurements of both over the total range of possible observations.

For instance, we might have medical records available giving the weight of children in the public school system. However, information on income of parents might be available only for children in the first few grades of school.

Sampling over a small and more restricted range for one variable has the unfortunate effect of decreasing the value of r. We can make a correction for that, however. Where r'_{xy} is an estimate of r_{xy} from a restricted sampling range, assuming that we know the true variation of X, s_x, we can compute the restricted variation s'_x, from our sample and correct r by

$$\text{corrected } r = \frac{\left(\dfrac{s_x}{s'_x}\right)}{\sqrt{1 - r'^2 + r'^2 \left(\dfrac{s_x}{s'_x}\right)^2}} \tag{27}$$

TESTING HYPOTHESES ABOUT CORRELATION AND REGRESSION

Very often we are concerned with the decision of whether or not a relationship exists between two variables so that predicting one from the other has any sense at all. Here again is a rather sharp distinction between the deterministic and the stochastic world. In the deterministic model, points fit along a curve with a small error (assumed to be due exclusively to measurements) so that the question of whether or not $Y = f(X)$ is a useful expression is very often settled by inspecting a graph.

The same is not true at all for the stochastic situation. If the trend is very pronounced so that the points obviously cluster very tightly about some best-fitting line, the decision that the relationship exists may be rendered almost by inspection. However, in many instances, the spread of points in the scattergram is wide enough that a satisfactory answer to the question "Is this a chance appearance in a scatter or is the apparent trend an estimate of some true tendency?" is a question that has no easy or immediate answer.

There is yet one other consideration that we must keep in mind at all times. The calculations for a best-fitting regression slope, associated error terms, and correlations can be done mechanically for any set of numbers. Because of sampling error, the values of a slope and of correlation will not necessarily be equal to 0 even if there is no correlation at all in the universe from which the sample was drawn. A small number of observations in the sample will give rise to large values of r almost by definition. Let us assume that we have only two observations. Since a straight line is defined by two points, we can draw a line of regression through these two points without any error at all. As a consequence, the value of r is equal to 1. Thus, for relatively small numbers of observations we may expect relatively larger values for rates of change and for correlations than is true for the reference population.

One way to resolve the problem of when a sample indicates a relationship and when it does not is to base decisions on the probability that the observed correlation (or slope) comes from a universe whose true correlation (or slope) is or is not equal to zero.

There are a number of ways in which this hypothesis can be tested. Our choices are between testing the hypothesis that the correlation coefficient is an estimate of a true correlation that is equal to zero or that the rate of change is an estimate of a true rate of change that is equal to zero. We shall discuss each approach separately.

Let us begin by testing hypotheses about r:

$$H_0: \quad r \rightarrow \rho_0, \qquad \rho_0 = 0$$
$$H_1: \quad r \rightarrow \rho_1, \qquad \rho_1 \neq 0$$

We state here the choice between H_0 and H_1 concerning the estimate of ρ or some true correlation. Our hypothesis is that ρ is or is not equal to 0. For large numbers of observations and for values of r smaller than .5

$$s_r = \frac{1}{\sqrt{n-3}} \tag{28}$$

so that we can construct a test based on the normal deviate

$$Z_\alpha \geq \frac{r}{s_r} \tag{29}$$

This test is restricted to instances where the observed value of r is less than .5. Since r has fixed boundary conditions, we cannot make the assumption that r is distributed normally for values that approach either $+1$ or -1. However, the distribution of values of r may be normalized by the following transformation:

$$z = .5 \log_e (1 + r) - .5 \log_e (1 - r) \tag{30}$$

or

$$z = 1.151 \log_{10} \left(\frac{1+r}{1-r} \right)$$

with the variation of these normalized scores given by

$$s_z = \frac{1}{\sqrt{n-3}} \qquad (31)$$

Although we would expect any program to develop the transformation of r to z automatically, a table of conversion values of r to z is given in Appendix B, Table 11.

We read this table either by entering the nearest value of r to find the appropriate z or by using the nearest value of z to find the appropriate r. Linear interpolations between the nearest values of r or z are quite sufficient for hand calculation purposes, whereas for more exact procedures, appropriate values of z can be obtained as part of the program.

If we wish to test the decision model above for values of r greater than .5, we find the value of the normal deviate as before by

$$Z_\alpha \geq \frac{z}{s_z} \qquad (32)$$

For the general linear model we can evaluate r by the use of the variance ratio. The probabilities for the basic decision model are computed from

$$F_\alpha \geq \frac{r^2(n-2)}{1-r^2} \qquad (33)$$

for 1 and $n-2$ degrees of freedom. The probability corresponding to the value of α is read from the table of percentile distributions of F.

We can construct an alternative model to test the hypothesis that a relationship is spurious or due to chance by

$$H_0: \quad a_1 \rightarrow \lambda_0, \quad \lambda_0 = 0$$
$$H_1: \quad a_1 \rightarrow \lambda_1, \quad \lambda_1 \neq 0$$

In this case we consider a_1 as an estimate of some true parameter λ such that λ is either equal or not equal to 0. The distribution of estimates of λ by a_1, where $\lambda = 0$, can be approximated by

$$s_{a_1} = \frac{s_{y|x}}{\sum (X - \bar{X})^2} \qquad (34)$$

so that we can test the hypothesis about a_1 by using the distribution of t.

$$t_\alpha \geq \frac{a_1}{s_{a_1}}$$
$$= \frac{a_1 s_x \sqrt{n-1}}{s_{y|x}} \qquad (35)$$

for $n-2$ degrees of freedom.

Example.   Let us assume that we have two scores each for ten individuals and that we wish to investigate the relation between them. Let the first score be referred to as X and the second as Y. We wish to establish $X = f(Y)$.

The scores are shown in Table 9.1.

Table 9.1.   Scores for 10 Individuals on X and Y

Individual	X	Y
A	0	−1
B	3	13
C	1	6
D	3	7
E	6	25
F	2	6
G	6	15
H	3	5
I	0	−1
J	4	16

$$\sum X = 28 \qquad \sum Y = 91$$
$$\bar{X} = 2.8 \qquad \bar{Y} = 9.1$$

Table 9.2.   Scores for 10 Individuals As Deviations from the Mean

$$x = X - \bar{X} \quad \text{and} \quad y = Y - \bar{Y}$$

Individual	x	y	ŷ	y − ŷ
A	−2.8	−10.1	−9.7	−0.4
B	0.2	3.9	0.7	3.2
C	−1.8	−3.1	−6.3	3.2
D	0.2	−2.1	0.7	−1.4
E	3.2	15.9	11.1	4.8
F	−0.8	−3.1	−2.8	−0.3
G	3.2	5.9	11.1	4.8
H	0.2	−4.1	0.7	−4.8
I	−2.8	−10.1	−9.7	−0.4
J	1.2	6.9	4.2	2.7

$$\sum x^2 = 41.6 \qquad s_x^2 = \frac{41.6}{9} = 4.62 \qquad s_x = 2.15$$

$$\sum y^2 = 594.9$$

$$\sum xy = 144.68 \qquad s_y^2 = \frac{594.9}{9} = 66.1 \qquad s_y = 8.13$$

$$a_1 = \frac{144.68}{41.6} = 3.478, \qquad a_0 = 9.1 - (3.478)(2.8) = -0.638$$

$$\tilde{y} = 3.478x \qquad \tilde{Y} = 3.478X - 0.638$$

$$\sum (y - \tilde{y})^2 = 99.26 \qquad s_{y|x}^2 = \frac{99.26}{8} = 12.41, \qquad s_{y|x} = 3.53$$

For a better understanding of regression analysis we shall rearrange our scores in terms of deviation from the mean, x and y. These scores are found in Table 9.2.

The x and y scores represent a deviation around the mean with the mean of the x and y's being equal to zero by definition. Table 9.2 shows the computation of s_x and s_y with which we are now familiar.

The best prediction of deviation scores is $\tilde{y} = 3.478x$ and for raw scores $\tilde{Y} = 3.478X - 0.638$.

The error variance around our best line of prediction is given by $s_{y|x}^2 = 12.41$, so that $s_{y|x} = 3.53$. Since $s_y = 8.13$ means that our best estimate of the deviations of Y from $\bar{Y}$ are distributed such that approximately 68 per cent fall within 8.13 units of the mean, we can reduce the error of estimation from 8.13 to 3.53 by using associated values of X to predict the outcome of observing Y. Our estimate will be 68 per cent of time within 3.53 units of the predicted value of the observations. Table 9.3 summarizes some of the other computations in which we might be interested.

Table 9.3. ADDITIONAL CALCULATIONS OF INTEREST
ON DATA FROM TABLES 9.1 AND 9.2

$$r = \frac{\sum xy}{\sqrt{\sum x^2}\sqrt{\sum y^2}} = \frac{144.68}{(6.45)(24.39)} = .9196$$

$$r = \sqrt{\frac{s_y^2 - s_{y|y}^2}{s_y^2}} = \sqrt{\frac{66.1 - 12.4}{66.1}} = .9015$$

$$a_1' = r\left(\frac{s_x}{s_y}\right) = \frac{(.9196)(2.15)}{8.13} = .243$$

$$a_0' = 2.8 - (.243)(9.1) = .59$$

$$\tilde{x} = .243y, \quad \text{or} \quad \tilde{X} = .243Y + .59$$

$$s_x \text{ (on larger sample)} = 5.6$$

$$\text{corrected } r = \frac{(.9196)(2)}{\sqrt{1 - .846 + (.846)(4)}} = .978$$

$$Z_\alpha = \frac{1.589}{.378} = 4.20$$

$$F_\alpha = \frac{6.768}{.154} = 43.948$$

$$t_\alpha = \frac{3.478}{.764} = 4.55$$

Note that the correlation coefficient computed in two different ways results in two values that are slightly different from each other. Direct calculation has fewer errors of approximations than using s_y^2 and $s_{y|x}^2$.

Thus, the first value of r is probably more correct. However, even here errors of approximation have had an effect. The student might at this point obtain a correlation coefficient program and compare the hand calculations in this example with double precision calculations. (The student will note also that the differences are really not that large to be of concern in most instances.)

Once the correlation coefficient has been obtained, the equation predicting $\tilde{X}$ from the knowledge of Y is easy to find.

At the bottom of Table 9.3 are three tests of the hypotheses that either the correlation or the slope are a departure from zero. Obviously, this hypothesis would be rejected for any one of the three tests with approximately the same level of statistical significance.

TESTING HYPOTHESES BETWEEN TWO VALUES OF r

If we have two different variables, each of which can be used to obtain a prediction, we may want to use only that variable which will give us the best correlation in the long run.

Assume that we have computed correlations between Y and variables U and W to obtain r_{yu} and r_{yw}. We wish to test the hypothesis that a difference between these two correlation coefficients is greater than may be expected by chance. To perform this test we make use of the distribution of t, where

$$t = \frac{\sqrt{n-3}\,(r_{yu} - r_{yw})\sqrt{1 + r_{uw}}}{\sqrt{2D}} \qquad (36)$$

where D is the determinant[1] of

$$\begin{vmatrix} 1 & r_{yu} & r_{uw} \\ r_{yu} & 1 & r_{yw} \\ r_{uw} & r_{yw} & 1 \end{vmatrix} \qquad (37)$$

with $n - 3$ degrees of freedom.

Example.   Table 9.4 shows an example output of a linear fit program from the MEDCOMP library format. The program has computed $\tilde{Y} = a_0 + a_1 X$ and all relevant measures pertaining to it. (Note, incidentally, that the slope in this figure is referred to as B rather than a_1 as we do here.) The standard output provides information for computing error terms around all estimates, and the result of testing the hypothesis that the slope a_1 is an estimate of a true slope of zero.

---

[1] A determinant is the value assigned to a matrix. The student may refer to almost any text on advanced high school algebra to learn how determinants are computed.

Table 9.4. LINEAR FIT WITH t TEST AND OTHER INFORMATION*

```
MEAN X                                               22.80692 +
MEAN Y                                                2.115 +
VARIANCE OF Y                                         1.320
STANDARD DEVIATION Y                                  1.148
VARIANCE OF X                                        57.26128
STANDARD DEVIATION X                                  7.56711
CORRELATION OF Y AND X                                0.574 +
CORRELATION SQUARED                                   0.330
VARIANCE OF Y GIVEN X                                 0.921
STANDARD DEVIATION OF Y GIVEN X                       0.960
VARIANCE OF B                                         0.00064
STANDARD DEVIATION B                                  0.025


B                                                     0.087 +
A                                                     0.127 +


T                                                     3.43
DEGREES OF FREEDOM                                   24
```

*Example printout from the MEDCOMP Program Library.

Table 9.5 shows a different example printout from the same library. The investigator started with a data file containing a number of items of information. The program provides a simple numerical description of each variable and also gives the correlation coefficients between all the variables that can be computed.

The information of sums, sums of squares, and sums of cross products are included as part of the output and are useful for further analysis.

Table 9.5. CORRELATION COEFFICIENT PRINTOUT*

SAMPLE RUN

VAR.NAME	MEAN	STD.DEV.	SUM X	SUM XSQ.	N
AGE IN YEARS AND MONTHS	13.94628	2.72471	488.12	7059.8800	35
WT. KG.	52.9257	13.2644	1852.4	104021.76	35
WT. LB.	116.257	29.150	4069.	501941.	35
HT. CM.	159.721	29.546	5592.	923122.	35
HT. INS.	63.028	11.663	2206.	143666.	35
TEMPERATURE	95.1400	16.5615	3329.9	326132.35	35
PULSE	60.628	13.095	2122.	134484.	35

VAR X	VAR Y	COR COEF	SUM X	SUM Y	SUM XY
AGE IN YEARS AND MONTHS	WT. KG.	.748	488.12	1852.4	26753.344
AGE IN YEARS AND MONTHS	WT. LB.	.745	488.12	4069.	58760.44
AGE IN YEARS AND MONTHS	HT. CM.	.904	488.12	5592.	80061.44
AGE IN YEARS AND MONTHS	HT. INS.	.904	488.12	2206.	31741.88
AGE IN YEARS AND MONTHS	TEMPERATURE	.884	488.12	3329.9	47796.788
AGE IN YEARS AND MONTHS	PULSE	.621	488.12	2122.	30146.80
WT. KG.	WT. LB.	1.000	1852.4	4069.	228499.8
WT. KG.	HT. CM.	.825	1852.4	5592.	306953.4
WT. KG.	HT. INS.	.825	1852.4	2206.	121090.9
WT. KG.	TEMPERATURE	.683	1852.4	3329.9	181341.02
WT. KG.	PULSE	.545	1852.4	2122.	115527.2
WT. LB.	HT. CM.	.825	4069.	5592.	674258.
WT. LB.	HT. INS.	.824	4069.	2206.	265990.
WT. LB.	TEMPERATURE	.683	4069.	3329.9	398335.6
WT. LB.	PULSE	.547	4069.	2122.	253796.
HT. CM.	HT. INS.	1.000	5592.	2206.	344170.
HT. CM.	TEMPERATURE	.936	5592.	3329.9	547588.6
HT. CM.	PULSE	.722	5592.	2122.	348528.
HT. INS.	TEMPERATURE	.935	2206.	3329.9	216019.5
HT. INS.	PULSE	.718	2206.	2122.	137476.
TEMPERATURE	PULSE	.811	3329.9	2122.	207865.2

*Example from the MEDCOMP Program Library.

ASSUMPTIONS FOR THE SIMPLE LINEAR STOCHASTIC MODEL

The model we have discussed so far is elegant and simple and also permits us to make a large number of inferences about the possible relationship that may hold between two variables. The price for this simplicity, however, is that we must make assumptions about the universe of numbers from which we draw our observations.

To begin with, we assume that the relationship between two variables is linear. Next we assume that the distribution of each variable is normal and that their joint distribution is also normal. We make one more assumption. Note that we have been looking at the distribution of Y as the values of another variable X increase or decrease. The requirement on our model is that the variation of values of Y remain stable and do not change with changes in X. This means that the distribution of weights, for instance, is the same for small children as it would be for tall children. This property is called *homoscedasticity*.

How reasonable is the expectation that these assumptions will be met and satisfied actually by experimental observations in the real world of science? If the linear model assuming bivariate normality and homoscedasticity is used, then this question is of considerable interest. The answer is not easy to come by.

It is clear that very little if any experimental data ever conform to these requirements. The assumption of linearity is not only contrary to experience, but very often also to expectation. Most biological and sociological processes are asymptotic; i.e., they tend to some limiting value. As a consequence, assuming linearity is seldom justified, and even when data do give the appearance of being linear it is probably only true because sampling has been done over a restricted range of values. Using a linear approximation to a function that is not linear will, of course, result in errors of estimates that will be increasingly larger in direct relation to the degree to which the true function departs from a straight line. One consequence is that a product moment correlation coefficient is usually an underestimate of the true correlation that holds between two variables rather than an overestimate. Thus for the conservative scientist the correlation coefficient may be an important index of the existence of a relationship between two variables, because it will tend to be an underestimate rather than an overestimate of the degree of correlation. The disadvantage of this "conservatism" is, of course, that a relationship may be overlooked because it departs far enough from linearity so that a linear correlation coefficient, computed as an estimate of true association, is so small that the possibility is discarded that two variables are associated.

Homoscedasticity is an assumption that also is very likely untrue in most instances. Variations in nature very often depend on absolute values. For instance, the weight of newborn infants or of small children may vary by a few grams or perhaps by a pound or two. The weight of grown animals, on the other hand, varies over a considerable range. Only the assumption of normality of distribution can be made with reasonable confidence in many instances.

If it is, then, so difficult to meet the assumptions for the linear model, why is this model used at all? Computations based on the linear model are easy to do, can be done at small cost, and, as we shall see later, can be extended to quite complex cases of multivariable relationships. On the other hand, computation in the nonlinear world becomes increasingly complex to the point where even high-speed computation may be of little help.

The second rationale for the use of linear models is that the size of errors that result from using a linear model for situations that are not linear depends directly on the extent to which the true situation is a departure from linearity. Over the range of phenomena of interest it is very often true that departure from linearity is not very large, so that errors are small enough to be tolerated.

For the investigator who is aware of the limitations and who can weigh these limitations against the needs of his experimental design and data processing requirements, the linear model thus offers a powerful tool even though it presumes a distorted view of reality.

INCREASING THE COMPLEXITY OF
THE PREDICTING MODEL

We can expand the uses of predictive models to instances that are clearly nonlinear and to instances in which more than one variable may have simultaneous effects.

NONLINEARITY

Chapter 8 developed a number of different methods to describe non-linear functions. We can use similar approaches to situations that are stochastic as well as nonlinear.

If we view $\tilde{Y}_i$ as the best estimate of Y_i when X_i is given, then if $f(X)$ is not linear, $\tilde{Y}$ will be predicted by a mathematical expression other than the straight line. Note that we bring together the stochastic and the deterministic model by simply seeking the line that best fits successive array means of Y, where the arrays are determined by intervals measured on the associated variable X. We may obtain, as before, an estimate of $\sigma^2_{y|x}$.

$$\sigma^2_{y|x} = \frac{\Sigma \, [Y_i - f(X_i)]^2}{N} \tag{38}$$

or estimated by

$$s^2_{y|x} = \frac{\Sigma \, [Y_i - f(X_i)]^2}{\text{d.f.}}$$

where $f(X_i)$ is not linear. Note that we divide by d.f. because the number of degrees of freedom will vary depending on the number of parameters that have to be estimated in the determination of $f(X)$. We define the correlation as before except it is now called (by convention) the *correlation ratio, η*.

$$\eta^2 = \frac{\sigma^2_y - \sigma^2_{y|x}}{\sigma^2_y} \tag{39}$$

or

$$\eta^2 = 1 - \frac{\sigma^2_{y|x}}{\sigma^2_y}$$

Note that the meanings of η and r are the same.

A test for the hypothesis that η is a chance deviation from zero is given by

$$F_\alpha \geq \frac{\eta^2(n - c)}{(1 - \eta^2)(c - 1)} \tag{40}$$

for $c - 1$ and $n - c$ degrees of freedom and where c is the number of arrays for which $f(X_i)$ is computed.

TEST FOR LINEARITY

The quantity r will be an underestimate of a true correlation if the relationship between two variables is not linear. Thus, $\eta \geq r$ if computed for the same set of data.

A test for linearity is thus useful in instances where η and r are not too far apart. This test is given by

$$F_\alpha \geq \frac{(\eta^2 - r^2)(n - c)}{(1 - \eta^2)(c - 2)} \tag{41}$$

for $c - 2$ and $n - c$ degrees of freedom.

If the hypothesis that the difference between η and r is due to chance cannot be rejected or, even, if rejected and the values of η and r are not too far apart, the linear model is preferable.

TRANSFORMATION OF DATA

Very often it may be convenient to use the linear model, but with transformed values of X or Y so that linearity, normalcy, or homoscedascity may be achieved. Since much of biological and sociological data is logarithmic, very often a log or a square root transformation will linearize a graph of Y on X. One other very useful transformation to normalize and develop homoscedascity is to convert all numbers to their arcsin equivalents. Of course, transformation entails a loss of information. But the added convenience of using a linear model usually outweighs the disadvantages of losing that small part of information that is eliminated by transformation. It is for these reasons that the program library should include a sufficient number of utility programs that will transform number scales with ease and at a small expenditure.

INSTRUMENTATION RELIABILITY

So far we have ignored measurement or instrumentation error and have commented on contributions from unknown variables. However, error of instrumentation or of measurement does indeed exist. Since high-speed data processing devices make it possible to analyze any data file rather comprehensively, corrections for unreliability can be included in the analysis of any set of relationships without adding to the costs of the job to any significant extent.

Error of measurement is an unpredictable complement of the total variation because misreading of instruments or misjudgments of events occur purely at random and with relatively unchanging frequencies. Thus we could look at any measurement as consisting of two components, a true value plus a random error

$$X_i = X_i' + d$$

or

$$x_i = x_i' + d$$

where X' or x' are the true scores. Since X' and d are obviously unrelated, their variances are additive [as in (15)] and we can write

$$\sigma_x^2 = \sigma_{x'}^2 + \sigma_d^2$$

where $\sigma_{x'}^2$ is the true variance.

σ_d^2 is the error variance.

If we were to measure the same phenomenon twice, we would obtain two scores each time such that

$$x_1 = x' + d_1$$
$$x_2 = x' + d_2$$

and a correlation between these two scores would be a measurement of the "reliability" with which we may make two such observations under the same conditions:

$$r_{x_1 x_2} = \frac{\sum (x' + d_1)(x' + d_2)}{N \sigma_{x_1} \sigma_{x_2}} \qquad (42)$$

Since we are dealing with the same phenomenon we may assume that

$$\sigma_{x_1} = \sigma_{x_2} \qquad (\text{i.e., } \sigma_{x_1} \sigma_{x_2} = \sigma_x^2)$$

and dividing through by N we get

$$r_{x_1 x_2} = \frac{\sigma_{x'}^2 + r_{x'd_1} \sigma_x \sigma_{d_1} + r_{x'd_2} \sigma_x \sigma_{d_2} + r_{d_1 d_2} \sigma_{d_1} \sigma_{d_2}}{\sigma_x^2} \qquad (43)$$

But if we are dealing with random events, all three correlation coefficients in (43) must be zero, so that

$$r_{x_1 x_2} = \frac{\sigma_{x'}^2}{\sigma_x^2} \qquad (44)$$

From this we can obtain an estimate of the true variance by

$$\sigma_{x'}^2 = r_{x_1 x_2} \sigma_x^2 \qquad (45)$$

It is often reasonable to assume that

$$\sigma_{d_1}^2 = \sigma_{d_2}^2$$

so that we can write the following relationship:

$$\frac{\sigma_{x'}^2}{\sigma_x^2} + \frac{\sigma_d^2}{\sigma_x^2} = 1 \qquad (46)$$

so that

$$r_{x_1 x_2} = 1 - \frac{\sigma_d^2}{\sigma_x^2} \qquad (47)$$

and

$$\sigma_d^2 = \sigma_x^2(1 - r_{x_1x_2}) \tag{48}$$

Thus, the expression

$$\sigma_d = \sigma_x\sqrt{1 - r_{x_1x_2}}$$

provides us with an estimate of the random error variance and standard deviation. If it were possible to obtain two replications of the same observation, we could make estimates of a true variance as well as of the random measurement error. Unfortunately, the determination of the reliability correlation is not always easy. In many physiological and other physical experiments it is possible to obtain two measurements of the same thing without any difficulty. In biological or sociological work this becomes extremely difficult, since carryover effects of one test to another do exist.

In some instances (especially for questionnaires) a split-half technique can be used. A correlation is computed between one-half the observations and the other, with the underlying assumption that both halves are essentially random repetition of the same thing. Where r_h is a correlation between halves, the Spearman Brown formula for determining the reliability correlation for split-half techniques is given by

$$r_{x_1x_2} = \frac{2r_h}{1 + r_h} \tag{49}$$

EFFECT OF UNRELIABILITY ON CORRELATION

The random effect on stochastic observations can be eliminated under proper conditions. As before, we think of any measurement we obtain as consisting of two parts:

$$x_i = x_i' + d_x$$
$$y_i = y_i' + d_y$$

One part of the measurement, x' or y', is the true measurement and the other part, d_x and d_y, is the random measurement error.

The correlation between variables x and y can then be written as

$$r_{xy} = \frac{\sum (x' + d_x)(y' + d_y)}{N\sigma_x\sigma_y}$$

$$= \frac{\sum x'y' + \sum x'd_y + \sum y'd_x + \sum d_xd_y}{N\sigma_x\sigma_y}$$

It is obvious that the sum of the cross products between $x'd_y$, $y'd_x$, and d_xd_y are all equal to 0, since they are uncorrelated. As a result,

$$r'_{xy} = \frac{\sum x'y'}{N\sigma_x\sigma_y} \tag{50}$$

where r'_{xy} is the correlation between the true scores x' and y'.

We know from before (44) that

$$\sigma_{x'} = \sigma_x\sqrt{r_{x_1x_2}}$$

$$\sigma_{y'} = \sigma_y\sqrt{r_{y_1y_2}}$$

so that we can now state our correlation coefficient as

$$r_{xy} = \frac{r'_{xy}\sigma_x\sqrt{r_{x_1x_2}}\,\sigma_y\sqrt{r_{y_1y_2}}}{\sigma_x\sigma_y}$$

$$= r'_{xy}\sqrt{r_{x_1x_2}}\,\sqrt{r_{y_1y_2}} \tag{51}$$

and from this we can then estimate the true correlation by

$$r'_{xy} = \frac{r_{xy}}{\sqrt{r_{x_1x_2}}\,\sqrt{r_{y_1y_2}}} \tag{52}$$

We see from (52) that the true correlation is always decreased by measurement error for each of the correlated variables. This means that the larger the error of measurement for each of the two variables separately, the smaller will be the observed correlation.

To obtain an unbiased and corrected value for correlation it is thus profitable to introduce into the data gathering scheme a provision to compute reliability coefficients. Before automatic data acquisition was possible and before computers enabled quick and easy computations to take place, corrections for measurement error as part of the routine computation of correlation was not practicable. It should be done now whenever possible.

This leaves open the question of how the reliability coefficients themselves are to be computed. It is clear that where data are gathered in such a way that replication is possible, it should be done routinely. In many instances, however, replication is not reasonable. This is true most often in the area of social phenomena.

When interviews or tests are being used and scaled and correlation is desired between a test question and some observation, tests can be constructed in such a way that questions, although different, may be considered to be measuring the same things. This pairing of questions introduces a split-half technique which is not as useful as repeated testing at different times but may be necessary if the replication of the experiment of observation is not possible or invalid. Replication of sets of questions should always be random throughout the observational scheme.

ESTIMATING THE CORRELATION COEFFICIENT
WHEN ONE OR BOTH VARIABLES
ARE TRUNCATED

The correlation coefficient assumes that the data are in the form of continuous measurements.

Sometimes this is not the case. For instance, it may not be possible to obtain age in any other way than in terms of voting or nonvoting. Weight may be obtained simply as heavy or light. It is thus possible for one or both variables to be expressed as being in one of two states. We may estimate the values of correlation coefficients when one of the variables remains continuous and the other one is truncated or when both are truncated. In the first case we speak of the *biserial correlation coefficient* and in the second case about *tetrachoric correlation.*

It is sometimes valuable to look at the purpose of a particular coefficient or measurement before undertaking further development of its computation. There are two reasons why we may wish to estimate a value of a correlation coefficient even in circumstances where one or two of the variables are not suitable for direct calculation. First of all, the correlation coefficient is a very efficient measurement. There are a great number of things it can tell us, especially about how much variance is accounted for by a particular relationship. The value of these statements is such that one would want to estimate the correlation even in instances where it may be difficult to do so.

There is one more cogent reason for estimating correlation. We shall see in the next section and in the next chapter that a number of very important multivariate techniques can be built on the correlation coefficient. Insofar as many of these techniques can be used only if correlation coefficients are computed between different variables in the file, it becomes useful to estimate what these correlations would have been had all the data been measured as continuously variable numbers. (This will become clearer as we go to multiple and stepwise regression.)

ONE VARIABLE DICHOTOMIZED: BISERIAL CORRELATION

Assume that we have one variable Y that is measured along a continuous scale and another variable X for which all measurements have been

grouped into one of two states. (These two states may be signified by yes
or no, true or false, 1 or 2, etc.)

Let us go back for a moment to one of the definitions of correlation

$$r_{yx} = a_1 \left(\frac{\sigma_x}{\sigma_y} \right) = a_1' \left(\frac{\sigma_y}{\sigma_x} \right)$$

Obviously we can estimate the value of σ_y. On the other hand, estimating
the value of a_1 or a_1' or that of σ_x will represent a difficulty. The definition
of a_1 is that of a rate of change. Actually, it represents a linear rate of
change of the variable Y as X changes. If we could determine two sets of
points along this line, we would be able to compute its slope.

First we divide all measures of Y into those for which X takes on state
1 and those for which X takes on state 2. This gives us two measures, $\bar{Y}_1$
and $\bar{Y}_2$. Thus, one set of points through which the line $a_1 x$ will go will be

$$P_1(\bar{X}_1, \bar{Y}_1) \quad \text{and} \quad P_2(\bar{X}_2, \bar{Y}_2)$$

Unfortunately, we do not know values of $\bar{X}_1$ and $\bar{X}_2$. If we did, we could
derive the equation of the straight line by finding a_1

$$a_1 = \frac{\bar{Y}_2 - \bar{Y}_1}{\bar{X}_2 - \bar{X}_1}$$

and then solving for Y. Therefore, we have to estimate $\bar{X}_2 - \bar{X}_1$ in some
way (see Figure 9.1).

Where $\bar{X}..$ is the mean of all observations of variable X,

$$\bar{X}_2 - \bar{X}_1 = A_2 + A_1 \tag{53}$$

where

$$\left. \begin{array}{l} A_2 = \bar{X}_2 - \bar{X}.. \\ A_1 = \bar{X}.. - \bar{X}_1 \end{array} \right\} \quad \text{for } \bar{X}_2 > \bar{X}_1$$

If X had been measured continuously, A_2 would be the mean deviation for
all measurements that fall in that tail of the distribution of X that is cut
off by the point of truncation between state 1 and state 2. Where H is the
value of the ordinate for the unit normal curve at the point where P proportion of cases is cut off, then the value of A_2 is equal to

$$A_2 = \frac{H}{P} \tag{54a}$$

and the value of A_1

$$A_1 = \frac{H}{Q} \tag{54b}$$

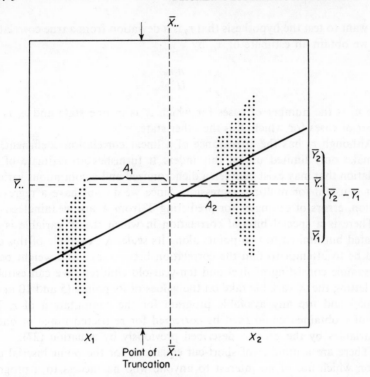

Fig. 9.1. Scattergram with one variable dichotomized.
Drawn after Computers and the Life Sciences, Columbia University Press, 1965.

where

$$P + Q = 1$$

Note that the values for H can be computed directly by finding that ordinate on the normal curve for which a percentage, P or Q, is cut off. (Obviously it makes no difference which proportion we call P and which proportion we call Q.)

If we measure X on the unit normal distribution for which $\sigma_x = 1$ by definition, we now have

$$r_b = a_1 \left(\frac{\sigma_x}{\sigma_y} \right) \tag{55}$$

$$= \frac{\bar{Y}_2 - \bar{Y}_1}{\left(\dfrac{H}{P} + \dfrac{H}{Q} \right) \sigma_y}$$

$$= \frac{(\bar{Y}_2 - \bar{Y}_1) PQ}{H \sigma_y}$$

If we want to test the hypothesis that r_b is a deviation from a true correlation of 0, we obtain an estimate of σ_{r_b} by

$$s_{r_b}^2 = \frac{n_1 n_2}{H^2 n^2} \qquad (56)$$

where n_1 is the number of cases for which X is in one state and n_2 is the number of cases for which X is the other state.

Although r_b has the appearance of a linear correlation coefficient, we can make only limited use of this index. It furnishes an estimate of the correlation that may exist between a dichotomized and a continuous variable and it is useful for multiple regression. Since we do not have a regression equation, errors of estimates for predicting Y from X are meaningless.

There is a special biserial correlation in which the X variable is not truncated but limited to two points along its scale. An example of this case would be to attempt to find the correlation between age and weight based on a sample consisting of five- and ten-year-old children. We can estimate r_b by letting the X variable take on the values of its points (5 and 10 in our example) and use any available program for the computation of r. The value of r obtained could then be corrected for restricted range of one of the variables by the process described previously by equation (27).

(There are a number of short-cut equations for the point biserial correlation which are of no interest to anyone who has access to a program that will compute a correlation coefficient on a computer.)

ESTIMATE OF CORRELATION WHEN BOTH VARIABLES ARE DICHOTOMIZED

Let us assume that both age and weight had been dichotomized in such a fashion that age was given for individuals older and younger than eight years and weight as heavier or lighter than 60 pounds. For our analysis of the biserial correlation we saw that we could translate proportions into distances from the mean to the mean deviation along the abscissca. We can take advantage of the same circumstance in the case where both variables are dichotomized. First we express the distribution of cases in terms of proportions, as shown in the following contingency table:

P_{11}	P_{12}	$P_{1\cdot}$
P_{21}	P_{22}	$P_{2\cdot}$
$P_{\cdot 1}$	$P_{\cdot 2}$	

so that P_{ij} stands for the proportion of the total number of cases found in the ith row and jth column of our contingency table, P_i. is the proportion of the ith row variables, and $P._j$ is the proportion of the jth column variables. It can be shown that

$$\frac{P_{21} - P_2.P._1}{H_1 H_2} = r_t + A_1 A_2 \frac{r_t^2}{2} + (A_1^2 - 1)(A_2^2 - 1)\frac{r_t^3}{6} + \cdots$$
$$+ [A_1^{i-1} - (i-1)A_1][A_2^{i-1} - (i-1)A_2]\frac{r_t^i}{i!} \qquad (57a)$$

expanded to as many terms as are desired for accuracy. The degree of expansion will usually depend on the type of program that is available at the computing center to find the roots r_t of an nth degree equation. The quantity r_t is known as the *tetrachoric correlation*.

The meaning of H_1 and H_2 are as before. The quantity H_1 is the ordinate of the unit normal curve where $P._1$ proportions of the cases are cut off, and H_2 is the ordinate of the unit normal curve where $P_2.$ cases are cut off. The quantities A_1 and A_2 are values along the abscissa corresponding to points for ordinates H_1 and H_2 expressed in terms of standard deviation units.

When an appropriate program for exact calculation is not available, r_t may be estimated with good accuracy. It is necessary to split both variables at the median. When n_{ij} are the frequencies in row i and column j of our contingency table, then if both variables are split near the median $n_1. \simeq n_2.$ and $n._1 \simeq n._2$. Then r_t is approximated by

$$r_t = \sin\left[90° \times \frac{(n_{11} + n_{22} - n_{12} - n_{22})}{n..}\right] \qquad (57b)$$

This approximation will be exact if the equality relation between the marginal frequencies is true. If the marginal frequencies are very different from each other, r_t may be approximated by

$$r_t = \cos\left[180 \frac{\sqrt{n_{12}n_{21}}}{\sqrt{n_{11}n_{22}} + \sqrt{n_{12}n_{21}}}\right] \qquad (57c)$$

The standard error of r_t can be approximated by

$$s_{r_t}^2 = \frac{n_1.n_2.n._1n._2}{H_1^2 H_2^2 n^2..} \qquad (58)$$

where again $n_i.$ is equal to the number of observations in the ith row and $n._j$ is equal to the number of observations in the jth column. The quantity $n..$ is equal to the total number of observations.

A special case of the tetrachoric correlation is the so-called four-point correlation. Similar to the biserial coefficient, it deals with instances in which the selected individuals come from a very restricted range. Assume that in the previous example, children had been selected only for ages five and eight and weighed either 45 or 90 pounds. If this had been the case we could simply use a standard program for the correlation coefficient. (Although it is reasonable to expect a point biserial correlation, it is difficult to visualize experimental observations in which four-point correlation occurs.)

OTHER MEASURES OF CORRELATION

There are a number of measurements of correlation available which depart from points of view that are similar or only slightly different from the explanation of reduced variance. They are in the form of "indices" or index values which somehow express preferences in the distribution of one variable depending on the state of associated variables.

One such example, of course, is χ^2. We may interpret χ^2 by saying that the larger its value with respect to a given number of degrees of freedom, the firmer the underlying association between the variables. It is questionable as to whether the value of χ^2 is enhanced to any extent by computing some other coefficient such as the so-called *contingency coefficient* given by

$$C = \sqrt{\frac{\chi^2}{N + \chi^2}} \tag{59}$$

The contingency coefficient tells us no more than χ^2 did to begin with. Neither do a number of other coefficients that are derived from the value of χ^2.

There are also a number of so-called nonparametric correlations that do not depend on the value of χ^2. Most of them are based on small samples. Computers are usually not necessary to calculate these statistics. We will give one such index which is very useful. It is the correlation between ranked differences. This technique is a quick and dirty method of estimating correlation and is independent of many assumptions required for estimating r. If individuals are assigned rank order positions with respect to each of two variables, and a difference between the two ranks is determined for each individual and given the value of d, then the rank correlation can be obtained by

$$RC = 1 - \frac{6 \sum d^2}{n(n^2 - 1)} \tag{60}$$

The standard error for the rank correlation is given by

$$s_{RC} = \frac{1}{\sqrt{n - 1}} \tag{61}$$

For large samples RC can be assumed to be normally distributed so that

$$z_d = RC\sqrt{n-1} \tag{62}$$

can be used to approximate the probability that an observed value of RC is larger than zero; Z is the normal deviate, which may be looked up in the table of normal values (Appendix B).

It is unlikely that single rank correlations will be computed on a high-speed processor. Very often, however, there are situations in which judgments made by several observers introduce a certain amount of computational difficulties that are resolvable on a high-speed machine. Let us assume that we had k judges, each ranking c observations or individuals. When the rank of the ith judge on the jth observation is equal to X_{ij} we can compute the sum of squared ranks

$$SR = \sum_{i=1}^{k}\sum_{j=1}^{c}(X_{ij}-\bar{X}..)^2 = \sum_{i=1}^{k}\sum_{j=1}^{c}X_{ij}^2 - \frac{(\sum\limits_{i=1}^{k}\sum\limits_{j=1}^{c}X_{ij})^2}{c} \tag{63}$$

where SR is equal to the sums of squared ranks and $\bar{X}..$ is the mean value of all ranks such that

$$\bar{X}... = \frac{\sum\limits_{i=1}^{k}\sum\limits_{j=1}^{c}X_{ij}}{c} \tag{64}$$

If agreement among all ranks were perfect, an expected value of SR would be equal to

$$\widetilde{SR} = \frac{k^2c(c^2-1)}{12} \tag{65}$$

Kendall has defined the coefficient of concordance as the ratio of SR and $\widetilde{SR}$, viz.,

$$W = \frac{SR}{\widetilde{SR}} \tag{66}$$

The quantity W is related to the average rank order coefficient $\overline{RC}$ by

$$\overline{RC} = \frac{kW-1}{k-1} \tag{67}$$

Testing the hypothesis that W deviates by chance from a value of 0 can be done for large values of k and c by the use of the variance ratio. The test is given by

$$F_\alpha \geq \frac{(k-1)W}{1-W} \qquad (68)$$

with degrees of freedom equal to $c - 1 - (2/k)$ and $(k = 1)\,[c - 1 - (2/k)]$.

If the values of k and c are small (k equal to or less than 5, c equal to or less than 12), a correction of the test can be had by subtracting one from $\tilde{S}R$ and adding two to SR.

(There are many other tests among ranks. One good test for a small number of ranks is given by Kendall's $\mathcal{T}$. Although one program for multiple ranking ought to be part of the computing center library, the many tests among ranks that are possible need not be. Many of them are computed easily by hand, and their statistical significance can be looked up in tables. The student who wishes to pursue this subject further is referred to M. G. Kendall, *Rank Correlation Methods*, Charles Griffin and Co., Ltd., London, 1948.)

MULTIPLE REGRESSION AND CORRELATION

We defined goodness of association by the amount of reduction in the variation of one variable resulting from using predictors based on values of another. This approach holds not only for the relation between two variables but presumes that there exist other variables which, if used as additional predictors, would decrease the variance still further. When Y is the predicted variable and X a predictor,

$$\tilde{Y} = f(X_1, X_2, \ldots, X_k) \qquad (69).$$

describes the relationship between a number of variables and a particular one about which we wish to make a prediction.

As before, we shall first consider the linear case because of its mathematical simplicity. Making the assumption that the relationship between all variables in a given set is linear permits us to develop a very simple model which is called multiple regression. As before, this model can be applied to more complex instances.

LINEAR MULTIPLE REGRESSION

We consider a situation in which a set of variables, denoted here as $X_1, X_2, \ldots, X_k$, is used to predict a variable which we shall denote here as Y. The expression we look for is linear, so

$$\tilde{Y} = a_0 + a_1X_1 + a_2X_2 + a_3X_3 + \cdots + a_kX_k \qquad (70)$$

By substituting deviation scores for actually observed values such that

$$y = Y - \bar{Y}$$
$$x = X - \bar{X}$$

we can rewrite expression (70) in such a way that we lose the constant term a_0:

$$\tilde{y} = a_1x_1 + a_2x_2 + a_3x_3 + \cdots + a_kx_k \qquad (71)$$

Since we have only relocated the coordinate system so that a line going through the means goes through the origin, the values of the coefficients are not changed, so that a_1 in equation (70) has the same value as a_i in equation (71).

We now proceed very much as we did in the case of regression having a single independent variable. First we define an error

$$D = \sum (y - \tilde{y})^2$$
$$= \sum [y - (a_1x_1 + a_2x_2 + \cdots + a_kx_k)]^2 \qquad (72)$$

Next we differentiate this expression with respect to the coefficients, $a_1, a_2, \ldots, a_k$. We end up with a set of equalities as shown below:

$$\frac{\partial D}{\partial a_1} = -2 \sum x_1(y - a_1x_1 - a_2x_2 - a_3x_3 - \cdots - a_kx_k)$$

$$\frac{\partial D}{\partial a_2} = -2 \sum x_2(y - a_1x_1 - a_2x_2 - a_3x_3 - \cdots - a_kx_k)$$

$$\vdots \qquad \vdots \qquad \qquad \vdots \qquad (73)$$

$$\frac{\partial D}{\partial a_k} = -2 \sum x_k(y - a_1x_1 - a_2x_2 - a_3x_3 - \cdots - a_kx_k)$$

We shall have found the minimum error when each line in (73) is equal to zero. Setting the values of each expression in (73) equal to 0 and dividing through by 2, we obtain

$$-\sum x_1y + a_1 \sum x_1^2 \; + a_2 \sum x_1x_2 + \cdots + a_k \sum x_1x_k = 0$$
$$-\sum x_2y + a_1 \sum x_1x_2 + a_2 \sum x_2^2 \; + \cdots + a_k \sum x_2x_k = 0$$
$$\vdots \qquad \vdots \qquad \vdots \qquad \qquad \vdots$$
$$-\sum x_ky + a_1 \sum x_1x_2 + a_2 \sum x_2x_k + \cdots + a_k \sum x_k^2 \; = 0$$

which can be rewritten as

$$a_1 \sum x_1^2 + a_2 \sum x_1 x_2 + a_3 \sum x_1 x_3 + \cdots + a_k \sum x_1 x_k = \sum x_1 y$$
$$a_1 \sum x_1 x_2 + a_2 \sum x_2^2 + a_3 \sum x_2 x_3 + \cdots + a_k \sum x_2 x_k = \sum x_2 y$$

$$
\begin{array}{ccccc}
\cdot & \cdot & \cdot & & \cdot & \cdot \\
\cdot & \cdot & \cdot & & \cdot & \cdot \\
\cdot & \cdot & \cdot & & \cdot & \cdot
\end{array}
\tag{74}
$$

$$a_1 \sum x_1 x_k + a_2 \sum x_2 x_k + a_3 \sum x_3 x_k + \cdots + a_k \sum x_k^2 = \sum x_k y$$

We can rewrite this expression in matrix format, obtaining

$$
\begin{pmatrix}
\sum x_1^2 & \sum x_1 x_2 & \cdots & \sum x_1 x_k \\
\sum x_1 x_2 & \sum x_2^2 & \cdots & \sum x_2 x_k \\
\cdot & \cdot & & \cdot \\
\cdot & \cdot & & \cdot \\
\cdot & \cdot & & \cdot \\
\sum x_1 x_k & \sum x_2 x_k & \cdots & \sum x_k^2
\end{pmatrix}
\begin{pmatrix}
a_1 \\ a_2 \\ \cdot \\ \cdot \\ \cdot \\ a_k
\end{pmatrix}
=
\begin{pmatrix}
\sum x_1 y \\ \sum x_2 y \\ \cdot \\ \cdot \\ \cdot \\ \sum x_k y
\end{pmatrix}
\tag{75}
$$

To make it easier for ourselves we shall give a label to each matrix so that we can rewrite (75) as

$$(XX) \ (A) = (XY) \tag{76}$$

To solve for matrix A, which is really a column vector, we simply multiply equation (76) by the inverse of the XX matrix

$$(A) = (XX)^{-1}(XY) \tag{77}$$

The result of this operation will be two column vectors of the form

$$
\begin{pmatrix}
a_1 \\ \cdot \\ \cdot \\ \cdot \\ a_k
\end{pmatrix}
=
\begin{pmatrix}
\text{value of } a_1 \\ \cdot \\ \cdot \\ \cdot \\ \text{value of } a_k
\end{pmatrix}
\tag{78}
$$

We can then write expression (71), putting down all the values for our coefficients.

$$\tilde{y} = a_1 x_1 + \cdots + a_k x_k$$

and since

$$\tilde{y} = Y - \bar{Y}$$
$$x = X - \bar{X}$$

we can rewrite equation (70).

$$\tilde{Y} = a_1 X_1 + a_2 X_2 + \cdots + a_k X_k + (\bar{Y} - a_1 \bar{X}_1 - a_2 \bar{X}_2 - \cdots - a_k \bar{X}_k)$$
(79)

with the intercept

$$a_0 = \bar{Y} - a_1 \bar{X}_1 - a_2 \bar{X}_2 - \cdots - a_k \bar{X}_k$$
(80)

To carry out this computation we must have for each value of Y a value for every one of the predictor variables. A more general solution for the coefficients of equation (74) uses values of the correlation coefficients rather than the sum of squares and cross products. Let

$$z = \frac{(X - \bar{X})}{\sigma}$$
(81)

We can then write a general prediction equation in a linear form for $\tilde{z}_y$.

$$\tilde{z}_y = a_1^* z_1 + a_2^* z_2 + \cdots + a_k^* z_k$$
(82)

Note that we have written our coefficients as a_i^*, since the coefficient in equations (70) and (71) and the coefficient in equation (82) differ from each other. In the former case, we moved the coordinate system but did not change the values along ordinate or abscissa. In equation (82) we are also changing the values along the coordinate axes by using the values of each standard deviation as the unit of measurements laid off along each coordinate axis.

We again define our error term in a manner similar to the way we did before;

$$D = \frac{\sum (z_y - \tilde{z}_y)^2}{n}$$
(83)

Next we find a solution that will give us the minimum error term:

$$\frac{\partial D}{\partial a_1^*} = \frac{-2 \sum z_1}{n} (z_y - a_1^* z_1 - a_2^* z_2 - \cdots - a_k^* z_k)$$

$$\frac{\partial D}{\partial a_2^*} = \frac{-2 \sum z_2}{n} (z_y - a_1^* z_1 - a_2^* z_2 - \cdots - a_k^* z_k)$$

$$\vdots \qquad \vdots \qquad \vdots \qquad \vdots \qquad \vdots \qquad \vdots$$
(84)

$$\frac{\partial D}{\partial a_k^*} = \frac{-2 \sum z_k}{n} (z_y - a_1^* z_1 - a_2^* z_2 - \cdots - a_k^* z_k)$$

Again the value of D will be a minimum for the case in which each line in expression (84) is equal to zero. Rearranging terms and dividing through by 2, we get

$$a_1^* \frac{\sum z_1^2}{n} + a_2^* \frac{\sum z_1 z_2}{n} + \cdots + a_k^* \frac{\sum z_1 z_k}{n} = \frac{\sum z_y z_1}{n}$$

$$a_1^* \frac{\sum z_1 z_2}{n} + a_2^* \frac{\sum z_2^2}{n} + \cdots + a_k^* \frac{\sum z_2 z_k}{n} = \frac{\sum z_y z_k}{n}$$

$$\vdots \qquad\qquad \vdots \qquad\qquad \vdots \qquad\qquad \vdots$$

$$a_1^* \frac{\sum z_1 z_k}{n} + a_2^* \frac{\sum z_2 z_k}{n} + \cdots + a_k^* \frac{\sum z_k^2}{n} = \frac{\sum z_y z_k}{n}$$

(85)

Since we can show that

$$\frac{\sum z^2}{n} = 1 \tag{86}$$

and

$$\frac{\sum z_i z_j}{n} = r_{ij} \tag{87}$$

we can rewrite the system of equation in (85) as

$$a_1^* \qquad + a_2^* r_{12} + a_3^* r_{13} + \cdots + a_k^* r_{1k} = r_{y1}$$

$$a_1^* r_{12} + a_2^* \qquad + a_3^* r_{23} + \cdots + a_k^* r_{2k} = r_{y2}$$

$$\vdots \qquad \vdots \qquad \vdots \qquad\qquad \vdots$$

$$a_1^* r_{1k} + a_2^* r_{2k} + a_3^* r_{3k} + \cdots + a_k^* \qquad = r_{yk}$$

(88)

Again we can rewrite (88) in matrix form

$$\begin{pmatrix} 1 & r_{12} & r_{13} & \cdots & r_{1k} \\ r_{12} & 1 & r_{23} & \cdots & r_{2k} \\ \cdot & \cdot & \cdot & & \cdot \\ \cdot & \cdot & \cdot & & \cdot \\ \cdot & \cdot & \cdot & & \cdot \\ r_{1k} & r_{2k} & \cdots & \cdots & 1 \end{pmatrix} \begin{pmatrix} a_1^* \\ a_2^* \\ \cdot \\ \cdot \\ \cdot \\ a_k^* \end{pmatrix} = \begin{pmatrix} r_{y1} \\ r_{y2} \\ \cdot \\ \cdot \\ \cdot \\ r_{yk} \end{pmatrix}$$

(89)

Again using a shorthand notation to designate our matrices, we get

$$(RR) \ (A^*) = (RY) \tag{90}$$

and multiplying through by the inverse of matrix RR, we obtain

$$(RR)^{-1}(RR) \quad (A^*) = (RR)^{-1}(RY)$$

$$(A^*) = (RR)^{-1}(RY) \tag{91}$$

The result of this operation will be two column vectors, the first of which will be the column of values of a_i^* and the second will be the solution or values for each a_i^*. We can then substitute the actual values of a_i^* into equation (82).

$$\tilde{z}_y = a_1^* z_1 + a_1^* z_2 + \cdots + a_k^* z_k$$

but we defined

$$z = \frac{(X - \bar{X})}{\sigma}$$

so that we can write a direct expression for $\tilde{Y}$ as

$$\tilde{Y} - \bar{Y} = a_1^*\left(\frac{\sigma_y}{\sigma_1}\right)(X_1 - \bar{X}_1) + a_2^*\left(\frac{\sigma_y}{\sigma_2}\right)(X_2 - \bar{X}_2) + \cdots$$

$$+ a_k^*\left(\frac{\sigma_y}{\sigma_k}\right)(X_k - \bar{X}_k) \tag{92}$$

so that

$$\tilde{Y} = a_1^*\left(\frac{\sigma_y}{\sigma_1}\right)X_1 + \cdots + a_k^*\left(\frac{\sigma_y}{\sigma_k}\right)X_h + \bar{Y} - \left[a_1^*\left(\frac{\sigma_y}{\sigma_1}\right)\bar{X}_1 + \cdots + a_k^*\left(\frac{\sigma_y}{\sigma_k}\right)\bar{X}_k\right]$$

If we let σ_1 equal the standard deviation of the first term, and σ_k equal the standard deviation of the kth variable, each coefficient a_i is now given by

$$a_i = a_i^*\left(\frac{\sigma_y}{\sigma_i}\right) \tag{93}$$

There are many advantages of solving the multiple regression equation by use of correlation coefficients. It is most important that we can include correlation coefficients that are not based on the same numbers of observations. It is unusual to find a complete matrix of observed values, i.e., one in which no values at all are missing. Computers make it possible to develop a value of a correlation coefficient between any pair of variables based on the number of observations contained in those two sets. When the computer is small, some short-cut estimation procedures become necessary. However, for the reasonably large machines that are commonly available today, separate correlation coefficients can be computed for any pair of variables based on the actual number of observations which exist. The value of a correlation can then be adjusted for number of observations by a simple method

$$r_{adj} = r\frac{n-1}{n-2} \tag{94}$$

where n is the number of cases on which the correlation coefficient has been based. One can also adjust r by making an estimate of the true value of r, using the correlation for restricted range of sampling of equation (63).

Another advantage of the use of correlation coefficients rather than sums of squares and cross products lies in that we many include truncated variables. In this case we can compute biserial and tetrachoric coefficients as estimates of r. In this way a variable whose effect is to be evaluated within a framework of other variables can be included even if it is not measured along a continuous scale.

We can take this procedure a step further and even include biserial and tetrachoric correlations computed for instances in which we can not make the assumption of an underlying continuous scale at all. For instance, if we wish to predict the weight of an individual from a set of variables which includes such continuously scaled measurements as height and age and also such nonscalable items as sex, maturity, obesity, and so on, we could make use of our multiple regression procedure to see whether or not the nonscalable items are related to weight, and even assign a value to their contribution. Although from a purely mathematical point of view we may not be justified in doing so, we could logically justify the use of multiple regression to tell us whether or not a nonscalable variable contributes to precision in prediction. Note that we are not really interested so much here in the actual amount of contribution, but in whether or not it acts to reduce the total variance.

THE MULTIPLE CORRELATION COEFFICIENT

In setting up a way to evaluate the effect of each variable by itself, we have anticipated a similar usage for multiple effects of several variables. To do so we shall define a multiple correlation coefficient in practically the same way as we defined the correlation between two variables. When $R_{y|123\ldots k}$ is the multiple correlation coefficient of variables $X_1, X_2, \ldots, X_k$ on some variable Y, then we define the square of this coefficient as

$$R^2_{y|123\ldots k} = \frac{\sigma_y^2 - \sigma_{y|123\ldots k}^2}{\sigma_y^2} \tag{95}$$

where the $\sigma^2_{y|123...k}$ is the variation of points around the best prediction defined as

$$\sigma^2_{y|123...k} = \frac{\sum [Y - f(X_1, X_2, \ldots, X_k)]^2}{N} \qquad (96)$$

It turns out that the multiple correlation coefficient can be computed easily by

$$R^2_{y|123...k} = a^*_1 r_{y1} + a^*_2 r_{y2} + \cdots + a^*_k r_{yk} \qquad (97)$$

so that

$$\sigma^2_{y|123...k} = 1 - R^2_{y|123...k} \qquad (98)$$

The standard error for the multiple correlation coefficient is given by

$$\sigma_{R_{y|123...k}} = \frac{\sigma_{y|123...k}}{\sqrt{N}} \qquad (99)$$

We are now ready to test the hypothesis that a particular value of a multiple regression coefficient is due to chance. We can use the variance ratio

$$F_\alpha \geq \frac{(R^2_{y|123...k})(n - k - 1)}{(1 - R^2_{y|123...k})k} \qquad (100)$$

for d.f. $= k/(n - k - 1)$.

We might also question whether the addition of yet one more predictor variable introduces a significant increment to prediction. Such a test could be derived, but, as will be seen in Chapter 10, there would be little profit in using it for a large data file.

Perhaps related but certainly of a somewhat lesser order is the question of what the multiple correlation for any given set of predictors would be if one of these predictors were left out. If we have a string of multiple predictors and wish to inspect the multiple correlation that would result if the ith predictor were left out, a convenient computational procedure exists:

$$R^2_{y|12...(i)...k} = (R^2_{y|12...k}) - \left(\frac{a^*_i}{C_{ii}}\right) \qquad (101)$$

where $R^2_{y|12...(i)...k}$ is the multiple R^2 with the ith predictor left out.

a^*_i is the regression weight of the ith predictor.

C_{ii} is the ith term in the diagonal of matrix RR^{-1} of equation (91).

The inclusion of the multiple correlation coefficient with the ith variable left out in a general printout for multiple regression analysis gives the investigator some basis for judging the relative importance of each predictor variable and its dependence or independence on or from other variables. When the multiple correlation coefficient with the ith variable left out drops sharply in value, this variable is strongly associated and adds an independent contribution to prediction not furnished by the other variables. On the other hand, if the elimination of the ith variable does not change the multiple correlation coefficient very much, then this variable is probably not very much associated or its contribution is not independent.

We shall see in Chapter 10 how equation (101) can be used to advantage in setting up automatic screening procedures for important variables.

DISPLAY

The printout for a multiple regression and correlation analysis should include a number of items of information.

1. The total regression equations should be stated.
2. The correlation matrix and the inverse of the correlation matrix should be stated.

Table 9.6. EXAMPLE OF MULTIPLE REGRESSION*

```
                    JOB             VELSICOL LIVER WEIGHTS - SAMPLE RUN

     ROW VARIABLES                                INVERTED CORRELATION COEFFICIENT MATRIX

BODY WEIGHT              1.0946418
LITTER SIZE               .28456816          1.0805819
BCCY WEIGHT SQUARED       .17520524          -.12708211          1.0346471
                        DETERMINANT OF ORIGINAL CORRELATION MATRIX =  .90754717



                                        MULTIPLE REGRESSION ANALYSIS
                    JOB             VELSICOL LIVER WEIGHTS - SAMPLE RUN

                    DEPENDENT VARIABLE IS LIVER WEIGHT
                    SQUARE OF MULTIPLE CORRELATION COEFFICIENT =  .90874802
                    VARIANCE OF DEPENDENT VARIABLE =             1.3779238
                    VARIANCE OF ESTIMATE =                        .12573830
```

INDEPENDENT VARIABLE	CORRELATION WITH DEPENDENT VARIABLE	NORMALIZED REGRESSION COEFFICIENT	REGRESSION COEFFICIENT	SQUARE OF MULTIPLE CORRELA COEFFICIENT WI VARIABLE OMIT
BODY WEIGHT	.93000000	.88750493	.47279219E-01	.18918387
LITTER SIZE	-.42600000	-.20241485	-.52954016E-01	.87083163
BCCY WEIGHT SQUARED	.53000000E-01	-.53967610E-01	-.33410874E-05	.90593305

```
                            CONSTANT =  .48227120
```

*Printout from the MEDCOMP Program Library.

3. The values of the multiple correlation coefficient should be shown, together with each regression weight (or coefficient).
4. The multiple correlation coefficient for the ith variable left out should be listed for each variable.

In addition, it may be well to obtain all the graphs among pairs of variables or at least all the graphs among the predicted variable and each predictor so as to check for linearity. An example of an appropriate printout is given in Table 9.6. This printout from the MEDCOMP program library predicts liver weight as a function of body weight (both simply and squared) and of liver size. The top of the printout shows the inverted matrix of correlation coefficients. (The determinant is given also, although we have not discussed its use here.) Next are given R^2, s_y^2, $s_{y|x_1 x_2 x_3}^2$. The value of R^2 is large ($R^2 = .9$). The values of s_y^2 and $s_{y|x_1 x_2 x_3}^2$ are given to round out the information supplied by R^2.

The final columns give information concerning the relation between liver weight and its predictor variables as well as the values of the regression coefficients.

PARTIAL CORRELATION

Sometimes we suspect that the correlation between two variables X and Y is influenced by multiple relationships that each variable may have with a common set of extraneous conditions. The set of extraneous conditions may enhance a correlation so as as to give a spuriously large value if the correlations of X and Y with each of these conditions are all positive or all negative. Conversely, the correlation between X and Y may be spuriously decreased if the correlation of each variable with the extraneous conditions is opposite in sign from that of the other variable.

Eliminating the effect of spurious variables is called *partialling out*; the effect of other variables and the resultant correlation coefficients are called *partial correlations*. The general expression for the partial correlation between X and Y eliminating the spurious effect of variables 1 through k is given below:

$$R_{xy|12\ldots k}^2 = (a_{x|y12\ldots k})(a_{y|x12\ldots k}) \tag{102}$$

where

$$a_{x|y12\ldots k}$$

is equal to the regression weight in the equation that predicts $\tilde{X}$ from k variables including variable Y and

$$a_{y|x12\ldots k}$$

is equal to a regression weight in the equation that predicts Y from k variables including X.

A simple equation for partialling for two variables with respect to a third is

$$r_{xy|z} = \frac{r_{xy} - r_{yz}r_{xy}}{\sqrt{1 - r_{xz}^2}\,\sqrt{1 - r_{yz}^2}} \qquad (103)$$

where $r_{xy|z}$ is the correlation between X and Y with the effect of z partialled out.

DISCRIMINANT FUNCTIONS

An important modification of the purpose of multiple regression can make this analysis useful for predicting differences between groups. We defined multiple regression as the case where a continuously scalable variable Y is related to a set of possible prediction conditions $X_1, X_2, \ldots, X_k$ such that

$$\tilde{Y} = f(X_1, X_2 \ldots X_k)$$

where the best-fitting function was selected such that

$$\sum (Y - \tilde{Y})^2 \text{ is a minimum}$$

Sometimes, however, we wish to obtain a difference between the way a set of predictors could be used to differentiate between two groups. We could restate this problem by asking if there is some value of a variable V such that for one group V takes on different values than for other groups. We want to find V, where

$$V = a_0 + a_1X_1 + a_2X_2 + \cdots + a_kX_k \qquad (104)$$

with the restriction that if we average V_1 for group one and V_2 for group two and obtain a difference between them D, the values of $a_0, a_1, \ldots, a_k$ are selected so that

$$\bar{D} = (V_1 - V_2) \text{ is a maximum} \qquad (105)$$

The student should note immediately that the formulations of the multiple regression and of the discriminant function problem are the same. He should not be surprised, therefore, to find that we shall seek very much the same solution to this problem as we did for the multiple regression problem.

We seek a solution to the system of equations stated in matrix form immediately below:

$$
\begin{pmatrix}
\sum x_1^2 & + \sum x_1 x_2 + \cdots + \sum x_1 x_k \\
\sum x_1 x_2 & + \sum x_2^2 \ \ + \cdots + \sum x_2 x_k \\
\vdots & \quad \vdots \qquad\qquad\qquad \vdots \\
\vdots & \quad \vdots \qquad\qquad\qquad \vdots \\
\sum x_1 x_k & + \sum x_2 x_k + \cdots + \sum x_k^2
\end{pmatrix}
\begin{pmatrix}
a_1 \\ a_2 \\ \vdots \\ \vdots \\ a_k
\end{pmatrix}
=
\begin{pmatrix}
d_1 \\ d_2 \\ \vdots \\ \vdots \\ d_k
\end{pmatrix}
\tag{106}
$$

where

$$
d_i = \bar{X}_{i1} - \bar{X}_{i2} \tag{107}
$$

or the difference between the values of the means for the ith variable for groups one and two, $\bar{X}_{i1}$ and $\bar{X}_{i2}$. We can solve for the values of the coefficients by

$$
(A) = (XX)^{-1} (D)
$$

The hypothesis that D is larger than would be expected by chance alone can be tested by the use of the variance ratio

$$
F_\alpha \geq \frac{n_1 n_2 (n_1 + n_2 - k - 1)\bar{D}}{k(n_1 + n_2)} \tag{108}
$$

for d.f. $= k/(n_1 + n_2 - k - 1)$.

The printout for a discriminant function analysis should be similar to that of multiple regression and include the cross-product matrix, the inverted cross-product matrix, and, if possible, the correlation matrix of all variables separated by the two groups. As in multiple regression, we shall discuss optimum research methods for automatic selection of best discriminants in Chapter 10.

NONLINEAR MULTIPLE REGRESSION

As with the relationship among two variables, the linear model is simple and mathematically elegant but unrealistic in the actual world. Linearity, homoscedasticity, and multivariate normal distributions are rare exceptions rather than the rule. However, as in the case of two variables, calculational difficulties for nonlinear multivariate models are immense. There are serious difficulties in solving them even with computers.

Nonlinear multiple regression is in many ways beyond the scope of this book. However, there are a number of approaches for developing some ideas of the relationships that might exist in any nonlinear universe by using simple approximating approaches. If the precise function of X_1, X_2 ... X_k is known, then of course the writing of an equation predicting $\tilde{Y}$ from a set of preconditions is defined. This is very seldom the case. Also, although it is simple to visualize a graph of Y versus a single variable, the multidimensional relationship between Y and a series of variables is difficult to picture, so the form of an equation describing a multidimensional surface cannot be clearly seen. Such an equation is usually known only in those instances in which a multivariate relationship is deduced from prior principles and definitions. Such events rarely happen even in the physical sciences and are almost unknown in the social or biological areas.

More usually, the form of the relationship between Y and a number of other variables is unknown. Perhaps the only assumption that can be made about this relationship is that it is not linear, not multivariate normal, and not homoscedastic. Under these circumstances there are three strategies that can be used.

We may simply accept the fact that the multivariate situation violates the linear model but use the linear model anyway. In most instances the linear model used in a nonlinear world will lead to an underestimate of the actual relationship that may exist. This type of reasoning is of comfort only to those who wish to find a significant correlation or wish to determine whether or not a significant correlation does indeed exist between certain antecedent conditions and their consequences. It is of lesser comfort to those who wish to predict a state of affairs in the best way possible, given a set of preconditions. Also, the actual importance of variables would be falsified to some extent, because those that tend to be less linear would have a smaller effect than those whose effect is more closely linear. However, in the absence of any knowledge about the possible linearity in a matrix of relationships, it might be simplest to proceed with the idea that violation of the linear hypothesis is essentially the same for all variables.

If we can obtain displays showing graphs between sets of variables, both among predictors and predicted and among all the predictors, we might be able to formulate some notions about how and to what extent linearity is violated by some variables. On the basis of these observations, we might use what we know about polynomial expansion to obtain a better prediction by choosing prediction equations of some alternate form such as

$$\tilde{Y} = a_0 + a_1 X_1 + a_2 X_1^2 + a_3 X_1^3 + a_4 X_2 + \cdots \tag{109}$$

In this case we are using a simple polynomial expansion to approximate the effect of one variable. Whether or not this procedure is useful can be determined by comparing the multiple correlation coefficient for the case where we use polynomial expansion and for the case where we do not. A related procedure may be to include the joint effect of two variables X_1 and X_2 by using a form such as

$$\tilde{Y} = a_0 + a_1 X_1 + a_2 X_2 + a_3 X_1 X_2 + \cdots \tag{110}$$

Joint effects and corrections for nonlinearity can be combined.

$$\tilde{Y} = a_0 + a_1 X_1 + a_2 X_2 + a_3 X_1^2 X_2 + \cdots \tag{111}$$

The models which best approximate nonlinear relationships are difficult to identify. Experience with shapes and forms of scattergrams will help the investigator find better ways of introducing corrections into a very general multiple regression model. Thus availability of display is extremely important.

This brings up another point. A computing facility should have a comprehensive *command language* that will enable the investigator to state how he wishes to expand the multiple regression model so as to include second order and higher terms as well as cross products, and combinations among them. This command language should be simple so that instructions concerning combinations and permutations of cross products and higher-order terms can be inserted in the over-all program procedure without undue difficulty. The command language ought to include provisions for producing or suppressing certain displays such as scattergrams, complete correlation matrices, (well labeled), inverted matrices, and so on.

PROBLEMS

1. Below are golf scores and measures of handgrip for a sample of athletes.

Subject	Handgrip Score	Golf Score
A	12	67
B	4	82
C	7	70
D	14	69
E	8	75
F	6	86
G	2	93
H	5	91
I	7	84
J	9	78

(a) Construct a scattergram of golf score versus handgrip.
(b) Find the best linear expression of golf score as a function of handgrip.
(c) What is the error of predicting golf scores if the handgrip is known?

(d) What is the value of the correlation between handgrip and golf score? How would you interpret this value?

(e) What is the expression predicting handgrip from golf score? Verify that $r = \sqrt{a_1 a_1'}$.

(f) You are interested in estimating the correlation between handgrip and golf score for the population at large, not just for athletes. It turns out that the standard deviation of handgrips is known for a large random sample of men and equal to 4.8. What is the corrected value of r?

(g) Test the hypothesis that the slope and the correlation coefficient are larger than they would be by chance alone.

2. Pair each of the scores for handgrip with a single integer selected at random from a table of random numbers. Answer questions 1(a) through 1(g) for this new set of pairs of numbers.

3. Below is a set of measures of size of a particular species of endocrine cells (in microns) and secretion of a particular hormone.

Cell	Cell Size (X)	Amount Secreted (Y)
A	27	18
B	64	47
C	98	88
D	80	71
E	71	52
F	33	21
G	23	17
H	74	56
I	99	98
J	90	78

(a) Construct a scattergram of amount secreted versus cell size.

(b) Find the best linear expression of $Y = f(X)$.

(c) Find the best linear expression for $Y = f(\log X)$.

(d) Compare the error terms and values of the correlation coefficients for the expressions in 3b and 3c.

4. Rank values from Problems 1, 2, and 3 from highest to lowest and compute the value of the rank correlation coefficient between each set of pairs.

5. Below are scores for handgrip for a group of males and females. Estimate the value of the correlation between handgrip and sex.

Handgrip of Males	Handgrip of Females
2	6
8	4
14	8
9	2
4	4
12	3
16	1

6. An experimenter wants to predict a dependent variable Y from the known state of three independent variables X_1, X_2, X_3. Below is the correlation matrix between all variables

$$\begin{pmatrix} r_{yy} & r_{yx_1} & r_{yx_2} & r_{yx_3} \\ r_{x_1y} & r_{x_1x_1} & r_{x_1x_2} & r_{x_1x_3} \\ r_{x_2y} & r_{x_2x_3} & r_{x_2x_2} & r_{x_2x_3} \\ r_{x_3y} & r_{x_3x_1} & r_{x_3x_2} & r_{x_3x_3} \end{pmatrix} \begin{pmatrix} 1.0 & 0.8 & -0.9 & -0.2 \\ 0.8 & 1.0 & -0.7 & -0.3 \\ -0.9 & -0.7 & 1.0 & 0.4 \\ -0.2 & -0.3 & 0.4 & 1.0 \end{pmatrix}$$

The other parameters are

$$\bar{Y} = 12 \qquad s_y^2 = 16$$
$$\bar{X}_1 = 22 \qquad s_{x_1}^2 = 25$$
$$\bar{X}_2 = 14 \qquad s_{x_2}^2 = 9$$
$$\bar{X}_3 = 16 \qquad s_{x_3}^2 = 16$$
$$n = 36$$

(a) Find the best linear expression for $\tilde{Y}$, given ($X_{1i}, X_{2i},$ and X_{3i}).

(b) Find the value of $R_{y|x_1x_2x_3}^2$ and the best estimate of $S_{y|x_1x_2x_3}$.

(c) Test the hypothesis that the multiple correlation and regression weights are significantly greater than zero.

(d) Compare $R_{y|x_1x_2}^2$ with $R_{y|x_1x_2x_3}^2$. What would you conclude?

(e) Which combination of variables ($X_1X_2X_3$) would you use in practice, assuming that you want to estimate Y as well as you can and at the same time keep the cost of estimating this value within reason? (Assume that a cost is connected with observing each of the associated variables $X_1, X_2,$ and X_3).

10 AUTOMATIC SEARCH TECHNIQUES

In the last two chapters we explored a variety of simple numerical techniques used to describe one variable as a function of one or a small number of other variables. These techniques have been tested and found useful throughout many decades and so predate automatic data processing by a considerable period of time. They are really independent of automation. Yet to a large extent it has been the advent of computers which has made them much more available to a larger circle of users. Computational aids offered by high-speed processors not only make it possible for the knowledgeable individual to undertake more complex calculations and execute them in a shorter period of time, but also open many numerical techniques to the mathematically unsophisticated person who, although able to understand the techniques conceptually, perhaps lacks some of the mathematical niceties requisite for doing his own computation.

By shifting the burden of computation completely onto the processor, the age-old problem of placing powerful mathematical tools into the hands of potential users who are not mathematicians may be successfully resolved. If this were not the case, then the many new expanded methods of analysis would be unobtainable to most scientists. As a matter of fact, very few fields have benefited more from high-speed processing machines than numerical computation. The development of more and more sophisticated methods to approximate parameters of complex situations or to optimize some of them has kept one step ahead of the development of larger and faster processors so that problems that may have many thousands of variables and constraints can be attacked. Many of these approaches could have powerful and revolutionary effects on developments in the biological and social sciences were it not for the obstacle that their execution demands,

444

by and large, a degree of mathematical sophistication which is beyond the scope of many workers in some fields. Automatic data processing can now bring many of these techniques within the grasp of most investigators.

We shall now turn to such a class of new data processing techniques, which are bound to automated procedures and which will have far-reaching consequences for the empirical sciences. They are methods by which clusters of related variables, multiple associations of interest to the investigator, and information about the morphology of relationships may be teased out from a welter of masking and interfering observations. They use the high-speed processor as a logical screening device or as a logical "filter" that lets through only those statements about data that may be of relevance to the investigator. Because these techniques share the property that automatic elimination or selection of variables is done by a program rather than by an individual, such terms as *robot data screening*, *data dredging*, *general inquirer*, and others have been used to describe them.

Before getting into the subject matter further, we draw the student's attention to the fact that we have not made a sharp distinction between numerical techniques in general and statistical techniques in particular. Although a practical division may be made between models that deal with deterministic or with stochastic situations, both are basically numerical tools. The unity of statistical and numerical techniques becomes very much more obvious as we turn to automatic search.

A PRACTICAL LOOK AT
THE MULTIVARIATE PROBLEM

We have treated the scientist's activities in designing experiments and analyzing data as aimed toward locating those variables that are related and determining those events in the environment that allow ultimate prediction and manipulation. Theory about natural phenomena is not necessarily involved in this search, nor is a discussion of the role of theory in science germane to our object here. Many investigators in the biological, medical, and social sciences are interested in almost any relationship that may be found in their data, because the chances are excellent that knowledge about such a relationship will lend itself to many interesting new formulations or useful activities. Often, the major concern of the investigator is to converge upon and isolate relevant associations among a welter and mass of possible relationships and let the theoretician worry why such relationships exist.

With automation of data collection and the ability to pool data from many sources into so-called data banks, large and multivariate data files can be created for a relatively small cost. These data files describe the behavior of materials, tissues, organs, social groups, or what have you, under a multitude of circumstances which can be defined as *associated variables*. The existence of such multivariate files is a new phenomenon, since such files were not practicable prior to the development of automatic data collection and data storage mechanisms. Therefore, methods of analysis of such multivariate files are not yet well established. In fact, prior to the existence of computers there was neither urge nor opportunity to develop analytic techniques for such multivariate data aggregations.

The motive behind gathering all this information and recording as much of the correlated environment as possible lies in the hope that somewhere within these data are crucial relationships that will somehow capture the investigator's attention. For medical-clinical data it may be that among a wide variety of seemingly aimless observations, a particular general characteristic, such as age, combined with a particular symptom, such as heat tolerance, and a specific treatment, such as chemotherapy, would lead to a very definite predictable aftereffect, such as palliation. In a quite different situation it may be that the size of a group, its racial composition, the age and educational level of its participants, particular outcomes on a number of personality tests, the occurrence and nonoccurrence of events in the history of the group, and other factors combine to shape this group toward a liberal or an authoritarian mold. These types of problems are inherent in the messy multivariate world of empiricists.

Let us assume that each variable in a multivariate file has a value, a code, or a number, which we shall denote by a letter, such as $A, B, \ldots, X, Y,$ or Z. Let us now select one of these variables for analysis. We are interested particularly if there is a constellation of variables in the data file that somehow determines the state or outcome of the variable of interest. Where we denote this variable of interest by Y, we state our problem as wishing to find $\tilde{Y} = f(X_i, \ldots, X_j)$, where X_i to X_j are that set of variables which, when combined, give a better prediction of the state of the dependent variable Y than any other combination of variables used as predictors. We are interested in a particular cluster of conditions that have the property that together they turn out to be the best "predictor" or most likely "antecedent" of a particular situation or event in which we are interested.

There is yet another way in which we may look at clustering variables along lines of interest. In any collection of variables, there are some which apparently covary or cofluctuate because they share a number of underlying conditions. Very often the isolation of these clusters enables the investigator or theoretician to postulate a general set of "factors" which determine much of the phenomenon with which he is concerned. His efforts are not directed so much toward finding sets of predictors but more toward isolating some unity and order within the mass and welter of observations. There are, however, some very practical problems that must be resolved before the clustering made potentially possible by high-speed processing of large integrated data files can become a reality.

Let us say that we are interested in factors associated with the effect of a treatment. We have reliably observed $N = 72$ different categories, such as sex, age, weight, I^{131} uptake, the effects of various treatments, and so on. Within each category there are several subcategories, such as age groupings, sexes, weight classes, or intervals of I^{131} uptake. We may be interested in the influence, if any, that some of these variables and their subcategories might have on treatment effect. Let us also assume that to judge the effects of various conditions on our variable of interest we make use of simple analytic devices, such as frequency tables that summarize the outcome of treatment by age, sex, diagnosis, or of graphs which depict the relation between a scale of improvement and weight, height, I^{131} uptake, and temperature. Indeed, the investigator would call for such tables and graphs as a first step in any analysis. However, he would be interested in the distribution of effects of treatment by more than one factor, specifically in such questions as: "Are there treatment effects which are somehow related simultaneously to age and sex or to age and type of treatment or to age and type of symptom? Are there effects of therapy somehow related simultaneously to weight and occurrence of menopause, to weight and age, to weight and the outcome of particular hemotological tests?" The number of such breakdowns, taken two at a time, is $N(N-1)/2$, where N is equal to the number of categories or variables. If we were working with a relatively small file of 72 such variables as an example, this would mean an inspection of 2485 frequency breakdowns or graphs. This is obviously a large number, but it is not impossible to conceive of an investigator actually inspecting that many graphs or tables. (We may form an idea of the magnitude of such a task by reflecting that in a city of million inhabitants, a telephone directory has approximately 850 to 900 pages. To inspect 2485 tables may be equivalent to reviewing, page by page, three such telephone directories.)

Yet it might be that the very significant associations exist on the level of interaction among three rather than two categories. Perhaps the effect of treatment is predicted best from a knowledge of age, sex, and a particular symptom. Perhaps one would have to know the average educational level of members of a teenage group, their need for security, and the presence of a single authoritarian-oriented individual to forecast delinquent actions. To find this triple association we would now have to inspect all possible three-way breakdowns contained in the data—whether these are in the form of tables or graphs is immaterial for the moment. The number of breakdown possibilities now increases very sharply. For the three-way break-down we have just described we would have to look at $[N(N-1)(N-2)/3!]$ combinations. For the example of 72 variables this would amount to 57,155 triple combinations of data breakdowns of frequency distribution or graphs.

Increasing the complexity to four breakdowns results in $[N(N-1)(N-2)$-$(N-3)/4!]$ combinations, or a total of 971,635 breakdowns in our example. In general, to find the number of breakdowns in groups of r would demand that we look at

$$\frac{N(N-1)(N-2)\ldots(N-r+1)}{r!}$$

combinations. It would take practically forever, even with uninterrupted use of fast computers, just to produce these breakdowns on magnetic tape for any reasonably sized collection of variables and observations. Certainly no investigator can expect to produce such tables or graph and inspect them within his lifetime.

Yet investigators in many empirical sciences hope that by collecting multivariate data of many types they will be able to find associations that will be of help to them in the treatment of disease, in understanding the formation of groups, in handling problems in delinquency or social aberrations, in formulating sane and safe policy for the nation, and so on. Such findings almost always result when the existence of a very striking cluster of predictor variables is unearthed, often more by a lucky accident and serendipity rather than through systematic search. Before computers came on the scene, making any sense out of clinical or sociological multivariate data was almost hopeless, and the invention of the computer itself certainly did not represent a solution to this problem.

The multivariate problem in the empirical sciences is made even more complex because of properties of numbers that are generated, by observations. In many cases observations may be missing. Even worse the properties of the numbers generated differ widely. Some are discrete, others continuous; some occur with a high frequency, others are observed only intermittently; some vary widely on the real number line, others remain relatively constant, and so on.

If solutions to these problems are going to come forth at all they will do so through one of two channels: either through very ingenious mathematical techniques that converge logically onto certain associations of scientific interests or through the creation of self-contained program systems and routines that simulate the intelligent activity of competent, perhaps also serendipitious investigators. This latter approach, for want of a better name, we call the *heuristic* type of solution.

THE HEURISTIC SOLUTION

We shall turn now toward the study of techniques that examine groups of variables according to set rules and eliminate from these clusters some variables as "uninteresting" or "irrelevant" and include others because they are "interesting" or "relevant" to an investigator according to very definitely stated criteria by which "uninteresting" and "interesting" are defined. None of these techniques are completely "formal" in the mathematical sense, nor are any of them completely devoid of mathematically based inference. Rather, they are a mixture of logic based on trial and error as well as on formal deduction and, in essence, operate very much as an educated investigator would under certain conditions. However, such a parallel would be very misleading if it were taken too literally. They are really large program systems which, in sequential actions, do the sort of things which well-trained investigators might do with their data to converge upon statements about different variables.

In this search or screening process, there are three important features. Each screening method must be examined on how it deals with them.

1. How suitable are the rules and definitions making up the criteria for selecting or rejecting a variable? Will the criteria really ignore uninteresting variables without overlooking interesting ones? Will the algorithms used in the program indeed execute the rules which define the selection criteria?

2. Quite independent from algorithms that define selection criteria are methods by which variables are selected. If variables are rejected or accepted by sequential application of a well-defined set of rules, then the selection process may require long or short periods of time, depending on the methods of screening that can be developed. This is a very crucial problem for some methods of screening which may demand excessive amounts of computer time. Since this is probably the major cost item in any automatic analysis, screening algorithms that will minimize computer time are important components of the analytic technique.

3. The sensitivity of the methods to actual numbers of observations is terribly important. Because large sample errors are more likely to occur with small samples rather than larger samples, searching techniques among large numbers of variables but based on small samples very often result in erroneous conclusions. The technique must be sensitive to the number of replications on which the data themselves are based.

It is obvious that any robot system may well have to be a compromise among criteria for selection, method of screening, and sensitivity to available numbers of observations. The adoption of one set of criteria rather than another could lead to excessive amounts of computer time for searching even with optimum methods. Certain automatic techniques may be completely unsuitable for small numbers of observations. Some methods of selection, although efficient in terms of selecting criteria, may be bound to the actual numbers of replications, so that they become unsuitable for large data files. Other methods of selection may become efficient only when large replicated data files exist. In our discussion, therefore, we shall point out where the analytic system is sensitive to compromises among the major features that determine the over-all suitability of any automatic search system.

ROBOT GRAPHING

In many life science problems, but also in some problems in the social sciences, a number of variables can be observed which are all scalable continuously or for which such a scale may be assumed even though measurements are taken along discrete intervals. These might be such values as age, weight, height, test scores, outcome of chemical or hemotological analysis, and so on. The number of scalable variables in a study may also be enlarged by the introduction of certain combinations among them or by the use of geometric and other criteria according to which some of these relations might be ordered.

One way of telling whether or not possible relationships may exist in this welter of information would be to graph each scalable variable against each other scalable variable. We saw before that when we have N such variables we could develop $N(N-1)/2$ graphs of two variables at a time. If we also have K discrete observations, each having M number of subclasses in our data files such as sex (male, female), social class (upper, middle, lower), and so on, the investigator may be interested not only in obtaining graphs for all pairs of scalable variables but also in producing these graphs for all possible subcategories for each of the K discrete variables. In this case, we would have $\sum_{i=1}^{k} \sum_{j=1}^{m} \frac{N(N-1)}{2}$ graphs, and a very large number of graphs could then be be developed for any data file.

A routine which may be very useful in these circumstances is one that automatically examines a large number of possible graphs contained in a data file and selects only those for presentation to the investigator which meet a reasonable criterion of "interest."

The problem of a robot grapher is comparatively simple, because the definition of "interest" in the selection of variables is relatively clear. Whenever it would appear from a graph that $\tilde{Y} = f(X)$ and where $f(X)$ is well behaved (that is, the data points are clustered very tightly around a best-fitting line or curve), then it can be concluded that a relationship exists between the two variables X and Y and that this relationship is of interest to the investigator.

In practice, however, there are a number of problems that have to be solved in determining whether or not a graph is well behaved and finding functions expressing a "best" fit.

CRITERIA FOR DEFINING FIT

Criteria for defining goodness of fit have been developed and used extensively in the last two chapters. We define the error of prediction or the spread of the actual observed points around the best line of fit by

$$\sigma^2_{y|x} = \frac{\sum (Y_i - \tilde{Y})^2}{N}$$

and from this error then find a measure of goodness of fit which we have referred to as the correlation, or

$$R^2_{yx} = \frac{\sigma^2_y - \sigma^2_{y|x}}{\sigma^2_y}$$

The quantity R^2 can be used to define a graduated scale of "better" or "worse" relationships.

We could, of course, also use the error term $\sigma^2_{y|x}$ or some similar measure. However, there are compelling reasons for the use of R^2 rather than $\sigma^2_{y|x}$ to scale goodness of fit. The spread of points around a predicted line is, in many ways, dependent on the number of data points. With a small number of points the fit may be quite good, so that the error variance around the best line of fit becomes very small and the value of R^2 may be quite large. For instance, using only two points, we can fit a line $f(X) = a_0 + a_1 X$ through them so that $\sigma^2_{y|x} = 0$ and $R^2 = 1$. However, as we saw before, the correlation coefficient is affected by numbers of observations, and the probability distribution for correlations based on small numbers of observations is known. We shall make use of this knowledge to develop a corrected measure to scale goodness of fit that is to a large extent independent of numbers of observations. For this purpose we use

$$\bar{R} = \frac{R^2}{r^2_\alpha} \tag{1}$$

where $\bar{R}$ is our scalable criterion measure of fit, R^2 is the square of the observed correlation, and r^2_α is that value of the correlation coefficient for the appropriate numbers of observations that would be used to reject the hypothesis that the true correlation is equal to 0 with probability of Type I error $= \alpha$. When $f(X)$ is linear, R^2 represents the Pearson product moment correlation coefficient. Consequently, $\bar{R} \leq 1$ if the fit is no better or worse than would be expected by chance alone, and $\bar{R} > 1$ if the fit of $f(X)$ to data points is better than would be expected by chance.

For N variables, $N(N-1)/2$ correlation coefficients can be computed, and a predictable number of over- and underestimates of true correlations may be expected by chance alone. However, we really need not be concerned with this dilemma here, as long as $\bar{R}$ represents purely a grading mechanism by which we decide that some functions are better behaved than others.

But what happens if $f(X)$ is not linear?

There are two reasons why $\bar{R}$ is also a useful measure in instances where R^2 is not based on a linear relationship. First, the definition of R^2 makes it independent of linearity. When R^2 is computed by comparing the two variances σ_y^2 and $\sigma_{y|x}^2$ each of which is found independently, then the actual shape of $f(X)$ is really immaterial. Also when $f(X)$ is not linear, using computations for linear correlation will be an underestimate of the true relationship that exists. (Why?)

The computed or estimated $\bar{R}$ always will be equal to or smaller than the true $\bar{R}$. Thus $\bar{R}$ becomes an adequate and perhaps even conservative method of ranking paired observations according to the criterion of goodness of fit.

There is only one reason why r_α could not represent a curvilinear correlation rather than a linear correlation. This is the necessary work and computer time involved in finding this value for every possible function that is included. Since $\bar{R}$ is used as a screening device, the accuracy with which r_α is stated is not really such a large factor. Thus considerations of cost and convenience make a linear r_α quite adequate and even preferable.

FINDING THE BEST-FITTING FUNCTION

We have a number of choices in finding $\bar{R}$ for each set of variables. These choices are very much determined by cost factors, where cost is defined by the time needed to do the necessary computations.

The simplest choice would be to compute R^2 as a linear correlation for all pairs of variables, the actual shape of $f(X)$ being ignored. The program would then display those pairs of variables for which $\bar{R}$ is larger than some predetermined value or print out a list of $\bar{R}$ values with their associated variables and let the investigator decide which graph or graphs he actually wants to see. The advantage of assuming linearity is that it makes fast screening possible. This is true especially if only R^2 is computed and not the coefficients for the best-fitting regression line.

The disadvantages of this method are, of course, obvious. Whenever a relationship between two variables is not linear, R^2 and $\bar{R}$ will be underestimates of the true relationship. The magnitude of underestimation will depend not only on the spread of the points around the best-fitting curve but also on the deviation of the actual curve from linearity. Nevertheless, this simple screening procedure may be a convenient and useful program for a first test run through a set of possible relationships, especially when the only processor available to the investigator is slow or has very limited memory.

A second method of approach is to approximate $f(X_i)$ where (X_i) is some value of X. This can be done without determining the actual shape of the function, simply by expanding the polynomial X_i.

$$f(X_i) = a_0 + a_1 X_i + a_2 X_i^2 + \cdots + a_n X_i^n$$

Each time the polynomial is expanded by one more term, R^2 and $s^2_{y|x}$ are computed. The decision on whether or not to expand $f(X_i)$ to $n + 1$ terms is based on the comparison of R^2 for n and $n + 1$ terms. The immediate advantage of this procedure is to free us from the problem of having to assume linearity of R^2. The obvious disadvantage, on the other hand, is that it increases computer time by requiring an additional criterion for deciding when to stop in the expansion of the series. There are simple criteria available for this choice. We can evaluate and compare the value for R^2_n with R^2_{n+1} and make a decision on whether the improvement by expanding the series by one more term is really large enough to justify going one step further. The problem here is that as we expand the series by a new term, the value of R^2_{n+1} will usually increase over R^2_n. However, we could decide at the beginning of the analysis that unless

$$\frac{R^2_{n+1} - R^2_n}{R^2_{n+1}} > K \tag{2}$$

the series will not be expanded any further.

An alternate method, just as good in the long run, is to expand the series to a specific number of terms (say four or five) and stop. Although in some instances the series will be expanded to more terms than is actually necessary to fit a good curve, a program that will expand a series to a set number of terms is not only simple to write but can be designed so as to consume a minimum amount of computer time. Expansion to four or five terms is generally sufficient to fit most nonlinear functions usually found in the many empirical sciences. (For a more exhaustive discussion of use of polynomial expansions, turn back to Chapter 8.)

The two procedures discussed so far for developing a robot grapher do not concern themselves with defining the actual shape of the function but are only concerned with locating those sets of variables that might show the best-behaved functions. In many ways, however, the shape of a function, when it is well behaved, is perhaps of greater interest to the investigator than the knowledge that such a function actually exists. When this is the case, it would be preferable to use a method that estimates the form of the best-fitting function at the same time as it ranks pairs of variables according to goodness of association. Such a process is actually less forbidding than it sounds. It is true that the definition of algorithms which isolate one particular function from another is not only difficult to devise but demands excessive amounts of computer time to execute. There are, however, less exact but simple solutions possible which may result in adequate first approximations.

Most data sets encountered in the empirical sciences exhibit essentially three different types of curves. These are exponential, sigmoid (probabilistic), or hyperbolic. As a first approximation to the type of shape inherent in the association between two variables, we could have a program fit the data to four possibilities (i.e., including linearity) and develop a value for R^2 for each. The results thus obtained would represent the best linear, probabilistic, exponential, and hyperbolic fits, with the largest R^2 pointing to the best over-all fit. Printouts showing each of these fitted lines superimposed on the data could be requested by the investigator.

The advantage of this particular method is that the investigator is also given some hint as to the shape of the function that best defines the association between sets of variables. The disadvantage is that it requires somewhat longer computer time than any of the other previous methods. However, by computational and programming shortcuts the time required to develop these multiple judgments need not be excessive. For instance, a hyperbolic fit need be computed only if the probabilistic and exponential fits are both very much superior to the linear approximation. Also the actual computation of four different fitting procedures to any set of data points can be done as a generalized routine in which many of the sums of squares and sums of cross products may be utilized by more than one calculational technique. As a consequence, the amount of computer time needed to find four fits is likely not much more than twice the time required to find one. (Computational procedures for fitting particular curves have been discussed in Chapter 8.)

DISPLAY OF ROBOT GRAPHER OUTPUT

There are any number of ways in which the results of the robot graphing program may be made available to the investigator. Some of the more obvious are hard copy produced on the high-speed printer or direct display through an online scope. In selecting a particular graph for display it may be useful to establish the capability for dialog between procedure and investigator. Although it is true that some pairs of variables could be selected for graphing because their "best" value of $\bar{R}$ is larger than for others, it may be best to give the investigator a list of variables, grouped according to the size of $\bar{R}$, together with additional information such as the associated value of R^2 and the kind of function selected for best fit. The investigator would then make his choice according to whether or not he wants to see a few or many of the selected graphs. With these displays at his disposal, and guided by the information supplied by the program, he could single out those associations which seem to be of greater interest to him than others.

It goes without saying that all graphs should be labeled clearly. The original data file should have been set up in such a way that complete labeling is possible (see Chapter 4). Also preferable are algorithms, suitable to each particular machine, that will result in graphs having "pleasant" numbers (see Chapter 5).

ELIMINATION OF EXTRANEOUS DATA POINTS

One source of error leading to underestimates of the computed value of R^2 lies in the existence of extraneous points which may be due to obvious errors of measurements or may represent conditions that do not happen very frequently. These are usually discerned by inspection, because they lie relatively far away from the cluster of other points. When the investigator sees a scatter in which most of the data points are clustered around a well-behaved function but one or two lie way off to the side, he may very often want to eliminate those deviate points because they represent either an error or a result which is not met often. Inclusion of such values with others during calculation will not only obscure any index of relationship but will also lead to errors in estimating parameters describing the distribution of all the other points. However, automatic fitting procedures provide no easy way of eliminating such points. One relatively simple algorithm for an elimination procedure is outlined below:

1. Group data into cells. This is done by dividing the area of the scatter into a convenient number of rows and columns.
2. Compute the value of $\bar{R}$.
3. Eliminate one observation in each cell. (This could be done by a random process, but the elimination criterion is really immaterial.)
4. Compute $\bar{R}$ for the remaining data.
5. Compare the resulting value $\bar{R}$ with the one obtained using all the data. If there is a sizable change, mark the set of observations for special attention and for further analysis.

There are a number of other algorithms possible. One most useful alternative is to eliminate not one observation in each cell but all those values which lie a given distance from best expectation. Sometimes this distance may be defined by a given number of standard deviations from the mean. Once this procedure is substituted for 3 (above), the program will work as before.

The only drawback to this elimination procedure is that all the data have to be read through again, best estimates for each point have to be computed, and a comparison between the actual value of the point and its best estimate has to be made. There is a certain computational nicety in eliminating one value in a matrix of locations which makes for easier computation. However, where the amounts of data are relatively small, the second method may be much more preferable.

The simplest way out, of course, is to alert the investigator that there appears to be a spurious point and ask him to review the scattergram and decide whether he wishes to eliminate such points or not. Development of automatic procedures for this purpose will be possible only after considerable research is performed.

We have done little more than touch on the possibilities for analysis of graphs opened up by automatic evaluation and screening procedures. Until experience accumulates, it will be well to concentrate on programs that permit investigators to interact with them. This type of man-machine dialogue will be explored more fully in the last chapter.

STEPWISE MULTIPLE REGRESSION
AND DISCRIMINANT FUNCTIONS

Let us begin by considering the analysis of a multivariate data file with variables that are measured by numbers for which an underlying continuous scale can be assumed. We want to find

$$\tilde{Y} = f(X_i \ldots X_k)$$

containing $(I, \ldots, K)$ out of N variables such that $\sigma^2_{y|x_i \ldots x_k}$ is a minimum or $R^2_{y|x_i \ldots x_k}$ is a maximum. In short, we want that K-tuplet of variables that will give the best prediction of Y.

We can lump this problem with that of finding the set of variables that can discriminate best between two states of some dependent variable. Here we try to find the maximum value of $\bar{V} = V_1 - V_2$ for which σ^2_d is a minimum (see Chapter 9). The problem in stating algorithms for automatic search in multiple regression and discriminant function analyses are so similar that we shall discuss them together.

THE BACKWARD SOLUTION

The backward solution starts with the largest possible set of variables as predictors and eliminates the least predictive variables one by one. We start by computing the best prediction of Y as a linear function of all the variables in the data file, viz.:

$$\tilde{Y} = a_0 + a_1 X_1 + a_2 X_2 + \cdots + a_n X_n$$

Next we estimate the values of the multiple correlation coefficients of all variables except the ith variable. We saw in Chapter 9 that we can estimate this multiple coefficient by

$$R^2_{y|x_1\ldots(x_i)\ldots x_n} = \frac{R_{y|x_1\ldots x_n}}{C_{ii}}$$

where $R^2_{y|x_1\ldots(x_i)\ldots x_n}$ is the square of the multiple correlation coefficient of all except the ith variable in a set of predictors.

Next we rank all the variables according to the value of the multiple correlation coefficient for which their effect has been partialled out. It is obvious that if the partialling effect is slight, the variable in question is of little consequence. On the other hand, if partialling out its effect results in a considerable drop in R^2, then this variable contributes considerably to the over-all prediction of Y.

After dropping the variable or variables with the smallest effect, we compute $\tilde{Y} = a'_0 + a'_1 X_1 + \cdots + a'_n X_n$ but not including X_i, where the a's are equal to the new regression weights and where X_i is that variable for which the partialling effect was the smallest. For discriminant function analysis we follow exactly the same rule.

This process is continued either until all variables have been used up or until the value of R^2 computed for the remaining variables takes a decided drop if any one of them is removed. Actually the method of continuing to step down the multiple regression procedure until all variables have been used up is preferable to stopping at one point in time, because it gives the investigator considerably more information about the relevant effect of the remaining variables.

The backward solution method has the advantage of converging on the best set of predictors (or discriminating) variables with a high probability. At this point it is important to realize that a set of variables that are independent of each other will have a relatively large combined effect, whereas a set of highly correlated variables will not predict much better as a group than taken one at a time. For instance, age, height, and weight are highly interdependent for children. Older children tend to be heavier as well as taller. Predicting "handgrip" can be done as well from the knowledge of age, weight, or height alone as from any combination among them. On the other hand, if we were to use specific gravity as another variable, we would increase predictability by a large margin, since specific gravity is an index of body type largely independent of weight, height, and age (within limits).

If each variable in such a set has a very small effect on prediction, then the set, as a group, may be overlooked as a collection of predictors. Partialling out a variable from a set of $X_1 \ldots X_n$ will lead to a decrease in R^2 which may be too small to be detected. However, the steady decline in each subsequent value of R^2 as each variable in the set of contributors is eliminated would tend to call attention to itself. This is even more true since the first set of variables to be eliminated will be those that are correlated highly to other predictors and contribute very little to prediction beyond that obtained by using the correlated variable as predictors.

In this way, variables which all predict because of some common factor will be eliminated first because their effect on R^2 is practically nil. Next will be a group of variables each of which has a small independent effect on predicting Y; the variables eliminated last will be those with a main effect on Y. The backward solution makes it more likely that the set of independent predictors is noticed as an important contributor. Whether or not this set will be isolated, however, depends largely on the absolute effect each one of these variables has on over-all prediction.

A disadvantage of the backward method is that it starts with the largest possible matrix. Since we solve the system of equations in multiple regression by the inversion of the matrix of cross products or correlation coefficients, the speed of the program and its accuracy depends on the size of the matrix to be inverted. Unfortunately, the time needed to invert a matrix is an exponential function of its size. Also, the larger the matrix, the larger the effect of approximation error. Thus it becomes necessary to increase considerably the precision of computation, as the matrix to be inverted is very large. As a consequence, the amount of computer time needed for the backward solution of stepwise multiple regression is always large. For these reasons another general method for stepwise multiple regression is designed to start with the smallest possible number of predictors and work its way through to a point at which further inclusion of variables seems to be pointless.

FORWARD SOLUTION

In this method we start with the intercorrelation matrix computed for all pairs of variables. When X_1 is that variable for which r_{yx} is largest, we arrange our variables internally in order from the largest to the smallest. Next we compute

$$r_{yx_1|x_i}, \qquad i = 2, 3, \ldots, n \text{ (excluding 1)}$$

and again arrange our variables so that X_2 represents that variable which, when added to X_1, gives the best prediction. This process is then repeated by computing

$$r_{yx_1x_2|x_j}, \qquad j = 3, 4, \ldots, n \text{ (excluding 1 and 2)}$$

For each step the program computes $R^2_{y|x_1x_2\ldots x_k}$, proceeding until $R^2_{y|x_1\ldots x_{n-k}}$ does not increase appreciably when yet another predictor is added.

This process has the advantage of making considerably lesser demands on calculation time and precision. It has the disadvantage that variables which exert a small but independent effect on prediction may be and probably are overlooked. This disadvantage may be corrected in part by deciding on stopping when the last set of m variables has not increased the value of R^2 by some prescribed amount. Although this procedure increases computer time, it is not nearly as demanding as the backward solution would be. The program logic is the same in the case where the judgment made is on the ability of the variables to discriminate rather than to predict.

USING CONTINUOUS AND DISCRETE VARIABLES

Chapter 9 described ways by which correlation coefficients can be estimated in situations in which one or both variables were discrete. We can see the value of such estimates now. There are instances in a multivariate situation when the investigator would like to evaluate the effect of such discrete variables along with those which are scalable continuously. For instance, in searching for predictors of weight, a data file could contain such obvious determinants as a judgment on "obesity" or information as to sex or whether an individual likes starchy foods or not. With the use of biserial and tetrachoric correlation coefficients, it is possible to include such variables in stepwise multiple regression screening procedures. From a practical point of view we may even want to do this when the discrete variables do not permit the assumption of an underlying continuous scale. Although this procedure might violate the basic assumptions on which correlations are computed, it may offer the investigator many useful hints about the relative importance of variables in a file.

PROBLEMS OF NUMBERS OF OBSERVATIONS

If we have many variables, each having relatively few replications, the chances are very good that some combination of factors may appear to give excellent prediction by chance alone. This is a problem that we shall meet again and again. We might look at it intuitively in this way.

If we have N variables, we can compute $[N(N-1)/2]$ correlation coefficients. For any value r_α for which we make a decision that correlation did or did not occur because of chance, we shall find a given proportion of correlations that will be larger than that value of r_α by chance alone. This means that if we had started with 100 variables and had assigned values to each variable by selecting numbers at random from a table of random numbers, we would expect that of the nearly 5000 correlation coefficients that can be computed from this file, all of which should really be an estimate of true correlations of zero, a given number will have magnitudes exceeding the value that could be expected to occur by chance α times in 100. In fact, the number of such spurious correlations is quite predictable.

Although this is true regardless of the number of observations on which r may be based, the absolute value of r_α becomes smaller and smaller for any value of α as the number of actual observations increases. However, although the value of r may decrease also for those instances in which there does exist a true correlation between two variables when numbers of observations are increased, it is more likely that its value will converge upon an estimate of the true correlation between them. Consequently, as we increase the numbers of replications on which all observations are based, we tend to decrease the absolute value of all coefficients that are large because of spurious chance factors, without similarly affecting those correlation coefficients which stem from a true relationship. If we search through a correlation matrix for specific patterns, these patterns will be masked and overshadowed by spuriously large correlations among unrelated variables when the numbers of replications on which each set of observations is based are small. This masking or misleading effect will decrease in importance as we increase the number of observations on which each variable is based.

This means, then, that for adequate use of stepwise multiple regression or discriminant function screening procedures, the numbers of observations available for each variable should be large. But how large is large? This is always a very difficult question. We might derive a rule for a minimum size of the data file, although it stands to reason that the larger the numbers of replications, the more certain we may be of our conclusions.

The error term for multiple R may be estimated by

$$\sigma_R = \frac{1}{\sqrt{M - N - 3}}$$

where M is the number of observations and N the number of variables. Thus M should be at least larger than the number of predictor variables plus 3. (This number should be considered the absolute minimum for serious work. It is preferred, however, that the number of observations be at least five times the number of variables in a study.)

This imposes an obvious constraint on any multiple data gathering scheme. If the investigator knows that he cannot obtain more than 500 replications of each set of observations, he should limit the number of variables he observes to the 100 most relevant and important. If he includes more than this number of variables in his data gathering scheme, he may arrive at erroneous and misleading conclusions. Although automatic data gathering procedures and high-speed computing have enlarged the scope of the investigator, they have not broken down completely some of the boundaries and limitations that always accompany research.

There are, however, instances in which the investigator finds it much simpler to develop a large number of variables rather than to observe a large number of replications. When the importance of finding relevant variables outweighs the risk of drawing spurious and unrealistic conclusions, the investigator can and should violate the restrictions imposed by numbers of replications. One excellent example is a study of factors which affect treatment outcome in leukemia. In this dreadful disease the number of cases available for study is always relatively small. Consequently, the investigator may not be able to obtain an exact description of many cases at any one time, even from large treatment centers. At the same time, the number of potentially relevant variables which can be and are observed with each patient are simply immense and number in the hundreds. Although robot screening techniques are probably useful in focusing the investigator's attention on some of the important relationships that determine treatment outcome, we must also keep in mind that this technique may distract the investigator by diverting his attention to relationships that are spurious.

WHAT ABOUT TESTS OF SIGNIFICANCE?

We have already examined the problem of evaluating outcomes of tests of significance in case of multiple comparisons (see Chapter 7). However, under these circumstances, we were dealing with a relatively small number of combinations to be tested. Robot screening applied to many variables raises a very serious question as to whether we should concern ourselves at all with evaluating the probability that some apparent association is or is not a result of random sampling error.

Let us assume that we select values for N variables from a table of random numbers. We now compute all correlations r_{xy} and test the hypothesis that each individual r is a chance deviation from 0. If α is the probability of rejecting H_0 incorrectly, the probability that we will not reject H_0 erroneously is given by

$$P_r = (1 - \alpha)^N \tag{4}$$

so that the probability that we shall reject H_0 erroneously at least once is given by

$$P = 1 - P_r = 1 - (1 - \alpha)^N \tag{5}$$

This means that as N becomes very large, we shall spuriously reject H_0 for at least one variable, regardless of how small we make α (or at least almost regardless of how small we make α). Similarly, we can compute the probability of rejecting H_0 incorrectly for 2, 3, up to K variables. Since N variables yield $N(N-1)/2$ correlation coefficients, the probability that at least one correlation coefficient in the matrix will be accepted as reflecting a true association when all correlations have actually been selected from a population for which the true correlation is 0 is given by

$$p = 1 - (1 - \alpha)^{N(N-1)/2} \tag{6}$$

And again the probability of spuriously selecting 2, 3, 4, and more correlation coefficients by chance is excellent, even for very small values of α.

We may turn these findings around and say that if we were to use tests of hypotheses and the logic of statistical inference to select combinations of variables as "interesting" to the investigator, we would definitely end up with a number of such combinations every time. This would be equally true whether the data collected were random numbers or whether they came from the real world. As a consequence, the investigator is no better off subjecting his best set of variables to statistical tests than he would be if he were not to perform this extra step. This does not mean that statistical inference is "bad," but rather that it is not suitable for robot screening procedures. A test of hypotheses here may be more misleading than useful.

It is best for the investigator to view the results that have been presented to him by the multiple regression screening program as a suggestion that a particular combination of variables is a good predictor for some dependent variable of interest. If this multiple set of relationships fits within existing theory, he may view his finding as bolstering the theoretical framework.

Table 10.1a. EXAMPLE OF FIRST PAGE STEPWISE MULTIPLE REGRESSION PRINTOUT*

```
                              MULTIPLE REGRESSION ANALYSIS
            JOB               VELSICOL LIVER WEIGHTS - SAMPLE RUN

   ROW VARIABLES                          INVERTED CORRELATION COEFFICIENT MATRIX
BODY WEIGHT            1.0649729
LITTER SIZE            .26304831          1.0649729
                      DETERMINANT OF ORIGINAL CORRELATION MATRIX = .93899102
```

```
                              MULTIPLE REGRESSION ANALYSIS
            JOB               VELSICOL LIVER WEIGHTS - SAMPLE RUN

DEPENDENT VARIABLE IS LIVER WEIGHT
SQUARE OF MULTIPLE CORRELATION COEFFICIENT =  .90593311
VARIANCE OF DEPENDENT VARIABLE =             1.3779238
VARIANCE OF ESTIMATE =                        .12961702
```

INDEPENDENT VARIABLE	CORRELATION WITH DEPENDENT VARIABLE	NORMALIZED REGRESSION COEFFICIENT	REGRESSION COEFFICIENT	SQUARE OF MULTIPLE CORRELATION COEFFICIENT WITH VARIABLE OMITTED
BODY WEIGHT	.93000000	.87836621	.46792380E-01	.18147600
LITTER SIZE	-.42600000	-.20904353	-.54688152E-01	.86489996
	CONSTANT = .47847600			

*From the MEDCOMP Program Library.

Table 10.1b. EXAMPLE OF SECOND PAGE STEPWISE MULTIPLE REGRESSION PRINTOUT*

MULTIPLE REGRESSION ANALYSIS

JOB   VELSICOL LIVER WEIGHTS - SAMPLE RUN

ROW VARIABLES   INVERTED CORRELATION COEFFICIENT MATRIX

Y WEIGHT	1.0649729	
TER SIZE	.26304831	1.0649729

DETERMINANT OF ORIGINAL CORRELATION MATRIX = .93899102

MULTIPLE REGRESSION ANALYSIS

JOB   VELSICOL LIVER WEIGHTS - SAMPLE RUN

DEPENDENT VARIABLE IS LIVER WEIGHT

SQUARE OF MULTIPLE CORRELATION COEFFICIENT =   .90593311

VARIANCE OF DEPENDENT VARIABLE =   1.3779238

VARIANCE OF ESTIMATE =   .12961702

INDEPENDENT VARIABLE	CORRELATION WITH DEPENDENT VARIABLE	NORMALIZED REGRESSION COEFFICIENT	REGRESSION COEFFICIENT	SQUARE OF MULTIPLE CORRELATION COEFFICIENT WITH VARIABLE OMITTED
Y WEIGHT	.93000000	.87836621	.46792380E-01	.18147600
TER SIZE	-.42600000	-.20904353	-.54688152E-01	.86489996

CONSTANT = .47847600

*From the MEDCOMP Program Library.

Table 10.1c. EXAMPLE OF THIRD PAGE STEPWISE MULTIPLE REGRESSION PRINTOUT*

MULTIPLE REGRESSION ANALYSIS

JOB   VELSICOL LIVER WEIGHTS - SAMPLE RUN

ROW VARIABLES   INVERTED CORRELATION COEFFICIENT MATRIX

JY WEIGHT	1.0000000

DETERMINANT OF ORIGINAL CORRELATION MATRIX = 1.0000000

MULTIPLE REGRESSION ANALYSIS

JOB   VELSICOL LIVER WEIGHTS - SAMPLE RUN

DEPENDENT VARIABLE IS LIVER WEIGHT

SQUARE OF MULTIPLE CORRELATION COEFFICIENT =   .86490000

VARIANCE OF DEPENDENT VARIABLE =   1.3779238

VARIANCE OF ESTIMATE =   .18615750

INDEPENDENT VARIABLE	CORRELATION WITH DEPENDENT VARIABLE	NORMALIZED REGRESSION COEFFICIENT	REGRESSION COEFFICIENT	SQUARE OF MULTIPLE CORRELATION COEFFICIENT WITH VARIABLE OMITTED
Y WEIGHT	.93000000	.93000000	.49543022E-01	0.

CONSTANT = -.56434180

*From the MEDCOMP Program Library.

If and when these multiple sets of relationships do not fit into an existing theory he ought to reevaluate his formulations of the phenomenological system that he is testing. When the investigator has no *a priori* theory, his task is made much easier. The multiple set of best predictors can be used

Table 10.1d. FINAL CHECK PAGE OF MULTIPLE STEPWISE REGRESSION PROGRAM*

```
                              VARIABLE LIST

                PREFERENCE       VARIABLE NAME


                     1       BODY WEIGHT
                     2       LITTER SIZE
                     3       BODY WEIGHT SQUARED


                TOTAL NUMBER OF VARIABLES =  3

                PRECISION = 20



                  DUMP OF CORRELATION MATRIX BEFORE INVERSION

 1.0000000000000000000

 -.24700000000000000000    1.0000000000000000000

  .13900000000000000000    .81000000000000000000E-01   1.0000000000000000000


                  DUMP OF CORRELATION MATRIX AFTER INVERSION AND REINVERSION

  .99999999999999999989

 -.24699999999999999998    .99999999999999999995

  .13899999999999999995    .81000000000000000043E-01   1.000000000000000000000
```

*From the MEDCOMP Program Library.

to estimate a value or a state of a dependent variable as long as it does so with a high degree of reliability. (An example of presentation of results is given in Table 10.1.)

The analysis shown in Table 10.1 tried to find the best combination of variables for determining liver weight of animals. Starting with three variables (body weight, the square of body weight, litter size) the program first defines the order of importance of all three (Table 10.1a), then the best two (Table 10.1b), and finally the best simple variable (Table 10.1c). Each table also shows all the information usually demanded of a multiple regression program as well as the inverted and reinverted matrices used for calculation.

PREPARATION OF DATA

It may be best to begin the multiple regression or discriminant analysis by first using the automatic grapher. This often allows the prior elimination of a number of variables that are quite obviously not related to anything in the total data file. In this way the total number of variables can be decreased, thus enabling the investigator to make a rational choice between a forward or backward solution. It may also permit the investigator to order his variables according to some educated guesses as to which are more important and which are the least important variables. Such an order may be of value, because very efficient stepwise regression programs can be written which take advantage of sequential prearrangements of variables according to their possible importance.

ROBOT DATA SCREENING

There are many instances in which large data files consist of numbers which might be described, at best, as a mixed bag. Some of these numbers may be discrete codes locating an individual in a census tract, a country, or a particular school. Other observations can be thought of as scalable in an ordinal sense, such as color codes for hemotological tests, observations that patients are better or worse after treatment, or social class positions of individuals. Still other measurements yield numbers that are akin to real numbers, such as height and weight.

Not only do some data files represent a mixed collection of numbers but many of these numbers have either a distribution that is known to be nonnormal, nonindependent, or in some other way irregular, or no information at all may be available about them. This collection of observations represents a very difficult background from which to tease out information about relationships and associations. This problem has thus far resisted a formal solution which makes assumptions about the parameters of distributions that may exist among measures or requires them to consist of numbers with specified scale properties.

Robot data screening is a technique that is almost completely free of assumptions about distributions of data. The purpose of robot data screening is to tease out from collections of variables those which determine a phenomenon under investigation or subjected to experiment. The fundamental approach on which robot data screening rests permits the automatic examination of possible combinations and permutations among variables. Variables that seem to be related to the outcome of the experimental observation are singled out automatically and presented to the investigator for further inspection and analysis. The system acts as an "intelligent" investigator does; i.e., it screens data to eliminate some variables of no further interest and pursues others for giving possible clues about relationships.

A number of basic problems must be resolved to realize this ambitious aim. Problem number one is to define "relationship" in such a way that an automatic process can decide whether such a relationship does or does not exist or, at least, attach a scalable value to the degree of association. The second problem concerns the necessity of setting up the systematic search so that all combinations and permutations in which variables can be classified need not be evaluated. Criteria are needed by which the search process can converge upon the most consistently related sets of variables without too many unprofitable combinations being searched through. Finally, the automatic searching process must be terminated when its continuation would seem fruitless.

MAXIMUM PREDICTABILITY

The criterion of maximum predictability reverts to a fundamentalist approach toward science in which the activities of the scientist in designing experiments and analyzing data are viewed as a search for deterministically related variables. A relationship is said to exist between antecedent conditions and their consequences if knowledge of antecedent values enables the investigator to classify correctly the resulting conditions. The criterion of maximum predictability selects among variables to find those of greater interest to the investigator, guided by a type of conditional probability computed according to the basic strategy that the variable is of importance if its knowledge leads to improved prediction of a second variable. For instance, if we are interested in the outcome of treatment Y, then we shall think of a variable as being related to that outcome (or of interest to the investigator) if, by knowledge of it, the investigator can improve his prediction of what the outcome of treatment is going to be. In that sense, this increase in predictability is an index of association. The statistic used to test the degree of association between a set of antecedent conditions and observed consequences is called the *predictability*.

Note that in a way we have restated the purpose of stepwise multiple regression. Here too our criterion for selecting the best set of variables is that they predict either the state of the variable or the difference in states between two alternatives. The measurement obtained as the basis on which judgment is made is the *reduction in variance*, for which R^2 is an index. Maximum predictability and reduction in variance are really two opposing sides of a simple coin. In this respect robot data screening and stepwise multiple regression are related. However, the relation ceases with this similarity.

The strategy for robot data screening rests predominantly on a taxonomical scheme. A variable is cross-classified by a number of other variables. The investigator is presumed to inspect this cross classification and to predict subsequent occurrences or nonoccurrences or outcomes of observations according to P, the highest relative frequencies with which particular events take place.

If A is a set of variables used for cross classification, we shall call P_A the predictability of A. If the classification is based on a representative sample of the parent population, P_A may be taken as an estimate of the probability of a correct prediction. A simple example will help to clarify this method. Let us take the consequence c to be the effect of treatment on some disease with classifications being cure, palliation, and no effect. Let A be the set (sex, age, duration of symptoms) with sets of values {male, female}, {≤ 40, > 40}, and {< 1 yr, 1–5 yr, ≥ 5 yr} respectively. We might have a distribution of subjects such as in Table 10.2.

Table 10.2. EXAMPLE WORK TABLE FOR ROBOT DATA SCREENING*

	Antecedent Variables			Effect			
β	Sex	Age	Duration	Cure	Palliation	No Effect	Total
(1, 1, 1)	Male	< 40	< 1	200	0	0	200
(1, 1, 2)	Male	< 40	1–5	150	50	0	200
(1, 1, 3)	Male	< 40	> 5	50	100	50	200
(1, 2, 1)	Male	$\leq$ 40	< 1	50	50	0	100
(1, 2, 2)	Male	$\leq$ 40	1–5	30	40	30	100
(1, 2, 3)	Male	$\leq$ 40	> 5	20	60	120	200
(2, 1, 1)	Female	< 40	< 1	100	75	25	200
(2, 1, 2)	Female	< 40	1–5	50	100	50	200
(2, 1, 3)	Female	< 40	> 5	0	0	100	100
(2, 2, 1)	Female	$\leq$ 40	< 1	75	100	25	200
(2, 2, 2)	Female	$\leq$ 40	1–5	25	75	100	200
(2, 2, 3)	Female	$\leq$ 40	> 5	0	0	100	100
				750	650	600	2000

*From Sterling, et al., " Robot Data Screening; A solution to multivariate type problems in the biological and social sciences," *Communications of the ACM* 9, 1966, pp. 529–552.

We would expect 100 per cent of those future patients in classification (male, ≤ 40, < 1 yr) to be cured. Similarly, if a patient is in classification (male, ≤ 40, ≥ 5 yr) the best guess would be that he will end with palliation of symptoms. The over-all predictability for the total set A would then be

$$P_A = \frac{[200 + 150 + 100 + 50 + \cdots + 100]}{2000} = \frac{1260}{2000} = 0.63$$

Thus, knowing the combination of variables in A yields 63 per cent over-all predictability.

The criterion of maximum predictability presents a rule by which a scale value R_A can be attached to a combination of variables reflecting the degree of association among them.

It would seem then that all we need is a program that will examine the predictive probabilities contained in different multiple cross classification schemes and select those for our attention that yield the largest over-all predictabilities. Unfortunately, this is not the case. Besides the near impossibility of examining the extremely large number of all possible cross classifications (with which we shall deal next), there are a number of defects in the use of a raw and unassisted measure of probability as the sole screening criterion.

One difficulty shared by P_A with correlation is that both R and P_A are spuriously made larger as the number of predictor variables is increased. In both instances, this increase is not a pure effect of the absolute number of variables used for prediction but rather an effect of this number of variables relative to the total number of observations. There is thus the need to find some measure which is a function of P_A but, at the same time, is also independent of (or less dependent on) the influence wielded by the number of classification categories relative to the number of observations.

There is yet one other defect P_A has as an unassisted screening criterion which is not shared by correlation. Thus, P_A is insensitive to shifts in the relationship among variables until the strength of the relationship reaches a certain value. Let us invent an example to demonstrate this. Assume that of 603 patients suffering from some disease, 83 are cured and 520 are not. Our best prediction for the outcome of the disease then is "no cure" with $P = \frac{520}{603}$. Let us say that a cross classification of disease outcome by treatment X yields the following breakdown (Table 10.3).

Table 10.3. CLASSIFICATION OF DISEASE OUTCOME AND TREATMENT X

Treatment	Disease Outcome		
	Cured	Not Cured	Total
Given X	80	120	200
Not Given X	3	400	403
	83	520	603

Where treatment with X is the variable set, A, used for classification, $P_A = \frac{520}{603}$ so that it would appear from comparing P_A to P that treatment X had no effect on disease outcome. In the present example, P_A would not change until the number of treated and cured was larger than the number treated and not cured.

What is needed then is a measure, based on P_A, that behaves better in the present instance and is also manageable with respect to numbers of classifications. We know by now that such functions can be derived. One of the most useful of such functions for our purposes is a measure called *entropy*.

ON ENTROPY AND CERTAINTY AND THE NUMBER
OF OBSERVATIONS AND CATEGORIES

The number P_A describes the over-all probability of correctly assigning a subject from a sample to a classification of c when only information about the past experience of subjects and observations relating c to the set

A is given. However, the interpretation of the importance of any classification depends not only on the value of P_A but also upon the number of available observations in relation to all the possible cross classifications.

As we compute the conditional probability that a particular subject having a variety of characteristics will be located in a particular cell of a cross classification table, we reach a point at which the number of available cases becomes small relative to the number of possible cells that result from cross classification. Eventually a point is reached where the number of cross classifications outnumber the number of subjects that can be assigned to them, so that the individual characteristics of each subject determine a unique position in the total cross classification table even when these individual characteristics are trivial.

We may look at this problem in another way. Let us assume a data file in which we have approximately six subcategories for each variable. If we develop cross classifications for one dependent variable c with respect to a number of independent variables, $(A_1 A_2 A_3 A_4)$, we may expect a large cross classification table. If each variable consists of six categories, a classification of c by four variables will result in a table having $6^5 = 46{,}656$ cells. To investigate the combined effect of many variables thus requires a large number of observations on all of them. If the number of observation is small, then they may be distributed so that each cell contains one or more of them with only a few cells containing an aggregate. As a consequence, each description of the multiple sets of conditions under which relative frequencies in subcategories occur in each of the cross classification arrays becomes less and less convincing, despite the fact that the value of P_A keeps on increasing steadily. We can easily see that once we have increased the number of subcategories far beyond the number of cases available, then each case is determined uniquely and P_A approaches unity as a limit. At the same time, it becomes a completely meaningless indicator.

A convenient measurement is available for evaluating a probability based on a finite number of observations distributed over a given number of cells. It is usually referred to as *entropy*. Entropy is essentially a measurement of the uncertainty that exists in a situation. Let us say that we have a variable, which we shall call a, with some set of classifications R^a, and that associated with each single classification α in R^a is a probability P_α. Let us also assume that some observation will occur in every class α. Let us label entropy, or the amount of uncertainty, by H. To be a useful measurement of uncertainty, H should have the following properties:

1. It should be continuous for the P_α's.
2. If $P_\alpha = 1/N$, each classification has the same probability, namely $1/|R^a|$; then if N increases, H should increase.
3. The uncertainty resulting from dividing a variable's subcategories into finer and finer partitions should be equal to the original uncertainty plus

the weighted uncertainty resulting in each original subcategory after the partition is made. It should be true, for example, that H (.25, .25, .25, .25,) $= H(.5, .5) = .5H(.5, .5) + .5H(.5, .5)$, since the final results are identical.

For a given set of classifications a, let $H(a)$ denote $H (\{P_\alpha \mid \alpha \varepsilon R^a\})$ Under these three conditions it turns out that

$$H(a) = -K \sum_{\alpha \varepsilon R^a} aP_\alpha \log P_\alpha$$

where $0 \log 0 = 0$ by convention and K is any constant greater than ₀0. The logarithm may be to any base. If no uncertainty at all exists, then for some α, $P_\alpha = 1$. In this case, H is 0, an intuitively reasonable result. For discrete variables a and b, where b has a set of classification R^b and associated to each single classification β, a P_β as before, the entropy function may be written

$$H(ab) = -\sum_{\alpha, \beta} P_{\alpha\beta} \log P_{\alpha\beta} \tag{8}$$

where $P_{\alpha\beta}$ is the probability that a has the value α and b has the value β. In the case where a and b are independent, it is easily verified that

$$H(ab) = H(a) + H(b) \tag{9}$$

This result also satisfies the intuitive notion of uncertainty. The greatest possible uncertainty concerning the value of the variable occurs when all values can be taken on with equal probabilities. When such is the case, H is found to reach its maximum value. Thus this entropy function provides a numerical realization of the intuitive notion of uncertainty.

Conditional uncertainty, the uncertainty concerning variable b when a is known, may also be given a numerical realization according to the following relations: Put

$$H(b \mid \alpha) = \sum_{\beta \varepsilon R^b} P(\beta \mid \alpha) \log P(\beta \mid \alpha) = \sum_{\beta \varepsilon R^b} \frac{P_{\alpha\beta}}{P_\alpha} \log \left(\frac{P_{\alpha\beta}}{P_\alpha} \right) \tag{10}$$

where $P(b \mid \alpha)$ is the probability of $b = \beta$ given that $a = \alpha$. Then let

$$H(b \mid a) = \sum_{\alpha \varepsilon R^a} P_\alpha H(b \mid \alpha) = \sum_{\alpha, \beta} P_\alpha \left(\frac{P_{\alpha\beta}}{P_\alpha} \right) \log \left(\frac{P_{\alpha\beta}}{P_\alpha} \right)$$
$$= \sum_{\alpha, \beta} P_{\alpha\beta} \log \left(\frac{P_{\alpha\beta}}{P_\alpha} \right) \tag{11}$$

Thus

$$H(b \mid a) = \sum_{\alpha, \beta} P_{\alpha\beta} \log (P_{\alpha\beta}) - \sum_{\alpha, \beta} P_{\alpha\beta} \log (P_\alpha) \tag{12}$$

Since $\sum_{\beta \varepsilon R^b} P_{\alpha\beta} = P_{\alpha}$ we can substitute and write

$$H(b \mid a) = H(ab) - H(a) \tag{13}$$

The equations given above can be extended to the case in which several variables have known values. These results strongly suggest that this $H(b \mid a)$ is a reasonable criterion with which to determine the effectiveness of a predictor.

For any real case the probabilities needed in these formulas are not actually known. The only values that are known are frequency counts. However, estimates of probability based upon frequency counts provide quite an accurate estimate of $H(b \mid a)$. Thus a practical criterion exists for rating variables according to their effectiveness as predictors.

A reasonable rejection criterion for a robot data screening program can be based upon the following considerations. If the addition of a variable to a previous variable combination (the null set is considered to be a variable combination in this context) does not "significantly" change the conditional entropy, the combination of the new variable and the old variable should not be used. The concept of "significant difference" can be made more exact by noting that the expression

$$2\hat{H}(b \mid a_1 a_2 \cdots a_n) - 2\hat{H}(b \mid a_1 a_2 \cdots a_{n-1}) \tag{14}$$

where b is the consequence and a_i is an antecedent and in which b has r values, a_n has d values, and the remaining a's have c values, has a χ^2 distribution with $(r-1)c(d-1)$ degrees of freedom. However, not all variables that pass this criterion can be used, since the amount of machine time available may frequently be limited. Consequently only the best variable or variable combinations passing this criterion ought to be retained for the purpose of stepwise accumulation of "significant" results.

The entropy will then tell us whether the increase in P_A, where $A = \{a_1 \text{ to } a_n\}$, resulting from our cross classification process is accompanied by an increase or at least not a decrease in the amount of certainty that we may have in these results.

However, entropy will do more than that. It is a much better behaved measure than is P_A with respect to numbers of classifying variables and observations. In addition, the distribution of H is known so that the significance of a change in H can be estimated. Also, H is sensitive to interval distributions that lie below the threshold at which values of P_A are affected. Thus, it solves many of the problems posed by the evaluation of discrete and even continuous, albeit nonlinear, distributions.

One note of caution is needed to prevent us from becoming ensnared in semantic confusion. Uncertainty as it is used here refers to a measurement of H, and has nothing to do directly with the amount of certainty or uncertainty that an investigator develops on the basis of inspecting his results. The quantity H is a guidepost which will tell him that, with respect to the total number of subcategories and observations, a particular value of P_A may mean more than a similar value of P_Z under a different situation in which the number of subcategories or observations is not the same. The usefulness of H is as a scaling device.

Perhaps we might get a better grasp of this notion by noting that H is not the only scaling number available. An alternate scale can be developed around the prediction quotient Q, which is given by

$$Q_A = \frac{\sqrt{N P_A}}{\sqrt{T-1}} \tag{15}$$

where T is the number of possible subcategories and N is the *total* number of observations that fall into the *various* subcategories. Although Q is not nearly as refined a measure as H and is affected considerably by the absolute value of N, it conveys very much the same meaning to the investigator. The advantages and disadvantages of H and Q lie precisely in that the computation of Q takes less machine time and the computation of H yields a more refined measurement of the importance of P_A with respect to numbers of observations and categories and that its distribution is known. The choice of which measure to use thus depends to some extent upon cost consideration, size of available machine, and so on. However the use of Q rather than H would be unreasonable where cost is not an overpowering factor.

OUTLINE OF A ROBOT DATA SCREENING PROGRAM

Despite the fact that we have a criterion by which we can group or select combinations of variables as more "interesting" or less so, and despite having additional criteria that will enable us to judge P_A with respect to its importance and applicability, we still have to face the problem that we could not possibly develop a measurement of P_A, H, or Q for all possible permutations and combinations of cross classifications that may be contained in a multivariate data file. Sequencing the search for related variables and rejecting some in favor of others will have to be done according to a reasonable scheme that maximizes the probability of isolating optimum sets of predictor variables and at the same time minimizes the number of passes through the data. Nowhere is the economic constraint on data processing as painfully visible as here.

We saw before that the number of combinations of cross classifications increases as $[N(N-1)(N-2) \ldots (N-r+1)]/r!$, where r is the number of variables combined in a cross classification table and N is the total number of variables in the study. This total number is relatively small for small values of r, but becomes excessively large as r increases. For instance, if 72 variables are available as potential predictors in a data file, there are 2485 combinations of pairs, 57,155 combinations of three, and 971,635 combinations of four variables at a time that could be evaluated for their ability to predict. Not only does the number of variable combinations increase, but also each cross tabulation becomes a more arduous sorting job, requiring appreciably larger amounts of computer time with each increase in the number of cross tabulation categories. It is clear, therefore, that a realistic search program must eliminate variables as it considers more complex groups of predictors. The selection or rejection procedures of the program thus become of major importance, as are its sorting algorithms.

The preferable mode of selection of clusters of predictors does not proceed according to the absolute value of P_A or how well variables predict, but according to a measurement of certainty or uncertainty which we have called Q or H. This makes a great deal of sense. We are selecting variables as being related according to how certain we are that the relationship will yield a useful prediction.

We must still deal, however, with the problem of how many variables to select for carry-over with each step. This question is far from easy to answer. It is clear that we must make a selection. We cannot possibly examine all three-way, four-way, and five-way combinations in a set of data. It is sensible, therefore, to select only those variables for which the difference between the Q's or the H's is the largest. But how many of these shall we select? The answer to this question actually depends on what the investigator can afford to spend in terms of computer time and funds. A choice of how deep a search to pursue will not only depend on the funds available, but also on the importance of the problem and the possible payoff that it may yield. Unfortunately the depth of search has to be decided prior to the analysis. Although we can obviously eliminate all variables for carry-over to the next level for which the value H does not decrease or Q does not increase as we go from less complex to more complex combinations of variables, we may still commit ourselves to too many breakdowns if we let an unrealistically small difference between successive values of Q or H dictate selection or rejection.

As an alternative we could decide beforehand to select only those variables for carry-over for which the increment in Q or in H goes beyond a realistic magnitude. It is here where the superiority of H over Q as a selection criterion makes itself felt. One can attach a number to a difference between two values of H that indicates the probability that a difference as large as the one observed can occur by chance. This probability has no meaning in terms of a statistical test. However, it becomes a useful criterion for selecting among predictors, because it evaluates a difference between

H's not as a static magnitude but as a flexible measure of how much the difference actually means. A useful measurement of cutoff is to specify to the program that it should keep only those major variables for which the probability of reducing H has a minimum value (such as .05, .01, .001). Where we would set this cutoff point would depend as before on the amount of computer time available. It is clear that as the specified value for this probability is lowered, the fewer variables will be carried over to each successive analysis and the faster the program will reach its conclusions. (One should not confuse the use of probability as a measurement as it is used here with a test of significance. The student should reflect for a moment on the use of scaling and measuring devices that are involved in this program.)

The investigator also should be able to specify to the program the number of best predictor variables to keep at each level of analysis. Such a course has many merits, since it allows approximations of the amount of computer time that will be required for an analysis.

DISPLAY

The result of robot data screening analysis is a clustering of those variables that may be assumed to be the best predictors. It does not say anything at all about how good these predictions are or how helpful they will be to the investigator. Before this can be done the results of the analyses have to be converted into a useful display. The processer has done much work so that a great deal of information can be kept for the investigator. However, not all this information is useful. The following printouts are recommended.

There should be a listing of names of variables, the number of subcategories each has, and the labels for the subcategories as well as the numbers of observations that are available for each subcategory. (Table 10.4 shows part of such a listing.)

The output should show the first step of the robot screening process. It should give the values for H_A, Q_A, and P_A that result from predicting the desired variable or state of affairs from each of the independent variables. It should also show the numbers of observations available at this step. This will enable the investigator to see that, using variable a, he can predict (on the basis of the cross classification of b by a) with a given probability which has a particular measure of uncertainty attached to it. This means the investigator should also have the numbers of observations which go with each subcategory. (Table 10.5 shows part of such a listing.)

There should also be a list of combinations of two, combinations of three, and so on, as they are carried over to each successive step. With each combination should be given the value of P, Q, or H, the numbers of

Table 10.4

VENEZUELAN ELITE STUDY - ROBOT DATA SCREENING

LIST OF VARIABLES AND SUBCATEGORIES

VARIABLE NAME	VAR. NO.	SUBCATEGORY NAME	NO.
CHURCH IN POL	1	KEEP OUT GUIDE VOTERS	0 1
AGE	2	JUNIOR MIDDLE SENIOR	0 1 2
MARITAL STATUS	3	MARRIED UNMARRIED WAS MARRIED	0 1 2
CHILDREN	4	NONE ONE OR TWO THREE OR MORE	0 1 2
LEVEL OF EDUCATION	5	PRIMARY SECONDARY UNIVERSITY	0 1 2
UNIV SPECIALIZATION	6	NAT SCI LAW SOC SCI HUMAN	0 1 2
PRESENT OCCUPATION	7	BUSINESS POL AND ADMIN OTHER PROFESSION UNIV TEACHER AGRICULTURAL	0 1 2 3 4
SECONDARY OCCUP	8	BUSINESS POL AND ADMIN OTHER PROFESSION	0 1 2

observations that were available for the categories, and the highest Q or lowest H from the previous less complex set of categories. In this way, the investigator can make a constant comparison and see how much certainty he has gained (or uncertainty he has lost), how well he can use this cluster of variables to predict, and how well he did at the lower level at which the cluster was smaller (see Tables 10.6 and 10.7).

Some of the information should be summarized in a different form. In this printout the highest combination and all its subcategories should be assembled, including all the associated values for P, H, Q, etc. The investigator can inspect this run and compare the best combination with some combinations made up of the same variables taken in smaller groups (Table 10.8).

Some of the breakdowns of interests to the investigator should be summarized in multiple form. (A possible and useful format is shown in Table 10.9.)

Table 10.5

VENEZUELAN ELITE STUDY - RODOT DATA SCREENING

DEPENDENT VARIABLE IS CHURCH IN POL
IT HAS 2 SUBCATEGORIES

PREDICTOR	PRESENT ENTROPY	LAST ENTROPY	ENTROPY CHANGE	CHI SQUARE	DEGREES OF FREEDOM	PROBABILITY	NUMBER OBSERVED	PRESENT NUMBER PRED.	PRESENT PRED.	LAST NUMBER PRED.	LAST PRED.
*CHURCH ATTEND	0.9566	1.0006	0.0439	76.126	3	0.0000	1201	711	0.5920	605	0.5037
*SOUR INFO TELEVISION	0.9884	1.0005	0.0122	27.301	7	0.0000	1205	678	0.5627	609	0.5054
*POL PARTICIPATION	0.9888	1.0006	0.0117	22.644	3	0.0000	1207	665	0.5510	608	0.5037
*SOUR INFO NEWSPAP	0.9945	1.0004	0.0060	12.066	2	0.0024	1214	654	0.5387	616	0.5074
UNIV SPECIALIZATION	0.9947	0.9983	0.0036	4.954	2	0.0840	596	324	0.5436	317	0.5319
*TALK TO POL LEADERS	0.9969	1.0005	0.0036	9.019	3	0.0290	1213	644	0.5309	614	0.5062
REGION OF BIRTH	0.9979	0.9986	0.0008	2.911	2	0.2333	870	462	0.5310	459	0.5275
VOL ASSO MEMB	0.9981	0.9981	0.0000	1.339	3	0.7198	952	511	0.5368	511	0.5368
PRESENT OCCUPATION	0.9981	1.0006	0.0024	8.055	4	0.0896	1199	644	0.5371	604	0.5038
PAREN PRIM OCCUP	0.9983	1.0005	0.0022	6.635	3	0.0845	1199	636	0.5304	608	0.5071
SECONDARY OCCUP	0.9983	1.0007	0.0025	4.750	4	0.3139	219	120	0.5479	116	0.5297
SIZE TOWN BIRTH	0.9984	0.9984	0.0000	2.507	3	0.4749	795	423	0.5321	423	0.5321
SOUR INFO MAG	0.9986	1.0004	0.0018	6.051	3	0.1092	1209	631	0.5219	615	0.5087
PARENT UNI SPEC	0.9986	1.0042	0.0056	3.190	2	0.2029	152	86	0.5658	78	0.5132
SAVING	0.9987	1.0005	0.0018	4.055	1	0.0440	1211	640	0.5285	612	0.5054
TALK TO MILITARY	0.9990	1.0005	0.0015	5.530	3	0.1369	1210	633	0.5231	611	0.5050
FIRST OCCUP	0.9996	1.0007	0.0012	4.228	3	0.2379	743	389	0.5236	378	0.5087
TALK TO BIG BUSIN	0.9997	1.0005	0.0008	4.334	3	0.2276	1216	639	0.5255	615	0.5058
AGE	0.9998	1.0005	0.0007	3.211	2	0.2008	1214	638	0.5255	614	0.5058
COMMUN PATT	1.0001	1.0005	0.0004	3.662	3	0.3004	1181	621	0.5258	596	0.5047
NUM YR PRES OCCUP	1.0002	1.0005	0.0003	3.461	3	0.3259	1210	633	0.5231	612	0.5059
FATHER YR SCHOOL	1.0003	1.0006	0.0003	3.442	3	0.3283	987	520	0.5268	500	0.5066

*Asterisk indicates variables carried over to next level of analysis.

Table 10.6

VENEZUELAN ELITE STUDY – ROBOT DATA SCREENING

DEPENDENT VARIABLE IS CHURCH IN POL
'T HAS 2 SUBCATEGORIES

PREDICTOR	PRESENT ENTROPY	LAST ENTROPY	ENTROPY CHANGE	CHI SQUARE	DEGREES OF FREEDOM	PROBA-BILITY	NUMBER OBSERVED	PRESENT NUMBER PRED.	PRESENT PRED.	LAST NUMBER PRED.	LAST PRED.
CHURCH ATTEND SECONDARY OCCUP	0.8861	0.9192	0.0331	25.834	16	0.0564	214	143	0.6682	131	0.6121
*SOUR INFO TELEVISION PARENT UNI SPEC	0.9297	0.9689	0.0392	14.258	6	0.0269	152	98	0.6447	93	0.6118
*CHURCH ATTEND POL PARTICIPATION	0.9422	0.9570	0.0148	36.380	12	0.0003	1188	716	0.6027	704	0.5925
*CHURCH ATTEND SOUR INFO TELEVISION	0.9459	0.9564	0.0106	25.402	8	0.0013	1187	723	0.6091	703	0.5922
*CHURCH ATTEND UNIV SPECIALIZATION	0.9468	0.9468	0.0000	4.799	8	0.7788	583	352	0.6038	347	0.5952
CHURCH ATTEND FATHER YR SCHOOL	0.9476	0.9541	0.0065	20.710	12	0.0548	971	595	0.6128	574	0.5911
CHURCH ATTEND TALK TO WORKERS	0.9479	0.9552	0.0073	23.957	12	0.0206	1189	727	0.6114	707	0.5946
*CHURCH ATTEND SOUR INFO NEWSPAP	0.9493	0.9575	0.0082	21.568	8	0.0058	1195	719	0.6017	706	0.5909
CHURCH ATTEND PAREN PRIM OCCUP	0.9531	0.9561	0.0030	16.874	17	0.1544	1180	710	0.6017	700	0.5932
CHURCH ATTEND SOUR INFO MAG	0.9533	0.9572	0.0038	18.349	12	0.1055	1190	707	0.5941	704	0.5916
CHURCH ATTEND PRESENT OCCUPATION	0.9535	0.9592	0.0057	25.411	16	0.0679	1181	707	0.5986	698	0.5910
CHURCH ATTEND TALK TO POL LEADERS	0.9546	0.9572	0.0026	16.249	12	0.1801	1195	718	0.6008	708	0.5925
CHURCH ATTEND TALK TO MILITARY	0.9550	0.9554	0.0003	12.533	12	0.4039	1192	709	0.5948	706	0.5923
CHURCH ATTEND LEAD POS VOL ASSO	0.9551	0.9551	0.0000	5.497	8	0.7033	432	259	0.5995	253	0.5856
CHURCH ATTEND COMMUN PATT	0.9552	0.9565	0.0013	14.083	12	0.2955	1164	696	0.5979	689	0.5919

Table 10.7

VENEZUELAN ELITE STUDY - ROBOT DATA SCREENING

DEPENDENT VARIABLE IS CHURCH IN POL
T HAS 2 SUBCATEGORIES

PREDICTOR	PRESENT ENTROPY	LAST ENTROPY	ENTROPY CHANGE	CHI SQUARE	DEGREES OF FREEDOM	PROBA-BILITY	NUMBER OBSERVED	PRESENT NUMBER PRED.	PRESENT PRED.	LAST NUMBER PRED.	LAST PRED.
*PARENT UNI SPEC SOUR INFO TELEVISION SOUR INFO RADIO	0.8571	0.9349	0.0779	34.296	18	0.0116	151	105	0.6954	97	0.6424
*PARENT UNI SPEC SOUR INFO TELEVISION TALK TO MILITARY	0.8649	0.9323	0.0674	41.021	27	0.0410	150	107	0.7133	96	0.6400
*PARENT UNI SPEC SOUR INFO TELEVISION TALK TO STUDENT LEAD	0.8674	0.9297	0.0624	40.141	27	0.0497	152	114	0.7500	98	0.6447
PARENT UNI SPEC SOUR INFO TELEVISION TALK TO WORKERS	0.8728	0.9077	0.0349	34.168	27	0.1612	148	109	0.7365	97	0.6554
SOUR INFO TELEVISION CHURCH ATTEND SECONDARY OCCUP	0.8817	0.9162	0.0345	58.197	48	0.1487	213	155	0.7277	139	0.6526
PARENT UNI SPEC SOUR INFO TELEVISION TALK TO POLICE	0.8839	0.9286	0.0447	36.354	27	0.1078	151	109	0.7219	98	0.6490
PARENT UNI SPEC SOUR INFO TELEVISION CHURCH ATTEND	0.8892	0.9307	0.0415	35.639	27	0.1234	150	108	0.7700	96	0.6400
PARENT UNI SPEC SOUR INFO TELEVISION REGION OF BIRTH	0.8927	0.8927	0.0000	16.507	18	0.5572	88	65	0.7386	59	0.6705
PARENT UNI SPEC SOUR INFO TELEVISION SOUR INFO MOVIES	0.8936	0.9295	0.0358	25.501	18	0.1117	151	106	0.7020	97	0.6424
PARENT UNI SPEC SOUR INFO TELEVISION INTIMACY GROUP EXP	0.8981	0.9296	0.0315	15.590	9	0.0760	151	103	0.6821	97	0.6424
PARENT UNI SPEC SOUR INFO TELEVISION	0.8986	0.8986	0.0000	22.503	27	0.7114	82	62	0.7561	57	0.6951

Table 10.8

VENEZUELAN ELITE STUDY — ROBOT DATA SCREENING

VARIABLE COMBINATION SUMMARY FOR LEVEL 3: BREAKDOWN INTO COMPONENTS

DEPENDENT VARIABLE IS CHURCH IN POL
IT HAS 2 SUBCATEGORIES

PREDICTOR	PRESENT ENTROPY	LAST ENTROPY	ENTROPY CHANGE	CHI SQUARE	DEGREES OF FREEDOM	PROBA- BILITY	NUMBER OBSERVED	PRESENT NUMBER PRED.	PRESENT PRED.	LAST NUMBER PRED.	LAST PRED.
PARENT UNI SPEC SOUR INFO TELEVISION CHURCH ATTEND	0.8892	0.9307	0.0415	35.639	27	0.1234	150	108	0.7700	96	0.6400
PARENT UNI SPEC SOUR INFO TELEVISION	0.9307	0.9708	0.0400	14.320	6	0.0263	150	96	0.6400	92	0.6133
PARENT UNI SPEC CHURCH ATTEND	0.9726	0.9936	0.0210	13.357	9	0.1471	150	96	0.6400	86	0.5733
SOUR INFO TELEVISION CHURCH ATTEND	0.9374	0.9708	0.0334	15.944	9	0.0681	150	98	0.6533	92	0.6133
PARENT UNI SPEC	0.9936	1.0037	0.0101	4.101	7	0.1287	150	86	0.5733	78	0.5200
SOUR INFO TELEVISION	0.9708	1.0037	0.0329	8.841	2	0.0120	150	92	0.6133	78	0.5200
CHURCH ATTEND	0.9991	1.0037	0.0045	3.944	3	0.2676	150	83	0.5533	78	0.5200

Table 10.9

VENEZUELAN ELITE STUDY – ROBOT DATA SCREENING

DEPENDENT VARIABLE IS CHURCH IN POL
IT HAS 2 SUBCATEGORIES

PARENT UNI SPEC SOUR INFO	TELEVISION CHURCH ATTEND	CHURCH IN POL KEEP OUT	GUIDE VOTERS	ROW SUM
NAT SCI LESS	DAILY OR NEAR	4 1.0000	0 0.0000	4 1.0000
NAT SCI LESS	SUNDAY	1 1.0000	0 0.0000	1 1.0000
NAT SCI LESS	FEW PER MONTH	10 1.0000	0 0.0000	10 1.0000
NAT SCI LESS	FEW PER YEAR	4 0.6667	2 0.3333	6 1.0000
NAT SCI FEW TIM MONTH	DAILY OR NEAR	1 0.5000	1 0.5000	2 1.0000
NAT SCI FEW TIM MONTH	SUNDAY	0 0.0000	2 1.0000	2 1.0000
NAT SCI FEW TIM MONTH	FEW PER MONTH	7 0.5385	6 0.4615	13 1.0000
NAT SCI FEW TIM MONTH	FEW PER YEAR	4 0.6667	2 0.3333	6 1.0000
NAT SCI EVERY DAY	DAILY OR NEAR	4 0.5714	3 0.4286	7 1.0000
NAT SCI EVERY DAY	SUNDAY	4 0.2667	11 0.7333	15 1.0000

ROBOT DATA SCREENING AND NATURAL LANGUAGE INFORMATION RETRIEVAL SYSTEMS

Now that we have a technique that permits us to search a large data file for useful combinations among many variables, the problem of comprehensive input takes on primary importance. The sources of information that may be subjected to a general search system such as robot data screening are observations made in a stochastic situation by such individuals as biological scientists, physicians, social scientists, managers, and others. The information is classified, coded, and labeled according to a pre-established taxonomical scheme. This is indeed the most common method that has been followed so far.

Coding is a laborious process. The clinical investigator must decide beforehand which of his observations are to be classified in which way and given what code. The same is true for the social scientist who tries to code materials such as transcripts of interviews or the content of editorials or other documents.

Although the investigator has traditionally had no choice but to classify and code such data manually if he wished to use automatic processing facilities, this situation is the subject of much concerted effort and is slowly beginning to change. In some instances, algorithms have been developed which search an entire document and, based on its word and phrase content, identify those terms which classify that document. Other techniques are available for identifying those sentences in a document which convey the most effective summary of its content. The aim is to develop techniques that will permit the investigator to use the source document as his actual data base from which meaningful descriptions of events will be automatically extracted.

Another and perhaps even more exciting connection between robot data screening and natural language information systems may be developed by using this screening technique to search for classification commonalities and differences that will furnish a basis for automating taxonomies.

A second disadvantage to preclassifying and coding is that it is almost never possible to provide a code for every shade of meaning that may be met in records or documents. Once a classification scheme has been set, it is static and unchanging. However, understanding of phenomena changes with time. This means that once a coding scheme has been adopted it eventually results in a loss of information or decreasing ability to answer questions about the data that were so pre-edited.

CLUSTERING AND FACTORIAL TECHNIQUES

The search and robot techniques that we have discussed so far are based predominantly on a heuristic approach to the taxonomical classification of data. There are also a number of techniques that are increasingly formal in their mathematical structure. One of the most important is a group of mathematical procedures called *factor analysis*.

Factor analysis can be used only where variables are measured continuously. It seeks to find variables that form a cluster or hang together when each of them describes very much the same properties about the environment or about observations. The techniques may be used to remove redundancies in a multivariate set of continuous observations by determining the minimum number of dimensions needed to account for most of the variance in the original set of variables.

Thus it is assumed that variables consist of factors in that groups of variables exist which share or measure these factors essentially in the same way. These may be common to all variables or represented in some groups of them, or they may be completely unique so that they are expressed by a single variable only. The advantage of classifying variables according to factors, of course, is that if a factor is found to be represented by a group of variables, i.e., each of several variables can be used for prediction, all but one may be removed from the data file and analysis limited to that one variable as a predictor. On the other hand, a variable that turns out to contribute a unique factor may be viewed as contributing an independent dimension to the total problem of establishing association.

Commonality of factors is defined basically by intercorrelations among variables. A common factor of a set of variables accounts for the inter-correlations of the variables, whereas unique factors represent the portion of a variance of each variable that is not correlated with other variables. If we have a sample of N individuals, each of which has been measured on M variables, which have been standardized, we can then write a *factor pattern formula* by assuming a possible decomposition of a standardized variable Z_{ij} into K weighted common factor scores and the unique weighted factor score.

$$\tilde{Z}_{ij} = \sum_{i=1}^{k} a_{j1}F_{i1} + c_jU_{ij}$$

where $\tilde{Z}_{ij}$ is the estimated value of Z_{ij}.

F_{i1} is the common factor score of individual i and factor 1.

a_{i1} is the coefficient of factor 1 in variable j (this coefficient indicates to what extent factor 1 is involved in this variable and is usually referred to as *loading*.

U_{ij} is the unique factor score specific to variable j and i.

c_j is the coefficient or loading of U_{ij}.

Common factors may be assumed to be correlated and uncorrelated among themselves. Depending on which assumption is made, different models can be constructed. Unique factors, of course, are assumed to be uncorre-lated among themselves and with common factors.

There are really many alternate techniques and models by which factor analysis may proceed. In each one of them an attempt is made to identify clusters of variables that share common factors. After such clusters have been found, the investigator by inspection and reference to a prior theoretical framework seeks to identify what these factors actually represent. Unfor-tunately, most solutions are indeterminate and not unique. This means that the grouping of variables according to their intercorrelations may be repro-duced in a number of ways. So far this arbitrariness of clustering has not been removed from factor analytic techniques or derivations of this type of analysis, such as the so-called *principal component solution* which is found very frequently in psychological work. In principal component solution the loadings a_{j1} are selected so that the sum of squared loadings is a maximum. Obviously, if factors can be found which consistently have the highest loading, they may be assumed to carry the major weight in predicting one variable from a group of others. Here, too, a number of solutions are possible, depending on what mathematical models are adopted.

Factor analysis is the oldest and first robot screening technique and should be mentioned for that reason. It is based on a considerable body of formal mathematical development. Because of the difficulty in calculation, factor analysis was used rather sparingly before computers came into the picture.

Before turning to a factor analytic program with his data, the student ought to consider the nature of data needed for successful factor analysis and the object that he wishes to accomplish. Factor analysis assumes that variables are related to each other linearly and that all multivariate distributions are normal. Also, the relationship between two variables is assumed to be homoscedastic. It is rather unrealistic to expect to find such relationships among many variables. However, we have learned to live with numerical techniques if their results give us at least an approximation of the possible relationships that may exist in nature. There is some question if factor analysis does even that. It is pointed out that sometimes there are no satisfactory or commonly approved criteria for estimating either the significance of factor loading or the composition of clusters. The type of clusters obtained will depend very much on the type of assumption the investigator is willing to make about the universe of intercorrelation with which he deals. The lack of uniqueness of solution makes for arbitrary choices of what may be selected as being related. Some users would reply to this that factor analysis may be used best to test already existing hypotheses. However, since we can change the groupings or clusterings of variables that result from different types of mathematical models, it is possible to force data so as to conform to any prior theory.

The method has been claimed to produce relatively relevant results in large samples dealing with intelligence theory. Indeed, its large application area lies in the testing of personality and intelligence.

Lately there have been developed a number of heuristic clustering techniques to find commonalities among observations. The object is to find clusters of subjects or objects which "look alike" but do not look much like subjects or objects outside this cluster. "Look alike" is, of course, the unspecified term that to some extent is left to the value judgment of the user.

Clustering procedures are motivated by different aims. The experimenter might be interested in knowing the individual members of a cluster or in the over-all description of the cluster, or in both. Also, objects or subjects may be permitted in only one of the clusters, or they may be members of different clusters. These clustering techniques have very much the same aim as has factor analysis. However, they are designed to deal with data that are not continuous and do not fulfill the assumptions about the numerical properties which underlie factor analysis. They also depart from simpler logical models.

The most common of these is to derive a similarity measurement among variables and group them according to similarity. For instance, if we have a number of subjects who were measured on a number of variables or *attributes* (such as age, sex, presence or absence of certain symptoms, and so on), we can define the presence or absence of an attribute by a 1 or a 0. If we now write down the attribute of a number of subjects such that each subject is represented by a string of 1's and 0's, a similarity measure may be defined, such as

$$S_{ij} = \frac{N_{ij}}{N_i + N_j - N_{ij}} \qquad (3)$$

where S_{ij} is the similarity measurement between subject i and j.
       N_i are the number of 1's for subject i.
       N_j are the number of 1's for subject j.
       N_{ij} are the number of 1's subject i and j have in common.

Techniques similar to factor analysis can be used to cluster subjects with high similarity scores. Subsequent inspection may then isolate the variables on which they have a large amount of agreement. Note that the measure S_{ij} considers only the number of 1's on which two subjects agree. Other measures can obviously be derived also.

This type of clustering technique has not yet gone beyond instances in which the truncation of variables has been beyond "yes" or "no," and it cannot handle incomplete sets of observations effectively. It has, therefore, some rather limited applications.

11 THE ANALYSIS OF VARIANCE

Early in the twentieth century the great Ronald Fisher developed a new technique for evaluating multidimensional experiments which has become known as *analysis of variance*. This technique has had a profound effect on all sciences, especially on agronomy, biology, and psychological and behavioral investigations. Because of the ability of analysis of variance to evaluate multidimensional experimental designs, it received much attention and underwent considerable growth and development even before computers became available. This proliferation has been sparked by relative ease of calculation, so that today the analysis of variance stands as a monumental series of interrelated techniques with demonstrated wide areas of applications.

In the real world of empirical investigations the types of studies that are often most useful are those which compare the effect of different dimensions of variables that are simultaneously applied to experimental situations. Not only does the experimenter wish to know whether or not some of his variables affected observations differently from others, but also how his observational material reacted in the presence of alternative dimensions of experimental controls and, especially, how it was affected by an "interaction" between different experimental conditions. In the treatment of leukemia, for instance, the investigator would not only like to know how patients react to the basic types of drugs used to bring about remissions, but also how these drugs affect patients in the presence or absence of different antibiotics, how different types of leukemic classifications are affected by the interactions between drugs and antibiotics, and how this complex of results differs for a variety of supportive strategies. Similarly, the agronomist is interested not only in differences between fertilizers, but also in how these fertilizers react under different conditions of irrigation and how fertilizer and irrigation affect different types of plants under different conditions of climate. Then there are related problems. Confounding variables may exist which cannot be controlled experimentally so that any observation is the result of interacting conditions. Sometimes "confounding" factors are discovered only after costly experiments have been performed. In other instances the number of available subjects may be very small so that they must be repeatedly used under different experimental conditions.

The analysis of variance is a technique that will handle many of these instances of multidimensional experimental design. It also possesses an analytic robustness which lies in the general insensitivity of the technique to violations of mathematical prerequisites and assumptions. It is hardly surprising, therefore, that it has become one of the major determinants in the design of laboratory studies.

The possibilities of high-speed calculation have had their effects not so much on the quantity but on the quality of this analysis. Perhaps the most important contribution of the computer has been the removal of the restriction on "missing" data. The death of a few animals could seriously vitiate a study designed for analysis of variance, since corrections for a number of missing observations are practically impossible to do by hand. The usefulness of the technique has also been greatly enhanced by expanded computing ability, since many confounding factors can be evaluated simultaneously. Because of the many modes of application, we are dealing with a group of techniques which, for the sake of convenience, are usually put under one common term. Yet the uses of this technique have proliferated until it is a large and complex topic. Quite contrary to correlation analysis, which can be introduced in a reasonable space, the analysis of variance cannot hope to receive complete discussion in this chapter. There are many alternate models and types of experimental situations to which the rationale and techniques of analysis of variance can be applied. We shall have to limit our discussion to the most widely used and fundamental of these models. We shall therefore examine the basic analysis of variance model, develop some of its most common uses, and try to gain an understanding of why some programatic attacks may be more advantageous than others.

THE BASIC MODEL OF
ANALYSIS OF VARIANCE AND
THE VARIANCE RATIO TEST

Let us begin by considering a large population of subjects from which observations will be taken. These observations might be the yields of plots of land, the temperatures or pulse pressures of patients after administration of a particular drug, or the magnitude of a nerve potential after a stimulation. We shall simply refer to each observation as X.

This population is divided by a random procedure into c groups. Each group consists of m instances. We may arrange our observations in a scheme such as that given in Table 11.1. Note that we do not assume that the groups have the same numbers of observations, nor have we stipulated whether or not these groups were subjected to different experimental conditions.

Table 11.1. EXPERIMENTAL DESIGN WITH VARIATIONS
IN A SINGLE DIMENSION

Group 1	Group 2	Group c	
X_{11}	X_{12}	X_{1c}	
X_{21}	X_{22}	X_{2c}	
.	.	.	
.	.	.	
.	.	.	
$X_{m_1 1}$	$X_{m_2 2}$	$X_{m_c c}$	
$\bar{X}_{\cdot 1}$	$\bar{X}_{\cdot 2}$	$\bar{X}_{\cdot c}$	$\bar{X}_{\cdot\cdot}$

$$\bar{X}.. = \left(\sum_{j=1}^{c} \sum_{i=1}^{m_j} X_{ij} \right) \Big/ n$$

where

$$n = \sum_{k=1}^{c} m_k$$

$$\bar{X}.j = \frac{1}{n_j} \left(\sum_{i=1}^{m_j} X_{ij} \right)$$

It is clear that for each group we can compute a group mean, $\bar{X}.j$ as well as a mean for the total population, $\bar{X}..$. We can also compute the sums of squares separately for each group

$$ss_j = \sum_{i=1}^{m_j} (X_{ij} - \bar{X}.j)^2 \tag{1}$$

where ss_j stands for the sum of squares of the jth group.

We can also obtain ss_t or the total sum of squares

$$ss_t = \sum_{j=1}^{c} \sum_{i=1}^{m_j} (X_{ij} - \bar{X}..)^2 \tag{2}$$

Next we define the difference between each score and the over-all mean as consisting of two parts

$$X_{ij} - \bar{X}.. = (X_{ij} - \bar{X}._j) + (\bar{X}._j - \bar{X}..) \tag{3}$$

Similarly, we can express the square of the difference as

$$(X_{ij} - \bar{X}..)^2 = (X_{ij} - \bar{X}._j)^2$$
$$+ (\bar{X}._j - \bar{X}..)^2 + 2(X_{ij} - \bar{X}._j)(\bar{X}._j - \bar{X}..) \tag{4}$$

so that the sum of squares for each group can be expressed as

$$ss_j = \sum_{i=1}^{m_j} (X_{ij} - \bar{X}..)^2$$
$$= \sum_{i=1}^{m_j} (X_{ij} - \bar{X}._j)^2 + m_j(\bar{X}._j - \bar{X}..)^2 \tag{5}$$

Note the following. The term $(\bar{X}._j - \bar{X}..)^2$ summed m_j times is simply equal to the product of $m_j(\bar{X}._j - \bar{X}..)^2$. Also the cross product term of expression (4) dropped out because

$$\sum (X_{ij} - \bar{X}._j)(\bar{X}._j - \bar{X}..) = 0, \quad \text{since,} \quad \sum (X_{ij} - \bar{X}._j) = 0 \tag{6}$$

We can now rewrite the total sum of squares as

$$ss_t = \sum_{j=1}^{c} \sum_{i=1}^{m_j} (X_{ij} - \bar{X}..)^2 = \sum_{j=1}^{c} \sum_{i=1}^{m_j} (X_{ij} - \bar{X}._j)^2$$
$$= n \sum_{j=1}^{c} (\bar{X}._j - \bar{X}..)^2 \tag{7}$$

or the sum of squares of all the measurements among different groups emerges as the sum of two components. We shall call these two components the within sum squares ss_w and the between sum squares ss_b. The definitions of ss_t, ss_b, and ss_w are summarized in Table 11.2.

Table 11.2. COMPONENTS OF THE SUM OF SQUARES FOR A ONE-DIMENSIONAL EXPERIMENTAL DESIGN

ss for group j	$ss_j = \sum_{i=1}^{m_j} (X_{ij} - \bar{X}._j)^2$
ss within all groups	$ss_w = \sum_{j=1}^{c} \sum_{i=1}^{m_j} (X_{ij} - \bar{X}._j)^2$
ss between all groups	$ss_b = n \sum_{j=1}^{c} (\bar{X}._j - \bar{X}..)^2$

$$ss_b = m_1(\bar{X}._1 - \bar{X}..)^2 + m_2(\bar{X}._2 - \bar{X}..)^2 + \cdots + m_c(\bar{X}._c - \bar{X}..)^2$$
$$= m_1\bar{X}._1^2 + m_2\bar{X}._2^2 + \cdots + m_c\bar{X}._c^2 + n\bar{X}..^2 - 2n\bar{X}..^2$$
$$= \frac{(\sum X._1)^2}{m_1} + \frac{(\sum X._2)^2}{m_2} + \cdots + \frac{(\sum X._c)^2}{m_c} - \frac{\left(\sum_1^c \sum_1^{m_j} X_{ij}\right)^2}{n} \tag{8}$$

We found an important identity in Chapter 6, namely,

$$\sigma_{\bar{x}}^2 = \frac{\sigma^2}{n} \quad \text{or} \quad \sigma^2 = n\sigma_{\bar{x}}^2$$

Verbally stated, if we were to take successive samples of n cases each and compute a mean, these means would be distributed with variance $\sigma_{\bar{x}}^2$ equal to the variance of population σ^2 divided by the number of cases in the sample. Consequently we could obtain two separate estimates of the variance of a population—the first estimate from the variation of observations around the individual sample means, the second from the variation of means around an over-all mean. This conclusion is summarized in Table 11.3.

Table 11.3. ESTIMATES OF THE VARIANCE OF A POPULATION
FROM TWO INDEPENDENT SOURCES

$$\sigma^2 \longrightarrow \frac{\sum\sum (X_{ij} - \bar{X}_{.j})^2}{m_1 + m_2 + \cdots + m_c - c} = s_w^2$$

$$\sigma^2 \longrightarrow \frac{m \sum_1^c (\bar{X}_{.j} - \bar{X}_{..})^2}{c - 1} = s_b^2$$

However, we saw from equation (7) that the total sum of squares can be divided into two separate components, the first of which we called ss_w, or the within sum of squares and the other of which we called ss_b, or the between sum of squares. Thus we can restate the summary of Table 11.3 in Table 11.4.

Table 11.4. ESTIMATES OF THE VARIANCE OF A POPULATION FROM TWO INDEPENDENT
SOURCES USING WITHIN AND BETWEEN SUMS OF SQUARES

$$\sigma^2 \longrightarrow \frac{ss_w}{m - c} = s_w^2$$

$$\sigma^2 \longrightarrow \frac{ss_b}{c - 1} = s_b^2$$

If (and this is important) we had done no more than to divide a population of measurements into c different groups, then we should be able to obtain two estimates of the variance of this population which we could call the between and within variance. Since the within variance is simply based on random variation within each group and the between variance on the random variations of the means, both of them should estimate the same variance. Hence, a ratio of the two should be equal to approximately 1.

$$1 \approx \frac{s_b^2}{s_w^2} = F \tag{9}$$

This ratio is called the *variance ratio* and was discussed briefly in Chapter 7. If we assume that the variable X_{ij} is distributed normally, then the sampling distribution of F is known and can be tabulated. Such a table appears in Appendix B, Table 9.

THE VARIANCE RATIO WHEN EXPERIMENTAL TREATMENTS HAVE BEEN APPLIED TO DIFFERENT GROUPS

Next we shall take a look at what would happen if factors other than random chance operated on the different groups. We shall begin by postulating a simple population model. Let us assume that each observation is an estimate of some true value μ from which it deviates by chance alone. We can write this as

$$X_i = \mu + \Delta_i \tag{10}$$

Let us now introduce some treatment on a subset of measurements of X which has a constant effect τ. We can rewrite our statement as

$$X_{ij} = \mu + \tau + \Delta_{ij} \tag{11}$$

This particular model is very often called the linear model. If we divide a population into different groups and subject each group to a particular treatment, we may or may not add some value τ to the mean of that population. Obviously, if the treatment itself has no effect at all, then the value of τ will be equal to zero.

We can think of τ as being either a fixed value or being itself a random variable. The analysis is called Model I or Model II, depending on which holds true. For our purposes we shall assume that τ is a constant quantity and does not vary. (Or we might view τ as an average quantity.)

What are our expectations of the values of within and between sums of squares when different groups have been exposed to different treatments during an experiment and when these treatments have had an effect on the measurements?

We begin by looking at each one of our groups separately. A group mean μ_i may be viewed as the sum of the over-all population mean and the treatment effect

$$\mu_1 = \mu + \tau_1 \tag{12}$$

The error for each score is

$$(X_{i1} - \mu_1) = \Delta_{i1} \tag{13}$$

and the average value of $(\Delta_{i1})^2$ is by definition the σ_1^2

$$E(\Delta_{i1}^2) = \sigma_1^2 \tag{14}$$

We also found in Chapter 6 that

$$E\left[\sum_{i=1}^{m_1} (X_{i1} - \bar{X}_{.1})^2\right] = E(ss_1) = (m_1 - 1)\sigma_1^2 \tag{15}$$

so that we can write the estimate variance for Group 1 as

$$s_1^2 = \frac{ss_1}{m_1 - 1} \tag{16}$$

It is common to refer to each of these variance estimates as *mean square*. The mean square is called an unbiased estimate of the variance, or

$$
\begin{aligned}
E[s_1^2] &= \sigma_1^2 \\
E[s_2^2] &= \sigma_2^2 \\
& \cdot \quad \cdot \\
& \cdot \quad \cdot \\
& \cdot \quad \cdot \\
E[s_c^2] &= \sigma_c^2
\end{aligned}
\tag{17}
$$

Since the within sum of squares is the sum of all the group sum of squares, we can write it as

$$
\begin{aligned}
E[ss_w] &= \sum_{j=1}^c (m_j - 1)\sigma_j^2 \\
&= (n - c)\sigma^2 \quad \text{if } \sigma_1^2 = \sigma_2^2 = \cdots = \sigma_c^2
\end{aligned}
\tag{18}
$$

The between sum of squares can be given as

$$ss_b = \sum_{j=1}^c \frac{\left(\sum_{i=1}^{m_j} X_{ij}\right)^2}{m_j} - \frac{\left(\sum_{j=1}^c \sum_{i=1}^{m_j} X_{ij}\right)^2}{n}$$

We can write

$$\sum_{j=1}^c \frac{\left(\sum_{j=1}^{m_j} X_{ij}\right)^2}{m_j} = \sum_{j=1}^c m_j \bar{X}_{.j}^2 \tag{19}$$

since this is an equivalent statement and

$$\frac{(\sum \sum X_{ij})^2}{n} = n\bar{X}_{..}^2$$

We saw from Chapter 6 that

$$E(m_1 \bar{X}_{.1}^2) = m_1 \mu_1^2 + \sigma^2 \tag{20}$$

so that

$$E(\sum m_j \bar{X}_{.j}^2) = m_1 \mu_1^2 + \cdots + m_c \mu_c^2 + c\sigma^2 \tag{21}$$

Similarly,

$$E(n \bar{X}_{..}^2) = n\mu^2 + \sigma^2 \tag{22}$$

so that we can express

$$
\begin{aligned}
E(ss_b) &= E\left(\sum_j m_j \bar{X}_j^2\right) - E(n \bar{X}_{..}^2) \\
&= \sum_{j=1}^{c} m_j \mu_j^2 - n\mu^2 + (c-1)\sigma^2 \\
&= \sum_{j=1}^{c} m_j(\mu_j - \mu)^2 + (c-1)\sigma^2
\end{aligned} \tag{23}
$$

We can now summarize the two independent estimates of mean squares from Table 11.4. This is presented in Table 11.5.

Table 11.5. THE TWO INDEPENDENT ESTIMATES OF σ^2
IF AN EFFECT EXISTS FOR SOME GROUPS

$$E\left[\frac{ss_w}{m-c}\right] = \sigma^2$$

$$E\left[\frac{ss_b}{c-1}\right] = m\sigma_\tau^2 + \sigma^2$$

where

$$\sigma_\tau^2 = \frac{\sum \tau^2}{c-1}$$

The two independent estimates of σ^2 if an effect τ exists for some groups are

$$E\left(\frac{ss_w}{n-c}\right) = \sigma^2$$

$$E\left(\frac{ss_b}{c-1}\right) = m\sigma_\tau^2 + \sigma^2$$

where

$$\sigma_\tau^2 = \frac{\sum \tau^2}{c-1}$$

Actually, we have already convinced ourselves in Chapter 9 that variances are additive. This means that if a score X is equal to the sum of two scores, $A + B$, then the variance of X will be equal to the variance of A plus the variance of B

$$\sigma^2_{A+B} = \sigma^2_A + \sigma^2_B \tag{24}$$

provided, of course, that the two measures A and B are not correlated.

As a consequence we now look at the variance ratio, where an experimental effect exists as

$$E[F] = E\left(\frac{s^2_b}{s^2_w}\right) = \frac{m\sigma^2_\tau + \sigma^2}{\sigma^2} > 1 \tag{25}$$

where m is an average sample size per group.

The basic notion of analysis of variance may then be summarized in this fashion. When we begin with a single population of individual measurements and divide these into groups, we may subject each of these groups to a different type of experimental condition. When these different experimental conditions have no effect on the measurements, we may expect that the two estimates of the variance of the population (obtained by using ss_w and ss_b) are equal to each other and differ by chance only. Thus the expected variance ratio F may be expected to be equal to unity and depart from unity only by chance.

When, however, some of the treatments have had an effect, then the variance estimate based on the within sum of squares will remain unchanged, whereas the variance estimate based on the between sum of squares will actually become the sum of two variances. Thus the variance ratio F may be expected to take on values larger than 1.

The basic hypotheses and decision model may be stated as follows:

$$
\begin{aligned}
H_0: &\quad \mu_1 = \mu_2 = \cdots = \mu_c = \mu \\
H_1: &\quad \text{some } \mu_j \neq \mu
\end{aligned}
\tag{26}
$$

and the decision model could be stated as

Rule: Accept H_0 if $F \leq k$; otherwise accept H_1 (27)

APPLICATION OF ANALYSIS OF VARIANCE
TO A SIMPLE EXAMPLE

Computational methods, especially those useful for calculating the components of the sum of squares with the help of semiautomatic calculators, are given in Table 11.6. Computer calculations may prefer to depart from the definition of each sum of square component for purposes of more efficient processing.

Computations may be performed automatically in a number of ways. Whenever possible the sums of squares should be computed with double or

Table 11.6. COMPUTATION FORMULAE FOR SUMS OF SQUARES, SIMPLE CASE

Source	Definition of Sum of Squares	Semiautomatic Computation Method
ss_t	$\sum\limits_1^c \sum\limits_1^m (X_{ij} - \bar{X}..)^2$	$\left[n \sum\limits_1^c \sum\limits_1^m X_{ij}^2 - \left(\sum\limits_1^c \sum\limits_1^m X_{ij} \right)^2 \right] \dfrac{1}{n}$
ss_b	$m_j \sum\limits_1^c (\bar{X}._j - \bar{X}..)^2$	$\left[c \sum\limits_1^c \left(\sum\limits_1^{m_j} X_{ij} \right)^2 - \left(\sum\limits_1^c \sum\limits_1^m X_{ij} \right)^2 \right] \dfrac{1}{n}$
ss_w	$\sum\limits_1^c \sum\limits_1^m (X_{ij} - \bar{X}._j)^2$	$ss_t - ss_b$

triple precision. If this is not done an occasional negative sum of squares might result. We have talked about this before. After each sum of squares has been computed, we arrange the sums of squares, label their sources, and list them, together with their appropriate degrees of freedom, in a table (like Table 11.7) to compute the necessary F ratios.

Table 11.7. SIMPLE ANALYSIS OF VARIANCE ARRANGEMENT

Source		d.f.	Expected Mean Square
Column	ss_b	$c - 1$	$\sigma^2 + m\sigma_\tau^2$
Residual	ss_w	$n - c$	σ^2
Total	ss_t	$n - 1$	

We shall pay special attention to the column indicating the composition of the mean square. Although this may not be important, we shall see as we go on that the complexity of possible components of the mean square will demand flexibility in handling of computer output.

A SIMPLE EXAMPLE

We shall gain practical understanding of the meaning involved in partitioning a sum of squares by analyzing examples in which experimental effects do or do not exert an influence.

We start by selecting 25 single-digit integers from a table of random numbers and arranging them in an array, as in Table 11.8. Let us assume that each number represents a score or a measurement taken on a particular individual. Each row or column can be viewed, then, as an arbitrary and random grouping of five scores at a time.

First we shall consider the five columns labeled A through E. We shall test the hypothesis that the means for these five columns come from a population in which $\mu_a = \mu_b = \mu_c = \mu_d = \mu_e = \mu$. In fact, we know this to be the case, since we arranged the numbers this way to begin with. We also know

Table 11.8. Twenty-five Random Integers Arranged
in a 5×5 Array

	A	B	C	D	E	Row Means
I	8	2	6	5	1	4.4
II	2	0	8	4	9	4.6
III	4	0	0	2	7	2.6
IV	4	4	0	4	8	4.0
V	2	5	9	4	0	4.0
Column Means	4.0	2.2	4.6	3.8	5.0	

that all observations are randomly selected from a known population with
homogeneous variance.

The calculations necessary for developing within and between sums
of squares are given in Table 11.9.

Table 11.9. Calculation to Test H_0: $\mu_a = \mu_b = \mu_c = \mu_d = \mu_e = \mu$
of Data from Table 11.8

	Column Groups						
	A	B	C	D	E		

$$\sum_1^r X_{ij} = \quad 20 \quad\quad 11 \quad\quad 23 \quad\quad 19 \quad\quad 25 \quad\quad \sum_1^c \sum_1^r X_{ij} = 98$$

$$\left(\sum_1^r X_{ij}\right)^2 = \quad 400 \quad\; 121 \quad\; 529 \quad\; 361 \quad\; 625 \quad\; \sum_1^c \left(\sum_1^r X_{ij}\right)^2 = 2036$$

$$\sum_1^r X_{ij}^2 = \quad 104 \quad\;\; 45 \quad\;\; 181 \quad\;\; 77 \quad\;\; 195 \quad\; \sum_1^c \sum_1^r X_{ij}^2 = 602$$

$$ss_t = \sum_1^c \sum_1^r (X_{ij} - \bar{X}..)^2 = \frac{1}{n}\left[n\sum_1^c \sum_1^r X_{ij}^2 - \left(\sum_1^c \sum_1^r X_{ij}\right)^2 \right]$$
$$= \tfrac{1}{25}[(25)(602) - (98)^2] \qquad\qquad = 217.84$$

$$ss_w = \sum_1^c \sum_1^r (X_{ij} - \bar{X}._j)^2 = \frac{1}{r}\left[r\sum_1^c \sum_1^r X_{ij}^2 - \sum_1^c \left(\sum_1^r X_{ij}\right)^2 \right]$$
$$= \tfrac{1}{5}[(5)(602) - 2036] \qquad\qquad = 194.8$$

$$ss_b = r\sum_1^c (\bar{X}._j - \bar{X}..)^2 \quad = \frac{1}{rc}\left[c\sum_1^c \left(\sum_1^r X_{ij}\right)^2 - \left(\sum_1^c \sum_1^r X_{ij}\right)^2 \right]$$
$$= \tfrac{1}{25}[(5)(2036) - (98)^2] \qquad\qquad = 23.04$$

There is no reason, of course, why we should have arranged our groups
by columns. We could just as easily undertake to test the hypothesis or row
means, i.e., $\mu_1 = \mu_2 = \mu_3 = \mu_4 = \mu_5 = \mu$. The necessary calculations for
testing these hypotheses are given in Table 11.10.

Regardless of which hypotheses we wish to test (i.e., that the column
means differ or that row means differ), we can arrange our results in an
analyses table as in Table 11.11. We can see from Table 11.11 that the total
sum of squares is the same whether we arrange our data by rows or by

Table 11.10. CALCULATION TO TEST H_0: $\mu_1 = \mu_2 = \mu_3 = \mu_4 = \mu_5 = \mu$ OF DATA FROM TABLE 11.8

Row Groups

	I	II	III	IV	V		
$\sum\limits_1^c X_{ij} =$	22	23	13	20	20	$\sum\limits_1^r \sum\limits_1^c X_{ij} =$	98
$\left(\sum\limits_1^c X_{ij}\right)^2 =$	484	529	169	400	400	$\sum\limits_1^r \left(\sum\limits_1^c X_{ij}\right)^2 =$	1982
$\sum\limits_1^c X_{ij}^2 =$	130	165	69	112	126	$\sum\limits_1^r \left(\sum\limits_1^c X_{ij}^2\right) =$	602

$$ss_t = \sum_1^c \sum_1^r (X_{ij} - \bar{X}..)^2 = \frac{1}{n}\left[n\sum_1^c \sum_1^r X_{ij}^2 - \left(\sum_1^c \sum_1^r X_{ij}\right)^2\right]$$
$$= \tfrac{1}{25}[(25)(602) - (98)^2] \qquad = 217.84$$

$$ss_w = \sum_1^c \sum_1^r (X_{ij} - \bar{X}_i.)^2 = \frac{1}{c}\left[c\sum_1^c \sum_1^r X_{ij}^2 - \sum_1^r \left(\sum_1^c X_{ij}\right)^2\right]$$
$$= \tfrac{1}{5}[(5)(602) - 1982] \qquad = 205.6$$

$$ss_b = c\sum_1^r (\bar{X}_i. - \bar{X}..)^2 = \frac{1}{rc}\left[c\sum_1^r \left(\sum_1^c X_{ij}\right)^2 - \left(\sum_1^c \sum_1^r X_{ij}\right)^2\right]$$
$$= \tfrac{1}{25}[(5)(1982) - (98)^2] \qquad = 12.24$$

columns. However, the partitioning of the total sum of squares into between and within components yields different values, depending on the type of grouping. In both instances the F ratio, which should have been close to unity, turns out to be smaller than 1. There is no significance to be attached to this.

Table 11.11. SUMMARY OF ANALYSIS OF DATA IN TABLE 11.8 BY COLUMNS AND ROWS

By Columns

Source	Sum of Squares	d.f.	Mean Squares	F	Estimates of
ss_t	217.84	24			
ss_b	23.04	4	5.79	0.59	$\sigma^2 + r\sigma_c^2$
ss_w	194.80	20	9.74		σ^2

By Rows

Source	Sum of Squares	d.f.	Mean Squares	F	Estimates of
ss_t	217.84	24			
ss_b	12.24	4	3.06	.30	$\sigma^2 + c\sigma_r^2$
ss_w	205.60	20	10.28		σ^2

The data in Table 11.8 may be viewed simply as the random variation of scores in the absence of any experimental effect. What will happen now if an experimental condition exerts an influence on these scores? (We shall assume that Model I prevails, i.e., that the experimental condition adds a constant value to all observations.)

We shall first view the column effect. Let us think of groups A through E as being subjected to five different experimental conditions. Each of these conditions has a definite effect on scores such that under condition A no value is added, condition B adds a 1 to each measure, condition C adds a 2 to each measure, condition D adds a 3 to each measure, and condition E adds a 4 to each measure. The resulting data are arranged as in Table 11.12.

Table 11.12. DATA OF TABLE 11.8 AFTER AN EXPERIMENTAL
EFFECT HAS BEEN ADDED FOR COLUMN TREATMENTS

	A	B	C	D	E	Row Means
I	8	3	8	8	5	6.4
II	2	1	10	7	13	6.6
III	4	1	2	5	11	4.6
IV	4	5	2	7	12	6.0
V	2	6	11	7	4	6.0
Column Means	4.0	3.2	6.6	6.8	9.0	

Note that while the column means from A through E progressively increase, the row means have simply increased by a constant but do not vary among each other to any greater extent now than they did before.

We now proceed with the same numerical calculations (as we did before) for a possible column effect. We obtain the calculations as summarized in Table 11.13. When we compare the calculations of Table 11.13 and Table 11.9, we see immediately that the total sums of squares have increased as have the between sums of squares, but that the within sums of squares have remained unchanged. The student will note that the experimental effect has added to the total variation between the means without modifying at all the natural variation that exists among individuals within each group.

Table 11.13. CALCULATION TO TEST H_0: $\mu_a = \mu_b = \mu_c = \mu_d = \mu_e = \mu$
OF DATA FROM TABLE 11.12

			Column Groups				
		A	B	C	D	E	
$\sum\limits_{1}^{r} X_{ij}$	=	20	16	33	34	45	$\sum\limits_{1}^{c}\sum\limits_{1}^{r} X_{ij} = 148$
$\left(\sum\limits_{1}^{r} X_{ij}\right)^2$	=	400	256	1089	1156	2025	$\sum\limits_{1}^{c}\left(\sum\limits_{1}^{r} X_{ij}\right)^2 = 4926$
$\sum\limits_{1}^{r} X_{ij}^2$	=	104	72	293	236	475	$\sum\limits_{1}^{c}\sum\limits_{1}^{r} X_{ij}^2 = 1180$

$$ss_t = 303.84$$
$$ss_w = 194.80$$
$$ss_b = 109.04$$

We can compare the result of partitioning the total sum of squares for columns (where an experimental effect does exist since we put it there) with the same analysis done for rows (where an experimental effect does not exist). The calculations for a possible row effect are given in Table 11.14.

Table 11.14. CALCULATION TO TEST H_0: $\mu_1 = \mu_2 = \mu_3 = \mu_4 = \mu_5 = \mu$
OF DATA FROM TABLE 11.12

Row Groups

$\sum\limits_1^c X_{ij}$ =	32	33	23	30	30	$\sum\limits_1^r \sum\limits_1^c X_{ij}$	= 148
$\left(\sum\limits_1^c X_{ij}\right)^2$ =	1024	1089	529	900	900	$\sum\limits_1^r \left(\sum\limits_1^c X_{ij}\right)^2$	= 4442
$\sum\limits_1^c X_{ij}^2$ =	226	323	167	238	226	$\sum\limits_1^r \sum\limits_1^c X_{ij}^2$	= 1180

$$ss_t = 303.84$$
$$ss_w = 291.60$$
$$ss_b = 12.24$$

In comparing Table 11.14 with Table 11.10 we see that changes in partition of the total sum of squares are reflected in the within sum of squares rather than in the between sum of squares. The reason for this should be clear to the student. The effect along columns has really done no more, as far as the rows are concerned, than to increase the variation along each row variable. However, since this increase was the same in each row group, the between sum of squares has remained unchanged, and the change in the total sum of squares has been absorbed by the within component.

The summary of the analyses by columns and rows is given in Table 11.15.

Table 11.15. SUMMARY OF ANALYSIS OF DATA IN TABLE 11.12
BY COLUMNS AND ROWS

Source	Sum of Squares	d. f.	Mean Squares	F
		By Columns		
ss_t	303.84	24		
ss_b	109.04	4	27.26	2.80
ss_w	194.80	20	9.74	
		By Rows		
ss_t	303.84	24		
ss_b	12.24	4	3.06	.21
ss_w	291.60	20	14.58	

Comparing Table 11.15 and Table 11.11, we can again see the effects of changing the means but not the variation within groups along columns and changing the variation within groups but not the difference between means among the rows. The value of F for the test of the hypothesis that the column means are different has now increased to 2.80, which for 4 and 20 degrees of freedom indicates a probability (of having sampled from a single population) of approximately one in twenty.

Display of printouts may vary depending on the taste of individuals who design program libraries. An example printout from the MEDCOMP library is given in Table 11.16.

Table 11.16. Example Printout Display for a Simple Analysis of Variance*

VARIABLE NAME	CELL COUNT	CELL MEAN	STANDARD DEVIATION	STANDARD ERROR
FIRST NAME	10	5.500	3.028	0.957
SECOND NAME	10	15.500	3.028	0.957
THIRD NAME	10	14.300	17.795	5.627
FOURTH NAME	8	10.000	4.899	1.732
FIFTH NAME	7	8.000	4.320	1.633
SIXTH NAME	15	811.000	447.214	115.470
SEVENTH NAME	5	28.660	17.501	7.827
EIGHTH NAME	12	3.500	1.784	0.515

SOURCE	SUM SQUARES	DEG. FREEDOM	MEAN SQUARE	F
TOTAL	12680605.0	76		2.799186
BETWEEN	2804555.3	7	400650.8	
WITHIN	9876049.7	69	143131.2	

*From the MEDCOMP Program Library.

ASSUMPTIONS UNDERLYING ANALYSIS OF VARIANCE AND WHAT TO DO ABOUT THEM

The mathematical model on which analysis of variance is based makes a number of crucial assumptions about the data.

Each measurement is thought to come from an independent source. This assumption can be modified by proper pooling of sums of squares, as we shall see later on.

The analysis of variance requires that the population from which measurements are drawn be distributed normally. This latter assumption may be tested in a number of ways. The investigator could inspect a histogram of his scores or even subject the frequency distribution to a test of goodness of fit to the normal distribution (see Chapter 7). When the assumption of normality of distribution is rejected, the investigator could take recourse to "normalization" by a number of transformation functions. (He could convert all his scores into logs, square roots, arcsins, etc.). It speaks for the robustness of analysis of variance, however, that although normalcy of distribution is required, the F ratio will not be affected appreciably unless

Table 11.17. EXAMPLE PRINTOUT DISPLAY OF BARTLETT'S TEST FOR HOMOGENEITY OF VARIANCE

GROUP NUMBER	MEAN SQUARE	CARD NUMBER
1	0.9089	1
2	0.4972	2
3	0.0756	3
4	0.1079	4
5	0.1460	5
6	0.0800	6
7	0.3940	7
8	0.3900	8

CHI SQUARE	DEGREE OF FREEDOM
20.24	7

*From the MEDCOMP Program Library.

there is a considerable skew in the distribution. For most normal uses of this analysis a rough fit of the data to the normal distribution suffices.

One other assumption is that within the group variances are of approximately equal size. If variances should differ considerably, it can be shown that the value of F will be increased spuriously. A number of tests are available to evaluate the degree of inhomogeneity that may exist between different variances. One well-known test has been developed by Bartlett, another one by Cochran. Either one of these two tests could be used routinely in any analysis of variance. Table 11.17 shows an example printout (from the MEDCOMP library) of Bartlett's test for homogeneity of variance. (An excellent listing of techniques for testing analysis of variance designs for homogeneities can be found in E. Eisenhart, M. W. Hastay, and W. A. Wallis, *Techniques of Statistical Analysis*, McGraw-Hill Co., New York, 1947).

If it is found that the variances for different subgroups do not fulfill the assumption of homogeneity, the investigator can again use an appropriate transformation of scores. There are also special procedures for analyses of variance which will weight mean squares and sums of squares for inhomogeneities and will adjust the F scores accordingly.

The general weighting factor is given by

$$w_j = \frac{m_j}{s_j^2} \tag{28}$$

where s_j^2 is the mean square for the jth group and w_j is the weighting factor for the jth group.

The weighted mean is given by

$$\bar{X}' = \frac{\sum_{i=1}^{c} (\bar{X}_j w_j)}{\sum_{1}^{c} w_j} \tag{29}$$

and the weighted sum of within squares is given by

$$ss'_w = \sum_{1}^{c} w_j(\bar{X}_{\cdot j} - \bar{X}')^2 \tag{30}$$

and finally the adjusted value of F is given by

$$F' = 1 + \left[\frac{2(c-2)}{c^2-1}\right] \sum_1^c \left[\frac{\left(1 - \frac{w_j}{\sum w_j}\right)^2}{m_j - 1}\right] \tag{31}$$

The degrees of freedom for this adjusted value of F' are

$$c - 1 \quad \text{and} \quad \left[\frac{3}{c^2-1}\right] \sum_1^c \left[\frac{\left(1 - \frac{w_j}{\sum w_j}\right)^2}{m_j - 1}\right] \tag{32}$$

Table 11.18 shows an example printout from the MEDCOMP Library.

Table 11.18. EXAMPLE PRINTOUT DISPLAY OF ANALYSIS OF VARIANCE WITH CORRECTIONS FOR HETEROGENEITY OF VARIANCE*

GROUP NUMBER	MEANS	NUMBER OF OBSERVATIONS	CARD NUMBER
1	2.84	10	1
2	2.66	8	2
3	3.18	10	3
4	2.98	8	4
5	2.37	6	5
6	2.90	4	6
7	1.98	6	7
8	2.35	4	8

WEIGHTED MEAN	WEIGHTED SUM OF SQUARES	DEGREES OF FREEDOM
2.89	39.36	DF 1 7
		DF 2 17

ADJUSTED F

4.53

*From the MEDCOMP Program Library.

It is obvious even from the simple analysis of variance examples that adjusting for inhomogeneity of variance and for lack of normality involves considerable computation. Prior to the invention of computers, correction for violations of underlying assumption was seldom undertaken. The amount of labor involved was simply too immense. Instead, the assumption was made with some justification that the analysis of variance technique is very robust. By this was meant that relatively large violations of the basic assumptions could be tolerated because they presumably produced relatively small errors in F. However, no satisfactory proof for this assumption was ever forthcoming. Like Don Quixote's helmet, it was a proposition better left untested.

Computer programs should include a test for homogeneity of variance as an option. Also, it may not be too inappropriate to have a double program in which F and F' are computed simultaneously. If there is no large difference between the two values, then the investigator simply accepts the larger value of F. However, if these two should differ considerably he is probably safer accepting the value of F'.

INCREASING THE COMPLEXITY
OF THE ANALYSIS OF VARIANCE

Because of the complexity of the mathematical model, we shall limit our analyses to a quick look at the manner in which the sums of squares can be partitioned and the meaning of the parts of the sums of squares and of the mean squares. It is especially important that we be clear about the components of the mean square. We shall see that different manipulations of sums of squares may sometimes be required to enable us to exploit the F ratio. We shall also introduce a new concept, that of interaction.

TWO-WAY ANALYSIS OF VARIANCE

We shall begin with an experimental design in which we wish to assess the effect of four drugs supported by one of five antibiotics. (see Table 11.19). The mean taken over the first row represents the average response to antibiotic 1 regardless of drug, and the average for any row represents the average response to any one of the antibiotics. Similarly, the average for column A represents the responses to drug A regardless of antibiotic, and the average for any column represents the response to any of the drugs.

Table 11.19. LAYOUT OF A DRUG-ANTIBIOTIC EXPERIMENT—
ONE SUBJECT PER CELL

Drugs

		A	B	·	·	c	
	I	X_{1a}	X_{1b}	·	·	X_{1c}	$\bar{X}_{1\cdot}$
	II	X_{2a}	X_{2b}	·	·	X_{2c}	$\bar{X}_{2\cdot}$
ANTIBIOTICS	·	·	·	·	·	·	
	·	·	·	·	·	·	·
	·	·	·	·	·	·	
	r	X_{ra}	X_{ra}	·	·	X_{rc}	$\bar{X}_{r\cdot}$
		$\bar{X}_{\cdot a}$	$\bar{X}_{\cdot b}$	·	·	$\bar{X}_{\cdot c}$	$\bar{X}_{\cdot\cdot}$

The difference between any score X_{ij} from the total mean $\bar{X}_{\cdot\cdot}$ is equal to the sum of the differences of row and column means from the total mean plus the remainder term, which represents a variation above and beyond that due to column and row effect. We can express this as

$$(X_{ij} - \bar{X}..) = (\bar{X}._j - \bar{X}..)$$
$$+ (\bar{X}_i. - \bar{X}..) + (X_{ij} - \bar{X}._j - \bar{X}_i. + \bar{X}..) \tag{33}$$

Summing and squaring expression (33), we get

$$\sum_1^c \sum_1^r (X_{ij} - \bar{X}..)^2 = r \sum_1^c (\bar{X}._j - \bar{X}..)^2 + c \sum_1^r (\bar{X}_i. - \bar{X}..)^2$$
$$+ \sum_1^r \sum_1^c (X_{ij} - \bar{X}._j - \bar{X}_i. + \bar{X}..)^2 \tag{34}$$

(Note that the sums of the cross product terms drop out. Why?)

The total sum of squares can then be broken into three parts. The first represents the sum of squared column means around the over-all mean, the second represents the sum of squared row means around the over-all mean, and the third represents that part of the sum of squares that remains after column and row effects have been eliminated. Table 11.20 shows source, degrees of freedom, and composition of mean squares.

Table 11.20. TWO-WAY ANALYSIS OF VARIANCE ARRANGEMENT

Source		d. f.	Expected Mean Square Is Estimate of
Row effect	$c \sum_1^r (\bar{X}_i. - \bar{X}..)^2$	$r - 1$	$\sigma^2 + c\sigma_r^2$
Column effect	$r \sum_1^c (X._j - \bar{X}..)^2$	$c - 1$	$\sigma^2 + r\sigma_c^2$
Remainder	$\sum_1^r \sum_1^c (X_{ij} - \bar{X}_i. - \bar{X}._j + \bar{X}..)^2$	$(r - 1)(c - 1)$	σ^2
Total	$\sum_1^r \sum_1^c (X_{ij} - \bar{X}..)^2$	$n - 1$	

The resulting two mean squares permit us to perform two separate tests —the mean square for rows and the mean square for columns against the remainder:

$$\text{For effect of row} \qquad F_r = \frac{\text{row mean square}}{\text{remainder}} \tag{35a}$$

$$\text{For effect of column} \qquad F_c = \frac{\text{column mean square}}{\text{remainder}} \tag{35b}$$

with degrees of freedom equal to $(r - 1)$ for the row effect and $(c - 1)$ for the column effect. The degrees of freedoms for the remainder are equal to $(r - 1)(c - 1)$.

A breakdown of preferable computational formulas is given in Table 11.21.

Table 11.21. COMPUTATIONAL PROCEDURES FOR TWO-WAY ANALYSIS OF VARIANCE, NO REPLICATION

Source	Definition of Sums of Squares	Semiautomatic
ss_t	$\sum\limits_1^r \sum\limits_1^c (X_{ij} - \bar{X}..)^2$	$\left[n \sum\limits_1^r \sum\limits_1^c X_{ij}^2 - \left(\sum\limits_1^r \sum\limits_1^c X_{ij} \right)^2 \right] \dfrac{1}{n}$
ss_r	$c \sum\limits_1^r (\bar{X}_{i\cdot} - \bar{X}..)^2$	$\left[r \sum\limits_1^r \left(\sum\limits_1^c X_{ij} \right)^2 - \left(\sum\limits_1^r \sum\limits_1^c X_{ij} \right)^2 \right] \dfrac{1}{n}$
ss_c	$r \sum\limits_1^c (\bar{X}_{\cdot j} - \bar{X}..)^2$	$\left[c \sum\limits_1^c \left(\sum\limits_1^r X_{ij} \right)^2 - \left(\sum\limits_1^r \sum\limits_1^c X_{ij} \right)^2 \right] \dfrac{1}{n}$
ss_w	$\sum\limits_1^r \sum\limits_1^c (X_{ij} - \bar{X}_{i\cdot} - \bar{X}_{\cdot j} + \bar{X}..)^2$	$ss_t - ss_r - ss_c$

It is extremely important that at least double if not triple precision be used in computation. Regardless of how small the errors of approximation might be, when effects of variables are very small it may be possible to obtain a negative sum of squares. As a corollary, if adequate multiprecision is not available, the investigator can interpret a negative sum of squares (or a negative mean square) simply as "no effect," providing, of course, that he has checked the accuracy of the program very carefully and is convinced that there are no procedural errors.

TWO-WAY CLASSIFICATION WITH REPEATED MEASUREMENTS PER CELL

Let us now assume that we have m measurements or replications for each combination of conditions (drug and antibiotic). For the moment we shall assume that the numbers of replications are equal for each cell. Our experimental layout would be as given in Table 11.22. It is obvious that we could treat each cell mean as we treated each single cell score in the case of two-way analysis without replication. Actually, this is what we shall indeed be doing.

If we write down the total sum of squares and its parts, we will obtain

$$\sum_1^r \sum_1^c \sum_1^m (X_{ijk} - \bar{X}...)^2 = mc \sum_1^r (\bar{X}_{i\cdot\cdot} - \bar{X}...)^2 + mr \sum_1^c (\bar{X}_{\cdot j\cdot} - \bar{X}...)^2$$

$$+ m \sum_1^r \sum_1^c (\bar{X}_{ij\cdot} - \bar{X}_{i\cdot\cdot} - \bar{X}_{\cdot j\cdot} + \bar{X}...)^2$$

$$+ \sum_1^r \sum_1^c \sum_1^m (X_{ijk} - \bar{X}_{ij\cdot})^2 \tag{36}$$

Table 11.22. LAYOUT OF DRUG—ANTIBIOTIC EXPERIMENT WITH m SUBJECTS PER CELL

Drug

	A	B	$\cdots$	c
I	X_{111} X_{122} $\cdot$ $\bar{X}_{11\cdot}$ $\cdot$ X_{11m}	X_{121} X_{122} $\cdot$ $\bar{X}_{22\cdot}$ $\cdot$ X_{12m}	$\bar{X}_{1c\cdot}$	$\bar{X}_{1\cdot\cdot}$
II	X_{212} X_{221} $\cdot$ $\bar{X}_{21\cdot}$ $\cdot$ X_{21m}	X_{221} X_{222} $\cdot$ $\bar{X}_{22\cdot}$ $\cdot$ X_{22m}	$\bar{X}_{2c\cdot}$	$\bar{X}_{2\cdot\cdot}$
$\cdot$	$\cdot$	$\cdot$	$\cdot$	
r	X_{r11} X_{r12} $\cdot$ $\bar{X}_{r1\cdot}$ $\cdot$ X_{r1m}		$\bar{X}_{rc\cdot}$	$\bar{X}_{r\cdot\cdot}$
	$\bar{X}_{\cdot1\cdot}$	$\bar{X}_{\cdot2\cdot}$ $\cdots$	$\bar{X}_{\cdot c\cdot}$	$\bar{X}_{\cdots}$

(ANTIBIOTICS, vertical label on left)

We shall now undertake a more detailed analysis of what these sums of squares and variance estimates imply (see Table 11.23).

Table 11.23. TWO-WAY ANALYSIS OF VARIANCE WITH REPLICATION

Source		d. f.	Expected Mean Square Is Estimate of
Row Effect	$mc \sum\limits_{1}^{r} (\bar{X}_{i\cdot\cdot} - \bar{X}...)^2$	$r - 1$	$\sigma^2 + m\sigma_i^2 + c\sigma_r^2$
Column Effect	$mr \sum\limits_{1}^{c} (\bar{X}_{\cdot j\cdot} - \bar{X}...)^2$	$c - 1$	$\sigma^2 + m\sigma_i^2 + r\sigma_c^2$
Interaction of Row and Column	$m \sum\limits_{1}^{r} \sum\limits_{1}^{c} (\bar{X}_{ij\cdot} - \bar{X}_{i\cdot\cdot} - \bar{X}_{\cdot j\cdot} - \bar{X}...)^2$	$(r - 1)(c - 1)$	$\sigma^2 + m\sigma_i^2$
Remainder	$\sum\limits_{1}^{r} \sum\limits_{1}^{c} \sum\limits_{1}^{m} (X_{ijk} - \bar{X}_{ij\cdot})^2$		σ^2
Total	$\sum\limits_{1}^{r} \sum\limits_{1}^{c} \sum\limits_{1}^{m} (X_{ijk} - \bar{X}...)^2$	$n - 1$	

Again we see our familiar division by row and column. However, the part of the effect which is not due to row and column has been divided into interaction of row and column and a remainder.

INTERACTION

If we look at the arrangement of observations in Table 11.23, it is clear that the variations of replications in each cell represent the best estimate of the true variation in the population quite independently of whatever effects are exerted by row and column. Our choice for the best estimate of the true error variance would thus be to take the sum of squares of the remainder and divide it by its appropriate degrees of freedom. This certainly makes good sense and would be the correct procedure.

What, then is the meaning of the term which we have labeled "Interaction?" Note that this term is actually the same one that we used previously to estimate the remaining error variance when we had no more than one observation per cell. Since observations are now replicated in each cell, the sum of squares of these replications becomes the best estimate for the true error variance. If we then subtract from the total sum of squares the contributions made by error variance and individual column and row effects, what remains represents the joint action of column and row effect. Experimental conditions presented by column and row together may act differently from what we might expect from knowing just either row or column effect separately. If this is true, then a source of variation is introduced which is due to the joint actions of column and row variables. This is the component of the sums of squares which we have labeled here as interaction. Interaction implies that the combination of two variables has a much more pronounced (or much less pronounced) effect than we would normally expect from looking at the individual effects. As such, it cannot be evaluated when only one observation is obtained per cell, since under those circumstances the interaction and true variance are inseparably combined.

TESTING HYPOTHESES

By using a two-way analysis of variance design, three separate hypotheses can be tested: whether or not there exist differences due to row effect, due to column effect, and due to the interaction between row and column variables. It is clear that if an interaction effect exists, then at least one of the two variables must exert an effect, but it is not necessary that both variables do so. We can see this clearly when we inspect the division of mean squares into their components in Table 11.23.

When an interaction exists, then the mean square for interaction consists of two parts. However, the row and column effect also contain part of this interaction effect.

Regardless of which hypothesis we are interested in to begin with, we must evaluate the interaction effect first. We test F for interaction effect by

$$F_I = \frac{\text{interaction mean square}}{\text{remainder}} \tag{37}$$

If this value of F should turn out to be so large that we would reject the hypothesis that it is due to chance, then we can conclude that the combination of row and column variables has joint enhancing or depressing effects which can be labeled as interaction. We can also conclude that either the row or the column variables or possibly both have an effect which exceeds that observable by chance.

In the event that F_I is so large that we reject the chance hypothesis, than we use the mean square for interaction to test the magnitude of row and column effects. The test then would be

$$F_r = \frac{\text{row mean square}}{\text{interaction mean square}} \tag{38a}$$

$$F_c = \frac{\text{column mean square}}{\text{interaction mean square}} \tag{38b}$$

In this way we test the row and column variables for an effect that transcends that due to interaction.

However, what should we do if the variables do not seem to produce a reasonably significant interaction?

If the interaction component for the joint effect of row and column is equal to zero (or very small), then the interaction mean square is just another estimate of the true variance. Thus it becomes possible to pool the two figures to obtain a more reliable estimate of the true variance. This is done by adding the sums of squares for interaction of row and column to the remainder sum square and dividing this sum by the combined degrees of freedom. This new sum of squares is given by

$$s_p^2 = \frac{ss_t - ss_r - ss_c}{rc(m-1) + (r-1)(c-1)} \tag{39}$$

The main effects are then tested by

$$F_r = \frac{\text{row mean square}}{\text{pooled remainder}} \tag{40a}$$

and

$$F_c = \frac{\text{column mean square}}{\text{pooled remainder}} \tag{40b}$$

The diversity of choices open for constructing different remainder terms for testing hypotheses has an important consequence for the format in which the results of the analysis should be displayed to the investigator.

It is important that the investigator obtain sums of squares and degrees of freedom for his analysis. It is not important, however, that the actual ratio between mean squares be computed for him. It is possible, of course, to set up a program in which the interaction mean square would first be tested for a given level of significance so that a decision could be made to pool or not to pool, depending on the value of F_I. However, different investigators may want to use different levels of probability for tests in different experimental situations. The amount of hand work involved here is so small that a presentation of sums of squares and degrees of freedom is really all that is required. The investigator can then pool sums of squares as he sees fit, especially when he evaluates more complex experimental schemes than a two-way design. Preferable computation formulas useful for minimizing errors of approximation are given in Table 11.24.

Table 11.24. COMPUTATIONAL PROCEDURE FOR TWO-WAY ANALYSIS OF VARIANCE WITH m REPLICATIONS PER CELL

Source		*Computational Method*
ss_t	$\displaystyle\sum_1^r \sum_1^c \sum_1^m (X_{ijk} - \bar{X}...)^2$	$\displaystyle\left[n \sum_1^r \sum_1^c \sum_1^m X_{ijk}^2 - \left(\sum_1^r \sum_1^c \sum_1^m X_{ijk} \right)^2 \right]\frac{1}{n}$
ss_r	$\displaystyle mc \sum_1^r (\bar{X}_i.. - \bar{X}...)^2$	$\displaystyle\left[r \sum_1^r \left(\sum_1^c \bar{X}_i.. \right)^2 - \left(\sum_1^r \sum_1^c \sum_1^m X_{ijk} \right)^2 \right]\frac{1}{n}$
ss_c	$\displaystyle mr \sum_1^c (\bar{X}._j. - \bar{X}...)^2$	$\displaystyle\left[c \sum_1^c \left(\sum_1^r \bar{X}_{ij.} \right)^2 - \left(\sum_1^r \sum_1^c \sum_1^m X_{ijk} \right)^2 \right]\frac{1}{n}$
ss_i	$\displaystyle m \sum_1^r \sum_1^c (\bar{X}_{ij..} - \bar{X}_i.. - \bar{X}._j. + \bar{X}...)^2$	$ss_t - ss_r - ss_c - ss_w$
ss_w	$\displaystyle\sum_1^r \sum_1^c \sum_1^m (X_{ijk} - \bar{X}_{ij.})^2$	$\displaystyle\left[m \sum_1^r \sum_1^c \sum_1^m X_{ijk}^2 - \sum_1^r \sum_1^j \left(\sum_1^m X_{ijk} \right)^2 \right]\frac{1}{m}$

AN EXAMPLE OF A TWO-WAY ANALYSIS

Let us assume that a treatment condition is applied to each group of scores defined by the five different rows and five different columns of our previous example problems. We shall also assume that Model I prevails and that the effects of the treatments are 0 for row one, -1 for row two, -2 for row three, $+1$ for row four, and $+2$ for row five. Column effects are as before. We then have experimental effects exerted along both row and column dimensions. Resulting scores are summarized in Table 11.25. The calculation to test two hypotheses simultaneously, namely, that the means for column groups come from the same population of measurements and that the means for row groups come from the same population of measurements is summarized in Table 11.26.

Table 11.25. Data of Table 11.8 After Experimental Effects Have Been Added for Column and Row Treatments

Row Groups	Column Groups A	B	C	D	E	Row Means
I	8	3	8	8	5	6.4
II	1	0	9	6	12	5.6
III	2	−1	0	3	9	2.6
IV	5	6	3	8	13	7.0
V	4	8	13	9	6	8.0
Column Means	4.0	3.2	6.6	6.8	9.0	

Table 11.26. Calculation to Test Simultaneously

$$H_a\colon \mu_A = \mu_B = \mu_C = \mu_D = \mu_E = \mu$$

$$H_b\colon \mu_{\text{I}} = \mu_{\text{II}} = \mu_{\text{III}} = \mu_{\text{IV}} = \mu_{\text{V}} = \mu$$

of Data from Table 11.25

$$\sum_1^c \left(\sum_1^r X_{ij} \right) = 148 \qquad \sum_1^r \left(\sum_1^c X_{ij} \right) = 148$$

$$\sum_1^c \left(\sum_1^r X_{ij} \right)^2 = 4926 \qquad \sum_1^r \left(\sum_1^c X_{ij} \right)^2 = 4802$$

$$\sum_1^r \sum_1^c X_{ij}^2 = 1252$$

$$ss_t = \frac{1}{n}\left[n \sum_1^r \sum_1^c X_{ij} - \left(\sum_1^r \sum_1^c X_{ij} \right)^2 \right] = 375.84$$

$$ss_c = \frac{1}{n}\left[r \sum_1^c \left(\sum_1^r X_{ij} \right)^2 - \left(\sum_1^r \sum_1^c X_{ij} \right)^2 \right] = 109.04$$

$$ss_r = \frac{1}{n}\left[c \sum_1^r \left(\sum_1^c X_{ij} \right)^2 - \left(\sum_1^r \sum_1^c X_{ij} \right)^2 \right] = 84.24$$

$$ss_w = \sum_1^r \sum_1^c X_{ij}^2 - \frac{\sum_1^c \left(\sum_1^r X_{ij}\right)^2}{c} - \frac{\sum_1^r \left(\sum_1^c X_{ij}\right)^2}{r} + \frac{\left(\sum_1^r \sum_1^c X_{ij}\right)^2}{n}$$

$$= ss_t - ss_c - ss_r = 182.56$$

The summary of the analysis is shown in Table 11.27. Note that although both F ratios are larger than unity, both of them fall short of a value that would ordinarily lead one to accept the hypotheses that the means came from a population of randomly selected numbers. However, we are not really concerned with this judgment, since we do know that the experiment has had an effect. The efficiency of the design, however, is such that for the size effect postulated, the number of observations were too small. Increasing the numbers of observations and doing the same analysis would yield larger F ratios.

Table 11.27. SUMMARY OF ANALYSIS OF DATA FROM TABLE 11.24

Source	Sum of Squares	d.f.	Mean Squares	F	Estimates of
Total	375.84	24			
Row Effect	84.24	4	21.06	1.85	$\sigma^2 + c\sigma_r^2$
Column Effect	109.04	4	27.26	2.39	$\sigma^2 + r\sigma_c^2$
Residual	182.56	16	11.41		σ^2

The student should compare Table 11.27 and Table 11.15. Note that the total sum of squares between columns is unchanged by the added row effect. If the student would do the same analysis for row effect only, he will find that the row effect by itself has a sum of squares identical to that found in Table 11.15. The student may do this as a homework exercise.

The display of the results of an analysis of variance program may take on many different forms. One pattern adopted by the MEDCOMP program library is shown in Table 11.28. Note that cell means, column means, and row means are given with the properly labeled sums of squares. In this way the investigator not only can evaluate the main effects and their interaction, but he can also inspect the relationship between means to evaluate the kind of effect that has occurred.

ANALYSIS OF VARIANCE
WITH CLASSIFICATIONS IN
THREE (OR MORE) DIMENSIONS

The analysis of variance model can be expanded to encompass any number of dimensions of experimental conditions. We began with an example in which an investigator was interested in the effect of drugs (Dimension I) in conjunction with different antibiotics (Dimension II) on patients in different stages of leukemia (Dimension III). (Note that our variables represent different types of numerical coding schemes. Different drugs or different antibiotics are nominal classifications. Differences in stages of diseases are essentially ordinal judgments.) We could have added other variables, such as amount of drug. In this case we would have kind of drug, amount of drug, kind of antibiotic, and stage of leukemia.

Let us suppose that we have three different dimensions consisting of five different drugs (including one placebo), six different antibiotics (including one placebo), and five different stages of leukemia. If we were to assign a single observation to each possible combination of conditions, we would have

Table 11.28. EXAMPLE PRINTOUT DISPLAY OF TWO-WAY ANALYSIS OF VARIANCE
WITH REPLICATIONS*

CELL MEANS

ROW	COLUMN 1	2	3						
1	25.61000+	22.80000+	42.49333+	0.	0.	0.	0.	0.	0.	0.
2	43.17166+	28.19166+	26.24666+	0.	0.	0.	0.	0.	0.	0.

COLUMN MEANS

COLUMN	1	2	3						
	34.39083+	25.49583+	34.37000+	0.	0.	0.	0.	0.	0.

ROW MEANS

ROW	1	2							
	30.30111+	32.53666+	0.	0.	0.	0.	0.	0.	0.

	DEGREES OF FREEDOM	SUM SQUARES	MEAN SQUARES	F
ANIMAL	2	631.4891722	315.7445861	1.758
DIET WITH OR WITHOUT CU	1	44.9793777	44.9793777	.250
CELLS	5	2435.7983163	487.1596632	2.712
INTERACTION	2	1759.3297663	879.6648831	4.898
WITHIN CELLS	30	5387.1562392	179.5718746	
TOTAL	35	7822.9545555	223.5129873	

*From the MEDCOMP Program Library.

$5 \times 6 \times 5$, or 150 different combinations of conditions. Since an average treatment center may see between 80 and 150 cases of leukemia a year, a single observation per cell may well involve us in an experiment lasting for three or four years. It is thus realistic to expect no more than a single observation per cell.

We arrange our data into r rows, c columns and b blocks (Table 11.29). Where there are b blocks, r rows, and c columns there will be

r means for row summed for all blocks and columns
c means for column summed for all blocks and rows
b means for all the scores in each block
rc means by rows and columns for each block

Table 11.29. ARRANGEMENT OF TRIPLE CLASSIFICATIONS

rb means by rows and blocks for each column
bc means by blocks and columns for each row

Finally there will be one total mean of all scores. We may get a better appreciation of the meanings of all these means if we arrange them into a figure (Figure 11.1) in which individual scores are thought of to be in the cubicles of a $5 \times 6 \times 5$ compartment box. Summing the box's contents in a vertical direction leads to the means on top; summing through the box in a traverse (left to right) direction leads to the means shown on the left edge of the box, and summing through the cubicles in a horizontal (forward to backward) direction leads to the means given on the side of the box facing the reader.

Inspection of this box will clarify to some extent the types of questions that we shall be able to ask of this design. The sources of the variations are relatively clear. Our major interest lies in the variation of row, column, and block means. We also have the interactions between rows and columns, rows and blocks, and between columns and blocks. Finally, a term remains which is the triple interaction or best estimate of the true variance. The source of the sum of the squares, degrees of freedoms, and estimates of the mean squares are summarized in Table 11.30. Note that we have simply broken down the sums of squares without going through the actual calculations. (The student may verify these for himself.)

In evaluating the effect of treatment we start by testing the hypothesis that the lower order interactions are larger than would be expected by

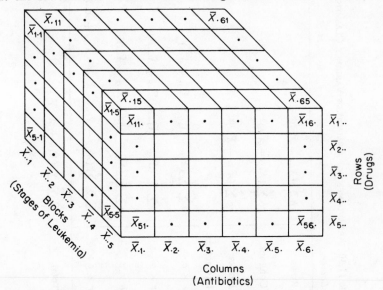

Fig. 11.1. Arrangement of means in a three-dimensional drawing.

Table 11.30. Arrangement of Analysis of Variance Classification for r Rows, c Columns, and b Blocks

Source	SS	d.f.	Expected Mean Square
Rows	$cb\sum_1^r (X_{i\cdots} - \bar{X}_{\cdots})^2$	$r-1$	$\sigma^2 + b\sigma_{rc}^2 + c\sigma_{rb}^2 + bc\sigma_r^2$
Columns	$rb\sum_1^c (\bar{X}_{\cdot j\cdot} - \bar{X}_{\cdots})^2$	$c-1$	$\sigma^2 + b\sigma_{rc}^2 + r\sigma_{bc}^2 + br\sigma_c^2$
Blocks	$rc\sum_1^b (\bar{X}_{\cdot\cdot k} - \bar{X}_{\cdots})^2$	$b-1$	$\sigma^2 + c\sigma_{br}^2 + r\sigma_{bc}^2 + rc\sigma_b^2$
Interactions			
$r \times c$	$b\sum_1^r\sum_1^c (\bar{X}_{ij\cdot} - \bar{X}_{i\cdots} - \bar{X}_{\cdot j\cdot} + \bar{X}_{\cdots})^2$	$(r-1)(c-1)$	$\sigma^2 + b\sigma_{rc}^2$
$r \times b$	$c\sum_1^r\sum_1^b (\bar{X}_{i\cdot k} - \bar{X}_{i\cdots} - \bar{X}_{\cdot\cdot k} + \bar{X}_{\cdots})^2$	$(r-1)(b-1)$	$\sigma^2 + c\sigma_{br}^2$
$b \times c$	$r\sum_1^c\sum_1^b (\bar{X}_{\cdot jk} - \bar{X}_{\cdot j\cdot} - \bar{X}_{\cdot\cdot k} + \bar{X}_{\cdots})^2$	$(b-1)(c-1)$	$\sigma^2 + r\sigma_{bc}^2$
$r \times c \times b$	$\sum_1^r\sum_1^c\sum_1^b (X_{ijk} - \bar{X}_{ij\cdot} - \bar{X}_{i\cdot k} - \bar{X}_{\cdot jk} + \bar{X}_{i\cdots} + \bar{X}_{\cdot j\cdot} + \bar{X}_{\cdot\cdot k} - \bar{X}_{\cdots})^2$	$(r-1)(b-1)(c-1)$	σ^2
Total	$\sum_1^r\sum_1^c\sum_1^b (X_{ijk} - \bar{X}_{\cdots})^2$	$n-1$	

chance. Testing the main effects (of row, column, block) will depend, of course, on whether or not any of the interaction terms turn out to be larger than chance would allow.

As we did in the case of two-dimensional analysis, we could use the interaction mean square to test the main effect if the former would be judged to be significant. For instance, if the row-column interaction effect is significant, this would mean that the effects of drug and antibiotic are such that the joint influence of drug-antibiotic combinations is more than would be expected. Since the main effects for drugs and antibiotics (rows and columns, respectively, in our case) contain the variation due to this interaction, the interaction variance or interaction mean square becomes the correct term against which to test both effects.

However, if none of the interactions are larger than would be expected by chance, then each of the interaction terms becomes an independent estimate of the true variance. Thus it would be possible to obtain a more accurate estimate of the true variance by pooling the sums of squares of all nonsignificant interaction terms and dividing by the sum of the degrees of freedom. (This is also true when only some of the interactions are not significant.) Again we see why an analysis of variance display should show the sums of squares and degrees of freedom without necessarily computing mean squares and F ratios.

What happens if there has been a replication in each cell?

By now the student should be able to realize that if the experiment had been replicated, the triple interaction $r \times c \times b$ could have been evaluated as an interaction term against a new remainder. This remainder would have been

$$\text{Remainder} = \sum_1^r \sum_1^c \sum_1^b \sum_1^m (X_{ijkl} - \bar{X}_{ijk.})^2 \qquad (41)$$

In testing hypotheses we would have tested the highest order interaction against the remainder first. If this interaction had been significant, it would be used as the best estimate of the true variance. If it had not been significant, it would have been pooled with the remainder variance estimate and the next order interaction would have been tested.

From our discussion so far it is obvious that additional dimensions of variables can be introduced into the experimental design and analysis of variance tables established to test hypotheses for main effect, interaction of variables taken two at a time, interaction of variables taken three at a time, and so on.

To how many levels or dimensions is it practical to take analysis of variance designs?

Although we can follow a simple interaction between two and perhaps even three variables, the interpretation of an interaction term involving more than three variables becomes very difficult. (Incidentally, the same holds true for the choice of the correct mean square.) Prior to the advent of computers, complexity of designs was kept within reason. The most effective limitation to complex design is not difficulty of calculation, but the number of cells that have to be filled with observations. This number rapidly becomes very large as more dimensions are included in the experimental design. Since the analysis of variance demands observations under very rigorously controlled conditions, changing the conditions of measurement from observation to observation for the many possible permutations and combinations of conditions make very severe demands on a laboratory. In terms of the need to provide multidimensional analysis of variance programs for a computing center, it may not be necessary, therefore, to go beyond programs for four or five levels of analysis. It is also possible to write a single program that can be used for multidimensional analysis of variance designs. Such a program may not always be practical, because there are wide ranges of problems in using analysis of variance under different conditions which are difficult to resolve by one set of algorithms.

First is the problem of correlated scores. Each observation has been treated so far as being independent from each other observation. However, in many instances such independence cannot be assumed. Repeated measurements are often obtained from the same subject. The effect of the correlation and order between successive scores requires special manipulations in the computation of sums of squares. The second problem is that of confounding effects within the experimental design. There are instances in which adjustments have to be made for confounding variables. (This type of design is generally called *covariance analysis*.) Although some analyses of covariance fit within the general mold of analysis of variance, others do not. Finally, there is the problem of missing data. Correcting for missing data represents severe computational demands.

We shall, therefore, defer the answer to the question of one or many programs until after a discussion of correlated means, covariance analysis, and analysis of variance with missing data.

ANALYSIS OF VARIANCE BETWEEN CORRELATED MEANS

It is very often advantageous to test the same individuals under different conditions because the number of available subjects is small or because variations between individuals for a particular treatment are very large.

Suppose we had r individuals, materials, or animals subjected to c experimental conditions. If we arrange our scores somewhat like those in Table 11.1 (except that now we would have the same number of observations in each column), the columns would stand for different groups and the rows for different individuals. The column means would be the means of all individuals for each particular experimental condition, and each row mean would be the mean score of an individual under all experimental conditions.

Let us begin by considering a limiting case where $c = 2$. The between treatment sums of squares may be written as

$$r \sum_1^c (\bar{X}_{\cdot j} - \bar{X}_{\cdot\cdot})^2 = r(\bar{X}_{\cdot 1} - \bar{X}_{\cdot\cdot})^2 + r(\bar{X}_{\cdot 2} - \bar{X}_{\cdot\cdot})^2 \qquad (42)$$

Within sum of squares can be written as

$$\sum_1^r \sum_1^c (X_{ij} - \bar{X}_{\cdot j})^2 = \sum_1^r (X_{i1} - \bar{X}_{\cdot 1})^2 + \sum_1^r (X_{i2} - \bar{X}_{\cdot 2})^2 \qquad (43)$$

It is also obvious that the over-all mean lies midway between the mean of the two treatment groups, so that

$$\frac{(\bar{X}_{\cdot 1} - \bar{X}_{\cdot 2})}{2} = \bar{X}_{\cdot 1} - \bar{X}_{\cdot\cdot} = \bar{X}_{\cdot 2} - \bar{X}_{\cdot\cdot} \qquad (44)$$

The between sum of squares can then be written as

$$r \sum_1^c (\bar{X}_{\cdot j} - \bar{X}_{\cdot\cdot})^2 = \frac{r}{2}(\bar{X}_{\cdot 1} - \bar{X}_{\cdot 2})^2 \qquad (45)$$

Finally we are left with the remainder term. This remainder term can be expressed as

$$\sum_1^r \sum_1^c (X_{ij} - \bar{X}_{i\cdot} - \bar{X}_{\cdot j} + \bar{X}_{\cdot\cdot}) = \sum_1^r (X_{i1} - \bar{X}_{i\cdot} - \bar{X}_{\cdot 1} + \bar{X}_{\cdot\cdot})$$
$$+ \sum_1^r (X_{i2} - \bar{X}_{i\cdot} - \bar{X}_{\cdot 2} + \bar{X}_{\cdot\cdot}) \qquad (46)$$

Since the mean of any row is the average of two scores

$$\bar{X}_{i\cdot} = \frac{(\bar{X}_{i1} + \bar{X}_{i2})}{2} \qquad (47)$$

it is also obvious that the total mean must be the average of the two treatment means

$$\bar{X}_{\cdot\cdot} = \frac{\bar{X}_{\cdot 1} + \bar{X}_{\cdot 2}}{2} \qquad (48)$$

If we now substitute these results into (46) we get

$$\sum_1^r \sum_1^c (X_{ij} - \bar{X}_{i\cdot} - \bar{X}_{j\cdot} + \bar{X}_{\cdot\cdot})^2$$

$$= \sum_1^r \left(X_{i1} - \frac{X_{i1} + X_{i2}}{2} - \bar{X}_{\cdot1} + \frac{\bar{X}_{\cdot1} + \bar{X}_{\cdot2}}{2} \right)^2$$

$$+ \sum_1^r \left(X_{i2} - \frac{X_{i1} + X_{i2}}{2} - \bar{X}_{\cdot2} + \frac{\bar{X}_{\cdot1} + \bar{X}_{\cdot2}}{2} \right)^2 \tag{49}$$

$$= \tfrac{1}{4} \sum_1^r (X_{i1} - X_{i2} - \bar{X}_{\cdot1} + \bar{X}_{\cdot2})^2 + \tfrac{1}{4} \sum_1^r (X_{i2} - X_{i1} - \bar{X}_{\cdot2} + \bar{X}_{\cdot1})^2$$

$$= \tfrac{1}{2} \sum_1^r [(X_{i1} - X_{i2}) - (\bar{X}_{\cdot1} - \bar{X}_{\cdot2})]^2$$

If we label the term in the first set of parentheses as the difference between any two scores D_i and the term in the second set of parentheses as $\bar{D}$ or the mean difference, we can express the remainder sum of square as

$$\tfrac{1}{2} \sum (D_i - \bar{D})^2 \tag{50}$$

(Note that this is really one-half the sum of squares of different scores around a mean difference from Case 2 in the discussion of the t test in Chapter 7.)

If we now compare column means by using F, we can write this as

$$F = \frac{s_b^2}{s_w^2} = \frac{\left(\frac{r}{2} (\bar{X}_{\cdot1} - \bar{X}_{\cdot2})^2 \right) / 1}{\tfrac{1}{2} \sum_1^r (D_i - \bar{D})^2 / r - 1}$$

$$= \frac{(\bar{X}_{\cdot1} - \bar{X}_{\cdot2})^2}{\sum (D_i - \bar{D})^2 / r(r - 1)} \tag{51}$$

Note that if we take $\sqrt{F}$ we get

$$\sqrt{F} = \frac{\bar{X}_{\cdot1} - \bar{X}_{\cdot2}}{s_{\bar{D}}} = t \tag{52}$$

so that we have also demonstrated that for two d.f., F is equal to t^2.

The same computational procedure would have been followed if we had had more than two treatments. The between mean square represents the variation between treatment means, and the within mean square is an expression of the variation of each subject with respect to his own over-all mean. A test of significance is based simply on the expansion of the remainder term (as indicated previously).

What should have been done if more than one measurement per subject per cell had been obtained?

There are two instances which could involve such replications by the same subject. Each subject could be assigned to a unique treatment and tested repeatedly. In this case it is simplest to take the mean for each subject as his score and treat the problem as an analysis of variance with one measurement per cell. If a number of subjects have been assigned to each cell and each tested repeatedly, it would be best to find the mean value for each subject and treat the design as an analysis of variance with repeated yet independent measurements. The advantage of repeated testing would lie in the improved estimate obtained for each individual's performance. An estimate of variation within individuals around treatment scores does not really contribute to the over-all analysis.

An individual can also be tested repeatedly in more than one cell. Replication would consist of repeatedly observing a number of subjects for a series of combinations of experimental conditions. The analysis of the problems may be performed by using the subject-treatment interaction as the correct estimate of the error term. This procedure permits us to use an existing program for the analysis of variance to evaluate treatment effects.

How about testing differences between subjects in such analyses?

In a design in which each row or block represents repeated measurements of a subject or group of subjects, testing the hypothesis that row conditions are from different universes of measurements makes very little sense. If the question relates to differences among individuals, the answer is obviously yes. We do know that there are different individuals and thus the variance test should yield a value of F large enough to reject the hypothesis of no difference among individuals. There are instances, however, when the population tested is extremely homogeneous so that the variance ratio is not large enough to warrant that conclusion. Should this be the case, then the experimental results lack generality. If no difference between individuals exists, it is obviously not necessary to test different individuals repeatedly, but observations on one individual will suffice. The investigator may be well advised to inspect the value of F between individuals, and if it leads him to reject the hypothesis that individuals differed, it might behoove him to re-evaluate his experiment.

Very much the same considerations hold when we go to triple and higher order experimental designs. In these situations, there are, as before, a number of options available. The same subject can be exposed to all possible sets of conditions. If we have r row conditions and c treatment conditions, we can think of the same subject being exposed to ($r \times c$) conditions. This could also be done by replicating the experiment a number of times by using more subjects. However, this type of design is better done in a counterbalanced order of the sort which we will discuss under the heading of Latin square.

An experimental design in which the same subjects make up a block of treatments might be looked at as a three-way design in which rows and columns stand for different treatments, and blocks stand for subjects. Again the highest order interaction sums of squares would be the interaction between treatments and subjects and would be suitable to test interaction effects of a lower order. However, the lower order interaction between subject and treatment (i.e., mean squares based on interaction between subject and row effect and subject and column effect) are always the correct error terms against which row and column treatments must be evaluated.

If the interaction between row and column effects is also very large, then the correct error term is the subject × row × column interaction or the row × column interaction, whichever is larger. However, it is likely that in this type of situation the subject × row × column interaction mean square will be considerably larger than any of the other lower order terms, so that this mean square will probably be the best error term to use.

LATIN SQUARES

Dealing with tissues, animal, and human subjects as well as with some organic and inorganic materials has taught the investigator the value of considering "order" as an experimental condition. Whatever the experimental substance from which observations were drawn, it could have been affected by previous manipulations. Even inert materials may have been fatigued by previous tests so that the application of different methods of measuring stress must be ordered in such a way that the factor of carry-over is somehow accounted for. This is true even more for organic matters or animal and human experiments. Giving the same person three or four questionnaires may very easily introduce a confounding effect by which the answers in a previous questionnaire affect answers in a subsequent interview. Experiments with drugs have demonstrated that not only may drugs have effects through residuals on subsequent drug experiments but individual experience with drugs may carry over so that even in situations where a placebo is given, a typical drug response may be observed.

It is customary to control such situations by *counterbalancing*. This is a simple procedure in which some conditions precede others in the experimental setup for some subjects or experimental materials whereas for other subjects the order in which conditions follow each other is reversed.

The analysis of variance may be extended to make such a counterbalance design extremely efficient. Let us suppose that we want to test the relative efficacy of four drugs on leukemic children. The measurement obtained after giving the drug could be signs indicating remission. Since there are a small number of children available for such experiments, we shall use the same subjects for all possible treatments. Although it is conceivable that most of the effect of one drug would wear off by the time we are ready to give a second drug, we shall nevertheless counterbalance the order in which drugs are given to different children so that carry-over effects can be evaluated.

Where the four drugs may be labeled as *A, B, C,* and *D,* we could arrange treatments for different children in blocks of four each in the way shown in Table 11.31. The design could be repeated with multiples of four children, each of whom is subjected to the same sequence.

Table 11.31. LATIN SQUARE DESIGN

| | | Sequence of Drugs | | |
Subject	First	Second	Third	Fourth
1	A	B	C	D
2	B	D	A	C
3	C	A	D	B
4	D	C	B	A

Partitioning the sums of squares proceeds in the conventional analysis of variance method according to source with degrees of freedom, as given in Table 11.32.

Table 11.32. ANALYSIS OF LATIN SQUARES

Source	d.f.	Expected Mean Square
Drugs	3	$\sigma^2 + 4\sigma_D^2$
Subjects	3	$\sigma^2 + 4\sigma_S^2$
Orders	3	$\sigma^2 + 4\sigma_O^2$
Residual	6	σ^2
Total	15	

In developing the sums of squares, the program should treat order as if it were another dimension in the experiment. Note that the mean squares are based on degrees of freedom that are subtracted from the remainder of the residual variance. If groups of four individuals are used, Table 11.32 would include a new remainder term, and the current remainder would become an interaction.

There are a number of problems in Latin square designs which are beyond our present scope. One issue is sufficiently important that it should at least be noted. It is clear that orders could be selected at random or in some counterbalanced scheme, such as the one in Table 11.32 in which each drug precedes and follows each other drug. When blocks of Latin squares are repeated, the investigator may or may not keep the same order. This choice is not part of the total analysis, and matters only insofar as a program has to be written for Latin squares that may or may not give the investigator the freedom of changing the order for repeated blocks in the same experiment.

The idea of a Latin square can be expanded. Let us suppose that we were interested not only in the effects of drugs, but also in the effects of antibiotics and, of course, in the joint effects of drugs and antibiotics. If we also had four different antibiotics, we could give these antibiotics Greek symbols such as α, γ, β, δ. We could now arrange our drugs and antibiotics in slightly different orders and still use the same group of subjects (see Table 11.33).

Table 11.33. GRAECO-LATIN SQUARE

Subject	Sequence of Drug and Antibiotic			
	First	Second	Third	Fourth
1	$A\alpha$	$B\gamma$	$C\beta$	$D\delta$
2	$B\delta$	$D\alpha$	$A\gamma$	$C\beta$
3	$C\gamma$	$A\beta$	$D\delta$	$B\alpha$
4	$D\beta$	$C\delta$	$B\alpha$	$A\gamma$

This arrangement is called *Graeco-Latin square* because it is customary to use Greek and Latin letters to designate treatments and their orders.

Because of the multiple possibilities introduced by Latin squares, the program should have an efficient command language or structure to specify conditions for the analysis.

COVARIANCE METHOD

The analysis of variance has an important application in instances where confounding variables exist. Suppose an investigator had divided a group of animals into four experimental samples to test the efficacy of four different chemical treatments that he suspects would protect the animal against the effects of radiation. After having conducted the experiment, he finds that some of his groups were heavier than others to begin with. Since the effect of a radiation protector is measured by weight loss and also since a heavy animal receives less radiation dosage per tissue unit than a lighter animal, the investigator is in a situation in which he has difficulty in deciding whether a particular effect could have been the result of the different initial weights of animals in his groups or of the workings of the chemical radiation protector. Although it is easy to say that the investigator ought to have checked group weights prior to experimentation, there are many situations in which a confounding variable does not appear until the results of experiments are evaluated.

There are yet other situations in which confounding cannot be avoided. An investigator may wish to compare differences in the aftereffects of anesthetics. Let us suppose that he can do this only by obtaining data from two different hospitals in which practices of applying types of anesthetics differ. It may also be that populations in each hospital differ in weight or in some other dimensions. Confounding of this type would ordinarily prevent an experiment from being evaluated or executed. There are, however, instances in which the analysis of variance combined with regression methods may be utilized to introduce a measure of mathematical control.

If weight is a confounding factor, then the contribution of weight could be eliminated by determining the best estimate of radiation effect as a function of weight, then treating the difference between the predicted and observed effect as containing both random variation and effect of chemical treatment. Where X_{ij} is the effect observed on the ith animal for the jth treatment and Y_i is the weight of the animal or subject at the onset of the experiment then, in essence, the investigator would seek to find

$$\tilde{X}_{ij} = f(Y_i) \tag{53}$$

and use as his new score

$$D_{ij} = X_{ij} - \tilde{X}_{ij} \tag{54}$$

Analysis of variance could then be performed upon the adjusted scores.

The investigator would have a choice in finding $f(Y_i)$. He could fit this function to all animals, or he could adjust each animal's score first for the mean of its group and then fit the function to that. The second procedure is, of course, much preferable, since fitting the function to all animals would confound the effect of the weight of the animal with the possible effect of the treatment for different groups.

It is clear that this method is very useful but that no specific program can be made available as a stock item in a program library. The analysis will depend very much on the type of function which has to be fitted. There is, however, an over-all program that makes the assumption that the effect of Y on X is linear. This program has two major advantages. It can be applied quickly and can give the investigator an indication as to whether or not there does indeed exist a confounding effect. It also lends itself to the elimination of multiple confounding effects. Where X_{ij} may be thought of as a function of $(Y_1, Y_2, Y_3, \ldots, Y_k)$, then, as we discussed in the previous chapters, the linear hypothesis is most convenient for evaluating multiple effects.

First we consider the covariance which we have already defined as

$$\text{Covariance} = \frac{\Sigma (X - \bar{X})(Y - \bar{Y})}{n}$$

$$= \frac{\Sigma xy}{n}$$

where

$$x = X - \bar{X}$$
$$y = Y - \bar{Y}$$

Let us suppose next that we have m pairs of X and Y scores in each of c groups. The product of deviation scores for the ith individual in the jth group is

$$(X_{ij} - \bar{X}..)(Y_{ij} - \bar{Y}..)$$

and the total sum of product is given by

$$\sum_1^m \sum_1^c (X_{ij} - \bar{X}..)(Y_{ij} - \bar{Y}..)$$

However, each deviation can be expressed in terms of two components

$$(X_{ij} - \bar{X}..) = (X_{ij} - \bar{X}._j) + (\bar{X}._j - \bar{X}..) \tag{55a}$$

$$(Y_{ij} - \bar{Y}..) = (Y_{ij} - \bar{Y}._j) + (\bar{Y}._j - \bar{Y}..) \tag{55b}$$

In this case, our sum of deviations becomes

$$
\begin{aligned}
\sum_1^m \sum_1^c & [(X_{ij} - \bar{X}._j) + (\bar{X}._j - \bar{X}..)][(Y_{ij} - \bar{Y}._j) - (\bar{Y}._j - \bar{Y}..)] \\
& = \sum_1^m \sum_1^c [(X_{ij} - \bar{X}._j)(Y_{ij} - \bar{Y}._j)] + n \sum_1^c [(\bar{X}._j - \bar{X}..)(\bar{Y}._j - \bar{Y}..)]
\end{aligned}
\tag{56}
$$

Note that only two of the four possible cross product terms remain after carrying out the multiplications in (56), since the other two terms vanish during summation. (Why?) The first of the remaining terms is the within group's sum of products and the second is the between group's sum of products. (We assume here that the number of observations are the same for each group. This is not necessarily true. If there happened to be an unequal number of observations per group, the n of the second term is simply converted to a summation sign for the c groups having m_j cases each.)

The degrees of freedom are $n - 1$ for the cross products of deviations, $c - 1$ for cross products of between groups sum of squares, and $n - c$ for cross products of within group sum of squares. Table 11.34 shows the sums of squares and sums of cross products arranged by total, within, and between group contributions.

We may use the sums and cross products of Table 11.34 to develop correlations slopes, and finally the adjusted sums of squares for total, within, and between groups, as shown in Table 11.35.

Actually the between groups correlation is the correlation between the means of the major and confounding variables. If this correlation is significant, then it indicates that one source of correlation of the total group is the heterogeneity resulting from throwing together groups with unlike means. (Of course, more than two groups must be involved; otherwise, this correla-

Table 11.34. Division of Sum of Squares and Products

	Within	Between	Total
Sums of squares for X (shorthand notation)	$\sum_1^m \sum_1^c (X_{ij} - \bar{X}_{\cdot j})^2$ (A_w)	$m \sum_1^c (\bar{X}_{\cdot j} - \bar{X}_{\cdot\cdot})^2$ (A_b)	$\sum_1^m \sum_1^c (X_{ij} - \bar{X}_{\cdot\cdot})$ (A_t)
Sums of squares for Y (shorthand notation)	$\sum_1^m \sum_1^c (Y_{ij} - \bar{Y}_{\cdot j})^2$ (B_w)	$m \sum_1^c (\bar{Y}_{\cdot j} - \bar{Y}_{\cdot\cdot})^2$ (B_b)	$\sum_1^m \sum_1^c (Y_{ij} - \bar{Y}_{\cdot\cdot})^2$ (B_t)
Sums of cross products (shorthand notation)	$\sum_1^m \sum_1^c (X_{ij} - \bar{X}_{\cdot j})(Y_{ij} - \bar{Y}_{\cdot j})$ (C_w)	$m \sum_1^c (\bar{X}_{\cdot j} - \bar{X}_{\cdot\cdot})(\bar{Y}_{\cdot j} - \bar{Y}_{\cdot\cdot})$ (C_b)	$\sum_1^m \sum_1^c (\bar{X}_{ij} - \bar{X}_{\cdot\cdot})(Y_{ij} - \bar{Y}_{\cdot\cdot})$ (C_t)

Table 11.35. Arrangement for Covariance Analysis

	Within	Between	Total
Correlation	$\dfrac{C_w}{\sqrt{A_w}\sqrt{B_w}}$	$\dfrac{C_b}{\sqrt{A_b}\sqrt{B_b}}$	$\dfrac{C_t}{\sqrt{A_t}\sqrt{B_t}}$
d.f. for r	$n - c$	$c - 1$	$n - 1$
Slope ($y = ay$)	$\dfrac{C_w}{B_w}$	$\dfrac{C_b}{B_b}$	$\dfrac{C_t}{B_t}$
Adjusted $\sum (X - \tilde{X})^2$	$\left(A_w - \dfrac{C_w^2}{B_w}\right)$	$\left[(A_t - A_w) - \left(\dfrac{C_t^2}{B_t} - \dfrac{C_w^2}{B_w}\right)\right]$	$\left(A_t - \dfrac{C_t^2}{B_t}\right)$
d.f. for Adjusted	$n - c - 1$	$c - 1$	$n - 2$

Table 11.36. EXAMPLE OF A COVARIANCE ANALYSIS PRINTOUT*

NATURE OF VARIANCE

		DEG. OF FREEDOM	VARIANCE SCORE
S1	GROUP REGRESSION COEFFICIENTS ABOUT COMMON COEFFICIENT (FIRST COMPONENT OF WITHIN TERM)	2	10.0000
S2	SCORES ABOUT REGRESSION LINE FOR THEIR OWN GROUP (SECOND COMPONENT OF WITHIN TERM)	9	47.5950
S3	GROUP MEANS ABOUT REGRESSION LINE BASED ON MEANS (FIRST COMPONENT OF BETWEEN TERM)	1	181.2000
S4	DIFFERENCE BETWEEN REGRESSION COEFFICIENT BASED ON MEANS AND COMMON REGRESSION COEFFICIENTS WITHIN GROUPS (SECOND COMPONENT OF BETWEEN TERM)	1	8.2150
SW	SCORES ABOUT REGRESSION LINE WITH COMMON SLOPE BW (WITHIN VARIANCE)	11	57.5950
SB	GROUP MEANS ABOUT REGRESSION LINE WITH SLOPE BW (BETWEEN VARIANCE)	2	189.4150
ST	SCORES ABOUT REGRESSION LINE FOR TOTAL GROUP (TOTAL VARIANCE)	13	247.0100

F TESTS		DEGREES OF FREEDOM NUM.	DEN.	
FI	TEST FOR A COMMON REGRESSION LINE	2	9	0.95
FW	TEST THAT THE WITHIN SLOPE, BW, IS ZERO		9	4.43
FB	TEST OF THE DIFFERENCE IN ADJUSTED MEANS	2	11	18.08

PREDICTER VARIABLE X   AGE

DEPENDENT VARIABLE Y   BLOOD PRESSURE

MEANS

	X	Y	ADJUSTED Y
GROUP 1	5.00	8.00	13.13
GROUP 2	15.00	10.00	9.43
GROUP 3	22.00	24.00	19.44
TOTAL	14.00	14.00	

	SUM SQUARES X	Y	SUM PRODUCTS	SLOPE	COR. COEF.
GROUP 1	20.00	20.00	15.00	.7500	0.75
GROUP 2	34.00	26.00	5.00	.1470	0.17
GROUP 3	34.00	40.00	30.00	.8823	0.81

	D.F.	SUM SQUARES X	Y	SUM PRODUCTS	SLOPE	COR. COEF.
BETWEEN	2	730.00	760.00	650.00	.8404	0.87
WITHIN	11	88.00	86.00	50.00	.5681	0.57
TOTAL	13	818.00	846.00	700.00	.8557	0.84

*From the MEDCOMP Program Library.

tion is completely meaningless.) If the between group correlation is large and statistically significant, then the total correlation is meaningless and the correct correlation between the major and confounding variable is given by the correlation coefficient computed from within groups. (The student should recall what he has learned about partial correlation at this point. The correlation computed from within cross products and sums of squares is actually the same as the correlation between X and Y variables with the effect of treatment partialled out.) Next we can take a look at the slopes. If the within slopes and between slopes are the same, this would indicate that different conditions of treatment did not affect the relationship between the major and confounding variable. We would start by testing the hypothesis that the within slope is equal to zero, using the methods developed in the last chapter. It is also obvious that if differences exist between slopes and within slopes then the treatment has an effect on the relationship between X and Y variables, so that we would at the same time conclude that the confounding variable had an effect. We might view this as testing for the interaction between the X-Y relationship and the treatment.

Finally, we can test the difference between the means of treatment variables, adjusted now for the effect of the confounding variable, by using our best estimates for within and between adjusted sums of squares, divided by the proper degrees of freedom. Table 11.36 shows an example of the printout of a covariance analysis from the MEDCOMP Computer Library.

THE PROBLEM OF MISSING DATA

One of the most serious restrictions in the application of analysis of variance was posed by missing data. To understand this difficulty better, we must realize that almost all the models examined so far assumed that the same numbers of observations exist for each cell.

For the simplest case where c treatments are being compared, the number of observations per treatment group may vary. However, this is not true for more complex multidimensional arrangements where sums of squares for row, column, block, and other subdivisions and combinations among them enter importantly into the comparison of means of different levels of effects.

In all empirical science research, it is very frequently true that observations are eliminated or lost. Starting with a group of animals, for instance, some might die; others may develop disease. Similarly, in selecting subjects for interviews some might refuse to answer certain questions or have to be disqualified for other reasons. The total experiment may be endangered unless an adjustment can be made for these missing values.

When replications exist, a simple method can often be used. In a multidimensional analysis of variance design with m replications per cell, we can substitute the mean value of the remaining observations in the cell for the missing value. Then the sums of squares within cells are minimally affected. Since the analysis between cells (that is, between columns, between rows, and between blocks) are based on cell means, no particular biasing factor would be introduced here. Since we have eliminated an observation, however, the degrees of freedom for which the error or remaining sums of squares are evaluated should be reduced by the number of observations which have been so estimated. Although there are more exact methods, this method remains the simplest approach to the problem of missing data in replicated experiments.

The problem of missing data becomes extremely severe in instances where the joint effect of rows, columns, and blocks is represented only by a single observation. To use the procedure of analysis of variance, missing observations have to be filled in with those values that will minimize the error sum of squares. We shall not derive the solutions but limit ourselves to describing the proper techniques.

Let us consider a two-way analysis of variance having r row and c column treatments with a missing observation in only one cell. Where T_r is the incomplete total of the row, T_c is the incomplete total in the column in which the observation is missing, and T_g is the incomplete grand total, the procedure of assigning a value and at the same time minimizing the error sums of squares is given by

$$\hat{X}_{rc} = \frac{rT_r + cT_c - T_g}{(r-1)(c-1)} \tag{57}$$

where $\hat{X}_{rc}$ is the most acceptable estimate for the missing observation. The rest of the calculations proceed in the same way as with complete data, except that the numbers of degrees of freedom for the total sum of squares and the remainder sums of squares should each be decreased by one. The estimate of the error variance is obtained in the usual way. The error variance between treatments will be inflated slightly, but this effect is minimal if the experiment involves many treatments.

A general solution for missing values for more complex designs proceeds in the same fashion. Where we have b blocks and T_b is the total for the block in which a missing value occurs, then the expression for a single missing value is given by

$$\hat{X}_{rcb} = \frac{rT_r + cT_c + bT_b - T_g}{(r-1)(c-1)(b-1)} \tag{58}$$

If there are two empty cells, the missing value would again be found in such a way that it would have the least effect on the sum of squares. For a two-dimensional design we may distinguish three different cases.

Case one is the instance in which the two values are missing in the same row treatment. *Case two* is the instance in which the two missing values are in the same column treatment. *Case three* is the instance in which the missing values are not in the same row or the same column treatment. We shall label $\hat{X}_1$ as the first missing value and $\hat{X}_2$ as the second missing value. For simplicity let T_{r_1} and T_{r_2} be the row totals and T_{c_1} and T_{c_2} be the column totals. For Case one, where the two missing values are in the same row, let $T_{r_{12}}$ be the total for the row effect in which both missing values occur. Then we find our missing values by

$$\hat{X}_1 = rT_{r_{12}} + (c - 1)T_{c_1} + T_{c_2}$$
$$\hat{X}_2 = rT_{r_{12}} + T_{c_1} + (c - 1)T_{c_2} \tag{59}$$

When both missing observations are in the same column, equation (59) would be modified accordingly:

$$\hat{X}_1 = cT_{c_{12}} + (r - 1)T_{r_1} + T_{r_2}$$
$$\hat{X}_2 = cT_{c_{12}} + T_{r_1} + (r - 1)T_{r_2} \tag{60}$$

There remains the case where the missing values occur in different row and column treatments. The solution for missing values in such situations is given by

$$\hat{X}_1 = \frac{(r - 1)(c - 1)(rT_{r_1} + cT_{c_1} - T_g) - (rT_{r_1} + cT_{c_1} - T_g)}{(r - 1)^2(c - 1)^2 - 1}$$
$$\hat{X}_2 = \frac{(r - 1)(c - 1)(rT_{r_2} + cT_{c_2} - T_g) - (rT_{r_2} + cT_{c_2} - T_g)}{(r - 1)^2(c - 1)^2 - 1} \tag{61}$$

Once we get beyond two missing values, the solution of the values for missing observations by minimizing the error sum of squares can still be obtained, but an explicit equation is no longer available. A good approximation for missing values may be obtained by an iterative calculation.

Suppose we have three missing values $\hat{X}_1$, $\hat{X}_2$, and $\hat{X}_3$. We proceed by first assigning an arbitrary numerical value to each of two of the missing values. A reasonable starting value might be the observed treatment mean or the over-all average for the rows and columns in which the missing values are found. Next we calculate $\hat{X}_1$, using the formula for one missing value. Adopting this value for $\hat{X}_1$, we calculate a value for $\hat{X}_2$ and $\hat{X}_3$ in sequence, using extensions of the equation in expression (61). The cycle is continued until such time as the new estimate of the missing value no longer changes appreciably for subsequent calculations. A similar procedure would assign a reasonable value to one missing observation and compute the other two by equations (59), (60), or (61), whichever may be appropriate. This same method could be expanded to more than three missing values. However, it is clear that as the number of missing values increases, the amount of computer time necessary to make adequate estimates in missing values increases disproportionately. The other problem, of course, is the relation between the number of missing values and the total number of treatments. If the total number of missing values increases with respect to the total number of treatments, less and less reliance can be placed on the over-all results. This problem is one with which the investigator must deal according to his best evaluation.

The ability to estimate missing values should not be confused with the freedom to do sloppy experimentation. Missing value estimation techniques are designed solely to solve an analytic problem for an experiment in which, for unavoidable reasons, some small number of treatment cells remain without adequate observations.

MISSING VALUES IN LATIN SQUARES

The same principles are used in deriving a missing value assignment technique for Latin square design. The missing value is assigned in such a way that the error sum of squares term is a minimum. Where T_r is the total in the incomplete row, T_c is the total in the incomplete column, and T_t is the total for the incomplete treatment, our best estimate for a single missing value is given by

$$\hat{X}_{rct} = \frac{r(T_r + T_c + T_t) - 2T_g}{(r-1)(r-2)} \tag{62}$$

(Note that in the Latin square, number of rows = number of columns = number of treatments.)

If there are several observations missing in a Latin square, then one good procedure is the iterative solution described before. All but one of the missing values are estimated by averaging the effect of treatment, row, and column. The one value is estimated by equation (62). The next value is then estimated, and so on until no further change in estimates results. Explicit solutions for two missing values are also available.

SUBSTITUTING FOR REJECTED OBSERVATIONS

Sometimes an experiment may not have a missing value, but one of the observations may be clearly so different from the others that its origin may be suspected. This is especially prevalent in situations where many instruments intervene between the observer and the phenomena he observes. The experienced investigator will very often feel that a particular value may be spurious and due to instrumentation error rather than to any particular effect. When such a decision can be defended, it is fully justifiable to eliminate that observation and use missing value estimation procedures to substitute a value for it. However, the investigator should keep in mind that this procedure is fraught with great danger. Missing value estimation does not substitute the value the investigator would have observed. Instead, it permits the evaluation of observed values to proceed using the analysis of variance design without negating a total experiment. Whether or not the particular combinations of conditions for which no observation was available would actually give rise to a particular value could only be determined by actual experimentation.

A SINGLE MONSTER PROGRAM
OR A SYSTEMATIC LIBRARY?

It is possible to approach the general program of analysis of variance by way of two avenues. The first method uses a general algorithm for an N-dimensional analysis of variance, with and without replication and with and without missing data. Such a model is possible and a number of general algorithms for it have been stated. The second approach utilizes a library of programs and a system which calls out the proper analysis of variance routine for different designs with and without missing data, replications, and so on.

Bainbridge, et al. ("Tabular Analysis of Factorial Experiments in the Use of Punch Cards," *J. American. Stat. Assos.* **51** (1956), pp. 149–158) developed a tabular method of analysis for any number of factors, each of which may have any number of levels. Although this method was developed for relatively small machines which could do little more than add numbers together, the tabular method has several appealing advantages. It can be used to calculate sums of squares for possible combinations of factors and present these in list form. The user pools the sums of squares in the appropriate manner to obtain main effects and interaction sum of squares for his particular analysis of variance table. Since the major interest lies in the pooled sums of squares, the factors along which sums of squares are computed need not even be meaningful and may be chosen for ease of computation and programming.

The major disadvantage of this tabular method is that the user must know quite a bit about the analysis of variance before he can avail himself of this all-purpose program. He must be able to break down his own design into the types of blocks, groups, or factors that can be handled by such a program and then recombine sums of squares in such a way that he can develop the proper analysis of variance table.

Another general program for the analysis of factorial experiments has been described by F. Yates and A. Anderson ("A General Computer Program for the Analysis of Factorial Experiments," *Biometrics* **22** (1966), pp. 503–524). The components of this analysis of variance are developed in a way that is very similar to the one suggested by Bainbridge. The components of the analysis are stored such that blocks can be printed out in any specified order with amalgamation of levels as required. Also, any subgroup of sum of squares can be designated as errors. The program described by Yates can deal with experiments using up to 512 blocks and up to seven factors including replications. The disadvantages of this design are similar to those discussed before. The user must know analysis of variance very well so that he can specify the way his design is to be broken into parts and sub-blocks and how the resulting sum of squares for each block is to be reassembled or pooled for meaningful comparisons.

Another approach has been suggested by T. Sterling and S. Pollack (*Computers and the Life Sciences*, New York: Columbia Press, 1965). It is based on a general linear model. Adjustments for missing data and a wide variety of factorial combinations can be treated with such a design. However, the user must again be very knowledgeable in manipulating analysis of variance blocks and components so as to specify and request proper computations.

But even with the most up-to-date general programs, it is difficult to include the many variations of analysis of variance which are possible and have not been treated here. Thus another alternative may be much more attractive. This is to create a library of different analyses of variance programs for varieties of combinations of factors and dimensions, with and without replication, missing data corrections, covariance, Latin and Graeco-Latin squares, etc. The user specifies the type of design he wishes to analyze and gives a general description of his data format. The system consists of two parts. The first part converts the data into the format necessary for the particular analysis of variance routine that will be utilized, and the second part pulls out the proper technique and does the necessary calculations. The display is then given very much in the format in which it has been described in this chapter.

The great merit of this approach is that it can be used by an investigator who knows little more about analysis of variance than the basic concepts and interpretations. It is also likely that such a system would be faster than an over-all program, since each component program could be planned with optimum efficiency. Although it might take longer and be costlier to program an over-all analysis of variance system consisting of many subprograms, faster running time and more convenient use may make such a system pay for itself quickly. Experience accumulated with generalized analysis of variance programs has shown that users are usually not comfortable with it and are not able to make use of it to the extent to which it is desirable.

PROBLEMS

1. Below are three groups of four numbers each, selected from a table of random digits.
   (a) Assume that the columns represent the results from three different samples. Develop a table of sum squares and mean squares, and test the hypothesis that the three groups are samples from the same universe of digits.
   (b) Add 5 to all digits in column *B* and 8 to all digits in column *C*. Recompute as in 1(a). Compare sums of squares, mean squares, and *F*.
   (c) Test for row effect in 1(a) and 1(b). What differences exist between sums of squares for rows as compared to columns?

		Column		
		A	*B*	*C*
	I	2	1	3
R	II	0	9	5
O	III	6	6	7
W	IV	8	4	4

2. A sample of prisoners convicted of three different categories of crime (theft, theft and assault, theft and aggravated assault) are subjected to four different discharge procedures. Group *A* gets a stern lecture from the warden, Group *B* is given a job in the city's health and welfare department, individuals in Group *C* get an $150 discharge allowance, and nothing at all is done to Group *D*.
   (a) Below are given the lengths of time elapsed in months to rearrest. Test the hypothesis that the treatment made a difference in keeping discharged convicts out of jail.

Convicted for	*A*	*B*	*C*	*D*
Theft	20	12	24	18
Theft and assault	21	15	21	11
Theft and aggravated assault	27	9	26	16

   Are there any effects on time to rearrest due to type of previous conviction?
   (b) Assume that two prisoners have been killed in a fight so that the resulting lengths of time to rearrest are

Convicted for	Groups			
	A	*B*	*C*	*D*
Theft	20		24	18
Theft and assault	21	15	21	11
Theft and aggravated assault	27	9		16

   Recompute sums of squares and *F* and compare the results to those of 2(a).

3. Another sample of 12 prisoners is added to the design in 2 so that the complete results are as below:

Convicted for	Groups			
	A	B	C	D
Theft	20	12	24	18
	24	8	31	17
Theft and assault	21	15	21	11
	19	10	21	14
Theft and aggravated	17	9	26	16
assault	14	16	25	11

Test the hypotheses that discharge procedure makes a difference and that previous conviction makes a difference. Is there an interaction between the two dimensions?

4. Assume that one prisoner of the pair in Group A convicted for theft was killed, so that the only entry in the cell was 20. What adjustment would you make? What correction would you use if both prisoners in this cell had been missing?

5. Time to rearrest prior to the previous conviction is known for the subjects in Problem 2 and is given below:

Convicted for	Time to Arrest for Previous Convictions Groups			
	A	B	C	D
Theft	14	15	12	18
Theft and assault	15	14	8	8
Theft and aggravated assault	12	4	14	10

Reanalyze the data in Problem 2, using this additional information.

The sample selected obviously was of prisoners serving at least their second sentence. What possible sources of bias are introduced by such a procedure?

6. If the student has access to a good library of analysis of variance programs, he may run the examples given here and others on the processor.

12

THE MAN-MACHINE COMBO:
THE INTELLECTUAL ROBOT

We have implied all along that the interaction between investigator and processor consists of a dynamic sequence of events. In the simple case the investigator might ask for some information from the machine (a histogram, graph, or table) and, on the basis of inspecting the printout, decide on a particular type of analysis (fitting a curve or determining a conditional probability). However, the ideal interaction between man and machine is usually much more complex. It might involve more than one machine, or it might involve more than one man. For instance, a number of sensing devices could keep track of the status of patients (temperature, blood pressure, heartbeat) and send a constant stream of information to a centrally located processor, which would monitor this information as it came in and activate some alerting device (a bell, a buzzer, a light) when the status of a patient warrants it. It could also type out or display on a screen the reason why an alarm was given and answer additional questions put to it by a doctor or nurse. In short, the relationship between man and machine may range from that between manager and clerk or investigator and technician to that which exists among a number of colleagues who labor together to bring forth a result or supervise a process.

UTILITY PROCEDURES FOR
AUTOMATIC DATA PROCESSING

The most fundamental form of a man-machine cooperation is through the use of a flexible library of programs designed to process information in a variety of ways, i.e., to describe graphically and numerically, to test hypotheses, to fit equations to curves, to estimate, to search, and to perform the many tasks which serve as the formulation for the scientific process.

The full exploitation of any existing library and the ease with which interplay will take place between the investigator and machine will depend in large part on the efficiency of the utility library available to the center.

A library of general procedures should be available for processing a wide variety of data from diverse sources, yet it is both inefficient and impractical to construct such procedures with built-in capabilities for accepting data without regard to the form in which they may arrive. Whoever designs general library procedures must be realistic about the investigator's needs in formulating and executing experiments or in collecting data from available sources. Data formats are dictated largely by circumstances arising from their collection rather than from processing considerations. Therefore, a procedure must expect to receive data in many different and often wondrously complex formats.

The number of preparatory steps in data manipulations which would have to be included in order to provide a truly general procedure would be so immense as to require considerably more design and planning than the algorithm for the actual procedure itself. This is especially true if a particular procedure is to be incorporated as one of a larger number of modules in some type of robot environment. Although a certain amount of data preparation is unavoidable in any procedure, it is usually highly desirable to keep it down to a minimum and to relegate it to separate routines which can be used as needed.

The general design philosophy behind such utility procedures is to construct them so that they will accept the widest possible variety of raw data forms. The type and degree of manipulations would then be directed towards producing output data of a form dictated by the user or by some other procedure in the system. A number of utility functions, such as the generation of label tables and data summaries, have been described in Chapter 4 in connection with the organization and maintenance of data files and data banks. Additional procedures, which constitute the nucleus of an adequate utility library, are described below.

HOUSEKEEPING ROUTINES

These straightforward but nonetheless important procedures do not effect any changes in the data themselves. Instead, they serve as conveniences which are useful for the physical handling of data files.

DUPLICATING PROCEDURES

A variety of routines are usually made available for transcribing the contents of a data file from one storage device to another. The process may involve a straight reproduction (where input and output media are similar) for purposes of creating a duplicate file (e.g., magnetic tape to magnetic tape), or the input and output media may be different, in which case the purpose is usually to store the file in a more convenient form (e.g., punched cards to magnetic tape, paper tape to disc, etc.). A third purpose for such duplication is that of display, i.e., the transmission of the data from machine readable to human readable form (such as from magnetic tape to line printer or cathode ray display). An additional function is to convert inactive files to compressed forms (blocking) for permanent storage or to reconvert them to expanded form (deblocking) for processing.

The actual form such procedures take depends on the size and type of the hardware constellation, as well as the ingenuity of the programming staff. In some cases it is appropriate to provide separate specialized procedures for each type of duplication. In others, a more general approach is taken by designing the procedure so that the input and output devices are specified as part of the instructions for each particular run, rather than being set as invariant parameters in the program.

FILE MAINTENANCE PROCEDURES

Two basic types of utility functions are usually performed on data files to keep them as current as possible.

UPDATING

The process of updating covers the three functions of addition, deletion, and modification of records in a data file. The most common (and efficient) type of updating procedure treats the complete data file, whose records are assumed to be in some convenient order, as one input source, and the updating information, arranged in the same order, as another. A record or set of observations from each source is brought in and a comparison is made. If the information on the updating record pertains to the record from the complete (master) file, the indicated processing is performed, the newly formed record is transmitted onto a new master file, and the next record is brought in from each input source. If the identifications on the two records do not match, it is concluded that the record from the master file is current as it stands, and it is transmitted to the new master file without further processing. The

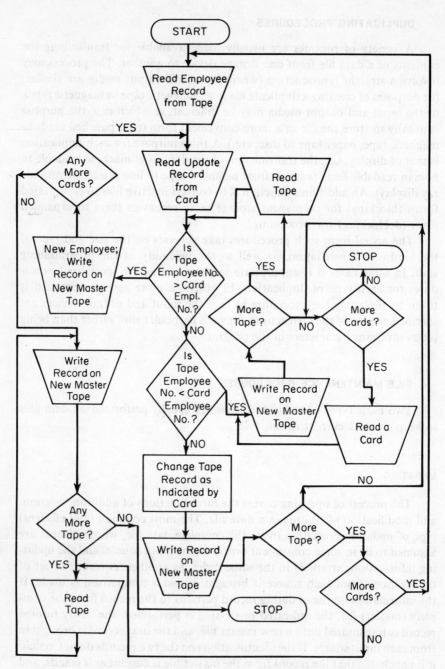

Fig. 12.1. Flowchart for processing example payroll.

next record is brought in from the master file, and the process is repeated until a match is found.

Example. Each record of a master payroll file, stored on magnetic tape, contains the name of an employee, together with various measurements and other coded data about that employee, including his rate of pay. These records are in numerical order according to the employees' badge numbers. At some particular time a number of these employees are to receive adjustments in pay rate and it is desired to update the file accordingly. A record for each affected employee, consisting of his badge number and new pay rate, is prepared on a punched card. The cards, also sorted in order by badge number, constitute the second source of input to the updating program. Processing then proceeds as is schematically shown in the flow diagram in Figure 12.1. The same type of process would be used to add a new employee to the master file, or to delete one who has left.

MULTIFILE MAINTENANCE

In order to conserve space and cut costs, it is a common practice to store several small data files on a single tape reel, disc, etc. When this is done, the physical storage medium itself assumes an identity that transcends the individual file contained on it, and a utility routine is used to generate information about its contents. In general, such a procedure scans all other information stored on the device, and produces an output report which indicates such information as the number of files on the device, the number of records in each file, and some indication of the amount of the device's capacity consumed or the amount of room still available for additional storage.

MANIPULATION OF INDIVIDUAL OBSERVATIONS

It is often convenient to rearrange the observations on each record of a data file. The most common reason for rearranging usually stems from the fact that similar observations may have been collected from many sources by a variety of people, with the result that each data collection group followed a different outline. This occurs in such cases as international studies, where each country controls the collection of its part of the over-all data network. The process of realignment, known as *column shifting*, requires a program which relocates any or all of the data fields in a group of records according to a set of input specifications. When several incoming files following different outlines are to be shifted to some common output format, each file, together with its specific input specifications, is submitted as a separate run.

TRANSFORMATION OF
INDIVIDUAL OBSERVATIONS

Certain analytical procedures may be designed for sets of observations in specific numerical or coded forms. To provide proper input, it is often necessary to change the actual values of some or all of the variables for each set of observations in a file.

RECODING OF VARIABLES

Displays such as frequency distributions and tables make use of observed values that are expressed as members of mutually exclusive categories. When such categories have to be formed from continuous numbers (such as age group from actual age), a utility program known as a *grouping procedure* is used. This type of routine operates with a set of input specifications which identify the variables to be grouped and, for each variable, define the range of values for each grouped code.

Example.   Suppose that a particular file was organized so as to include a label table. A typical input request to a grouping program for such a file might look as follows:

HEIGHT GROUP: $< 30 = 1,$ $30–39 = 2,$ $40–49 = 3,$ $50–59 = 4$
$\qquad\qquad\qquad\; 60–69 = 5,$ $70–79 = 6,$ $> 79 = 7$

AGE GROUP: $< 20 = A,$ $21–30 = B,$ $31–40 = C,$ $41–50 = D$
$\qquad\qquad\;\; 51–60 = E,$ $61–70 = F,$ $> 70 = G$

The grouping program would interpret these commands and add two new variables to each set of observations in the data file, naming them HEIGHT GROUP and AGE GROUP, with the coded values designated appropriately. This type of procedure also finds extensive use in multivariate analyses, such as robot data screening.

MATHEMATICAL TRANSFORMATIONS

Many analyses may not be appropriate for data in their original form, but will work quite nicely when those data are transmuted into another form by some consistent mathematical function. Thus, for example, the values for a particular variable may not be distributed normally, but their logarithms may fit such a distribution very well. Utility routines should be available to produce a variety of standard transformations by means of simple input commands. Usually included are such transformations as logarithm, sine, cosine, square, square root, inverse sine, and reciprocal.

MANIPULATIONS OF DATA FILES:
SORTING AND MERGING

Procedures for rearranging the order of individual sets of observations in a data file are usually designed to operate in stages, since it is usually impractical with present hardware to provide memories large enough to accommodate the entire file at one time. These stages consist of sort phases, during which a number of records are rearranged according to input specifications and are stored with other ordered portions, followed by merge phases, during which two or more of these partially ordered streams are combined. The number of such stages required for sorting a particular file, of course, depends on such factors as the number of records in the file, the size of each individual record, the size of the processor's memory, and the number and type of peripheral devices available for storing various portions of the file. With the exception of the most complex mathematical/logical analytical procedures, sorting is the most time-consuming data processing operation. The time required for a sort on a particular data file using a given configuration depends on the number of criteria used in determining the order (sorting level). Sequencing a number of records according to a four-digit identification number will obviously not take nearly so long as their rearrangement in alphabetical order by subject name.

Another important factor influencing the time required for a particular sorting operation is the type of algorithm used. A number of techniques have been developed, and the careful choice of the proper one for a given configuration can produce sizable savings in time and cost. Unfortunately, there are no general rules that can be applied to the selection of an algorithm for a particular installation. The choice must be made based on a careful evaluation of the available equipment and the range of sorting requirements for that installation.

SORTING TECHNIQUES

The sorting techniques described below represent illustrations of several algorithms in wide use today. We shall concentrate on the actual internal manipulations themselves, having assumed the availability of a logical mechanism which, based on record and memory size, determines the number of records to be handled at a particular time.

THE SIMPLE SORT (INSERTION TECHNIQUE)

The most straightforward type of sort occurs when each record of a subset is brought into memory, compared with those already there, and inserted in its proper place. The process is initiated by bringing in the first record and arbitrarily placing it in the portion of memory reserved for the lowest (i.e., the first) record of the subset in its final order. Then, when the second record in the stream is brought in, it is compared to the first one and placed either directly after it or in its location, pushing it one position further back. Each succeeding record is then brought in and inserted in its proper

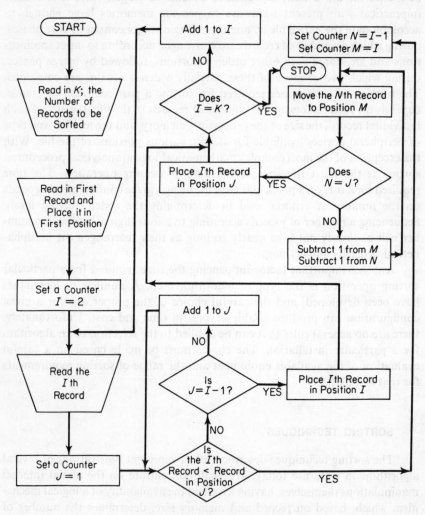

Fig. 12.2. Flowchart for simple sort.

place. The flow chart for this general procedure is shown in Figure 12.2.

A refinement of the insertion technique is achieved by introducing the binary searching procedure. An arbitrary number of records (say six) are introduced and sequenced as before. Each subsequent record, upon introduction into the processor, is immediately compared to the midpoint of that part of the file already in memory. This initial comparison eliminates one-half of the subset. The next comparison is made with the midpoint of the remaining half, and so on until the proper insertion is made. The time savings realized by the binary search techniques become very substantial when the internal sort operates on a large string of records. In general, if N records at a time can be accommodated in memory, then the number of compare operations C required to sort these records would be $\log_2 N$. Thus, for a subset of 128 records, C would be 7, compared to 64 for a simple insertion procedure.

INTERNAL SHIFTING TECHNIQUE

This procedure, sometimes referred to as the *bubble sort*, requires that the entire subset of records be brought into memory before any rearranging takes place. All the records to be sorted are brought in regardless of the order in which they happen to be. A series of operations ensues in which the first record is compared to the second one. If the latter is lower, the positions are exchanged. The procedure continues in this fashion until the lowest record in the subset ends up in the first position, and so on. This technique is of particular advantage when the configuration being used is capable of overlapped operations, since each value can be transmitted to an external storage device as soon as it becomes available, without waiting for the entire sort to be finished.

SEGMENTED SORT TECHNIQUE

This procedure, often referred to as the *tournament technique*, starts as the one described above in that all of the records in the subset are brought into storage before any manipulating is started, with the restriction that the number of records to be used is some integral power of two (say 32 or 64). The records are paired off, and the lower one of each pair is selected by comparison. The half of the subset thus identified is again divided into pairs and again halved by the same procedure. This process continues until the lowest record is identified and transmitted to external storage. Now the operation is somewhat faster than it was in the previous case, because the second lowest record is immediately identified as the "loser" in the last contest which determined the lowest one. The order of subsequent records in the subsets can then be determined fairly easily by looking back through the series of individual contests. It turns out that the number of comparisons can be substantially reduced in this manner.

Example.   Suppose we had a subset of eight records which were initially stored in the following order:

$$05 \quad 02 \quad 03 \quad 08 \quad 06 \quad 07 \quad 01 \quad 04$$

The segmented technique would then proceed as follows:

1. The initial set of comparisons would identify number 1 as the lowest record (first to be sent out) as shown in Figure 12.3.

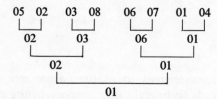

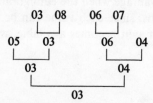

Fig. 12.3. Segment sort technique example, first stage.

2. The second lowest record would then be immediately identified as the loser of the contest in which the lowest was the winner.

3. The comparison structure would then be rearranged by shifting the level of those branches that originally contained the lowest records. The shift is schematically depicted in Figure 12.4.

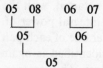

Fig. 12.4. Segment sort technique example of re-arranging branches.

4. A new winner and runner-up are selected as before and sent out. Step 3 is repeated, giving the new comparison structure shown in Figure 12.5.

Fig. 12.5. Segment sort technique example of re-arranging branches.

5. Step 4 is repeated, leaving one more comparison to be made for completion of the sort.

Improvements in the tournament technique can be introduced by using a more complex procedure. Instead of completing a sort on a subset of records before bringing in the next group, single records are brought in as particular locations in the tournament are vacated. If the newly introduced record is lower than the winner or the runner-up, it is identified as belonging to the next subset (i.e., tournament). If not, it is entered in the current tournament, which continues, with a full set of contestants, until all of the replacements are lower than the initial winner. At that point a new tournament is begun.

A VERY FAST SPECIALIZED SORT

When a set of records is to be sorted according to a single numerical criterion, there are some special conditions under which this type of sort can be performed without any comparisons at all. This very efficient technique, which requires no more than half of the sorting time used for other procedures, works only when the numerical sorting criteria are of a certain type and sufficient memory is available to accommodate them.

Example. Suppose we have 467 records, each identified by a unique three-digit number whose value could be anything from 000 to 999, and we wish to sort these records in order according to that number. Assuming that each record is short enough, and our memory is large enough, we can do this very quickly by allocating sufficient memory for 1000 records. Then, as each record is brought in, its identification number is used as the address to which that record is transmitted. Thus, for an example, the 242nd record is sent to the 242nd position, the Nth record is sent to the Nth position, etc. Of course, this leaves a number of blank record positions, but if the storage is available and if the existence of blank records on a file does not affect the outcome of subsequent analyses, then the time savings incurred usually justify this lavish use of space.

GENERAL MERGING TECHNIQUES

The merging operation, i.e., the process of successive amalgamation of sequenced subsets of records until a single ordered file is produced, is very strongly dependent on the number and type of input/output units available. However, since such considerations unduly complicate the understanding of the principles, we shall limit our discussion to a description of the basic techniques involved.

SIMPLE (BALANCED) MERGE

The most straightforward type of merge procedure starts with an even number (call it $2N$) of input/output devices (we shall assume them to be tape drives for simplicity). Half of these (i.e., N) are initially unused and available for output. Each of the other N tape drives contains N sequenced strings of records stacked behind each other. The first string is brought in from each of the input tapes, and this group is merged to produce a single sequenced string of records, as schematically shown on the flow chart of Figure 12.6. This string is transmitted to the first available output tape.

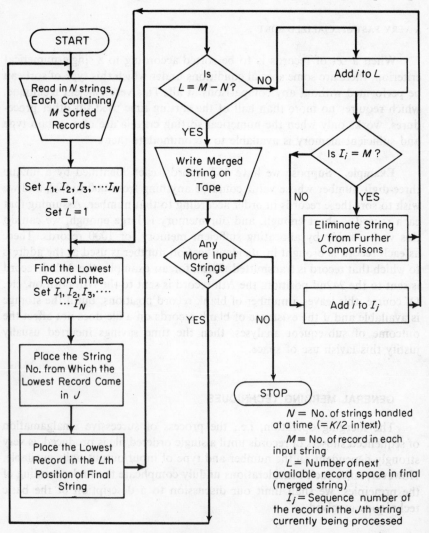

N = No. of strings handled at a time ($= K/2$ in text)

M = No. of record in each input string

L = Number of next available record space in final (merged string)

I_j = Sequence number of the record in the Jth string currently being processed

Fig. 12.6. Flowchart for simple merge.

This process is repeated until all N output units contain data strings. At this point, the procedure has produced sequenced strings on the same number of tape units as were used previously (i.e., $N/2$), but each string is now $N/2$ times as long, meaning that there are now $1/N$ times as many strings as there were before. This process continues until the final result is one sequenced string containing all of the records.

Example. Let us consider a system that has six tape drives available. The sort routine is designed to produce initial output on three of these tape drives. Let us assume further that each of these three units contains three sequenced strings, each consisting of four records. This initial condition is shown in Table 12.1. As a result of the first phase of the merge procedure,

Table 12.1

Tape 1	Tape 2	Tape 3	
3	1	9	
7	6	12	first string
10	20	19	
31	27	35	
8	13	2	
14	16	17	second string
22	28	21	
24	33	29	
4	5	18	
11	15	23	third string
32	26	25	
34	36	30	

the nine individual strings have been amalgamated into three longer ones, as shown in Table 12.2. An additional merge operation will produce the single string in the desired sequence.

Table 12.2

Tape 4	Tape 5	Tape 6
1	2	4
3	8	5
6	13	11
7	14	15
9	16	18
10	17	23
12	21	25
19	22	26
20	24	30
27	28	32
31	29	34
35	33	36

ADVANCED MERGING TECHNIQUES

Considerable merge time can be saved by using more complicated tape allocation algorithms during the sort operations and employing a more involved type of merge. One of these, for example, assigns usage of a system of N tape drives such that all but one drive contains output from the sort operation and only one tape drive is initially available for output from the first merge operation. The sort routine is equipped with logical steps that allocate sequenced strings of records to the N-1 tapes such that each tape contains a different number of subsets according to a prescribed relationship. The merge is then initiated by amalgamating the first N-1 strings, one from each input tape, and writing the resulting string on the single available output unit. This process is repeated, that one unit being used, until the input tape with the smallest number of strings has been exhausted. That tape then becomes the next output tape and the N-2 remaining input tapes are used in the next merge phase, which continues until the next input tape has been fully processed. That tape now becomes the next output unit and the merge continues with the remaining N-3 tapes, etc., until all of the input has been processed. Depending on the number of available drives and the initial number of strings, this process is repeated until the final merge of N-1 strings produces the single desired sequence.

An additional complication, resulting in further time savings, can be introduced by conducting the initial merge with N-1 input tapes and a single output tape as before. Then, instead of following this with a merge of strings from N-2 tapes, the newly produced tape is included as part of the input, so that strings from N-1 tapes are always being merged. The resulting time savings increases very sharply with the size of the data file and the number of strings originally produced by the sorting operations. In addition to requiring some fairly sophisticated programming, the successful implementation of such techniques also hinges on the hardware's ability to read from and write on several input/output units simultaneously.

Sort and merge times are being reduced even further by taking advantage of many new hardware features. For example, random access devices, such as discs, drums, and data cells, are playing more and more significant roles in such operations. In addition, many tape units are now being built with the ability to read a record backwards so that it is not necessary to rewind a sorted tape in order to use it in a succeeding phase. This feature alone is causing some basic restructuring in sorting algorithms (such as sorting some tapes in reverse sequence).

MAN-MACHINE INTERACTION

There seems little doubt that the most useful interplay between investigator and machine will be based on direct conversation between these two.

It should be clear by now that we can create any amount of collaborative substance by building a proper hardware/software complex. When properly connected and programmed, such a complex serves as the ultimate in tools— the intellectual robot.

CONCEPTUAL CHANGES IN PROCEDURES

Any examination of the properties and implications of the intellectual robot must begin with a redefinition of the data processing procedure. We can no longer view such a procedure solely in the traditional context, i.e., an episode consisting of a user request that instigates some type of processing in which the various alternative pathways are predetermined and internally controlled. Under this scheme, any subsequent user action, though dictated by the nature of the output, constitutes a new procedure. The discrete nature of such procedures is a characteristic which persists regardless of the physical time separation between successive episodes. Such a time lag may be very short, as in the case of the user who examines his output, adjusts his input appropriately, and initiates the new procedure minutes or even seconds later. On the other hand, the user may be part of a so-called closed shop environment in which he submits his request and must wait for one turnaround cycle (which may be several hours or several days) before output is available to help him define his next step.

In sharp contrast, the type of procedure provided by a robot complex is structured to allow the user to shape the procedure, and even change it substantially, at various points during its operation. Such changes may consist of alterations in the sequence of instructions, entry of additional input, deletion or modification of current input, etc. Furthermore, the frequency with which the user can intervene in a given procedure can be variable and virtually without constraint, being limited only by the smallest procedural element (viz., the individual machine instruction). Because of this mutual participation, procedures involving these intellectual robots have been termed *man-machine communication, interactive processing, conversational mode*, etc.

BASIC REQUIREMENTS FOR A RESPONSIVE SYSTEM

The concept of an intimate partnership between man and machine arose with the installation of the first computer (whatever it is that may be identified as such) and has been a reality since that time, albeit for a very small population. In almost all instances the use of this mode of operation was restricted to people who debugged programs by tracing their logical pathways directly from the processor's console. This type of process can be outlined as follows: With the program (and perhaps some test data as well) constantly residing in memory, the user allows processing to proceed to some desired point, at which time he stops the machine and produces a display of that portion of memory containing the current results. Should they indicate some error in the procedure, the programmer can then devise a possible change in the procedure, implement that change directly by altering the appropriate instructions, and then manually direct the processor to repeat that portion of the procedure.

Such interaction is obviously very limited for several reasons. Use of the computer in this fashion requires a thorough knowledge of its operation and the basic machine language for which it was designed. Thus, the communication occurs strictly on the processor's terms. More basically, this type of interaction, though most direct, occurs at the barest minimal level. The responses evoked from the processor are results of direct contact with the circuitry. There is no intervening software to elevate the type of response beyond this level.

We can identify the basic features that define the metamorphosis of this primitive interactive structure into a responsive intellectual robot:

1. A prime attribute is immediacy. In order for the interaction to proceed as a dialogue, the user's request must be processed as soon as it is submitted, and the results must be available to him as soon as they are generated. At the same time, the necessary logical mechanisms must be ready to accept and act on the user's response to these results, which may come at any time.

2. Such a system must be accessible on the user's terms, or as close to them as current technology permits. This will require a "language" structure that is "natural" for the user. It is excessively distracting and, as a matter of fact, quite discouraging for a user to have to concern himself more with protocol for interaction than with the proceedings and results of the dialogue itself.

3. The communicative structure must be flexible. A machine response may be required after the execution of only one instruction, or not until several thousand instructions have been processed without interruption. At either extreme, or at all intermediate stages, the system must be able to produce the required response with what appears to the user to be equal ease. Furthermore, such flexibility implies a spectrum of obtainable responses ranging from a straightforward display of results to a complex derivative of those results stemming from further processing, which they automatically triggered.

Note that we are discussing only the technical attributes required of such an interactive system. Economy is not a technical attribute and was therefore not mentioned as such. From a practical viewpoint the speed of immediate access, convenient natural language, and flexibility of communication which an actual user may buy will probably always be a compromise between cost, need, and technical feasibility. Building and exploring interactive systems for man-machine dialogue will never be inexpensive undertakings. However, the control over business, military, and scientific enterprises which is the result of this interaction assures that this work will flourish. Of course, human curiosity will continue to supply the most vital fuel for the exploration of what intellectual promises such robots may hold forth.

HARDWARE REQUIREMENTS

An interactive system needs equipment specifically designed for its purposes. Its components fall into groups consisting of processors, transmission devices, and input and display units that must be able to communicate with each other cohesively and rapidly.

CENTRAL PROCESSORS

A considerable effort has gone into the expansion of central processor capabilities. It is often difficult to identify those features whose development was undertaken with the exclusive purpose of providing more efficient means for man-machine communication. Consequently, the basic features that make the man-machine system possible are simply those attributes that are essential for implementing and controlling such activity independent of their initial reason for development.

The introduction of larger and faster central memories has been crucial in furthering the exploration of interactive systems. In order to build and maintain an adequate logical base for the processing of requests and generation of meaningful responses, it is necessary to supply software structures that are considerably larger and more complex than was previously required. Furthermore, if response times are to be kept short enough to establish and maintain a feeling of a dialogue, it is necessary for much of the software to reside permanently in memory.

Closely allied with the enlargement of the memory is the incorporation of memory protect circuits, which, under software control, make it impossible to destroy the contents of designated locations in storage by inadvertently moving information in over them. Implementation of this capability facilitates the stupendous job of preserving the integrity of information and releasing it from such protected status as the logistics of the procedure demand.

Another contributor to the minimization of response time is overlapped processing, i.e., the ability to perform input/output operations while internal processing continues. This is particularly helpful in instances where the generation of a particular response requires a considerable amount of processing. When this occurs it may be possible to design the procedure in such a way that the initial portion of the response is transmitted to the user while the remainder is still being generated. (The existence of several overlapped input/

output channels employed here is also crucial if the configuration is to support several users operating from several different terminals.)

Since most operating or contemplated man-machine systems are designed to accommodate more than one user station (though not necessarily on a time-shared basis), any enumeration of basic hardware requirements should include some type of priority interrupt provisions that will allow a hierarchy to be established so that work coming in from one station can curtail another job already in progress. This hierarchy may be more finely adjusted in that it may allow different levels of priority to be defined for each individual job rather than for all jobs emanating from an individual station. In either event this requirement is tied very intimately to the supporting software that must manipulate the various jobs and handle the interruptions.

The installation of one or more online terminals for interactive use must, of course, be supported by a full complement of interface components to regulate the transmission of information to and from the central processor as well as effect whatever conversions may be necessary. This hardware, although strictly no part of the central processor, also includes transmission and communication equipment to support such terminals at remote locations.

The entire list of processor features required to support the variety of terminals and interactive software for a man-machine complex include a large number of additional components and features that, however, are of much more direct concern to the designer of such complexes as opposed to the investigator who is to engage in an actual dialogue with them. Consequently, their exclusion from subsequent discussions will not interfere with developing an understanding of the intellectual robot's range of application and possibilities.

INPUT/OUTPUT EQUIPMENT

The immediate and obvious response to queries about an appropriate input device for man-machine dialogues would be to suggest the typewriter. (Our thinking along these lines is sufficiently preconditioned by some knowledge of the present state of the art with regard to signal recognition that we would not consider the human voice.) Despite its very limited input speed, the typewriter has a tremendous twofold advantage in that much of the technology associated with its development is already accumulated and available for use; furthermore, the typewriter is a familliar instrument. A large number of people are relatively skilled in its use, and others can acquire adequate proficiency with little difficulty.

Even when information on a typewriter is generated by a processor and not a human, mechanical limitations restrict rate of exchange to modest speeds. Consequently, the typewriter as an output device suffers from severe speed limitations. This shortcoming is presently outweighed, however, by its economic advantages, which lie in the relatively low cost of the terminal itself and the comparative ease with which a central processor can be equipped to accept such devices. Furthermore, the typewriter emerges as a much more powerful and flexible component if we divorce ourselves from the constraint of considering it merely as a recording device and begin thinking of it as a communications vehicle accessible by both man and machine. (The realization of this flexibility is basically a software problem and will be discussed later.)

The problem of output speed (but not input speed) is resolved when the traditional typewriter keys and carriage are abandoned and the keyboard is combined with a cathode ray display unit. This arrangement suffers from the disadvantage that its use makes it inconvenient to obtain permanent copies of the output. However, in an interactive system the user is interested in a particular display (perhaps with the exception of the final one) for only as long as it takes him to examine it, work out an appropriate response, and continue the "conversation." Since it is the user who ultimately determines when a display is to be removed from the screen, such output is, in that sense, permanent. In many cases this "permanency" of display is maintained with no inconvenience to the course of activity in the main processor, since many cathode ray units are designed with sufficient self-contained memory to retain whatever information is required to preserve the current output.

The interactive user can be provided with a quick and convenient method of input by augmenting the keyboard/cathode ray display unit with a light pen or electronic stylus. The light pen's similarity to a pencil makes it a more natural instrument for transmitting input, especially since the user can literally write on the display screen. Although present light pens are somewhat bulkier and more cumbersome to handle than pencils, it is expected that the introduction of units that duplicate pencils in both size and weight is close at hand.

We spent an entire chapter (Chapter 5) exploring techniques whereby it is possible to direct a computing system to produce and transmit meaningful information in forms other than words or numbers. Without such devices as the light pen, however, this type of activity has been strictly a one-way proposition, reserved for the processor and denied to the user. Now, with this capability available, we can design useful and powerful software that will allow the processor to read, interpret, store, and manipulate graphical, pictorial, diagrammatic, and other nonalphameric types of input in their basic forms, i.e., without requiring the extremely difficult and often impossible job of restating this input in symbolic terms.

The light pen may be used as an eraser as well as a pencil. With the proper control setting, the user can point the light pen at the screen and direct the processing system to delete a character or graphical symbol not only from the screen but from memory as well. Thus it becomes quite easy and very natural to transmit and implement the equivalents of requests such as "Delete these points from the set of input values. Then add these other points, run through the analysis again, and let's see what the resulting display looks like." The discussion on software for interactive systems will reveal further implications of the use of the light pen.

A very imaginative variation on the light pen/cathode ray communicating device is seen in the Rand Tablet (Figure 12.7). The input portion of this versatile instrument, i.e., the tablet itself, consists of a horizontally mounted plate having an effective "writing" surface of 10 by 10 inches. This plate is actually a large printed circuit containing a grid of 1000 horizontal lines of conducting material, each of which intersects with 1000 vertical lines (both sets equispaced 100 to the inch). With the appropriate interface circuits, it is thus possible for the processor to pick up signals at each of 1,000,000 points on the grid. The cathode ray screen, mounted vertically, is used to display the processor's output. In addition, it, rather than the tablet, displays the input as the user generates it with his stylus. Interestingly enough, it turns out that the provision of the capability for the user to write horizontally rather than vertically, as he does with conventional cathode ray terminals,

Fig. 12.7. Rand Tablet. *Courtesy Rand Corporation.*

represents a considerable contribution to naturalness. The behavioral adjustment required to write on a surface and see what has been written on a
screen at right angles to it rather than on the surface itself has been found
to be a very minor one, taking no more than a few minutes. (The developers
of this device have ingeniously added icing to the cake by weighting the stylus
and providing it with a pressure switch set so that the production of an image
on the display screen requires the same movements and efforts used in
manipulating a pencil.) Since all the components are interconnected, it is
possible to display a processor-generated picture, diagram, etc., on the screen
and superimpose additional images transmitted from the tablet. With this
type of resolution the user is able to transmit, manipulate, and display
lines, curves, drawings, or any other graphical information. Should it be
necessary, enough is known about the design and construction of such circuits to allow the resolution to be doubled, thus reducing the distance between
adjacent points on the grid to 0.005 inch.

We need not think of input as being restricted to information written
on a two-dimensional tablet. An independent free-swinging arm whose tip's
position is translated constantly into sets of coordinates may be constructed so that its swing through three-dimensional space will be recorded
as proper sequences of coordinates. This way the user can not only write
or sketch information to be recorded and acted upon, but he can also describe objects that are difficult to portray in two dimensions. For instance, there
may be a need to record a portion of a patient's contour in three dimensions
and transmit these data to the central processor for the purpose of producing
a plan for radiation therapy. A free-swinging transducer can be utilized to
trace and send the information on patient contours to the processor. It is
even possible to build a system that will respond to visual cues. However,
such input systems are still much too cumbersome to be practicable, nor does
the conversation between man and machine really require such complexities
except on special occasions when part of the man-machine interaction may
also be the input information on changes in a complex perceptual field.

Some of the exploratory work on interactive software began prior to
the availability of suitable equipment. Experimental systems, such as the
UCSORE structure (described in Chapter 3), although developed on computers without appropriate terminals, have provided valuable basic information regarding some of the crucial logical components required to support
conversational data processing. By slowing down the time scale and simulat-
ing direct user response, it was possible to explore the design of procedure
modules and the underlying software for providing the user with the capability of combining them in various ways to produce new procedures. Such
investigations also concerned themselves with the design of routines for
generating responses to users' queries and for producing convenient output.

To obtain a clearer picture of the required capabilities of such software it will be very helpful to dispense with our traditional concept of what a type-writer is and how it functions, and to realize that the analogy between light pen and pencil is all right for physical considerations only. Specifically, we need no longer think in terms of a one-to-one correspondence between the typewriter key that the user presses and the symbol that appears on the paper or on the connected cathode ray screen. Because the processor can and does intervene between the depression of the key and the appearance of the display, it is possible to establish any desired relationship between these two occur-rences, regardless of its complexity. Similarly, the drawing or diagram that appears on a display screen can be a direct representation or a very complex derivative of what was drawn by the user with his light pen. Also, in approch-ing these concepts from the user's viewpoint, it is really of secondary impor-tance to distinguish between the user who captures the continuous and undivided attention of the intellectual robot and the one who uses it for fleeting moments as a member of a time-shared complex. (If both are properly designed and administered, the person sitting at the terminal should not be able to tell the difference in most instances.)

INTERACTIVE LANGUAGES

The development of interactive processes and the encouragement of investigators to participate in them hinges around the formulation and implementation of languages that are heavily user oriented. To fulfill this qualification they must allow him to set the pace and tone of the dialogue, change it at will, define and redefine a variety of conveniences for himself, and control the type and extent of the system's responses. For example, an investigator may wish to make frequent and repeated use of certain words, phrases, sentences, or even groups of sentences in a particular interactive procedure and would like to avoid typing their complete text each time he refers to them. Instead, he would like to define an abbreviation (perhaps one or two characters) that will always represent and be interpreted as the longer string of characters (i.e., until such time as this relationship is rescinded by the user). At the same time, however, he requires that the entire string be maintained in or accessible to the system's memory so that it can be mani-pulated, and, every time he types the abbreviation, he wishes to have the entire string displayed. Furthermore, a simple request should bring forth a complete listing of the abbreviations and their corresponding character strings defined by the user up to that point in the procedure. Such a feature can certainly enhance the naturalness of an interactive language considerably.

This ability to ad-lib must extend to the definition of procedures as well as terms. If a user finds that he is consistently combining certain opera-tions in a particular sequence, he should be able to define a convenient term that will invoke the entire procedure. (A typical response to such a definition would consist of a search of the system's vocabulary to determine whether such a term is already there and to indicate the redundancy or lack of it.) In a way this implies the ability for the user to expand the language as it suits his purpose while the dialogue proceeds.

The qualities of spontaneity and convenience are both increased substantially when the language includes commands whose specific purpose is to help the user learn the language while he is actually engaging in useful dialogue with the machine. The responses elicited by these commands are not restricted to diagnostic messages or error indicators. Instead, they may be guide lines or instructions designed to lead a user to increased fluency and familiarity with greater sections of the software structure. Thus, for example, a new user with minimal instructions could bootstrap himself to a higher level of proficiency with a typewritten dialogue such as follows:

Man: HELLO

Machine: I AM READY; WHAT WOULD YOU LIKE?

Man: HELP

Machine: WHICH NUMBER DO YOU WISH?

    1. DESIGN A NEW PROCEDURE (WRITE A PROGRAM).

    2. SYNTHESIZE A PROCEDURE FROM EXISTING MODULES.

    3. EXECUTE A PREVIOUSLY DEFINED PROCEDURE.

Man: 3.

Machine: OKAY. HERE'S HOW TO START:

The machine then displays a set of instructions among which would be included guide lines for requesting further help. Several interactive structures, such as System Development Corporation's TINT, already contain such aids, and active exploration is in progress to determine the directions in which such features should be expanded.

Inclusion of devices such as the Rand Tablet in man-machine systems adds a new dimension to the meaning of the term "user-oriented language" by allowing the command structure to include nonverbal elements. Not only can the user transmit graphic and other difficult or impossible-to-verbalize data to the machine, but he can also ask for certain operations to be performed on such data. A typical example is seen by considering a situation involving two men and a blackboard. One man, wishing to illustrate a point, draws a line on the board. He means it to be straight, but produces instead a nearly straight line having some bumps and wiggles. His partner in the dialogue, however, knows his intent and accepts it as representing a straight line. On a tablet with 0.01 inch resolution, the steadiest of hands will produce lines with unintentional but nonetheless detectable and measurable bumps and wiggles. By a software provision the user can conveniently (and option-ally) inform the system that it should store the points along his drawn line, but not before the bumps are ironed out. The same holds true for circles that are not quite round, perpendicular lines that do not make right angles, etc.

Along these same lines, the user can circle or point to particular por-tions of a display with a light pen and instruct the system to erase or retain the data in that region. Thus, the user, with complete clarity, can issue other-wise vague instructions such as "Take out this line over here and substitute this other one and let's see what the whole thing looks like now." It is unlikely that the user will ever employ such free-swinging language in actual input words. It is more reasonable that for a long time to come such commands as the one quoted above will be in a semicoded form. For instance, the keyed word DORTEN might alert the input system (and with it the processor) that the user will require action on a part of a screen that is circumscribed or pointed to by the light pen. In this case the command might say "ELIMI-NATE DORTEN," coupled with the user's physically pointing to a line on the screen.

COMPILERS AND TRANSLATORS

Adequate support of such interactive languages requires compilers whose level of sophistication transcends that employed in most problem-oriented or other high-level languages. In order to provide the user with the capability of issuing simple yet extremely powerful commands, the underlying compiler must be equipped to inspect these commands and, from the minimal number of indicators imbedded in them, synthesize a rather formidable struc-ture of sequential logic for their excution. To do this, the compiler must be able to pull together a variety of modules ranging from subroutines to large complexes of instructions that are procedures in themselves, as well as to generate additional instructions where needed. While all this is going on, the system must also fulfill its function as a concientious participant in a dialogue by keeping the user informed of its activities. This means that each of these activities must be coupled with the generation and display of an infor-mative and meaningful response indicating that the activity has been per-formed and, where appropriate, reporting the results of that process. When the activity occupying the man-machine combination happens to be the con-struction of a program in the interactive language, these responses take the form of diagnostic messages after each command or statement in the pro-gram. In many systems of this type, the actual compilation process does not take place until all of the statements have been entered and found to comply with the syntactical rules of the language.

EXECUTIVE PROGRAMS

Perhaps the most formidable problems in constructing and maintaining an effective interactive system lie in the design and implementation of the executive routines for its supervision and control. Since flexibility is such a crucial requirement, it is obviously necessary to conceptualize the system as a large network of very small modules, so that they can be strung together in virtually infinite numbers of ways. To make this type of structure possible, each module must carry with it a complete set of what can figuratively be described as terminals or connectors, so that they can be located, retrieved, and strung together in any sequence.

One of the most effective techniques developed for handling such operations efficiently is dynamic storage allocation. Although it was initially implemented as software, a number of newer processors are providing this function, at least in part, as a hardware feature. Its basic task is to provide the system with the capability of shifting sequences of instructions and/or data from one section of memory to another without the user's knowledge. During the execution of a particular procedure, the executive programs can shuffle the contents of memory around to produce the arrangement that is most efficient for that particular portion of the procedure. A major benefit of this capability is that it allows routines that are no longer needed to be wiped out, followed by an amalgamation of areas of core that are currently available so that additional routines which the system knows will soon be required can be brought in and readied. Without this type of capability the only hope for an effective interactive system would be in having a main memory large enough to accommodate all of the software (including the library of procedures) and the user's entire data file simultaneously so that all required ingredients would always be available.

DATA REQUIREMENTS

In our discussion of conversational systems we have examined some of the operational concepts around the assumption that the typical interactive episode involves the processing of data that are submitted along with the user's requests. This is generally true for work with deterministic models, where the amount of data involved is sufficiently limited to allow them to be submitted via a keyboard device, light pen, or perhaps a slow, inexpensive card reader, without undue inconvenience. In many empirical sciences, however, an interactive request is much more likely to involve operations on a considerably larger body of data which must already be available to the system. In order for the interchange between man and machine to proceed smoothly in such cases, it is necessary for the organization and internal identification of such data files to be sufficiently standardized that they can be retrieved in part or in full, moved around, rearranged, and merged with or protected from other files without user intervention. The most effective schemes for basic data matrix and label table arrangement are described in Chapter 4. It is unreasonable (and really unnecessary) to impose rigidities on the user's data collection efforts. Instead, the standardization process can be effected by means of a series of utility routines which examine the raw input data, perform the necessary transformations, and generate the various identifiers and labels along with the reorganized data file required by the interactive software for future use.

USES OF SOME INTERACTIVE SYSTEMS

In many areas the development of hardware/software complexes have already demonstrated their value as active and highly effective aids in generating new knowledge; others are serving effectively as impediments in their users' first steps towards effective dialogue. Some of these structures have paid for themselves many times over in terms of time saved, establishment of new consequence/antecedent rules, or increases in efficiency; still others are hardly more than expensive though fascinating toys, with no tangible payoff in sight. In discussing some of the areas in which such dialogues are taking place, we shall not concern ourselves with economic factors but, rather, focus our attention on the conceptual and operational aspects.

INTERACTIVE DESIGN AID

One of the first areas to receive the attention of users and computerniks interested in man-machine dialogues was the development of graphical hardware/software structures for interactive design procedures. Systems have been devised which allow the user to specify the shape and dimensions of an object by an appropriate series of command words, whereupon the machine produces the corresponding drawing. In other configurations, the user can draw a mechanical structure, call for a certain analytical procedure by pressing a particular console button, and receive a display giving a schematic representation of the stress distribution throughout the structure under specified loading conditions. The interaction then proceeds as the user changes the loading conditions or modifies the shape of the structure and the robot designer responds by displaying the new stress diagram resulting from the change. Although the particular language and procedure set may change to suit a particular application, the graphical/pictorial nature of the dialogue is basically the same whether a mechanical designer is looking at the stress distribution on a complex beam or a radiotherapist is inspecting dose distribution in a patient.

One system developed as a design aid is in use at General Motors Corporation. Known as the DAC-1 (Design Augmented by Computer), this system consists of a large general-purpose digital processor equipped with additional external memory (discs and drum) and a number of special components. Communication is effected via a cathode ray display and light pen, supplemented by a keyboard on which each key triggers the execution of a particular procedure or set of routines. Once a particular drawing is displayed on the screen, whether generated by a combination of machine procedures or drawn by the user, the system presents a number of options to the user for manipulating and altering the display, such as adding or deleting lines and other forms. In addition, several instructions are shown on the screen along with the actual display. By pointing to a particular instruction with his light pen, the user can trigger the execution of that particular procedure. These options allow him to perform such operations as shifting the display to one side; circling a particular portion of the display results in having its scale changed by a specified factor. Additional features are imbedded in the system to enhance the conversational nature of these design procedures. For example, if a particular procedure is requested by the user, its completion is followed by a system-generated message that indicates that the request has been fulfilled. Similarly, if the duration of the procedure extends beyond some preset maximum time criterion, another message is displayed indicating that processing is still in progress.

A number of special components are included for producing permanent copies of those displays that the user wishes to retain. For this purpose, the user activates a microfilm camera. In addition, the resulting photograph can be projected on a screen from which an enlarged permanent copy can be produced.

THE ANALYTICAL ASSISTANT

The analytical and display techniques discussed in Chapters 5 through 11 form the basic ingredients for a very powerful and useful analytical robot which can help the user to string together a series of steps leading to the identification of useful relationships in his network of data. A user looking for particular patterns in a pictorial or grey-shaded display, for example, can ask for various adjustments of the grey shading or suppression of points below some specified value, or can enhance the image by other manipulations and, by inspecting the resulting displays, may be in a better position to locate a pattern or determine that it is not present. Similarly, a curve-fitting robot, by displaying scattergrams of various combinations of variables, can guide the user towards identification of the most consistently associated variables. Furthermore, it can offer the user a choice of function types, each of which can be fitted to a particular set of data by pointing to its name with the light pen or pressing a particular button on the keyboard.

Some analytical robots are already in use, although their orientation is still predominantly numerical rather than graphical. On systems such as IBM's Quiktran the user is able to apply a complete stochastic procedure (such as multiple regression) to his data by giving a single command. The results of the processing (in this case a multivariate equation together with some parameters indicating its goodness of fit) are displayed as soon as they are generated, and the system is available for additional requests. The language available to the user is constructed in such a way that when the investigator wishes to use the interactive system to write a program, it will respond to each statement in that program as it is submitted, producing appropriate error messages and adding that statement to the others in the program only after such procedural and syntactic discrepancies are corrected.

THE EDUCATIONAL ROBOT

A number of investigators have become interested in the idea of providing an interactive system with a set of procedure modules which, in effect, comprise some type of organized syllabus. By having the robot determine the direction in which the dialogue proceeds, the user becomes a student and the machine takes the role of a completely attentive, infinitely patient instructor. The information to be imparted is divided into small modules (perhaps a paragraph or even a sentence in which an attempt is made to contain a single idea or concept). This material is displayed for a prescribed time interval or until the student decides to proceed and signals the machine appropriately. At this point the robot produces one or more questions about the material just displayed, to which the student must respond by typing on the keyboard or selecting the proper answer from a set of alternatives displayed on the screen by pointing to it with his light pen. If the answer is correct (as determined internally by a simple check against a table of correct answers) the machine displays the next module of wisdom, then the next question or questions, etc. Should the student fail to answer a particular question correctly (he must supply some kind of answer to every question), the machine will either go back and display the previous module or will call in an alternative presentation of this information (presumably simplified), followed by its question or questions. If the student gets through these properly, the original module is displayed for him again and the procedure resumes its normal flow. When the student decides to call it a day, he tells the machine goodbye by pressing the appropriate button, whereupon the robot records the student's identification and the point at which the interaction ceased. Thus, when the student identifies himself at the start of the next interactive episode, the machine can check his record and resume at the proper stage.

This type of educational robot is being used in a very imaginative way as an effective therapeutic device for aphasic individuals. Each subject, working through a keyboard terminal, is directed by the procedural system to exercise his cerebromuscular coordination by typing words of increasing complexity. The infinite patience of the device is exploited very effectively by allowing the student to repeat a procedure as many times as necessary. When the student is working on that phase of therapy which involves the improvement of his speed and fluency in responding to requests for correctly spelled and typed words, a very clever feature is introduced by having the system calculate and display the amount of time the student takes to respond, so that he has an ongoing record of his progress. With this system in operation, it is possible for a single therapist to monitor the over-all performance of several individuals effectively, without serious loss in personal contact.

A large number of educational robots are being explored for a variety of subjects ranging from preschool word-picture associations to foreign languages to technical courses at the graduate level. In addition, several physical configurations have been prepared for commercial use and are under experimental evaluation for full classes at several schools. The general effectiveness of such teaching devices for standard courses of study is a rather controversial issue among educators. There is still insufficient conclusive evidence to allow the generation of anything more than opinions, and these range from the contention that such devices will successfully and painlessly produce assimilation and permanent retention of information by individuals where all other means would fail to the claim that these machines constitute an exercise in gimmickry and much of the funds being poured into it could be put to better use by attracting better teachers.

TOWARDS MORE INVOLVED DIALOGUES

The changes in the computer's role from a rapid accounting machine to an informative and active participant in some of man's most imaginative pursuits has taken place in less than a decade, and extensions in interactive uses are emerging faster than they can be reported. Although many of these represent the automation of increasingly complex but previously known and used procedures, others are presenting us with information handling concepts and operations whose effects will necessitate a reexamination of some of our basic dealings with information.

One direction in which the development of interactive systems is being pursued is in the development of software for expanding the flexibility of the machine's side of the conversation. The intention is to reproduce a more dynamic dialogue by analyzing the input, together with the available information in storage, and actually producing (i.e., synthesizing) a response based on prevailing conditions. This is a rather basic departure from most current interactive procedures in which the system determines which of its available vocabulary of responses is most pertinent and appropriate for the situation at hand. In support of such activity, though not exclusively for that reason, an entire field of inquiry has grown around the development of algorithms for analyzing the content and meaning of written text. Some of the findings in this field are proving very useful in the exploration of "ad-lib" interactive systems. One of the areas receiving attention in this connection is the simulation of interview situations in which the robot takes the role of a prospective employer or counselor, seeking to draw out information from the subject by deciding when to respond declaratively and when to prod the subject into further disclosure by synthesizing and displaying a question. In addition to being a most fascinating exercise in complex programming logic, such interactive systems may provide some very valuable insight into human information transfer and learning processes.

More basic and more widespread is the continued exploration and use of interactive systems that will be more effective in helping the user to dredge more information out of an existing corpus. Faced with a growing body of information which is already too large even to scan for a given field, the investigator must presently ignore most of it and operate on the somewhat optimistic assumption that he has some *a priori* criteria for defining that small subset of the total which will be most valuable to him. The present state of interactive hardware and software, together with some plausible projections as to future developments, points to the formulation of systems in which such valuable subsets can actually be culled from entire information networks. In fact, some fairly plausible extrapolations indicate that man's basic interaction with a library, unchanged in form for hundreds of years, may eventually be supplanted, at least in technical areas, by a series of bibliographical robots. The very rapid development of larger, more compact, and more economical memories introduced the very real possibility of storing entire libraries of documents in machine-readable form. Concurrently, processing systems equipped to accept large numbers of online terminals are becoming more common, and the expense of acquiring and maintaining such terminals is expected to decrease sharply. Consequently, there is no foreseeable physical deterrent to the availability of large masses of information to an online user. Insofar as the software is concerned, current work with interactive languages and procedures encourages us to look forward to proficiency in content analysis to a sufficient degree to allow the user, acting in concert with the robot, to guide the latter into producing the document or sections of documents which give him the information he seeks, in basically the same way that robot data screening techniques help the user to converge on the most informative subset of their variables in his data.

As the dialogue between man and computer grows, a curious change in definition of this dialogue takes place. The computer serves as the dominant communication link between an investigator, scholar, executive, or leader and information that has been gathered, digested, molded, and shaped by other investigators, scholars, executives, and leaders. It brings to each of us what man has done at other places and in other times. The dialogue, then, is not between man and machine but ultimately between man and man.

APPENDIXES

A REVIEW OF FUNDAMENTAL MATHEMATICAL MANIPULATIONS

It is the purpose of this appendix to furnish the basic manipulative mathematics necessary to understand the introductory concepts presented in this book. We consider a knowledge of flowcharting, scientific and mathematical notation, approximations through series, slopes and rates, areas under a curve, counting principles, some notions about probability, and introductory matrix manipulations the minimum amount of applied mathematics which the student in the empirical sciences ought to have as his background before he does any serious analysis of data.

For the student who perhaps has had introductory courses covering the material in this appendix in his dim educational past, this part of the book will serve as a refresher. For those unfamiliar with the material in this appendix, the topics are laid out in such a way that the ideas necessary to deal successfully with the rest of the material in this book can be picked up without delving further into mathematics.

FLOWCHARTING

Workable solutions to mathematical, logical, and other practical problems can be stated as sequences of specific procedures. Such a collection of rules is very often referred to as an *algorithm*.

Most of us are familiar with methods of dividing one number by another, multiplying numbers together, or finding a square root. The arithmetic by which solutions are developed are examples of sequences of procedures, devices, and executions which, when properly followed, produce the desired result. The total action sequence or method of solution is called an algorithm.

We do not have to think of algorithms as limited to mathematics. Life contains many instances in which we act according to well-defined rules. One instance is the sequence of actions that we (and other survivors of modern traffic) go through before crossing a busy intersection. A much more complex algorithm is used in a missile launch countdown, to fill out an income tax report, or to light the pilot flame on a heater. In most instances there are alternatives among algorithms which could be used. Some procedures are simpler, others faster, others less expensive, and so on.

Knowledge of methods for devising and describing algorithms have taken on extreme importance for solutions of data processing problems on high-speed computers. The algorithm has to contain only such terms, rules, and procedures as can be executed by the logic circuitry of a machine. The best way of making sure that the sequence of instructions will indeed yield a solution requires a diagram of the flow of procedures.

When a technique is developed for handling some type of data processing situation, it becomes extremely useful to prepare a concise yet detailed description of the sequence of events required for its execution so that others can learn to make proper use of it or to modify it for their own purposes. The most effective method for presenting this documentation is in the form of a *flow chart*. This descriptive vehicle has found wide use in an endless variety of situations which involve a sequence of events. In chemical processing, for example, it takes the form of a process flow sheet showing each major step in proper sequence from the introduction of raw materials to the recovery and purification of final products.

For computational and other information handling procedures the flow diagram depicts the stepwise development of a general problem solution. Since the sequential nature of data processing holds true whether or not a computer is involved, virtually any procedure can be diagrammed in this manner.

The basic symbols used in general flowcharting are quite straightforward: A slot (Figure A.1a) is used to denote the beginning and end of a procedure; a rectangle (Figure A.1b) indicates a processing or manipulative step; the rhombus (Figure A.1c) depicts a decision step phrased in such a way that there are two alternative causes of action (yes or no). Regardless of the complexity of a given decision, it is always possible to reduce it to

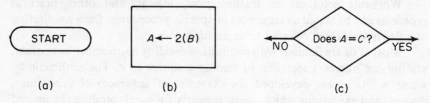

(a)　　　　　(b)　　　　　(c)

A.1. Flowchart.

a sequence of several yes-or-no choices; finally, the arrow is used to connect the various boxes and indicate the flow of logic and data.

As an example of flowcharting refer to Figure A.2 or to the method of solving the equation

$$Y = \log_{10} X + 5$$

described in Chapter 1. Note that the amount of detail shown in a flow chart cannot be prescribed by any definite rules but must be governed, rather, by the individual process to be shown and the intended use of the flow chart. Thus, the degree of detail for illustrative purposes will differ from that used when it is expected that the reader will adapt and use the procedure.

NOTATION

Mathematical statements and outlines for analyses are usually given in general terms. The student ought to be familiar with the notation used in these descriptions so that he can apply a general statement of analysis to his own particular case.

SCIENTIFIC NOTATION FOR NUMERICAL VALUES

Analysis of scientific data often involves the calculation of very large or very small numbers. A convenient way to keep track of decimal point locations is to treat each number as having two components: a convenient-sized fraction or mixed number and an integral power of 10. Thus, the operations indicated by the expression

$$\frac{366,000 \times .0004647}{2,511,048 \times .000009}$$

are much more easily handled by rewriting the numbers as

$$\frac{3.66 \times 4.647}{2.511048 \times 9} \times \frac{10^5 \times 10^{-4}}{10^6 \times 10^{-6}} = \frac{3.66 \times 4.647}{2.511048 \times 9} \times 10^1$$

On computers, this is more than a convenience. By partitioning numbers in this manner it becomes possible to extend the range of magnitudes which can be handled, and many processors are actually organized to do calculations in this manner automatically. Numbers expressed this way are termed *floating point numbers*, and operations on them are classified as *floating point arithmetic*.

Many people have found it useful and convenient to report as well as calculate numerical results in this form. When used for display, this is called *scientific notation*. The following forms are all equivalent:

$$24{,}713 = 2.4713 \times 10^4 = .24713 \times 10^5 = .24713 + 05 = .24713E5$$

LABELS AND SUBSCRIPTS

Numbers or judgments that are variable (that is, may take on a range of values) are usually indicated by such letters as X, Y, or Z. We shall use lower case letters such as a, b, c to indicate constants (that is, numbers which will remain unchanged regardless of the conditions of measurement). It is also usual to use Greek letters for "true" values or parameters, and the corresponding English letters for estimates of these true parameters (e.g., s is an estimate of σ).

The student should keep in mind that he has ultimate freedom in labeling. He may be accustomed to computer programming conventions that allow multicharacter labels, such as TIME or RATE2. We shall use single letters for all labels here.

Observations to be analyzed are usually arranged in arrays of numbers and subscripts are used to distinguish between different observations of variables in such arrays. The symbol X_1 refers to the first observation of the variable to which we have given the label X. More generally, X_i refers to the ith observation of the variable labeled X. The symbol a_3 may mean the third coefficient or constant, and b_i may mean the ith coefficient labeled b.

A variable may have more than one referent. For instance, if X is the answer to a questionnaire item asked of males and females in various social classes, we would have to know two things (sex and class) to identify a particular X uniquely. Assuming six classes and two sexes, we can arrange the combination of class and sex in a matrix consisting of two rows and six columns:

Social Class

	I	II	III	IV	V	VI
M	X_{11}	X_{12}	X_{13}	X_{14}	X_{15}	X_{16}
F	X_{21}	X_{22}	X_{23}	X_{24}	X_{25}	X_{26}

The symbol X_{23} represents the answer given by the female in Class III, X_{15} stands for the reply of the man in Class V, and so on. If more than one individual of a given sex and class respond, the subscripts are enlarged to differentiate between individuals. Thus, X_{152} would uniquely identify the second male in Class V, etc. More generally, X_{ijk} would refer to the reply of the kth individual in the ith row of the jth column. Any number of additional subscripts can be used in this manner to delineate other attributes. For example, the element X_{ijkm} could mean the response given by informant k in the ith row and jth column when queried for the mth time.

SUMMATION

It is a usual practice to make many observations. Although varied operations can be performed on them, they almost always entail summing procedures. The symbol for this operation is one of the most important shorthand notations we will use:

$$\sum_{i=1}^{N} X_i \tag{1}$$

The symbol $\sum$ stands for the operation of "adding together." The exact meaning of expression (1) is: "Add together all measurements to which the label X has been given. Start with that that is subscripted 1 and continue until you come to the Nth instance." The equivalent longhand statement would be as below:

$$\sum_{i=1}^{N} X_i = (X_1 + X_2 + \cdots + X_i + \cdots + X_n) \tag{2}$$

which can also be written $\sum_{1 \leq i \leq N} X_i$ or $\sum_{i} X_i$ or simply $\sum X_i$. In the last two cases the set of values that i may assume is presumed to be clear from the context.

Summing need not start with the first observation nor end with the last. It is perfectly permissible to sum only a small number of items from a total population

$$\sum_{d=5}^{22} X_d = (X_5 + X_6 + \cdots + X_d + \cdots + X_{22}) \tag{3}$$

In this case we add together all values of X that are subscripted from 5 to 22. The segment to be summed can also be stated very generally as

$$\sum_{i \leq k} X_t = (X_1 + X_2 + \cdots + X_t + \cdots + X_k) \tag{4}$$

This means, "Sum all values of X_t for which t is smaller than k." This is not the same as adding all values of X which are smaller than a given number, or

$$\sum (X < P) \tag{5}$$

This statement means, "Add all values of X which are smaller than P regardless of their subscript."

Use of Σ as a shorthand symbol in conjunction with subscripts or powers is accompanied by simple common sense. A sum of squares will be written as follows:

$$\sum_{i=1}^{c} X_i^2 = X_1^2 + X_2^2 + \cdots + X_i^2 + \cdots + X_c^2 \tag{6}$$

On the other hand, the sum squared would be written

$$\left(\sum_{i=1}^{c} X_i\right)^2 = [X_1 + X_2 + \cdots + X_i + \cdots + X_c]^2 \tag{7}$$

There is a simple rule that can be derived for adding or summing a constant. If the constant a is added N times, the result is the same as the product of Na:

$$\sum^{N} a = \overset{N\ \text{times}}{a + a + \cdots + a} = Na \tag{8}$$

If variable numbers are multiplied by a constant and summed, we can write the result as

$$\sum_{i=1}^{r} aX_i = aX_1 + aX_2 + \cdots + aX_i + \cdots + aX_r$$

$$= a[X_1 + X_2 + \cdots + X_i + \cdots + X_r]$$

$$= a\sum_{i=1}^{r} X_i \tag{9}$$

If a constant is to be added or subtracted from a variable quantity each time, we can write this as

$$\sum_{i=1}^{c} (X_i \pm a)$$

$$= [(X_1 + X_2 + \cdots + X_i + \cdots + X_c) \pm (a + a + a + \cdots + a)]$$

$$= \sum_{i=1}^{c} X_i \pm ca \tag{10}$$

Sometimes it is the coefficient rather than the variable that is subscripted. Also it may be that for each power of the variable quantity there exists a different constant. If we wish to sum over a series having different powers of a variable and different constants, we would write this as

$$\text{Sum of series} = a_0 + a_1 X + a_2 X^2 + \cdots + a_c X^c + \cdots + a_n X^n$$

$$= \sum_{c=0}^{c=n} a_c X^c \tag{11}$$

This series is called a polynomial expansion, and we will find it to be of great use later on.

If we add different variables together, then the sum of the sum of the variables can be written as

$$\sum_{i=1}^{N} (X_i + Y_i + \cdots + Z_i) = \sum_{i=1}^{N} X_i + \sum_{i=1}^{N} Y_i + \cdots + \sum_{i=1}^{N} Z_i \qquad (12)$$

This formula is very important and is sometimes referred to as the *distributive law*.

The same or similar law does not hold for products.

$$\sum_{i=1}^{N} X_i Y_i \neq \sum_{i=1}^{N} X_i \sum_{i=1}^{N} Y_i \qquad (13)$$

However, we can write an expanded term, taking advantage of the distributive law.

$$\sum_{i=1}^{k} (X_i - a)(Y_i - b) = \sum_{i=1}^{k} [X_i Y_i - bX_i - aY_i + ab]$$

$$= \sum_{i=1}^{k} X_i Y_i - b \sum_{i=1}^{k} X_i - a \sum_{i=1}^{k} Y_i + kab \qquad (14)$$

If a variable is referenced by more than one subscript and we wish to sum for more than one classification, we use a double summation sign.

$$\sum_{i=1}^{r} \sum_{j=1}^{c} X_{ij} = X_{11} + X_{12} + \cdots + X_{1c} + X_{21} + X_{22} + \cdots$$

$$+ X_{2c} + \cdots + X_{r1} + X_{r2} + \cdots + X_{rc} \qquad (15)$$

This expression means that we sum all X's which have their first subscript from 1 to r and their second subscript from 1 to c. This can also be written $\sum_{i,j} X_{ij}$ or $\sum_{\substack{1 \leq i \leq r \\ 1 \leq j \leq c}} X_{ij}$. The summation sign can be used similarly if each variable is referenced to more than two categories.

For double and higher order summation signs, the distributive law holds as before, and so do the manipulations with constants.

PRODUCTS

The upper case pi (Π) has been adopted as a shorthand notation for products, its use being analogous to that of Σ for sums:

$$\prod_{i=1}^{n} X_i = X_1(X_2)(X_3)(X_4)(X_5) \cdots (X_n) \qquad (16)$$

If b is a constant, the expression

$$\prod_{i=1}^{i=n} bX_i = b^n \prod_{i=1}^{i=n} X_i \qquad (17)$$

FACTORIALS

In the derivation of many useful mathematical expressions, one frequently develops quantities of the general type

$$1\,(2)\,(3)\,(4)\,\cdots\,(a-1)a \qquad (18)$$

Since this is quite commonly encountered, a convenient short form has been adopted to denote it:

$$1\,(2)\,(3)\,(4)\,\cdots\,(a-1)a = a! \qquad \text{or sometimes also as A} \qquad (19)$$

When factorials appear as ratios, we can state a general rule to the effect that

$$\text{if } a > b, \qquad \frac{a!}{b!} = a(a-1)(a-2)\cdots(b+1) \qquad (20)$$

To provide consistency in dealing with factorials, the convention has been adopted (not derived) that $0! = 1$.

BINOMIAL COEFFICIENTS

Another useful notation is the symbol

$$\binom{n}{r} = \frac{n!}{r!(n-r)!} = \frac{n(n-1)(n-2)\cdots(n-r+1)}{r(r-1)\cdots 2\cdot 1} \qquad (21)$$

This quantity is called the nth binomial coefficient of degree r, since it is the coefficient of the term of degree r in the expansion of the binomial $(X+1)$ to the nth power. That is,

$$(X+1)^n = X^n + nX^{n-1} + \frac{n(n-1)}{2}X^{n-2} + \cdots + \binom{n}{r}X^r + \cdots + 1$$

$$= \sum_{i=0}^{n} \binom{n}{i} X^i \qquad (22)$$

Notice that $2^n = (1+1)^n = \sum_{i=0}^{n} \binom{n}{i}$.

APPROXIMATIONS BY POLYNOMIAL EXPANSIONS

Polynomial expansions are very often used in scientific work because they are the simplest method of approximating a function. Any continuous function on a finite interval $[a, b]$ can be approximated as closely as one wishes by a polynomial expansion of high enough degree, and in some cases an exact match can be obtained. In other cases it can be made to approximate the function with an error or remainder as small as desired.

A polynomial expansion has been defined before (11) as a series of the form

$$a_0 + a_1 X + a_2 X^2 + \cdots + a_i X^i + \cdots + a_n X^n$$

in which

$$\sum_{i=0}^{n} a_i X^i = \text{SUM}$$

We now assume that with the proper choice of coefficients and using a sufficiently large number of powers of X, any value of a function may be approximated by SUM. There are a number of ways to find the proper values. We shall look at some of the most common as well as simple procedures.

METHOD OF UNDETERMINED COEFFICIENTS

We shall start off by finding the value of $\sum_{D=1}^{D=K} D$, where K is an integer greater than zero. The quantity $\sum_{D=1}^{D=K} D$ is, of course, the arithmetical progression $1 + 2 + 3 + 4 \cdots + K$. Let us denote $\sum_{D=1}^{K} D$ by $S(K)$. We wish to find a closed formula for $S(K)$—that is an expression which has the same form for all values of K. We notice that for all K's

$$S(K + 1) - S(K) = K + 1 \tag{23}$$

Now let $F(K)$ denote the closed formula we seek and suppose F has the form

$$F(K) = \sum_{i=0}^{n} a_i K^i = a_0 + a_1 K + a_2 K^2 + \cdots + a_n K^n \tag{24}$$

Then $F(X)$ is a polynomial expression; and if $x = K$ an integer, then $F(K) = S(K)$. Also $H(X) = F(X + 1) - F(X) - (X + 1)$ is a polynomial expression and for each integer K, $H(K) = 0$ by the remarks above. But any polynomial of degree n has only n roots (i.e., values of x such that the polynomial is zero), so $H(X)$ must be the zero polynomial, or for all X

$$F(X + 1) - F(X) = X + 1 \tag{25}$$

Recalling that $F(X) = \sum_{i=0}^{n} a_i X^i$, we compute

$$F(X + 1) - F(X) = \sum_{i=1}^{n} a_i[(X + 1)^i - (X)^i] = X + 1$$

Using the binomial expansion, we get

$$X + 1 = \sum_{i \geq 1} a_i(\sum_{j < i} \binom{i}{j} X^j) \qquad 0 = a_{n+1} = a_{n+2} = \sum_{j \geq 0} X^j(\sum_{i > j} \binom{i}{j} a_i) \tag{26}$$

If we put $b_j = \sum_{i > j} \binom{i}{j} a_i$ and observe that $0 = b_n = b_{n+1} = b_{n+2} = \cdots$, we see that $X + 1 = \sum_{j=0}^{n} b_j X^j$ and hence

$$b_0 = b_1 = 1, \qquad b_2 = b_3 = \cdots = b_{n-1} = 0$$

Writing out these equations, we have

$$b_0 = 1 = a_1 + a_2 + a_3 + \cdots + a_n \tag{27a}$$

$$b_1 = 1 = \qquad 2a_2 + 3a_3 + \cdots + na_n \tag{27b}$$

$$b_2 = 0 = \qquad\qquad 3a_3 + \cdots + \binom{n}{2} a_n \tag{27c}$$

$$\cdots$$

$$b_{n-1} = 0 = \qquad\qquad\qquad\qquad \binom{n}{n-1} a_n \tag{27d}$$

Thus

$$a_n = a_{n-1} = \cdots = a_3 = 0$$

and we have

$$a_1 + a_2 = 1 \tag{28a}$$

$$2a_2 = 1 \tag{28b}$$

or

$$a_1 = a_2 = \tfrac{1}{2}$$

Thus we get

$$F(X) = a_0 + \tfrac{1}{2}X + \tfrac{1}{2}X^2 \tag{29}$$

What we know so far is that if such an expression exists it must have this form. We must now check that F indeed satisfies

$$F(K) = S(K) \qquad \text{for all integers } K$$

We must have

$$1 = F(1) = a_0 + \tfrac{1}{2} + \tfrac{1}{2}, \quad \text{so} \quad a_0 = 0$$

Now since both S and F satisfy the relationship

$$F(K+1) - F(K) = K + 1$$

we know that $F(K) = S(K)$ for all K. Thus we have

$$\sum_{D=1}^{K} D = \tfrac{1}{2}K + \tfrac{1}{2}K^2 = \frac{K(K+1)}{2} \tag{30}$$

The student is probably already aware that we can derive this formula much more easily by the following counting argument:

Consider $\sum_{D=1}^{K} D = S(K)$ and a $K \times K$ checkerboard in which the total number of shaded squares is precisely $S(K)$. But the total number of unshaded squares is $S(K-1) = S(K) - K$.

Thus $S(K) + S(K) - K = K^2$, the total number of squares, so $S(K) = (K^2 + K)/2 = [K(K+1)]/2$.

The reason for giving this longer, more difficult argument is to introduce the student to a new method by applying it to an example which is already familiar.

The student should attempt to use the same technique to obtain the formula

$$\sum_{D=1}^{K} D^2 = \frac{K(K+1)(2K+1)}{6}$$

Let us take a number of simple examples of how we can use the power of expansion to estimate the value of a function. Let

$$f(X) = \sqrt{X}$$

We wish to find a method to approximate this function.

We saw before that

$$\sum_{D=1}^{D=X} D = \frac{X(X+1)}{2}$$

From this it follows that

$$\sum_{D=1}^{D=X} (2D-1) = 2\sum_{D=1}^{D=X} D - X$$

$$= \frac{2X(X+1)}{2} - X$$

$$= X^2 + X - X = X^2 \qquad (31)$$

This means that X^2 can be approximated by a series

$$X^2 = [1 + 3 + 5 + \cdots + (2X-1)] \qquad (32)$$

or that the sum of the first X odd integers equals X^2. In order, then, to find the square root of X^2 we merely need to count the number of odd integers that add up to this amount. Thus, we will find the square root of 25 by adding up how many odd integers starting with 1 are needed to obtain 25.

$$25 = 1 + 3 + 5 + 7 + 9$$

and hence $\sqrt{25} = 5$.

Though this method might seem more laborious than finding a square root by the usual trial and error method, it turns out to be a very quick and easy way of writing a program that will let a computer find a square root.

Procedures by which calculations are performed automatically have to be based on precise rules. It often turns out that rules that are very easy for man to follow are difficult, if not impossible, to implement on computers. Such actions as "guessing" or "recognizing a pattern," which come naturally to man's sensorium, represent some of the most difficult actions to duplicate automatically. On the other hand, many laborious and time-consuming trial and error or iterative methods that are generally eschewed by man are simple matters for computers.

An excellent example of the use of iterative trial and error techniques can be based on the proposition credited to Newton that if the right answer is selected for the square root of N, then

$$\frac{N}{\sqrt{N}} = \sqrt{N} \qquad (33)$$

which means that if we divide the number N by its square root (or a close approximation of it) then the quotient would be precisely the same as the divisor (or a close approximation of it). To find the square root by one automatic method, we would proceed by the algorithm flowcharted in Figure A.2. This iterative method will enable a computer to converge very quickly on the square root of any number to any desired degree of accuracy. The tremendous speed of the machine makes this iterative method practicable. The simplicity with which it can be programmed makes it highly desirable.

Note that there are different iterative procedures possible, all based on the basic proposition in (33). For instance, we could simply take our number N and start dividing it first by 1, then by 2, then by 3, and so on until we have reached the desired square root. Obviously, this type of

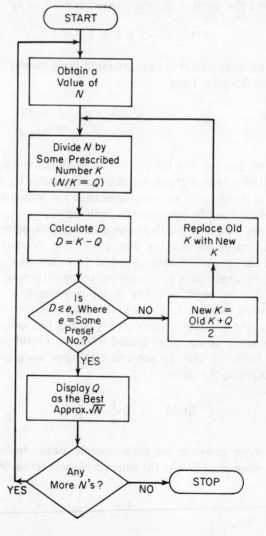

A.2. Flowchart for square root procedure.

situation will always take longer than the one outlined before. We can shorten the number of iterations needed in our method by letting the program take a "guess" at the first divisor. (We leave it for the student to think of rules for such guesses.)

What are we to do, however, if $\sqrt{X}$ is not a rational number (that is, if the square root is not an integer, such as $\sqrt{2}$ or $\sqrt{5}$)? Although we cannot find the exact value of the square root, we can use a series or iteration to obtain a reasonably good approximation. Let us say that we want to find $\sqrt{2}$. Instead of approximating $\sqrt{2}$ we will approximate $\sqrt{200}$, which can be written $10\sqrt{2}$, and then move the decimal. To find $\sqrt{200}$ we find the number of odd integers needed to add up to 200.

$$200 \cong 1 + 3 + 5 + 7 + 9 + \cdots + 27 = 196$$

The quantity $\sqrt{200}$ is approximated fairly closely by the sum of the first 14 odd integers. Thus,

$$\sqrt{200} = 10\sqrt{2} \approx 14$$

$$\sqrt{2} \approx 1.4$$

We can see that the error of approximation may be reduced by finding $\sqrt{20,000} = 100\sqrt{2}$ and decreased even further by using $\sqrt{2,000,000}/1000$.

In deciding on an iterative method for finding a numerical answer, two problems must be satisfactorily analyzed.

The first one concerns the accuracy and precision of the results. We have seen before that the precision of our iterative procedure would vary if we were to use our method to find the square root of 2, $10\sqrt{2}$, or $100\sqrt{2}$. The next question is, how many iterations are needed to get desired or needed accuracy or precision? The major problem here is that the number of iterations could be so many as to make a solution economically impossible (we might not have enough money to pay for computer time). Even worse, the number of iterations needed to derive a result could be infinite. This is true for series that do not converge upon an answer but are infinite. As an example, the series

$$\text{SUM} = 1 + \frac{1}{2} + \frac{1}{3} + \cdots + \frac{1}{X} + \cdots \tag{34}$$

will never converge on some specific value. Instead, the sum will keep increasing steadily with the addition of more terms. We express this by saying

$$\lim_{X \to \infty} \sum_{D=1}^{D=X} \frac{1}{D} \longrightarrow \infty \tag{35}$$

As X approaches infinity as its "limit," the sum of the series approaches infinity. (The meaning of limit will be discussed in greater detail further on. We use it here in its simple and intuitive sense.)

Another type of series that does not converge upon an answer would be

$$\text{SUM} = 1 - 1 + 1 - 1 + 1 - \cdots \tag{36}$$

The sum of this series is either 1 or 0, depending on the last item in the series.

An infinite series need not have a sum that is indeterminate or infinite. The sum of an infinite series can also converge on a specific value as the number of summed values in the series approaches infinity as a limit. This series is called *convergent*. The series

$$\text{SUM} = 1 + \frac{1}{2} + \frac{1}{2^2} + \frac{1}{2^3} + \cdots \frac{1}{2^N} \tag{37}$$

converges in the sense that

$$\lim_{X \to \infty} \sum_{N=0}^{N=X} \frac{1}{2^N} \longrightarrow 2 \tag{38}$$

In other words, the sum of the series approaches 2 as N approaches infinity.

We can now define a converging series. A series is convergent if the absolute difference between its sum and a constant E approaches 0 as a limit as the number of terms summed becomes infinite.

$$\lim_{N \to \infty} \left| \sum_{D=0}^{D=N} D - E \right| = 0 \tag{39}$$

As seen from (39) the constant E represents the limiting value. Where this difference is not equal to 0 it is called the *remainder*. If, instead of a complete series, summing is done over a truncated portion of a series up to the Nth term, the remainder is often called the *error of truncation*. To a large degree, it is the business of numerical analysis to estimate errors caused by using only a partial series.

Before we can continue our discussions on series and how to use and deal with errors and remainders, we shall have to review some fundamental ideas in calculus. The student who wishes to pursue approximation by series further should turn to the appropriate section in the review of slopes and rates of change of functions.

BASIC MANIPULATIONS WITH FUNCTIONS

Sciences are concerned predominantly with two types of manipulations of functions which provide precise descriptions of the association between antecedent and consequent conditions. One is to find the rates with which quantities in the consequent conditions are changing with respect to changes in the quantities in the antecedent conditions (or vice versa). The investigator might be concerned with questions which ask how long it will take for a process to be completed or how fast a process rate changes at any point in time. The second type of manipulation is that in which the rate of change of antecedent or consequent conditions can be observed, and statements are made about the underlying function between these conditions that can account for the observed rate of change. The investigator observes only the effect a group of variables has on each other, and he uses the tools of mathematics to construct the form of this relationship. In effect, he is resurrecting the function from observing something about its rate of change. It is little wonder that because of its importance the study of rates of change of functions has received a great deal of attention.

COORDINATES

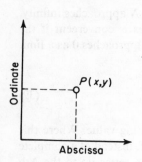

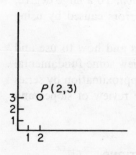

A.3. (X, Y) coordinate system.

To find a point in any space (where "space" may be a plane, a volume, a time period, etc.) we have to establish a one-to-one correspondence between the location of a point and a set of numbers. The set of numbers that locate the point are called *coordinates*. In the memory of a computer, the location of a point may be given by a single number (consisting of one or more characters) that indicates the specific address. On the other hand, if the point is located on a disk, then two or three numbers may be needed to locate it.

Insofar as we shall use a graphic representation of functions, we shall be concerned predominantly with a point on a plane. Any point P is located by a pair of numbers (X, Y) that represent distances from two basic reference lines. These lines are set up at right angles to each other and are oriented so that one extends vertically (ordinate or Y axis) and one extends horizontally (abscissa or X axis). The point at which the two lines meet is called the *origin of the coordinate system* and therefore has the coordinates (0, 0), as shown in Figure A.3.

Both abscissa and ordinate values for any point are represented by real numbers, i.e., integers or integers plus frac-

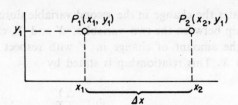

A.4. Graph showing horizontal line.

tions, including nonterminating fractions. The X coordinate reflects the distance of the point from the origin along a line parallel to the X axis and, similarly, the Y coordinate gives the distance along a line parallel to the Y axis.

To illustrate this system further, let us draw a line parallel to the X axis and Y_1 distance units away from it (Figure A.4). The extremities of this line (P_2 and P_1) have the coordinates (X_1, Y_1) and (X_2, Y_2). Note that the ordinate value stays the same along the entire line. The length of the line, i.e., the distance between P_1 and P_2, is given by $X_2 - X_1$. By the same token, the extremities P_3 and P_4 of a line drawn parallel to the Y axis (Figure A.5) will have the same X coordinate, as will any point on that line, and the distance between any two points will be merely the difference in Y values ($Y_2 - Y_1$). We can then denote distances

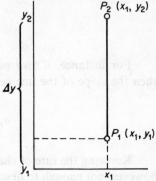

A.5. Graph showing vertical line.

along these lines as ΔX and ΔY:

$$\Delta X = X_2 - X_1$$

$$\Delta Y = Y_2 - Y_1 \qquad (40)$$

THE STRAIGHT LINE

Let us begin by considering a straight line that is not parallel to either of our reference lines (see Figure A.6). We now take two points on this line and call them P_1 and P_2. The coordinates for our points are (x_1, y_1) for P_1 and (x_2, y_2) for P_2. The quantity ΔX represents a change in the X coordinate(or in one variable) as we move along the line from P_1 to P_2, whereas

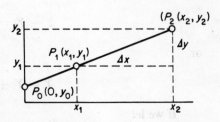

A.6. Graph showing straight slanting line.

ΔY indicates the change in the second variable during this movement. The relationship between the two variables, X and Y, can be described by expressing the amount of change in Y with respect to a given amount of change in X. This relationship is stated by

$$a_1 = \frac{\Delta Y}{\Delta X} \tag{41}$$

or the rate with which Y changes as X changes. The quantity a_1 is called the *slope* or the rate of change of Y with respect to X. It is computed simply by

$$a_1 = \frac{Y_2 - Y_1}{X_2 - X_1} \tag{42}$$

For instance, if two points on a line have coordinates (5, 7) (7, 11), then the slope of the line connecting them is given by

$$a_1 = \frac{11 - 7}{7 - 5} = \frac{4}{2} = 2$$

Knowing the rate of change of one variable with respect to the other is, however, not enough to describe the straight line completely. This line needs one reference point. One such convenient point may be selected where the line intercepts the ordinate (or the abscissa).

Since the purpose of the straight line equation is to help us find the location of any point $P(X, Y)$, we shall start with that. If we take any other point, $P_1(X_1, Y_1)$ we can state rate of change of this line in terms of these two sets of coordinates:

$$a_1 = \frac{Y - Y_1}{X - X_1} \tag{43}$$

This is called the point slope form of the equation of the straight line. It can be rewritten as

$$Y - Y_1 = a_1(X - X_1) \tag{44}$$

or

$$Y = Y_1 + a_1(X - X_1)$$

If we let

$$a_0 = Y_1 - a_1 X_1$$

then

$$Y = a_0 + a_1 X \tag{45}$$

The equation of a straight line is usually written in this form. The quantity a_0 is the Y coordinate of the point at which the line intercepts the ordinate axis (also known as the intercept) and a_1 is the rate of change.

FINDING THE SLOPE OF CURVES

Let us take a line that is not straight (see Figure A.7). Suppose we keep P fixed and move P_1 toward P. It is obvious that the rate with which P_1 will move along the X or Y axis will differ, depending on which part of the curve it is located. We can say, therefore, that the rate of change of Y with respect to X is not constant. It is precisely this criterion which defines a line that is not straight. (It would be more accurate to say that the straight line is defined by a constant relationship between Δy and Δx.)

Let us now draw a straight line between P and P_1 and consider the slope of this line. When the coordinates of P are (X, Y) the coordinates of P_1 can be given as $(X + \Delta X, Y + \Delta Y)$.

Now we shall find a rule by which we can determine the slope at any locale from the given value of X at that point. Where Y is a function of X we can denote the existence of a relationship by

$$Y = f(X) \tag{46}$$

and consequently

$$Y + \Delta Y = f(X + \Delta X) \tag{47}$$

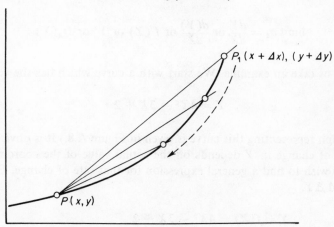

A.7. Graph showing progression of secants converging to tangent at a point.

so that

$$\Delta Y = f(X + \Delta X) - f(X) \tag{48}$$

and the slope of the line P to P_1

$$a_1 = \frac{\Delta y}{\Delta x} = \frac{f(X + \Delta X) - f(X)}{\Delta X} \tag{49}$$

What would happen now if we were to move P_1 closer and closer to P? This would be the same as holding X fixed and making ΔX smaller and smaller, approaching zero. As we do this, a_1 approaches some value which we call its limit and define as the slope of the tangent to the curve at P (Figure A.7). The mathematical symbols which summarize this discussion are

$$\lim_{P_1 \to P} a_1 = \lim_{\Delta X \to 0} \frac{\Delta Y}{\Delta X} = \lim_{\Delta X \to 0} \frac{f(X + \Delta X) - f(X)}{\Delta X} \tag{50}$$

Carrying out this operation produces a number which we have called a_1 because we labeled it a slope of the line connecting P to P_1. Actually, where we have a curve which is not a straight line, we will not obtain a single number but rather a more complex function describing the change in Y with respect to the change in X. It is customary to call this function the *derivative of Y with respect to X*. The process of finding derivatives is called *differentiation*. The derivative can be symbolically expressed in a number of ways as shown below.

$$\lim_{P_1 \to P} a_1 = \frac{dY}{dX} \text{ or } \frac{d(Y)}{dX} \text{ or } f'(Y) \text{ or } Y' \text{ or } D_x(Y)$$

Let us take an example. We start with a curve which has the equation

$$Y = 4X^2 - 3X + 2$$

(The graph representing this curve is given in Figure A.8.) It is obvious that the rate of change in Y depends on the actual value of the coordinate X. We now wish to find a general expression for that rate of change. First we shall find ΔY.

$$Y = f(X) = 4X^2 - 3X + 2$$
$$Y + \Delta Y = f(X + \Delta X) = 4(X + \Delta X)^2 - 3(X + \Delta X) + 2$$
$$= 4X^2 + 8X\Delta X + 4\Delta X^2 - 3X - 3\Delta X + 2$$

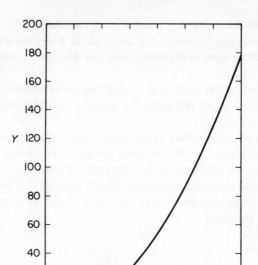

A.8. Graph of $Y = 4X^2 - 3X + 2$.

So that

$$\Delta Y = f(X + \Delta X) - f(X) = 8X\,\Delta X + 4\,\Delta X^2 - 3\,\Delta X$$

We can now express the slope of the line tangent to the curve at a point (X, Y) by dividing both sides by ΔX:

$$\frac{\Delta Y}{\Delta X} = 8X + 4\,\Delta X - 3$$

Now as we make the interval defined by ΔX on the X axis smaller and smaller until it approaches zero, we obtain the general statement of the slope at any point:

$$\lim_{\Delta X \to 0} \frac{\Delta Y}{\Delta X} = \frac{dY}{dX} = 8X - 3$$

This expression states the rule that the slope of the curve in our example of any point P (having coordinates X, Y) is given by $8X - 3$.

LIMITS

The quantity $\Delta Y/\Delta X$ is more commonly called the derivative of Y with respect to X and involves the calculation of a limit. As we keep one point fixed and let the quantity ΔX approach zero, the function of X, i.e.,

$f(X)$, must be defined at any point $X + \Delta X$ so that $f(X + \Delta X)$ makes sense. More importantly, however, ΔX must at all times be different from zero. Obviously, if we were to divide by zero, our quotient would be a meaningless number.

Therefore, when we divide by ΔX, we really divide before ΔX is zero. No matter how small ΔX gets, the division is performed while it is larger than zero.

Now as we are dividing by quantities of ΔX that are smaller and smaller, the quotient which we obtain tends toward a particular value. This value is referred to as the limit as ΔX approaches zero.

A detailed discussion of limits would take us too far afield. However, the concept is so important that we ought to clarify it by an example. Let us take the function

$$Y = \frac{X^2 + X - 6}{X - 2}$$

This can be simplified and written as

$$Y = \frac{(X + 3)(X - 2)}{(X - 2)}$$

(We could simplify this further, but we shall not do this here.)

We shall now consider what the value of Y is when X is equal to 2. When X is equal to 2, it is obvious that we both multiply and divide by zero so that Y is either zero or not determined. However, while Y may not have a value when X is equal to 2, what is the value of Y when X is almost equal to 2? There are, obviously, values that exist for Y if X takes on values that are either larger or smaller than 2. Some of the values are given below:

if		then	
$X = 0,$		then	$Y = 3$
$X = 1,$			$Y = 4$
$X = 1.5,$			$Y = 4.5$
$X = 1.999,$			$Y = 4.999$
$X = 2,$			Y is not determined
$X = 2.111,$			$Y = 5.111$
$X = 3,$			$Y = 6$

We can see here that as X approaches 2, from above or below that value, Y approaches a limit. The limit in this case is equal to 5. We can write this as

$$\text{limit } Y = 5$$
$$X \to 2$$

It is important to note that the value of the limit of Y, which depends on X and ΔX, can be made as nearly equal to 5 as is desired, providing we take ΔX to be sufficiently close to zero. It does not really matter whether X or Y ever gets to the limit. We simply answer the question of what happens to Y as X comes as close as we please to a given value.

DERIVATIVES OF POLYNOMIAL FUNCTIONS

We shall consider a function of the form

$$f(X) = a_0 + a_1 X + a_2 X^2 + a_3 X^3 + \cdots + a_i X^i \qquad (51)$$

This function, which is the sum of a finite number of small monomial terms, is called a polynomial in X. We shall now derive some simple rules which shall enable us to find the derivatives of polynomials easily.

THE DERIVATIVE OF A CONSTANT

Let us take the function

$$f(x) = C \qquad (52)$$

which simply says that we are dealing with a straight line parallel to the X axis. The coordinates at any point P are (X, C). If we now take some other point P_1, it will have coordinates $(X + \Delta X, C)$. Thus for all cases,

$$\frac{dY}{dX} = \lim_{\Delta X \to 0} \frac{\Delta Y}{\Delta X} = \frac{0}{\Delta X} = 0 \qquad (53)$$

Thus, it is true that the derivative of a constant with respect to X is always equal to zero. Or

$$\frac{dC}{dX} = 0 \qquad (54)$$

THE DERIVATIVE OF aX^n

We start with a function of the form

$$f(X) = aX^n \qquad (55)$$

The coordinates at any point P will be (X, aX^n). If we now take any other point P_1, its coordinates will be $[X + \Delta X, a(X + \Delta X)^n]$. We then obtain a value for ΔY.

$$\Delta Y = a(X + \Delta X)^n - aX^n \tag{56}$$

To solve this we have to remember the binomial theorem:

$$(X + \Delta X)^n = X^n + nX^{n-1} \Delta X + \frac{n!}{(n-2)!\,2!} X^{n-2} \Delta X^2$$

$$+ \frac{n!}{(n-3)!\,3!} X^{n-3} \Delta X^3 + \cdots \tag{57}$$

$$+ \frac{n!}{(n-r)!\,r!} X^{n-r} \Delta X^r + \cdots + \Delta X^n$$

where

$$\frac{n!}{(n-r)!\,r!} \tag{58}$$

is the binomial coefficient. If we now perform the subtraction indicated above, we get an expression for ΔY as follows:

$$\Delta Y = anX^{n-1} \Delta X + a\frac{n!}{(n-2)!\,2!} X^{n-2} \Delta X^2 + \cdots$$

$$+ a\frac{n!}{(n-r)!\,r!} X^{n-r} \Delta X^r + \cdots + \Delta X^n \tag{59}$$

If we now divide each term by ΔX, we obtain

$$\frac{\Delta Y}{\Delta X} = anX^{n-1} + a\frac{n!}{(n-2)!\,2!} X^{n-2} \Delta X + \cdots + \Delta X^{n-1} \tag{60}$$

Now as ΔX approaches zero and P_1 approaches P, the only term not affected in the expression above is the first. Thus,

$$\lim_{x \to 0} \frac{\Delta Y}{\Delta X} = \frac{dY}{dX} = anX^{n-1} \tag{61}$$

We can now write a general derivative of a polynomial expression. If this polynomial expression is simply indicated as $f(X)$, then

$$\frac{df(X)}{dX} = a_1 + 2a_2X + 3a_3X^2 + \cdots + ia_iX^{i-1} \tag{62}$$

is the derivative of any polynomial in X.

HIGHER DERIVATIVES

It is clear that the derivative of a function is itself a function describing what happens to the slope of a line tangent to any point of a curve as X changes. This function may be analyzed further and its derivatives found. In fact, we may proceed in this fashion in finding higher order derivatives until no more derivatives can be found.

For instance, we might take the function

$$f(X) = x^3 - 6x^2 + 9x - 6$$
$$f'(X) = 3x^2 - 12x + 9$$
$$f''(X) = 6x - 12 \tag{63}$$
$$f'''(X) = 6$$
$$f''''(X) = 0$$

The uses of higher order derivatives are many. We shall examine two applications that are especially important. One of them is to find the high and low points of a function, the other is to give us a better approximation for the value of a function by the use of a series.

MAXIMA AND MINIMA

Differentiation enables us to solve problems in which we want to find the maxima or minima of a function. Let us take the curve expressed in (63). As the curve rises and falls, the slope of the line tangent to the curve rises and falls. We can tell, therefore, if the curve is increasing or decreasing at any particular point by looking at the first derivative. For instance, where X is equal to 2, the value of the first derivative is equal to

$$f'(2) = 12 - 24 + 9 = -3 \tag{64}$$

or negative. Therefore, the curve is falling at the point at which the X coordinate is equal to 2. On the other hand, for a point that has an X coordinate equal to 4, the first derivative is

$$f'(4) = 48 - 48 + 9 = 9 \tag{65}$$

or the slope at the point is positive or rising.

We can now go one step further. At the point at which the curve changes from rise to fall or from fall to rise, the slope should be 0. Therefore, if a maximum or minimum exists at any point, then the slope at that point will have a value of 0. We can often find maxima and minima by the simple process of setting the first derivative equal to 0.

$$\frac{df(X)}{dx} = f'(X) = 0 \tag{66}$$

In our example

$$f'(X) = 3X^2 - 12X + 9 = 0 \tag{67}$$

This relationship is satisfied when $X = 1$ or when $X = 3$. We have, then, two points at which the curve changes from rise to fall or fall to rise.

There are two methods of finding out whether maxima or minima occur at each of these points. To do that, we could find the slope at adjacent values of X. For instance, we could find the slope for the point at which the X coordinate is equal to .9 and 1.1 as well as 2.9 and 3.1. If the sign of the slope changes from positive to negative, then we have a maximum; if it changes from negative to positive, we have a minimum.

A more expedient method for deciding whether maxima or minima are involved is to evaluate the second derivative at the point in question and look at the sign. If the second derivative is positive, then the curve is concave upward, or the point at which the first derivative is equal to 0 locates a minimum. Where the second derivative is negative, the curve is concave downward, and the point at which the first derivative is 0 locates a maximum. If the second derivative equals 0, the test fails. Instead we know that the function defining the slope is itself changing. This point is called the *point of inflection*.

In our present example, for $x = 1$, the second derivative is negative, so that the curve forms a maximum at that point. Where $x = 3$, the second derivative is positive, so that the curve forms a minimum at that point. We can, of course, also evaluate points of inflection for the function describing the first derivative, or the second, and further on.

Finding maxima and minima is terribly important in the natural sciences and engineering, but used to be less of a necessity in social and biological areas. However, with automatic data processing in the empirical sciences, the location of maxima and minima on a curve has become extremely important for very practical reasons. When continuous data describing curves are read into the machine and automatically analyzed, it is necessary to find the points at which the curve has relative or absolute minima and maxima. Obviously, the simplest method of finding those is to define first and second derivatives. Another important application of minima is to develop methods for best-fitting equations, as in Chapters 10, 11, and 12.

FINDING THE SUM OF A SERIES

Using higher order derivatives, the method of undetermined coefficients can be applied to any function that can be differentiated over and over. (It is necessary, of course, for the function to be differentiable; that is, the limit of $\Delta y/\Delta X$ must exist when $X \rightarrow 0$.) Let us begin by taking the polynomial

$$\text{SUM} = f(X) = a_0 + a_1 X + a_2 X^2 + \cdots + a_i X^i \tag{68}$$

for finite values of i.

Let us now differentiate this function successively.

$$
\begin{aligned}
f'(X) &= a_1 + 2a_2 X + 3a_3 X^2 + \cdots \\
f''(X) &= 2a_2 + 2\cdot 3a_3 X + 3\cdot 4a_4 X^2 + \cdots \\
f'''(X) &= 2\cdot 3a_3 + 2\cdot 3\cdot 4a_4 X + 3\cdot 4\cdot 5a_5 X^2 + \cdots \\
f''''(X) &= 2\cdot 3\cdot 4a_4 + 2\cdot 3\cdot 4\cdot 5a_5 X + 3\cdot 4\cdot 5\cdot 6a_6 X^2 + \cdots
\end{aligned}
\tag{69}
$$

Substituting 0 for X, we find

$$
\begin{aligned}
f(0) &= a_0 \\
f'(0) &= a_1 \\
f''(0) &= 2a_2 \\
f'''(0) &= 2\cdot 3a_3 \\
f''''(0) &= 2\cdot 3\cdot 4a_4 \\
&\quad\vdots \\
f^i(0) &= i!a_i
\end{aligned}
\tag{70}
$$

From this we can see that the coefficients can be expressed as follows:

$$
\begin{aligned}
a_0 &= \frac{f(0)}{0!} = f(0) \\
a_1 &= \frac{f'(0)}{1!} \\
a_2 &= \frac{f''(0)}{2!} \\
&\quad\vdots \\
a_i &= \frac{fi(0)}{i!}
\end{aligned}
\tag{71}
$$

As a consequence, we can now write SUM as

$$\text{SUM} = f(X) = f(0) + \frac{f'(0)}{1!} + \frac{f''(0)}{2!} + \cdots + \frac{f^i(0)}{i!} \tag{72}$$

This type of series, erroneously called a Maclaurin series, is easy to remember because the order of the higher order derivatives, the power of X, and the number taken factorial are all the same number when applied to a general function f, which is not a polynomial, and this leads to an infinite series providing all the derivatives exist. Of course, this series can be used only if it converges and the remainder (defined below) tends to zero.

The Maclaurin series is said to be an expansion about 0 because it starts with $f(0)$ and modifies this first estimate by a number of additional terms.

The method of undetermined coefficients can also be used to find SUM by defining SUM as a series involving X and some constant C:

$$\text{SUM} = f(X) = a_0 + a_1(X - C) + a_2(X - C)^2 + \cdots \tag{73}$$

If we apply the method of undetermined coefficients to this series, we find that

$$\text{SUM} = f(X) = f(C) + \frac{f'(C)}{1!}(X - C) + \frac{f''(C)}{2!}(X - C)^2 + \cdots$$
$$+ \frac{f^i(C)}{i!}(X - C)^i \tag{74}$$

This expression is called Taylor's series. If the constant C is well chosen, the amount of calculation required to find SUM through the Taylor series will be reduced greatly from that needed to use the Maclaurin series.

ERROR OF TRUNCATION (FORMAL SOLUTIONS)

How far shall we take such a series? As we develop coefficients for higher and higher powers of X, it may happen that our estimate of SUM approximates the true value of the function more and more closely. However, there is still a difference between the actual value of $f(X)$ and our estimate, which we call the error of remainder or E_i. The correct way to write down the Maclaurin series (or Taylor's series) is to hang the error of truncation on the end.

$$\text{SUM} \approx f(0) + \frac{f'(0)}{1!}X + \cdots + \frac{f^{i-1}(0)}{(i-1)!}X^{i-1} + E_i \tag{75}$$

where E_i represents the difference between the truncated series and the true functional value.

An important discovery was made by LaGrange which is called the LaGrange theorem. There is some value θ between zero and 1 such that

LaGrange form $= \dfrac{f^i(\theta X)}{i!} X_i = E_i \dfrac{f^i(\theta X)}{i!} X^i(1 - \theta)^{i-1} =$ Euler form

$$(76)$$

Although it is in general impossible or impractical to calculate the value of θ, it is not really necessary. What we are interested in is not so much the value of E_i but an estimate of the largest value of E_i that could possibly exist. From this we can come to a general statement for the error of truncation.

For any infinite Maclaurin series, the error of truncation E_i can be estimated by

$$0 \leq E_i \leq \left[\frac{|f^i(X_1)|}{i!} |X|^i \right] \qquad (77)$$

where X_1 is in the interval from 0 through X, and $f^i(X_1)$ is the largest value of the ith derivative of f_i between 0 and X.

Let us now illustrate how we would use the remainder theorem.

Let us say we want to find e (the natural logarithm base) with great accuracy (say, to the nearest .00001). We select e for simplicity because it works out that

$$\text{If } f(X) = e^x, \quad \text{then} \quad f'(X) = e^x, \quad f''(X) = e^x, \text{ etc.} \qquad (78)$$

and, therefore,

$$f(0) = f'(0) = f''(0), \text{ etc.} = 1 \qquad (79)$$

Then from (75)

$$e^x = 1 + X + \frac{1}{2!} X^2 + \frac{1}{3!} X^3 + \cdots + \frac{1}{(i-1)!} X^{i-1} + E_i \qquad (80)$$

We start with the knowledge that e is a number somewhere between 2 and 3 (to make life easy for ourselves) and we shall evaluate the e^x series with X equal to 1:

$$e = \text{SUM} = 1 + 1 + \frac{1}{2!} + \frac{1}{3!} + \cdots + \frac{1}{(i-1)!} + E_i \qquad (81)$$

We must now estimate E_i to have some idea of how many terms are needed. Expression (78) for our function is

$$E_i \leq \left[\frac{e^{x_1}}{i!} X^i \right], \qquad (82)$$

since we know that $f'(X) = e^x$ for all values of X. Moreover, since we are interested in evaluating e^x for $X = 1$, X^i is always 1, and (82) simplifies further to

$$E_i \leq \left[\frac{e^{X_1}}{i!} \right] \tag{83}$$

We must now find the value of X_1 that gives the largest E_i. Since we started with the knowledge that e is somewhere between 2 and 3, and a stipulation of (77) is that X_1 is from 0 through X (1 in our case), we can say that e^{X_1} lies somewhere between 2^0 and 3^1. Taking the "worst" case, let us say that e is 3 and X_1 is 1. Then (83) becomes

$$E_i \leq \left[\frac{3^1}{i!} \right] \tag{84}$$

where i, of course, is the number of terms used in our series.

When i is 9, E_i can be no larger than 3/9!, or .000008267, which is below the .00001 we set for ourselves, and (81) carried to nine terms works out to 2.718282, which is not bad under any conditions.

If we use Taylor's series, (76) becomes

$$E_i = \frac{(X - C)^i}{i!} f^i(C + \theta(X - C)) \quad \text{or} \quad \frac{(X - C)^i}{i!}(1 - \theta)^{i-1} f^i \tag{85}$$

where C is a constant as in (74) and θ falls between 0 and 1. Expression (77) becomes

$$0 \leq E_i \leq \left[\frac{(X - C)^i}{i!} f^i(X_1) \right] \tag{86}$$

where X_1 lies between C and X and is chosen so that:

$$|f^i(X_1)| \geq |f^i(Y)| \text{ for all } Y \text{ between } C \text{ and } X \tag{87}$$

The advantage of using Taylor's series is that it requires fewer terms to obtain the same accuracy as with Maclaurin's.

Again we must remind ourselves why we wish to find such approximations. We can tell quite a few things about a curve from cursory visual inspection. We can see its maxima and minima, its relative minima and maxima, and values that the various points on the curve might have in relation to other scales. If we introduce the same data into a computer and let it decide on some action, depending on what values are presented to it, the computer must have a method by which it can determine the same minima and maxima or rescale certain values. The approximations of functions by series and the use of derivatives are some of the tools used to describe curves and fix key points on them through an automatic process.

ERROR OF TRUNCATION (HEURISTIC SOLUTION)

Finding the minimum number of terms to give an acceptable approximation to a solution was much more important when no high-speed processors were available than it is now, when the expansion of a series to a few more terms may not really involve much additional effort. For instance, the flow chart for finding a square root shown in Figure A.2 depicts a process by which the error of approximation is checked against a predetermined value e. As long as the error (approximated by $D/2$) is larger than e, the program loops back for one more iteration. This process stops when $D < e$. For the user who can avail himself of a high-speed machine that can complete as many as 100,000 full cycles of such operations per second, it is easier to let the machine work until e is as small as desired for most practical purposes rather than to evaluate the number of cycles needed to obtain a value of D that is acceptable.

INTEGRALS OF POLYNOMIAL FUNCTIONS

Very often, problems present themselves in which a function's rate of change is known and the function itself is to be determined. This is handled by a process which is the reverse of differentiation and is termed *integration*.

Let us take the relation

$$\frac{dY}{dX} = 3X^2 \qquad (88)$$

and evaluate it at $X = 2$. The quantity dY/dX comes out to 12, telling us that for this function when X is 2, Y changes 12 times as fast as X does. We can restate this in a more convenient form by rewriting (88) as

$$dY = 3X^2\,dX \qquad (89)$$

This says that if a particular point on this curve $P(X_i, Y_i)$ moves a very small distance in the horizontal direction dX, the approximate amount of movement in the vertical direction dY required to keep it on the curve would be approximately $3X_i^2\,dX$. The relation between the values of Y and X, as opposed to the relation between the amounts they change, is written

$$Y = f(X) = \int 3X^2\,dX \qquad (90)$$

$\int$ is the integral sign, read as "the function for which the rate of change is . . . ."

We can work our way back to the original function by using (61), which said that if $Y = aX^n$

$$\frac{dY}{dX} = anX^{n-1}$$

Combining (61) with (88), we have

$$3X^2 = anX^{n-1}$$

$$(an) = 3 \tag{91}$$

$$n - 1 = 2$$

Then

$$n = 3 \quad \text{and} \quad aX^n = \frac{anX^n}{n} = \frac{3X^3}{3} = X^3 \tag{92}$$

Differentiating X^3 gives us $3X^2$, thus establishing consistency. However, if we look at (54), it is clear that if we differentiate $X^3 + 47$, $X^3 - 6$, $X^3 + 1758$, or, more generally stated, $X^3 \pm C$, we will get the same derivative. Consequently, if we have some function that we wish to integrate, we must indicate the possible presence of some constant in the result. Thus in our example

$$Y = \int 3X^2 \, dX = X^3 + K \tag{93}$$

where K is termed the constant of integration. Thus, the results of such an integration process are a family of curves, one for each value of K, (Figure A.9) rather than a unique one. In general,

$$\int bX^m \, dX = \frac{b}{m+1} X^{m+1} + K \tag{94}$$

Therefore, for a polynomial consisting of several such terms, viz.,

$$f(X) = a_0 + a_1 X + a_2 X^2 + a_3 X^3 + \cdots + a_i X^i$$

$$\int f(X) \, dX = a_0 X + \frac{a_1 X^2}{2} + \frac{a_2 X^3}{3} + \frac{a_3 X^4}{4} + \cdots + \frac{a_i X^{i+1}}{i} + K \tag{95}$$

It is apparent that we must know more than this equation for a derivative in order to pin down the specific function from which it came. Usually, what is known is the value of a point on the original curve. Going back to our example in (93) and augmenting it with the information that when X is 6, Y is 234, we can evaluate K as

$$K = 234 - 6^3 = 18 \tag{96}$$

and define the specific function $Y = X^3 + 18$

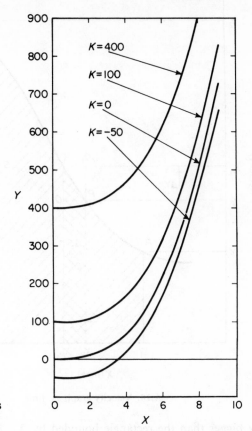

A.9. Family of curves $3X^2\,dx$.

CALCULATION OF AREAS VIA INTEGRATION

When a curve is drawn depicting the consequent-antecedent relationship $Y = f(X)$, it is often of value to determine the area under some portion of that curve. For example, if Y were the velocity of some moving object and X represented time, then a graph of $Y = f(X)$ would depict the history of the velocity (Figure A.10), and the area under the curve between $X = X_1$ and $X = X_2$ would indicate the distance traveled by the object during the elapsed time between t_1 and t_2. Since such areas are usually irregular shapes, they cannot be determined by ordinary geometric formulas. It is possible, however, to relate them to integrals:

Referring to Figure A.10, let us denote the area bounded by X_1, X_2, Y_1, and Y_2 as S. Suppose we take a point P on the curve and advance along the curve to point P_1. The piece of area covered by this movement (ΔS) is

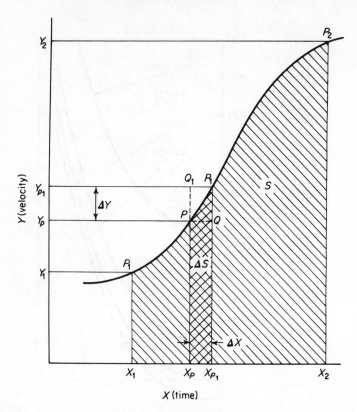

A.10. Velocity graph vs. time.

obviously bigger than the rectangle bounded by X_P, P, Q, and X_{P1} [whose area is $Y_P(\Delta X)$] and smaller than the rectangle bounded by X_P, Q_1, P_1, and X_{P1} [whose area is $Y_{P1}(\Delta X)$]. We can express this symbolically by saying

$$Y_P(\Delta X) < \Delta S < Y_{P1}(\Delta X) \tag{97}$$

Now, since $Y_{P1} = Y_P + \Delta Y$, (97) becomes

$$Y_P \Delta X < \Delta S < (Y_P + \Delta Y)\,\Delta X \tag{98}$$

Dividing this by ΔX does not change the order of the inequality, and

$$Y_P < \frac{\Delta S}{\Delta X} < Y_P + \Delta Y \tag{99}$$

If the increment ΔX approaches zero, so does ΔY. Therefore, $Y + \Delta Y$ approaches Y and

$$\lim_{\Delta X \to 0} \frac{\Delta S}{\Delta X} = \frac{dS}{dX} = Y \tag{100}$$

Thus,

$$dS = Y\,dX = f(X)\,dX \tag{101}$$

If we integrate,

$$S = \int f(X)\,dX = F(X) + K \tag{102}$$

The constant K in this case can always be evaluated because we know that when X is X_1, the area is zero. Hence we have $F(X_1) + K = 0$ or $K = -F(X_1)$. The total area then is $F(X_2) + K = F(X_2) - F(X_1)$. This is written $\int_{x_1}^{x_2} f(X)\,dX$. Observe that if $G(X)$ is some other function such that $(dG/dX)(X) = f(X)$, then $S = G(X) + K'$, and just as before, we find $K' = -G(X_1)$ and total area $= G(X_2) - G(X_1)$. The expression $G(X_2) - G(X_1)$ is denoted $\int_{x_1}^{x_2} G(X)$.

Suppose the velocity Y in miles per hour is related to X, the time in hours, by the function

$$Y = f(X) = 12X^2 + 7X - 3 \tag{103}$$

and we wished to determine the distance S covered over the first three hours ($X_1 = 0$, $X_2 = 3$).

$$S = F(X) = \int f(X)\,dX = \left[4X^3 + \tfrac{7}{2}X^2 - 3X \right]_0^3 = 130.5 \tag{104}$$

Since $S = 0$ when $X = 0$, K in this case is also 0, and $S = 4(27) + \tfrac{7}{2}(9) - 3(3) = 130.5$ miles. If we wanted to determine S for the hour from $X_1 = 2$ to $X_2 = 3$, then we would get

$$\left[4X^3 + \tfrac{7}{2}X^2 - 3X \right]_2^3 = 130.5 - 40 = 90.5$$

SYSTEMS OF EQUATIONS

One of the powerful aids which mathematics has offered is the ability to represent associations symbolically and to resolve questions concerning consequent conditions or values of unknowns by algebraic manipulations.

The vast importance of these algebraic manipulations is by no means limited to science or engineering. Business and manufacturing problems can be and are, indeed, resolved by very much the same methods.

We have already reviewed the concept of a function in the first chapter. The importance of symbolic representation of an association lies in the fact that it permits us to manipulate, with paper and pencil, the interaction of variables and conditions and provide two types of answers. Where $f(X)$ is the symbolic representation of the way the antecedent condition X exerts an influence, then two types of manipulations are basically possible.

1. If a particular value of the antecedent variable is known, then the total effect of $f(X)$ can be evaluated.
2. If the effect of a particular result of the workings of antecedent conditions is known and if $f(X)$ can be stated, then it is possible to find the actual value of the antecedent variable which gave rise to the particular result.

For example, let us take the hypothetical case where

$$f(X) = 4X^2 - 16X \tag{105}$$

What this relationship states is that there exists some consequence Y that is associated with some antecedent condition X, in such a manner as described by $f(X)$. If we can now state the value for the antecedent condition under a particular set of circumstances as X_1, then a precise solution for the consequence, $Y_1 = f(X_1)$, can be obtained easily. For instance, when $X_1 = 2$,

$$Y_1 = 4X_1^2 - 16X_1 = 4 \cdot 2^2 - 16 \cdot 2 = -16 \tag{106}$$

Conversely, we might not have been able to state the exact value for the antecedent condition X_1, but we may have been able to measure the results. In this case, we might have knowledge of the following conditions:

$$f(X_1) = 4X_1^2 - 16X_1 = -16 \tag{107}$$

We can find a solution for this expression by the types of manipulations permissible with equations. Basically, we would do certain operations to the right and left sides of the equation in such a way that we isolate the unknown X_1 on one side and all other terms on the other.

$$4X_1^2 - 16X_1 = -16$$
$$4X_1^2 - 16X_1 + 16 = 0 \tag{108}$$

Dividing by 4 gives

$$X_1^2 - 4X_1 + 4 = 0$$

$$X_1 = \frac{4 \pm \sqrt{16 - 16}}{2}$$

$$X_1 = 2$$

In most instances, the relationships in biological and social sciences are not dependent on a single antecedent condition but on many. In principle, the methods of recovery of precise values of antecedent conditions from their results are the same whether we deal with one variable or many. However, the number of variables introduced raises considerable problems for symbolic manipulations.

Let us say that a consequence Y is the result of the interaction of two antecedent conditions X and Z. If it were now known that

$$Y_i = f(X, Z) = 2X_i + 3Z_i \qquad (109)$$

then for any value of one of the antecedent conditions or variables there are an infinite number of possible values for Y, depending on the value given to the other antecedent condition or variable. To be able to resolve questions concerning Y for this relationship, we must know another set of conditions that holds true and ties Y to variable X and Z. If it were also known that another relationship existed, such that

$$Y_i = g(X_i, Z_i) = 2X_i + Z_i \qquad (110)$$

a unique solution for Y_i is possible. For instance, if we could measure Y_i under the two types of relationships so that

$$f(X_i, Y_i) = 8 \quad \text{and} \quad g(X_i, Y_i) = 4 \qquad (111a)$$

then

$$2X_i + 3Y_i = 8$$
$$2X_i + Y_i = 4 \qquad (111b)$$

Expressing Y as

$$Y = 4 - 2X$$

we can rewrite (111a) as

$$2X_i + 3(4 - 2X_i) = 8$$
$$2X_i - 6X_i + 12 = 8 \qquad (112)$$
$$4X_i = 4$$
$$X_i = 1$$

and since

$$Y_i = 4 - 2X_i$$
$$Y_i = 4 - 2 = 2 \qquad (113)$$

We can verify this since it is true that

$$2 \cdot 1 + 3 \cdot 2 = 8$$
$$2 \cdot 1 + 2 = 4 \qquad (114)$$

These types of equations are called linear because they do not contain powers of X higher than 1. Many problems of great importance in science, business, and industry lead to statements in terms of sets of linear equations. It turns out that solutions to large sets of linear expressions get to be cumbersome (although still much simpler than if the equations would be nonlinear). There do exist very efficient procedures by which systems of linear equations can be resolved.

SYMBOLIC REPRESENTATION OF A SYSTEM OF LINEAR EQUATIONS

A general statement for a system of linear equations can be written in the following form:

$$a_{11}X_1 + a_{12}X_2 + \cdots + a_{1c}X_c = b_1$$
$$a_{21}X_1 + a_{22}X_2 + \cdots + a_{2c}X_c = b_2$$
$$\vdots \qquad (115)$$
$$a_{r1}X_1 + a_{r2}X_2 + \cdots + a_{rc}X_c = b_r$$

where the a's and b's are known constants and the X's are unknown. Note that there are r rows and c columns in this system. We might call this an r by c system. This system is said to be of r equations and c unknowns. Such systems, which may also be considered as arrays of numbers that can be written and manipulated in various ways, form the subject of study known as *matrix algebra*.

MATRIX NOTATION

A matrix is a rectangular array of numbers. We shall let A, B, and C stand for such matrices or arrays of numbers. Such arrays can be written as follows:

$$B = \| b_{11} \quad b_{12} \quad b_{13} \quad \cdots \quad b_{1n} \|$$

$$C = \begin{pmatrix} c_{11} \\ c_{21} \\ \cdot \\ \cdot \\ \cdot \\ c_{m1} \end{pmatrix} \tag{116}$$

$$A = \begin{pmatrix} a_{11} & a_{12} & \cdots & a_{1n} \\ a_{21} & a_{22} & \cdots & a_{2n} \\ a_{m1} & a_{m2} & \cdots & a_{mn} \end{pmatrix}$$

A matrix consists of $m \cdot n$ numbers, a_{ij}. The quantities m and n are, respectively, called the height and width of the matrix. Matrix A is said to be an m by n matrix, meaning that it has m rows and n columns. The quantity a_{ij} is the element or member of the matrix in the ith row and jth column. In the general (rectangular) matrix $m > 1$, $n > 1$. A special case is the square matrix in which $m = n$. If m or n should be 1, the resulting matrix is termed a row-vector or a column-vector.

The elements $a_{11}, a_{22}, \cdots, a_{ii}, \cdots$ form the principal diagonal of a matrix:

$$\begin{pmatrix} a_{11} & & & & & \\ & a_{22} & & & & \\ & & \cdot & & & \\ & & & \cdot & & \\ & & a_{ij}(i = j) & & \cdot & \\ & & & & & \cdot \end{pmatrix} \tag{117}$$

The terms in the diagonal are called diagonal elements of A. If we now interchange the rows and columns of A, we obtain an n by m matrix called A^T, the transpose of the matrix A. Matrix A^T has the same principal diagonal as A, but all the elements are interchanged, so that they can be linked by the relation

$$a_{ij}^T = a_{ij} \tag{118}$$

If the only terms that exist in a matrix are diagonal terms and all others are zero, the matrix is called a diagonal matrix; viz.,

$$\begin{pmatrix} a_{11} & \cdot & \cdot & 0 & \cdot & \cdot & \cdot & \cdot & \cdot & \cdot & \cdot & \cdot & \cdot & 0 \\ 0 & & a_{22} & & \cdot & \cdot & \cdot & \cdot & \cdot & \cdot & \cdot & \cdot & \cdot & 0 \\ \cdot & & & & & & & & & & & & & \cdot \\ \cdot & & & & a_{ij} & & & & & & & & & \cdot \\ \cdot & & & & & & & & & & & & & \cdot \\ 0 & \cdot & \cdot & \cdot & 0 & \cdot & \cdot & \cdot & \cdot & \cdot & \cdot & \cdot & \cdot & a_{mn} \end{pmatrix} \qquad (119)$$

If all elements a_{ii} in a diagonal matrix are equal to k, the matrix is called a *scalar*.

There is a special kind of scalar matrix in which all elements in the diagonal are equal to 1. This is called the identity matrix I, and has many important properties.

$$I = \begin{pmatrix} 1 & 0 & \cdot & \cdot & \cdot & \cdot & \cdot & \cdot & \cdot & \cdot & \cdot & \cdot & \cdot & 0 \\ 0 & 1 & \cdot & \cdot & \cdot & \cdot & \cdot & \cdot & \cdot & \cdot & \cdot & \cdot & \cdot & 0 \\ \cdot & & & & & & & & & & & & & \cdot \\ \cdot & & & & & & & & & & & & & \cdot \\ \cdot & & & & & & & & & & & & & \cdot \\ 0 & 0 & \cdot & \cdot & \cdot & \cdot & \cdot & \cdot & \cdot & \cdot & \cdot & \cdot & \cdot & 1 \end{pmatrix} \qquad (120)$$

If all elements of a matrix are zero, it is a zero matrix.

BASIC MATRIX ARITHMETIC

The rules for adding, subtracting, multiplying, or dividing matrices are in many ways similar to the arithmetic operations we can do on individual real numbers. There are, however, also some important differences.

MATRIX ADDITION

Let us say we have two matrices, A and B, and are interested in matrix C such that

$$C = A + B$$

The required operation, i.e., matrix addition, is defined as:

$$\begin{pmatrix} a_{11} & a_{12} & \cdot & \cdot & a_{1n} \\ \cdot & \cdot & & & \cdot \\ \cdot & \cdot & & & \cdot \\ \cdot & \cdot & & & \cdot \\ a_{m1} & a_{m2} & \cdot & \cdot & a_{mn} \end{pmatrix} + \begin{pmatrix} b_{11} & b_{12} & \cdot & \cdot & b_{1n} \\ \cdot & \cdot & & & \cdot \\ \cdot & \cdot & & & \cdot \\ \cdot & \cdot & & & \cdot \\ b_{m1} & b_{m2} & \cdot & \cdot & b_{mn} \end{pmatrix}$$

$$\begin{pmatrix} (a_{11} + b_{11}) & (a_{12} + b_{12}) & \cdot \ \cdot \ \cdot & (a_{1n} + b_{1n}) \\ (a_{m1} + b_{m1}) & (a_{m2} + b_{m2}) & \cdot \ \cdot \ \cdot & (a_{mn} + b_{mn}) \end{pmatrix} = C \qquad (121)$$

Thus, matrix C has elements c_{ij} such that

$$c_{ij} = a_{ij} + b_{ij} \ . \qquad (122)$$

Obviously, we can add matrices together only if they are of the same size.
Matrix addition is associative in that

$$(A + B) + C = A + (B + C) \qquad (123)$$

The operation is also commutative, so that

$$A + B = B + A \qquad (124)$$

which means that it does not matter in which order matrices are added
together.

MULTIPLICATION OF MATRICES

Matrices can also be multiplied with each other so that we can write
expressions like

$$AB = C$$

Although matrices must have the same number of rows and columns to be
added, in multiplication the first factor must have as many columns as the
second factor has rows. If A is an m by n matrix and B is a p by q matrix,
then a product of A and B can be developed only if $n = p$. The resulting
matrix C will be an m by q matrix such that each term

$$C_{ij} = \sum_{k=1}^{m} a_{ik} b_{kj} \qquad (125)$$

The operation described here may be stated as follows: Each row of matrix
A has as many elements as each column of matrix B. To obtain an element
in matrix C located at the ith row and jth column we take the ith row from
matrix A and the jth column from matrix B.

$$\begin{pmatrix} a_{i1} & a_{i2} & \cdot \ \cdot \ \cdot & a_{in} \end{pmatrix} \begin{pmatrix} b_{1j} \\ b_{2j} \\ \cdot \\ \cdot \\ \cdot \\ b_{pj} \end{pmatrix} \qquad (126)$$

We multiply the first element in the ith row of A by the first element in the jth column of B, the second element in the ith row of A by the second element in the jth column of B, and so on, and then add all these products together.

$$
C =
\begin{pmatrix}
(a_{11}b_{11} + a_{12}b_{21} + \cdots + a_{1n}b_{p1}) \cdots (a_{11}b_{1q} + a_{12}b_{2q} + \cdots + a_{1n}b_{pq}) \\
(a_{21}b_{11} + a_{22}b_{21} + \cdots + a_{2n}b_{p1}) \cdots (a_{21}b_{1q} + a_{22}b_{2q} + \cdots + a_{2n}b_{pq}) \\
\vdots \qquad\qquad\qquad\qquad\qquad\qquad \vdots \\
(a_{m1}b_{11} + a_{m2}b_{21} + \cdots + a_{mn}b_{p1}) \cdots (a_{m1}b_{1q} + a_{m2}b_{2q} + \cdots + a_{mn}b_{pq})
\end{pmatrix}
$$

$$(127)$$

For example,

$$
A =
\begin{pmatrix}
1 & -2 & 3 \\
2 & 1 & 3 \\
-3 & 2 & 1
\end{pmatrix}, \qquad
B =
\begin{pmatrix}
3 & 2 \\
1 & -2 \\
2 & 1
\end{pmatrix}
\tag{128}
$$

and where $C = AB$

$$
C =
\begin{pmatrix}
[1(3) - 2(1) + 3(2)] & [1(2) - 2(-2) + 3(1)] \\
[2(3) + 1(1) + 3(2)] & [2(2) + 1(-2) + 3(1)] \\
[-3(3) + 2(1) + 1(2)] & [-3(2) + 2(-2) + 1(1)]
\end{pmatrix}
$$

$$(129)$$

$$
=
\begin{pmatrix}
(3 - 2 + 6) & (2 + 4 + 3) \\
(6 + 1 + 6) & (4 - 2 + 3) \\
(-9 + 2 + 2) & (-6 - 4 + 1)
\end{pmatrix}
=
\begin{pmatrix}
7 & 9 \\
13 & 5 \\
-5 & -9
\end{pmatrix}
$$

Matrix multiplication is not commutative. The order in which matrices are multiplied will result in different products, so that

$$
AB \neq BA \tag{130}
$$

(multiplication of individual numbers, of course, is commutative).

On the other hand, matrix multiplication is associative, i.e.,

$$
A(BC) = (AB)C \tag{131}
$$

provided that A is an m by n matrix, B is an n by p matrix, and C is a p by q matrix.

There are two more properties of matrix multiplication that are important. Matrix multiplication is distributive over addition, or

$$(A + B)(C + D) = AC + BC + AD + BD \tag{132}$$

Also, the transpose of the product of two matrices will be the same as the product of the transpose of the two matrices.

$$(AB)^T = B^T A^T \tag{133}$$

The product of an identity matrix I and any other matrix A (provided I is of the proper height and width) is always commutative, so that

$$IA = AI = A \tag{134}$$

(I thus plays a role very much like that which 1 does in real numbers.)

MATRIX INVERSION

If we have an expression such that

$$aX = 1 \tag{135}$$

$X = \dfrac{1}{a} = a^{-1}$, where a^{-1} is called the inverse of a such that

$$a^{-1}a = 1$$

Similarly, we define A^{-1}, the inverse of matrix A, such that

$$A^{-1}A = I \tag{136}$$

or the product of A and its multiplicative inverse is equal to the identity matrix.

Before showing the importance of the inverse in a solution of systems of equations, we shall first show how we can express a system of equations in matrix form.

EXPRESSING A SYSTEM OF EQUATIONS IN MATRIX FORM

In expression (115) we wrote out a system of equations in symbolic form. This expression can be considered to be the product of two matrices to the left of the equal sign and a column matrix or column on the right. Rewriting (115), we have

$$\begin{pmatrix} a_{11} & a_{12} & \cdots & a_{1c} \\ a_{21} & a_{22} & \cdots & a_{2c} \\ \cdot & & & \\ \cdot & & & \\ \cdot & & & \\ a_{r1} & a_{r2} & \cdots & a_{rc} \end{pmatrix} \begin{pmatrix} X_1 \\ X_2 \\ \cdot \\ \cdot \\ \cdot \\ X_r \end{pmatrix} = \begin{pmatrix} b_1 \\ b_2 \\ \cdot \\ \cdot \\ \cdot \\ b_r \end{pmatrix} \qquad (137)$$

or

$$AX = B$$

Matrix A is called the *matrix of coefficients*. Matrix X is called the *matrix of unknowns*. Matrix B is called the *matrix of constants*.

SOLVING A SYSTEM OF LINEAR EQUATIONS

Let us return to (135) and generalize it so that

$$aX = b$$

We resolve this statement in principle by finding the multiplicative inverse of a and multiplying both sides of our equations by it.

$$a^{-1}aX = a^{-1}b \qquad (138)$$

and since

$$a^{-1}a = 1$$
$$X = a^{-1}b$$

Similarly, we can define the principle of solution for a system of equations, where

$$AX = B$$
$$A^{-1}AX = A^{-1}B \qquad (139)$$

and since

$$A^{-1}A = I$$

we have

$$IX = A^{-1}B$$

and since

$$IX = X$$

we have

$$X = A^{-1}B$$

where A, B, and X are matrices of coefficients, constants, and unknowns, respectively. The product $A^{-1}B$ will be a column vector in which each element will be equal to each element in the column vector of matrix X.

Let us take an example. We start with a system of linear equations

$$
\begin{align}
2X - Y + 3Z &= 9 \\
X - Y \quad\;\; &= -1 \\
-X + Y - Z &= -2
\end{align}
\tag{140}
$$

This system appears in matrix form as

$$
\begin{pmatrix} 2 & -1 & 3 \\ 1 & -1 & 0 \\ -1 & 1 & -1 \end{pmatrix}
\begin{pmatrix} X \\ Y \\ Z \end{pmatrix}
=
\begin{pmatrix} 9 \\ -1 \\ -2 \end{pmatrix}
\tag{141}
$$

Next we find the inverse of matrix A. (For the moment, we shall just give the inverse for this problem.)

$$
A^{-1} =
\begin{pmatrix} 1 & 2 & 3 \\ 1 & 1 & 3 \\ 0 & -1 & -1 \end{pmatrix}
$$

(The student can convince himself that this is the inverse by showing that $A^{-1}A = I$.) We can now rewrite our equations:

$$
\begin{pmatrix} X \\ Y \\ Z \end{pmatrix}
=
\begin{pmatrix} 1 & 2 & 3 \\ 1 & 1 & 3 \\ 0 & -1 & -1 \end{pmatrix}
\begin{pmatrix} 9 \\ -1 \\ -2 \end{pmatrix}
\tag{142}
$$

so that

$$
\begin{pmatrix} X \\ Y \\ Z \end{pmatrix}
=
\begin{pmatrix} 1 \\ 2 \\ 3 \end{pmatrix}
$$

and hence

$$X = 1$$
$$Y = 2$$
$$Z = 3$$

FINDING THE INVERSE OF A MATRIX

A rectangular matrix can have left or right inverses or none (136) but not both. On the other hand, if a square matrix has an inverse it is unique; however, there are cases in which a square matrix has no inverse. When this occurs, the matrix is called a *singular* matrix. The fact that the matrix is singular means that one or more rows can be written as a linear combination of two or more other rows.

Finding the inverse of a matrix may be simple when the matrix is small but becomes somewhat more complex when the matrix is large. One way is to solve the equations for the unknown elements in the inverse matrix. For instance, where A is equal to

$$A = \begin{pmatrix} 1 & 2 \\ 2 & 3 \end{pmatrix} \tag{145}$$

we can set up a system of equations to find the inverse

$$\begin{pmatrix} a_{11}^{-1} & a_{12}^{-1} \\ a_{21}^{-1} & a_{22}^{-1} \end{pmatrix} \begin{pmatrix} 1 & 2 \\ 2 & 3 \end{pmatrix} = \begin{pmatrix} 1 & 0 \\ 0 & 1 \end{pmatrix}$$

so that

$$a_{11}^{-1} + 2a_{12}^{-1} = 1, \qquad a_{21}^{-1} + 2a_{22}^{-1} = 0$$
$$2a_{11}^{-1} + 3a_{12}^{-1} = 0, \qquad 2a_{21}^{-1} + 3a_{22}^{-1} = 1$$

Solving, we get

$$a_{11} = -3, \qquad a_{21} = 2$$
$$a_{12} = 2, \qquad a_{22} = -1$$

and

$$A^{-1} = \begin{pmatrix} -3 & 2 \\ 2 & -1 \end{pmatrix} \tag{146}$$

while the statements above are certainly true, we should notice that they lead nowhere. We started out with two equations and two unknowns. These equations led to a 2×2 matrix. To describe the inverse of this 2×2 matrix required four equations and four unknowns. This would lead to a 4×4 matrix. To describe its inverse would require 16 equations, etc.

A number of manipulations of a matrix leave the solution of a system of equations unchanged. The reader might think of these as the operations that are permissible on systems of equations. Multiplying both sides of an equation by the same number or adding the same number to both sides of some or all equations will not change the solution of such a system. Since both sides of an equation have the same value, adding or subtracting one equation to or from another will not change the solution of the system. The algorithm of inverting a matrix proceeds by analogous steps and operates on both the matrix and the identity matrix until the former has been converted into an identity matrix. The same operations, performed on the identity matrix, convert this array into the desired inverse. Although this explanation of the "arithmetic" of matrix inversion is not wholly accurate, it will suffice to take us through an example.

It would be inappropriate to prove the validity of these operations here, and we shall tacitly make use of them as procedural arithmetic conveniences.

The arithmetic operations which are allowed (i.e., they do not change the solutions of the system) and which we shall use are that we can multiply one or more rows of the matrix by a constant and that we can add (or subtract) one row to (or from) another. We shall apply these operations on the matrix to be inverted and on an identity matrix until the matrix is converted into an identity matrix. If we parallel the same operations step by step on the identity matrix, this will become the inverse of our original matrix.

We can start by generating an array of values and writing it next to its identity matrix:

$$\begin{pmatrix} 2 & -1 & 3 \\ 1 & -1 & 0 \\ -1 & 1 & -1 \end{pmatrix} \begin{pmatrix} 1 & 0 & 0 \\ 0 & 1 & 0 \\ 0 & 0 & 1 \end{pmatrix} \qquad (147)$$

We shall perform a series of operations on both matrices designed to convert the matrix on the left to an identity matrix. The same operations, when applied to the matrix on the right, will result in the inverse of the matrix on the left.

We start by adding three times the third row to the first row.

$$\begin{pmatrix} -1 & 2 & 0 \\ 1 & -1 & 0 \\ -1 & 1 & -1 \end{pmatrix} \begin{pmatrix} 1 & 0 & 3 \\ 0 & 1 & 0 \\ 0 & 0 & 1 \end{pmatrix} \qquad (148)$$

By this operation we manage to replace the 3 in the upper right with a zero and the 2 at upper left with a -1. Note the changes the same operation produces on the identity matrix.

Next, we add two times the second row to the first row.

$$\begin{pmatrix} 1 & 0 & 0 \\ 1 & -1 & 0 \\ -1 & 1 & -1 \end{pmatrix} \begin{pmatrix} 1 & 2 & 3 \\ 0 & 1 & 0 \\ 0 & 0 & 1 \end{pmatrix} \tag{149}$$

We add the second row to the third row and multiply the results by -1, obtaining

$$\begin{pmatrix} 1 & 0 & 0 \\ 1 & -1 & 0 \\ 0 & 0 & 1 \end{pmatrix} \begin{pmatrix} 1 & 2 & 3 \\ 0 & 1 & 0 \\ 0 & -1 & -1 \end{pmatrix} \tag{150}$$

Finally, we subtract the first row from the second row and multiply the result by -1.

$$\begin{pmatrix} 1 & 0 & 0 \\ 0 & 1 & 0 \\ 0 & 0 & 1 \end{pmatrix} \begin{pmatrix} 1 & 2 & 3 \\ 1 & 1 & 3 \\ 0 & -1 & -1 \end{pmatrix} \tag{151}$$

On the left side we now have the identity matrix and on the right side we find the inverse of the matrix with which we started. (The student can convince himself that it is indeed the inverse of the original matrix.)

OTHER MATRIX MANIPULATIONS

Finally, we shall list a number of very important theorems in matrix manipulations without giving the necessary proofs.

The product of two identity matrices is itself an identity matrix.

$$II = I \tag{152}$$

The inverse of an inverse is the original matrix.

$$(A^{-1})^{-1} = A \tag{153}$$

If A and B each has an inverse, then

$$(AB)^{-1} = B^{-1}A^{-1} \tag{154}$$

If A has an inverse, then

$$(A^T)^{-1} = (A^{-1})^T \tag{155}$$

In manipulations with probabilities a specific type of matrix is used for which the sum of a row of elements always equals one. Such a matrix is called a *Markov matrix.*

AN INTRODUCTION TO PROBABILITY

The scientist usually has a number of scales for measurement. He uses "length" to determine the distance between two points. He uses "weight" to determine the mass of an object. These two very familiar measures rest essentially on the arbitrary choice of some unit of measurement, such as a meter or a pound, and the determination of how often this unit can be divided into some observed distance or mass. The very day-to-day familiarity with measuring distance or mass tends to hide the basic circularity of such measurements. Length is defined by length, and weight is defined by weight. Familiarity also tends to make us forget the arbitrariness of selecting one particular method of defining distance or mass over some other. Distance could be expressed, for instance, in terms of the time needed to traverse a distance at a standard velocity or by the pitch of sound, which, after all, is determined by the length between two symmetrical points, or the wave, and so on. The units and procedures of measurement are determined, however, not so much by the possibilities of choice (which are almost endless) or by any "natural" fitness of one measure over another, but by the final arbiter of all choice in science—usefulness.

With this short introduction we shall turn to the discussion of a particular scale of measurement, that of probability. To the scientist, probability is the measurement of certainty or likelihood or, if this sits better, of uncertainty or lack of likelihood. The definition of probability is no different from that of distance or weight in principle. It, too, is circular. We define an arbitrary unit likelihood as the base. It is also the result of "counting." The probability of a situation is assessed by counting how often the basic unit can be applied to a situation of certainty very much like measuring distance by how often a unit length can be laid off between two points.

The definition of probability may be stated as follows: If there are N outcomes possible for some observation and if some event E can happen in n possible ways, and if each of the outcomes of observations can be considered equally likely, the probability P of the event E is the ratio of n to N.

$$P(E) = \frac{n}{N} \tag{156}$$

For example, if we are tossing a die, we can assume that there are six equally likely outcomes for any roll. These outcomes are the face of the die that lies looking upward after the toss, having the value of 1, 2, 3, 4, 5, or 6. Theoretically, there are other outcomes possible. The die could end up standing on edge, the die could fall apart, a bird could dart from the sky, grab the die, and disappear with it, and so on. However, all these outcomes happen so infrequently that for practical consideration they are simply discounted. We have then a situation in which $N = 6$. The value for n would depend on the definition of the event E. We could define E variously as 1, any odd number, or the number 3 or larger. Depending on this definition, the value of n is equal to 1, 3, or 4. The relative probabilities are then

$$
\begin{aligned}
&P\ (\text{value} = 1) = \tfrac{1}{6} \\
&P\ (\text{value} = \text{odd}) = \tfrac{3}{6} \\
&P\ (\text{value} = 3 \text{ or larger}) = \tfrac{4}{6}
\end{aligned}
\tag{157}
$$

We may express this idea more rigorously by defining the collection of outcomes of observations as a *fundamental probability set*. (The term "set" is usually used to denote a collection of numbers or objects.) Subsets of this fundamental probability set are called *events*. Note that we consider an event to be a subset, that is, also a collection of numbers or occurrences within the larger collection. As we saw in the previous example, an event could be called "odd" and consist of a number of observations. To each event E_i there is attached a number which is called the *probability* of E_i, $P(E_i)$. This number has the properties that

$$0 \leq P(E_i) \leq 1 \tag{158}$$

We begin by being interested in the probability with which some value of a variable X may occur. If X is related to E, then the probability of event E_i automatically defines the probability of the values of X_i. In this case, X is called a *random variable*. If X consists of individual numbers, such as the number of patients in a hospital, or the number of dollars earned, it is said to be *discrete*. If X represents a variable measured along some numerical scale, such as height or weight, it is said to be *continuous*.

If we go back and look at our problem of tossing a die, we might say that to each event E, there is associated a number called the *probability* of E. Also associated with each event there is the random variable of the number of dots on the face of the die.

There are a number of concepts in the definitions of events which are useful.

A set of events is *exhaustive* if it includes every event that could possibly happen.

Events are called *independent* if the probability of one is not affected by whether or not the other events occur. This is stated symbolically as

$$P(E_1 \mid E_2) = P(E_1)$$

i.e., the probability of event E_1, given that E_2 occurs, is equal to the probability of event E_1. If, on the other hand, event E_1 will have associated with it different probabilities depending on the state of E_2, we talk about a *conditional* probability. The probability, for instance, that an individual will be six feet or larger will differ considerably, depending upon whether this individual is a male or female.

Events are thought to be *complementary* if they are in an either/or relationship. The event "odd" and the event "even" are complementary. The event "1 or less" and the event "larger than 1" are similarly complementary. It is axiomatic that for each event we can find its complement.

Finally, we may think of some events as being exclusive and others as not. For instance, a person can only be male or female. He cannot be both. On the other hand, a male can be a baker or a tailor as well. The events "male" and "tailor" are not exclusive.

There are a number of general statements about probabilities of events which are important.

Where E_1 and E_2 are mutually exclusive,

$$P(E_1 \text{ and } E_2) = 0 \tag{159}$$

Where E_1 and E_2 are not mutually exclusive but are independent of each other,

$$P(E_1 \text{ and } E_2) = P(E_1)P(E_2) \tag{160}$$

Where E_1 and E_2 are not independent, then

$$P(E_1 \text{ and } E_2) = P(E_1)P(E_2 \mid E_1) = P(E_2)P(E_1 \mid E_2) \tag{161}$$

Where E_1 and E_2 are complementary,

$$P(E_1 \text{ or } E_2) = 1 \tag{162}$$

Where E_1 and E_2 are mutually exclusive,

$$P(E_1 \text{ or } E_2) = P(E_1) + P(E_2) \tag{163}$$

More common is the case where E_1 and E_2 are not mutually exclusive, so that the alternative of either/or can be stated more generally

$$P(E_1 \text{ or } E_2 \text{ or both}) = P(E_1) + P(E_2) - P(E_1 \text{ and } E_2) \qquad (164)$$

$$\begin{aligned}
P(E_1 \text{ or } E_2 \text{ or } E_3 \text{ or any combination}) = {} & P(E_1) + P(E_2) + P(E_3) \\
& - P(E_1 \text{ and } E_2) \\
& - P(E_1 \text{ and } E_3) \\
& - P(E_2 \text{ and } E_3) \\
& - P(E_1 \text{ and } E_2 \text{ and } E_3)
\end{aligned}$$

DETERMINING PROBABILITY

Probabilities may be used to predict the outcome of experiments, observations, or experiences. The justification of using probabilities to predict experimental outcomes rests on two propositions. The first is randomness. We can predict the outcome of the toss of a die or of the fall of a coin or of the selection of an individual of a given height as long as tossing of coins or the selection of individuals is done at random. Randomness entails the idea that each event has an equal chance of being selected. If this is not true, if the die should be loaded or if our selection procedures are biased, then we cannot apply probabilities to expectations of outcomes of observations. The second proposition is that probabilities form approximations of the outcome of observations which will generally become better the larger the number of observations is. This is a very rough statement of the law of large numbers and important especially for processing of large data files. What the law of large numbers says is that although it may be true that the probability of attaining a head or tail in tossing a coin is one-half, it will work best in predicting the outcome of tosses when we toss two tons of coins. In this case, we should expect one ton of heads and one ton of tails (give or take a few pounds). The law of large numbers is especially important to the investigator who has large data files at his disposal. He may be able to estimate probabilities with a high accuracy.

For certain games of chance, such as cards or dice, and for other limited situations, probabilities can be computed by making simple assumptions about the combination of randomly selected events. In most scientific situations, probabilities cannot be computed, but must be deduced from observed distributions of random variables. The empirically developed probability distributions of such observations as age at death, weight at birth, and so on, serve as a basis for determining or approximating the probabilities of certain events (such as the probability of surviving for more than 70 years, or weighing less than five pounds at birth). However, the use of relative frequencies without reasonable reasons for assuming randomness without large numbers may be a hazardous undertaking.

In this book we shall be working largely with tables of probabilities based either on calculation or on observations. The actual computation of these values is largely beyond the scope of this book. However, we shall occasionally indicate how computers may be used to develop nonstandard tables of probability distributions.

So far we have talked about the probability of discrete events. Many observations, however, are continuous. Discrete numbers may be N or $N + 1$, but no number between N and $N + 1$. The number of patients in a hospital or the number of deaths from a specific disease in a given year are discrete counts. Continuous numbers have the property of density. Between any two values N and $N + K$ there exists some number M such that $N < M < (N + K)$. For instance, between the weight of 165.35 lb and 165.34 lb there lie such weights as 165.345, 165.34001, 165.3499, etc. Thus, the number of possible values between any two numbers is infinite.

This raises a problem in the computation of probabilities, since the probability of observing a specific continuous value approaches zero [i.e., $P(3.8502) \approx 0$].

We can get around this difficulty by computing probabilities as functions of areas rather than counts. Let the rectangle in Figure A.11 (of length 10 and width 1) represent all continuous numbers from 1 to 10.

Imagine that a random device points to some place in this rectangle. The total event space, comprising all numbers at which the pointer may stop, is given by

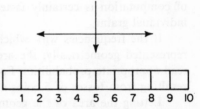

A.11. Rectangular description represented by area.

the total area of the rectangle, i.e., 10. The event space of interest is given by the appropriate area of the subspace A_i.

$$P(E_i) = \frac{A_i}{10}$$

For example, the probability that the pointer will stop at random between 3.5 and 3.8 is given by the ratio of the areas in Figure A.12.

$$P[3.5 < E < 3.8] = \frac{.3}{10} = .03$$

Also

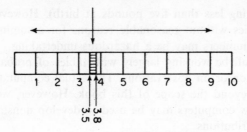

A.12. Probability represented as part of an area of a rectangular description.

$$P[E > 2.5] = \frac{7.5}{10} = .75$$

$$P[E < 9.35] = \frac{9.35}{10} = .935$$

However, the probability that E is equal to exactly 2.5 or any other value is still equal to zero.

It usually is more convenient to compute probabilities by area than by counts. For instance, gray beach sand consists of black and white grains which are completely identical except for color. If we know that 25 lb of gray sand are made up of 10 lb of black and 15 lb of white sand then the probability of picking a single black grain at random is $\frac{10}{25} = .4$. This method of computation is certainly faster and more convenient than a count of individual grains.

If the frequencies with which events occur in the event space can be represented geometrically, the area of the resulting figure can be used to read appropriate probabilities. For instance, the different numbers of heads resulting from tosses of 5 coins are pictured in Figure A.13.

Letting the area of the geometric figure (a histogram) equal to unity, the proportions of the area corresponding to 0, 1, 2, 3, 4, and 5 heads are approximately .03, .15, .32, .32, .15, and .03. We can now read directly the desired probabilities as (where X is the number of heads in a toss of 5 coins)

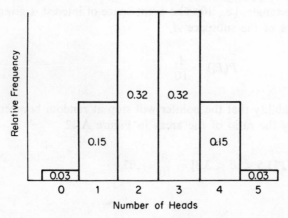

A.13. Number of heads.

$$P(X > 2) = .5$$
$$P(X < 2) = .18$$
$$P(0 < X < 3) = .47$$

The same procedure can be followed for continuous numbers, providing the shape of the frequency distribution is known. For an example, let us assume that the frequency of misses from a target is distributed triangularly, (Figure A.14). The distance of misses ranges from 0 cm to 10 cm. We can let the area of the triangle, A, represent the event space and set it equal to unity.

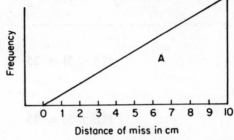

A.14. Description of frequency of misses.

Suppose we want to compute the probability that a shot misses the target by less than 5 cm. This probability is given by the area, a, of the triangle with base 5 and height, h, of Figure A.15. Since

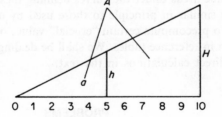

A.15. Schematic representation of the probability of missing target by less than 5 cm.

$$A = 1 = \frac{BH}{2}$$

where A is the area of larger triangle.
  B is its base $= 10$.
  H is its height.

$$H = \frac{2}{B} = \frac{2}{10} = .2$$

By the law of similar triangles,

$$\frac{h}{b} = \frac{H}{B}$$

$$h = \frac{Hb}{B}$$

$$= \frac{.2 \times 5}{10} = .1$$

so that

$$a = \frac{hb}{2} = \frac{.1 \times 5}{2} = \frac{.5}{2} = .25$$

or

$$P(E < 5) = .25$$

Similarly,

$$P(E > 5) = .75$$

In the text we shall deal with a number of distributions described as "normal, t, χ^2, F," and so on. These are simply descriptions of the geometric shape taken on by a specific measure. When the geometric shape of a density distribution is known, it is then possible to find desired probabilities by finding specific areas under the curves defining these geometric dispositions by methods similar in principle to those used by us here. Most often it is customary to precompute certain "crucial" values of probabilities and summarize them in reference tables. We shall be dealing with such tables rather than with direct calculations in the text.

PROBLEMS

1. State algorithms for:
   (a) Second move in Tic-Tac-Toe game.
   (b) Finding the area of the largest circle that can be inscribed in a rectangle, given the length and width of the figure.
   (c) Finding the $\log_{10} 40.5$, given $\log_{10} 2$ and $\log_{10} 3$.

2. Flowchart the procedures stated in Problem 1, (a), (b), and (c).

3. Flowchart a procedure for arranging a list of numbers in descending order.

4. Express the following numbers in scientific notation.
   (a) 20,210.35.
   (b) $\sqrt{0.0036}$.

(c) $-.000047$.
(d) 868, 331, 564, 229.1.
(e) $\frac{1}{12}$.
(f) 5!

5. Convert the following floating point numbers to decimal notation.
    (a) 1.758×10^4.
    (b) $.317 \times 10^{-5}$.
    (c) $2.98 \times 10°$.
    (d) $3.602 + 07$.
    (e) 1.7E02.

6. You have the following array for values of variable Y (where rows and columns are labeled 1, 2, or 3).

		Sex		
		A (1)	B (2)	C (3)
Age Group	Young (1)	26.4	12.2	-28
	Adult (2)	17.4	-8	0
	Old (3)	12.5	-14	1

   (a) Give subscripts for Y with largest value.
   (b) Give subscripts for Y with largest absolute value.
   (c) What are the values of Y_{23}, T_{31}, and Y_{12}?

7. For Problem 6 give

   (a) $\sum\limits_{i=1}^{3} Y_{i2}$ (c) $\sum\limits_{i=1}^{2} \sum\limits_{j=1}^{3} Y_{ij}$

   (b) $\sum\limits_{j=1}^{2} Y_{1j}$ (d) $\sum\limits_{i=1}^{j-1} \sum\limits_{j=2}^{3} Y_{ij}$

8. For Problem 6 multiply all numbers in Column A by b, in Column B by p, and in Column C by m. Express the resulting sum of all numbers in general notation.

9. Approximate $\sqrt{7}$ and $\sqrt{18}$ by numerical solution.

10. Find the slope to the following curve at $x = 5$:
    (a) $y = 2$.
    (b) $y = x + 3$.
    (c) $y = x^4 + 3x^2 + x + 1$.

11. Find the slope and write the equation for the line through the points $(7, 0)$ and $(7, 7)$. For the points $(-1, 5)$ and $(0, 10)$, do the same thing.

12. Make a table of values for $y = 1/x$ for $x \to 0$ from the positive side of 0. Does $\lim\limits_{x \to 0} y$ have a value? What is it? On a sheet of graph paper plot the pairs of x's and y's, and see if you can determine the slope as $x \to 0$.

13. Find the maximum or minimum of the following curves and associated value of x. Is the function at maximum or minimum?
    (a) $y = 4$.
    (b) $y = x - 3$.
    (c) $y = x^2 - 4x + 4$.
    (d) $y = -x^2 + 4x - 4$.
    (e) $y = x^3$.
    (f) $y = \frac{1}{3}x^3 - 2x^2 + 4x + 1$.

14. In steps of $\frac{1}{2}$ make a table of x versus y and plot these pairs for $x = 0$ to $x = 3$ for the function $y = x^2 + 4x + 4$. Do the same thing on a separate piece of paper for the steps $\frac{1}{4}$, $\frac{1}{10}$, $\frac{1}{20}$. Draw straight lines between each of the points and for each of the four plots cut out the area bounded by the curve and the x axis from $x = 0$ to $x = 3$. Find a scale and weigh one square inch of the graph paper. Now weigh each of the four graphs. Divide these four weights by the weight of the square inch. Now integrate the area under the curve by the method given in class. Which of the four weights is closest to the integrated area? Does taking more and more points help the approximation? Are there drawbacks to this method of taking more points?

15. Find the inverse of

$$A = \begin{pmatrix} 1 & 4 & 3 \\ 2 & 7 & 9 \\ 10 & 1 & 0 \end{pmatrix}$$

16. Find the solution to

$$x_1 + 4x_2 + 3x_3 = 6$$
$$2x_1 + 7x_2 + 9x_3 = 10$$
$$10x_1 + x_2 \quad\quad = 9$$

17. The matrix associated with the equations

$$x_1 + x_2 = 5$$
$$2x_1 + 2x_2 = 40$$

is singular. Graph the lines associated with each equation. What do you notice about them?

18. The matrix associated with the equations

$$x_1 + x_2 = 5$$
$$x_1 - x_2 = 4$$

is nonsingular. Graph these lines also. What do you notice about the lines? Compute the inverse and find the solution. What can you conclude about singular matrices and the associated equations?

19. Where K is the total number of dots resulting from the throw of a pair of dice, make up a frequency distribution for possible outcomes and compute the following probabilities.
    (a) $P(K = 7)$.
    (b) $P(K < 10)$.
    (c) $P(6 < K < 11)$.

20. Compute the probabilities that hold when two cards are drawn from a standard deck.
    (a) P (2 jacks).
    (b) P (2 face cards—not including a 10 or ace).
    (c) P (2 hearts).
    (d) P (at least one ace).

21. Use the triangular distribution of the example in the appendix to compute the following probabilities.

$$P(K < 1)$$

$$P(1 < K < 4)$$

B   SOME COMMONLY USED STATISTICAL TABLES

TABLE 1
COMPUTER GENERATED RANDOM NUMBERS

```
0571297781   0825125145   8080685680   4840800032
0825125145   4840800032   2565564205   1052480773
8080685680   2565564205   3626025627   9982904947
4840CC032    1052480773   9982904947   7645121979
0583494307   8546915580   3590546147   0386349601
2565564205   9982904947   4445504513   4853793622
3173124825   3835726256   5215679893   3507342019
1052480773   7645121979   4853793622   6929136959
3626025627   4445504513   8012852165   4180018750
8546915580   0386349601   6627043140   2452847237

0825125145   4840800032   2565564205   1052480773
4840800032   1052480773   9982904947   7645121979
2565564205   9982904947   4445504513   4853793622
1052480773   7645121979   4853793622   6929136959
8546915580   0386349601   6627043140   4180018750
9982504947   3507342019   4180018750   2452847237
3835726256   4180018750   5117164687   5764925148
7645121979   6929136959   4493925055   8778207201
4445504513   4180018750   6166889484   1002185181
C386349601   2452847237   1299720027   5017578696

R08068568C   3626025627   9982904947   7645121979
2565564205   4445504513   4853793622   6929136959
3626025627   8012852165   4180018750   4853793622
9982904947   4180018750   9982904947   6929136959
3590546147   8969308815   5145818903   8778207201
4445504513   6166889484   1299720027   5017578696
5215679893   1118767985   5507261605   0244510436
4853793622   1002185181   0244510436   8288348501
8012852165   0244213409   8361450545   4775312929
6627043140   9895033505   9839766996   2128499762

484C800032   1052480773   9982904947   7645121979
1052480773   7645121979   4853793622   6929136959
9982904947   4853793622   4180018750   4180018750
7645121979   6929136959   4493925055   4493925055
C386349601   2452847237   1299720027   2452847237
4853793622   4493925055   1002185181   4493925055
3507342019   5764925148   6507261605   5764925148
6929136959   8778207201   0244510436   8778207201
4180018750   1002185181   8361450545   1002185181
2452847237   5017578696   9839766996   4567879819
```

```
0583494307   4840800032   1052480773   2565564205
8546915580   1052480773   7645121979   9982904947
3590546147   9982904947   4853793622   4445504513
0386349601   7645121979   6929136959   4853793622
2726313457   0386349601   2452847237   6627043140
6627043140   4853793622   0426134921   4180018750
0832543171   3507342019   1299720027   5117164687
2452847237   6929136959   6409588753   4493925055
8969308815   4180018750   5017578696   6166889484
0426134921   2452847237   9985302693   1299720027

8546915580   1052480773   9982904947   9982904947
0386349601   7645121979   4853793622   4853793622
6627043140   4853793622   4180018750   4180018750
2452847237   2452847237   4493925055   4493925055
0426134921   2452847237   1299720027   1299720027
1299720027   4493925055   1002185181   1002185181
6409588753   5764925148   5507261605   5507261605
5017578696   8778207201   0244510436   0244510436
9895033505   1002185181   8361450545   8361450545
9985302693   5017578696   9839766996   9839766996

3590546147   9982904947   4445504513   4445504513
6627043140   4853793622   4180018750   4180018750
8969308815   4180018750   6166889484   6166889484
1299720027   1299720027   1002185181   1002185181
5145818903   5145818903   9895033505   9895033505
9895033505   9895033505   8361450545   8361450545
4550103661   5507261605   2078156597   2078156597
9839766996   0244510436   2128499762   2128499762
8751943761   8361450545   1800093248   1800093248
4804582051   9839766996   0139045751   0139045751

0386349601   7645121979   4853793622   4853793622
2452847237   6929136959   4493925055   4493925055
1299720027   4939925055   1002185181   1002185181
5017578696   5017578696   0244510436   0244510436
9837766996   8778207201   9839766996   9839766996
4367443921   0244510436   2128499762   2128499762
4567879819   8288348501   2141684757   2141684757
0139045751   4775312929   0569476756   0569476756
          2128499762   1729940595   1729940595
5634565316   4567879819   6537900703   6537900703
```

TABLE 1
COMPUTER GENERATED RANDOM NUMBERS

0825125145	8563921335	2284266894	0571297781
4840800032	0044363510	9826639073	0825125145
2565564205	0583494307	4840800032	8080685680
1052480773	3957386902	1632379892	4840800037
8546915580	8535555261	3957386902	0583494307
9982904947	8546915580	1052480773	2565564205
3835726256	7811989759	6087122162	3173124825
7645121079	9822554367	0787594595	1052480773
4445504513	3590546147	9982904947	3620025627
0388349601	3008366528	9822554367	8546915580

4840800032	0044363510	9826639073	0825125145
1052480773	3957386902	1632379892	4840800032
9982904947	8546915580	1052480773	2565564205
7645121979	9822554367	0787594595	1052480773
0386349601	3008366528	9822554367	8546915580
4853793622	0386349601	7645121979	9982904947
3507342019	0671892328	3464739822	3835726256
6929136959	0419262021	0431279807	7645121979
4180018750	6627043140	4853793622	4445504513
2452847237	5260322716	0419262021	0388349601

2565564205	0583494307	4840800032	8080685680
9982904947	8546915580	1052480773	2565564205
4445504513	3590546147	9982904947	3626025627
4853793622	0386349601	7645121979	9982904947
6627043140	2726311457	0386349601	3590546147
4180018750	6627043140	4853793622	4445504513
5117164687	0832543121	3507342019	5216678833
4493975055	2452847237	6929136959	4853793622
6166689484	8969308R15	4180018750	8012852165
1299720027	0426134921	2452847237	6627043140

1052480773	3957386902	1632379892	4840800032
7645121979	9822554367	0787594595	1052480773
4853793622	0386349601	7645121979	9982904947
6929136959	0419262021	0431279807	7645121979
2452847237	5260322716	0419262021	0386349601
4493925055	2452847237	2327847502	4853793622
5764925148	5177053684	7029212564	3507342019
8778207201	6229953648	7029212564	0431279807
1002185181	1299720027	4493925055	4953793622
5017578696	0292929526	6229953648	0419262021

2243449921	3460391178	0571297781	2284266894
3460391178	2284266894	0825125145	9826639073
0571297781	0825125145	8080685680	4840800032
7262266894	9826639073	4840800032	1632379892
8563921335	0044363510	0583494307	3957386902
0825125145	4840800032	2565564205	1052480773
7875641033	3540954085	3173124825	6087122162
9826639073	1632379892	1052480773	0787594595
8080685680	2565564205	3620025627	9982904947
0C443A3510	3957386902	8546915580	9822554367

3460391178	2284266894	0825125145	9826639073
2284266894	9826639073	4840800032	1632379892
0825125145	4840800032	2565564205	1052480773
9826639073	1632379892	1052480773	0787594595
0044363510	3957386902	3590546147	9822554367
4840800032	1052480773	5982904947	7645121979
3540954085	6087122162	3835726256	3464739822
1632379892	0787594595	7645121079	0431279807
2565564205	9982904947	4445504513	4953793622
3957386902	9822554367	0388349601	0419262021

TABLE 1
COMPUTER GENERATED RANDOM NUMBERS

4860800032	0044363510	9988904947	7645121979
1052480773	3957386902	4853793622	5929136959
9982904947	8546915580	4180018750	4493925055
7645121979	9822554367	4493925055	8778207201
0386349601	3008366528	1299720027	5017578696
4853793622	0386349601	1002185181	0244510436
3507342019	0671892328	6507261605	8288348501
6929136959	0419262021	0244510436	4775312929
4180018750	6627043140	8361450545	2128499762
2452847237	5260322716	9839766996	4567879819

1052480773	3957386902	8546915580	9822554367
7645121979	9822554367	0386349601	0419262021
4853793622	0386349601	6627043140	2452847237
6929136959	0419262021	2452847237	6229553648
2452847237	5260322716	0426134921	0292929526
4493925055	2452847237	1299720027	5017578696
5764925148	5177053684	6409588253	1202908596
8778207201	6229553648	5017578696	3666882274
1002185181	1299720027	9895033505	9839766996
5017578696	0292929526	9985302693	3357884337

COMPUTER GENERATED RANDOM NUMBERS

9826639073	1632379892	1052480773	0788594595
1632379892	0787594595	7645121979	0431279807
1052480773	7645121979	4853793622	6929136959
0787594595	0431279807	6929136959	7029212564
9822554367	0419262021	2452847237	6229553648
7645121979	6929136959	4493925055	8778207201
3464739822	2327847502	5764925148	7673219907
0431279807	7029212564	8778207201	4662638689
4853793622	4493925055	1002185181	0244510436
0419262021	6229553648	5017578696	3666882274

2284266894	9826639073	4860800032	1632379892
9826639073	1632379892	1052480773	0787594595
4860800032	1052480773	9982904947	7645121979
1632379892	0787594595	7645121979	0431279807
3957386902	9822554367	0386349601	0419262021
1052480773	7645121979	4853793622	6929136959
6087122162	3464739822	3507342019	2327847502
0787594595	0431279807	6929136959	7029212564
9982904947	4853793622	4180018750	4493925055
9822554367	0419262021	2452847237	6229553648

3460391178	2284266894	0825125145	9826639073
2284266894	9826639073	4860800032	1632379892
0825125145	4860800032	2565564205	1052480773
9826639073	1632379892	1052480773	0787594595
0044363510	3957386902	8546915580	5822554367
4840800032	1052480773	9982904947	7645121979
3540954085	6087122162	3835726256	3464739822
1632379892	0787594595	7645121979	0431279807
2565564205	9982904947	4445504513	4853793622
3957386902	9822554367	0386349601	0419262021

TABLE 2

TABLE OF SQUARE ROOTS

	0	1	2	3	4	5	6	7	8	9
1.0	1.0000	1.0050	1.0100	1.0149	1.0198	1.0247	1.0296	1.0344	1.0392	1.0440
10.	3.1623	3.1780	3.1937	3.2094	3.2249	3.2404	3.2558	3.2711	3.2863	3.3015
1.1	1.0488	1.0536	1.0583	1.0630	1.0677	1.0724	1.0770	1.0817	1.0863	1.0909
11.	3.3166	3.3317	3.3466	3.3615	3.3764	3.3912	3.4059	3.4205	3.4351	3.4496
1.2	1.0954	1.1000	1.1045	1.1091	1.1136	1.1180	1.1225	1.1269	1.1314	1.1358
12.	3.4641	3.4785	3.4928	3.5071	3.5214	3.5355	3.5496	3.5637	3.5777	3.5917
1.3	1.1402	1.1446	1.1489	1.1533	1.1576	1.1619	1.1662	1.1705	1.1747	1.1790
13.	3.6056	3.6194	3.6332	3.6469	3.6606	3.6742	3.6878	3.7014	3.7148	3.7283
1.4	1.1832	1.1874	1.1916	1.1958	1.2000	1.2042	1.2083	1.2124	1.2166	1.2207
14.	3.7417	3.7550	3.7683	3.7815	3.7947	3.8079	3.8210	3.8341	3.8471	3.8601
1.5	1.2247	1.2288	1.2329	1.2369	1.2410	1.2450	1.2490	1.2530	1.2570	1.2610
15.	3.8730	3.8859	3.8987	3.9115	3.9243	3.9370	3.9497	3.9623	3.9749	3.9875
1.6	1.2649	1.2689	1.2728	1.2767	1.2806	1.2845	1.2884	1.2923	1.2961	1.3000
16.	4.0000	4.0125	4.0249	4.0373	4.0497	4.0620	4.0743	4.0866	4.0988	4.1110
1.7	1.3038	1.3077	1.3115	1.3153	1.3191	1.3229	1.3266	1.3304	1.3342	1.3379
17.	4.1231	4.1352	4.1473	4.1593	4.1713	4.1833	4.1952	4.2071	4.2190	4.2308
1.8	1.3416	1.3454	1.3491	1.3528	1.3565	1.3601	1.3638	1.3675	1.3711	1.3748
18.	4.2426	4.2544	4.2661	4.2778	4.2895	4.3012	4.3128	4.3243	4.3359	4.3474
1.9	1.3784	1.3820	1.3856	1.3892	1.3928	1.3964	1.4000	1.4036	1.4071	1.4107
19.	4.3589	4.3704	4.3818	4.3932	4.4045	4.4159	4.4272	4.4385	4.4497	4.4609
2.0	1.4142	1.4177	1.4213	1.4248	1.4283	1.4318	1.4353	1.4387	1.4422	1.4457
20.	4.4721	4.4833	4.4944	4.5056	4.5166	4.5277	4.5387	4.5497	4.5607	4.5717
2.1	1.4491	1.4526	1.4560	1.4595	1.4629	1.4663	1.4697	1.4731	1.4765	1.4799
21.	4.5826	4.5935	4.6043	4.6152	4.6260	4.6368	4.6476	4.6583	4.6690	4.6797
2.2	1.4832	1.4866	1.4900	1.4933	1.4967	1.5000	1.5033	1.5067	1.5100	1.5133
22.	4.6904	4.7011	4.7117	4.7223	4.7329	4.7434	4.7539	4.7645	4.7749	4.7854
2.3	1.5166	1.5199	1.5232	1.5264	1.5297	1.5330	1.5362	1.5395	1.5427	1.5460
23.	4.7958	4.8062	4.8166	4.8270	4.8374	4.8477	4.8580	4.8683	4.8785	4.8888
2.4	1.5492	1.5524	1.5556	1.5588	1.5620	1.5652	1.5684	1.5716	1.5748	1.5780
24.	4.8990	4.9092	4.9193	4.9295	4.9396	4.9497	4.9598	4.9699	4.9800	4.9900
2.5	1.5811	1.5843	1.5875	1.5906	1.5937	1.5969	1.6000	1.6031	1.6062	1.6093
25.	5.0000	5.0100	5.0200	5.0299	5.0398	5.0498	5.0596	5.0695	5.0794	5.0892

TABLE 2

TABLE OF SQUARE ROOTS

	0	1	2	3	4	5	6	7	8	9
2.6	1.6125	1.6155	1.6186	1.6217	1.6248	1.6279	1.6310	1.6340	1.6371	1.6401
26.	5.0990	5.1088	5.1186	5.1284	5.1381	5.1478	5.1575	5.1672	5.1769	5.1865
2.7	1.6432	1.6462	1.6492	1.6523	1.6553	1.6583	1.6613	1.6643	1.6673	1.6703
27.	5.1962	5.2058	5.2154	5.2249	5.2345	5.2440	5.2536	5.2631	5.2726	5.2820
2.8	1.6733	1.6763	1.6793	1.6823	1.6852	1.6882	1.6912	1.6941	1.6971	1.7000
28.	5.2915	5.3009	5.3104	5.3198	5.3292	5.3385	5.3479	5.3572	5.3666	5.3759
2.9	1.7029	1.7059	1.7088	1.7117	1.7146	1.7176	1.7205	1.7234	1.7263	1.7292
29.	5.3852	5.3944	5.4037	5.4129	5.4222	5.4314	5.4406	5.4498	5.4589	5.4681
3.0	1.7321	1.7349	1.7378	1.7407	1.7436	1.7464	1.7493	1.7521	1.7550	1.7578
30.	5.4772	5.4863	5.4955	5.5045	5.5136	5.5227	5.5317	5.5408	5.5498	5.5588
3.1	1.7607	1.7635	1.7664	1.7692	1.7720	1.7748	1.7776	1.7804	1.7833	1.7861
31.	5.5678	5.5767	5.5857	5.5946	5.6036	5.6125	5.6214	5.6303	5.6391	5.6480
3.2	1.7889	1.7916	1.7944	1.7972	1.8000	1.8028	1.8055	1.8083	1.8111	1.8138
32.	5.6569	5.6657	5.6745	5.6833	5.6921	5.7009	5.7096	5.7184	5.7271	5.7359
3.3	1.8166	1.8193	1.8221	1.8248	1.8276	1.8303	1.8330	1.8358	1.8385	1.8412
33.	5.7446	5.7533	5.7619	5.7706	5.7793	5.7879	5.7966	5.8052	5.8138	5.8224
3.4	1.8439	1.8466	1.8493	1.8520	1.8547	1.8574	1.8601	1.8628	1.8655	1.8682
34.	5.8310	5.8395	5.8481	5.8566	5.8652	5.8737	5.8822	5.8907	5.8992	5.9076
3.5	1.8708	1.8735	1.8762	1.8788	1.8815	1.8841	1.8868	1.8894	1.8921	1.8947
35.	5.9161	5.9245	5.9330	5.9414	5.9498	5.9582	5.9666	5.9749	5.9833	5.9917
3.6	1.8974	1.9000	1.9026	1.9053	1.9079	1.9105	1.9131	1.9157	1.9183	1.9209
36.	6.0000	6.0083	6.0166	6.0249	6.0332	6.0415	6.0498	6.0581	6.0663	6.0745
3.7	1.9235	1.9261	1.9287	1.9313	1.9339	1.9365	1.9391	1.9416	1.9442	1.9468
37.	6.0828	6.0910	6.0992	6.1074	6.1156	6.1237	6.1319	6.1400	6.1482	6.1563
3.8	1.9494	1.9519	1.9545	1.9570	1.9596	1.9621	1.9647	1.9672	1.9698	1.9723
38.	6.1644	6.1725	6.1806	6.1887	6.1968	6.2048	6.2129	6.2209	6.2290	6.2370
3.9	1.9748	1.9774	1.9799	1.9824	1.9849	1.9875	1.9900	1.9925	1.9950	1.9975
39.	6.2450	6.2530	6.2610	6.2690	6.2769	6.2849	6.2929	6.3008	6.3087	6.3166
4.0	2.0000	2.0025	2.0050	2.0075	2.0100	2.0125	2.0149	2.0174	2.0199	2.0224
40.	6.3246	6.3325	6.3403	6.3482	6.3561	6.3640	6.3718	6.3797	6.3875	6.3953

TABLE 2

TABLE OF SQUARE ROOTS

	0	1	2	3	4	5	6	7	8	9
4.1	2.0248	2.0273	2.0298	2.0322	2.0347	2.0372	2.0396	2.0421	2.0445	2.0469
41.	6.4031	6.4109	6.4187	6.4265	6.4343	6.4420	6.4498	6.4576	6.4653	6.4730
4.2	2.0494	2.0518	2.0543	2.0567	2.0591	2.0616	2.0640	2.0664	2.0688	2.0712
42.	6.4807	6.4885	6.4962	6.5038	6.5115	6.5192	6.5269	6.5345	6.5422	6.5498
4.3	2.0736	2.0761	2.0785	2.0809	2.0833	2.0857	2.0881	2.0905	2.0928	2.0952
43.	6.5574	6.5651	6.5727	6.5803	6.5879	6.5955	6.6030	6.6106	6.6182	6.6257
4.4	2.0976	2.1000	2.1024	2.1048	2.1071	2.1095	2.1119	2.1142	2.1166	2.1190
44.	6.6332	6.6408	6.6483	6.6558	6.6633	6.6708	6.6783	6.6858	6.6933	6.7007
4.5	2.1213	2.1237	2.1260	2.1284	2.1307	2.1331	2.1354	2.1378	2.1401	2.1424
45.	6.7082	6.7157	6.7231	6.7305	6.7380	6.7454	6.7528	6.7602	6.7676	6.7750
4.6	2.1448	2.1471	2.1494	2.1517	2.1541	2.1564	2.1587	2.1610	2.1633	2.1656
46.	6.7823	6.7897	6.7971	6.8044	6.8118	6.8191	6.8264	6.8337	6.8411	6.8484
4.7	2.1679	2.1703	2.1726	2.1749	2.1772	2.1794	2.1817	2.1840	2.1863	2.1886
47.	6.8557	6.8629	6.8702	6.8775	6.8848	6.8920	6.8993	6.9065	6.9138	6.9210
4.8	2.1909	2.1932	2.1954	2.1977	2.2000	2.2023	2.2045	2.2068	2.2091	2.2113
48.	6.9282	6.9354	6.9426	6.9498	6.9570	6.9642	6.9714	6.9785	6.9857	6.9929
4.9	2.2136	2.2159	2.2181	2.2204	2.2226	2.2249	2.2271	2.2293	2.2316	2.2338
49.	7.0000	7.0071	7.0143	7.0214	7.0285	7.0356	7.0427	7.0498	7.0569	7.0640
5.0	2.2361	2.2383	2.2405	2.2428	2.2450	2.2472	2.2494	2.2517	2.2539	2.2561
50.	7.0711	7.0781	7.0852	7.0922	7.0993	7.1063	7.1134	7.1204	7.1274	7.1344
5.1	2.2583	2.2605	2.2627	2.2650	2.2672	2.2694	2.2716	2.2738	2.2760	2.2782
51.	7.1414	7.1484	7.1554	7.1624	7.1694	7.1764	7.1833	7.1903	7.1972	7.2042
5.2	2.2804	2.2825	2.2847	2.2869	2.2891	2.2913	2.2935	2.2956	2.2978	2.3000
52.	7.2111	7.2180	7.2250	7.2319	7.2388	7.2457	7.2526	7.2595	7.2664	7.2732
5.3	2.3022	2.3043	2.3065	2.3087	2.3108	2.3130	2.3152	2.3173	2.3195	2.3216
53.	7.2801	7.2870	7.2938	7.3007	7.3075	7.3144	7.3212	7.3280	7.3348	7.3417
5.4	2.3238	2.3259	2.3281	2.3302	2.3324	2.3345	2.3367	2.3388	2.3409	2.3431
54.	7.3485	7.3553	7.3621	7.3689	7.3756	7.3824	7.3892	7.3959	7.4027	7.4095
5.5	2.3452	2.3473	2.3495	2.3516	2.3537	2.3558	2.3580	2.3601	2.3622	2.3643
55.	7.4162	7.4229	7.4297	7.4364	7.4431	7.4498	7.4565	7.4632	7.4699	7.4766

TABLE 2

TABLE OF SQUARE ROOTS

	0	1	2	3	4	5	6	7	8	9
5.6	2.3664	2.3685	2.3707	2.3728	2.3749	2.3770	2.3791	2.3812	2.3833	2.3854
56.	7.4833	7.4900	7.4967	7.5033	7.5100	7.5166	7.5233	7.5299	7.5366	7.5432
5.7	2.3875	2.3896	2.3917	2.3937	2.3958	2.3979	2.4000	2.4021	2.4042	2.4062
57.	7.5498	7.5565	7.5631	7.5697	7.5763	7.5829	7.5895	7.5961	7.6026	7.6092
5.8	2.4083	2.4104	2.4125	2.4145	2.4166	2.4187	2.4207	2.4228	2.4249	2.4269
58.	7.6158	7.6223	7.6289	7.6354	7.6420	7.6485	7.6551	7.6616	7.6681	7.6746
5.9	2.4290	2.4310	2.4331	2.4352	2.4372	2.4393	2.4413	2.4434	2.4454	2.4474
59.	7.6811	7.6877	7.6942	7.7006	7.7071	7.7136	7.7201	7.7266	7.7330	7.7395
6.0	2.4495	2.4515	2.4536	2.4556	2.4576	2.4597	2.4617	2.4637	2.4658	2.4678
60.	7.7460	7.7524	7.7589	7.7653	7.7717	7.7782	7.7846	7.7910	7.7974	7.8038
6.1	2.4698	2.4718	2.4739	2.4759	2.4779	2.4799	2.4819	2.4839	2.4860	2.4880
61.	7.8102	7.8166	7.8230	7.8294	7.8358	7.8422	7.8486	7.8549	7.8613	7.8677
6.2	2.4900	2.4920	2.4940	2.4960	2.4980	2.5000	2.5020	2.5040	2.5060	2.5080
62.	7.8740	7.8804	7.8867	7.8930	7.8994	7.9057	7.9120	7.9183	7.9246	7.9310
6.3	2.5100	2.5120	2.5140	2.5159	2.5179	2.5199	2.5219	2.5239	2.5259	2.5278
63.	7.9373	7.9436	7.9498	7.9561	7.9624	7.9687	7.9750	7.9812	7.9875	7.9937
6.4	2.5298	2.5318	2.5338	2.5357	2.5377	2.5397	2.5417	2.5436	2.5456	2.5475
64.	8.0000	8.0062	8.0125	8.0187	8.0250	8.0312	8.0374	8.0436	8.0498	8.0561
6.5	2.5495	2.5515	2.5534	2.5554	2.5573	2.5593	2.5612	2.5632	2.5652	2.5671
65.	8.0623	8.0685	8.0747	8.0808	8.0870	8.0932	8.0994	8.1056	8.1117	8.1179
6.6	2.5690	2.5710	2.5729	2.5749	2.5769	2.5788	2.5807	2.5826	2.5846	2.5865
66.	8.1240	8.1302	8.1363	8.1425	8.1486	8.1548	8.1609	8.1670	8.1731	8.1792
6.7	2.5884	2.5904	2.5923	2.5942	2.5962	2.5981	2.6000	2.6019	2.6038	2.6058
67.	8.1854	8.1915	8.1976	8.2037	8.2098	8.2158	8.2219	8.2280	8.2341	8.2401
6.8	2.6077	2.6096	2.6115	2.6134	2.6153	2.6173	2.6192	2.6211	2.6230	2.6249
68.	8.2462	8.2523	8.2583	8.2644	8.2704	8.2765	8.2825	8.2885	8.2946	8.3006
6.9	2.6268	2.6287	2.6306	2.6325	2.6344	2.6363	2.6382	2.6401	2.6420	2.6439
69.	8.3066	8.3126	8.3187	8.3247	8.3307	8.3367	8.3427	8.3487	8.3546	8.3606
7.0	2.6458	2.6476	2.6495	2.6514	2.6533	2.6552	2.6571	2.6589	2.6608	2.6627
70.	8.3666	8.3726	8.3785	8.3845	8.3905	8.3964	8.4024	8.4083	8.4143	8.4202

TABLE 2

TABLE OF SQUARE ROOTS

	0	1	2	3	4	5	6	7	8	9
7.1	2.6646	2.6665	2.6683	2.6702	2.6721	2.6739	2.6758	2.6777	2.6796	2.6814
71.	8.4261	8.4321	8.4380	8.4439	8.4499	8.4558	8.4617	8.4676	8.4735	8.4794
7.2	2.6833	2.6851	2.6870	2.6889	2.6907	2.6926	2.6944	2.6963	2.6981	2.7000
72.	8.4853	8.4912	8.4971	8.5029	8.5088	8.5147	8.5206	8.5264	8.5323	8.5381
7.3	2.7019	2.7037	2.7055	2.7074	2.7092	2.7111	2.7129	2.7148	2.7166	2.7185
73.	8.5440	8.5499	8.5557	8.5615	8.5674	8.5732	8.5790	8.5849	8.5907	8.5965
7.4	2.7203	2.7221	2.7240	2.7258	2.7276	2.7295	2.7313	2.7331	2.7350	2.7368
74.	8.6023	8.6081	8.6139	8.6197	8.6255	8.6313	8.6371	8.6429	8.6487	8.6545
7.5	2.7386	2.7404	2.7423	2.7441	2.7459	2.7477	2.7495	2.7514	2.7532	2.7550
75.	8.6603	8.6660	8.6718	8.6776	8.6833	8.6891	8.6948	8.7006	8.7063	8.7121
7.6	2.7568	2.7586	2.7604	2.7622	2.7641	2.7659	2.7677	2.7695	2.7713	2.7731
76.	8.7178	8.7235	8.7293	8.7350	8.7407	8.7464	8.7521	8.7579	8.7636	8.7693
7.7	2.7749	2.7767	2.7785	2.7803	2.7821	2.7839	2.7857	2.7875	2.7893	2.7911
77.	8.7750	8.7807	8.7864	8.7920	8.7977	8.8034	8.8091	8.8148	8.8204	8.8261
7.8	2.7928	2.7946	2.7964	2.7982	2.8000	2.8018	2.8036	2.8054	2.8071	2.8089
78.	8.8318	8.8374	8.8431	8.8487	8.8544	8.8600	8.8657	8.8713	8.8769	8.8826
7.9	2.8107	2.8125	2.8142	2.8160	2.8178	2.8196	2.8213	2.8231	2.8249	2.8267
79.	8.8882	8.8938	8.8994	8.9051	8.9107	8.9163	8.9219	8.9275	8.9331	8.9387
8.0	2.8284	2.8302	2.8320	2.8337	2.8355	2.8373	2.8390	2.8408	2.8425	2.8443
80.	8.9443	8.9499	8.9554	8.9610	8.9666	8.9722	8.9778	8.9833	8.9889	8.9944
8.1	2.8460	2.8478	2.8496	2.8513	2.8531	2.8548	2.8566	2.8583	2.8601	2.8618
81.	9.0000	9.0056	9.0111	9.0167	9.0222	9.0277	9.0333	9.0388	9.0443	9.0499
8.2	2.8636	2.8653	2.8671	2.8688	2.8705	2.8723	2.8740	2.8758	2.8775	2.8792
82.	9.0554	9.0609	9.0664	9.0719	9.0774	9.0830	9.0885	9.0940	9.0995	9.1049
8.3	2.8810	2.8827	2.8844	2.8862	2.8879	2.8896	2.8914	2.8931	2.8948	2.8965
83.	9.1104	9.1159	9.1214	9.1269	9.1324	9.1378	9.1433	9.1488	9.1542	9.1597
8.4	2.8983	2.9000	2.9017	2.9034	2.9052	2.9069	2.9086	2.9103	2.9120	2.9138
84.	9.1652	9.1706	9.1761	9.1815	9.1869	9.1924	9.1978	9.2033	9.2087	9.2141
8.5	2.9155	2.9172	2.9189	2.9206	2.9223	2.9240	2.9257	2.9275	2.9292	2.9309
85.	9.2195	9.2250	9.2304	9.2358	9.2412	9.2466	9.2520	9.2574	9.2628	9.2682

TABLE 2

TABLE OF SQUARE ROOTS

	0	1	2	3	4	5	6	7	8	9
8.6	2.9326	2.9343	2.9360	2.9377	2.9394	2.9411	2.9428	2.9445	2.9462	2.9479
86.	9.2736	9.2790	9.2844	9.2898	9.2952	9.3005	9.3059	9.3113	9.3167	9.3220
8.7	2.9496	2.9513	2.9530	2.9547	2.9563	2.9580	2.9597	2.9614	2.9631	2.9648
87.	9.3274	9.3327	9.3381	9.3434	9.3488	9.3541	9.3595	9.3648	9.3702	9.3755
8.8	2.9665	2.9682	2.9698	2.9715	2.9732	2.9749	2.9766	2.9783	2.9799	2.9816
88.	9.3808	9.3862	9.3915	9.3968	9.4021	9.4074	9.4128	9.4181	9.4234	9.4287
8.9	2.9833	2.9850	2.9866	2.9883	2.9900	2.9917	2.9933	2.9950	2.9967	2.9983
89.	9.4340	9.4393	9.4446	9.4499	9.4552	9.4604	9.4657	9.4710	9.4763	9.4816
9.0	3.0000	3.0017	3.0033	3.0050	3.0067	3.0083	3.0100	3.0116	3.0133	3.0150
90.	9.4868	9.4921	9.4974	9.5026	9.5079	9.5131	9.5184	9.5237	9.5289	9.5341
9.1	3.0166	3.0183	3.0199	3.0216	3.0232	3.0249	3.0265	3.0282	3.0299	3.0315
91.	9.5394	9.5446	9.5499	9.5551	9.5603	9.5656	9.5708	9.5760	9.5812	9.5864
9.2	3.0332	3.0348	3.0364	3.0381	3.0397	3.0414	3.0430	3.0447	3.0463	3.0480
92.	9.5917	9.5969	9.6021	9.6073	9.6125	9.6177	9.6229	9.6281	9.6333	9.6385
9.3	3.0496	3.0512	3.0529	3.0545	3.0561	3.0578	3.0594	3.0610	3.0627	3.0643
93.	9.6437	9.6488	9.6540	9.6592	9.6644	9.6695	9.6747	9.6799	9.6850	9.6902
9.4	3.0659	3.0676	3.0692	3.0708	3.0725	3.0741	3.0757	3.0773	3.0790	3.0806
94.	9.6954	9.7005	9.7057	9.7108	9.7160	9.7211	9.7263	9.7314	9.7365	9.7417
9.5	3.0822	3.0838	3.0854	3.0871	3.0887	3.0903	3.0919	3.0935	3.0952	3.0968
95.	9.7468	9.7519	9.7570	9.7622	9.7673	9.7724	9.7775	9.7826	9.7877	9.7929
9.6	3.0984	3.1000	3.1016	3.1032	3.1048	3.1064	3.1081	3.1097	3.1113	3.1129
96.	9.7980	9.8031	9.8082	9.8133	9.8184	9.8234	9.8285	9.8336	9.8387	9.8438
9.7	3.1145	3.1161	3.1177	3.1193	3.1209	3.1225	3.1241	3.1257	3.1273	3.1289
97.	9.8489	9.8539	9.8590	9.8641	9.8691	9.8742	9.8793	9.8843	9.8894	9.8944
9.8	3.1305	3.1321	3.1337	3.1353	3.1369	3.1385	3.1401	3.1417	3.1432	3.1448
98.	9.8995	9.9046	9.9096	9.9146	9.9197	9.9247	9.9298	9.9348	9.9398	9.9448
9.9	3.1464	3.1480	3.1496	3.1512	3.1528	3.1544	3.1559	3.1575	3.1591	3.1607
99.	9.9499	9.9549	9.9599	9.9649	9.9700	9.9750	9.9800	9.9850	9.9900	9.9950

TABLE 3

BINOMIAL PROBABILITY FOR C(N,R) * P**R * (1-P)**(N-R)
FOR DIFFERENT VALUES OF P, R, AND N.

VARIOUS VALUES OF P

N	R	.10	.20	.30	1/3	.40	.50
N= 4	0	.6561	.4096	.2401	.1975	.1296	.0625
	1	.2916	.4096	.4116	.3951	.3456	.2500
	2	.0486	.1536	.2646	.2963	.3456	.3750
	3	.0036	.0256	.0756	.0988	.1536	.2500
	4	.0001	.0016	.0081	.0123	.0256	.0625
N= 5	0	.5905	.3277	.1681	.1317	.0778	.0312
	1	.3280	.4096	.3602	.3292	.2592	.1562
	2	.0729	.2048	.3087	.3292	.3456	.3125
	3	.0081	.0512	.1323	.1646	.2304	.3125
	4	.0004	.0064	.0284	.0412	.0768	.1562
	5	.0000	.0003	.0024	.0041	.0102	.0312
N= 6	0	.5314	.2621	.1176	.0878	.0467	.0156
	1	.3543	.3932	.3025	.2634	.1866	.0938
	2	.0984	.2458	.3241	.3292	.3110	.2344
	3	.0146	.0819	.1852	.2195	.2765	.3125
	4	.0012	.0154	.0595	.0823	.1382	.2344
	5	.0001	.0015	.0102	.0165	.0369	.0938
	6	.0000	.0001	.0007	.0014	.0041	.0156
N= 7	0	.4783	.2097	.0824	.0585	.0280	.0078
	1	.3720	.3670	.2471	.2048	.1306	.0547
	2	.1240	.2753	.3177	.3073	.2613	.1641
	3	.0230	.1147	.2269	.2561	.2903	.2734
	4	.0026	.0287	.0972	.1280	.1935	.2734
	5	.0002	.0043	.0250	.0384	.0774	.1641
	6	.0000	.0004	.0036	.0064	.0172	.0547
	7	.0000	.0000	.0002	.0005	.0016	.0078
N= 8	0	.4305	.1678	.0576	.0390	.0168	.0039
	1	.3826	.3355	.1977	.1561	.0896	.0312
	2	.1488	.2936	.2965	.2731	.2090	.1094
	3	.0331	.1468	.2541	.2731	.2787	.2188
	4	.0046	.0459	.1361	.1707	.2322	.2734
	5	.0004	.0092	.0467	.0683	.1239	.2188
	6	.0000	.0011	.0100	.0171	.0413	.1094
	7	.0000	.0001	.0012	.0024	.0079	.0312
	8	.0000	.0000	.0001	.0002	.0007	.0039
N= 9	0	.3874	.1342	.0404	.0260	.0101	.0020
	1	.3874	.3020	.1556	.1171	.0605	.0176
	2	.1722	.3020	.2668	.2341	.1612	.0703
	3	.0446	.1762	.2668	.2731	.2508	.1641
	4	.0074	.0661	.1715	.2048	.2508	.2461
	5	.0008	.0165	.0735	.1024	.1672	.2461
	6	.0001	.0028	.0210	.0341	.0743	.1641
	7	.0000	.0003	.0039	.0073	.0212	.0703
	8	.0000	.0000	.0004	.0009	.0035	.0176
	9	.0000	.0000	.0000	.0001	.0003	.0020
N=10	0	.3487	.1074	.0282	.0173	.0060	.0010
	1	.3874	.2684	.1211	.0867	.0403	.0098
	2	.1937	.3020	.2335	.1951	.1209	.0439
	3	.0574	.2013	.2668	.2601	.2150	.1172
	4	.0112	.0881	.2001	.2276	.2508	.2051
	5	.0015	.0264	.1029	.1366	.2007	.2461
	6	.0001	.0055	.0368	.0569	.1115	.2051
	7	.0000	.0008	.0090	.0163	.0425	.1172
	8	.0000	.0001	.0014	.0030	.0106	.0439
	9	.0000	.0000	.0001	.0003	.0016	.0098
	10	.0000	.0000	.0000	.0000	.0001	.0010

TABLE 4

BINOMIAL COEFFICIENTS

N	C(N,0)	C(N,1)	C(N,2)	C(N,3)	C(N,4)	C(N,5)	C(N,6)	C(N,8)	C(N,9)	C(N,10)
0	1									
1	1	1								
2	1	2	1							
3	1	3	3	1						
4	1	4	6	4	1					
5	1	5	10	10	5	1				
6	1	6	15	20	15	6	1			
7	1	7	21	35	35	21	7	1		
8	1	8	28	56	70	56	28	8	1	
9	1	9	36	84	126	126	84	36	9	1
10	1	10	45	120	210	252	210	120	45	10
11	1	11	55	165	330	462	462	330	165	55
12	1	12	66	220	495	792	924	792	495	220
13	1	13	78	286	715	1287	1716	1716	1287	715
14	1	14	91	364	1001	2002	3003	3432	3003	2002
15	1	15	105	455	1365	3003	5005	6435	6435	5005
16	1	16	120	560	1820	4368	8008	11440	12870	11440
17	1	17	134	680	2380	5188	12376	19448	24310	24310
18	1	18	153	816	3060	8568	18564	31824	43758	48620
19	1	19	171	969	3876	11628	27137	50388	75582	92378
20	1	20	190	1140	4345	15504	38760	77520	125970	167960

C(N,7) column:

N	C(N,7)
7	1
8	8
9	36
10	120
11	330
12	792
13	1716
14	3432
15	6435
16	11440
17	19448
18	31824
19	50388
20	77520

C(N,10) column continued:

N	C(N,10)
10	1
11	11
12	66
13	286
14	1001
15	3003
16	8008
17	19448
18	43758
19	92378
20	184756

TABLE 5

DIFFERENT VALUES RELATED TO A PROPORTION P.

P	P(1-P)	(P(1-P))**1/2	1-P**2	1-(1-P)**2
.01	.0099	.09950	.9999	.0199
.02	.0196	.14000	.9996	.0396
.03	.0291	.17059	.9991	.0591
.04	.0384	.19596	.9984	.0784
.05	.0475	.21794	.9975	.0975
.06	.0564	.23749	.9964	.1164
.07	.0651	.25515	.9951	.1351
.08	.0736	.27129	.9936	.1536
.09	.0819	.28618	.9919	.1719
.10	.0900	.30000	.9900	.1900
.11	.0979	.31289	.9879	.2079
.12	.1056	.32496	.9856	.2256
.13	.1131	.33630	.9831	.2431
.14	.1204	.34699	.9804	.2604
.15	.1275	.35707	.9775	.2775
.16	.1344	.36661	.9744	.2944
.17	.1411	.37563	.9711	.3111
.18	.1476	.38419	.9676	.3276
.19	.1539	.39230	.9639	.3439
.20	.1600	.40000	.9600	.3600
.21	.1659	.40731	.9559	.3759
.22	.1716	.41425	.9516	.3916
.23	.1771	.42083	.9471	.4071
.24	.1824	.42708	.9424	.4224
.25	.1875	.43301	.9375	.4375
.26	.1924	.43863	.9324	.4524
.27	.1971	.44396	.9271	.4671
.28	.2016	.44900	.9216	.4816
.29	.2059	.45376	.9159	.4959
.30	.2100	.45826	.9100	.5100
.31	.2139	.46249	.9039	.5239
.32	.2176	.46648	.8976	.5376
.33	.2211	.47021	.8911	.5511
.34	.2244	.47371	.8844	.5644
.35	.2275	.47697	.8775	.5775
.36	.2304	.48000	.8704	.5904
.37	.2331	.48280	.8631	.6031
.38	.2356	.48539	.8556	.6156
.39	.2379	.48775	.8479	.6279
.40	.2400	.48990	.8400	.6400
.41	.2419	.49183	.8319	.6519
.42	.2436	.49356	.8236	.6636
.43	.2451	.49508	.8151	.6751
.44	.2464	.49639	.8064	.6864
.45	.2475	.49749	.7975	.6975
.46	.2484	.49840	.7884	.7084
.47	.2491	.49910	.7791	.7191
.48	.2496	.49960	.7696	.7296
.49	.2499	.49990	.7599	.7399
.50	.2500	.50000	.7500	.7500

TABLE 6

SELECTED PERCENTILE VALUES OF THE CHI-SQUARE DISTRIBUTION

D.F.	PERCENT LARGER THAN .1	.05	.01
1	2.71	3.84	6.63
2	4.61	5.99	9.21
3	6.25	7.81	11.34
4	7.78	9.49	13.28
5	9.24	11.07	15.09
6	10.64	12.59	16.81
7	12.02	14.07	18.48
8	13.36	15.51	20.09
9	14.68	16.92	21.67
10	15.99	18.31	23.21
11	17.28	19.68	24.73
12	18.55	21.03	26.22
13	19.81	22.36	27.69
14	21.06	23.68	29.14
15	22.31	25.00	30.58
20	28.41	31.41	37.57
30	40.26	43.77	50.89
40	51.81	55.76	63.69
50	63.17	67.50	76.15
60	74.40	79.08	88.38
70	85.53	90.53	100.42
80	96.58	101.88	112.33
90	107.57	113.14	124.12
100	118.50	124.34	135.81

TABLE 7

SELECTED AREAS OF THE NORMAL DISTRIBUTION

Z	AREA	ORDINATE	Z	AREA	ORDINATE
0.25	.0987	.3867	1.75	.4600	.0863
0.50	.1914	.3521	2.00	.4772	.0540
0.75	.2735	.3011	2.25	.4878	.0317
1.00	.3414	.2420	2.50	.4938	.0175
1.25	.3944	.1827	3.00	.4986	.0091
1.50	.4332	.1295	4.00	.4999	.0001

VALUES OF Z AND P FOR FREQUENTLY USED REGIONS OF REJECTION

P	AREA	Z
.10	.40	1.282
.05	.45	1.645
.01	.49	2.326
.001	.499	3.090

TABLE 8

SELECTED PERCENTILE VALUES OF THE STUDENT T DISTRIBUTION

D.F.	PERCENT LARGER THAN .1	.05	.01
1	3.078	6.314	31.821
2	1.886	2.920	6.965
3	1.638	2.353	4.541
4	1.533	2.132	3.747
5	1.476	2.015	3.365
6	1.440	1.943	3.143
7	1.415	1.895	2.998
8	1.397	1.860	2.896
9	1.383	1.833	2.821
10	1.372	1.812	2.764
11	1.363	1.796	2.718
12	1.356	1.782	2.681
13	1.350	1.771	2.650
14	1.345	1.761	2.624
15	1.341	1.753	2.602
20	1.325	1.725	2.528
30	1.310	1.697	2.457
40	1.303	1.684	2.423
INFINITY	1.282	1.645	2.326

TABLE 9

PERCENTILES OF THE DISTRIBUTION OF R ON THE ASSUMPTION THAT THE TRUE CORRELATION IS ZERO

NUMBER OF OBSERVATIONS	R .95	R .99	R .995
5	.805	.934	.959
6	.729	.882	.917
7	.669	.833	.875
8	.621	.789	.834
9	.582	.750	.798
10	.549	.715	.765
11	.521	.685	.735
12	.497	.658	.708
13	.476	.634	.684
14	.457	.612	.661
15	.441	.592	.641
16	.426	.574	.623
17	.412	.558	.606
18	.400	.543	.590
19	.389	.529	.575
20	.378	.516	.561
22	.360	.492	.537
24	.344	.472	.515
26	.330	.453	.496
28	.317	.437	.479
30	.306	.423	.463
40	.264	.366	.402
50	.235	.328	.361
60	.214	.300	.330
80	.185	.260	.286
100	.165	.232	.256
250	.104	.147	.163
500	.074	.104	.115
1000	.052	.074	.081
INFINITY	0	0	0

SELECTED PERCENTILE VALUES OF THE F DISTRIBUTION FOR UPPER 5 PERCENT POINTS

C.F. OF DENOM.	D.F. OF NUMERATOR														
	1	2	3	4	5	6	7	8	9	10	15	20	30	40	INFINITY
1	161.43	199.50	215.71	224.62	230.21	234.05	236.83	238.91	240.50	241.92	245.94	248.05	250.09	251.13	254.28
2	18.51	19.00	19.16	19.25	19.30	19.33	19.35	19.37	19.38	19.40	19.43	19.45	19.46	19.47	19.50
3	10.13	9.55	9.28	9.12	9.01	8.94	8.89	8.85	8.81	8.79	8.70	8.66	8.62	8.59	8.53
4	7.71	6.94	6.59	6.39	6.26	6.16	6.09	6.04	6.00	5.96	5.86	5.80	5.75	5.72	5.63
5	6.61	5.79	5.41	5.19	5.05	4.95	4.88	4.82	4.77	4.74	4.62	4.56	4.50	4.46	4.36
6	5.99	5.14	4.76	4.53	4.39	4.28	4.21	4.15	4.10	4.06	3.94	3.87	3.81	3.77	3.67
7	5.59	4.74	4.35	4.12	3.97	3.87	3.79	3.73	3.68	3.64	3.51	3.44	3.38	3.34	3.23
8	5.32	4.46	4.07	3.84	3.69	3.58	3.50	3.44	3.39	3.35	3.22	3.15	3.08	3.04	2.93
9	5.12	4.26	3.86	3.63	3.48	3.37	3.29	3.23	3.18	3.14	3.01	2.94	2.86	2.83	2.71
10	4.96	4.1C	3.71	3.48	3.33	3.22	3.14	3.07	3.02	2.98	2.85	2.77	2.70	2.66	2.54
11	4.84	3.98	3.59	3.36	3.20	3.09	3.01	2.95	2.90	2.85	2.72	2.65	2.57	2.53	2.40
12	4.75	3.89	3.49	3.26	3.11	3.00	2.91	2.85	2.80	2.75	2.62	2.54	2.47	2.43	2.30
13	4.67	3.81	3.41	3.18	3.03	2.92	2.83	2.77	2.71	2.67	2.53	2.46	2.38	2.34	2.21
14	4.60	3.74	3.34	3.11	2.96	2.85	2.76	2.70	2.65	2.60	2.46	2.39	2.31	2.27	2.13
15	4.54	3.68	3.29	3.06	2.90	2.79	2.71	2.64	2.59	2.54	2.40	2.33	2.25	2.20	2.07
20	4.35	3.49	3.10	2.87	2.71	2.60	2.51	2.45	2.39	2.35	2.20	2.12	2.04	1.99	1.84
25	4.24	3.39	2.99	2.76	2.60	2.49	2.40	2.34	2.28	2.24	2.09	2.01	1.92	1.87	1.71
30	4.17	3.37	2.92	2.69	2.53	2.42	2.33	2.27	2.21	2.16	2.01	1.93	1.84	1.79	1.62
40	4.08	3.23	2.84	2.61	2.45	2.34	2.25	2.18	2.12	2.08	1.92	1.84	1.74	1.69	1.51
INFINITY	3.84	3.00	2.60	2.37	2.21	2.10	2.01	1.94	1.88	1.83	1.67	1.57	1.46	1.39	1.00

SELECTED PERCENTILE VALUES OF THE F DISTRIBUTION FOR UPPER 1 PERCENT POINTS

C.F. OF DENOM.	D.F. OF NUMERATOR														
	1	2	3	4	5	6	7	8	9	10	15	20	30	40	INFINITY
1	4052.	4999.	5403.	5625.	5764.	5859.	5928.	5982.	6022.	6056.	6157.	6209.	6261.	6287.	6366.
2	98.50	99.08	99.17	99.25	99.30	99.33	99.36	99.37	99.39	99.40	99.43	99.45	99.47	99.47	99.50
3	34.12	30.84	29.46	28.71	28.24	27.91	27.67	27.49	27.35	27.23	26.87	26.69	26.50	26.41	26.13
4	21.20	18.00	16.69	15.98	15.52	15.21	14.98	14.80	14.66	14.55	14.20	14.02	13.84	13.75	13.46
5	16.34	13.25	12.06	11.39	10.97	10.67	10.46	10.29	10.16	10.05	9.72	9.55	9.38	9.29	9.02
6	13.75	10.92	9.78	9.15	8.75	8.47	8.26	8.10	7.98	7.87	7.56	7.40	7.23	7.14	6.88
7	12.25	9.55	8.45	7.85	7.46	7.19	6.99	6.84	6.72	6.62	6.31	6.16	5.99	5.91	5.65
8	11.24	8.65	7.59	7.01	6.63	6.37	6.18	6.03	5.91	5.81	5.52	5.36	5.20	5.12	4.86
9	10.56	8.02	6.99	6.42	6.06	5.80	5.61	5.47	5.35	5.26	4.96	4.81	4.65	4.57	4.31
10	10.04	7.56	6.55	5.99	5.64	5.39	5.20	5.06	4.94	4.85	4.56	4.41	4.25	4.17	3.91
11	9.65	7.21	6.22	5.67	5.32	5.07	4.89	4.74	4.63	4.54	4.25	4.10	3.94	3.86	3.60
12	9.33	6.93	5.95	5.41	5.06	4.82	4.64	4.50	4.39	4.30	4.01	3.86	3.70	3.62	3.36
13	9.07	6.70	5.74	5.21	4.86	4.62	4.44	4.30	4.19	4.10	3.82	3.66	3.51	3.43	3.17
14	8.86	6.51	5.56	5.04	4.69	4.46	4.28	4.14	4.03	3.94	3.66	3.51	3.35	3.27	3.00
15	8.68	6.36	5.42	4.89	4.56	4.32	4.14	4.00	3.89	3.80	3.52	3.37	3.21	3.13	2.87
20	8.10	5.85	4.94	4.43	4.10	3.87	3.70	3.56	3.46	3.37	3.09	2.94	2.78	2.69	2.42
25	7.77	5.57	4.68	4.18	3.85	3.63	3.46	3.32	3.22	3.13	2.85	2.70	2.54	2.45	2.17
30	7.56	5.39	4.51	4.02	3.70	3.47	3.30	3.17	3.07	2.98	2.70	2.55	2.39	2.30	2.01
40	7.31	5.18	4.31	3.83	3.51	3.29	3.12	2.99	2.89	2.80	2.52	2.37	2.20	2.11	1.80
INFINITY	6.83	4.61	3.78	3.32	3.02	2.80	2.64	2.51	2.41	2.32	2.04	1.88	1.70	1.59	1.00

TABLE 11

VALUES OF THE R TO Z TRANSFORMATION

(FOR EACH VALUE OF R GIVEN IN THE FIRST COLUMN AND FIRST ROW, THE APPROPRIATE VALUE OF Z IS IN THE BODY OF THE TABLE.)

R	.00	.01	.02	.03	.04	.05	.06	.07	.08	.09
.0	.00000	.01000	.02000	.03001	.04002	.05004	.06007	.07012	.08017	.09024
.1	.10034	.11045	.12058	.13074	.14093	.15114	.16139	.17167	.18199	.19234
.2	.20273	.21317	.22366	.23419	.24477	.25541	.26611	.27686	.28768	.29857
.3	.30952	.32055	.33165	.34283	.35409	.36544	.37689	.38842	.40006	.41180
.4	.42365	.43561	.44769	.45990	.47223	.48470	.49731	.51007	.52298	.53606
.5	.54931	.56273	.57634	.59014	.60415	.61838	.63283	.64752	.66246	.67767
.6	.69315	.70892	.72500	.74142	.75817	.77530	.79281	.81074	.82911	.84795
.7	.86730	.88718	.90764	.92873	.95048	.97295	.99621	1.02033	1.04537	1.07143
.8	1.09861	1.12703	1.15682	1.18813	1.22117	1.25615	1.29334	1.33308	1.37577	1.42192
.9	1.47222	1.52752	1.58902	1.65839	1.73805	1.83178	1.94591	2.09229	2.29756	2.64665

TABLE 12

FACTORIALS (1 TO 100)

N	N FACTORIAL	N	N FACTORIAL	N	N FACTORIAL	N	N FACTORIAL
1	1.0000	26	4.0329E026	51	1.5511E066	76	1.8855E111
2	2.0000	27	1.0889E028	52	8.0658E067	77	1.4518E113
3	6.0000	28	3.0489E029	53	4.2749E069	78	1.1324E115
4	2.4000E001	29	8.8418E030	54	2.3084E071	79	8.9462E116
5	1.2000E002	30	2.6525E032	55	1.2696E073	80	7.1569E118
6	7.2000E002	31	8.2228E033	56	7.1100E074	81	5.7971E120
7	5.0400E003	32	2.6313E035	57	4.0527E076	82	4.7536E122
8	4.0320E004	33	8.6833E036	58	2.3506E078	83	3.9455E124
9	3.6288E005	34	2.9523E038	59	1.3868E080	84	3.3142E126
10	3.6288E006	35	1.0333E040	60	8.3210E081	85	2.8171E128
11	3.9917E007	36	3.7199E041	61	5.0758E083	86	2.4227E130
12	4.7900E008	37	1.3764E043	62	3.1470E085	87	2.1078E132
13	6.2270E009	38	5.2302E044	63	1.9826E087	88	1.8548E134
14	8.7178E010	39	2.0398E046	64	1.2689E089	89	1.6508E136
15	1.3077E012	40	8.1592E047	65	8.2477E090	90	1.4857E138
16	2.0923E013	41	3.3453E049	66	5.4435E092	91	1.3520E140
17	3.5569E014	42	1.4050E051	67	3.6471E094	92	1.2438E142
18	6.4024E015	43	6.0415E052	68	2.4800E096	93	1.1568E144
19	1.2165E017	44	2.6583E054	69	1.7112E098	94	1.0874E146
20	2.4329E018	45	1.1962E056	70	1.1979E100	95	1.0330E148
21	5.1091E019	46	5.5026E057	71	8.5048E101	96	9.9168E149
22	1.1240E021	47	2.5862E059	72	6.1234E103	97	9.6193E151
23	2.5852E022	48	1.2414E061	73	4.4701E105	98	9.4269E153
24	6.2045E023	49	6.0828E062	74	3.3079E107	99	9.3326E155
25	1.5511E025	50	3.0414E064	75	2.4809E109	100	9.3326E157

647

TABLE 13

LOGARITHMS OF FACTORIAL N (1 TO 100)

N	LOG N	N	LOG N	N	LOG N	N	LOG N
1	0.00000	26	26.60562	51	66.19064	76	111.27543
2	0.30103	27	28.03698	52	67.90665	77	113.16192
3	0.77815	28	29.41249	53	69.63092	78	115.05401
4	1.38021	29	30.94654	54	71.36332	79	116.95164
5	2.07918	30	32.42366	55	73.10368	80	118.85473
6	2.85733	31	33.71502	56	74.85187	81	120.76321
7	3.70243	32	35.42017	57	76.60774	82	122.67703
8	4.60552	33	36.93869	58	78.37117	83	124.59610
9	5.55976	34	38.47016	59	80.14202	84	126.52038
10	6.55976	35	40.01423	60	81.92017	85	128.44980
11	7.60116	36	41.57054	61	83.70550	86	130.38430
12	8.68034	37	43.13874	62	85.49790	87	132.32382
13	9.79428	38	44.71852	63	87.29724	88	134.26830
14	10.94041	39	46.30959	64	89.10342	89	136.21769
15	12.11650	40	47.91165	65	90.91633	90	138.17194
16	13.32062	41	49.52443	66	92.73587	91	140.13098
17	14.55107	42	51.14768	67	94.56195	92	142.09476
18	15.80634	43	52.78115	68	96.39446	93	144.06325
19	17.08509	44	54.42460	69	98.23331	94	146.03638
20	18.38612	45	56.07781	70	100.07840	95	148.01410
21	19.70834	46	57.74057	71	101.92966	96	149.99637
22	21.05077	47	59.41267	72	103.78700	97	151.98314
23	22.41249	48	61.09391	73	105.65032	98	153.97437
24	23.79271	49	62.78410	74	107.51955	99	155.97000
25	25.19065	50	64.48307	75	109.39461	100	157.97000

ANSWERS TO NUMERIC PROBLEMS

CHAPTER 6

PAGES 264–265

3: 5; 5; 5.33; 9; 3.4; 7.1; 3.7; 2.1

4: 6.22; 2.49

5: 47

6: 3.125; 2; .5; .125

8: 4; 5

9: .1056; .5987; .8944; .04; .8944; .15; .7358; .2901; .0821

10: .75; .8125; .4374; .8542

11: $\frac{3}{400}$; $\frac{1597}{1600}$; $\frac{7}{16}$; $\frac{41}{48}$

12: $\frac{1}{27}$; $\frac{7}{27}$; $\frac{19}{27}$

13: $\dfrac{1}{3} - \dfrac{\sqrt{3}}{4\pi}$; $\left(\sqrt{12} + \dfrac{\sqrt{15}}{2} + \dfrac{4\pi}{3} + 8 \arcsin \dfrac{1}{4} \right) / 8\pi$;

$$\left(\dfrac{3\sqrt{7} - \sqrt{15}}{16} + \arcsin \dfrac{3}{4} - \arcsin \dfrac{1}{4} \right) / \pi$$

CHAPTER 7

PAGES 286–287

2: .2241; .0781; .4744

4: (approximately) .16; .07; .64

5: 1,239; reject H_0 if $X \geq 346$

6: .0074; .0083; between 202 and 203

649

PAGES 301–305

1: .1; .09; .95
2: $\chi^2 = 6.95$ so that $P(\chi^2 \geq 6.95 \mid H_0,$ d.f. = 2) $\leq$ .05
3: $\chi^2 = 3.93$ so that $P(\chi^2 \geq 3.93 \mid H_0,$ d.f. = 1) $\leq$ .05
4: $\chi^2 = 7.28$ so that $P(\chi^2 \geq 7.28 \mid H_0,$ d.f. = 2) $\leq$ .02
8: expected frequencies are: 189.28, 503.62, 1,562.41, 2,965.95, 2,022.93, 927.27, and 280.54; $\chi^2 \geq 200$ so that assumption is not reasonable

PAGES 326–327

1: .6915; .5; .9878; .0062; .0928; .1385
2: .8413; .5; .9999; approximately zero; .1517; .6687
  .8413; .6915; .7823; .0228; .6147; .5319
3: (for $\mu = 96$, $\sigma = 8$) 100.20, 98.02, and 93.98;
  (for $\mu = 96$, $\sigma = 4$) 98.10, 97.01, and 94.99;
  (for $\mu = 100$, $\sigma = 8$) 104.20, 102.02, and 97.98
4: (for $\mu = 96$, $\sigma = 8$) .8413 and .4772;
  (for $\mu = 96$, $\sigma = 4$) .9772 and .5;
  (for $\mu = 100$, $\sigma = 8$) .1587 and .3413
6: .2420; .1922; .0808
7: .3085; .1587; .0668; .3085; .1587; .0068;
  .0228; < .01
9: (a) $\overline{D} = 6.06$, $s_{\overline{D}} = 3.5$, $t = 1.73$, d.f. = 15;
  (b) $\overline{D} = 6.06$, $s_{\overline{D}} = 5.48$, $t = 1.1$, d.f. = 30
10: $\overline{D} = 2.95$, $s_{\overline{D}} = 1.633$, $t = 1.81$, d.f. = 7
11: .6513; .2639

CHAPTER 8

PAGES 393–394

1: $Y = 1.2X - .01$
2: $Y = 1.9X - 533$
3: $Y = .75X + 4$
4: $Y = -17X + 114$
5: $Y = .62X - 6.9$
6: $Y = -.745X + 445$
7: $Y = .96X - 8$
8: $Y = 3.2X - 41$
9: $Y = -7X^2$
10: $Y = .24X^2 - 5$
11: $Y = 18X^2 + 4X$
12: $Y = 3X^2 - 2X + 400$

13: $Y = 1.1X^2 + 2.2X + 3.3$
14: $Y = 1.5 X^{1.5}$
15: $Y = .3X^{1.8}$
16: $Y = 2X^{.6} - 4$
17: $Y = -X^{.5} + 10$
18: $Y = 3 \times 10^{.5X}$
19: $Y = 2.2 \times 10^{x+4}$
20: $Y = 3 \times 4^x$
21: $Y = \dfrac{4}{1.1 + 5X}$
22: $Y = \dfrac{-4}{3 + 3X} + 6$
23: $Y = 18 - \dfrac{5.5}{X}$

CHAPTER 9

PAGES 441–443

1: $\bar{Y} = 95.27 - 2.13X$; $s_{y \cdot x}^2 = 28.49$; $r = -.83$ so that approximately 70 per cent of the variance in golf scores can be accounted for by whatever "handgrip" is an index of; $\bar{X} = 33.23 - .3254$; $r \approx 1.0$
3: $\bar{Y} = -11.498 + 1.003X$, $r = .982$
5: $r_b = .703$
6: $\bar{Y} = 4.6466 + .273X_1 - .987X_2 + .199X_3$; .8995 and 1.608

CHAPTER 11

PAGES 533–534

1(a):

Source	Sum Square	d.f.	Mean Square
Columns	2.2	2	1.1
Rows	30.9	3	10.3
Residual	51.8	6	8.6
Total	84.9	11	

1(b):

Source	Sum Square	d.f.	Mean Square
Columns	160.2	2	80.1
Rows	30.9	3	10.3
Residual	51.8	6	8.6
Total	242.9	11	

2(a):

Source	Sum Square	d.f.	Mean Square
Category of crime	12.7	2	6.3
Discharge procedure	295.3	3	98.4
Residual	72.7	6	12.1
Total	380.7	11	

2(b):

Source	Sum Square	d.f.	Mean Square
Category of crime	10.5	2	5.3
Discharge procedure	200.6	3	66.8
Residual	80.9	5	16.1
Total	292.0	10	

3:

Source	Sum Square	d.f.	Mean Square
Category of crime	37	2	18.5
Discharge procedure	583	3	194.3
Interaction	88	6	14.7
Residual	102	12	8.5
Total	810	23	

5:

Source	Sum Square	d.f.	Adjusted Sum Squares	d.f.	Mean Square
Category of crime	12.7	2	30.6	2	15.3
Discharge procedure	295.3	3	256.5	3	85.5
Residual	72.7	6	25.6	5	5.1
Total	380.7		312.7		

APPENDIX A

PAGES 624–627

4: $.2021035 \times 10^5$; $.6 \times 10^{-1}$; $-.47 \times 10^{-4}$; $.8683315642291 \times 10^{12}$; $.833 \times 10^{-1}$; $.12 \times 10^3$

5: 182.832; .00000317; 2.98; 10.602; 170

6: 1, 1; 1, 3; 0, 12.5, and 12.2

7: -9.8; 38.6; 20; -23.8

8: $\sum_{i=1}^{3} (bY_{i1} + pY_{i2} + mY_{i3})$

11: not determined; 5

13: at any point; none; min at $X = 2$; max at $X = 2$; none; max at $X = 2$

15: $\begin{pmatrix} -.0612 & .0204 & .1020 \\ .6122 & -.2040 & -.0204 \\ -.4625 & .2653 & -.0068 \end{pmatrix}$

16: $X_1 = .7548$, $X_2 = -5.8968$, and $X_3 = -.1832$

19: $\frac{1}{16}$; $\frac{1}{12}$; $\frac{1}{2}$

20: $\frac{1}{231}$; $\frac{11}{231}$; $\frac{1}{7}$; $\frac{33}{231}$

21: .01; .15

INDEX